D0438833

THE NEAR EAST IN HISTORY

Courtesy of the Metropolitan Museum of Art,
Gift of Alexander Smith Cochran, 1913

PAGE OF A MANUSCRIPT OF NIZAMI, *KHAMSAH*, DATED 1525

(See page 300)

THE
NEAR EAST
IN HISTORY
A 5000 YEAR STORY

By PHILIP K. HITTI

Professor Emeritus of Semitic Literature on the
William and Annie S. Paton Foundation, Princeton University

D. VAN NOSTRAND COMPANY, INC.

Princeton, New Jersey · New York, N. Y.
Toronto, Canada · London, England

D. VAN NOSTRAND COMPANY, INC.
120 Alexander Street Princeton, New Jersey

D. VAN NOSTRAND COMPANY, INC.
24 West 40th Street, New York 18

D. VAN NOSTRAND COMPANY (Canada), LTD.
25 Hollinger Road, Toronto 16, Canada

D. VAN NOSTRAND COMPANY, LTD.
358, Kensington High Street, London W. 14

Copyright © 1961 by D. Van Nostrand Company, Inc.
Published simultaneously in Canada by
D. Van Nostrand Company (Canada), Ltd.

All rights in this book are reserved
No reproduction in any form of this book
in whole or in part (except for brief quotation in
critical articles or reviews), may be made with-
out written authorization from the publishers.

Designed by Lewis F. White

09623a30
Printed in the United States of America

TO
MY DAUGHTER (*'umruh*)
VIOLA H. WINDER

Preface

Mounting interest in Near Eastern peoples prompted the compilation of this volume for the benefit of non-specialists—students and laymen. It tries to bring out the high-water marks in the careers of these peoples, their contributions to the progress of mankind and their contacts with the rest of the world, particularly the West. That part of the past which has become integrated with the present and promises to pass on to the future has been primarily sought. The author, however, does not claim to have done justice to an area (what is today Turkey, Iran, Iraq, Syria, Lebanon, Jordan, Israel, Egypt and Arabia), which was the cradle of our civilization and has experienced a longer history than any other area, and to a people who, with no ancestors to guide them, lifted mankind from barbarism to the highest cultural stage in antiquity, attained in the spiritual realm unprecedented, unsurpassed heights and, in scientific and artistic fields, levels unmatched by their medieval contemporaries. Nor does he claim specialization in all the countries and periods covered. He, therefore, had to draw on other works and heavily on his own, particularly *History of the Arabs, History of Syria Including Lebanon and Palestine,* and *Lebanon in History.* In the interest of clarity and brevity—as in all such works—he had on controversial matters to take a definite but seemingly vulnerable stand and, in other cases, to make generalizations without protective reservations.

The chapters on the ancient Semites were submitted to the critical consideration of his colleague Professor John H. Marks, on Roman and Byzantine history to Professor Glanville Downey of Dumbarton Oaks Research Library (Harvard University in Washington), those on Persia and Turkey to two other colleagues Professors T. Cuyler Young and Lewis V. Thomas respectively. Credit should be given these scholars for their valuable contribution to the improvement of the text but none should be blamed for any defects. I also acknowledge with appreciation the cooperation of Dr. George C. Miles of the American Numismatic Society in the choice of illustrative coins, of Dr. M. S.

Dimand and Mr. Charles K. Wilkinson of the Metropolitan Museum in the choice of illustrations of Persian art.

The items in the list of Books to Read at the close of each chapter, it should be remembered, were chosen with a view to comprehensibility —not comprehensiveness—readability and availability.   If they serve to amplify the text, give a varied point of view and whet the appetite of the reader for further study they would have served their primary purpose.

P. K. H.

Princeton, N. J.
August 1960

Table of Contents

Period of conquest — Enter Saladin — Ayyubids —
Mamluks — The impact of the Crusades — Ayyubid
and Mamluk contributions — End of the Mamluks.

CONTENTS

List of Illustrations

List of Maps

List of Coins

PART ONE

THE PRELITERARY AGE

I *The Near East in Its World Setting*

SCHOLARS may disagree on the location of the cradle of the human race, but on the cradle of its civilization there is no disagreement. It lies in the area which, in this study, is called the Near East and is comprised of the Fertile Crescent—with its two horns of Mesopotamia (modern Iraq), Syria, and Palestine—Egypt, Anatolia (Asia Minor, Turkey), and Persia or Iran. The "Near East," originally a European geographical term loosely used to designate that part of southwestern Asia nearest Europe, was borrowed by America, parts of which are nearer the Far East. This was the prevailing usage until the second World War, when the British Government created a military province extending from Iran to Libya and named it the Middle East, a term until then traditionally applied to India and adjacent territory. A Middle East supply center was thereupon established in Cairo and later became an Anglo-American project, thus giving sanction to the new terminology.

CLAIMS ON OUR INTEREST

The area's geographic and historic significance stems from its position athwart the international highways linking Africa, Europe, and Asia; its having provided the stage for some of the earliest, most spectacular and enduring discoveries and achievements of man; and its having been the original homestead of our three monotheistic religions. The Near East passed on to later generations a matchlessly rich heritage of science, art, literature, and philosophy—all the fruits of which we still enjoy. The area encompasses not only the world's earliest centers of civilization but also those with the best records and the longest lives. No other region can display a record of civilization as a going concern for over five thousand years.

PREHISTORIC ECONOMIC REVOLUTIONS

Long before the curtain rose on written records, Near Easterners had developed urban life with ordered governments, religions, and social and economic institutions. Still earlier, those who occupied the arch of the Fertile Crescent and nearby territory had discovered metal, realized its potentialities, and worked it into tools and weapons that replaced the more primitive stone implements of the preceding generations. In those crude tools of flint and copper lay a dim vision of the gigantic machines and engines so vital to our modern life. Even earlier, and probably in that same general area, primitive man learned through long and sustained experience, initiated by chance, that certain wild plants could be cultivated and certain wild animals could be domesticated. He then lifted himself from the status of a food gatherer—wandering from place to place in quest of sustenance—to that of a food producer, with a dependable reservoir of food which made possible a settled life with its accumulation of wealth, an increase in population and leisure time part of which could be devoted to the cultivation of the higher things of life. Civilization first developed where it did because this was the one region of the globe that provided the climate, vegetation, and fauna necessary for transition from a life of nomadic grazing and hunting to a settled one.

Through migration, invasion, or cultural osmosis these remarkable accomplishments eventually found their way into the Eastern Mediterranean and the Aegean islands and thence into the European mainland where they provided a prelude to the classical civilization of Greece and Rome, parent to our civilization. After all, Europe is but a peninsular projection of Western Asia. The ancestor of the wheat and barley cultivated in early Europe seems to have been the wild cereals that still grow in north Syria, al-Biqa' of Lebanon and Palestine. The domesticated sheep of Europe have evidently descended from the animal that once roamed wild on the plateaus extending from Anatolia to Iran. Crete in the Mediterranean and Mycenae in southern Greece served as the main stepping stones; Anatolia, Phoenicia, and Egypt provided the bridges. In its metallurgy Crete followed the Egyptian and north Syrian tradition. Similarity marks certain of the ceramics of Western Asia and Eastern Europe. That ancient Near East culture formed the background of the early European civilization was a fact barely realized a hundred years ago. Nor was the debt that Greece and Rome owed this area fully appreciated until recently, a debt that does not necessarily make the grandeur that was Greece less grand, or the greatness that was Rome less great. In fact, it was not until the early nineteenth century that scholars began to rediscover the empires of Egypt, Babylonia, and Assyria and to reconstruct their cultural institutions. As for the Hittites and their empire in Anatolia, their discovery began as late as the twentieth century.

But Europeans were not mere borrowers and imitators. They adopted, adapted, and originated. The measure of energy, inventiveness, and independence which they introduced into the old world enabled them to set the old on new paths and subsequently to create institutions of government and bodies of science, philosophy, and art which far excelled what had preceded them.

SCIENTIFIC DEBT

Domestication of plants and animals, metallurgy, pottery, and other material objects are not the only gifts from the Near East. Our seven-day week stems from the story of creation as recorded in Genesis and from an early Semitic system of numeration in which the number seven figured. The Babylonians considered seven celestial bodies to be planets. To the first of these they dedicated the first day of the week, hence our Sunday; to the second, the moon, the second day was devoted, whence comes our Monday. The seventh, Saturn, gave us Saturday. From those same Mesopotamians we inherited the sexagesimal system represented today by our division of the hour into sixty minutes, the minutes into sixty seconds and the circle into three hundred and sixty (a multiple of sixty) degrees. The division of the day into twelve hours comes from Egypt. From Egypt also comes the solar calendar introduced by Julius Caesar and reformed by Pope Gregory.

SPIRITUAL LEGACY

Great as all these cultural contributions in our heritage may be, still greater are the spiritual and intellectual elements initiated by Palestine and Phoenicia. Islam, the third great monotheistic religion, was an historical outgrowth of Judaism and Christianity. All three are the products of the religious experience of one people, the Semitic-speaking people, living within an area of a few-hundred-miles square. Long after those palaces, temples, towers, and pyramids that were built by Egyptians, Assyrians, Babylonians, and Chaldaeans shall have crumbled into dust (and most of them have already done so), the prophetic voice of ancient Israel, emphasizing for the first time in the history of mankind the virtues of mercy, justice and righteousness, and the record of the life and teachings of Jesus of Nazareth, laying stress on love as a fundamental law of life—all recorded in letters derived from those developed and disseminated by Phoenicians on the coast of Lebanon—shall remain a source of inspiration and enlightenment to numberless men and women throughout the world. The clocks we see, the calendar we use, the religions we profess, the ethical and legal codes we apply, the art we cherish, the writing we employ, the languages we speak, the names we give our children all bear witness to the debt we owe the ancients of the Near East. Uncountable, indeed, are the elements in that composite body of practices and beliefs constituting Western civilization which were earlier gleaned from the vanished cultures of Western Asia, enriched and transmitted to later generations.

Nor did the Near Eastern contributions cease in later times. As the medieval representatives of the Semitic peoples and heirs of the Hellenistic civilization, the Arabs held aloft the torch of enlightenment for centuries throughout the world. From their Syrian capital, Damascus, they ruled an empire extending from the Atlantic to the confines of China. In their later capital, Baghdad—heir of Ctesiphon, Babylon, and Ur—they translated Greek, Persian, and Hindu works of science and philosophy which were subsequently enriched by original contributions. Between the middle of the eighth and the early thirteenth centuries, Arabic was the medium for the expression of the highest and richest thought in philosophy, literature, art and science. Such words as algebra, zero and the Arabic numerals in mathematics; zenith, nadir and the names of stars in astronomy; alcohol, alkali, alchemy in medicine; sugar, coffee, candy, orange, lemon, atlas, satin in agriculture and industry; divan, mattress, sofa and jar in everyday vocabulary testify to the height and extent of Arab culture.

UNIQUE GEOSTRATEGIC POSITION

Such free transmission and dissemination of cultural elements from the cluster of civilizations centered in that area would not have been possible but for the geography of the region, both as to local physical characteristics and global setting. The entire area may be considered as one super-peninsula, mostly arid and partly sandy. A minor but distinct unit within the larger one is the Fertile Crescent, a semicircular belt of arable land enclosed on all sides by deserts, mountains and seas. The eastern end constitutes the fertile plain of Mesopotamia, the western the equally fertile valley of Egypt. Assyria, Syria, Lebanon and Palestine may be considered the arc of the Crescent framing the Desert, itself a continuation of the Arabian peninsula. Deserts were primitive man's thoroughfares and did not within certain limits greatly impede his movements. As the scene of some of man's greatest cultural achievements, the Fertile Crescent is the most significant part of our area.

The Anatolian plateau is continued into the Iranian, with intervening but not impassable mountains. Globally the whole region is so strategically posed as to form a link between Europe, Asia and Africa and a bridge between two oceanic areas, the one washed by the Atlantic and its long Mediterranean projection and the other by the Arabian-Indian Ocean and its Red Sea and Persian Gulf arms. When the known world was much smaller and its people had not ventured beyond the Pillars of Hercules (Gibraltar), the Mediterranean appropriately acquired its name "the Middle of the Earth." Across the bridges of the eastern islands of this sea, which unites and divides the three historic continents, Eastern civilization first advanced to Europe.

Somewhere in this intercontinental, interoceanic region whenever a man in the course of history—from Alexander to Napoleon—dreamed of a world empire, he found himself sooner or later fighting for the realization of his dream. Its military history is epitomized in those multi-lingual inscriptions at the mouth of the Dog River on the Lebanon coast memorializing the passage, among others, of the Egyptian Pharaoh Ramses, the Assyrian invader Esarhaddon, the Neo-Babylonian empire builder Nebuchadnezzar and the Roman emperor Marcus Aurelius. The semi-legendary Trojan wars were fought some 1200 years before Christ for the control of the Dardanelles; the Anglo-Egyptian clashes of the mid-twentieth century were occasioned by the desire for the control of the Suez Canal. In the nineteenth century, rivalry between the three great European powers—Russia, Great Britain, and France—for spheres of influence in the declining Ottoman Empire resulted in more than one armed conflict. In the terminology of modern geostrategists the Near East is "the heart land of the Euro-Asian-African world island."

The story of the Near East is, therefore, not only the story of Moses and Christ, Zoroaster and Muhammad, but also of Darius and Alexander, Caesar and Cleopatra, Chingiz Khan and Hulagu, Napoleon and Allenby. Its Eastern Mediterranean waters served as a Phoenician and then as a Greek lake before becoming a part of Rome's *mare nostrum* (the control of which was contested by Carthage); subsequently it became the center of the Ottoman crescent empire and lastly as the scene for the clashing of rival ambitions of Great Britain, France, and Russia.

The recent discovery and exploitation of petroleum, vital for industry in peace and even more vital in war, has greatly enhanced the strategic importance of the area. Sixty-two per cent of the total oil reserves of the world is estimated to be embedded in the soil of Arabia, Iraq, and Iran. Meantime the advent of the age of air navigation turned such cities as Cairo and Beirut into centers of communication for the all-weather round-the-world trips. The contemporary struggle between the great powers of democracy and of communism has brought the states of the area into the international limelight, as both contending parties realized that the political orientation of Turks, Persians, and Arabs may have a decisive effect on the shape of things to come.

To the different states of the Near East which in the last few years have embraced the Western European doctrine of nationalism, the rediscovery of their past glory and ancient history has been a source of infinite pride and inspiration. The contemporary Arabs never tire of reciting the story of the caliphate centered in Damascus, where it attained unprecedented heights, and later in Baghdad, when it enjoyed the golden age of Arabic literary activity. The Iranians, whose memory of the greatest period in their historic career—that of Cyrus, Darius, Xerxes and others of the Achaemenid dynasty—had been dimmed by the vicissitudes of time, did not awake to the full realization of that heritage and to the claim of superiority based on descent until the late nineteenth century. Even the Kemalist Turks began to evoke the ghost of the Hittite past and take national pride in the archeological finds in the terrain not occupied by them until later times. Surely the ancient Near East is still living in modern Europe and America as well as in the hearts and minds of modern Near Easterners.

II   *The Setting of the Stage*

THROUGH the near endless changes of states, peoples, and cultures, one relatively unchanging factor continued with its determining effect on the course of men and events—the geographical factor. Physical geography was the open stage on which was enacted the earliest scene in the great drama of man's evolution from savagery and his triumph over nature. Not only is the history of the Near East a part of universal history but it is also a part of the history of the earth upon which it happened.

Ten millenniums or so before Christ, while northern Europe was still blanketed with ice and the Alps and the Pyrenees were still capped with glaciers, the Near East must have enjoyed more hospitable weather than Europe and received more bountiful and more widely distributed rain over the whole year than it has in historic times. Trees and grass grew where the desert rules today. Desiccation accompanied the final retreat of the ice cap in Eurasia in the centuries immediately preceding the dawn of history. River beds, now wadies, in the Egyptian desert, the Arabian peninsula, and the Iranian plateau testify to an early pluvial period. But within historic times the desiccation must be attributed to the destruction of irrigation works by wars, invasions, or negligence. The cutting down of trees and promiscuous grazing deprived the soil of plant roots to hold it together, thus facilitating erosion and the denudation of the hillsides by winds and running rain water. Such phenomena as dried-up springs, choked cisterns, ruined settlements on the fringe of the Syrian Desert and in north Syria, as well as deserted villages bordering neglected caravan routes in the Iranian plateau, can be explained as man- rather than nature-produced.

PHYSICAL AND CLIMATIC FEATURES

The stretch of mountain ranges along the western border of this area intercept the passage of the moisture-laden winds from the Atlantic or Mediterranean, tap their resources, and leave the hinterland in a rain shadow zone. The entire interior is therefore marked by dryness bordering on aridity which is reflected in the barren soil. Other than the coastland and river valleys no extensive tracts receive sufficient precipitation in winter and relief from prolonged intrusive heat in summer to sustain agricultural activity. What rain falls is normally crowded into the months of December to February. Corresponding to this twofold nature of the land the population falls into two main categories: settled agriculturists and nomadic wanderers. The interiors of Asia Minor, Iran, Syria, Arabia and the fringes of Egypt are barren waste or desert land inhabited by Bedouins.

Such climatic conditions and topographical characteristics have through the ages determined the general occupation of the population, set rigid limits to its size, and fixed its distribution. While the intercontinental, interoceanic position of the land made of it a broad corridor linking several major parts of the globe, the alternation of mountain ranges and barren or desert lands created geographical pockets where minorities could in isolation maintain their identity and pursue their own way of life unmindful of the general course of events. Until recent years such has been the case of the Armenians and Kurds in the highlands between Anatolia and Iran, the Maronites and Druzes in Lebanon, and innumerable other secluded groups in different recesses of the area. Sectarianism contributed its share to the crystallization of the communities. The ethnic result is admixture in the corridor and comparative purity of blood in the recesses.

THE ANATOLIAN-IRANIAN PLATEAU

The core of both Anatolia and Iran is an enclosed inner plateau ringed by mountain ranges. The Anatolian plateau rises 3000 to 3500 feet above the sea; the one in Iran, occupying about half of the land, rises from 1000 to 3000 feet. Iran is shielded on the north by the Elburz Mountains and on the west and south by the Zagros massif, which further drains any left-over moisture of the westerlies. On both plateaus the climate is one of relatively extreme cold in winter and extreme heat in summer. On the Anatolian plain 10 to 17 inches of rain fall annually; in Tehran, capital of Iran, the average is 9.2 inches. The average January temperature in central Anatolia is 30°F, rising to an average of 86° in July. In Tehran it is 35°F in January and 85°F in July.

The barrier of the Taurus and the Anti-Taurus ranges in southern Anatolia retarded but did not stop communication with the Semitic (later Arab) lands to the south. Together with the climate and the soil of the plateau behind, they contributed to keeping Asia Minor

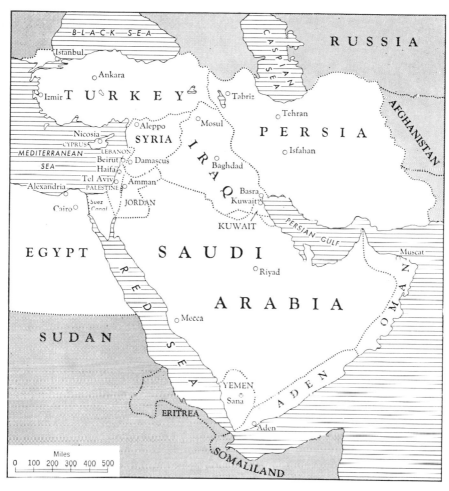

THE NEAR EAST TODAY

The above map shows the modern countries covering the area that is meant by the term Near East as used in this book.

un-Semitic, un-Arabic.   In Iran the bulk of the population gravitates westward.   Throughout history the cultural and commercial orientation has also been westward, toward the Fertile Crescent, rather than eastward toward Central Asia or India.   When the time for imperial expansion came under Achaemenids, Sasanids, and Safawids the lines of least resistance led to Mesopotamia, Syria, and Asia Minor despite the Zagros barrier.   Following the same route in reverse direction the Arabian Moslems overran Persia, temporarily Arabicized and permanently Islamized it.

THE ARABIAN PENINSULA

The ranges of Anatolia and Iran frame a more elevated and less arid plateau than that enclosed by the ranges of Arabia.   The Arabian plateau reaches a height of 2000 to 3000 feet above the sea, dips as it extends eastward.   It is an extension of the African Sahara, from which it is separated by the rift of the Nile and the chasm of the Red Sea. Cupped between the two horns of the Fertile Crescent, the Syrian Desert is structurally a continuation of the sandy core of the Arabian peninsula. The highlands of the peninsula stretch all the way along the sea, attain a height of 9000 feet in Hejaz, the holy land of Islam, and an estimated height of 14,000 feet thirty miles west of Sana, modern capital of Yemen.   So complete is the drainage of the westerlies during their passage over the mountains that the hinterland is left almost rainless. Even the favored coastal area does not receive more than ten inches a year.   Only in the southwestern region, Yemen, are there sufficient periodic rains to warrant systematic cultivation of the land.   The nucleus of the northern interior is Nejd, a pastoral tableland.   As the nursery of the warlike Wahhabis, represented today by the Saud (Suʻud) royal family, it is the only region that has figured in history.   Otherwise the entire interior of the peninsula is almost a barren land whose monotony is relieved by only an occasional oasis.   The average summer temperature in Dhahran, headquarters of the Arabian American Oil Company (Aramco), is 118°F, reaching 165° in the sun.   The peninsula, the largest single unit in the Near East, does not possess a single river that could be called perennial.   Its south central part, an area of 400,000 square miles called al-Rabʻ al-Khali (the empty quarter), had not been traversed by Westerners until the last score of years or so.

THE VALLEY OF THE ONE AND THAT OF THE TWO RIVERS

The valley at the eastern horn of the Fertile Crescent is largely created by the twin rivers, the Tigris and the Euphrates; the one at the extremity of the western horn is likewise created by the Nile.   Both cultivatable,

Egypt and lower Mesopotamia are literally the gifts of the rivers that flow through them; their soil is the alluvium deposited year after year on a substratum of sand or rock, except at the lowest courses of the rivers where the build-up has been from the sea. In Egypt the rich deposit is about forty feet deep. The irrigation and drinking waters of both almost rainless countries also come from these rivers. Because they are annually replenished, the valleys are almost inexhaustibly fertile. The three-hundred-mile stretch south of present-day Baghdad must have been reclaimed, Delta-wise, from the sea partly in historic times. The site of Eridu, an early Sumerian capital and seaport, now lies some hundred and fifty miles from the head of the Persian Gulf. The present rate of reclamation is estimated at one and a half miles per century.

In Mesopotamia and Egypt spring and autumn are short transitional periods between summers of intense heat and winters of insufficient rain, leaving all tracts outside the range of irrigation unfit for settled life. In Cairo the mean July temperature is 84°F; over the whole country the summer heat reaches a maximum of 100°F, but the nights are cooler. The winter is mild; Cairo's mean January temperature is 53°F. Rain does not on the average exceed 8 inches and falls mostly along the coast. The average temperature in Basra at the head of the Persian Gulf in July is 97°; in January it is 52°. Baghdad receives an average rainfall of 5.5 inches, but Mosul gets 13 inches. Both countries, being alluvial, are almost stoneless and timberless (except for the date palm of Mesopotamia), necessitating incursions or trips into Syria and Lebanon for a supply of wood for monumental structures. Originally a wild plant which no doubt served as a main attraction to that valley for the early man, the date palm now provides a highly nutritious and reliable fruit crop that under the label of Basra enjoys world reputation. The dryness of climate in lower Mesopotamia has been responsible for the abundance and the state of preservation yield of the vestigial mounds of ancient cities in it.

It was likewise the dryness in Egypt which gave the country its unique preservative character and enabled archeologists to win some of their earliest and most sensational triumphs in its soil. Last among the dramatic finds was the barge of the pyramid builder Cheops which for days in the spring of 1954 usurped front page space in the world's press. It was largely through its Egyptian experience that archeology developed into a science, acquiring techniques and methods that were later applied in other fields.

Similarities in climate and topography between the valley of the Nile and that of the Tigris-Euphrates do not make the two situations exactly identical. In Egypt there is more regularity and unity. For thousands of miles its life-giving stream traverses an almost flat surface, having no sizable tributaries on either side. Its floods are therefore steady and predictable. From a plane the river looks like a snake stretching snugly through a patch of green, extending about seven miles on either side, beyond which the desert is resumed. The twin rivers of Mesopotamia begin in the Armenian mountains, where they are fed by snowfall and from which they thread their paths irregularly and tortuously southward. As they proceed, they receive a number of flows, especially the Tigris lying close to the Zagros. The banks of the Tigris have had no considerable settlement between Mosul and Baghdad—a medieval city—and hardly any worth mentioning between Baghdad and the gulf. In its upper course the Euphrates suddenly turns southeast, belying its promise to continue southwest and to empty into the Mediterranean. Both rivers have within historic times shifted their courses, a disturbing factor. Lower Mesopotamia has thus been subjected to a more radical change than has Egypt. The differing nature of the Tigris-Euphrates and the Nile valleys has been reflected in the two civilizations cradled on these river banks. In the Sumero-Babylonian society man felt somewhat helpless vis-à-vis capricious gods and tended toward pessimism in his philosophy of life. In contrast, the Egyptian became imbued with a sense of the benignity of nature and developed an optimistic outlook.

Mesopotamia is less homogeneous in its configuration and is less sheltered than Egypt, the long valley of which is practically insulated on all sides. Being easily accessible on different sides Mesopotamia has had a history punctuated by invasions from Elam and Iran in the east, migrations and invasions from Arabia in the south, and raids from Hittiteland in the northwest. The valley of the two rivers was more widely open to outside influences both militarily and culturally. Politically it was not completely unified until the age of Hammurabi in the eighteenth century, some one thousand years later than the valley of one river had become a political unit. Egypt on the other hand, flanked by desert on three sides and the sea on the fourth, was not so accessible and was more easily defensible. Its isolation for a long stretch of its early history enabled it to develop a stable civilization which was on a consistently high level. The physical unity of the land with a sharply defined habitable valley found expression in the marked homogeneity of its cultural development and in the traditionally conservative character of its population. Security, unity, self-assuredness, love of nature, and *joie de vivre* became the main springs of life. It was not until after a steady, peaceful career of over a thousand years that the first major invaders, in the person of the Hyksos from Syria, came knocking at its gates. More than another thousand years had to elapse before the country experienced another invasion, this time from the Assyrians in the seventh century.

SYRIA-LEBANON

The Syria-Lebanon area is also marked by mountains fronting on the west. They rise to a height of about 5000 feet in the Nusayri region, and to 11,000 feet in the Maronite district of Lebanon to the south. These ranges, paralleled in Lebanon by the Anti-Lebanon which culminates in Mount Hermon (Jabal al-Shaykh), catch most of the precipitation from maritime winds, leaving but little for the Syrian hinterland. The coastland of Lebanon and its western slope, ancient Phoenicia, receive enough rain to make it the garden of the Near East. In summer, however, absolute drought rules. Beirut receives an annual average of 35.9 inches of rain, more than parts of Great Britain, but all normally crowded into the months of November to March. But Damascus, behind the double rain screen of the Lebanon, gets only 10 inches; Aleppo receives 14.6, and Gaza 16. The mean annual temperature in Beirut is 68°F; in Jerusalem, which is 2550 feet high, the average temperature of July—generally the hottest month—is 75°F; in January it is 47°F.

PALESTINE

Palestine is geologically a continuation of Lebanon, and Transjordan proper is a continuation of Anti-Lebanon and Syria. The Lebanese maritime plain continues through the plain of Sharon, which extends from Mount Carmel southward and connects with the littoral of Philistia. The highlands in Upper Galilee north of Safad attain an elevation of 3935 feet, the highest in Palestine. The earliest human skeletal remains discovered in the area and among the earliest found anywhere else were recently unearthed at the caves of Carmel. They range from the Neanderthal type (so called from a cave in Germany excavated in 1856) through progressive forms to some that are almost human. The Neanderthal man of Palestine was short in stature, about five feet and five inches, not quite erect, stocky in build, with a thick and heavy head, low sloping skull, and chinless lower jaw. He still lived in caves, subsisted on plants and animals in their natural condition, and evidently knew how to make fire. His tools consisted of irregular flakes and rough chunks of flint which he employed as hand-axes, scrapers, choppers and hammers. He had not yet passed from savagery.

BOOKS TO READ

Childe, V. Gordon, *The Dawn of European Civilization,* 5th ed. (London, 1950); *New Light on the Most Ancient East,* 4th ed. (London, 1952).

Field, Henry, *Ancient and Modern Man in Southwestern Asia* (Coral Gables, Florida, 1956).

Fisher, W. D., *The Middle East,* 3rd ed. (London, 1956).

Hogarth, D. G., *The Nearer East* (London, 1902).

Semple, Ellen C., *The Goegraphy of the Mediterranean Region* (London, 1932).

Smith, George A., *The Historical Geography of the Holy Land,* 11th ed. (New York, 1934).

III *From Savagery to Civilization through Barbarism*

I<small>N HIS</small> arduous and steady evolution the preliterary man passed, from the standpoint of mode of living, through three main cultural stages of momentous significance: food gathering, food production, and craftsmanship The first stage was the oldest and by far the longest, lasting for at least half a million years. Throughout that period of man's existence on earth, he sustained life by the gathering of plant and animal food in its natural and wild condition. Toward the end of that period he took the steps which ended in changing the basis of his economy from gathering to producing food. This was achieved through the domestication of plants and animals which gave him for the first time in his career control over his sources of livelihood and freed him from total bondage to his physical environment. This second stage was of relatively short duration, lasting only a few thousand years. The two economies, of course, overlapped in part and were not entirely exclusive. The story of Esau, the hunter, and Jacob, the farmer (Gen. 25:27 *seq.*), illustrates that point. From the standpoint of industry, the first stage, in which a roughly chipped stone hand-ax was the predominant tool, has been called the Old Stone Age (Palaeolithic). The second stage—in which more polished stone tools were devised and used as knives, saws, chisels, awls, and axes—has been called the New Stone Age (Neolithic).

In the third stage of man's evolution pottery was developed. weaving was discovered, the wheel was invented and metal was utilized for tools and weapons. The wide use of copper and then its alloy, bronze, ushered in a new era of metallurgy. The earliest stage was one of savagery, the second of barbarism, and the third of civilization. All three are well recorded through tools, weapons, pottery sherds, as well as skeletal and other remains. All three preceded the dawn of history, whose break was signalized by a fully developed system of writ-

17

ing, heralded by the cuneiform of Mesopotamia and the hieroglyphic of Egypt, at the turn of the fourth millennium before Christ.

MAN AS FOOD GATHERER

Before the sixth pre-Christian millennium, when both valleys of the lower Nile and of the Tigris-Euphrates were still marshy and probably uninhabitable, other parts of the Fertile Crescent, as well as the Anatolian-Iranian plateau, were receiving a more generous supply of rain more widely distributed over the seasons. That area must have looked like a park land rich in trees, animals, and grass. Climatically, zoologically, and botanically it fulfilled the conditions for a mode of life based on wild plants and animals.

For hundreds of thousands of years, perhaps ninety-eight per cent of his age on earth, man lived on uncultivated grains, berries, seeds, fruits, and vegetables, and on such wild animals as deer, gazelle, boar, goats, and sheep. He gathered and ate his food where and when he could find it. In its quest our savage ancestor had to roam from place to place and struggle for existence against the natural elements and animate foes. Life indeed was precarious. It was mobile. The source of supply was unreliable.

At some point in his struggle for survival this man sought the aid of nodules which were all ready or which he himself chipped on both sides (hence the name bifaces) and which he used as hand- or fist-axes. The arc of the Fertile Crescent abounds in flint. These crude almond- or pear-shaped stone cores were gradually improved in shape and roughly given a fine edge. Further advance was made when a flake knocked off from a core was so polished as to render it serviceable as a scraper, a chisel, or an awl and later as a blade with parallel edges that cut. Flakes may have been struck off from flint nodules with the express purpose of making them tools. As such polished implements came to prevail, man passed on into the Neolithic Age. Thus did the Old Stone Age shade off into the New and merge into it. Complete sequence of stone industries has been discovered in different sites of the Near East, particularly the Syria-Lebanon-Palestine part.

The early Palaeolithic man must have experienced fires engendered by lightning or other natural occurrences, but he had to wait for generations before he pondered over that strange phenomenon and tried to generate and control it himself. When he did, he initiated one of the earliest and most significant revolutions in his progressive march toward ultimate civilization. The earliest fragments of coal thus far discovered come from one of the lowest levels in a Carmel cave. They are probably some 150,000 years old. Charcoal, which continued in

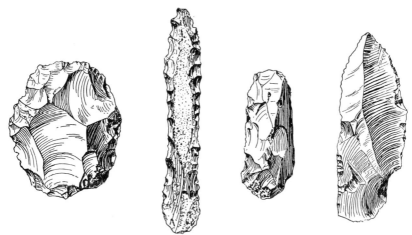

Garrod and Bates, THE STONE AGE OF MOUNT CARMEL (Oxford University Press, 1937)

EARLY STONE IMPLEMENTS FROM A CAVE AT MOUNT CARMEL

use as the most convenient fuel until it was replaced in modern times by gas and electricity, comes back today as a luxury cooking fuel for which restaurants charge extra.   An equally dynamic achievement of early Palaeolithic times was the development of language—that distinctive means of communication between one human being and another and contributed to the welding of isolated individuals into groups.

Man was then still living under a crude herd or tribal system in natural or artificial caves.   Later on he learned to protect his body with the skins of the animals he killed.   The luxury for which the present-day husband toils and saves to offer to his wife as a present was readily acquired by his primitive ancestor in the pursuit of his daily occupation.   Settlements on a considerable scale could not have been possible before man became a food producer—a farmer.

MAN, THE FOOD PRODUCER

Sometime in the twilight zone between the Stone Age and the Metal Age the initial steps were taken leading to the purposeful cultivation of plants and the domestication of animals.   It probably all began when some wild grain included in man's food happened to spill near the camping ground and was noticed as a dense growth in the following year.   Some man or woman must have realized that by refraining from consuming all the seeds gathered at a certain time and then scattering some over the ground a new crop might be expected.   The cultivation of wheat and barley opened the way for other cereals and other vegetables and culminated in the cultivation of such fruits as olives, grapes, and figs. The date palm was native to Arabia as it was to Mesopotamia. Progressive desiccation, following the retreat of the last ice sheet from the north, may have provided further stimulation toward the adoption of a food-producing economy.

The discovery of the domesticability of animals, like other great discoveries of that age, was more by chance rather than by design. Its development was dictated by necessity and need rather than by speculation or superiority of intellect. The process involved more than taming; it included learning to breed the new stock. Of the wild animals the dog, a relative of the wolf, was presumably the first to be brought into such close relationship with man. It all started when one of these

TEMPLE SERVANTS MILKING COWS, STRAINING, AND STORING MILK   From a Frieze
of the Temple at Tell al-Ubaid, *ca.* 3100 B.C.

wild beasts was attracted to, and then attached to, a camp. "Throw the poor dog a bone" may have first been prompted by a sentimental urge but later by utilitarian considerations. Taming was the first step toward domestication, the second being breeding under human control. Besides his services in hunting, guarding and acting as garbage disposer, the dog developed from being man's first mute slave to becoming his ally and most loyal of animal friends. It has also become the most widely domesticated animal. In ancient Egypt it was commonly respected and mummified. The strata of a Carmel cave provide the first evidence of the domestication of the dog. Pigs, nature's scavengers, were evidently attracted by refuse food around camps and dwellings and gradually tamed and bred. Other animals were domesticated in due course during the agricultural era. The ass was the first beast of burden to be tamed. The horse came later and was followed by the camel. In historic times not a single animal is known to have been added to the domesticated list.

With the full adoption of crop and stock raising, man tended to give up his nomadic life and become a settler, a farmer, or a shepherd. The settlements grew into villages. Land ownership, personal property, and the accumulation of wealth became possible. The germs of capitalism were thus laid. With the enlargement and enrichment of diet and with a more secure economy, population increased and a more complex social order began to evolve. A larger measure of leisure became available and could be utilized for the pursuit of the higher things of life such as speculation, religion, and art. Elbowroom in time is as essential for growth as elbowroom in space. What many an overworked man of today, on snatching a little leisure, covets by way of entertainment—hunting and fishing—so preoccupied his primitive ancestor as to leave him no leisure. The face of the Near East is dotted with human settlements dating back to the fifth millennium and antedating any other settlements in the world. Nuzi (near Kirkuk) in Iraq, Tell (mound of) al-Judaydah in north Syria, Byblus (Gebal, modern Jubayl) in Lebanon, and Jericho in Palestine may be cited as illustrations. Of these the last two could claim the honor of being the oldest living towns. Uruk in lower Mesopotamia has yielded the earliest evidence of a full-fledged urban settlement with a temple, city wall, and brick houses.

THE ORIGINAL CENTER

The arc and segment of the Fertile Crescent which comprise Assyria, Syria, Lebanon, and Palestine meet the necessary requirements for passage from a food-gathering to a food-producing economy. This must have been accomplished in the first half of the last pre-Christian millennium. Here the relatives of the wild cereals and animals that were first pressed into the service of humanity are native. Wild barley also grows in Anatolia and Iran and wild wheat in western Persia. Flint sickles from Natuf, northwest of Jerusalem, are among the earliest thus far found, suggesting the practice of some form of agriculture there. From a Carmel cave come circular basins with raised rims which might have been used for pounding grain. From no other people, excepting north Syrian contemporaries of the Natufians, come such evidence of possible early agricultural practice. A variety of sheep that gave rise to the domestic one inhabits the highlands from Asia Minor to north Persia. The earliest representation of a domestic sheep occurs on a Sumerian vase of the fourth millennium before Christ. Other edible plants and domesticable animals abound in that general area. Such facts point to it as the nursery of stock breeding and deliberate plant cultivation. Emigrants from Syria-Palestine presumably introduced wheat as well as viniculture into Egypt. The invention of the plow raised hoe culture to a higher stage. The pictures of the Sumerian plow, the Assyrian plow, and the Egyptian plow

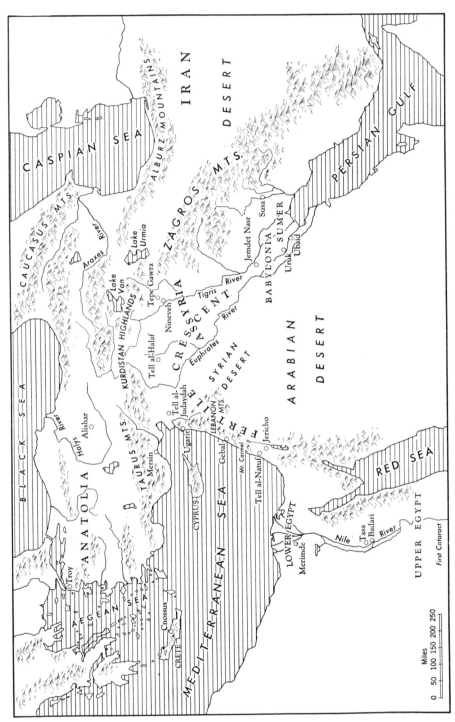

STONE AGE SITES IN THE NEAR EAST

Macmillan and Co., Ltd.

Fig. 1. SUMERIAN PLOW   Fig. 2. ASSYRIAN PLOW   Fig. 3. EGYPTIAN PLOW   Fig. 4.
MODERN ARAB PALESTINIAN PLOW

found on the monuments look strikingly alike; they do not radically differ from the ones used in Syria, Lebanon, or Palestine today.

Philologists contribute to the argument. The word for wheat and the word for vineyard in ancient Egyptian are unmistakable loan words from Sumero Akkadian. They are the words used today in Arabic.

There is reason to believe that agriculture, animal domestication and other elements of Neolithic culture developed in one general center and spread thence in successive waves to the ends of Asia, Africa, and Europe. Whether the spread was due to actual migration of tribes, cultural diffusion, or both cannot be ascertained. The Neolithic Age of Western Asia was in full progress by 6000 B.C.; that stage did not begin in Europe until 3000 B.C.; in other parts of Asia and Africa it came even later. The parents of Europe's domesticated animals seem to have been the same as those of Western Asia. The same holds true in the case of the early cultivated European plants. Such a wide distribution of similar plants and animals, as well as of similar core implements and of types of pottery, strikingly similar in shape and technique, argue in favor of cultural penetration from some focal point as against their evolving independently at different times and places.

AS A CRAFTSMAN: POTTERY

While Palaeolithic hunters of Western Europe were still chasing the reindeer, the Neolithic man of the Near East was making notable advances in farming, cattle raising, and polishing or grinding flint implements.   More than that he was beginning to make pottery, develop weaving, and work metals into tools more serviceable for his purpose. He was, in brief, paving the way for the age of metallurgy and of writing.

Early in his agricultural experience man must have felt the need for storing or transporting that part of his foodstuff which he could not consume at a certain time.   This need presumably led to the invention of receptacles which perhaps first took the form of baskets made simply and roughly by plaiting stems of reed or grass which were then daubed with mud, and of bags produced by folding animal skins. Bags were especially useful for holding surplus water.   It was probably by chance that he discovered clay hardened and kept its form when it was subjected to heat.   This must have been accomplished by sun drying first, but later it was baked in an open fire, and still later in an oven.   This is the art of ceramics in its infancy.   The technique was greatly improved with the discovery that covering the surface of clay with sand produced a glaze which rendered the vessel waterproof.

Pottery made its first appearance in the lower strata of Tell al-Halaf (ancient Gozan, on a tributary of the Euphrates), Tell al-Judaydah (northeast of Antioch), Jericho, and other cities in the Near East dating back to about 5000 B.C.   All hand-fashioned and monochrome, it was invented independently in different places and as it developed and

Courtesy of Oregon State System of Higher Education

PAINTED POTTERY VESSELS FROM THE PREHISTORIC AGE IN MESOPOTAMIA spread acquired technical and artistic qualities, a far cry from the first clay pots shaped like baskets or leather bags. Especially attractive was its polychrome variety. Sherds of dishes, bowls, platters, jars and cups from Syria, Palestine and Mesopotamia rank among the finest relics of ancient days. In pottery as in flint working, Egypt developed its industry along indigenous lines. While easily breakable, pottery is virtually indestructible. Long after wood and metal had decayed to the vanishing point fragments of vessels remain to tell their story. In the absence of written records and other relics of the past they serve as a boon to the archeologist and as a valuable criterion for measuring the level of culture and its interrelationship with neighboring cultures.

THE WHEEL

A strong forward push was given to the art of ceramics after 4000 B.C. when the wheel made its debut. This was indeed an epoch-making technical invention, resulting in symmetrically rounded pottery,

Smith, EARLY HISTORY OF ASSYRIA (London)

A REPRESENTATION OF A WAR CHARIOT FROM PREDYNASTIC UR The chariot is drawn by asses (?) and guided by a footman. Its wall is covered with a skin. The weapons of the charioteer's "second man" are shown.

wheeled carriages and carts, finer fabrics and better wrought metals. It made possible the war chariot. The wheel established long distance communication by land and sea and revolutionized the transportation of men and goods. By the third pre-Christian millennium this

device had spread from the Indus to the Orontes. Vehicular wheels
from this area and millennium are so identically constructed as to suggest diffusion from a common center. The potter's wheel reached
Hamah in Syria and Byblus in Lebanon about 2800 B.C. and even
Egypt in the pyramid age. Our modern economy runs on wheels whose
origins can be traced into round blocks of wood invented in Mesopotamia. The earliest vehicles were evidently sleds. A royal sled of an
early queen of Ur (of biblical association with Abraham) has survived
in her tomb. Meantime woodworkers (future carpenters) were busy
making boats first propelled by oars, then by sails and later capable of
navigating seas. The earliest boats on the Euphrates were simply inflated animal skins of the type still used there. Those of Egypt were
pieces of papyrus bound together. The largest and best seafaring boats
were made by Phoenicians. Hitherto primarily a discoverer, the hero
of our story is now well on his way to becoming an inventor.

METALLURGY: COPPER

An adequate wheel implies the use of metal tools and consequently
the existence of professional smiths. With potters, carpenters and
smiths began specialization in labor. Smiths appear early in Uruk
(biblical Erech, modern Warka) associated with the wheeled vehicles.
For making a wheel the saw is essential, and the saw cannot be made
of stone or wood. Extensive utilization of copper and bronze was
possible only in a settled society where regular trade had developed.
In Neolithic times native metals and precious stones were used for
ornamentation or magical effect, as indicated by finds in Mesopotamian
tombs of the early fourth pre-Christian millennium. But the first
important metal that served as a conclusion to barbarism and prelude
to civilization was undoubtedly copper. Deposits of copper ore were
found in Armenia, Asia Minor, southeastern Arabia and Sinai. The
metal was first used in Mesopotamia between 4000 and 3500 B.C.,
after the introduction of pottery, but it did not gain widespread use till
about 3000 B.C. It could not have displaced stone at once. Mining,
extracting, smelting and shaping were some of the processes necessary
before the possibility of wide distribution. The use of copper did not
reach Europe until about a thousand years later (*ca.* 2000 B.C.),
possibly introduced by Near Eastern traders in search of the metal.
In the second half of the fourth millennium B.C. other Near Easterners,
Armenoids, had evidently settled in Crete, the Aegean islands and parts
of Greece, crossed the Bosporus and advanced through the Danube

valley into Central Europe, introducing other cultural elements relating to the domestication of plants and animals. Prior to that time Semites from Syria, originally from Arabia, were doing the same in Egypt.

BRONZE

The discovery that copper could be hammered into shape was seconded by the realization that that could be more readidly achieved if the metal was heated. Another important step was made forward when it was learned that copper could be hardened when tin is added. This was bronze, which heralded a new era in technology. By 3000 B.C. bronze was in use in Sumer. The period between 3000 and 1200 B.C., at which time iron began its wide career, has been designated the bronze age. The first certain development of iron occurred in Asia Minor, land of the Hittites, during the fourteenth pre-Christian century. It did not reach Europe until the eleventh or tenth century before Christ and the New World until the sixteenth after Christ.

The employment of metal tools rendered men's tasks easier, increased their efficiency and in time of war gave them a decided advantage over conservative foes that clung to stone weapons. The advantage thus introduced must have been no less than that bestowed by the invention of firearms vis-à-vis bow and arrow arms. Without metal tools the digging of canals for the exploitation of wider areas of the river valleys, the building of boats capable of negotiating the Persian Gulf, Red Sea and the Mediterranean and the erection of monumental structures for royalty and deity would not have been possible. Besides facilitating irrigation, canals served as highways for communication. The use of copper, bronze, iron and other metals has been responsible for the greatest recorded advances in industry and, until the advent of the airplane, for the largest measure of progress in transportation.

BOOKS TO READ

Albright, William F., *The Archaeology of Palestine* (London, 1952); *From the Stone Age to Christianity* (Baltimore, 1940).

Braidwood, Robert J., *The Near East and the Foundations for Civilization* (Chicago, 1952).

Childe, V. Gordon, *New Light on the Most Ancient East*, 4th ed. (London, 1952).

Coon, Carleton S., *Caravan: The Story of the Middle East*, rev. ed. (New York, 1958).

Field, Henry, *Ancient and Modern Man in Southwestern Asia* (Coral Gables, Florida, 1956).

Frankfort, Henri, *The Birth of Civilization in the Near East* (London, 1951).

Turner, Ralph, *The Great Cultural Traditions,* vol. I, *The Ancient Cities* (New York, 1941).

IV *The Dawn of History*

CERAMICS and metallurgy opened the way for urban civilization. With them man passed from prehistory to protohistory. The invention of writing marks the passage from a preliterary into a literary area. With adequate writing history begins. Through this invention man was at last enabled to record his experience, preserve his knowledge, and transmit the whole to later generations. Writing continues to be the criterion for distinguishing civilizations from lower cultures.

The duration of the historic period of mankind, 5000 years, is but a small fraction of the prehistoric period. If we could compress man's age on earth into one single day of 12 hours, his literary period would begin at about 11:53 P.M., the Crusades would have been fought about 1 minute and 44 seconds ago, and America discovered 55 seconds ago. But man's existence is in turn out of all proportion to the history of the earth itself. If the earth's age could be compressed into one single year, the first eight months would be completely devoid of life; mammals would not make their appearance until the second week of December; man would make his debut on December 31 at 11:45 P.M., writing would have been invented less than a minute ago, Christ would have been born 22 seconds ago, and America discovered six seconds ago.

WRITING: CUNEIFORM AND HIEROGLYPHIC

The oldest extant written remains come from Mesopotamia, more specifically Uruk, from shortly before 3000 B.C. They represent temple accounts with conventional numerals. The language is Sumerian, the pre-Semitic tongue of the valley, later superseded by Babylonian (Akkadian) and Assyrian both members of the Semitic family. The script is called cuneiform (wedge shaped) because of the arrowheaded characters produced by a stylus pressed on a soft clay tablet. Egyptian writing came shortly after its appearance in Mesopotamia and has been designated hieroglyphic (sacred). For material it

29

first used papyrus and a sort of ink.   Both cuneiform and hieroglyphic appear full fledged at the very dawn of history, presupposing a long period of growth.

Though originating independently and developing separately, both scripts indicate a beginning in picture drawing.   Even today illiterate cooks, when marketing, roughly sketch ovals for eggs, pendent clusters for grapes or bananas and round figures for apples or pears.   In its first stage the rude picture represented an object; by a slight variation it could express an idea.   A representation of a human body with uplifted arms conveyed the idea of prayer; with hand at the mouth , the idea of eating.   The pictograph then became an ideograph.   But whether pictograph or ideograph, the pictorial sign expressed no word.

In the second stage, the phonetic, the sign was used for a sound or group of sounds.   The sound was a syllable consisting of a consonant and a vowel.   A monosyllabic word then could be represented by one symbol.   By that time pictures had become so conventionalized and formalized as to lose all pictorial qualities.   More, however, of those qualities have been retained in hieroglyphics.   It was left for the Phoenicians to take the last step and employ syllabic symbols exclusively, thus developing a true alphabet.[1]   In the alphabet the script, which started with pictographs and developed into syllables, reached its climax.

Though superseded as a spoken language around 1800 B.C. by Akkadian (Babylonian), Sumerian remained the classical language which was used in ritual, magic, and the legal code for the entire Mesopotamian area.   Its script survived until the first Christian century, a record thus far unmatched by Greek, Latin, or Arabic.   The latest dated cuneiform tablet was written in A.D. 57.   Cuneiform writing was adopted by Babylonian, Assyrian and Hurrian (Horite in the Old Testament), Hittite, Ugaritic (Phoenician of Ras al-Shamrah), and Old Persian.   Old Persian, which appeared with Elamite and Assyrian in a trilingual inscription of Darius I (*ca.* 520 B.C.) on a rock near the ruined town of Behistun (Bisutun), provided the key for the nineteenth century deciphering of Akkadian and ultimately Sumerian with their undreamed-of literary and scientific treasures.   No more difficult crossword puzzle had ever faced linguists and no more spectacular intellectual feat in this field had ever been achieved.   The decipherment of ancient Egyptian at about the same time, from a clew provided by a bilingual

---

[1] See below, p. 102.

inscription (including Greek) found near the Rosetta (Rashid) mouth of the Nile during the Napoleonic invasion of Egypt, was of almost equal importance in the history of thought.

SOCIAL ORGANIZATION

The Stone Age folks lived in caves, huts, or humble dwellings under a somewhat self-sufficient economy. In the nomadic society, still represented by Arab Bedouins and portrayed on the pages of the Old Testament in the case of the early Hebrews, social organization was of the patriarchal type, in which the unit was the tribe really or fictitiously descended from the same male ancestor. This unit was fundamentally an expanded family and functioned as an economic and political body under the control of its senior member. Members of the tribe and all its retainers were under his jurisdiction. Members could no doubt claim small portable possessions as their own, but flocks and herds were held in common.

In lower Mesopotamia the Sumerians created urban settlements with an economy appropriate to the land and with a socio-political structure fitting for the development of the community. The city was normally nucleated around a temple whose patron deity theoretically owned the land. The rights of ownership were exercised by priests, as the deity's representatives, and the work was done by day laborers and by share-cropper tenants. Priests were the one learned class in the society. They were wealthy and influential, and at times exercised magical powers for exorcising evil spirits and thus curing disease. Often the priest was the ruler with his palace adjoining the temple. The city was a city-state, normally surrounded by a sun-dried brick wall. A ruler who combined the functions of royalty and priesthood was later called patesi. Before the close of the fourth pre-Christian millennium Uruk, Eridu, Ur, and Lagash had figured among the powerful Sumerian city-states. A powerful city might annex a weaker neighbor. Cities could coalesce by conquest or pact to form larger political units. The head god of the conquering city would then be acknowledged as superior by all concerned; the mere fact that his worshipers had won argued in his favor. One monarch, Lugal-zaggisi of Uruk (*ca.* 2255 B.C.), claimed to have "conquered the lands from the rising of the sun to the setting of the sun" and to have "made straight his path from the Lower Sea [Persian Gulf] unto the Upper Sea [Mediterranean]." His westward path must have been made as a raider rather than as a conqueror.

Before the opening of the third pre-Christian millennium similar processes of urbanization and coalescing in Egypt had reached the point at which the habitable part of the valley was divided into districts called nomes, each centering around a capital city which in turn was centered around a temple dedicated to the local god. City-states in Egypt tended to unite into larger units more readily than they did in other parts of the Near East.[1] By 2900 B.C. the two kingdoms of Upper and Lower Egypt are thought to have merged under one rule, that of Menes, founder of the First Dynasty. Menes and his successors styled themselves Horus, claiming personification of the god of that name who was principal deity of Lower Egypt. By that time the basic elements of the economic, social, and political institutions of the land had been firmly laid. Agriculture had passed the incipient stage; basic technology had progressed from its formative level; and urbanization had expanded over the riverine alluvium of the classic valley. The division of labor had given rise to such professional classes as soldiers, priests, carpenters, and masons. All of these conditioned the development of formal political states with official laws, public projects, and monumental works anchored in a society with classes and hierarchies.

ETHNIC RELATIONSHIPS

The principal actors in this urban development were Sumerians in Mesopotamia and Hamites in Egypt. The Sumerians were the pre-Semitic people whose social, religious, and legal ideas and institutions, together with their scriptural and artistic conventions dominated the whole Tigris-Euphrates valley and spread throughout the neighboring lands. Such terms as Sumerians, Hamites, Semites, Hittites, Arabs—used in connection with the population of the Near East, past and present—should be considered linguistic rather than racial. The Sumerians were simply those pre-Semitic people whose tongue can be easily differentiated from the Semitic or Indo-European family of languages. Its agglutinative feature relates it to the type exemplified by Turkish, Hungarian, and Finnish; but Sumerian displays no other affinity to these or other members of the Ural-Altaic or Mongolian family. In fact it does not seem to be a cognate of any other tongue, living or dead. As they appear on the monuments, those who used this language look like a mixture of the long-headed Mediterranean people and the broad-headed mountaineers from the northeast called Armenoid. The Armenoid general features are round-headedness, heavy build, and moderate height. From Western or Central Asia, Armenoid tribes must have reached Europe in prehistoric times to form the bulk of the population of Central and Eastern Europe, where they are designated

[1] See above, p. 14.

Alpine.　Others reached Anatolia, Syria, and Lebanon and intermarried with Mediterraneans passing on to their descendants the large aquiline nose and thick lips wrongly styled Semitic.　Recent Danish excavations (1959-1960) point to Bahrain as having been the possible site of Dilmun, whence legend brings the Sumerians to lower Mesopotamia.

The Hamites, who acquired their traditional name from Noah's second son, originally lived in North Africa as a part of the Mediterranean division of the white or Caucasian race.　From there Mediterraneans spread throughout southern Europe to become ancestors of the bulk of the population of Spain, southern France, Italy, the islands of the East Mediterranean, and even parts of Britain and Germany.　The features generally associated with the Mediterranean type include long-headedness, brunetteness, and relatively small stature.　Another group of Mediterraneans migrated, probably through Bab al-Mandab, into the Arabian peninsula, whence successive migratory movements into the Fertile Crescent and intermixture with earlier populations produced the Assyro-Babylonians, Amorites of north Syria, Canaanites (Phoenicians) of Lebanon, Aramaeans of inner Syria, and Hebrews—all considered Semites.　Last among those "waves" was the Moslem Arabian one of the seventh Christian century.　In fact seepage from the Arabian reservoir must have been perennial.　The different tongues these peoples spoke share many basic characteristics that differentiate them from other languages and that justify the conclusion of common descent from one mother tongue.　That mother passed away long before it was recorded, but we can reconstruct parts of it from what is common among its surviving daughters.　In the case of the Romance languages, the Latin mother has been immortalized in written records.　It should be noted, however, that the imposition of Semitic dialects in all that wide area presupposes preponderance in numbers or superiority in strength or in culture on the part of those who introduced it.

BOOKS TO READ

Barton, George A., *Semitic and Hamitic Origins* (Philadelphia, 1934).

Caldwell, Wallace E., *The Ancient World*, rev. ed. (New York, 1951).

Coon, Carleton S., *Caravan: The Story of the Middle East*, rev. ed. (New York, 1958).

Kramer, Samuel N., *From the Tablets of Sumer* (Indian Hills, Colorado, 1956).

Swain, Joseph W., *The Ancient World* (New York, 1950), vol. I.

PART TWO

ANCIENT SEMITIC TIMES

V   *The Dynastic and Imperial Periods*

Semitic hegemony in the lower Mesopotamian valley was established by Sargon (*ca.* 2350), builder of Akkad (Accad of Gen. 10:10, Agade of inscriptions) and founder of the dynasty named after him. His was the first great name in Semitic history. No one before him is known to have written in a Semitic language. For over a thousand years before his time uncultured Bedouins from the Syrian-Arabian Desert had been infiltrating into the valley to the east, there to learn from the highly civilized Sumerians how to construct and inhabit homes, till the land, acquire varied techniques and skills, and above all learn to read and write.

SARGON, FIRST EMPIRE BUILDER

Sargon destroyed Sumerian power represented by Lugal-zaggisi;[1] unified and consolidated the Mesopotamian realm under his sway; and in a series of remarkable campaigns, extended its boundaries eastward through Elam and westward into north Syria. The motivation for his western campaigns was manifestly the acquisition of copper, stone, and coniferous wood from the Amanus rather than the control of the area. That he reached the Lebanon is doubtful. This first empire builder was apparently the son of a sacred prostitute attached to the temple of Ishtar.[2] A late inscription ascribed to him anticipates Moses' infant experience. It reads: "My father I knew not. My mother, who was poor, conceived me and secretly gave birth to me. She placed me in a basket of reeds; she shut up the mouth of it with bitumen. She abandoned me to the river which did not overwhelm me" to be picked up by a gardener in the temple of Ishtar.

[1] Mentioned above, p. 31.
[2] For more details see below, p. 105.

37

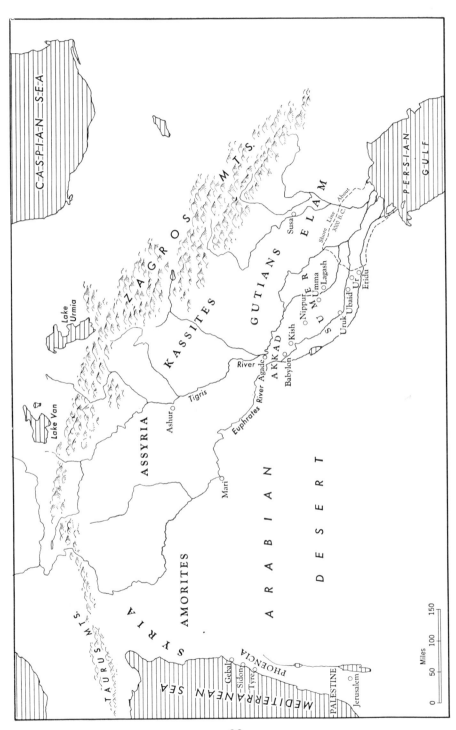

WESTERN ASIA WHEN BABYLON WAS SUPREME: EARLY SECOND MILLENIUM B.C.

Sargon's grandson and successor Naram-Sin (r. *ca.* 2270-2233) wielded even greater power. He extended his realm northward through Assyria, which validated his title "king of the four quarters of the world." His world was indeed so small that the claim is less of an exaggeration than it sounds today.

Elam (today roughly Luristan and Khuzistan, Susiana of classical geographers after its capital Susa—biblical Shushan) was the mountainous district east of the lower valley. It came piecemeal under the domination of its Sumerian and Akkadian neighbors, but later rose to prominence and remained a threat to the Mesopotamian kingdoms until incorporated into the Assyrian empire about the mid-seventh pre-Christian century. Originally not highly cultured mountaineers, the Elamites assimilated Sumerian civilization and adopted the cuneiform script. Hebrew tradition brings a conquering Elamite monarch, Chedorlaomer (Gen. 14:1-10), as far as Palestine in the days of Abraham.

EGYPT UNDER EARLY PHARAOHS

Egypt developed its dynastic and political institutions long before such institutions appeared in Babylonia. Adequate utilization of the fertile land by the Nile, second longest river in the world, and the exploitation of the river stream as a public highway called for an unusual degree of centralization of power and of cooperation among the ruling class, feudal chiefs, and peasantry. Menes heads the Pharaonic list.

The first distinguished personage after him was Zoser (Djoser, r. *ca.* 2650), first of the Third Dynasty and builder of the step pyramid at present-day Saqqara, once the necropolis of Memphis, his capital. Zoser's vizir, counselor, and architect was Imhotep, whom later Egyptian tradition considered so skilled in medicine and magic as to deify him. Zoser recorded expeditions to Lebanon for cedar wood and to Sinai for copper or turquoise. Snefru (r. *ca.* 2600), founder of the Fourth Dynasty, followed Zoser's example in promoting navigation and pyramid building. The record of his expeditions includes Libya and Nubia. As a builder, however, he was surpassed by his successors of the Fourth Dynasty who erected the colossal pyramids at Gizeh (now a suburb of Cairo). The greatest of these pyramids is that of Cheops (Khufu, *ca.* 2550 B.C.), whose barge was recently found.[3] A successor of Cheops, Khafre, built the second of the greatest pyramids and carved from the living rock the spectacular sphinx still gazing mutely at the sands of the desert. The Greeks were so impressed by the pyramids that they counted these monumental structures first among the "seven

[3] See above, p. 13.

wonders" of the world. As the sole survivor of those wonders, the pyramids still attract tourists from all lands into the land of the Pharaohs.

After a period of Pharaonic decline, civil wars, and social disintegration, in which autonomous nomes reasserted themselves, a great dynasty arose. The Twelfth Dynasty (r. *ca.* 1991-1792) ushered in a new era, that of the Middle Kingdom. The Old Kingdom, a formative period of Egyptian civilization, ended about 2200 B.C. The Twelfth Dynasty, whose capital was Thebes, consisted of four Amenemhets and three Sesostrises (Senwosrets), almost all of whom were energetic, progressive, and far sighted rulers. As they curbed the power of the provincial feudal chiefs, they centralized authority in royal hands and even aimed at expansion. Nubia was conquered and Palestine was invaded. Sesostris III (r. *ca.* 1878-1840) is credited with establishing maritime navigation between the Mediterranean and the Red Sea through a canal from the Nile. As the country enjoyed peace it entered upon an era of prosperity. The reclamation of the marshy Fayum (Lake Moeris) district, one of the remarkable hydraulic feats of antiquity, and the commercial expeditions to Punt (roughly Somaliland and perhaps parts of Yemen) for obtaining ivory, ebony, leopard skins, and frankincense, contributed to this prosperity. It was reflected in the flourishing of architecture and the plastic arts. The period also marks the classical age of Egyptian literature and the birth of new genres. Among the examples extant is Sinuhe's travel story.[4] The splendor ended abruptly with the advent of foreign invaders called Hyksos.[5]

HAMMURABI, THE GREAT LAWGIVER

Akkadian hold on Mesopotamia was broken under the impact of Semitic newcomers from the west, designated Amorites, and others from the east, opening the way to a resurgence of the power of the Sumerians, who had not been fully assimilated by the Semites. The Amorites succeeded in establishing a dynasty in Babylon the most distinguished member of which was Hammurabi (r. *ca.* 1728-1686). The capital gave its name to the country. The sixth monarch of the first Babylonian dynasty, Hammurabi, drove the Elamites out of the land, reunited the valley, unified Mesopotamia, and extended his realm west toward the Mediterranean. Mari (now Tell al-Hariri), Amorite capital in north Syria, was reduced. To his title of king of Babylon, Hammurabi added the old titles of king of Sumer and Akkad and king

---

[4] Discussed below, p. 71.
[5] Treated below, p. 44.

of the four quarters of the world. His public works involved building temples and palaces, digging new canals, and reopening old ones. His deeds corroborated his words: "Lasting water I provided for the land of Sumer and Akkad. Its separated people I united. With blessings and abundance I endowed them; in peaceful dwellings I made them live." Under his rule Babylonia attained a position of height and prosperity that was not again experienced until the days of Nebuchadnezzar a thousand years later. Its merchandise reached as far as Egypt and Crete.

The patron deity of Babylon and Hammurabi, Marduk, was elevated to the head of the pantheon, his cult becoming a sort of state religion. Hammurabi replaced the old priestly rulers with appointed magistrates and official judges. The crowning achievement of his reign, however, was a compilation of existing and earlier laws which he engraved and set up in cities, thus giving his code wide publicity. A copy of one of these was found on a diorite stele in 1901 in the ruins of Susa. The stele is topped by a bas-relief representing the king in a suppliant attitude receiving the code, Moses-like, from the sun-deity Shamash, god of justice who is seated on a mountain. In its prologue Hammurabi calls himself the shepherd of his people. The code throws a flood of light on the political, economic, and social organization of Babylonia. Striking similarities to the Mosaic code can be explained by a common Semitic background.[6] The code reveals the family as the basis of a society in which distinction is made between three classes. Members of the upper class filled the high political and religious offices and enjoyed special rights and responsibilities. An intermediate one consisted of shopkeepers, merchants, artisans, and other common people. A slave class constituted a substantial part of the population. Provision was made for marriage contracts, breach of promise, divorce, and concubinage. In general the rights of women were safeguarded as in no other code until the Roman Empire. The wages of doctors, boatmen, and other skilled laborers were fixed but varied in accordance with the social class of the patient or customer. They were often paid in kind. In criminal law the time-honored principle of retaliation was maintained; theft from a temple or palace and adultery were punishable by death. Punishment for injuring an aristocrat could be more severe than for injuring a commoner; but a guilty aristocrat could be punished more severely than a commoner committing the same offense.

Hammurabi's successors were unable to hold the empire for long. In 1530 an army from Carchemish (modern Jarabulus on the Eu-

[6] Cf. below, p. 61.

phrates), Hittite stronghold in north Syria, moved against Babylon, sacked it, and put an end to its first dynasty.   Thus the way was opened for the advent of an alien people from the east, called Kassites, who assimilated Babylonian culture and lorded it over the valley for over four centuries.   In that period the horse, probably tamed by Indo-Europeans around the Caspian Sea, became common in Western Asia.   Until then the ass had been the chief means of transport.   The camel did not make its debut until late.   The horse, which was first used for war chariots, revolutionized the art of war and the economy of peace. From Western Asia it found its way into Egypt in the south and into Greece in the west.

The royal Kassite family established matrimonial and commercial relations with the Egyptian royal family.   Pharaoh Amenhotep (Amenophis) III (d. 1377) of the Eighteenth Dynasty included a sister and a daughter of a Kassite king in his harem.

HITTITES

Judging by language and physique the people called Hittites, who dominated Asia Minor between 1800 and 1200 B.C., were an admixture of Indo-Europeans and Armenoids or Alpines.   The Halys River (now Kizil Irmak) valley was their homeland, and Hattushash (now Bogazköy, ninety miles east of Ankara, capital of Turkey), was their capital.   In writing they used a double script composed of Akkadian cuneiform and pictographs comparable to Egyptian hieroglyphs. Hittite written records bear the earliest marks of linguistic relationship to Sanskrit, Persian, Greek, Latin, and consequently to English and other European and Asiatic languages.

With the brusque raid on Babylon in 1530, the Hittites made their debut on the military stage.   In the first half of the fourteenth century their empire had become the strongest in Western Asia.   North Syria was already theirs.   In Phoenicia they wrested from the Pharaohs the coast to a point south of Gubla (Byblus, modern Jubayl).   Egypt had passed its heyday and Babylonia was under foreign rule.   What gave the Hittites military advantage was their effective use of horses and chariots.   These weapons of warfare, used earlier by Sumerians, must have had an effect much like that of the tank in the first World War.

The struggle for suzerainty between the two would-be world powers over the East Mediterranean area ended in a treaty signed in 1280 in which north Syria was recognized as Hittite and south Syria (Palestine) remained under Egypt.   This earliest of international pacts, professing to bring "peace and good brotherhood between the contending parties for ever," has been preserved in both Egyptian hieroglyphic and Hittite

EGYPTIAN AND HITTITE EMPIRES

In the mid-fourteenth century B.C. the Egyptian empire and that of the Hittites stood face to face as the two mightiest powers of the age. Centered in Anatolia the Hittite kingdom had by then pushed the frontier of its domain south of the Taurus, expanding at the expense of the Pharaohs. Southern Phoenicia and Palestine became the bone of contention between the two rival powers.

cuneiform inscribed on a silver tablet.   In it a thousand of the Hittite
"male and female gods" are invoked.

Following a period of decline the Hittite empire fell around 1200
B.C. under the attacks from Assyrians on the east and the invasions of
hordes from the Aegean whose movements were connected with the
Trojan war.   The Hittite people slipped into obscurity and their empire
into oblivion.   Classical writers had nothing to say about either; biblical references were inadequate, and local records were unknown.   It
was not until the second decade of the twentieth century that a Czech
scholar succeeded in deciphering the Hittite cuneiform inscriptions
on clay tablets excavated by a German archeologist in the ancient
Hittite capital.   Neo-Hittite hieroglyphics on stone, found in southern
Anatolia and north Syria, were deciphered in the 1940's.   With these
developments, the story of a forgotten empire was rediscovered, and a
most sensational episode in modern Oriental scholarship was enacted.

IMPERIAL EGYPT

Egypt entered upon its imperial stage with the founding of the
Eighteenth Dynasty—one of the most brilliant in Egyptian annals—in
Thebes by Ahmose (Amosis, r. *ca.* 1570-1545).   With him the change
from a complacent, isolationist policy to one of dynamic activity and
aggression began.   The New Kingdom, an imperial one, followed the
Middle Kingdom.   The move was prompted by the driving out of the
Hyksos (commonly called Shepherd Kings, but more accurately "kings
of foreign lands") after a hated rule of about a century and a half.   The
Hyksos were mostly Semites from the Syria-Lebanon area.   Their
Egyptian capital was Avaris (classical Tanis, Arabic Tinnis, today San
al-Hajar echoing biblical Zoan).   The settlement of Israel in Egypt
and Joseph's rise to power may have taken place during Hyksos' rule.
They are credited with the introduction of the horse and war chariot
into the Nile valley and the instituting of Semitic deities who in due
course became identified with Egyptian ones.

Ahmose was not content with chasing the Hyksos out of the land.
He followed them into their original homeland, thus setting his country
upon its military career.   The new foreign policy pursued by Ahmose
and his successors resulted in the incorporation into the Egyptian empire of the neighboring Mediterranean coast and north Nubia.   The
actual conquest was accomplished largely by Thutmose III (r. *ca.* 1502-
1448), the Napoleon of ancient Egypt, who undertook no less than
sixteen campaigns and carried his arms victoriously to a point east of the
Euphrates.   He inscribed on the walls of the Theban temple lists of
cities he had conquered in Palestine, Phoenicia, and Syria, and catalogs

of spoils he carried away—ivory, ebony, jewelry, silver, precious stones and carob wood wrought with gold.[7]   During his early reign the real ruler was Thutmose's sister-wife Hatshepsut, first among the celebrated women of history.   On some of her monuments this queen appears with a false beard, simulating masculinity.   Her and her brother-husband's obelisks decorate public squares and parks in Istanbul, Rome, London, and New York.   The empire established by the Eighteenth Dynasty was the most extensive one the ancient world had seen.   Its glittering capital, Thebes, became the opulent cultural center of that world.

DECLINE IN POWER

Thutmose's successors were able to preserve the integrity of the Asiatic empire until the time of Amenhotep (Amenophis) IV[8] (*ca.* 1377-1361), who was more interested in theology and religious reform than in conquest and diplomacy.   In the face of opposition from the Theban priests of Amon-Re, this extraordinary monarch who may be considered the "first personality" in history but not the "first mono-theist," [9] raised his favorite god Aton (the sun disk with its life-giving rays) into a position of preeminence in the Egyptian pantheon, changed his own name to Ikhnaton (splendor of Aton) and moved his capital to a new site Akhetaton (the horizon of Aton), now known as Tell al-Amarna and noted for its royal archives of cuneiform tablets.   Cities of Phoenicia and Syria started to slip away from Egyptian control through internal disaffection or outside pressure from Hittite and Amorite aggression.   Ikhnaton's son-in-law and successor, Tutankhamon (r. *ca.* 1361-1352), restored the worship of Amon, as his name in-dicates, and moved the seat of government back to Thebes.   He was buried by priests with such lavish display of furnishings that the dis-covery of his unviolated tomb in 1922 provided one of the great sensa-tions in archeological annals.   His buried art treasures, now in the

[7] See below, p. 90.
[8] Pharaohs of Dynasty XVIII with approximate dates:
    Ahmose 1580-1545 B.C.
    Amenhotep I 1545-1525
    Thutmose I 1525-1508
    Thutmose II 1508-1504
    Queen Hatshepsut 1504-1482
    Thutmose III (sole ruler) 1482-1447
    Amenhotep II 1447-1421
    Thutmose IV 1421-1413
    Amenhotep III 1413-1377
    Amenhotep IV (Ikhnaton) 1377-1361
    Tutankhamon 1361-1352
[9] See below, p. 63.

Cairo museum, are considered technically the finest that Egypt ever produced. The bust of his predecessor's beautiful wife Nefertiti, the most quietly regal of all sculptured ladies, was found by American troops in Germany during the second World War and cached for safekeeping in a salt mine. It is now in the Berlin Museum.

Courtesy of the Metropolitan Museum of Art, Rogers Fund, 1925

PORTRAIT BUST OF QUEEN NEFERTITI, WIFE OF IKHNATON   Painted on limestone, the queen wears a high conical blue headdress and around her neck a beaded collar.   Bust was found at Tell el Armarna.   Original now in Berlin.

Pharaohs of the Nineteenth Dynasty attempted to restore the Asiatic province but all they got was Palestine. A non-aggression and mutual assistance pact[10] was signed by Pharaoh Ramses II (r. *ca.* 1301-1234)[11] and Hattushilish which maintained a balance of power and temporary stability. The cordial relations between the two royal houses were solemnized by Ramses' marriage to Hattushilish's daughter. The

[10] Cited above, pp. 42, 44.
[11] Pharaohs of Dynasty XIX with approximate dates:
   Ramses I 1319-1318
   Seti I 1318-1301
   Ramses II 1301-1234
   Merneptah 1234-1215

Hebrew exodus probably took place under Ramses' son Merneptah (r. *ca.* 1234-1215).

The downward curve in Egyptian prestige continued. In 945 a Libyan chief, Shishak of Hebrew history (1 Kings 14:25, 26), established himself in the seat of the Pharaohs and started a new dynasty with a new capital in the Delta. An Ethiopian dynasty followed. One of its members, Tirhaka (r. 688-663) of 2 Kings (19:9), was defeated by the Assyrian army under Esarhaddon in 671 at which time Egypt was incorporated into a far-flung empire controlled from distant Nineveh on the upper Tigris.

ASSYRIA

The Assyrians evidently belonged to the same Semitic migration that settled the Akkadians in the southern half of the valley. In their hilly terrain with its unyielding soil and relatively cold climate those early Semitic migrants intermarried with the indigenous people and later with Hurrians (biblical Horites) from whom they inherited Armenoid features. There they developed those hardy, rugged traits of character that made Assyrians the greatest military people of the ancient world down to the time of the Romans. Their image differs somewhat from that of their more peace-loving plain-dwelling cousins of the Euphrates valley to the south and contrasts sharply with that of the Nile valley dwellers who enjoyed more fertile soil and benevolent elements of nature.[12] Assyrian culture was heavily indebted to the Sumero-Baby lonian; in fact it was its heir and continuer. The Assyrian language was written in cuneiform borrowed from its Akkadian sister. In religion these people contributed Ashur, originally a sun-deity who gave his name to the first capital (now Sharqat) and through it to the country. In certain fields, however, particularly those of sculpture, architecture, military equipment, and imperial administration, Assyria excelled.

With the eclipse of Babylonia and Egypt and the elimination of Hittite power the chance of the Assyrians came. They had experienced centuries of precarious and obscure existence mainly under Sumerian and Babylonian control. Their first great warrior, Tiglath-pileser I (1116-1093), attempted westward expansion, but the move proved to be premature. The new Semitic people, the Aramaeans, who established petty states in north Syria and the upper Euphrates, stood in the way. It was not until the rise of Ashur-nasir-pal (r. 884-859) that an Assyrian essay at world power was successful. This warrior king received piecemeal the submission of Aramaean states in his way,

---

[12] Cf. above, pp. 14-15.

conquered north Syria, reached the Mediterranean, and exacted tribute
from wealthy and prosperous Phoenician cities along the Lebanese
coast.   Those cities were ever ready to purchase immunity from interference in their commercial activity which formed the very basis of
their economic existence.   From this time on the cardinal point in
Assyrian foreign policy was a westward push for control of the sources
of copper, silver, other metals, stone, timber, and the trade routes of
Western Asia.

THE IMPERIAL AGE

Ashur-nasir-pal's son and successor, Shalmaneser III (r. 859-824),
after having "washed his weapons" in the Mediterranean, penetrated
inland to face a formidable coalition on the battlefield of Qarqar (853)
in the Orontes valley.   Headed by the Aramaean king of Damascus,
Ben-Hadad, the allied forces included those of Ahab, king of Israel;
of Jundub, an Arabian shaykh; and of Phoenician city-states.   The first
contact between Assyrians and Israelites was therewith established, and
the first identifiable Arab name in recorded history emerges.   That the
victory was not as decisive as represented by Shalmaneser in his inscriptions may be inferred from the repeated returns of the Assyrian army
to the Syro-Palestine war sector.   It was not until the time of Tiglath-
pileser III (r. 745-727) that Israel was forced into submission (733),
Damascus was captured (732), and the Assyrian foothold on the
coast was firmly established.

Tiglath-pileser then embarked upon a policy of incorporating the
conquered territories into the empire as provinces.   Until this time
such territories had been treated as objects of loot and sources of booty.
Between raids, they were generally under their own dynasts.   By way
of further consolidating the realm and reducing the chances of rebellion,
Tiglath-pileser made more effective the policy of transplanting conquered
populations and replacing them with alien peoples.   Damascus experienced such a deportation and received an Assyrian governor.   But
Samaria, capital of Israel, was subjected to a three-year siege by his
successor Shalmaneser V (r. 726-722).   Toward Babylon he introduced a new policy by "taking the hands of Marduk," seeking thereby to
ingratiate himself with its people as he installed himself as their king.

NINEVEH, MISTRESS OF WESTERN ASIA

Under the Sargonid dynasty, founded by a usurper, Sargon II (r. 722-
705), Assyria entered its best known and most brilliant period.   Sargon
received the submission of Samaria, carried off the flower of its popula-

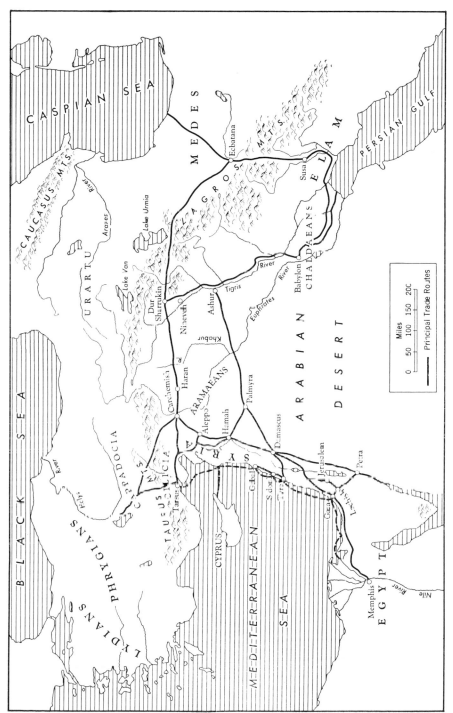

ASSYRIAN EMPIRE

tion to Media and Assyria and replaced them with an alien population.[13]
His son Sennacherib (r. 705-681) put down an insurrection fomented
by Egypt, took Sidon and Ascalon, devastated Judaea (701), and raised
Assyrian prestige to a new height.   However, he made one blunder, for
which he was never forgiven; he destroyed proud Babylon, a city that
had never ceased to be restless under Assyrian domination.   But his
son Esarhaddon (r. 681-668) tried to rectify the mistake by rebuilding
the former capital and giving it a native ruler.   Esarhaddon carried his
predecessors' military policy one step further by attacking Egypt and
reducing its Delta (671).   In two campaigns his successor Ashur-bani-
pal (r. 668-626) carried the Assyrian arms victoriously into Upper
Egypt.   The fame of this monarch, however, rests more on his patronage of arts and letters.   The library he had established at Nineveh—
when unearthed by the British last century—provided the world with
much of what it knows today about Assyro-Babylonian civilization.
Some 25,000 tablets of his and Sennacherib's collection are now in the
British Museum.

With Ashur-bani-pal Assyria hit the zenith of its power, and Nineveh
(near present-day Mosul) assumed its position as the undisputed mistress
of Western Asia.   But the fall was precipitous and soon.   Fourteen
years after the death of this monarch, his city was surrounded by a
joint army of Medes and Neo-Babylonians.   The Neo-Babylonians (or
Chaldaeans), originally brought to lower Mesopotamia by a late
Semitic migration, were led by Nabopolassar, the rebellious governor
of Babylon.   The Indo-Iranian Medes of northwestern Persia were led
by their king, Cyaxares.   The alliance had been cemented by the marriage of Cyaxares' daughter to Nabopolassar, son of Nebuchadnezzar I.
After bitter resistance the haughty Assyrian capital fell and was so wiped
out that a Greek general, Xenophon, passing by the site two centuries
later, failed to recognize it.   Nahum's prediction against the "bloody
city," "full of lies and robbery," scene of "the rattling of wheels, and of
the prancing horses, and of the jumping chariots" was literally fulfilled.
With it one of the mightiest powers of the ancient world disappeared
from the scene.

NEO-BABYLONIA

With the destruction of Nineveh and the decay of Thebes, Babylon
once again emerged as the mistress of the civilized world.   It achieved
this position under Nabopolassar's son Nebuchadnezzar II (r. 605-562),
who at Carchemish when still a crown prince administered to Pharaoh
Necho of the Twenty-Sixth Dynasty such a defeat as to leave no doubt

---

[13] See below, pp. 99-100.

as to whether Babylonia or Egypt was to be supreme in Western Asia. This victory was followed by the destruction of Jerusalem, capital of Judah, in 586 and the reduction of Tyre in 572 after one of the longest sieges on record.[14]   Therewith was terminated Egypt's ambition in the area and her chance to stir up revolt among Hebrew and Phoenician kinglets was lost.

Great as Nebuchadnezzar's conquests were, they do not appear from the inscriptions to have pleased him as his public works and monumental structures did.   These comprised irrigation canals, roads for caravans, temples, and palaces.   Babylon was rebuilt and made worthy of its new imperial role.   It began to boast one of the seven "wonders of the world," the "hanging gardens," evidently a pyramidal terraced structure with trees and flowers on its terraces.   It was said to have been erected by the monarch to relieve the nostalgia of his Median queen, as she longed for the hills of her native country.   Babylonia must have achieved a new level of high prosperity.

ENTER THE PERSIANS

But the end was not far off.   Neo-Babylonian (Chaldaean) supremacy was shorter lived than the great periods of Assyria or old Babylonia.   By the mid-sixth century a new people was rising farther east, the Persians.   Indo-Iranian in language and Zoroastrian in religion, these people differed ethnically from Mesopotamians, Phoenicians, Hebrews, and Egyptians.   With their rise, Semitic hegemony in Western Asia gave way; it was not reestablished till the birth of Islam in the seventh Christian century.

The leader who made Persia a new world power was Cyrus of Anshan in Elam (r. 550 529), real founder of the Achaemenid dynasty, named for a royal predecessor of Cyrus.   Cyrus began his career by rebelling against his Median master Astyages, son of Cyaxares, capturing his capital Ecbatana (modern Hamadhan), and taking Astyages prisoner (550).   Having united Medes and Persians under his scepter, Cyrus stood ready to face an unusual and formidable coalition which brought together Nabonidus of Babylon, Amasis (Dynasty XXVI) of Egypt, even Croesus of Lydia on the western coast of Asia Minor, and Spartans from across the sea.   This was the Croesus of the simile "rich as Croesus."   To his kingdom is ascribed the invention of coinage, the oldest coins having been found therein.   Before the opening of hostilities, Croesus had consulted an oracle and been assured "he would destroy a great empire."   A great empire he indeed did destroy, but it was his own.   Cyrus directed the army from his capital, Pasargadae,

[14] Discussed below, p. 100.

first against Croesus whom he overthrew in 546 and whose capital, Sardis, he seized.

Nabonidus' turn came next. This Neo-Babylonian king was more interested in archeology than in rule. He had chosen to live on an oasis in northern Hejaz, leaving state affairs in the hands of his incompetent son, Belshazzar. The young crown prince, who resided in the sumptuously built palace of Nebuchadnezzar, was given to frivolity, luxury and drink. On his palace wall the writing was clear to all those with vision: "Thy kingdom is divided, and given to the Medes and Persians" (Dan. 5:28). In 539 the Babylonian army was crushed: and in the following year the capital was occupied. Cyrus allowed exiled Jews to return to Palestine and was hailed by them as the divinely appointed savior (Is. 44:28; 45:1).[15] Syria-Phoenicia-Palestine readily acknowledged the new suzerainty. All Western Asia from the Aegean to the borders of Egypt was for the first time united under one emperor, Cyrus the Great. Though Pasargadae was maintained as a royal residence, the seat of government shifted to Susa, a more central position.

Egypt was next on the list. Its conquest was left to Cyrus' son Cambyses (r. 529-521), who achieved it after a memorable march through the desert. Cambyses even planned to push westward against Carthage in what is today Tunisia, but the plan was frustrated by the refusal of his Phoenician allies, who provided the fleet, to bear arms against a daughter colony. Instead, Cambyses pushed up the Nile into the "dark continent" (525). The Persian emperor literally "reigned, from India even unto Ethiopia" (Esther 1:1).

CONFLICT WITH ATHENIANS AND SPARTANS

The Achaemenid line of energetic and able rulers did not end early. Darius I (r. 521-485) had first to quell serious domestic revolts, but he resumed the work of expansion extending the realm beyond the Indus. More than a warrior, he was a builder and an administrator. He established two royal residences. There was one at Susa; but the grandest one at Persepolis matched, if it did not surpass, Nebuchadnezzar's in Babylon. The establishment at Persepolis went up in flames when Alexander burned the city in 330 B.C. Darius linked cities with roads; utilized Phoenicians in developing a fleet; and, in anticipation of the Suez Canal, dug a waterway from the Nile to the Red Sea which provided a sea route between Egypt and Persia. Trade began to flourish and public security improved. But a new development was in store. It was to open the first chapter in the history of a Near Eastern-European political conflict that was continued by Alexander, Pompey,

[15] See below, p. 100.

Julius Caesar, Muʻawiyah, Saladin (Salah-al-Din), Salim and Sulayman the Magnificent down to Napoleon and Allenby.

A revolt among the Ionian Greeks, on the shore of Asia Minor, led to a prolonged war with the European Greeks and culminated in the oft-described battles of Marathon (490), Thermopylae (480), and Salamis (off Piraeus, 480). The first of these battles was lost by Darius, the third by his son and successor Xerxes I (biblical Ahasuerus, r. 485-465). Salamis was a sea battle, with the Phoenician fleet forming the core of the Persian navy. Greek poets, storytellers and historians covered the battlefields of victory with honor and glory; those who laid their lives thereon were raised to the rank of national and immortal heroes. The issue, according to Greek interpretation, was between the preservation of liberty and subjection to Oriental despotism. Persian culture then was no lower than Greek culture, and Persian religion was certainly higher than Greek religion.[16] To Darius and Xerxes the Athenians and Spartans represented a nation of barbarians and sea pirates, a source of constant trouble to the Persian coastal domain of Asia Minor.

The Perso-Greek war was the first serious setback in the advance of Persian military power. Its phenomenal success had been due to able generalship, effective employment of lances and arrows, and long experience in the use of the war horse which provided unmatched mobility. The fame of the imperial bodyguard of ten thousand "immortals" spread far and wide. But the Greek phalanx, with its heavy-armed infantry formed in close and deep ranks, proved more than equal to the Persian troops. Then there was the question of morale. The Athenians and Spartans were fighting for their own homes, which could not be said of their invaders. The conflict marked a turning point in Persian history.

EMPIRE ORGANIZATION

To Darius fell the colossal task of putting the vast empire on a firm basis. Babylonia and Egypt were placed under his direct rule; but the rest of the empire was divided into twenty provinces (satrapies), each under its own governor (satrap) who exercised considerable authority. This was a variation of the earlier system of Assyrian administration. But Persian policy toward subject peoples was much more enlightened and tolerant than anything the Assyrians or Babylonians had ever practiced. It involved less interference with the cultural life of the conquered and permitted a larger measure of autonomy. No imposition of religion or language was attempted. Vanquished kings were usually

[16] See below, p. 67.

honorably dealt with; and enemy towns, except in special cases, were spared.   All preceding empires had been held primarily by the power of conqueror over conquered, but Persian emperors displayed some concern regarding the welfare and security of the people under their control.   They introduced stamped coinage, facilitated communication, and organized postal service by relays of couriers primarily, of course, for royal messages.   The journey from Sardis to Susa is said to have taken no more than ten days.   Trade was further enhanced by the general use of Aramaic, the language of the Aramaens (later Syrians), as a commercial tongue.   It was also used as an official language[17] thus contributing a measure of economic and political cohesion.   The Persians reversed Assyro-Babylonian policy of deporting troublesome subject peoples; they allowed all deportees to return to their homes. Besides Jews from Babylon,[18] they allowed other Jews to return under Nehemiah (445 B.C., Neh. 2-6) to rebuild the walls of Jerusalem and shortly after that under Ezra (Ezra 5, 6) to build a new temple.   The title of "king of kings," which Persian emperors assumed, was borrowed by the Christians and applied to Christ (I Tim. 6:15).   It has survived to modern times in shahanshah, used by the Persian shahs and Ottoman sultans.

THE DOWNFALL

In less than a century and a half after Xerxes' death, the grand empire founded by Cyrus and enlarged and consolidated by Darius breathed its last at the hands of a new enemy from Greek quarters.   Xerxes' son, Artaxerxes I (r. 465-424), found himself on the defensive vis-à-vis the Greeks, whose troops had aided rebels in Egypt and attacked Cyprus. The peace treaty he signed with the Greeks in 446 ended Asiatic aspirations in Europe.   On his death the succession to the throne was disputed.   This Artaxerxes was the king who permitted groups of Jewish exiles to return to Jerusalem (Ezra 7:11-26).

The last Achaemenids were faced by repeated rebellions on the part of powerful satraps.   The state was further weakened by corruption in the court.   Dissension and harem intrigue and degeneration in the royal family in the royal household contributed their share to the ultimate fall.   Sensing that the Persian sun was setting, Phoenician city-states, headed by Sidon, began to break away in the mid-fourth century.   Artaxerxes III (Ochus, r. 359-338) dealt severely with them and with other rebellious centers in Egypt.   He was poisoned by his

[17] See below, pp. 105-106.
[18] As mentioned above, p. 52.

chief minister, a eunuch, who installed Darius III (r. 336-330) in his place.[19]

Meantime Philip of Macedon, who had consummated plans to liberate the remaining Greek cities in Asia from Persian control, was also assassinated. But his work was carried on by his more illustrious son Alexander, who in three years of brilliant successes swept through Asia Minor and completely demolished the empire of the "king of kings." [20] The last of the Achaemenids was pursued into the mountains and murdered en route to Bactria by his own satrap. Europe was avenged on Asia.

BOOKS TO READ

Cameron, George G., *History of Early Iran* (Chicago, 1936).

Finegan, Jack, *Light from the Ancient Past* (Princeton, 1946).

Garstang, John, *The Hittite Empire* (New York, 1930).

Ghirshman, R., *Iran* (Harmondsworth, Middlesex, 1954).

Gurney, Oliver R., *The Hittites* (Melbourne, 1952).

Hall, H. R., *Ancient History of the Near East*, 8th ed., rev. (New York, 1952).

Hrozny, Bedrich, *Ancient History of Western Asia, India and Crete*, tr. Jindrich Prochazka (Prague).

Moscati, Sabatino, *Ancient Semitic Civilizations* (London, 1957).

Olmstead, A. T., *History of Assyria* (New York, 1923); *A History of the Persian Empire* [Achaemenid Period] (Chicago, 1948).

Smith, Sidney, *Early History of Assyria* (London, 1928).

Steindorff, George and Seele, Keith C., *When Egypt Ruled the East*, 2nd ed. (Chicago, 1957).

Wilson, John A., *The Burden of Egypt* (Chicago, 1951).

Woolley, C. Leonard, *The Sumerians* (Oxford, 1928).

[19] List of the Achaemenid emperors:
    Cyrus 550-529
    Cambyses 529-521
    Darius I 521-485
    Xerxes I 485-465
    Artaxerxes I 465-424
    Xerxes II 424-423
    Darius II 423-404
    Artaxerxes II 404-359
    Artaxerxes III 359-338
    Arses 338-336
    Darius III 336-330
[20] See below, pp. 113 *seq.*

VI *Religion and Literature*

SUCH problems as those relating to the origins of man and the universe, the mysteries of nature, the inevitability of death, the natural desire for eternal youth, and man's suffering and its relation to righteous living must have agitated the mind of early man. The formulation of these problems and attempts at interpretation found expression in myths, legends, and folk tales which have their counterpart in our theology, history, and popular science. Religion then played a central role in the life of man; it permeated his varied activities.

IN MESOPOTAMIA

In its earliest and simplest form Mesopotamian religion must have been nature worship. Its basic concepts were and continued to be Sumerian, which were rooted in primitive ideas. Semitic ideology was imposed as an upper layer. Over the three great divisions of the universe—heaven, earth, and water presided a triad of great gods—Anu, Enlil, and Ea (Enki). With the rise of Babylon to power, under the dynasty of which Hammurabi was a distinguished member, Enlil was replaced by Babylon's god Marduk ("the young one") styled Bel, lord. When in due course Nineveh achieved supremacy, its god, Ashur, naturally became the head of the pantheon. On the whole the Assyrians revered the same gods and observed the same ceremonials and prayers as did the Babylonians. Sin, the moon-god, was a favorite in Ur, whence Hebrew tradition brings Abraham, as well as in Haran his stopping place. Ishtar, the mother goddess, was a favorite throughout. She represented fertility and reproduction.[1]

When abstraction became possible the sun-god Shamash was made guardian of justice. Minor gods presided over the minor operations of nature. Each of the city gods was considered the private owner of the city, with the king acting as his steward, the priests as his agents, and the cultivators as his laborers. The Sumerians regarded their kings as

---

[1] Treated below, p. 105.

56

agents of the gods; the Egyptians regarded theirs as gods incarnate. The "good life" consisted of obedience to family, ruler, and god. Those who led good lives were rewarded with earthly favors, chief among which were prosperity and health. Following the human family pattern, gods were provided with consorts and children and given a retinue of minor deities, some four thousand in all, who served as messengers. The world was populated with a host of malevolent spirits and demons who caused disease and were subject to exorcism by spells and incantations in which a class of priests specialized. In his more primitive period man endowed every tree, stone, river, mountain and all other objects of nature with wills and characters. These spirits had to be propitiated. Religious thought is, by its very nature, so conservative as to tend to persist once it is formulated.

Other priests specialized in other functions. Before a king would launch a campaign, a builder start a construction, a businessman undertake a new enterprise, a traveler venture on a journey, he would be sure to ascertain through a priest whether the omens were propitious. The priest could determine this by varied means; but the most favorite was through the observation of the liver or entrails of a sacrificial animal, a practice well known later among Greeks and Romans. An elaborate system of warding off evil influences by magical practices and incantations, of interpreting omens by divination, and of foretelling events by the movement and positions of the heavenly bodies (astrology) became a prominent feature of religion.

As the chief custodians of learning the priests in Mesopotamia, as in Egypt and other lands of the area, were the teachers par excellence. Temple schools, like the schools of medieval monasteries, were practically the only places of learning. But perhaps the most conspicuous function of a priest was the correct performance of religious ceremonies and festivals, with their elaborate ritual, intended among other things to keep the gods propitiated. These festivals normally coincided with the plowing of the fields and the reaping of the harvest. The unfailing cycle involving the apparent death of vegetation in winter and its reappearance—vivified and refreshed—in spring must have impressed the population of Western Asia and Egypt as no other physical phenomenon did. Agriculture, it should be remembered, was the core of their entire economic life.

EPIC OF CREATION

Most important among the seasonal rituals was that of the New Year festival, intended to insure fertility for the ensuing year. The basic element in this ritual was the dramatization of the death and resurrection of Marduk.   Passages from the epic of creation were chanted as a part of the ritual.   The epic was the form which the accepted interpretation of the origin of the universe had taken.   The Akkadian version, a literary masterpiece coming from the second millennium, makes Marduk the author of the present world order.   In the earlier Sumerian version, Enlil was the hero and central figure, in the later version it was Assyrian Ashur.

In the beginning:
When a sky above had not yet even been mentioned
And the name of firm ground below had not yet even been thought of,[2] two deities come into existence: Marduk and the rebellious dragon goddess Tiamat.   With his mace Marduk cleaves Tiamat's body in two.   With the upper half of the carcass he forms the sky.   On it he sets up constellations of stars to determine time.

He bade the moon come forth; intrusted night to her.[3]   Finally the creator fashions man from the blood of a god (cf. Koran 96:2) so that he may work for the gods.

Several points invite comparison with the Hebrew story.   Both accounts start with a watery chaos, proceed to a division of the world into heaven and earth, and lead to the creation of man as the capstone of the entire structure.   In both stories the number seven figures.   That Mesopotamia, rather than Palestine, was the origin of the story may be inferred not only from the superior antiquity of the Babylonian account but from geographic considerations too.   An early version of the epic comes from Eridu, where people could observe the process of "creation" in the form of land rising from the deep.[4]   But in its simplicity and dignity the biblical account excels all other ancient cosmogonies.   Tiamat, the name of the female personification of the primeval ocean, may be identified with the Hebrew *tehom* (Gen. 1:2; 7:11), where it is rendered "deep" and denotes chaos.   It occurs in its plural form in Proverbs (3:20).   In a Ras al-Shamrah tablet, the term is used for ocean.   The low coastal land of western Arabia is still known by the name Tihamah. This dark watery abyss was represented as a dragon or serpent and called by various names.   Echoes of the conflict between the great creator and hostile elements are repeated in Old Testament passages.   In one place (Ps. 75:13) God breaks the head of the dragons of the deep; in another (Ps. 75:14; cf. Job 41) he breaks the heads of leviathan in pieces.   In still another (Ps. 89:10; cf. Is. 51:9-10) he breaks Rahab in pieces,

[2] H. and H. A. Frankfort *et al., The Intellectual Adventure of Ancient Man* (Chicago, 1946), p. 170.
[3] Frankfort, p. 181.
[4] See above, p. 13.

as one that is slain. In Isaiah (7:1; Job 26:13) the Lord with His sword pierces the crooked serpent. This monster of the sea appears later as the nine-headed Hydra slain by Hercules.

EPIC OF GILGAMESH: THE DELUGE

Longer and more interesting than the story of creation is the epic extolling the heroic deeds of Gilgamesh, his search for immortality, and his interview with Ut-napishtim, the Sumero-Babylonian Noah. Composed at the beginning of the second millennium and translated into Hittite and other foreign languages, this literary masterpiece, with its emphasis on the dangerous adventures of a national hero and his final return home, set the pattern for later epics, possibly including that of Homer. Its Egyptian literary counterpart is the tale of Sinuhe,[5] whose odyssey in Palestine and Lebanon is one of the most delightful of its kind coming from antiquity.

The central figure in the epic of Gilgamesh is a tyrannous king of Uruk who undertakes an adventurous journey to a deep cedar forest in the west whose god is guarded by a fearful dragon. Gilgamesh kills the dragon but then has to face an awesome bull sent against him by a goddess whose love advances he did not reciprocate. With the aid of his companion, Gilgamesh kills the bull but on the return journey the companion dies. So grieved was the hero that he set out in quest of eternal life. On an island he meets the only man who, with his wife, had escaped a devastating flood which the gods in days of old had sent to destroy mankind. Forewarned, the Mesopotamian Noah had built a large boat and occupied it with his wife and pairs of all living things. As a reward for saving life on earth, he received the universally desired gift of eternal life. Finally he divulges the secret: a plant at the sea bottom which rejuvenates him who partakes of it. Gilgamesh discovers the plant in the Persian Gulf but on the way back home stops at a pool to refresh himself and a snake carries it away. (Hence this reptile's ability to slough off its skin every year and be reborn in youthful vigor.)

The efforts of the ancient Mesopotamian seeker to escape the nightmarish concept of oblivion and to achieve perpetual youth were no more successful than those of the medieval alchemist seeking the elixir of life or the modern scientist experimenting with hormones.

While the analogies with the Hebrew story of the deluge are striking and include such details as fixing the dimensions of the ark, sending forth the dove, and finally landing atop a mountain, the differences are significant. The story undoubtedly had its origin in Mesopotamia

[5] Discussed below, pp. 71-72.

where, unlike Palestine, river floods were, and are, a common occurrence. Even as recently as March 1954, flood damage was estimated at $80,000,000 and complete evacuation of Baghdad had to be considered. Two years later a huge flood-control system—involving dams, conduits, and reservoirs—was put into operation at Samarra on the Tigris and at Ramadi on the Euphrates. The twin project, it is expected, will not only protect the area against its greatest natural menace but will add greatly to its prosperity. The Hebrew version, however, is more rational, less intricate, and introduces an ethical element and a monotheistic concept that are lacking in the Babylonian. In the Babylonian version the sending of the flood was an arbitrary act on the part of the deities, whose multiplicity complicates the narrative.

The extent of parallelism between biblical and Babylonian stories was not realized until less than a century ago. In the 1870's, while an Assyriologist of the British Museum was trying to piece together and read fragments of tablets excavated in the ruins of the ancient royal library outside of Mosul, his eye caught the statement "the ship rested on the mountain." [6] There was only one such notable case in literature. Any doubt about its significance must have been expelled when a later passage described the sending forth of a dove and its return on finding no resting place. A public lecture by the Assyriologist aroused so much interest that the *Daily Telegraph* subsidized an expedition to reopen the excavations on the site of the ancient capital with the hope of finding other fragments and tablets that would complete the story and provide other material bearing upon the Book of Genesis. The hope was realized by the expedition led by him.

Echoes of the Gilgamesh legendary exploits resounded in those of the Greek Hercules and of the Arab Iskandar (Alexander). Alexander's koranic name, dhu-al-Qarnayn (the two-horned, surah 18:84-98), and his reaching the setting place and the rising place of the sun connects him also with the sun-god.

Other cuneiform narratives treat the same problem of immortality. In one the hero is Adapa who, like the Hebrew Adam, was the first man. While fishing in his boat, Adapa encountered the South Wind which upset his boat and so infuriated him that he attacked and broke the wind's wing. Summoned by Ea to render an account of his violent conduct and forewarned not to partake of the food and drink to be offered him on the ground that it would be the food of death, Adapa refused to eat although in reality the food offered him was that of life. Thus did the progenitor of the human race let the one opportunity to secure eternal life slip by.

[6] George Smith, *The Chaldean Account of Genesis* (New York, 1876), p. 4.

Another short story deals with the righteous sufferer and raises the question of whether man is entitled to receive justice as a right or simply as a favor. What constituted righteousness then was the observance of the ceremonies of the cult rather than social conduct. In this moralizing poem the Babylonian Job laments:

> I only heeded prayer and supplication,
> my very thought was supplication, sacrifice habitual to me.

Nevertheless:

> *Alu*-disease covers my body like a garment;
> sleep in a net enmeshes me;
> my eyes stare, but see not,
> my ears are open, but hear not,
> weakness has seized my body.[7]

HAMMURABI'S CODE

Parallelism extends to the legal field. The code compiled by Hammurabi[8] (r. *ca.* 1728-1686) on the bases of old Sumerian and Semitic practices and laws, being imperial and written, superseded all others in the area and for over a thousand years was studied as the codification of "judgments of righteousness." Like the Mosaic code, Hammurabi's was considered of divine origin. In both the time-honored principle of *lex talionis* involving "eye for eye, tooth for tooth," itself an improvement on the earlier practice of unlimited revenge, is accepted and incorporated. The Hammurabi code reflects a more industrial and commercial society than the pastoral and agricultural Hebrew society. Though half a millennium older, the Mesopotamian legislation on the social, political, and economic issues was generally in advance of the Hebrew legislation. Hammurabi frees the slave in the fourth year, Moses in the seventh. Smiting a parent is punishable, according to Hammurabi, by mutilation; according to Moses it results in death. In Hammurabi the restitution ranges from two- to threefold, in the covenant from four to five. In both codes adultery is punishable by death.[9]

The Mosaic code, however, strikes an ethical note in its Decalogue that is unequaled in the Hammurabi code or any other ancient system. No one but Christ has ever been able to improve on those Ten Commandments.[10]

[7] Frankfort, pp. 213-214. See below, p. 76.
[8] See above, p. 40.
[9] Most of the biblical references can be found in Ex. 20-22; Deut. 15, 19; Lev. 20, 24. For the latest translation of the Babylonian code consult James B. Pritchard, ed., *Ancient Near Eastern Texts* (Princeton, 1950), pp. 163-180.
[10] See Matt. 5:28.

The Egyptian religion was more than one religion. Stretching over thousands of years and covering an extensive area, it came to embrace some of the most primitive elements along with some of the most highly developed ones to be found in any ancient form of paganism. From totemic clans, with ancestral animals for patrons, come weird animal deities. From those small predynastic political units termed city-states were added local deities. Foreign conquerors introduced new deities. Others were personifications of natural forces. The processes of synthesis and amalgamation started early and continued. Gods came to be represented in three forms: animal, human, and a combination of animal and human. Of all the animals the sacred bull Apis, considered an embodiment of Ptah, the creator god of Memphis, was most and for the longest time revered. His dead body was embalmed and ceremoniously buried while a search was being made for a successor born upon his death and recognized by certain marks. Conservatism was the rule in a land where climatic and environmental conditions were relatively uniform. Pyramid texts and the Book of the Dead mention no less than fourteen hundred deities. When a city-state conquered another, its god assumed suzerainty; but the conquered one did not necessarily cease to exist. He was relegated to a secondary position and left in charge of local affairs. Horus rose to a royal position when Lower Egypt was consolidated.[11] He developed into a god of both Lower and Upper Egypt when the two kingdoms were united and was thereupon depicted as a falcon-headed man. Eventually he was identified with the rising sun and had no difficulty in merging into one with Horus the Child, son of Osiris and Isis.

The ibis-headed god Thoth functioned as scribe of the gods and taught men to write. Anubis, who shared with Thoth the office of ushering the dead to the judgment hall and was later identified by the Greeks with Hermes, took the form of a jackal-headed man. Amon (Amen) of Thebes, who achieved supremacy with the rise of the Eighteenth Dynasty, was represented as a ram. When he merged with the sun, the sun disk was added between his horns—as simple a process as that. Hathor, goddess of love and reproduction—the Aphrodite of the Greeks—was appropriately represented by a cow.

Re belonged to a different category. He made his appearance—evidently imported—after the collapse of the First Dynasty, gave his name to the sun and assumed a universal, but not exclusively universal, position in the country. His symbol was the sun-ward pointing obelisk.

[11] See above, p. 32.

Centering in the ancient capital Heliopolis, where influential priests worked out the first theological system, the cult of Re became a state religion under the Fifth Dynasty. He was later compounded with Amon, the local deity of Thebes and originally a god of fertility and reproduction. Of all the gods, this Amon-Re ultimately attained the greatest power. Thus did the solar religion finally achieve prevalence throughout the land. Even the deity of Ikhnaton, "heretic" rebel against Amon-Re, was a sun deity.[12] A hymn ascribed to this Pharaoh in praise of Aton endows the sun disk with universality, beneficence, and creativeness, but not to the exclusion of other deities. The hymn makes Akhetaton "the beloved son" of Aton and makes his chief wife Nefertiti "living and youthful forever." So striking is the similarity in spirit and wording between this hymn and Psalm 104 that actual borrowing by the Psalmist has been maintained by some.

> Thou appearest beautifully on the horizon of heaven,
> Thou living Aton, the beginning of life!
> When thou art risen on the eastern horizon,
> Thou hast filled every land with thy beauty.
> Thou art gracious, great, glistening and high over every land;
> Thy rays encompass the lands to the limit of all that thou hast made.

> Darkness is a shroud, and the earth is in stillness,
> For he who made them rests in the horizon.[13]

> How manifold it is what thou hast made!
> They are hidden from the face (of men).[14]

> Everyone has his food, and his time of life is reckoned.[15]

Another god of foreign extraction and with universal pretensions was Osiris. Associated with fertility and agriculture, Osiris was introduced presumably from Syria-Lebanon[16] and soon established close connections with the Nile, the source of all Egyptian fertility. Osiris became head of a triad embracing his wife-sister Isis and their son Horus. But the happiness of this family was destroyed when an enemy deity, Set, attacked its head, murdered him, cut his body into pieces, and dumped them into the Nile. A late version makes Gubla (Byblus) the scene of his interment in a cedar chest. Lamenting his loss, Isis and

[12] See above, p. 45.
[13] Cf. Ps. 104:20.
[14] Cf. Ps. 104:24.
[15] Cf. Ps. 104:27. Pritchard, James B., ed., *Ancient Near Eastern Texts* (Princeton, 1950), p. 370.
[16] See above, pp. 21, 23; below p. 105.

Horus set out to hunt for the dismembered body, found the pieces and thus brought Osiris back to life, a patently Semitic idea. He then became, like Tammuz of Babylonia and Phoenicia,[17] a dying and rising god, symbolizing the annual sequence of the death and vivification of vegetation in a land dependent for its livelihood on agriculture. As one who had suffered death and risen to immortal life, he became the center of the cult of immortality, god of the underworld, and judge of the dead. Through him the cult of the dead and the institution of mummification became firmly established.

Naturally a favorite among peasants, the Osiris cult permeated all strata of Egyptian society. Horus became the symbol of the dutiful child, Isis that of the faithful wife and mother. The domestic bliss of this heavenly family mirrored general Egyptian life. Even on the tomb walls Egyptians in their multifarious activities are depicted as a merry and contented people.

Unlike Mesopotamia, where the fitful Tigris and Euphrates often wrought havoc, Egypt possessed a tame and dependable river.[18] Unlike the Fertile Crescent its valley was not exposed to foreign invasions and sheltered even against the cloudbursts that infested the neighboring desert. The Egyptian Pharaoh, who had hitherto proclaimed himself son and incarnation of Re as well as of Horus and claimed to have sucked at Isis' breasts, began to cite Osiris as his father, enhancing thereby his authority and hoping for dynastic stability. The god-king institution lingered throughout Egyptian dynastic history, some three thousand years. As late as the mid-first century before Christ, Cleopatra, the last of the Ptolemies, masqueraded as Isis. The concept appealed to Alexander and his successors,[19] and after them to the Roman emperors, and in a modified form to their European successor.

In addition to these major gods and goddesses, the Egyptians, no less than the Babylonians, filled their world with minor deities, spirits, and supernatural beings with roles reminiscent of those performed by jinnis and afreets of the *Arabian Nights*. Traces of such beliefs can be detected in the contemporary Moslem and Christian religions of the area.

BOOK OF THE DEAD

No other people of antiquity, the Hebrews included, manifest such absorbing interest in future life and hold such clear and firm beliefs as to its details as do the Egyptians. The preservation of the dead body

---

[17] See below, pp. 104-105.
[18] See above, pp. 13-14.
[19] Treated below, pp. 114; 128 typescript.

in the dry soil of the land may have prompted the conviction that life continued after death. Life on earth was too good to be discontinued when one "goes west" to his burial place. The summer rise of the Nile from its bed and its annual rebirth contributed to the conviction. Even in predynastic days, fear of annihilation haunted the dweller of the Egyptian valley. In the pyramid age celestial bliss was evidently considered a monopoly of the royalty and nobility, but as new upper classes emerged the privilege was extended and heaven was more democratized. Huge pyramids and later rock-hewn chambers were initiated as a safeguard against the destruction of the body, whose preservation was considered a prerequisite for immortality. As a double safeguard embalming, first with salt treatment and sun drying, was devised and gradually developed into that unique institution of mummification. The personal existence of the disembodied spirit depended on the preservation of the body. Provision of an adequate supply of food, drink, and furniture was essential, though statuary and mural paintings would do as a replacement for articles of nourishment and comfort. The vital principle of the departed, termed *ka* and corresponding to the soul in our terminology, could as well utilize the representation of the body in case of its destruction. Hence the first impetus given to representational art in Egypt. Writings on the wall offered instructions for the benefit of the dead and served as a miniature Baedeker for the afterlife.

The judgment of the dead, worked out with unmatched elaborate details as recorded in the Book of the Dead, constitutes a unique contribution to early religious thought. In this book, the chief monument of the religious literature of ancient Egypt, the funeral ritual is described in mystical language and the hazardous adventures after death are treated in detail. On the walls of the Egyptian room in the British Museum spreads a sumptuously illustrated papyrus roll containing the finest copy of this book extant. It was compiled in the mid-fifteenth century for a Theban scribe Ani and his wife. Most impressive among the scenes is that relating to the judgment. In a worshipful posture the deceased enters into the judgment hall followed by his wife Tutu. As he proceeds, he recites a formal repudiation of forty-two sins in the presence of forty-two judges, each one of whom could challenge him on his specialty. "I have not stolen"; "I have not told falsehoods"; "I have not blasphemed"; "I have not made conspiracies"; "I have not made to weep, I am not a land-grabber, I committed no adultery, I am not a slayer of man, I tamper not with the balance, I do not cheat." This negative confession is followed by a positive one introduced by "I am pure." "I am pure." "I am pure." "I gave bread to the hungry, water to the thirsty, clothing to the naked, and a ferry to him who was

Courtesy of The Bettmann Archive

A JUDGMENT SCENE FROM THE BOOK OF THE DEAD (Page 3695)

without a boat." [20]   Acquitted, Ani and his wife who is identified with him, is presented to Osiris, enthroned within a shrine, and supported by Isis and her sister Nephthys.   In the fields of blessedness the couple proceed to enjoy a lighthearted, easygoing life in continuation of that on earth.

The notion of a triumphant afterlife partially dependent upon social behavior undoubtedly helped to detract from emphasis on rites in favor of right living and on cult in favor of conduct.   However, the concept of sin, as failure to observe ceremonial law, remained intact in Egypt as in Mesopotamia and Iran.   Formulas embodying the social precepts illustrated in the confession of the dead can be traced back to the pyramid age through wise sayings and inscriptions on tombs, coffins, and mortuary statues.   They mark what Breasted has termed "the dawn of conscience" and the emergence of an ethical order.[21]   In a brief word of counsel, addressed by Amenemhet I (*ca.* 2000 B.C.) to his son who succeeded him as Sesostris I, the aged monarch proclaims:

> I gave to the beggar, I nourished the orphan,
> I admitted the insignificant as well as him
>   who was of great account.[22]

[20] Cf. E. A. Wallis Budge, *The Book of the Dead: The Papyrus of Ani* (London, 1913), pp. 573, 574, 575, 587.

[21] James H. Breasted, *The Dawn of Conscience* (New York, 1933), pp. 123 *seq.*

[22] James H. Breasted, *Development of Religion and Thought in Ancient Egypt* (New York, 1912), p. 203.

ZOROASTER AND THE AVESTA

In theology and morality the Persian religion yields to no other religion of the ancient world, with the exception of Judaism and Christianity, and far excels those of Mesopotamia, Egypt, and Greece. The founder of the national religion that prevailed from the early Archaemenid to the close of the Sasanid period was Zoroaster, a Median reformer of about 600 B.C. whose life has been shrouded in legend and mystery. The new faith he taught was rooted in the old Iranian folk beliefs related to those of the early Hindus. The sacred book of Zoroastrianism, the Avesta, is the oldest literary monument of Persia. It is a collection of archaic sayings attributed to the Prophet Zoroaster, sacrificial hymns and prayers, priestly codes, and liturgical works.

The essence of Zoroastrianism is a dualism which personifies the two opposing principles of good and evil, light and darkness, in two major deities Ahura Mazda (Ormazd) and his antithesis Ahriman. Both possess creative powers. As the omniscient, omnipresent, uncreated, and creator of what is pure and living, Mazda reminds us of the Hebrew Jehovah, Ahriman is reflected in the Satan of later epochs. Life is conceived as a ceaseless struggle between the two opposing forces, with the ultimate triumph on the side of the good spirit. It is the ethical and religious duty of the believer to contribute his share. All thoughts, deeds, and words of man are entered and itemized in the book of life to be checked against his wicked actions, of which none can be remitted or forgiven. On death the soul is conducted to the "accountant's bridge" which leads to the heavenly realms. If the balance is on the side of good works crossing over the bridge is assured; otherwise the deceased falls down into the hellish realm. The bridge idea corresponds to the Egyptian balance that was later adopted by Islam. Indeed the koranic and the New Testament concepts of the afterlife and the dependence of its state upon deeds committed on earth is more akin to Avestan and Book of the Dead concepts than to Old Testament ones. The prohibition of burning or burying the dead and the centering of worship on the holy fire of the altar which grew into fire temples was later Zoroastrian developments. The profession of faith required from new converts illustrates the lofty quality of the code of ethics:

I forswear henceforth all robbing and stealing of cattle and the plundering and destruction of villages belonging to worshippers of Mazda. To householders I promise that they may roam at will and abide unmolested wherever upon the earth they may be dwelling with their herds. Humbly with uplifted hands to Asha[23] I swear this. Nor will I hereafter bring plunder or

[23] Member of the heavenly council, corresponding to archangels in Judaeo-Christian terminology.

destruction on the Mazdayanian villages, not even to avenge life and death. I confess myself a worshipper of Mazda, a follower of Zarathushtra [Zoroaster], professing and confessing the same. I profess good thoughts, good words, good deeds.[24]

The last sentence embodies the motto of the religion.

After the onslaught of Islam in the thirties of the seventh Christian century, only a handful of believers survived in Persia. Those who sought refuge in and near Bombay are represented today by a small community called Parsi (Persian) who, by laying less stress on Ahriman, have become practically monotheistic.

BOOKS TO READ

Frankfort, H., *Ancient Egyptian Religion* (New York, 1948).

Glanville, S. R. K., *The Legacy of Egypt* (Oxford, 1947).

Jastrow, Morris, Jr., *The Civilization of Babylonia and Assyria* (Philadelphia, 1915).

Oesterly, W. O. E., *The Wisdom of Egypt and the Old Testament* (London, 1927).

Peet, T. Eric, *A Comparative Study of the Literatures of Egypt, Palestine, and Mesopotomia* (London, 1931).

Rogers, Robert W., *Cuneiform Parallels to the Old Testament* (New York, 1912).

Steindorff, George and Seele, Keith C., *When Egypt Ruled the East,* 2nd ed. (Chicago, 1957).

Wilson, John A., *The Burden of Egypt* (Chicago, 1951).

[24] Zénaïde A. Ragozin, *Media, Babylon and Persia* (New York, 1900), p. 111.

VII   *Secular Writings*

Secular literature has been transmitted to us from Mesopotomia on hundreds of thousands of tablets and from Egypt on innumerable papyri. At the beginning of the dynastic period some mutual influence between Babylonia and Egypt is noticeable, but Egyptian literature developed its own characteristics and, as in the case of art and architecture, excelled its rival. The creative literary and artistic effort of Egypt attained superior proportions in the quality and quantity of its product.

Cuneiform tablets record sales, receipts, accounts, contracts, and other business transactions, letters, administrative documents, deeds, legal decisions and other private and official correspondence, lists of kings, royal annals, reports of campaigns and other political and military information. From these records we gain much of our knowledge of the economic and social structure of the Assyro-Babylonian society. Then there is a large body of texts relating to omens, astrology, mathematics, and medicine which provides us with information about science. There are also specimens of the so-called wisdom literature and of short stories, but there are not many of these and they are not of a high order. At least two of the fables ascribed to Aesop, the sixth century writer to whom the Greeks attributed the invention of fables, have been traced back to Sumerian collections of the early second millennium.

WISDOM LITERATURE

In Egypt wisdom literature makes its early appearance with the semi-legendary Imhotep, vizir of the Third Dynasty,[1] who for some thousand years was revered as the incomparable sage, but from whose maxims practically nothing is extant. Egyptian wisdom, like the Semitic and unlike Greek philosophy, aimed at good manners and at achieving worldly success. Its concern was more with "how to make friends and

---

[1] Mentioned above, p. 39.

influence people" than with securing a passport into the blessed here-after. To another sage-vizir of the pyramid age, Ptahhotep (fl. in Fifth Dynasty), is ascribed the oldest collection of maxims. While ad-dressed to his son, Ptahhotep's precepts are applicable to any schoolboy interested in good conduct:

Magnify not thy heart because of thy knowledge, and fill not thy heart with the thought about it because thou hast knowledge. Hold converse with the ignorant man as well as with the learned.

. . . . A thousand men seeking what is beautiful [in outside women] are destroyed by them. A man is made a fool of by their shining limbs, but they turn into things that are harder than quartzite sandstone. The pleasure is only for a little moment.

If thou wouldst be wise (or, prosperous) establish thyself in a house (*i.e.,* get married). Love thou thy wife in the house wholly and rightly. Fill her belly and clothe her back; oil for anointing is the medicine for her limbs.

Have no intercourse with a woman-child.[2]

In the teachings of Amenemapt this genre of Egyptian writing reaches its most perfect poetical form and its highest ethical point. This sage flourished around 1100 B.C., but his work no doubt enshrines the teachings of the Heliopolitan priesthood of the Old Kingdom. His counsels are reminiscent of the Book of the Dead confession and of the maxims ascribed to Ptahhotep. Amenemapt admonishes against ar-rogance, covetousness, intellectual snobbery, ill temper, and oppressing the poor; he also counsels courtesy, deference, contentment, tolerance, and kindness. He implies that virtue is its own reward. The apparent dependence of certain Hebrew Proverbs on this Egyptian model is especially interesting. Egyptian wisdom became celebrated throughout the ancient world.

> Better is poverty in the hand of God,
> Than riches in the storehouse.
> Better are loaves when the heart is joyous,
> Than riches in unhappiness.
>> (Cf. Prov. 15:16-17.)
> Incline thine ears to hear my sayings,
> And apply thine heart to their comprehension.
> For it is a profitable thing to put them in thy heart,
> But woe to him who transgresses them.
>> (Cf. Prov. 12:17-18.)
> Fraternise not with the hot-tempered man,
> And press not upon him for conversation.
>> (Cf. Prov. 22:24.)

[2] A. E. Wallis Budge, *The Teaching of Amen-em-Apt* (London, 1924), pp 53-62.

> Remove not the landmark on the boundary of the fields.
> (Cf. Prov. 23:10.)
> A scribe skillful in his office,
> He shall find himself worthy of being a courtier.
> (Cf. Prov. 22:29.)
> Weary not thyself to seek for more
> When thy need is (already) secure.
> If riches be brought to thee by robbery,
> They will not abide the night with thee. . . .
> They have made themselves wings like geese,
> And they have flown to heaven.[3]
> (Cf. Prov. 23:4-5.)

Egyptian influence can also be detected in Job, Ecclesiastes, and certain books of the Apocrypha. Job's protestations of innocence are reminiscent of items in the negative confession of the dead.

The century and a half of social disintegration, feudal disorder, and civil war (*ca.* 2000-1850 B.C.) between the Old Kingdom and the Middle gave rise to a sage of a different brand, a sage whose admonitions were framed as a social prophecy. Deeply stirred by the existing turmoil, Ipuwer delivered in the presence of an unidentified monarch an oration expressing the anguish of the times and embodying a passionate arraignment of existing conditions. The oration was concluded with wise admonitions daring to hope for the regeneration of society, the advent of a righteous ruler with "no evil in his heart" who like a "shepherd" would gather his decimated flock and thus usher in a golden age. Here is the earliest messianic voice in the pre Hebrew world.

An Egyptian tale from Rameside times, the story of the Two Brothers, has the same moral motif as that underlying the experience of Joseph with Potiphar's wife, but the possibility of borrowing on the part of the biblical narrator is remote. The wife of the elder of the two brothers makes advances to the unmarried younger one, and when he refuses her—exemplifying the wise precepts of the sages of his land—she makes her husband believe a perverted version of the episode.

STORYTELLING

In narrative no less than in wisdom literature, Egyptians made a major contribution. They were among the earliest to endow random tales with a permanent literary form, as illustrated by the story of Sinuhe, an acknowledged masterpiece of world literature. This story was so popular that five hundred years after its composition it was still copied and studied in schools.

The hero, a high official in the court of Amenemhet I, overhearing

---

[3] Breasted, *Dawn of Conscience*, pp. 372-81.

the news of the violent death of the Pharaoh (*ca.* 1960) flees away through Palestine and settles in what is probably today al-Biqa' of Lebanon.   There he goes native, identifies himself with a Bedouin tribe, marries the daughter of the shaykh, and then succeeds him.   He hunts game with dogs, gives water to him who is athirst, guides the wayfarer, and participates in tribal raids.   Finally overcome by homesickness and shuddering at the thought of burial among "sand-dwellers" in a strange land, Sinuhe heeds the summons of Senusret I and returns to the land of his birth to indulge in the luxury of a bath and a real bed.

The story, antedating biblical narratives, gives us our first glimpses of life in Palestine and adjacent lands.   In its characterization and psychological portrayal it has no contemporary peer.   It exemplifies the attachment of the ancient and modern Egyptian to his land of nativity, a characteristic expressed in the still often-repeated adage: Once you drink from the water of the Nile, you will be satisfied with nought else. Even today hardly any Egyptian emigrants can be found permanently settled in other lands.   In its extant form the story looks like a conscious literary performance based on some experience as in the case of the story of Sindbad in the *Arabian Nights*.   It is neither fiction nor history.

A similarly composed story vividly relates the misadventures of an Egyptian envoy to fetch wood for the sacred barge of Amon from Lebanon.   After a hazardous journey Wenamon lands at Byblus but is snubbed by its prince.   The time is around 1100 B.C., when Egyptian influence in the area had greatly declined.   The Egyptian is brought to the brink of despair when he sees the birds of passage migrating for the second time to Egypt, while he lingers in Lebanon, his mission unfulfilled.   At last the haggard and anxious envoy of the effete Twentieth Dynasty is given an audience by the prince who "sits in his upper chamber, his back leaning against a balcony and the waves of the sea beating behind him."   But even then no wood is released until more money is produced.   No sooner does the ship of the ill-starred emissary set sail than it is attacked by Byblian ships and he is taken prisoner.   In conversation, atmosphere, production, and psychological treatment of the hero, this story compares favorably with Sinuhe's.

SCIENCE

When dealing with what is termed Babylonian or Egyptian science, which at its best was still primitive, it is hardly legitimate to project current conceptions of science, with its conscious observation, experimentation and implementation.   Nonetheless what that antique body of knowledge bequeathed to our present culture is still obvious and important.   This is especially true in mathematics, astronomy, and medi-

Courtesy of The British Museum

CLAY MODEL OF A LIVER USED IN THE BABYLONIAN ART
OF MEDICAL DIAGNOSIS BY DIVINATION

cine. That they had other areas of knowledge but of which we have found few traces may be illustrated by a recently discovered Babylonian clay tablet from about 2500 B.C. Cartographers believe it depicts the Euphrates valley.

MATHEMATICS AND ASTRONOMY

Early Sumerians and Egyptians, like all other primitive peoples, started counting on the fingers of the hand. Counting lies at the root of all arithmetical processes. Ten—the fingers of both hands—a most convenient figure, yielded the basis of the decimal system, which became the Egyptian notation. A multiple of ten, sixty, and a factor of sixty, twelve, became respectively the basis of the sexagesimal and the duodecimal systems which were developed and widely used in Mesopotamia. The sexagesimal is still used for the division of the hour into sixty minutes and the minute into sixty seconds. A multiple of sixty is apparent in the division of the circumference of the circle into three hundred and sixty degrees; the degree is again divided into sixty minutes. The unit of weight was called *mina* and divided into sixty shekels. A continuous tradition may be assumed to have connected Mesopotamian mathematics with Islamic and Hindu mathematics through Greek and Aramaic writings.

At an early date the Babylonians divided the week into seven days, resulting from associating a day with each of the gods identified with the seven movable heavenly bodies. Each day was under the rule of and dedicated to one of these seven heavenly bodies in the following order: sun, moon, Mars, Mercury, Jupiter, Venus and Saturn. This is still the sequence of the days of our week with its first, second and last days named respectively after the sun, the moon, and Saturn. The seventh day (*sabbath*) was fixed as a day of rest. The Babylonian names of the planets, translated into Latin, have come down to our English language.

These people also bequeathed the notion of the zodiac, that imaginary belt in the heavens which included the paths of the sun, the moon, and all the principal planets. The zodiac, with its twelve signs, each thirty degrees, was used as a frame of reference for solar, lunar, and planetary motions. Consistent observations of heavenly bodies led to a general knowledge of the movements of stars and planets and culminated in the accurate prediction of lunar eclipses and their recurrence. These were the earliest scientific observations permanently recorded. Babylonian astronomy thus became the fountainhead of its European counterpart. Hipparchus, born in Asia Minor about the mid-second century before Christ and considered founder of scientific astronomy, used Babylonian observations. Ptolemy, who flourished at Alexandria in the first half of the second Christian century and whose systems of astronomy and geography were universally accepted until the sixteenth century, recorded those observations.

THE SOLAR CALENDAR

The Egyptians also began early the study of the incomparably clear celestial world above their valley. They soon established in their minds an association between the rise of the Nile water and the appearance of certain heavenly bodies. The determination of the exact length of a year was in response to farming. The farmers were dependent upon an annual water phenomenon that was so regular the interval between one flood and the other could be counted. The only intelligent calendar of antiquity therefore originated on practical grounds. As in Babylonia the moon was first used for dividing the year, but the Egyptians took a step further and divided each month into thirty days, adding five feast days at the end of the year. By about 2000 B.C. a three-hundred-sixty-five-day year was official. This solar calendar was an outstanding astronomical achievement; it became Egypt's most conspicuous bequest to the civilized world. Introduced into Rome by Julius Caesar and reformed by Pope Gregory XIII (1582), this is the calendar still in use throughout the West today. The second Egyptian astronomical contribution was the twelve-division of daytime and night still used in our system. This division of the day into twenty-four hours, used by late Babylonia, was of Egyptian origin. The watches and clocks in use today are a constant reminder of this legacy.

In Mesopotamia and Egypt where the landmarks were liable to obliteration by the rivers' flow, there was a need for surveying that led to scientific geometry. The pursuit of geometrical and mathematical studies led to elaborate calculations of areas and cubic contents even beyond the requirements of practical affairs. In engineering, as indicated by the Nile-Red Sea canal and the Fayum reclamation project,[4] Egyptians were superior.

ASTROLOGY

Interest in planets and stars, which the early Near Easterners considered powers controlling the fortunes of man, led to a pseudo-science, astrology (etymologically science of the stars). Certain great gods of the pantheon became identified with the planets: Marduk with Jupiter, Nebu (the announcer) with Mercury, Nergal (god of war) with Mars, Ninib (patron of agriculture) with Saturn, and Ishtar (goddess of love) with Venus. Particularly the late Babylonians, or Chaldaeans, distinguished themselves in this field. In Hellenistic and Roman usage, "Chaldaean" was equated with astrologer or magician. Astronomy and mathematics played but a small role in daily life, but astrology played a major part. By relating men's actions to the will of gods, manifested through heavenly bodies, the ancients hit upon the profound philosophical principle of universal causation. The principle implied the rule of divine order, as opposed to caprice, in the universe and brought human life and heavenly phenomena into a harmonious relationship.

The professed purpose of the astrologer was to foresee and foretell, by drawing a horoscope, a person's fate. It is still his purpose today as he poses in his strange garb and gathers fees from curious or innocent passers-by on the boardwalks of a resort like Atlantic City. Arab caliphs employed court astrologers. The founders of Baghdad and Cairo would not begin operations until assured of a favorable horoscope. Cairo (al-Qahirah, the triumphant) acquired its name from Mars (the triumphant of heaven), who was then ascendant.

Among other pseudo-scientific procedures aimed at predicting future

[4] See above, p. 40; below, pp. 92-93.

events, there was divination. Special priests in both Babylonia and Egypt claimed that by inspecting a sheep's liver and entrails, observing the casual behavior of birds, and studying other omens they could foresee what was to happen.

Our language has preserved such fossilized expressions as ill-starred, lucky stars, and Latin words such as consider ("with the stars") to indicate how deeply rooted astrology was in our ancient heritage. "Influence" was considered an ethereal fluid flowing from the stars and affecting the actions of men; "influenza" was given as a name to a disease attributed to the influence of heavenly bodies; and "lunatic" shows that the moon was blamed for what modern psychologists blame on the subconscious psyche.

MEDICINE

In their notion of the cause of disease, the Near Easterner posited demons and evil spirits where we now posit viruses and microbes. The diagnostic method took the form of consulting omens; the treatment consisted of exorcisms. It was the business of the physician-priest to determine and then exorcise those strange dwellers of the body by incantations, spells, and magic formulas. The antique notion survives in our use of a "possessed person."

A description of the work of the demon we now call rheumatic arthritis has been detailed for us on a clay tablet from Nippur. It is in the poem of the "righteous sufferer," the Job of Babylonian literature. It was composed by a paralyzed bed-ridden, totally helpless ruler who asserted:

> An evil demon has come out of his (lair);
> From yellowish, the sickness became white.
> It struck my neck and crushed my back.
> It bent my high stature like a poplar;
> Like a plant of the marsh, I was uprooted, thrown on my back.
>
> The house became my prison;
> As fetters for my body, my hands were powerless,
> As pinions for my person, my feet were stretched out,
> My discomfiture was painful, the pain severe.
> A strap of many twists has struck me,
> A sharply pointed spear pierced me.
> All day the pursuer followed me,
> At night he granted me no respite whatever,
> As though wrenched, my joints were torn apart.[5]

[5] Morris K. Jastrow, *The Civilization of Babylonia and Assyria* (Philadelphia, 1915), p. 479.

A sample incantation, to be repeated by the ailing person, specifically commands the demon to leave the body and closes by invoking certain gods:

Away, away, far away,
Be ashamed, be ashamed! Fly away!
Turn about, go away, far away,
May your evil like the smoke mount to heaven!
To my body do not return,
To my body do not approach,
To my body draw not nigh,
My body do not afflict.

By Ea, the lord of the universe, be ye forsworn,
By Marduk, the chief diviner of the great gods, be ye forsworn,
By the fire-god who consumes you, be ye forsworn,
From my body be ye restrained.[6]

Starting from a base of magic and folk practice, medicine lifted itself by its bootstrap to a higher level, but remained throughout entangled in primitive conceptions. It added the use of massage, poultices, and particularly herbal remedies on the assumption that if the demon of the disease does not like the smell or taste of a plant he is likely to run away. This led to the rule that the filthier and less available the remedy the more efficacious. Mice blood, human urine and excrement, as well as fleas' excrement, figure in the prescriptions. Assyrian medical texts, preserved by the hundreds, combine old women's treatments with magical formulas and experience-proved remedies.

If a man is sick of anus trouble, and his anus picks him [hemorrhoids?], pine turpentine, fir-turpentine, opopanax, the husks of barley, in oil or beer into his anus thou shalt pour, and he shall recover.
If a man is sick of a painful swelling and his feet are full of blood, the rind of pomegranate and gazelle dung thou shalt bray, with rose-water in a small copper pan thou shalt mash, bind on.[7]

In one field of medicine, surgery, remarkable advance was made. Babylonian divination involving the study of animal entrails furnished, by analogy, vague knowledge of human anatomy and helped in the development of the surgeon's art. Progress was made especially in the treatment of eye diseases, still prevalent in those semi-tropical lands. Hammurabi's code punishes, by cutting off his fingers, a surgeon who opens an abscess in a man's eye (cataract?) and blinds him; it prescribes death for quack surgery.

Egyptian surgeons excelled the Babylonian. The earliest known

[6] Jastrow, pp. 245-246.
[7] Cf. *Journal of the Royal Asiatic Society* (1937), pp. 276, 284-285.

scientific treatise is the Edwin Smith surgical papyrus, copied in the seventeenth pre-Christian century and now in the collection of the New York Historical Society.   The long-standing practice of mummification, involving as it did removal of the viscera, gave them the advantage of direct study of human anatomy.   It also acquainted them with the preservative properties of salts and resins used in the process.   Medical papyri discuss surgical treatment of cysts, boils, carbuncles, wounds, fractures, and gynecological conditions.   The inclusion of incantations shows that magic never lost its hold.   Mummies show evidence of advanced dental surgery.   The delicate operation of trepanning was not beyond the specialists' skill.   The impact of Egyptian medical lore is recognizable in Greek, Latin, Syriac, and Persian systems.   Its patron god, Imhotep,[8] was later identified by the Greeks—with whom we associate the beginnings of this and other sciences—with their Asclepius. Many of the drugs and their properties mentioned by Pliny, Dioscorides, and Galen are clearly borrowed from Egyptian sources.   Young Greek practitioners must have frequented Egyptian medical centers, particularly those of Alexandria, as young American specialists of the nineteenth century frequented schools of Western Europe.

ART

Mesopotamian art was cradled in Sumeria, developed in Babylonia, and brought to maturity in Assyria.   In art, as in science and religion, Assyrians started as pupils of their southern neighbors.   In this field, however, the pupils soon outstripped the teachers.   The abundance of raw materials in the form of alabaster, marble, and minerals gave them a decided advantage.   Booty from Syria, Phoenicia, and other conquered lands enriched the capital and enabled its monarchs to patronize munificently artists and artisans.

Limited by the use of clay and brick, the Euphrates valley produced no massive structures comparable to the mighty pyramids, elaborate rock-hewn tombs, and huge stone columns of the Nile valley.   Stone for use in Babylonia had to be imported from neighboring lands, and wood came from the Taurus or Lebanon.   Elaborate and monumental buildings made their appearance in the early second millennium taking the form of royal palaces and temples.   Columns were presumably modeled after the palm tree, native to the land.   Architects and artists bestowed their most lavish care on these residences for kings and deities.   Temple towers, introduced by Sumerians, developed into lofty pyramidal structures a hundred or more feet high.   They were built in successive stages, usually seven, ending in a shrine atop and having a staircase on the

[8] Cited above, p. 39.

Courtesy of The Oriental Institute, University of Chicago

SARGON II HOLDING A MACE BEFORE A GOD WITH AN OFFICIAL STANDING BEHIND THE
KING Wall painting found in Khorsabad, city of Sargon outside of Ninevah.

outside. The seven stages of these ziggurats (high places), as they
were called, may have represented the sun, the moon, and the five known
planets. The writer of the biblical Tower of Babel must have had some
such picture in mind. The impress of this strange structure is noticeable in a ninth century minaret built by Moslems at Samarra (on the
Tigris).

In Babylonia and Assyria it became customary to cover the exterior of temples and palaces, as well as the gates leading thereto, with decorative designs, geometrical figures, and pictorial representations in animal and floral forms. Geometrical patterns became and remained a favorite motif in Islamic ornamental art. The decoration was extended to interior halls and doors. Sculpture was promoted by this means and reached its pinnacle on the imperial palace walls of Ashur-nasir-pal, Sargon II, Sennacherib, and Ashur-bani-pal. The bas-reliefs represented the kings in sacred rituals, military campaigns, and hunting scenes. The portrayal of men and animals ranked the artist high in realistic representation. It shows intimate study of the living form, and success in conveying the impression of pain and terror endured by the arrow-struck lion. Likewise animal figurines—usually cows, bulls, asses and lions —at palace doors are executed with exquisite detail and admirable approach to reality. The bas-reliefs display kings and nobles wearing robes brightly colored, richly patterned and elaborately embroidered. Though on hard limestone the embroidery and tassels look real.

The art of jewelry had its beginnings in Sumerian days. The earliest examples of metalwork are gold beads. Engraved gems also come very early. Smiths worked chiefly with copper and bronze to produce vases and vessels many of which have been unearthed. Houses were embellished with metalwork and with carved, inlaid, and outlaid articles of furniture and with transparent and colored glass vessels.

A distinctive product of practical Mesopotamian art were the cylinder

Courtesy of The Oriental Institute, University of Chicago

IMPRESSION OF CYLINDER SEAL FROM BABYLONIA   The sun-god Shamash is shown rising with one foot on the mountain. In front of him is a worshipper with a sacrificial kid and behind him Ishtar in her guise as war-goddess with ornamental mace.

seals. These were usually made of stone on which a dedicatory inscription to a deity or the owner's name was engraved to authenticate documents by impressing the seal on the clay tablet. Seal cylinders were usually executed with grace and delicacy and display beauty of design.

Music was not neglected as evidenced by a variety of instruments—harps, lyres, flutes, cymbals and drums—which appear on relics from Mesopotamia. They were used singly or in orchestral combination. Epics seem to have had refrains indicating that they were sung, at least on festive occasions.

What dramatizes Egyptian civilization and in our day attracts thousands of annual visitors is not the spiritual or scientific legacy but the architectural ruins and artistic relics on which the eyes can feast from Cairo north of Memphis to Luxor and Karnak on the site of Thebes. The twenty-two major pyramids, mostly strictly oriented by the four points of the compass and representing the oldest monumental edifices in stone; the countless temples, obelisks and pylons; the colonnades rising in the form of papyrus sheaves; the rock-hewn tombs; the gracefully and delicately executed sculptures; and the gorgeously colored paintings seem to form a part of the imperishable and in some respects inimitable legacy of antiquity. A visit to any important museum in Europe or America, with their specimens of Egyptian jewelry, vases, and vessels suffices to impress the beholder with the glory that was Egypt. A visit to the national museum at Cairo, especially to the gallery housing the dazzling treasures of Tutankhamon's tomb, is the nearest thing to witnessing an *Arabian Nights'* fantasy.

Egyptian architecture, painting, and sculpture had their start in religion and never divorced themselves completely from it. As in Mesopotamia, the architectural tradition sprang from mud-and-sand construction; but the residences of gods and kings naturally deserved and received more permanent and elaborate treatment. Moreover the burial places of the royalty and aristocracy had to be so solidly constructed as to contribute to the preservation of the body. The deceased was at first liberally provided with weapons, furnishings, and food for the long and hazardous journey but later with their replacements in form of representation.[9] Statues of wives and of attendants carrying water pots on their heads served as substitutes for living mates and servants. Primarily executed for their magical values, sculptured and painted images were later aimed at aesthetic values. Memphis had a craftsman-god in Ptah. His protégés wrought exquisite pieces in every medium from wood to black diorite. In the sanctuary of Amon at present-day

[9] See above, p. 65.

Karnak the highest point in Egyptian, indeed in the ancient world's, craftsmanship was attained.

The beauty of the Egyptian landscape, the unbounded bounty of the Nile, the sense of sufficiency and security enjoyed and the extension of the country's military, political, and cultural contacts into lands far beyond its boundaries combined to give the artists of the Eighteenth Dynasty the opportunity to excel, and they seized it. The beauty of nature in its characteristic aspects, involving the river and its barges, the canals and lakes with their wild flower and bird life, and the desert with its variety of wild animals and plants was extended to interior adornment of homes. Decorative designs on the walls of Ikhnaton's palace at Tell al-Amarna display a veritable garden with flower plants, running water and multicolored birds and fish. Domestic furnishing and utensils were enriched with carvings hinting at the splendor and luxury of aristocratic life. The representation of agricultural life, industrial work and other aspects of daily life were not neglected. Glass vessels and vases leave no question about the steady progress of this art, invented in Egypt. Rings, bracelets, pectorals, jewel boxes, and

Courtesy of The Metropolitan Museum of Art

A HARVESTING SCENE   The owner sits in a booth watching his workers prepare the soil and cut a tree.   In the upper register, men with sickles cut tops of grain and force them into a carrier by a bar while two women at the left pull flax.

Courtesy of The Metropolitan Museum of Art, Rogers Fund and contribution from Henry Walters, 1916

PECTORAL OF PRINCESS SAT-HATHOR-IUNIT OF THE TWELFTH DYNASTY

perfume caskets stand comparison with the best products of Paris and New York jewelers of today.

In February 1923 near Luxor there was opened the rock-hewn tomb of Tutankhamon (r. 1358-1349), son-in-law of Ikhnaton and restorer of the worship of the Theban deity Amon.[10] This was one of the rare burial places to escape detection and plunder of tomb robbers. The gorgeous and impressive collection, on which Theban priests and artisans lavished an unusual measure of expense and care, comprised golden beds, couches, chariots, caskets and garlands of flowers wrought in silver—all in a state of admirable preservation. The gem of the collection was a throne encrusted with gold and silver and sparkling with jewels. Almost equally impressive was the outer coffin made of gold. The mummy shows that the king was a mere youth of eighteen at his death after a reign of nine years. His was the unique case of a monarch whose mortuary furniture, rather than political significance, made his name a household word.

In art no less than in medicine the Egyptian impact is noticeable in other lands of the Near East. Isis' representation as nursing the infant god Horus became a model for the Christian Madonna.

IN PERSIA

The dwellers of the Iranian plateau offered no competition in science to those of the Euphrates and Nile valleys, but in aspects of art they

[10] See above, p. 45.

Photograph by Harry Burton, The Metropolitan Museum of Art

TUTANKHAMON STANDING IN HIS CHARIOT CHARGES GAZELLES AND OSTRICHES   The herd is shown fleeing before the king's hounds in a field of desert flora.   Taken from his tomb in Thebes, now in Cairo Museum.

even excelled.   Their artistic feeling and expression emerged as early as it had in those two other localities—3000-4000 B.C.—but it maintained a rather unique, uninterrupted continuity throughout the ages. As Indo-Europeans, Iranians have generally manifested higher aesthetic talents than their Semitic neighbors.   For forty centuries these dwellers never ceased to produce works of note and excellence in varied media. Besides, having established control over the Fertile Crescent early in their imperial history, Egypt and the former Hittiteland, including the Greek colonies on its western shore, they had the advantage of benefiting from the arts and crafts of their subjects.   In fact long before the empire their Kassite kinsmen had seized Babylon and ruled it for over four centuries.[11]   The so-called Luristan bronzes, in the form of weapons, trinkets, mirrors, and horse trappings mostly made of copper hammered into shape, reached an unusual stage of stylization and naturalism in the mid-second millennium.   Other types of bronzes of this millennium included axes, daggers, diminutive animals, garment pins, and votive

[11] See above, p. 42.

Victoria and Albert Museum

GOLD ARMLET WITH GRIFFIN FINIALS   Fifth century B.C.

staves.   In painted pottery pieces they assumed first rank among the artistic products of Western Asia from the fourth millennium on.

In a remarkably short time under the Achaemenids (r. *ca.* 550-330 B.C.) a vigorous youthful nation brought all the major centers of the ancient civilization under its sway.[12]   Its rulers were open-minded enough to utilize the artistic traditions of their subjects.   Foreign workmen took part in the construction of those symbols of a world empire, the royal palaces of Persepolis and Susa, begun by Darius the Great (r. 521-485), completed and embellished by Xerxes and his successors, and burned by Alexander the Great.   We even know some Greek architects by name.   The elevated terraces on which palaces arose follow Assyrian models; the colossal stone columns suggest Egyptian inspiration; the capitals of the columns display Greek influence; but the ensemble is purely Iranian in conception and execution.   It is a creation of indigenous and harmonious character.   Themes, techniques, materials, and workmen were indeed borrowed but the product remained Iranian.

In sculpture the Assyrian tradition predominates.   Fragments of relief sculpture from the audience hall of Pasargadae, residence city of Cyrus of which but little now remains, show tribute bearers similar to those of Persepolis.   The human beings on these stone reliefs look more

[12] See above, pp. 5, 52.

Courtesy of The Oriental Institute, University of Chicago

A SCULPTURED FRIEZE AT PERSEPOLIS   Tribute-bearing subjects at the Archae-
menids.   Sardinians are bringing a humped bull, shields, and lances.   The Bac-
trians are bringing gold vessels and a camel.

alive and the animals they lead—camels, horses, and rams—more
individualized than their Assyrian predecessors.   Persian cylinders also
betray Assyro-Babylonian patterns.   Achaemenid architecture was necessarily royal and aristocratic, but sculpture had a wider base in society.
It is almost entirely relief, whereas Nineveh and Babylon have left us
specimens in the round, portrait statues.   Especially noteworthy are
the glazed brick friezes of Susa.   In the field of painting hardly any
specimens have survived.   In metalwork the products evince long and
intimate familarity with the processes of casting, embossing, and inlaying gold and silver articles with pearls, precious stones, and lapis lazuli.
Figurines show jewelry worn by men as well as women and at times by
horses.

From the bright morning of their civilization, Iranians began to
propitiate the powers of the sky with fine and brilliant symbols which
they continued to use down to the present day.   Abstraction rather than
strict reproduction became a dominant motif.   Their art has never lost
sight of its main objective—decoration rather than literal representa-

tion. Its value has consistently lain in the aesthetic rather than in the utilitarian. Utensils, weapons, and garments received artistic treatment that transformed the humblest material of which they were made into something beautiful. This decorative intent and quality constitutes a perseverant trait in Persian art. Throughout its long course it embraced interaction with Greek tradition, subsequent to Alexander's conquest, and with the later Mongol and the Moslem traditions resulting in exquisite manuscript miniatures, designs on rugs, and mosaics on mosque walls that have not ceased to exercise their fascination on onlookers.

BOOKS TO READ

Breasted, James H., *Development of Religion and Thought in Ancient Egypt* (New York, 1912).

Erman, Adolf, *The Literature of the Ancient Egyptians*, tr. A. M. Blackman (London, 1927).

Kramer, Samuel N., *From the Tablets of Sumer* (Indian Hills, Col., 1956).

Moscati, Sabatino, *Ancient Semitic Civilizations* (London, 1957).

Peet, T. Eric, *A Comparative Study of the Literatures of Egypt, Palestine, and Mesopotamia* (London, 1931).

Pritchard, James B., ed. *Ancient Near Eastern Texts* (Princeton, 1950).

Rogers, Robert W., *Cuneiform Parallels to the Old Testament* (New York, 1912).

Wilson, John A., *The Burden of Egypt* (Chicago, 1951).

VIII   *Canaanites, Aramaeans and Hebrews*

T HE second major Semitic group after the Assyro-Babylonian to establish a new abode in the Fertile Crescent was the Amorite,
of whom the Canaanites formed the southern branch. Canaanites
covered the bulk of what is today Syria, Lebanon, and Palestine. Before Palestine was so named, it was a part of the land of Canaan.
Canaan lay at the hub of a circle of a highly civilized area including the
Tigro-Euphrates valley on the east, Egypt on the south, Crete and
Mycenae on the west, and Hittiteland on the north. In the thirteenth
and twelfth centuries Semitic hordes, later identified as Aramaeans and
Israelites, and Indo-European Sea Peoples, called Philistines (whence
the name Palestine), swept into Canaan, occupied the bulk of its south,
and parts of its north and east, and turned the eyes of its people sea-
ward. For centuries the narrow but prolific land of Phoenicia, with an
energetic and restless population, remained a theater of significant
events—economic and cultural—that left their imperishable stamp on
the civilization of Europe. Those of the Canaanites with whom the
Greeks traded were called by them "purple red" after the color of their
cloth which they sold or exchanged. Those traders were mostly from
what is today the Lebanese coast.

PHOENICIAN CITY-STATES

The ancestors of the Canaanites must have occupied the entire area
from the beginning of the third millennium before Christ, but their language and religion did not begin to emerge as distinct Semitic entities
until a thousand years or so later. Hemmed in between mighty empires to the north, east, and south and occupying a land fragmented by
mountains, they never succeeded in establishing a strong unified state.
Their political organization took the form of city-states extending from

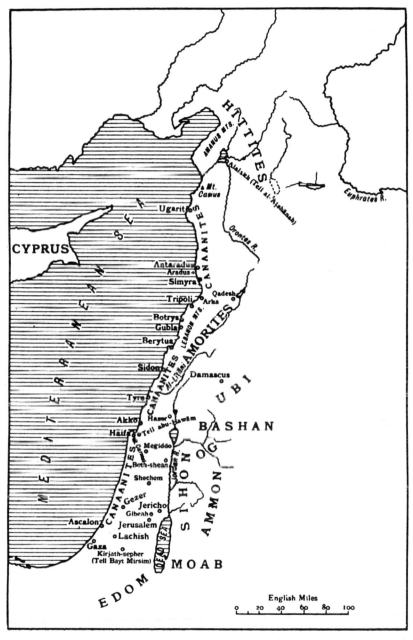

CANAAN BEFORE ISRAEL

Ugarit and Aradus along the shore through Gubla, Sidon, and Tyre to Ascalon and Gaza in the south. Jericho, Gezer, Jerusalem, and Shechem were among their inland centers. Many of these and other cities figure prominently for the first time in the campaign reports of Thutmose III (1490 B.C. *seq.*)[1] and in the Tell al-Amarna correspondence (1370 B.C. *seq.*). Some are described in the Books of Joshua and Judges. Among them Aradus, Sidon, and Tyre had two settlements each, one on the mainland for trading and agriculture and the other on close-by inlets for resort for protection against Egyptian, Assyrian, or Neo-Babylonian assaults.

The organization of the city-states mirrored the physical dismemberment of the land. At times a city might succeed in extending its hegemony over the hinterland and neighboring city-states, as did Ugarit in the late sixteenth century, Gubla in the fourteenth, Sidon in the twelfth to the eleventh, and Tyre thereafter. Such cities would then become city-based states. But throughout, the Canaanites proved to be peace- rather than military-minded, with the center of their interest in trade, art, and religion. Their usual procedure was to bow their heads before the Egyptian, Hittite, Mesopotamian, or Persian storm of conquest; buy security by paying tribute; and hope for partial compensation by an enlarged market for their wares.

INDUSTRY

Ceramics was one of the earliest and most successful of Canaanite industries attaining its pinnacle prior to 1500 B.C. In metallurgy, especially as it related to copper and bronze, Canaanites were probably unexcelled from about 2100 to 1200 B.C. In quest of gold and silver, of tin for hardening copper into bronze, and of other metals for hardening iron into alloy steel, they undertook long and hazardous journeys into little-known lands. Tradition ascribes the invention of glass— in reality an Egyptian performance—to Phoenicians who in reality perfected this art and trafficked in its product. A graphic description of the land and sea traffic of early sixth century Phoenicians has been preserved in Ezekiel (27). The three centuries beginning about 1000 B.C. encompass the most brilliant and prosperous period in their history.

PURPLE CLOTH

But it was through textiles, particularly those dyed purple, that the Phoenician name became known throughout the world. Tyre was the

[1] See above, pp. 44-45.

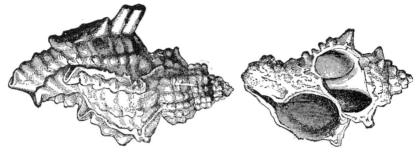

Courtesy Rawlinson, PHOENICIA (Longmans Green)

SHELL OF THE MUREX TRUNCULUS, WHICH YIELDED THE PURPLE DYE Large heaps of these shells can be seen near Tyre and outside the south gate at Sidon.

principal center of this industry. In its and Sidon's vicinity flourished a superior variety of the murex from which the purple fluid was extracted. So considerable and painstaking were the labor and skill required in extracting the few drops of liquid from the tiny mollusk and in applying it to the cloth that only the wealthy could afford it. Hence the expression "born in the purple." Helen of Troy, Cleopatra of Egypt, Jewish high priests, Jupiter priests in Asia Minor, and later Roman emperors took pride wearing purple garments. The red robes of Catholic cardinals and of Oriental Church patriarchs perpetuate the tradition.

MARITIME ACTIVITY

Large-scale trade in textiles, metalwork, pottery, glass, timber, wheat, oil, wine and other native products necessitated the discovery or creation of new markets. From modest beginnings involving coastwise sailings, the Canaanites developed into the first maritime nation in history. Their high mountain hindered intercourse with the hinterland, but the sea at their feet invited them to chart routes across its surface. The deep held no deterring terrors for these early Lebanese, and the horizon beckoned them to the unknown behind it. Their earliest international routes led from Gubla to Egypt; later ones connected Sidon and Tyre with the islands of the Mediterranean and with their settlements on the northern and southern shores of this sea. Night navigation was facilitated by the discovery and utilization of the Pole Star, which the Greeks named after the Phoenicians. Phoenician ships, for the construction of which the Lebanon provided its durable coniferous and resinous trees, served as a model for the early free ships. They were represented in bas-relief on the palace wall of Sennacherib (*ca.* 700 B.C.). Centuries before this Assyrian monarch, Solomon resolved to build a fleet to be based at the head of the Red Sea. He turned to his friend King Hiram of Tyre for "shipmen who had knowledge of the sea" (I Kings 9-27).

PHOENICIAN COLONIES

Canaanites settled wherever they went, and the settlements grew into colonies. Their colonies were first planted in Egypt, Cilicia, Cyprus, and other islands of the Eastern Mediterranean, then in Sicily, Sardinia and other islands of the mid-Mediterranean. Later, colonies were established on the southern shores of France and Spain and in North Africa. All were linked together and with the mother cities, mainly Sidon and Tyre, by navigation. Gades (Cadiz) beyond the Pillars of Hercules was founded around 1000 B.C. It introduced the Phoenicians into the Atlantic Ocean, whose discovery by them ranks next to the invention of the alphabet and to the dissemination of Near Eastern material and spiritual culture, as their greatest contribution to the progress of mankind. Voyages on the Atlantic may have landed them in Cornwall, southwestern England, in quest of tin. Tarshish in Spain, Tarsus (birthplace of Paul), Corinth in Greece, and other cities bearing Canaanite names or revering Semitic deities owe their origins to Canaanite commercial activity. Legend asserts that Europe received its name from Europa, daughter of a Phoenician king, and Libya, the Greek name for North Africa, is said to have the name of his mother. A brother of Europa, Cadmus, is credited with introducing the alphabet into the Greek world.

In what is now Tunisia, the Phoenicians planted their most distinguished colony, Carthage (Phoenician for "new town") about 814 B.C. This illustrious daughter of Tyre established its hegemony from the borders of modern Libya to the Straits of Gibraltar. It contested the supremacy of the sea with rising Rome, and in 218 B.C. sent its world-renowned general Hannibal across Spain and the Alps to battle with the Romans for years on their own soil. Defeated (202) he fled (196) to Tyre. Fifty years later his capital was wiped out from the slate by its unrelenting enemy.

The crowning achievement of Phoenician navigation was the circumnavigation of Africa under Pharaoh Necho (600-593 B.C.), over two thousand years before Portuguese navigators rounded the Cape of Good Hope, with the discovery of which they are generally credited. The feat was made possible by Necho's redigging of the canal connecting the eastern arm of the Nile with the head of the Red Sea. Greek writers ascribe the first linking of the two bodies of water to Sesostris.[2] As an inscription still preserved in a garden in al-Ismailiyah indicates, however, the canal had become silted up again and was redug by Darius the Great.

ARAMAEANS

Like the Canaanites, the Aramaeans were originally Bedouins from the desert. Before the mid-second pre-Christian millennium their tribes settled on the banks of the middle Euphrates, where they developed their distinct nationality and language, originally a Semitic dialect. There, in that corridor between Syria and Mesopotamia, they set up their first state, Aram Naharaim (Aram of the two rivers, the Khabur and the Euphrates). Another state centered in Haran (later Harran). Hebrew tradition brought its patriarchs from that region before settling them in Palestine, sent Abraham's servant to Haran in quest of a wife for Isaac, and dispatched Jacob there to marry Leah and Rachel.[3] Abraham himself was called Syrian,[4] the Greek term for Aramaean. Evidently the forefathers of the Hebrew people were with the Aramaean migration first into Syria[5] and spoke Aramaic before settling in Palestine and adopting the local Canaanite dialect, which became the Hebrew of the Old Testament.

ARAM DAMASCUS

Aramaean groups drifted southward in the fourteenth and thirteenth centuries into inland Syria. Before long the entire area behind the Phoenician coastline was dominated by Aramaean states of changing size. Mount Lebanon blocked their penetration into the coastal plain already peopled by Phoenicians. By 1200 B.C. Damascus, capital-to-be, was already in Aramaean hands. In due course the newcomers assimilated the higher culture of their Semitic cousins, the Amorites and Canaanites, among whom they had settled. They preserved, however, their dialect which developed into an international medium of expression and was the mother tongue of Christ.[6]

Of the numerous states established by Aramaeans Damascus was

[2] Cited above, p. 40.
[3] Gen. 24:4; 29:21-28.
[4] Deut. 26:5.
[5] Cf. below, p. 94.
[6] See below, pp. 105-106.

the most distinguished.   It is the one referred to in the Old Testament
as Aram.   Their capital's position at the head of the caravan route
across the desert enabled them to gain control over the inland trade.
Established in the late eleventh century, the kingdom of Damascus extended its frontiers to the Euphrates in the north and the Yarmuk
(confluence of the Jordan) in the south.   It maintained hostile relations
with its southern neighbor the kingdom of Israel for over a century.
For a time, beginning about 875 B.C., in King Omri's last days, Israel
became a vassal of Damascus.   When Omri's son and successor, Ahab,
refused to pay the tribute or join the federation against a threatening
Assyrian attack, headed by Ben-Hadad of Damascus (*ca.* 879-843)
the Aramaean king suddenly appeared before the capital Samaria to
coerce him.[7]

HEBREWS

Of all the peoples of antiquity the Hebrews, mainly because of the
Old Testament, are the ones best known.   They entered the land of
Canaan in two major, if ill-defined, movements, one connected with
the Aramaeans beginning in the fourteenth century and the other from
Egypt in the late thirteenth century.   Entering as wanderers, adventurers, and nomads the future Hebrews settled among the highly
civilized Canaanites, learned from them the practice of agriculture,
the techniques for living in homes, and more importantly the art of
reading and writing.   Gradually they gave up their old Semitic tongue
in favor of the Canaanite.   The Hebrew of the Old Testament differs
only dialectally from Phoenician.   Their oral tradition, as later recorded
in their scriptures, brings their first ancestor Abraham from Mesopotamia.   It stretches their history and connects it wtih the story of the
creation of man, drawing upon Assyro-Babylonian sources.[8]

With the Exodus from Egypt (*ca.* 1234-1215), involving only
Rachel's tribe, the real history of the Hebrews begins.   While en route
to Palestine under Moses' leadership, the tribesmen picked up a north
Arabian deity, the Jehovah of Israel.   Originally a tribal god abiding
in a tent and favoring feasts and sacrifices from the herd,[9] this desert
deity was radically transformed later by the Prophets.   He was endowed
with noble attributes of mercy, righteousness, and justice and raised
to a position of universality.   He became the one and only God of Jews,
Christians and Moslems.

[7] 1 K. 20:1 *seq.*
[8] Treated above, pp. 57 *seq.*
[9] Ex. 3:18; 18:12; 51; Num. 10:35-36.

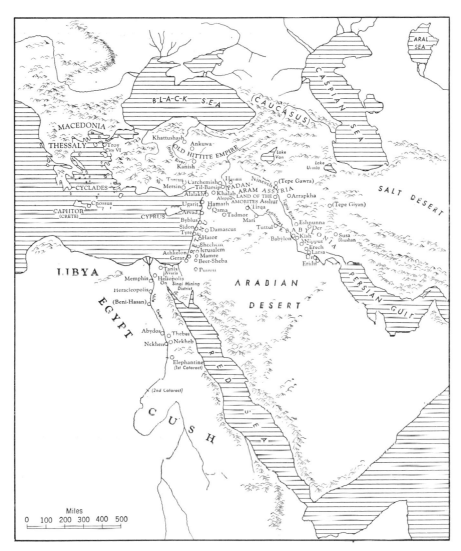

THE NEAR EAST *ca.* 1600 B.C.

The Hebrew occupation of the promised land of "milk and honey" was in part military conquest and in part peaceful penetration. Reinforced by intermarriage with the natives and by coalescing with their kinsmen who had remained in the land, the newcomers struck root in the early twelfth century, mainly in the sparsely populated hilly country west of the Jordan. This is the period called that of the Judges. Their community, Israel, was an association of twelve tribes bound together by a common belief in one god, Yahweh. Central to their creed was the notion that their god had chosen them as a special instrument for carrying out his purposes here on earth. The Hebrews encountered a formidable adversary, besides the Canaanites, in the Philistines[10] who had just established themselves along the Palestine coast. The Philistine five cities, organized into city-states, stretched from south of Jaffa to Gaza. Their superiority in arms, which involved knowledge of smelting and the use of iron, gave them the upper hand over the Israelites. In that general area only the Hittites had, prior to this time, made some military use of this metal. Both peoples naturally tried to maintain a monopoly on that knowledge. In due course the Canaanites acquired the knowledge and with it the use of iron chariots. Some of the most picturesque military exploits of Hebrew tradition relate to such national heroes as Samson and David as they struggled against Philistines. It was not until David's reign that the Philistine grip on the land was loosened.

THE MONARCHY

The Hebrew-Philistine rivalry for the possession of the land provided the occasion for the creation of the Hebrew monarchy; the neighboring kinglets of Canaan furnished the model. Saul's anointment (*ca.* 1020) as the first king was tantamount to a challenge to Philistine suzerainty. But Saul, who lived in a tent and conducted himself more like a Bedouin chief, was weak in character and melancholy of temperament. It was left for David, who succeeded him in about 1004, to shake off the Philistine yoke. Additionally David extended his domain in all directions and established the most powerful state Palestine ever produced. Its control of the great trade route that linked Aram and Phoenicia with Arabia and Egypt insured unprecedented prosperity. Under David's son and successor, Solomon (r. *ca.* 963-*ca.* 923), the Hebrew monarchy attained dazzling heights of glamor and pageantry.

[10] See above, p. 88.

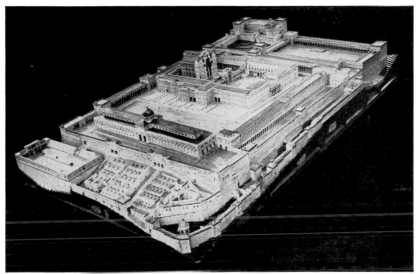

Courtesy of The Bettmann Archive

SOLOMON'S TEMPLE

In addition to proceeds from commerce maintained by Phoenician built- and manned-ships, Solomon fed the treasury on extensive mining projects also initiated if not conducted by Phoenicians. Smelting was carried on in a refinery at Elath (Ezion-geber) at the head of today's Gulf of al-Aqabah, where his fleet was likewise based. Naval expeditions along the Arabian and African coasts exchanged native-produced ingots of copper and iron for frankincense, spices, ivory, gold, and jewels. Solomon "in his glory" followed the pattern of autocratic, voluptuous monarchs of Assyria and Egypt and to that extent depleted the treasury. His one great architectural monument was the temple bearing his name.

Upon Solomon's death at about 923, the united monarchy split into a northern kingdom, Israel, based on ten tribes and having Shechem (near the modern village of al-Balatah), and a southern one, Judah, based on the remaining two tribes and using Jerusalem as capital.

The two tiny kingdoms fell into the complex political and belligerent developments of the general area and became rivals, at times enemies. Repeated uprisings and mounting intrigues in both states contributed to their final undoing. Israel experienced nine dynastic changes, involving nineteen kings, in its two-century existence. The throne of Judah was occupied by twenty kings, but the southern kingdom out-

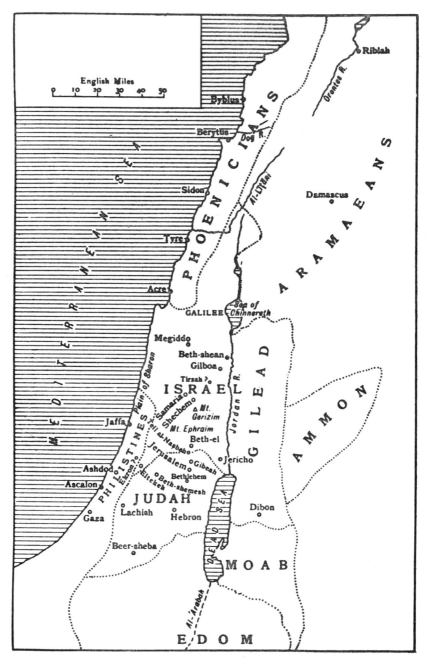

PALESTINE IN THE PERIOD OF THE HEBREW MONARCHIES

lived the northern by about a century and a third.[11]   The way was paved for their final destruction one by Assyria and the other by Neo-Babylonia.

DECLINE AND FALL: THE ARAMAEANS

Such petty states as the Canaanite, the Aramaean, and the Hebrew could enjoy an Indian summer only during an interval when aggressive and expansive empires in the vicinity were in a state of suspended animation.   This was the case in the centuries immediately preceding and succeeding 1000 B.C.   But once suspension was replaced by activity, threatening clouds begin to thicken and darken on the horizon of the minor states.

Under Ashur-nasir-pal II (r. 884-858) and his son Shalmaneser III (r. 859-824), Assyria built up a formidable war machine and started on its career as an imperial world power.   Ashur-nasir-pal conducted the first full-dress invasion of the area from Mesopotamia (879), an invasion comparable to that of Thutmose III from Egypt.[12]   The immediate objective was the control of the east-to-west trade route; the

[11] List of the Hebrew kings of the divided monarchy with their approximate dates (the spaces indicate the changes of dynasties):

ISRAEL		JUDAH	
Jeroboam I	923-907	Rehoboam	926-910
Nadab	907-906	Abijam	910-908
		Asa	908-872
Baasha	906-883	Jehoshaphat	872-852
Elah	883-882	Jehoram	852-845
		Ahaziah	845-844
Zimri	882		
		Athaliah	845-839
Omri	882-871		
Ahab	871-852	Joash	839-800
Ahaziah	852-851	Amaziah	800-785
Jehoram	851-845	Uzziah	785-747
		Jotham	758-743
Jehu	845-818	Ahaz	742-725
Jehoahaz	818-802	Hezekiah	725-697
Joash	802-787	Manasseh	696-642
Jeroboam II	787-747	Amon	641-640
Zechariah	747-746	Josiah	639-609
		Jehoiahaz	609
Shallum	747-746	Jehoiakim	608-598
		Jehoiachin	598
Menahem	746-737	Zedekiah	598-587
Pekahiah	736-735		
Pekah	734-733		
Hoshea	732-724		

[12] Discussed above, pp. 44-45, 48.

ultimate, a showdown with the traditional rival, Egypt, for supremacy in Western Asia.[13] A coalition of twelve kings under Ben-Hadad of Damascus was defeated, but not decisively, by Shalmaneser (853) at Qarqar on the Orontes.[14] But there was no follow-up until after a century had passed. In 733 Tiglath-pileser forced Israel to submit and in the following year he overthrew Damascus, center of Aramaean power. His successor, Shalmanese V (r. 727-722), overran the Phoenician states, employed the navies of Sidon and Acre against the island city of Tyre, and won its surrender after five years of struggle. He also started the siege of Samaria, then capital of Israel, which after two years yielded (721) to Sargon II.[15] Israel lost its independence forever. Its twin sister Judah meantime became a vassal of Assyria until the Neo-Babylonian power replaced the Assyrian (612). In 587 Nebuchadnezzar swept over this kingdom, devastated Jerusalem and other towns, and converted the area into a Neo-Babylonian province.[16] Following the example of Sargon II, he deported the cream of the upper classes into Mesopotamia. Their descendants were permitted to return to Palestine in 538, when the Persian Cyrus brought Neo-Babylonia under his rule. With the fall of Aram, Israel, and most of the Phoenician city-states, including Sidon, all hope of survival for heroic Tyre was gone. After a siege of thirteen years ending in 572 the city yielded to Nebuchadnezzar.

Aram, Phoenicia, Israel, and Judah disappeared as political entities, but as cultural influences they endured as an integral part of the heritage of man.

BOOKS TO READ

Albright, William F., *From the Stone Age to Christianity,* 2nd ed. (New York, 1957).

Baramki, D. C., *Phoenicia and the Phoenicians* (Beirut, 1961).

Bright, John, *A History of Israel* (Philadelphia, 1959).

Gordon, Cyrus H., *Introduction to Old Testament Times* (Ventnor, 1953).

Hitti, Philip K., *History of Syria including Lebanon and Palestine,* 2nd ed. (New York and London, 1957).

Kenyon, Kathleen M., *Archaeology of the Holy Land* (London, 1960).

Meek, Theophile J., *Hebrew Origins* (New York, 1936).

Noth, Martin, *History of Israel* (London, 1958).

[13] Consult above, p. 50.
[14] See above, p. 48.
[15] See above, pp. 48, 50.
[16] 2 K., ch. 25; Jer., ch. 39.

O'Callaghan, Roger T., *Aram Nahraim* (Rome, 1948).

Olmstead, A. T., *History of Palestine and Syria to the Macedonian Conquest* (New York, 1931).

Robinson, Theodore H., *A History of Israel,* vol. I (Oxford, reprinted 1948).

Weill, Raymond, *Phoenicia and Western Asia,* tr. Ernest F. Row (London, 1940).

Wright, George E. and Filson, Floyd V., *The Westminster Historical Atlas of the Bible,* 2nd ed. (Philadelphia, 1956).

IX *Cultural Contributions: Literary and Religious*

THE millennium beginning around 1500 B.C. was one of cultural pluralism and cross-fertilization in which Mesopotamia, Egypt, Phoenicia, Aram, and Palestine freely exchanged scientific, literary, religious, artistic, and other cultural ideas. Phoenician ships and Aramaean caravans carried more than cargoes; they carried intangibles of equal if not greater significance to the progress of man. The Mediterranean and its eastern basin became a wide base for multiform cultural influences involving Crete and Greece. The spotlight which first brilliantly illumined Mesopotamia and Egypt shifted then to Phoenicia and Palestine. It is a paradox of world history that the two countries destined to give birth one to the most accomplished system of writing and the other to the noblest system of religious beliefs were not extensive, mighty and opulent Mesopotamia or Egypt but relatively small, poor, and militarily weak Phoenicia and Palestine. They lay at the crossroad of the nations and on the narrow cultural bridge linking Western Asia with Africa.

THE ALPHABET

The alphabet was the most significant of the boons conferred upon mankind by Phoenicia. It is generally considered the greatest invention ever made by man. The Egyptians had phonologically developed from their hieroglyphics forty signs which were consonantal, but they did not go so far as using them as independent signs. It was the Canaanites who made exclusive use of a well-developed alphabetic system, and disseminated it throughout the world. The basis of this system, consisting of twenty-two letters, was evidently the Egyptian language employed in Sinai, where Egyptians maintained copper and turquoise mines. The earliest Canaanite inscriptions in this linear alphabet date from the fourteenth century. The Phoenicians passed

102

Sinaitic	Form represents	South Arabic	Phoenician	Ra's al-Shamrah	Later Greek	Latin	Arabic
	ox-head				A	A	ء
	house				B	B	ب
					Γ	CG	ج
					Δ	D	د
	man praying				E	E	ذ
					Y	FV	و
	= (?)				I	…	ز
	double loop				θ	H	ح
	…				⊗	…	ط
	hand				⌐	I	ى
					K	…	ك
	oxgoad?				LΛ	L	ل
	water				M	M	م
	serpent				N	N	ن
	fish				Ξ	X	…
	eye				O	O	ع
					Γ	P	ف
					…	…	ص
					φ	Q	ق
	human head				P	R	ر
	bow				ξ	S	سش
	cross				T	T	ت

Courtesy of The Macmillan Co., Ltd.

A TABLE OF ALPHABETS SHOWING THE DEVELOPMENT OF LATIN AND ARABIC LETTERS
FROM THE SINAITIC THROUGH PHOENICIAN

their alphabet westward to the Greeks (850-750 B.C.), who transmitted it to later Europeans; and eastward to the Aramaeans, who transmitted it to the Hebrews to record in it their Old Testament; to the Persians to employ it as their official language; to the Arabians, who used it for their Koran, and to other peoples in Asia.

It is the irony of fate that the people who developed and spread the first effective system of writing did not leave much literature behind them. Their literature dealt largely with business transactions and was recorded on papyrus, a perishable material; fortunately, however, much of the literary and religious output has found its way into the sacred writings of the Hebrews. Unmistakable Canaanite mythological compositions are embedded in Genesis and the Prophets; while Canaanite lyric pieces and wise sayings are noticeable in the Proverbs, Job, the Psalms and the Song of Songs. Psalm 29 is in its entirety of Canaanite origin. Parallelism constitutes the basis of both Canaanite and Hebrew poetry. The remarkable discoveries at Ugarit (Ras al-Shamrah) in and after 1929 reveal close analogies in both language and thought between the Canaanite literature of the fourteenth century and the later Hebrew literature. "Rider of the clouds" is applied in Ugaritic to Baal and in Hebrew (Ps. 68:4) to Jehovah. Thunder is applied to the voice of Baal in Ugaritic as well as to the voice of Jehovah (Ps. 29:3-5; Job 37:2-5). Baal slays leviathan; so does Jehovah (Is. 27:1). Daniel is a Ugaritic hero closely resembling the Daniel of the Story of Susanna in the Apocrypha.[1]

FERTILITY CULT

Worship of the forces of growth and reproduction on which depended the very existence of an agricultural, stock-raising community was basic in Canaanite religion, a Semitic system of practices and beliefs. The outstanding feature of this Semitic cult was mourning for the periodical death of the vegetation deity through the summer heat, rites for his overcoming of the god of death and the underworld, and for his revival in spring with the renewed vigor of the sun emerging from its defeat in winter. As a result of the marriage of the restored god, Baal, with the goddess of fertility, Ishtar, the earth once more puts out its green foliage and bursts forth with flowers and blossoms. This episode of nature was first embodied in an ancient Babylonian myth centering on Tammuz, whom the Canaanites entitled Adhon and who was borrowed by the Greeks as Adonis. The Canaanites localized the Tammuz-Ishtar (Lady of Byblus) cult at the source of the river in Lebanon now called Nahr Ibrahim. In connection with the Ishtar rites at Byblus, as in Babylon earlier and in Greece, Cyprus, and Sicily later, there was practiced a sacred form of prostitution. The Hebrews,

[1] Cyrus H. Gordon, *The Loves and Wars of Baal and Anat* (Princeton, 1943), pp. XI-XIV.

too, maintained "temple harlots." [2]   The cult of the dying and rising god became central in the Christian system.   By his resurrection Christ established the belief that death was not the end but a beginning, not only an exit but also an entrance.

GODS

Being essentially nature worship, Canaanite religion had two central gods who bore different names among different Semites but were fundamentally the Father Sky and the Mother Earth.   The sky god, generally known as Baal (lord), controlled the rain and crops, enjoyed festivals and feasts, and was propitiated by sacrifices.   The mother goddess went by the name Ashtart (Ishtar of Babylonia, Ashtoreth of the Hebrews) and was borrowed by the Greeks and fused with their Aphrodite to become the celebrated goddess of fertility.   By the Romans she was identified with the brightest of the planets, Venus.   Through Ovid and Shakespeare the story of Venus and Adonis reached us.   The rite entered Egypt very early as the worship of Isis and Osiris.   The Semitic name of this goddess has been preserved in Esther.   Her title was Baalat (mistress, lady).   The Canaanite god had his abode in a temple featuring a rock altar on which sacrifices were offered, a sacred pillar representing the male deity and suggesting phallic origin, and a sacred pole standing for the evergreen plant in which resided the female deity's fertility.   The pillar and pole generally obviated the necessity of setting up idols in the temples.

THE EXTRAORDINARY CASE OF ARAMAIC

The peaceful penetration of Aramaic culture, and with it the Aramaic language, survived Aramaean political and military penetration.   This was mainly due to Aramaean merchants who monopolized overland trade as their Phoenician neighbors had monopolized the maritime trade.   Purple and glass from the Lebanese coast; oil and wine from Palestine; jasper, coffee, ivory, and ebony from Africa constituted the main articles of exchange.   With no imperial background, Aramaic became the vehicle of international commerce from India to Ethiopia.   Even the Assyrians, who deprived the Aramaeans of their political independence for all time, were Aramaicized.   Aramaic enjoyed the advantages of simpler script.   It also succeeded Akkadian as the international language of diplomacy,[3] and was used by the Persian Achae-

---

[2] Consult Ezek. 8:14; Mic. 1:7; Deut. 23:18.
[3] See above, p. 54.

menids.[4]   By about 500 B.C. it had become, with local variations, the vernacular of the entire Fertile Crescent.   Its triumph over Hebrew made it the language in which Christ communicated his message.   His last words "Eloi, Eloi, lama sabachthani" [5] have been transmitted through a fossilized Greek text, which is the only text that has been preserved.

Before Greek or Latin, Aramaic was the language of the Christians. Syriac, its eastern branch, is still used in the liturgy of the Maronite and other Oriental churches.   As a colloquial it has survived among a few remnants of the Syrian Church.

THE ARAMAEAN PANTHEON

Aramaic literature, like its Phoenician counterpart, was used mainly for business literature and was lacking in enduring quality.   From the extant religious pieces we gather that the storm-god Hadad headed the pantheon.   A god of rain and thunder, Hadad was both beneficent, as he sent rain to fructify the earth, and maleficent, when he sent destructive floods.   He was a special favorite with an agricultural society.   Hadad's cult was later merged with that of the sun and his head was ornamented with rays, as in his Baalbak representation. Under the Romans he was metamorphosed into Jupiter Damascenus. His consort, a fertility goddess, was worshiped under the name Atargatis, the "Syrian goddess" of the Greeks and Romans.   After the conquest of Alexander her cult spread westward to Greece and Rome. Besides this divine couple, the Aramaean temple displayed an assortment of minor deities charged with specific functions.

HEBREW LITERATURE

In art, architecture, pottery, metalwork, crafts, and in other industries, the Hebrews, we have learned,[6] generally followed Canaanite models and offered little of originality.   Nor did their contribution to world progress lie in the fields of politics or commerce; it lay rather in literature and religion.   Through their religious literature they acquired the envious position of the ethical and moral teachers of a large section of mankind.   The Old Testament is their unsurpassed literary monument; monotheism is its unique contribution.   Throughout the ages this literary bequest has remained a dynamic force in the lives of men and women throughout the world.   Writers, speakers, poets, artists in ancient, medieval and modern times have resorted to it for inspira-

[4] See above, p. 54.
[5] Mark 15:34.
[6] Above, pp. 91-92, 97.

tion and guidance. Hardly a modern tongue does not bear the stamp of Old Testament allusions. Hebrew, the language of the Old Testament, though supplanted in Palestine by Aramaic after the fifth pre-Christian century, continued in partial use in religious literature.

The authorship of this book is composite. The lawgiver, personified by Moses, spoke as the mouthpiece of Jehovah. Although the Mosaic code mirrors a lower stage of industrial and commercial development than its Hammurabi counterpart,[7] Hebrew legislation, as expressed in the Decalogue, surpasses anything the ancients had ever enacted. Another Hebrew author-teacher was the priest, who at times turned historian. As historian his sources were materials worked out by Babylonians and Assyrians; he added a moral touch that was brand new, in fact unique.[8] Then there was the wise man, personified by Solomon, who like the Egyptian sage addressed himself to the individual—rather than the society. His message was on achieving success in earthly terms. Quite often the wise man, as in the case of the author of the Book of Job, was a poet. Other poets, represented by the Psalmist, composed devotional songs and hymns of such tender and exalted feeling as to continue in use by Jews and Christians to the present day.

PROPHETISM

The prophet whose main interest was to speak for Jehovah, not to foretell the future was especially significant among Hebrew teachers and authors. Starting as Jehovah's champions against the Baals and other foreign gods, the prophets of Israel worked their way to lofty and sublime spiritual thinking. They effected a virtually new religion, centering on one and only one supreme and universal deity. This one god, they insisted, was an ethical and righteous being, who did not rejoice in his worshipers' sacrifices but in their righteous living.

The concept of an exclusive, ethical monotheism was at the core of Hebraic teaching. The old gods had been jealous and cruel; they ordered their followers to slaughter other peoples mercilessly and held tribes responsible for the sin of one of its members. In a world and at a time when polytheism dominated religious thinking and when the performance of certain rites was considered essential for securing the gods' favor or averting their anger, the Hebrew prophets introduced a new interpretation of God, and of man, and of their interrelations. Their God exacted justice but loved mercy. It was on this prophetic

[7] P. 61.
[8] Consult above, pp. 58-59.

foundation that Christ built and on the joint Judaeo-Christian structure that Muhammad established his system. The revolutionary enthusiasm of the prophets in support of the needy inspired much of the
idealism of medieval Christianity. The claim then that Hebrew
prophetism "ushered in the greatest movement in the spiritual history of
mankind" [9] is no exaggeration.

MONOTHEISM

Ethical monotheism was the capstone of the Hebrew structure of
religious thought. Amos (fl. *ca.* 750) is considered its first theoretical
exponent.[10] That a shepherd and dresser of sycamore trees, perhaps
illiterate, from an insignificant village[11] in Judah should achieve that
distinction is one of those inexplicable facts of history. Amos was
the first to entertain a clear idea of Jehovah as god of peoples other
than the Israelites and as a god of social justice.[12] To Isaiah, who
shared the same view,[13] all rival gods were worthless, the creation of
man. Living in a turbulent period which witnessed Samaria's destruction by Sargon (721) and Jerusalem's siege by Sennacherib (701),
Isaiah furnished a shining example of the type of patriotism that, inspired by an unfailing faith in a holy God, shrinks from no sacrifice.
"Holy, holy, holy, is the Lord of hosts: the whole earth is full of his
glory" [14] was the song which he heard the angels chant in the temple.
With the eye of that faith this Hebrew prophet saw a vision of a new
and different world, one in which universal peace shall prevail under
a "Prince of Peace" and in which wolves shall dwell with lambs and
leopards with kids[15]—a noble dream that refuses to die.

Like Isaiah Jeremiah, who prophesied from 626 to 586, was a Messianic prophet envisioning a utopia in which full justice would be executed.[16] Such utterances served to bolster the morale of an oppressed
and depressed community by holding up the prospects of better times
and personifying hope in a forthcoming deliverer. In his monotheism
Jeremiah was more thorough and practical. To him all other deities
were sheer vanities.[17] Jeremiah advanced the thinking of his age by

[9] Julius A. Bewer, *The Literature of the Old Testament* (New York, 1926),
p. 87.
[10] Amos 9:5-7.
[11] Tekoa, name retained in Khirbat (ruins of) Taqu'ah, 6 miles south of
Bethlehem.
[12] Amos 5:21-24.
[13] Is. 2:8, 18; 10:10.
[14] Is. 6:3.
[15] Is. 2:2-4; 9:6-7; 11:1-9.
[16] Jer. 23:5.
[17] Jer. 5:7; 10:10-12; 14:22; 16:17-21.

representing Jehovah as entering into a new covenant with his people, one involving inwardness and inscribed on human hearts, rather than on stones as in the case of their fathers.[18] This new covenant doctrine was appropriated by Jesus in the Last Supper and was quoted in the Epistle to the Hebrews.[19] In this connection Jeremiah enunciated a new doctrine, that of individual responsibility as against group responsibility, marking a degree of moral sensitiveness unattained even in our day by certain societies. Group responsibility was a heritage of the times when the tribe was the unit of social organization. No more shall it be said: "The fathers have eaten a sour grape, and the children's teeth are set on edge;" but rather "everyone shall die for his own iniquity."[20] In his remarkable chapter (18) Ezekiel, a contemporary of Jeremiah, elaborated on this theme.

Other prophets made other original contributions or reiterated and emphasized earlier ones. From a tragic experience in his domestic life Hosea, who flourished between 745 and 735 in the northern kingdom, worked out the sublime idea that God was love.[21] God persisted in his love to Israel despite their iniquity. Shortly after Hosea flourished Micah (730-722), who struck the same note of a "new deal," when swords shall be beaten into plowshares and weapons into pruninghooks, that was struck by Isaiah and Jeremiah. As champion of the poor and oppressed Micah[22] summed up the entire code of justice and expressed the concept of social righteousness in terms that have become immortal (chapter 6):

> 6 Wherewith shall I come before the Lord,
>   And bow myself before the high God?
>   Shall I come before him with burnt offerings,
>   With calves of a year old?
> 7 Will the Lord be pleased with thousands of rams,
>   Or with ten thousands of rivers of oil?
>   Shall I give my firstborn for my transgression,
>   The fruit of my body for the sin of my soul?
> 8 He hath showed thee, O man, what is good;
>   And what doth the Lord require of thee,
>   But to do justly, and to love mercy,
>   And to walk humbly with thy god.[23]

In such utterances the Hebrew prophets attained a level of morality and spirituality that had not been attained by any teachers of antiquity

[18] Jer. 31:31-4; 32:40.
[19] Matt. 26:28; Lk. 22-20; Heb. 10:16-17.
[20] Jer. 31:29-30.
[21] Hos. 14:4.
[22] Mic. 4:1-8.
[23] Passages set in poetic form are quoted from the Westminster Study Edition.

and has not been surpassed except by the teachings of the founder of Christianity and of its chief propagator.[24]   The intrusion of Greek thought and language between the two periods was a direct result of the conquest of the Near East by Alexander the Great.

BOOKS TO READ

Albright, W. F., *From the Stone Age to Christianity,* 2nd ed. (New York, 1957).

Bentzen, Aage, *Introduction to the Old Testament,* 4th ed. (Copenhagen, 1958).

Bevan, Edwyn R. and Singer, Charles, eds., *The Legacy of Israel* (Oxford, 1928).

Graham, William C., *The Prophets and Israel's Culture* (Chicago, 1934).

Hitti, Philip K., *Lebanon in History* (New York, 1957).

Lods, Adolphe, *The Prophets and the Rise of Judaism* (New York, 1937).

Noth, Martin, *History of Israel* (London, 1958).

Pfeiffer, Robert H., *Introduction to the Old Testament* (New York, 1948).

Scott, Robert B. Y., *The Relevance of the Prophet* (New York, 1944).

[24] See below, pp. 155-156.

PART THREE

THE GRECO-ROMAN AGE

X   *Alexander and His Successors*

IN THE spring of 334 B.C. a twenty-one-year-old Macedonian, at the head of some 30,000 foot and 5000 horse, crossed that arbitrary line called the Hellespont (Dardanelles) which separates Europe from Asia.   He routed the Persian satrap near the mouth of the Granicus River emptying into the Sea of Marmora and swept through Asia Minor, setting off a chain reaction destined to change the course of Near Eastern history.   Western Asia and Egypt were ushered into the European sphere of political and cultural influence—Macedonian, Greek, Roman, and Byzantine—and there remained until the rise of Islam a thousand years later.   The legacy of Greece and Rome has not ceased to be a living force in the area today.

ALEXANDER IN THE EAST

Alexander's father had raised Macedon to the headship of the Greek states, laid plans for the "liberation" of the Greek territory in Asia Minor, and repaying the visits paid Greece by Darius and Xerxes.[1] Youthful love of adventure and devotion to Pan-Hellenic ideals undoubtedly contributed to the son's motivation.   As the invader emerged from the Cilician Gates and crossed the lowlands, he encountered Darius III (r. 336-330) with a motley host of about three times as large as his. In the ensuing battle at the narrow defile of Issus (333) numerical superiority was outweighed by training and discipline.   The Persian emperor, most powerful monarch of the day, who watched the fight from a gorgeous chariot drawn by four horses abreast, took to flight eastward, leaving his treasures and harem behind.   All Syria lay at the feet of the victor.   The city Iskandarunah (Alexandretta) commemorates the site.

With a view to insuring command of the sea and all lines of communication behind him, Alexander pushed southward.   Of all the Phoenician cities, only Tyre, confident of its tested strength, dared

[1] See above, pp. 52-53.

113

close its gates in his face. A special mole built from the mainland to the two-mile island city and a seven-month siege yielded its surrender in 332. Ships were provided by Tyre's rivals to the north. Two thousand of its unhappy population were hanged and thirty thousand were sold into slavery. Gaza, once chief among the five Philistine cities, offered an equally heroic but not equally long resistance; it shared the same fate. The way was then open to Egypt. Weary of the Persian rule, its people willingly exchanged masters. Alexander ordered his architect to found at the northwestern extremity of the Delta a city which proved to be of greater significance than the sheer conquest of the land. Alexandria (al-Iskandariyah) developed into an eminent seat of Hellenistic culture, an Oriental successor of Athens. In the Roman period it ranked next to Rome in learning and intellectual attainment.

The dashing general thence struck south to the oasis of Siwa, seat of a cult of Amon (Ammon of the Greeks) whose priest welcomed the conqueror with the traditional salutation given a Pharaoh as the son of god. The Macedonian acquiesced and later expected his courtiers to follow the Persian custom of prostration in his presence. Through his successors, the concept of the divine right of rule became firmly fixed in the European mind and through Rome made its way into the rest of Europe.

With that vast territory from the Hellespont to the western arm of the Nile stripped from the Persian empire Alexander flung himself again, but in a new spirit, against the might of its emperor. On a plain between Arbela (now Irbil) and Nineveh he again routed the enemy. Babylon and Susa, treasure houses of the East, opened their gates. Persepolis with its royal palaces of Darius and Xerxes was burned. At last Xerxes' destruction of the Athenian temples was avenged. In the following year Darius was mortally wounded by conspirators in his own camp. The Macedonian considered himself the legitimate successor of the last Achaemenid.[2]

The path of victory led farther east. The Oxus was crossed and Soghdiana (Bukhara) occupied. From Bactra (now Balkh in Afghanistan) the road led to the conquest of the northwestern part of India. Murmuring generals and mutinying soldiers, all weary if not exhausted, compelled the retreat (326). In Babylon the palace of Nebuchadnezzar provided the scene for a gala banquet after which the hero fell suddenly ill and died (323), leaving behind him a singular record of physical courage, unwavering determination, and military achievement. In

[2] See above, pp. 54-55.

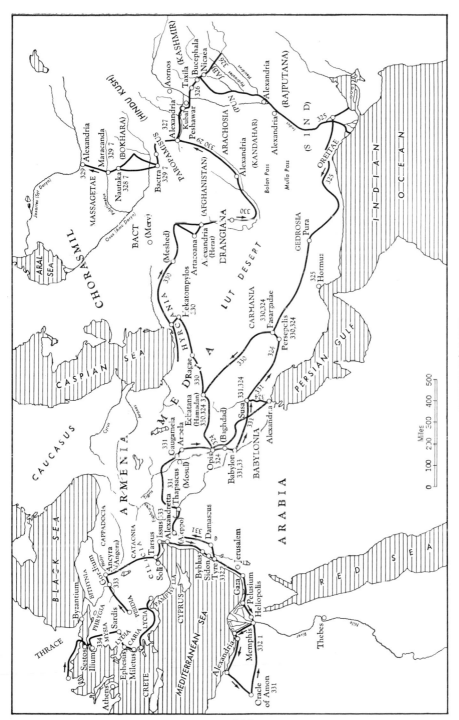

ALEXANDER'S ROUTE

115

Courtesy of The Oriental Institute, University of Chicago

ALEXANDER COINS FOUND AT PERSEPOLIS

Egypt and elsewhere he was accorded divine honors. The Koran (18:82) invested him with a divine mission. His name has been immortalized in multilingual cycles of romances spread throughout Eurasia.

Among the contributions Alexander the Great made to the progress of man, the practical steps he took toward the harmonizing and fusion of Greek and Near Eastern ideas and institutions was especially significant. "He was the pioneer of one of the supreme revolutions in the world's outlook, the first man known to us who contemplated the brotherhood of man or the unity of mankind." [3] His plan stands out among those rare historic ones in which the borderline between reality and dream seemed momentarily effaced. Contracting intermarriages and planting colonies were two means of implementation. He himself adopted Persian dress and court etiquette; married Darius' daughter; and encouraged officers, eighty of them, and soldiers, 10,000, to take Persian wives. Prior to his time visionary prophets had, albeit imperfectly, transcended the boundaries of nationality in their utterances; but here was the first man of affairs, a student of Aristotle, who sought a society with no barrier between Greek and barbarian.

THE BREAK-UP OF THE EMPIRE

Such a hastily assembled and far-flung empire as that left by Alexander was sure to fall to pieces on its founder's death. His comet-like rise and disappearance left a vacuum that could not be filled. Nor could his world-shaking exploits be continued. After a protracted

[3] W. W. Tarn, *Alexander the Great and the Unity of Mankind* (London, 1933), p. 28.

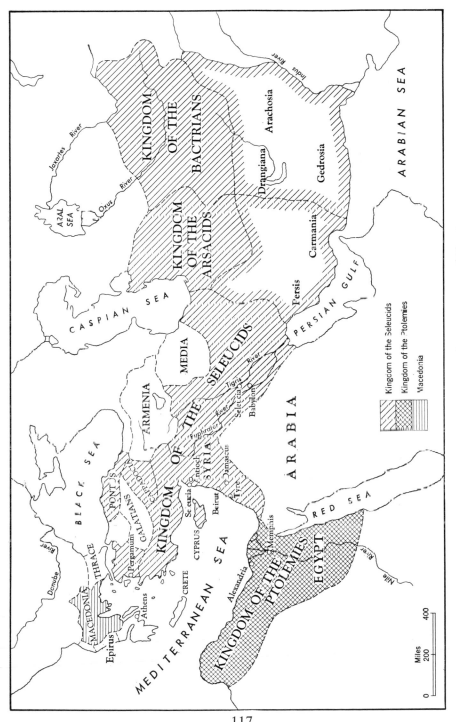

THE KINGDOMS OF ALEXANDER'S SUCCESSORS *ca* 200 B.C.

period of jockeying and struggle for power among heirs and would-be heirs scrambling for the largest chunks, four states emerged headed by four of Alexander's generals: Seleucus in the satrapy of Babylonia, Ptolemy in Egypt, Antigonus in Asia Minor, and Antipater in Macedonia. "The great horn was broken; and for it came up four notable ones toward the four winds of heaven" (Dan. 8:8). Of these Seleucus was the ablest and acquired the lion's share. As a result of the battle of Ipsus (301), he added Syria and much of Asia Minor to his realm, which eastward reached India. Palestine, Coele-Syria, and southern Phoenicia were contested by the Ptolemies and often went with Egypt.

THE SYRIAN KINGDOM

This Syrian kingdom founded by Seleucus I (r. 312-280), surnamed Nicator (conqueror), nearly coincided with the Asiatic part of the Alexandrine empire. Following the example of his predecessor, who had founded twenty-five cities to Hellenize the East, Seleucus founded no less than sixty cities. Chief among them was Antioch on the Orontes, named after his father; Seleucia-on-the-Tigris, bearing his own name; Laodicea (al-Ladhiqiyah, Latakia, on the Syrian coast) perpetuating his mother's name; and Apamea honoring his Bactrian wife Apama. Seleucia (Saluqiyah), seaport of Antioch, was built either by him or by an immediate successor. Antioch became the capital of the kingdom, while Seleucia-on-the-Tigris served as the capital of the eastern part. Apamea (Afamiyah of classical Arabic, now Qal'at al-Madiq) housed the Seleucid army, the war treasury, a national stud of mares and stallions, and a stock of war elephants. Fifteen other Antiochs, four Seleucias, eight Laodiceas, and two Apameas were sprinkled from the Hellespont to the Indus. Such cities, founded by Seleucus and his successors, served as foci for radiating Greek culture and the Greek language throughout the East. Christ's message, delivered in Aramaic,[4] survived in its Greek rendition and thus became available to the then civilized world.

Next to colonization, the establishment of a standard calendar for the entire realm was perhaps the greatest achievement of this dynasty. The Seleucid calendar was reckoned from 312 B.C. when Seleucus was firmly established as a king and continued in general use until the rise of Islam. Called Greek by Syrians and Jews, it is still in limited use today.

None of Seleucus' immediate successors was comparable to him in

---

[4] See above, pp. 105-106.

ability or performance. The reign of his great-grandson Seleucus II [5] (Callinicus, gloriously victorious, r. 246-226) witnessed the surrender of the coasts of Syria and Asia Minor (241) to Ptolemy III of Egypt. This marked the zenith of Ptolemaic power, and the complete loss of Parthia (248-240), northeastern Persia corresponding to modern Khurasan, to a rebel leader, Arsaces, who claimed descent from the early Persian royal family. Parthia received its name from an Iranian tribe which has survived in Pahlawi, and is applied to Middle Persian and to the present Shah family. The Parthians were especially skillful in cavalry battle involving notably the use of pretended flight in the course of which they could shoot their unerring arrows backward. The expansion of the Parthian kingdom to the Euphrates under the Arsacids brought on its inevitable collision with Rome expanding eastward, but the dynasty survived until superseded in A.D. 226 by another Persian dynasty, the Sasanid.

Twenty years of incessant fighting by Antiochus III (r. 223-187) won back most of the territory lost under his father and grandfather and carried him the epithet of Great. Eastward his troops reached India through the Kabul valley; southward they scored a clear victory over the Egyptian army at Pancas (now Baniyas, Caesarea Philippi of the Gospels) with the aid of a fresh supply of war elephants from India. Drunk with victory, Antiochus ventured to strike westward against Greek and Roman territory and met signal defeat at the hands of the Romans near Magnesia in Asia Minor. Therewith was established

[5] The tree below shows the genealogical relationship of the early members of the Seleucid house:

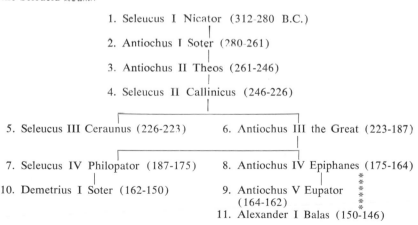

1. Seleucus I Nicator (312-280 B.C.)

2. Antiochus I Soter (280-261)

3. Antiochus II Theos (261-246)

4. Seleucus II Callinicus (246-226)

5. Seleucus III Ceraunus (226-223) 6. Antiochus III the Great (223-187)

7. Seleucus IV Philopator (187-175) 8. Antiochus IV Epiphanes (175-164)

10. Demetrius I Soter (162-150) 9. Antiochus V Eupator (164-162)

11. Alexander I Balas (150-146)

Note—Starred line indicates pretended father and son relationship.

Courtesy of The Macmillan Co., Ltd.

ANTIOCHUS III THE GREAT   From a bust in the Louvre

the first fateful contact with the rising giant of the West. In 188
Antiochus was forced to cede to Rome all his dominion beyond the
Taurus and pay a heavy war indemnity. Asia Minor's natural resources
and trade routes were forever lost to the Seleucids.

Enfeebled Syria was still strong enough to strike another and harsher
blow at her rival to the south. At the frontier fortress of Pelusium
(al-Farama) the army of Ptolemy IV Philopator (father-loving),[6] a

[6] Genealogical tree of the early Ptolemies:

Ptolemy I (323-285)
|
Ptolemy II Philadelphus (309-246)
|
Ptolemy III Euergetes (246-221)
|
Ptolemy IV Philopator (221-203)
|
Ptolemy V Epiphanes (203-181)

Ptolemy VI Philometor (181-145) Ptolemy VII Energetes (145-116)

weak debaucher, was crushingly defeated in 169 by Antiochus IV (r. 175-164) and Ptolemy himself was captured. Lower Egypt was overrun and Alexandria besieged. But under pressure from Rome, to whom Antiochus was still paying indemnity, the siege was lifted and the army withdrawn.

By this campaign against Egypt, Antiochus satisfied one of the two ambitions of his life, the second being the furtherance of the traditional policy of his house and of Alexander the Great involving the Hellenization of the Near East. Hellenism was the common denominator to which all Near Eastern subjects were to be reduced. In an effort to induce religious uniformity he proclaimed himself Theos Epiphanes (god manifest), thus associating himself with Zeus Olympus, who then became as much the Oriental Baal as the Occidental Zeus. The Greek god was endowed with semi-Semitic attributes, worshiped in quasi-Semitic temples, and dressed in half-Oriental clothes. Antiochus encouraged the identification of Zeus with Jehovah and set up an altar for him at the temple of Jerusalem. That was the "abomination that makes desolate" referred to in Daniel (11:31). While Syrian polytheism could tolerate such compromise, Hebrew monotheism could not. In Judas of the priestly Hasmonaean family, the Jews found a hero-rebel who, with his brothers, succeeded in capturing Jerusalem and cleansing the temple. Judas was surnamed Maccabeus, which probably means "the hammerer," in allusion to the telling blows he inflicted on the Syrian army. In 164 the Jewish community attained religious freedom and in 140 political independence. Under the Maccabean dynasty of priest-kings, the realm expanded and lasted until the advent of the Romans about eighty years later. The stone, known later as the Rosetta Stone, which furnished the key for the decipherment of ancient Egyptian contained an inscription—in hieroglyphic, demotic,

Courtesy of American Numismatic Society

A TETRADRACHM OF ANTIOCHUS IV Struck in Tyre 175-164 B.C. Obverse shows the diademed head of the monarch; reverse shows Apollo seated on omphalos holding an arrow in his right hand. The inscription reads BASILEOS [King] ANTIOCHUS

and Greek—celebrating the coming of age of Ptolemy Epiphanes in 196.

LAST CONVULSIONS OF SELEUCID KINGDOM

Intrigue, corruption, incompetence, and internecine warfare characterized the remaining years of the Seleucid monarchy. The concomitant loss of territory, beginning with the independence of Bactria and Parthia; Asia Minor's annexation by Rome; and the intrusion of Arabian tribes into Syria and Palestine reduced the Seleucid empire to a local state in north Syria. It had once stretched from the lower Mediterranean and the Aegean to Turkestan and India. The house which for generations had stood before the world as the imperial house of the East progressively lost in dignity, prestige, and power.

Outstanding among the intruding tribes were the Nabataeans. From their multicolored rock-hewn capital-fortress Petra ("rock," today in southern Jordan), these Arabians extended their sway as far north as Damascus. Around 85 B.C. they wrested the fertile plain of Coele-Syria from Seleucid hands. It was an ethnarch of theirs who came near arresting Paul in Damascus.[7] By 130 B.C. the Parthian kingdom stretched from the Indus to the Euphrates and from the Indian Ocean to the Oxus. Westward the progress of its arms was checked by rising Armenia. Originally centering on the Ararat Mountain, Armenia— with a brachycephalic population speaking an Indo-European language akin to Iranian—attained its height of power under King Tigranes.

Between 83 and 69 B.C., Tigranes established himself as the most powerful monarch in Western Asia. He first united Armenia Major (east of the upper Euphrates) with Armenia Minor (mostly Cilicia) and then annexed Syria and eastern Asia Minor. He built a new capital in the upper Tigris region and styled himself "king of kings." In his ambitious plans he had an ally in his father-in-law, Mithradates of Pontus (on the southern shore of the Black Sea), who was meantime carving out a domain for himself from the client states of Rome in Asia Minor. At the age of twenty-one, Mithradates killed his brother, married his sister, mounted the throne of Pontus, and started bedeviling imperial Rome. Through three wars the Pontic king, who claimed descent from the Achaemenids, made himself master of the Roman possession in Asia Minor. Next to Hannibal he was the most formidable opponent Rome had.

But at last the Roman legions caught up with him and his equally aggressive son-in-law. Under the brilliant generalship of Pompey, the

[7] 2 Cor. 11:32.

Romans chased Mithradates out of the land and forced Tigranes to withdraw from Syria, surrender eastern Asia Minor, and content himself with a contracted Armenia as a vassal of Rome. Meantime Antioch was reoccupied by Antiochus XIII Asiaticus (r. 69-65), whose claim was acknowledged by Rome but contested by another Seleucid Philip II (r. 68-64). These two were the last to wear the royal diadem of the Seleucid house.

Egypt's turn came next. There the decline had begun with Ptolemy IV (r. 221-203)[8] and hit the bottom with Cleopatra. Cleopatra first ruled (51-49) jointly with her brother-husband Ptolemy XII and then (r. 48-30, mostly as a Roman vassal) with her younger brother Ptolemy XIII, whom she also married and later murdered to make room for her infant son Caesarion, so named after his probable father Julius Caesar. Julius had come to Egypt (48) not to conquer, but to capture his principal contestant for supreme power, Pompey. Charmed by the Egyptian queen, who became his mistress in more than one sense, he lingered there for three months before advancing through Syria to meet a son of Mithradates.

At Zela in Pontus, Caesar defeated the new enemy and announced his victory in the memorable words "Veni, vidi, vici" (I came, I saw, I conquered). Master of the East, Caesar returned to Rome late in 47. After his death Cleopatra met Antony, who had received Asia as his command. Antony also succumbed to her charms and followed her to Alexandria. Shorn of his authority by the Roman senate, defeated by the future Augustus Caesar—Antony's rival for supreme power— and deserted by his own men, Antony at last committed suicide. Failing to influence the new conqueror Cleopatra likewise killed herself (30) by poison—legend says by an asp. Her son Caesarion was disposed of by order of Augustus. The Macedonian kingdom of Egypt, following its sister of Syria, was wiped out of existence.

BOOKS TO READ

Bevan, Edwyn R., *The House of Seleucus,* 2 vols. (London, 1902); *History of Egypt under the Ptolemaic Dynasty* (London, 1927).

Burn, A. R., *Alexander the Great and the Hellenistic Empire* (London, 1947).

Cary, Max, *The Legacy of Alexander: A History of the Greek World from 323 to 146 B.C.* (New York, 1932).

Debevoise, Neilson C., *A Political History of Parthia* (Chicago, 1938).

[8] See above, p. 120.

Downey, Glanville, *A History of Antioch in Syria* (Princeton, 1961).

Elgood, P. G., *The Ptolemies of Egypt* (Arrowsmith, 1938).

Hitti, Philip K., *History of Syria including Lebanon and Palestine,* 2nd ed. (London, 1957).

Mahaffy, J. P., *The Empire of the Ptolemies* (London, 1895).

Robinson, Charles A., *Alexander the Great: The Meeting of East and West in World Government and Brotherhood* (New York, 1947); *The History of Alexander the Great* (Providence, 1953).

Tarn, W. W., *Alexander the Great* (Cambridge, England, reprinted, 1951); *Hellenistic Civilization,* 3rd ed. (London, 1952).

XI   *Hellenistic Culture*

T HE interpenetration of Greek and Semitic civilizations, initiated by Alexander's conquests and enhanced by Seleucid and Ptolemaic policies, gave rise to a new culture known as Hellenistic in contradistinction to the Hellenic or purely Greek. Hellenism became the dominant feature of the Near East in the three pre-Christian centuries. It did not, however, supersede the native culture, which remained predominant especially outside the Hellenized cities. Sandwiched in between two indigenous layers, the preceding Egypto-Semitic and a succeeding Arabic-Islamic, Hellenism remained an effective force for a thousand years and left an enduring legacy thereafter. In Persia it was not much less effective and enduring; in Asia Minor it was more.

GREEK CITIES

The nursery of this eclectic culture was, of course, in the scores of cities planted by Alexander and his Macedonian successors at strategic spots of intercourse all the way from the Sea of Marmara to the Oxus and the Indus. Greek in population and in speech, these cities generally enjoyed constitutions of their own with privileges, rights and a measure of democracy and civic independence. The cities had theaters, baths, gymnasiums and forums, thus differing conspicuously from native establishments. Their original population of soldiers, mercenaries, traders, artists, and scholars often married native wives. The process of ethnic integration, consciously launched, continued with less consciousness but with more vigor as the cities attracted other settlers. In several cases Seleucids and Ptolemies took over old towns which they colonized and renamed. Rabbath-Ammon (today Amman, capital of Jordan) was called Philadelphia in honor of Ptolemy II Philadelphus (r. 285-247).

The policy of admitting properly qualified natives into government positions contributed to integration. The concept that Hellenic culture could be acquired and was not entirely hereditary made the gymnasiums, where athletic and aesthetic as well as academic training was practiced,

125

the melting pot of the emerging society. Alexander conquered by his arms, Hellenism by its institutions. Certain artistic, architectural, and other cultural elements introduced by the new settlers made themselves especially manifest in the Roman period. The Corinthian capital, for instance, continued to gain vogue down to Byzantine days.

PHOENICIAN CITIES HELLENIZED

Different areas responded in varying degrees to Greek stimuli. Cities along the Phoenician coast, with a record of contact with the Greek world going back to the eleventh century,[1] struck coins with Greek

Courtesy of American Numismatic Society

A COIN OF BEIRUT   Obverse and reverse of a bronze coin of Berytus, second century B.C.   On the obverse is a bust of Tyche with turreted crown; on the reverse, Baal-Beroth in a car drawn by four hippocampi.   The inscription is in Phoenician and Greek.

legends alongside the Phoenician ones and introduced Greek as the language of poetry, science, and philosophy. Sidon and Tyre contributed a number of Epicurean and Stoic philosophers. A Cypriote Phoenician, Zeno (333-261), founded the Stoic school of philosophy, considered the greatest creation of the age and probably the noblest philosophy of the ancient world. The system got its name from the Painted Porch (*stoa poikile*) in Athens, where Zeno began his teaching in 302. In a sepulchral epigram the following was said of him:

> And if thy native country was Phoenicia,
> What need to slight thee. Came not Cadmus[2] thence,
> Who gave to Greece her books and art of writing? [3]

From the outset Stoicism maintained close connection with the Semitic conception of life. In its stress on universal brotherhood, virtue, and ethical living and in its consideration of health and sickness, wealth and power as matters of no great concern, it was a precursor of Christianity.

Like Stoicism, its contemporary Epicureanism concerned itself primarily with human conduct. The question it tried to answer was:

---

[1] Discussed above, p. 92.
[2] Cited above, p. 92.
[3] Diogenes Laertius, *Lives of Eminent Philosophers*, tr. R. D. Hicks (London, 1925), Bk. VII, § 30.

How should a wise man conduct his life? But its founder Epicurus (d. 270), who taught in Athens, laid the basis of his ethical system on the material world and its values rather than on the gods and their values. The system was later attacked by both pagan and Christian writers as "pig philosophy," emphasizing pleasure as the only good and the end of all morality.

ANTIOCH

In north Syria the intrusive Greek elements made themselves so much at home that the region was referred to as a "new Macedonia." Antioch was the nucleus. Four miles to its south lay Daphne, its pleasure park. Here the nymph by the same name was pursued by Apollo, when charmed by the nymph's beauty, and metamorphosed into a laurel tree. Apollo's temple on the site, standing amidst a laurel grove and with copious water,[4] was invested with the right of asylum. Antiochians and visitors from all over the region made it a center of pilgrimage and licentiousness. The Daphne-Apollo legend was transplanted from Thessaly.

Seleucid political institutions presented a strange picture of Greco-Macedonian and Syro-Persian elements. Provincial administration and the system of communication were based on Persian antecedents. Even the Persian name, satrapy, was preserved. The monarch's head was surrounded by a divine halo. His court, with its chamberlains and eunuchs, looked more oriental than occidental. Its highest official, minister of affairs, was a continuation of the Persian office of vizir. Seleucids and Ptolemies were generally monogamous but kept concubines. Slaves were a conspicuous feature of the Hellenistic society.

Hellenism, it should be remembered, was and remained highly urban. The educated few studied Greek; aspired for government positions; and wrote their poetical, scientific and philosophical works in the language of the conquerors. But the native peasantry everywhere remained untouched, persisting in its ancestral way of life and in the use of its vernacular—Aramaic, Egyptian or Persian. Baalism in Syria-Mesopotamia and Judaism in Palestine sustained their Semitic traditions. The religions of the East held special fascination for the Asiatic Greeks. local cults, with their emotional rituals and exotic mysteries, were readily adopted. Native deities were Hellenized; Baal became Zeus.[5] Two major Hebrew works of the age found their way into the Old Testament: Ecclesiastes, written about 200 B.C. by a Hellenized aristocratic Jew, and Daniel, composed shortly after that.

[4] Daphne is called today Bayt al-Ma', home of the water.
[5] Cf. below, p. 142.

ALEXANDRIA

We know more about Hellenism in Egypt—thanks to papyri found in the last fifty years—than in any other region. Here it had an easier course due to the homogeneous character of the population, the relatively limited area and the munificent patronage of the early Macedonian rulers. By accepting the traditionally Egyptian god-king concept and adopting the practice of marrying their own sisters,[6] the Ptolemies early in their career identified themselves with the Pharaohs and integrated their families into the existing order. Ptolemy II (r. 285-246) deified his parents and his sister-wife as Philadelphus (brother-lover), a title which was later given him.

The Ptolemies administered Egypt, as had the Pharaohs, as a state monopoly. The economic life of the area was stimulated by unification in Greek hands, improved navigation and communication, and an expanded world market. Egypt especially benefitted by maritime trade with South Arabia and India. Ptolemy Philadelphus explored the upper Nile, for commercial purposes and reopened the Nile-Red Sea canal originally dug by the Pharaohs and redug by Darius I.[7] The country's resources were, however, largely depleted by its foreign policy based on contesting with the Seleucids the possession of the southern part of Syria. This may have been justified on defensive grounds and on creating an Aegean empire which was largely offensive.

Enough royal income, however, was left to make of Alexandria one of the most magnificent capitals of the age. In it public buildings reached a high level. Outstanding among them was the museum (temple of the Muses), which was in fact an academy of scholars; the library, which at one time is said to have housed 700,000 rolls and had office facilities for transcribing and writing books; and the Pharos, the lighthouse on the island by the same name whose reflection of the sunrays by day and special lights by night for the benefit of mariners made it one of the "seven wonders" of the world. The islet is today joined to the mainland. The public building program was launched by the first Ptolemy and carried on by his successors. These facilities coupled with personal royal patronage made of Alexandria a conspicuous literary, scientific, and philosophic center that attracted scholars from Asia Minor, Rhodes and other parts of the Greek world. Philology, textual criticism, and kindred subjects, rather than creative writing, marked the literary products.

[6] See above, p. 45.
[7] See above, pp. 92-93, 52.

Eratosthenes, born (*ca.* 276) of Greek parents in Cyrenaica (today east Libya), came to Alexandria and worked as chief librarian under Ptolemy III. His geographical writings reveal that he believed the earth to be round. He invented the zones still used in our geographical vocabulary and was the first to mark maps with lines indicating longitude and latitude. Still more brilliant was his achievement in calculating the earth's circumference at 24,-662 miles, only 195 miles less than the exact measure. Another librarian was Aristophanes, who came from Byzantium (*ca.* 197) and edited among other works those of Hesiod, Homer, and Pindar. In mathematical science the name of Euclid shines with conspicuous brilliancy. He founded a school in Alexandria (*ca.* 300), where he wrote *Elements of Geometry* that became the basis of all later works in this field, not excluding today's textbooks in plane and solid geometry.

Especially munificent in his patronage of scholarship and art was Ptolemy III (r. 246-221), called Euergetes (benefactor). He added to the collection of books in the library and erected other buildings

Courtesy of University of Pennsylvania Museum

HEAD OF A PTOLEMAIC KING

elsewhere. Under him the fleet, based in Alexandria, attained primacy in the Eastern Mediterranean. The port and its Pharos helped to make Egypt the dominant naval power. His reign was generally one of peace during which the kingdom enjoyed its greatest prosperity. Alexandria boasted another building, the Serapeum, ranked by ancient writers as one of the finest temples of the world. The temple was erected by Ptolemy I for the worship of Serapis—a synthetic god of Osiris and Apis—who was endowed with the healing power of Asclepius and represented in a human form not unlike that of Poseidon or even Zeus. It became the home of a national cult in which both Greeks and Egyptians shared. Alexandrian intellectual and spiritual activity experienced no decline after the assumption of full control by the Romans (30 B.C.).

Hellenism did not sink deep in Parthian soil. The kingdom which arose there, in the territory of modern Khurasan, was founded by Arsaces I (r. 249-247 B.C.) who gave it his name. Lying between the Seleucid and the Bactrian kingdoms, the Parthian became a real empire under Mithradates I (r. 171-138) covering, besides almost all modern Iran, parts of Bactria and Babylonia. The acquisition of the lower Mesopotamian valley necessitated the removal of the capital to a village on the left bank of the Tigris opposite the Greek city of Seleucia. The peak of power was attained under Mithradates II the Great (r. 124-88), who annexed part of India. As Parthia expanded westward and Rome eastward a clash became inevitable. After 64 B.C. the two powers came into frequent collision with each other, one outstanding bone of contention being the possession of Armenia. Parthia may be credited with having set limits to the Roman Empire's expansion in the East, but after this it was almost always on the defensive side.

The Arsacids claimed descent from the Achaemenid Artaxerxes II, assumed the old title of "king of kings" (*shahanshah* of modern Persia), but did not attain the stature of their predecessors nor that of their successors, the Sasanids. Sprung from a predatory nomadic tribe with no national basis, the Arsacids inherited the Achaemenid system, borrowed Seleucid institutions, and inscribed Greek legends on their coinage. Pahlawi, middle Persian written with Aramaic characters, became their official language. Mithradates I assumed the title Philhellene (friend of the Greeks), which was retained by certain successors. Others took as surnames Epiphanes (the revealed god), Euergetes (benefactor), and other Greek surnames used by Seleucids and Ptolemies. In fact no people with aspirations for playing a role in world affairs could afford to dam the ripples of the tidal wave of Hellenism which then represented the dominant world culture. Insulation spelled isolation and that meant deterioration. The indigenous population, as in other Eastern lands, hardly participated in the operation of the new culture. Its centers were in cities, particularly those with Greek populations, and those were relatively few.

In Asia Minor Hellenism sank its roots deeper than on the Iranian plateau. Here, too, cities worshiped their kings as founders or benefactors. The ruling houses of many provinces—such as Bithynia, Cappadocia, and Pontus—adopted the language and manners of the Greeks and founded and protected Greek cities. Some of the dynasts were partly Greek in blood. On the western shore such cities were preponderant and many. Two of these, Ephesus and Smyrna, antedate the Macedonian conquest. Here Pergamum (now Bergama), though smaller than Antioch or Alexandria, provided the hearth from which the torch of Hellenism burned with a brighter and perhaps purer flame. This was particularly true under the Attalids, the dynasty founded by Attalus (r. 241-197), who on defeating a group of Gauls who had penetrated Asia Minor and settling them in the district henceforth designated Galatia, assumed the title of king.

Paul's epistle to the Galatians, in which he took a firm stand against Peter and others who stood for admission into the new religion through the gateway of Judaism, set Christianity on its path of becoming a world religion instead of remaining a Jewish sect. Other declarations in the epistle make it a Magna Charta of Christian liberty. Attalus' son Eumenes (r. 197-159) adorned the capital with several public buildings, noteworthy among which was the library. With its 200,000 rolls, the library ranked next to that of Alexandria. Half Greek themselves, the Attalids claimed divinity and posed as champions of democracy and Hellenism. Their capital lay at the terminus of the main road from the East and served as the natural outlet for much of the commerce of the area. Minerals, wool, textiles, vegetable oils, and parchment stood high on the list of exports.

After annexing the region in 133 B.C., the Romans made Pergamum capital of the extensive province of Asia, embracing such cultural centers as Ephesus and Smyrna. Mark Antony gave thousands of the rolls of the library collection to Cleopatra, who had them removed to Alexandria. Parchment, next to papyrus the most important writing material of that age, was first obtained from Pergamum, whence the term is derived. The Greco-Roman ruins of the city show its adequate equipment in the institutions of that culture. The acropolis was crowded with temple, theater, circus, and library buildings. The style of the celebrated Pergamese school of art is best illustrated in the friezes of the enormous altar to Zeus erected by Eumenes. The altar was reconstructed by German archeologists in Berlin, but it was carried away by the Russians during the second World War. The statue of the Dying Gaul carved to glorify Attalus' victory over the Gauls is a masterpiece of sculpture. It displays considerable technical ability and knowledge of anatomy. The city was such a stronghold of anti-Christian idolatry that it is referred to as "Satan's seat" in Revelation (2:13).

Courtesy of The Bettmann Archive

THE DYING GAUL   Carved to commemorate victory over the Gauls.   Copy in
Capitoline Museum, Rome.

ECONOMIC PROSPERITY

Progress in the Hellenistic age was not only intellectual.   Despite the
international conflicts, civil disturbances, and the quasi-chaotic conditions that marked the disintegration of the Seleucid and Ptolemaic
regimes, there is reason to believe that the curve of prosperity tended
generally upward.   The fact that the Hellenistic world, fragmented
though it was, had a measure of uniformity of general culture, including
a common speech, similar coinage, and analogous laws, gave impetus
to trade on both the domestic and foreign levels.   New roads were
constructed and old ones repaired.   In the Syrian kingdom the main
highways were guarded by chains of colonies, some with fortresses and
garrisons, providing safety, resting places for caravaneers, and relay
centers for their camels.   Dura-Europos (al-Salihiyah today), founded
by Seleucus I on the desert road halfway between the capitals of Syria
and Mesopotamia, was such a colony.   It soon developed from a
strong fortress to an important emporium, reaching its height as a
caravan city under the Parthians.   Petra was a caravan city on the
Arabian route.   Palmyra flourished later in the Syrian Desert.

Syrian trade was in such agricultural and industrial products as
fruits, cereals, oil, wine, purple, glass, and slaves.   The slave
market was supplied with prisoners of war, victims of kid-

naping, and at times with those who had been purchased. India offered war elephants, minerals, precious stones, pepper, cinnamon, and other semi-tropical products which went by sea to depots in Yemen. From there they were transported by caravan to Petra and thence to Egypt and Syria. Sometimes the goods went by sea to the Persian Gulf, up the Tigris to Seleucia, and thence in different directions, particularly northwestward through Dura-Europos. A Seleucid fleet in the Persian Gulf kept its trade with fabulous India lively. The Ptolemies established ports on the Red Sea in the interest of their South Arabian and East African trade. Silk from China reached Mediterranean ports either by overland routes through Bactria and Iran or partly by sea routes through India. Egyptian commodities were mostly salt, papyrus, linen and other textiles, glassware, and brewed beverages, practically all manufactured by the state. In a sense the Ptolemaic was a social state exercising control over trade and industry. In wheat the valley of the Nile was unsurpassed; it acted as a granary for the East in the Hellenistic and the Roman period.

SOUTH ARABIA

Of special importance in this international exchange of products was southwestern Arabia, the Arabia Felix of classical writers and the Yemen of today. This is the only part of the peninsula favored with sufficient rain to make systematic agriculture possible.[8] Occupying the territory across the path to India and producing commodities highly prized in the market to the north—frankincense, myrrh, cinnamon, and other spices—the South Arabians were the middlemen of the southern seas, as the Phoenicians had earlier been of the Mediterranean. Frankincense was in great demand for embalming, fumigating, and temple use. The entry of the Egyptian merchant marine into the Red Sea, subsequent to the enterprises of Ptolemy II,[9] was the beginning of the end for the South Arabians' monopoly of the trade in those waters. They, however, held on jealously to their commercial supremacy until the first pre-Christian century.

Of the South Arabians, the Sabaeans were best known. Their civilization, based on trade and agriculture rather than military power, had flourished for some fifteen centuries beginning in the thirteenth century B.C. The renowned Queen of Sheba, said to have visited Solomon, bears their name. Their capital Marib—east of the modern capital Sana—with its stupendous dam considered one of the great

[8] As noted above, p. 12.
[9] Above, p. 128.

hydraulic feats of antiquity, has left remains that when excavated may yield finds as sensational as some of those in Babylonia or Egypt.

Late Ptolemaic and early Egyptian mariners were gradually initiated into the mysteries of the southern sea routes with their hazards and periodic monsoons. The entry of Roman-Egyptian shipping into the Indian Ocean sounded the knell of South Arabian prosperity. Economic decline brought in its wake political ruin. One by one of the caravan cities—Petra, Palmyra, Dura-Europos—fell under the paws of the Roman wolf—paws large enough to cover a large part of the civilized world.

BOOKS TO READ

Bury, J. B., *et al. The Hellenistic Age* (Cambridge, 1923).

Bell, H. Idris, *Egypt from Alexander the Great to the Moslem Congress* (Oxford, 1948).

Bevan, Edwyn, *Hellenism and Christianity* (London, 1921).

Croiset, Maurice, *Hellenic Civilization* (New York, 1925).

Elgwood, P. G., *The Ptolemies of Egypt* (Arrowsmith, 1938).

Grant, Frederick C., ed., *Hellenistic Religions* (New York).

Jouquet, Pierre, *Macedonian Imperialism and the Hellenization of the East* (New York, 1928).

More, Paul E., *Hellenistic Philosophies* (Princeton, 1923).

Murray, Gilbert, *Hellenism and the Modern World* (London, 1953).

Rostovtzeff, M. I., *The Social and Economic History of the Hellenistic World,* 3 vols. (Oxford, 1941).

Tarn, W. W., *Hellenistic Civilisation,* 3rd ed. rev. (London, 1952).

XII   *Under Roman Rule*

T̲HE progress of Roman arms, commencing on the
battlefield of Magnesia in 190 B.C., proceeded in a crescendo to the
conquest of Syria in 64 B.C. and ended in the annexation of Egypt in
30 B.C.[1] The victory of Octavius (future Augustus, commemorated
in the name of the eighth month of our calendar) at Actium in Greece
over his two adversaries, Antony and Cleopatra, marked the end of the
Roman Republic as well as the end of the last Hellenistic state. The
center of political history for the first time shifted from Asia to Europe
where, except for a short period of the Arab caliphate, it has since
remained. A new order, the Roman Empire, arose. Its natural limits
had been reached: the Atlantic on the west; the Rhine, the Danube and
the Black Sea on the north; the Syro-Arabian desert on the east; and
the Mediterranean on the south. The Roman world—the Hellenistic
world and the Near East, Persia excluded—were for the first time
united under one scepter. History holds no other example of so many
races, languages, cultures, and peoples brought and held together for
so long in a firm political union. Augustus succeeded where the
Greek generals had failed. What had haunted a Macedonian conqueror
as a dream of world unity and was worked out into a philosophical
concept by a Phoenician-Greek thinker[2] seemed at last to have been
realized by a Roman emperor.

IN A WORLD EMPIRE

The question then arose as to how to manage a domain with a con-
glomerate population of some seventy million claiming to constitute
the civilized world and looking upon all beyond its defensible frontiers
as barbarians. In contrast to its western wing—Gaul and Spain, which
was sparsely populated and still at a low stage of culture—its eastern
wing—Asia Minor, Syria, and Egypt—was densely peopled, highly

[1] Treated above, pp. 122-123, 119-120.
[2] Cited above, p. 126.

135

cultured, and deeply rooted in a centuries-old tradition. In between were the Greeks, to whom the Latins owed the basic elements of their civilization. It was easy to colonize and Latinize the west. In the Near East the Romans were naturally inclined to favor Greeks against natives and natives with a tinge of Hellenism against the rest. Only a few Roman colonists settled in the area.

The policy of unification initiated by Augustus was carried on by his successors. To Hadrian (r. 117-138), ex-legate of Syria, fell the task of perfecting the defenses of the empire by a system of frontier fortifications and watchtowers which were strategically placed and connected by roads provided with inns at convenient spots. With this went the process of consolidating the area within. But before unifying, leveling was imperative. Pompey, Caesar, Antony and other generals had conferred Roman citizenship, considered hereditary, upon provincials as a reward for signal services. Besides social distinction, such citizenship carried with it legal rights and economic privileges. Hence the challenge made by Paul to a Roman officer in Jerusalem, "Is it lawful for you to scourge a man that is a Roman?" [3] Paul further boasted that he was a born citizen as against the captain who had purchased his citizenship. Provincials were allowed voluntary enlistment in the army leading to full citizenship. The gradual extension of the franchise, with its purposeful assimilative effect, culminated in the proclamation of Emperor Caracalla in 212 that all freeborn men within the realm were equal citizens of the state. Caracalla himself was a member of the Syrian dynasty in Rome.[4] With the assimilating influence of a common nationality went that of commercial and social intercourse. The result was the gradual disappearance of linguistic distinctions in important urban centers and surrender to the seductive influence of the fusion of Roman ideas and Greek cultural elements. Urbanization accompanied the growth of a wealthy class of merchants, shopkeepers, and landowners and became a cardinal point in Roman policy. Italian engineers improved old roads, some dating back to the royal system inaugurated by the early Persians; they also opened new ways which linked the far-flung parts of the empire. Augustus (r. 27 B.C.-A.D. 14) inaugurated a postal service to bring the central government in contact with its provincial agents. Meant primarily for facilitating troop movements and carrying imperial post through horse relays, these roads nevertheless enhanced the flow of merchandise and promoted trade and industry. Travelers were provided with maps and roadbooks as well as lodging facilities. Roman armies saw that the highways were

[3] Acts 22:25.
[4] See below, p. 143.

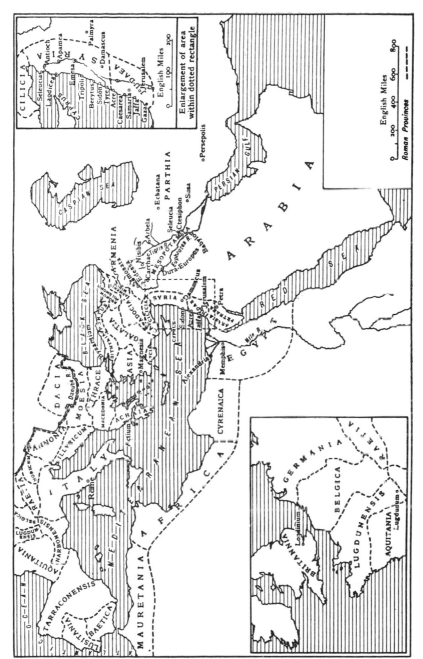

THE ROMAN EMPIRE IN IMPERIAL TIMES

kept safe from robbers, as the Roman fleet kept the Mediterranean safe from pirates, robbers of the sea highways.   Paul's early autumn sea voyage to Rome from Palestine is related by Luke in Acts (1-2:16) with singular accuracy of detail.   Routes were further enriched when Trajan (r. A.D. 98-117) restored the canal connecting the Nile with the extreme northwest arm of the Red Sea.[5]   Ordinarily the voyage from Alexandria to Puteoli, Rome's port before Ostia, must have taken about eighteen days.   The value of easy and safe communication to the province more than outweighed the tribute exacted by Rome, though at times rapacious officials overtaxed the populace.   In these provinces Roman governors and legions maintained order, established security, quelled rebellions and civil wars and thus contributed to the prosperity and general welfare of the area.

ASIA MINOR

The western coast of Asia Minor was conquered by Rome as early as the second century before Christ,[6] the rest in the first century after Christ.   Pompey reorganized the territory into three provinces: Bithynia-Pontus (excluding eastern Pontus) in the north, Asia in the west, and Cilicia in the south.   East Pontus, Cappadocia, Galatia, and Lycia were accepted as client kingdoms.   With the new acquisitions alterations in the boundaries and status became necessary.   Lycia, for instance, in the southern part of the peninsula which was annexed in the first Christian century, was later united with Pamphylia, the narrow strip on the coast stretching between it and Cilicia.   A bishop of Lycia, tortured during the reign of Diocletian (284-305), became known as Saint Nicholas, our Santa Claus.   The custom of giving presents in secret on the eve of his feast was later transferred to Christmas Day and, tradition asserts, originated in his surreptitious bestowal of dowries on three daughters of an impoverished parishioner who was on the point of giving them up to a life of shame.   Roman Asia Minor was in the main a land of peace.   Its inner districts were largely wild and sparsely populated; but the coast, especially its western sector, swarmed with populous cities.

The extensive province of Asia, first formed in 133 B.C. on the basis of the Attalid kingdom,[7] continued as the leading state.   Its cities— Ephesus, Sardis and Smyrna, headed by the capital Pergamum—enjoyed the advantage of being the main outlets for the hinterland and the connecting link with Greece, Italy, and the West.   The entire penin-

[5] See above, pp. 92-93.
[6] See above, pp. 119-125.
[7] See above, p. 131.

sula shared in the ensuing prosperity. In certain cities the possession of a national cult added prestige. The "great Diana of the Ephe-sians," [8] also known as Cybele, was the mother-goddess of Asia Minor. Her Greek counterpart Artemis had her principal shrine at Pergamum. Cybele had another famous temple at Sardis, once capital of the king-dom of Lydia and seat of rich Croesus. Of Ionic style the temple was 300 feet long and 150 feet wide. After an earthquake (A.D. 17), Sardis was rebuilt with imperial funds and continued to prosper under the Byzantines. It was one of the "seven churches" of Asia Minor (Rev. 3:1).

ALL THAT REMAINS OF THE GREAT TEMPLE OF CYBELE AT SARDIS

Such a province was basically a league of cities with a joint represent-ative assembly. Long before the advent of the Romans, that whole western coast had already been populated by Greeks.[9] The Hellenizing influences released by Alexander's successors proceeded at a more rapid pace under the empire. Italian businessmen and soldiers, government officials and their trains, travelers and visitors carried with them the Latin language and Roman customs and laws, but Greek remained the

[8] Acts 19:28, 34.
[9] See above, pp. 53, 113.

commercial, literary and to a large extent the legal medium of exchange. In the Byzantine period the whole peninsula acquired a Greek name, Anatolia ("the rising of the sun") which the Turks and Arabs have perpetuated to the present day (Anatul, Anadul). Christianity, introduced into the region about the middle of the first century, must have made rapid progress there. In his first missionary journey Paul penetrated inland into Galatia and in one of its chief synagogues delivered the first recorded specimen of his preaching.[10] In his third journey, the apostle reached Ephesus, where he settled for over two years.[11] Ephesus was number one among "the seven churches which are in Asia," to which John addressed his revelations (Rev. 1:4, 11).

SYRIA

The organization and administration of the province of Syria, with its basically Semitic culture, presented more difficult problems, despite the fact that in the interweaving of Hellenistic and native cultures there was no interruption. The first Roman proconsuls could not exercise their authority beyond the capital Antioch with its environs and such other Greek cities as Seleucia, Laodicea and Gaza. Ten Greek cities, mostly east of the Jordan, formed a league known as Decapolis. Multitudes from Decapolis followed Jesus in his early ministry.[12] The rest of the country was allowed to remain in the hands of a large number of petty kings who paid tribute. Twenty-three such states were still in power in Augustus' days. The client kings of Judaea and Nabataea were the outstanding ones. Native rulers and aristocrats with a veneer of Hellenistic culture were favored. As they became more Romanized their territories were annexed as provinces. Thus were the kinglets gradually eliminated and imperial power extended and consolidated.

The military potential of the province of Syria and its focal importance in the Asiatic possessions was from the outset fully realized and diligently exploited. The country was put under the direct rule of a Roman proconsul with authority to levy troops and engage in war. Syria was of unique strategic value to the empire as a military base for operations against Armenia, Mesopotamia, unwieldy Arabian tribes, and, more importantly, against Persia, the only serious rival remaining in the East. Syria's governorship, no less than that of Gaul, was coveted as the most honored and highly prized one in the realm. More than one of its incumbents ended his political career wearing the purple robe of the Caesars. With Syria as a focus of Roman power in the Near

[10] Acts 13:16-41.
[11] Acts 19:1, 8, 10.
[12] Matt. 4:25; Mk. 5:20.

East, Roman administration established a chain of posts along the fringe of the desert to protect the more settled and civilized area.   Protection from external enemies, immunity from civil disturbances, and the opening of a world market for native products, ushered in a new era for the land.

ECONOMY FLOURISHING

In the first century and a half of imperial rule, beginning in 30 B.C., Syria lifted itself up from the deep depression into which it had sunk and achieved a hitherto unattained degree of prosperity.   Its population had probably doubled before the Ottoman period, when it dwindled to about three millions.   Syria became one of the wealthiest provinces in the empire.   Its merchants—including Lebanese, Palestinians, Mesopotamians—all Syriac (Aramaic) speaking and therefore known as *Syri*— were sprinkled over Europe, reaching as far as Gaul and Spain. There were no more adventurous or successful traders in the empire. They revived the ancient Phoenician activity—serving as the middlemen between East and West—a function in which they were replaced by Genoese and Venetians in the Middle Ages.

Technical inventions including an improved plow and a more efficient water wheel, effective administration of the water supply, and an increased number of reservoirs for irrigation promoted agriculture and gave rise to villages and towns.   The ruins of these towns are still conspicuous in the Orontes valley east of Aleppo and east of Hims and along the frontier of the Syrian Desert where only barrenness rules today.   A system for the protection of wild plants and the methodical felling of trees was applied at least in the case of the cedars of Lebanon, which then still crowned the summits.   A legate of Tiberius (r. A.D. 14-37) is credited with the introduction of the pistachio and varieties of the fig tree into Italy.   Other trees then introduced were the Damascus plum and the jujube.   Phoenician cities exported wheat, dates, frankincense, and other products of South Arabia as well as perfumes, drugs, and other aromatic and medicinal products of Western Asia. They imported pottery from Greece and Italy, dried fish from Egypt and Spain, papyrus from Egypt, myrrh and incense from South Arabia, spices and jewels from India, and silk from China.   Syria and Egypt were the main sources of linen goods for the empire.   Vessels bearing the signature of a Sidonian glassmaker of the first Christian century have been unearthed in Egypt, Cyprus, Italy, and south Russia.   Syria's traffic reached its peak when the caravan cities of Petra, Palmyra, and Dura-Europos became flourishing centers of transit trade.

INFLUENTIAL CITIES: ANTIOCH

Syria was the home of city life in almost as high a degree as western Asia Minor.   In fame, splendor, and luxurious living the Syrian capital yielded only to the imperial one; in population it vied with Alexandria for second place in the empire.   It may have had half a million inhabitants.   With its suburb and pleasure park Daphne,[13] a sort of consecrated Coney Island, cosmopolitan Antioch attracted pilgrims and visitors from the East and the West.   Early it became the recipient of special imperial and royal favors.   Julius Caesar enriched it with a theater; Herod the Great[14] with a colonnade; Caligula (r. A.D. 37-41), Trajan, and Hadrian with public baths.   Caracalla raised its status to that of a colony and Commodus (r. 180-92) reorganized its Olympian games.   Lamps illuminated its streets and public squares making its nights almost as bright as its days.   The four-mile road between it and Daphne was bordered by gardens, fountains, and villas providing an appropriate framework for the gay procession that led from the capital to the scene of its festive pleasures, Daphne.   The site itself, with its flowing waters, shady parks, towering cypresses, and beautiful laurel trees dedicated to Apollo, was no less world renowned.   As late as the sixth century the law forbidding the cutting of those trees was enforced. A Greek-writing Antiochene rhetorician of the fourth century, Libanius, called Daphne "the purest gift of the queen of nymphs."   Here resided the oracles consulted by emperors.   Here also was the site of the greatest celebration of games in Syria, the Daphnean festival, consisting of Olympian sports, dances, dramatic performances, chariot racing, gladiatorial contests, and incidentally moral irregularities.

HELIOPOLIS

Not much is left to remind the spectator of the glory of Roman Antioch; the remains of Heliopolis (Arabic Baalbak, Balabakk) are second to none, not excluding those of Rome itself.   The Greek name, "city of the sun," was superimposed by Seleucids when the Semitic Baal-Hadad was identified with the sun.   The name was retained under the Romans and the chief deity was Latinized as Jupiter Heliopolitanus.   The ancient Semitic name of the town, however, reasserted itself in modern Arabic.   Made a colony by Augustus, Heliopolis remained less Roman than Berytus, less Greek than Antioch, and more Semitic than both.

The city owes its distinction to an ancient Semitic temple which antedated the Seleucids.   It was elaborately enlarged to majestic dimen-

---

[13] See above, p. 127.
[14] Treated below, pp. 149-150.

sions by Romans and converted to a castle by Arabs. The Arabs counted it among the seven wonders of the world. Its oracle early acquired wide repute. In 116, before he launched his campaign against Parthia, Trajan consulted the Heliopolitan oracle and received in response a bundle of wood wrapped in a cloth. His death the following year in Cilicia, whence his bones were transmitted to Rome, contributed to a plausible though belated interpretation of the oracular response.

It was probably Antoninus Pius (r. 138-161) who embarked on the elaborate enlargement of the temple. The work progressed slowly to its completion under Caracalla (r. 211-217) and other members of the Syro-Lebanese dynasty. Caracalla's mother, Julia Domna, was a talented and beautiful daughter of the high priest in the temple of a Semitic deity at Emesa (Hims). She had met her husband Septimius Severus (r. 193-211) when he was commander of a legion stationed in Syria.

Courtesy of American Numismatic Society

A COIN OF SEPTIMIUS SEVERUS   Obverse and reverse of a bronze coin of Heliopolis struck in the name of Septimius Severus *ca.* A.D. 211. The reverse displays a front and side view of the temple of Jupiter Heliopolitanus.

Septimius' coins display a part of the temple as do those of a later Roman emperor of Syrian origin, Philip the Arab (r. 244-249) who was born in a small village in Hauran. Glorying in her title of Augusta, Julia collaborated with her husband in the conduct of state affairs and wielded even greater political power immediately after his death. For chief counselor she had a relative, Papinian, an eminent jurist and law professor at the law school of Berytus. Julia's salon embraced a number of historians, sophists, and other learned men among whom was the great Greek physician Galen. Her work was carried on by her younger and abler sister Julia Maesa, grandmother of Elagabalus (r. 218-222) whose name perpetuates that of the Semitic god of Emesa, and of Alexander Severus (r. 222-235), the last and best of this line. Alexander's father was born at Arka (Arqah), Lebanon.

Within the Heliopolitan temple area lie the ruins of two temples: the larger and older one is that of Jupiter-Hadad; the smaller but more

richly ornamented one is that of his consort Atargatis (Ashtart). The
temple of Jupiter housed his statue in gold, representing him as a beardless youth in the garb of a charioteer holding in his right hand a whip
and in his left thunderbolts and ears of grain. The temple of Atargatis
is commonly attributed to Bacchus. The temple area, 300 by 200
yards, probably exceeds that of any cathedral in medieval Christendom
and is surpassed by only a few modern ones like St. Peter's in Rome.
The remaining six of Jupiter's columns proudly lift their heads erect,
defying earthquakes and storms to this day. Each one consists of only
three blocks, rises to a height of 62 feet, and boasts a diameter of
seven and one-half feet. Porphyry columns, quarried in Egypt, were
removed from this temple by Justinian and used in building St. Sophia,
his splendid cathedral in Constantinople.[15] The spaciousness of the
temple area, the massiveness of the stone blocks in the walls and
columns, the wealth of detail in ornamentation, and the figure work in
the frieze have combined to make of Baalbak a magnet of tourism today.

Under the appellation Jupiter Heliopolitanus, the ancient Semitic
Baal-Hadad was carried by Syrian merchants and Roman veterans into
many lands of the West to be worshiped in grand style. This was the
period in which Italian gates were opened to Syrian cultural, economic,
and social influences. In Rome itself the worship of the sun deity of
Emesa and Baalbak became virtually supreme. Not content with the
easily accessible Mediterranean coasts, Syriac-speaking settlers followed

[15] Described below, p. 180.

Courtesy of The Bettmann Archive

THE TEMPLE OF JUPITER AT BAALBAK

inland commercial highways and courses of the great rivers. Even before this time Syrian musicians, dancers, singers, circus players, and professional performers must have flooded Italy prompting the Roman satirist Juvenal (d. A.D. 140) angrily to exclaim: "The Syrian Orontes has long since poured its water into the Tiber, bringing with it its lingo and its manners, its flutes and its slanting harp strings."

BERYTUS

If Antioch gloried in its political activity and Heliopolis in its religious achievement, Berytus (modern Beirut) gloried in its intellectual attainments. In this, Berytus also differed from all other maritime cities, which were centers of trade and industry. Early in the third century it became the seat of a school of Roman law which to the end of its existence in the mid-sixth century functioned as one of the most renowned provincial schools of the empire. It made of Berytus a mecca for the best minds of the Near East, just as the American University and the Jesuit University do in the Beirut of today.

The school was presumably founded by Septimius Severus (r. 193-211) and promoted by his successors of the Syro-Lebanese

Courtesy of The Macmillan Co., Ltd.

JUPITER HELIOPOLITANUS, BAALBAK

dynasty. The two names which shed luster on the academy and the city were those of Papinian and Ulpian, who held chairs of jurisprudence before they were called as imperial counselors to Rome. Papinian was born at Emesa and Ulpian at Tyre. No less than 595 excerpts from Papinian's legal writings were later incorporated in Justinian's *Digest*. At the age of thirty-seven (212) he was beheaded by the tyrannical Caracalla, who could not tolerate such an honest counselor and stern monitor. His successor Ulpian (d. 228) was more fortunate in serving a more benevolent master Alexander Severus. One-third of the body of the *Digest* was extracted from this jurist's writings. No wonder that Justinian, whose name the Code bears, styled Berytus "the mother and the nurse of the laws." Law was the greatest and most enduring achievement of the empire.

The city itself offered an appropriate setting for such a seat of learning. Augustus honored it by making it a colony and naming it Colonia Julia Augusta Felix after his daughter. It was then made the seat of a detachment of a Roman legion. Several kings of Judaea, eager to ingratiate themselves with Roman emperors by bestowing gifts on colonies, enriched Beirut with theaters, amphitheaters, baths, and porticoes. It early became an islet of Romanism in a sea of Hellenism.

CARAVAN CITIES: PETRA

The Nabataean capital Petra[16] owed its birth and flourish to the geographical fact that it was the only place with abundant and invitingly pure water between Hejaz and Palestine. As the town was hewn in the bosom of a rock, it became impregnable on three sides. Caravaneers from spice-producing South Arabia seeking a market in the towns of the Fertile Crescent or returning thence with textiles, grains, vessels, and other products of the Mediterranean region found in Petra a haven of rest and refuge and a place for relaying their camels. This continued for over four centuries, beginning about 300 B.C. Petra served as a key city in the south-to-north trade route.

Originally a north Arabian tribe, the Nabataeans became adept in hydraulic engineering and in husbanding the little rain water that annually fell around their desert city. They must have inherited that magic rod which an earlier Semite, Moses,[17] had wielded in that same territory to bring water out of a dry rock. As the people grew in number and wealth their kings, whose favorite name was Harithath (Aretas), grew in might and extended their domain. Though they early repulsed an attack by Pompey, they gradually succumbed to the lure of Hellenism, the dominant culture of the day, and finally found themselves in the embrace of Rome. The Harithaths assumed the title of client, ally of Rome. The capital took on all the aspects of a Hellenistic city with public buildings—including a theater, a temple, and a treasury—in Greco-Roman style. At its height in the first Christian century the kingdom embraced north Arabia, Palestine, Transjordan, and southeastern Syria.

[16] See above, p. 122.
[17] Ex. 17:6.

But the end was not far off. After having absorbed all the petty kingdoms of Syria-Palestine and poised itself to measure swords with that remaining great Near Eastern power, Parthia, Rome could not tolerate the existence of such a semi-independent power in between. In A.D. 106 Trajan's legate in Syria captured and destroyed Petra. The picturesque and opulent capital was pushed into the limbo of history. Its ruins, though difficult to reach, are today a source of tourist revenue to the Kingdom of Jordan. Arabia Petraea gave way to the province of Arabia. The Roman Empire then and there reached its farthest limits.

PALMYRA

As the sun of Petra began to set, another caravan city, Palmyra, began to rise. Originally an Arab hamlet in an oasis named Tadmor (surviving in the modern Arabic name), Palmyra like Petra owed its existence to a copious spring of drinkable water on the east-to-west trans-desert route. The new orientation in world empires and the shift in international trade routes gave it its chance. For a time the desert city lay safe beyond the easy reach of Roman legions and Parthian cavalry. In due course the bulk of the Mediterranean trade with Persia, India, and the Far East came to be funneled through it. In a Palmyrene tomb of A.D. 83, pieces of Chinese silk have recently been discovered. The desert town steadily grew to a position of dazzling opulence and power among the cities of antiquity.

Early in the Roman imperial period Palmyra must have acknowledged Rome's suzerainty. Trajan incorporated it in the new province he created on the destruction of Petra. Its Westernization was steady and sure. Prominent citizens began to adopt Roman names; one family had Septimius prefixed to its Semitic name. Meantime the city was extending its sway into neighboring lands. Dura-Europos on the mid-Euphrates (now in Iraq) was reduced and used as a fortress to protect Palmyra's growing trade. By the mid-third century Palmyra's role in international affairs had become considerable. When the Sasanid Shapur I in 260 inflicted a shameful defeat on the Roman army at Edessa and captured Valerian,[18] Odenathus (Udaynath), the Palmyrene ruler, led his Syro-Arabian army to the rescue of the emperor. He pursued the Persians to the very walls of their capital Persepolis and even captured some of the royal harem, but Valerian died in captivity. Udaynath was rewarded for his loyalty by being given the title of *dux Orientalis,* which virtually recognized him as vice-emperor of the eastern

[18] Treated below, p. 172.

part of the empire. The empire was then in a feeble and confused state as a result of harassment from numerous enemies from the West and East.

On the death of Udaynath his minor son Wahab-al-Lath ("gift of the goddess al-Lat," Latin translation Athenodorus) succeeded, but his ambitious and beautiful widow Zenobia (Bath-Zabbay, "daughter of the gift") held the reins of authority tight in her hands. Zenobia modeled her court after that of the Persian emperors and conducted herself with royal dignity and pomp. She claimed descent from her early Egyptian counterpart, Cleopatra. She patronized Greek and studied it under the celebrated philosopher Longinus, who became her adviser. With her authority acknowledged throughout Syria, north Arabia, and east Mesopotamia, Zenobia dispatched her troops against Egypt, where they established a garrison at Alexandria, and into Anatolia, where they penetrated as far as Ancyra (Ankara). She then shook off her Roman tutelage and behaved as an independent sovereign carrying the honorific title of Augusta.

At last Rome under a vigorous emperor bestirred itself. Early in 272, Aurelian reduced the Palmyrene garrison in Anatolia, pushed on to the occupation of Antioch and Hims, and thence pursued Zenobia's army to the gates of her capital. The queen sought safety in flight on a dromedary by night. Pursuing horsemen overtook her just before she reached the Euphrates. Shortly afterwards Aurelian returned to Palmyra, put its inhabitants to the sword, and destroyed it. Only the temple was spared.

What is left of Palmyra stands out today as the most imposing sight in the Syrian Desert. Like the remains of Baalbak they bespeak the prosperity once enjoyed in Syrian cities. Conspicuous among the ruins are the colonnade and the temple. In the avenue of columns, which extended 1240 yards, stood some 375 columns each 55 feet high. About 150 are partly or wholly extant. A few are of Egyptian granite. Until 1929 an Arab village was housed within the enclosure of the temple of Bel, a Semitic solar deity, the dwellers were then evacuated and the village was turned into a museum. Palmyrene busts, many of which may be found in European and American museums, are usually frontal with an inscription in Aramaic above the shoulder.

JUDAEA

North of the client kingdom of Nabataea stood a better-known one, Judaea, centering around Jerusalem and Samaria. Judaea was the name given to Roman Palestine. This kingdom attained its greatest territorial extent under Herod the Great, who by the grace of Rome

From Chabot, INSCRIPTIONS DE PALMYRE (Imprimerie Nationale, Paris)

A PALMYRENE FATHER AND THREE CHILDREN, *ca.* A.D. 170   The father, beardless and with uncovered head, holds a vase in his left hand and a bunch of dates or bananas in his right.   His son, between the two daughters, holds a bird in his left hand and a cluster of grapes in his right.   The two girls wear veils which do not cover the face.   The inscription near the left arm of the man gives his name and the names of his children.

ruled for thirty-three years ending with his death in 4 B.C., two years after the birth of Christ (*ca.* 6 B.C., as reconstructed by scholars). Herod had inherited his authority from his father, an Idumaean (Edomite) whom Pompey had appointed. The Edomites were Judaized Arabians. This makes the Jewish king a couple of generations removed from the desert. Herod promoted agriculture, encouraged industry, inaugurated irrigation projects, refortified Jerusalem, and rebuilt its temple on a magnificent scale. The temple was known to Jesus. On the coast he rebuilt a small place, destined to become the port of Roman Palestine, and named it Caesarea in honor of his patron Augustus Caesar. Herod's beneficence extended to neighboring provinces.[19] This generosity aroused the hostility of his conservative Jewish subjects and he was accused of favoring Hellenism and of promoting Romanism at the expense of national interests. Of all the multitudinous peoples who constituted the Roman world, the Jewish

[19] As noted above, pp. 142, 146.

Courtesy of The Bettmann Archive

RELIEF FROM THE ARCH OF TITUS, ROME, SHOWING THE TRIUMPHAL PROCESSION
CARRYING THE SEVEN-BRANCHED CANDLESTICK

—due to their nationalistic and religious peculiarities—were undoubtedly the most difficult for the Romans to govern. Herod repressed the outbreaks against his authority with bloody fury. The "massacre of the innocents," reported by Matthew (2:13-16), vaguely echoes the repressive measures taken by him.

After Herod the Judaeans continued restive under Roman rule. In A.D. 67 Vespasian, future emperor, moved against them from Syria at the head of 50,000 troops and dealt them telling blows. His son Titus carried on the operations against Jerusalem, which after a few months' siege was starved to surrender (A.D. 70). The Judaean capital was razed and thousands of its inhabitants were slaughtered. Titus' triumphal entry into Rome featured the seven-branched candlestick which he had removed from the temple.

EGYPT

The province of Egypt, Augustus' most important territorial acquisition, presented even more difficulty of administration than the province of Syria. Its control had been in the hands of an elaborate and traditionally entrenched bureaucracy of Egyptianized Greeks and Hellenized Egyptians. The first problem facing Rome was to penetrate and take over this bureaucracy. The Romans shared in the Ptolemaic—and behind it the Pharaonic—theory that the land was the king's estate. As the principal grain supply of Rome, Egypt was actually brought under the direct control of the emperor. It received a prefect for governor and was garrisoned with a powerful force. The house-to-house census of property and persons demonstrates the importance attached by the government to the country. While keeping the Ptolemaic institutions, Roman officials injected new life and efficiency into the old system. For a century and a half after the annexation, Rome had but little trouble with the natives.

The inherited capital, Alexandria, was one of the most imposing cities of the world. One fourth of its area is said to have been covered with temples, palaces, and public buildings. Chief among these was the museum,[20] which by this time had developed into a Greek university. The population was of course cosmopolitan with a preponderance of Greeks and Hellenized natives and a large Jewish element. In fact there were more Jews in this city than in Jerusalem. In the Augustan age, the estimated free population of Alexandria was three hundred thousand. Those of Hellenic culture enjoyed such privileges as a reduced poll tax and a popular assembly. The city, a center of Hellenism and of Semitism, was crucial to the new commerce between Europe and the Arabian-Indian east. The Nile-Red Sea canal [21] diverted into Egypt some of the traffic which would have otherwise gone overland in Western Asia.

The country's industry and agriculture contributed the general prosperity, which though considerable was quite below the Ptolemaic mark. The management of commerce and industry remained in local hands, though a limited number of Italian businessmen had moved to the country in quest of new markets. Under Roman aegis industrialization advanced, giving the country a continuing preeminence in its traditional products of fabrics, glassware, and metalwork. Italian irrigation engineers cooperated with native ones in improving the system on which the fertility of the land depended. Besides grain the main exports continued to be foodstuffs, metalware, textiles, and pottery.

Egypt differed markedly from its neighbor to the north in that it was almost a one-city country. Egyptians also differed from Syrians in not sending businessmen, merchants, agents and skilled workers into Western markets. Throughout the ages Egyptians have been more closely bound to their land than their eastern neighbors. Whatever

[20] Treated above, p. 128.
[21] See above, pp. 128, 136.

contributions Egypt made to Western life were made on its own soil or through Westerners.

COUNTRY LIFE

While in such cities as Antioch, Berytus and Alexandria theaters, forums, temples and public buildings embellished the scene, aqueducts supplied water, sewers provided drainage and elegantly furnished mansions housed the wealthy, the countryside remained unimpressed. It was mostly in coastal towns, Greco-Roman colonies and caravan cities that the wealthy and the Westernized flourished. In such centers slavery enabled a "white collar" class, too proud to work, to rise. Certain members of this class undoubtedly made good use of their leisure and devoted themselves to the Muses and other high callings of life, but the majority became addicted to sports, amusements and diverse entertainments.

Throughout, the general aspects of country life in the provinces of Syria and Egypt followed the earlier patterns unaffected. The villages were populated mostly by peasants who were as little impressed by the Romanizing process as they had been by the Hellenizing one. Especially those far removed from urban centers tenaciously clung to the old faiths, languages and practices. The Syrian villager did not give up his Aramaic tongue, nor did the Egyptian his Coptic. An analogous situation obtains today vis-à-vis the impact of the English and French languages. The poor—and the bulk of the population was poor—did not share in the abundant life. Many, especially among Egyptians, were bound to the soil, overworked, overtaxed, undernourished, subject to recurring plagues and unaware of any possibility of escape.

As the third century advanced the decay that had beset the empire began to manifest itself increasingly in the provinces. To corruption, civil discord and other signs of decadence was added religious dissension. Persia was meanwhile passing through a similar stage in its history.

PARTHIA

The eastern wing of the Roman eagle, as it spread itself over Europe and Western Asia, reached but failed to cover Parthia. Parthia's frontier was the only one which confronted Rome with an opponent who could be considered a match. This country's distance from the main center of authority, its cherished tradition of independence and the arms of the Arsacids[22] spared it the fate of its neighbors. Of all the

[22] Treated above, p. 119.

attempts on it Trajan's came nearest to winning a permanent victory over it. For Rome the real East remained there.

Before the close of the first Christian century, however, confusion begins to prevail in the Parthian kingdom. At times two or more kings rule simultaneously and are constantly challenged by other claimants. A splinter Arsacid dynasty is established in Armenia. Repeated hostilities with Romans and intermittent nomad incursions from north and east, going back to Scythian pre-Christian days, at last began to tell. The destruction of Seleucia by a Roman general in 164 and of Ctesiphon by Septimius Severus in 199 hastened final disintegration. But the mortal blow came from inside, culminating a series of civil disturbances and domestic feuds. It was administered by Ardashir (Artaxerxes), a vassal king ruling in Fars (Persia proper). Ardashir defeated and slaughtered Artabanus V, last of the Arsacids, and in 226 started a new line named Sasanid after an ancestor of his. Ardashir I reasserted as "king of kings" the claim of hegemony over all lands that belonged to the Achaemenids. His dynasty lasted till the advent of the Moslem Arabs in 651.[23]

Parthia was gradually alienated from the Greek world as that world became more closely affiliated with Rome. In art the Arsacid is called the dark age, one in which Hellenistic classical types and motifs were modified generally in the direction of simplification. Hostility to Rome had no doubt its cultural repercussion. Coins with Aramaic initials of kings by the side of the usual Greek legend make their appearance after the mid first Christian century. Like Egypt Parthia was not a country of many cities. The destruction of Seleucia, western half of the capital and the most vital source of Western culture, sealed the fate of Hellenism east of the Euphrates. Greek culture gave way to Aramaic. The ever-advancing progress of Christianity in Western Asia engendered a new Aramaic literature with headquarters at Edessa. Henceforward Greek literary treasures were to become available to Near Easterners, even to the Moslem Arabs, through translations from Greek.

BOOKS TO READ

Bailey, Cyril, *The Legacy of Rome* (Oxford, 1928).

Bell, Harold I., *Egypt from Alexander the Great to the Arab Conquest* (Oxford, 1948).

Bouchier, E. S., *Syria as a Roman Province* (Oxford, 1916).

Chapot, Victor, *The Roman World* (New York, 1928).

[23] To be treated later, p. 211.

Gibbon, Edward, *The History of the Decline and Fall of the Roman Empire,* ed. J. B. Bury, 7 vols. (London, 1896-1900).

Hitti, Philip K., *Lebanon in History* (New York, 1957).

Jones, A. H. M., *The Herods of Judaea* (Oxford, 1938); *The Cities of the Eastern Roman Provinces* (Oxford, 1937).

Mattingly, Harold, *Roman Imperial Civilisation* (New York, 1957).

Mommson, Theodor, *History of Rome,* tr. William P. Dickson, 4 vols. (New York, 1894); *The Provinces of the Roman Empire,* tr. William P. Dickson (London, 1909), vol, II.

Ramsay, William M., *The Social Basis of Roman Power in Asia Minor* (Aberdeen, 1941).

Rostovtzeff, M., *The Social and Economic History of the Roman Empire,* 2nd ed., P. M. Fraser, 2 vols. (Oxford, 1957).

XIII   *Intellectual and Religious Activity: Christianity*

WHILE the eyes of the world were turned toward Rome as its mistress and hub of its activity and were there bedazzled by the resplendent throne of the august Caesar, a child was born in the manger of a small town in a remote corner of a province of the empire. The manger outlasted imperial Rome. The child's name was Jesus, a Hellenized form of the Hebrew word which gave us Joshua ("Jehovah is salvation"). Only one contemporary Latin historian (Tacitus) mentions "Christus" (a translation of Aramaic "anointed," which gave us Messiah) with the casual remark that he "had undergone the death penalty in the reign of Tiberius, by sentence of the procurator Pontius Pilatus." This must have been about A.D. 27.

None of the outstanding features of Christ's life—virgin birth, miracle performance, crucifixion, exaltation to heaven—lacked a parallel in earlier Near Eastern religious experience. Hardly a teaching of his was not anticipated by former teachers in the area. The Golden Rule, pride of the new teaching, had an Assyrian parallel of the seventh pre-Christian century: "As for him who doeth evil to thee, requite him with good." [1] The Christmas message (Lk. 2:14) echoes not only the message of the Hebrew prophet but that of the Phoenician god Aliyan:

> Remove war from the earth!
> Do away with passion!
> Pour out peace over the earth,
> Loving consideration over the fields! [2]

In this respect Christianity came as a superior synthesis of the highest and noblest spiritual thoughts of the Near East. In it Semitic religious genius reaches its climax. Yet there was much that was new in the

[1] Samuel H. Langdon, *Babylonian Wisdom* (London, 1923), p. 90, 1. 6.
[2] Albrecht Goetze, "Peace on Earth," *Bulletin, American Schools of Oriental Research,* No. 93 (1944), p. 20.

teaching and the teacher: emphasis on love, love of God and love of men, by one who completely practised what he preached and laid down his life for it. In general the new teaching gave mankind a new outlook on the world, placed the stress on the duty of unselfish devotion to God and humanity, and provided it with a shining example of a human life that could embody these ideals.

Starting as a Semitic religion at the crossroads of the Greco-Roman world the new religion had to incorporate into itself certain features to make it palatable. The operation began with Paul, himself a Hellenized convert from Judaism, and was further pursued by early Christian Fathers. Before that Paul struggled successfully to free the nascent church from the shackles of Jewish legalism. By its reconciliation with Greek philosophy Christianity developed its world potential. It thus transcended its Semitic origin, and, after serving as a bridge between East and West, it took firm hold of the Eastern Mediterranean and thence resolutely went forth addressing its message to mankind.

This it could not have done had it not offered answers to universal questions regarding the inner meaning of life and death to the intellectual and spiritual satisfaction of inquirers. For this was an age in which such questions and those regarding the riddle of the universe were being fervently asked. Old answers were no more acceptable. The old gods had disappointed their worshipers. None of the existing creeds had a satisfying vital message for the maltreated, the unfortunate, the discontented, the poor, the outcast, the sinner. To all these the new faith offered the hope of a future life more blessed than the earthly one. The Greco-Roman system accorded immortality only to the few, the benefactors of their peoples. The mystery cults of the East made religion a monopoly of the initiated elite. Thus did Christianity in its ideology, ethics, dogmatic certainty and eschatology stand in a class by itself.

SLOW PROGRESS

But at first progress was slow and success uncertain. Until the end of the first Christian century this Near Eastern cult must have looked to the casual observer like one of those many which had been mushrooming for some time. Not until the early second century did it seriously challenge the older faiths. Professors of those polytheistic faiths, by the very nature of their beliefs, were relatively more tolerant of others. Their policy was one of "live and let live." But the professors of the new faith were different. As monotheists they could not compromise their position; they had to assume an aggressive attitude toward all others. They could not very well participate in the worship of the emperor and other religious functions of the community amidst which they lived. A clash was inevitable.

PERSECUTIONS

First in the series of severe persecutions authored by Roman emperors was that of Nero in A.D. 64. It was, however, local and motivated not by religious but by incendiary considerations. An accidental conflagration had destroyed the center of the capital but the Christian community was made to blame. On many other occasions, national and provincial, Christians were conveniently made the scapegoat. The most eminent victim of the Neronian decree was supposedly Paul, who died in Rome in 67. The persecution undertaken by Domitian (95) was likewise local and not directed primarily against Christians as such but against the Jews, with whom Christians were still confused. By the end of the first century the threat of the new religion had not evidently been keenly felt. More serious was Trajan's decree of 112, which made Christians unwilling to pay homage to the emperor and the gods of the state traitors. For the next two years the entire Christian community was theoretically outlawed. The mob and the provincial governors, actuated by personal and local motives, took advantage of the opportunity to impose upon Christians all kinds of penalties. In 250-251 Decius reactivated the provisions of Trajan's decree and six years later Valerian not only required the offer of public sacrifice by Christians but forbade their reunions. The list of martyrs, "whose blood is the seed of the Church," mounted higher and higher.

More devastating than all these was the persecution inaugurated by Diocletian in 303. His edict ordered that churches be razed, books burned, and civil and military officers dismissed. Issued by an emperor whose wife and daughter were supposedly Christians and who himself had sympathy with the new religion, this edict is difficult to explain. Evidently the heathen priesthood had by then become fully conscious of the challenge and the threat offered by Christianity, and spread rumors that churches were used as meeting places for secret societies conspiring against the security of the state. By that time civil and military government officials must have felt the competition of their Christian colleagues and become jealous of their success.

For ten years persecution raged with unabated fury. Heavy penalties, including executions, were administered on a large scale. New means of torture were devised. In Antioch and vicinity, Church historians tell us men were toasted on gridirons and women threw themselves into the Orontes to escape rape. In Arabia people were butchered by the ax. So sure were the imperial executioners of the success of their work that they then erected a triumphal column with an inscription boasting that they had exterminated the Christian name and superstition. In a few years Christianity was to become under Constantine an official state religion. Diocletian's persecution was the last to be decreed by a Roman emperor.

THE STOIC SYSTEM

With two influential Greek systems of philosophy, Stoicism and Neo-Platonism, the Christian system established a give-and-take relationship. As the two assumed the functions of a religion, Christianity had to contend with them.

Paul was the first intermediary between Christianity and Stoicism.[3] The tone and contents of several theses in his Epistles, for instance those relating to human nature and to the analysis of the body as earthy or natural, heavenly or spiritual,[4] are largely Stoic. Stoic principles readily recommended themselves to Roman political and intellectual aristocracy. In Roman literature beginning with the Christian era the validity of those principles was taken for granted. Most good administrators under the early empire were imbued with them. Emperors, like Marcus Aurelius (d. 180), identified themselves with this philosophy. Its concept of the unity of the world and the universality of the state under the rule of the wisest seemed to have been realized in the Roman merger of Syrians, Phoenicians, Egyptians, Phrygians, Greeks, Iberians, Gauls, and countless others into one organic structure owing common allegiance to the Caesars' throne. Through Stoicism the Roman Empire, an indirect successor of Alexander's, may be said to have found its soul. But in due course Stoic devotees discovered that their "perfect man" was not to be found in the degenerated Greco-Roman society. By the third century Christianity had overtaken Stoicism, reconciled itself with it and absorbed many of its features. The discourses of Epictetus, the poor lame Phrygian who taught in Rome (*ca.* 90), became to all practical purposes Christian manuals. Epictetus' "golden sayings" recur in Marcus Aurelius' meditations.

NEO-PLATONISM

This third century was for the empire a turbulent one indeed, featuring domestic strife, foreign attacks and economic depression. In it

[3] On Stoicism, consult above, pp. 126-127.
[4] I Cor. 15:44-9, 52-4; 2 Cor. 5:1-4; Ro. 8:5-13, 6:12; Col. 3:5; I Cor. 6:13, 9:27.

the intellectual center of the world shifted from Athens and Rome back to the East, and the philosophical leadership was provided by Hellenized Anatolians, Syrians, Egyptians and other Near Easterners. Even before that some of the outstanding Greek-writing scholars had been born in Western Asia or Egypt. In the second century flourished Galen of Pergamum whose treatise on medicine was accepted as authoritative by Greeks, Romans and medieval Arabs. His contemporary Ptolemy of Alexandria worked out a mathematical astronomy which was accepted until the seventeenth century. Strabo (d. A.D. 24), whose geography provides a mine of information on the Mediterranean world, was born in Pontus about 63 B.C. In its seventeen books, he describes the European and Asiatic ports as well as those of Egypt and Libya. The decay of classical philosophies prepared the way for the advent of syncretistic systems of Greek and Oriental thought and the final triumph of Christianity.

Neo-Platonism was such a system. Its endeavor was directed toward reconciling Plato and Aristotle with Oriental ideas. Under Near Eastern influence it developed the Platonic dualism of "idea" and "matter" into a form of pantheism which reappears in medieval Sufi Islam. The physical world became an emanation of the immanent divinity, "the one," from whom human souls are arisen and with whom they may be reunited through trance or ecstasy. Contempt for the world of matter and belief in the purification of the soul through asceticism and mystic revelation have since been echoed by Christian monks and Moslem Sufis.

All three exponents of Neo-Platonism were Near Easterners. Plotinus (d. 270), who was born in Egypt of Roman parents and educated at Alexandria, taught in Rome. Alexandria was the cradle of Neo-Platonism and the Alexandrian academy was its nurse. Among those attracted to study under Plotinus in Rome was Porphyry ("clad in purple," d. ca. 305) whose real name, Melik (king), betrays his Semitic origin. Porphyry was probably Tyrian by birth and certainly by education. It was he who expounded and popularized Plotinus' views and thus inaugurated a system that for centuries dominated European philosophical thought. Based on Platonism but with interpretations that could hardly be accepted or even understood by Plato, the new system was farther removed from its basis by Porphyry.

Porphyry had a distinguished pupil Iamblichus (Jamblichus, d. ca. 333), who was born in Syria. Iamblichus did not follow other philosophers' precedent and migrate but lived and taught in his native land. Following the Neo-Pythagorean pattern Iamblichus ascribed to numbers higher significance than they possessed in scientific mathematics and modified his masters' views in the direction of mysticism. The collection of ideas strung together loosely in what is termed Neo-Pythagoreanism, had its formulation also at Alexandria in line with the Orientalizing tendencies of the age. It revived many ideas ascribed to Pythagoras, the sage of Samos (sixth pre-Christian century) and his followers and gave them mystical interpretation. To Pythagoras is ascribed the doctrine of metempsychosis and the doctrine that earthly life is only a purification of the soul. Pythagoreans advanced astronomical and mathematical studies.

ALEXANDRIAN SCHOOL OF THEOLOGY

The Christian system, which inherited Neo-Pythagorean—as it did Neo-Platonic—ideas was fortunate in attracting from the outset some of the brilliant minds of the Roman Hellenistic world. In Alexandria, where the waves of Jewish, Christian and pagan thought met, clashed or were reconciled, flourished the catechetical school to whose work was due much of the intellectual progress of early Christianity. Between 190 and 203 the school was headed by Clement, generally considered founder of the Alexandrian school of Christian theology. Originally a pagan deeply read in Greek philosophy and apparently an initiate into one of the mysteries, Clement attempted to harmonize the best in the antique culture with Christian thought. He was succeeded in 211-232 by his more celebrated pupil Origen. Origen was born in Egypt (*ca.* 185) to a father who was at the time pagan, as indicated by the name he gave his son meaning begotten of Horus. In the persecution of 202 young Origen must have coveted martyrdom, for his mother tried to keep him home by hiding his clothes. After quarreling with the bishop of his native city he established his residence at Caesarea in Palestine, where he continued his teaching and writing. In his commentaries on the books of the Bible, he made extensive use of allegorical interpretation. During Decius' persecution[5] he was tortured and died shortly after his release from prison (253).

These two theologians were followed in the next century by a third saint and Greek Father of the Church, the Alexandrian-born Athanasius (d. 373). He was a stalwart opponent of paganism and heresy and generally known as father of orthodoxy. Athanasius' fight was directed against Arianism, which again had its rise in Alexandria and owed its name to a Greek ecclesiastic Arius (d. 336). Arius taught that God was unknowable, separate from any created being and that Christ, as a created being, was not God in the full sense. His theology

[5] Discussed above, p. 157.

was condemned at Nicaea (325), where Athanasius figured in the formulation of what became the Nicene creed, featuring the Trinity. In medieval times the Visigoths embraced Arianism, and today the Unitarians may be regarded as heirs of its Christology. As patriarch of Alexandria Athanasius refused to obey emperors' commands favoring Arianism and was deposed and reinstated, expelled and repatriated several times. On one occasion he lived in exile with hermits.

A work ascribed to Athanasius describes the life of a hermit, personally known to him, named Anthony. This Egyptian-born ascetic spent twenty years in the desert, where he gathered a circle of disciples around him but visited Alexandria during the great persecution[6] to fortify his brethren in the faith. Colonies of hermits subsequently grew in Lower Egypt. From Egypt monastic life soon found its way into Sinai, whence it entered Palestine and spread throughout Christendom. Monasticism and theology were Egypt's principal contributions to ecclesiastical history.

LATIN FATHERS

While early Fathers in Alexandria were enriching and embellishing Christian theology with Greek philosophical thoughts, Latin Fathers and saints were introducing into the Church government and administration Roman legal ideas and juridical concepts. But these men belonged mainly to the North African Church, on the periphery of the Near East. First among them was Tertullian, a pagan practitioner of law born in the ancient Phoenician colony Carthage (*ca.* 155), who embraced Christianity at the age of thirty. His pupil Cyprian was also pagan born (*ca.* 200), in Carthage, where he professed rhetoric and was not converted till he attained his late forties. Cyprian was elevated to the bishopric of his native city, where he suffered a martyr's death by decapitation during Valerian's persecution.[7]

Towering above all these saints and writers stands the gigantic figure of Augustine, probably greatest among all Church Fathers. Augustine was born in 354 in Numidia (west of Carthage) and was not converted till 387, after having been a votary of Manichaeism[8] and Neo-Platonism. Seven years after his conversion he was elected bishop of Hippo, another Phoenician colony in North Africa. This position he held till his death in 430. He is popularly known for his *Confessions,* an interesting autobiographical work, and his *The City of God,* in which he envisaged the Christian Church as a new empire rising over the

[6] See above, pp. 157-158.
[7] Treated above, p. 157.
[8] See below, pp. 181-182.

ruins of old Rome, but one that has existed from the beginning of time. A contemporary of Augustine and another ornament of the Latin Church was Jerome (340-420), who migrated to Bethlehem. There in the quiet of a monastery he devoted himself to a life of devotion and study. His Latin translation of the Bible, the Vulgate, is still used as the official text in the Roman Catholic Church.

The Church Fathers of Alexandria, heirs of a Greek heritage which stressed belief in reason, love of learning and pursuit of knowledge for its own sake, built up the early intellectual Christian system. It was Clement, Origen and Athanasius who laid the doctrine of the Trinity. Thanks to their efforts love of knowledge became a part of Christian tradition but took the form of dogmatic belief. For the first time in the history of thought, correct belief became so essential as to render deviation sinful. Greek councils held in Asia Minor reflect such thinking. The Greek Fathers also stressed the Neo-Platonic distinction—introduced by Paul—between the world of tangibles that is changeable, transient and the world of ideas that is stable and eternal. This made clear the distinction between matter and spirit, the body and the soul. The world became a "vale of tears" leading to the next world, and a premium was placed on asceticism as a way of life.

By contrast the Latin Fathers, heirs of the Roman tradition which interested itself more in organizing human society and regulating it by law, worked toward the institutional organization of the Church. The Romans were more practical than the Greeks. Their councils reflect the contributions of Tertullian and Augustine. The medieval Christian Church became the institution which embodied elements of Hebrew justice, Christian love, Greek belief in intellect, Roman organization and Hellenic asceticism.

PHILO

The reaction of Judaism to Greek philosophy was personified in Philo Judaeus of Alexandria (*ca.* 20 B.C.-A.D. 40), the earliest and one of the greatest of Jewish philosopher-theologians. To Philo the Pentateuch had absolute divine authority implying revelation, a principle unknown to Greek philosophers. Meanwhile Philo accepted the dualistic doctrine of man derived from Plato. The body is a prison of the soul, from which it seeks to return to God. To Philo God was infinite, transcendent; but matter was finite, limited. Hence the necessity of positing a mediating power between the two. This is the logos (the word),[9] whom he identifies as the first-born son of God, the

---

[9] Cf. John 1:1.

second God. Philo exercised profound influence on Christian theological thought.

MYSTERY CULTS

The decline of Greek science and the trend away from classical philosophy—both Greek and Roman—which marked the third century, landed the seeker after reality in the embrace of Eastern mystery and mystic cults, which then enjoyed their golden age. In the embrace of Eastern religions the Western ones expired. Dependence upon reason alone failed man. He learned that man could not live by knowledge alone. The intellectual bankruptcy of the West provided the opportunity of the East. Chief among the Eastern cults were those connected with Cybele, originally the Mother Goddess of Phrygia, Isis of Egypt and Mithras of Persia. As possessors of something "mysterious," something that cannot be explained, these cults demanded initiation on the part of devotees. "Mystic" has the same derivation from Greek as "mystery." The underlying assumption in mystic religions was that knowledge of the divine, of spiritual truth, was not attainable through reasoning or the ordinary sense perception but rather through intuition, insight, emotion. The ultimate goal was communion with the saving god. This communion must have been the special longing of the time with its contempt for reason and philosophy.

All mystery religions guaranteed happiness in this world and a favorable reception in the world to come. Though offering, in competition with each other, a better way of life, they had so many features in common that they interacted and at times overlapped. Primitive Christianity shared in the process as a contributor and receiver. But, unlike Christianity, mystery religions belonged to only those who were initiated and held secret doctrines and practices which they were forbidden to reveal. Initiation presupposed special preparation. Being held in secret little is known about the initiatory ceremonial and ecstatic rituals. Priests held the keys tight in their hands.

In Mithraism, initiation involved seven degrees. Admission into the society of votaries was through some rite of purification, by water or blood, a parallel of baptism. Magic here played its part. Communion with the deity was accomplished by participation in a ceremonial meal. Once achieved, this communion with the deity was followed by enlightenment to the votary, leading in certain cases to visions. Illumination reappears in Moslem Sufism. Isis was wont to appear to her devotees and hold discourse with them. Early Christian missionaries must have operated in an atmosphere imbued with Stoic and Neo-Platonic as well as mystic beliefs and practices.

From the cult of Cybele the orgiastic rites in honor of the goddess and her youthful divine lover had long before this been borrowed by Greeks and Romans. The revelries of the worship of the Phoenician Ishtar and Adonis[10] had also been taken over, and these goddesses and their lovers had by now become fully identified with Greco-Roman deities. The maternal loveliness of Isis endeared her to men and women alike. The fascination of her mysteries, the effectiveness of her ceremonies, the absorption into herself of the virtues of all other goddesses, the rewards she offered the initiate in terms of purification, forgiveness, communion and regeneration—all these gave her cult a universality of appeal. The Isis-Osiris cult enjoyed in the Roman period an even larger measure of success than it did in the Hellenic.[11] In the first two Christian centuries Isis' shrines and temples could be found in Sicily, Sardinia and Italy. From the second century on the cult was the most bitter antagonist of Christianity. In the short period of the revival of pagan religion at Rome in 394 Isis, the Mother Goddess and Mithras occupied the foreground. Isis was finally identified with the Virgin Mary and Horus with Christ. The process was to a certain extent one of blending rather than displacement.

But of all the Near Eastern rivals of Christ Mithras was no doubt the strongest. An ancient Iranian deity conceived of as the chief aid of Ahura Mazda[12] and therefore as a god of light, Mithras was engaged in constant struggle with the powers of darkness. Central in his worship was sacrifice, the sacrifice of a bull, with Mithras himself slaying the animal as protagonist. His chief appeal was to Roman legionaries fighting for life and empire under the god as heroic leader. Through soldiers, slaves and traders his cult was diffused not only in Italy but in the empire, reaching Gaul and Germany. The seats of Mithraic worship were caves and underground shrines, to insure secrecy. Such cave temples can still be seen in the baths of Caracalla at Rome. The feast of the *sol invictus* (invincible sun), celebrated on December 25 at the vernal equinox, when the victory of light over darkness begins to become apparent in the lengthening of the day, was especially cultivated by votaries of Mithraism and probably determined our date of Christmas.

In the third century it was a toss between Mithras and Christ. In the fourth victory was assured.

[10] See above, p. 105.
[11] See above, p. 129.
[12] Treated above, p. 67.

BOOKS TO READ

Angus, S., *The Mystery-Religions and Christianity* (London, 1925).

Cumont, Franz, *The Mysteries of Mithra*, tr. Thomas J. McCormack (New York, reprint 1956); *The Oriental Religions in Roman Paganism* (New York, reprint 1956).

Foakes-Jackson, F. J., *History of the Christian Church from the Earliest Times to A.D. 481* (New York, 1933).

Hatch, Edwin, *The Influence of Greek Ideas on Christianity* (New York, 1957).

Hyde, Walter W., *Paganism to Christianity in the Roman Empire* (Philadelphia, 1946).

Murray, Gilbert, *The Stoic Philosophy* (New York, 1915).

Patterson, L., *Mithraism and Christianity* (Cambridge, Eng., 1921).

Pfeiffer, Robert H., *History of New Testament Times* (New York, 1949).

XIV   *In Byzantine Days*

When Constantine in 324 chose the site of an old Greek colony, Byzantium on which he subsequently founded his new capital, he could not have foreseen the full consequences of his deed. Admirably situated on a hilly promontory separated from the Asian bank by a narrow channel—the Bosporus—commanding the entrances to two seas and the gateways of two continents and not far removed from the ancient seats of culture in Europe and Asia, Constantinople ("the city of Constantine," since 1923 Istanbul) was destined to exercise on the course of human affairs an influence comparable to those exercised by Jerusalem, Athens and Rome. Dedicated in 330 as the seat of the eastern half of the Roman Empire, which reached its zenith between the ninth and the eleventh centuries, it became known as the New Rome. The chief patriarch of the Greek Orthodox Church, who still resides in it, signs himself "archbishop of Constantinople, New Rome." Its magnificent harbor contributed to making the new city a leading center of trade. Its site rendered the city a natural citadel, difficult to approach by land or sea and to invest. The remains of the mighty walls built around it by Constantine's successors are still included in tourists' itineraries.

As the new Rome on the Bosporus rose in power, importance and prestige, the old Rome on the Tiber sank. The "eternal city" did not prove to be so eternal. Rome fell in 476 before the onslaught of Germanic barbarians, but Constantinople served until 1453 as imperial seat of the Eastern Roman Empire and until 1922 as capital of the Ottoman Empire—in all 1592 years. It survived attacks from Goths and other Germanic hordes, Huns and other Mongolian barbarians, Arabs from Damascus and Baghdad and witnessed the birth and rise of most of the modern nations of Europe. Its span of Roman imperial life covers roughly medieval times (400-1500), of which the first six

166

centuries are loosely called the dark ages of Western Europe. But Constantinople experienced no comparable black-out; it remained almost throughout a center of the civilized world.

CONSTANTINE

The establishment of Constantinople, which paved the way for the final division of the empire into two halves, and the recognition by Constantine (joint emperor 306, sole emperor 324-337) of Christianity as a tolerated and even favored religion, which led the way to its becoming the official religion, entitle this emperor to a unique niche in the Roman hall of fame. Probably no other Byzantine emperor approached him in impact on the course of historical events. His title the Great was certainly well deserved. For years after Constantine the external and theoretical unity of the Roman Empire was maintained, though in practice the two halves were separated more than once and ruled by different emperors. But in 395, when Theodosius the Great died and one of his sons succeeded him over the western part and the other over the eastern, the final separation was complete. Constantine's successors, with the exception of Julian "the Apostate" (r. 361-363), professed Christianity. Julian's attempt to restore paganism to its place as a state religion was unsuccessful.

THE BYZANTINE EMPIRE

In two chief respects the Eastern Roman Empire differed from the Western: it was Greek in language and Christian in religion. Latin, however, remained in official use until the reign of Heraclius (r. 610-641), when it yielded to Greek as the natural medium of the people and the Church. The empire was the first Christian one in Europe. Its orientation was eastward, with its back toward the west. The center of world gravity had by this time shifted back to the Near East. The transference of the capital to the shore of Europe fronting on Asia was a recognition of the mounting importance of the Eastern provinces. As in earlier times these provinces were still then richer, more resourceful, more densely populated and more highly cultured than the Western.[1] The official permission given Christianity by Constantine to exist and develop was an acknowledgment of the political importance attached to the Christian element in the population. Then there was Persia, rejuvenated under Sasanids and posing a new menace to the integrity of the realm. The disintegration and final collapse of the Roman administration in the West left the Empire of the East as the sole representative of imperial power.

[1] Cf. above, p. 135-136.

Thus did the Byzantine state embark upon its career—rooted in Greek culture, inspired by Roman imperial tradition and enriched by those Oriental Hellenistic elements that had by this time become an integral part of the Greco-Roman world.

ASIA MINOR

Byzantine power was based for centuries in Asia Minor. Syria and Egypt were not only far removed but had maintained their respective Semitic and Hamitic aspects. Anatolia was by this time almost thoroughly Hellenized. This now could mean Byzantinized. Greek was its language. Any traces of the old tongues, if left, must have been limited to a few out-of-the-way places. And when Christianized, the country adhered to the orthodox form of the faith. Arianism, Nestorianism,[2] Monophysitism[3] and other so-called schisms and heresies found their way into the country but achieved no permanent lodging. As these Christological controversies raged, the country served as host for a number of church councils beginning with that at Nicaea (325)[4] and continuing through the one at Chalcedon (451).[5] Likewise group migrations left no permanent mark on its ethnic structure. Toward the end of the fourth century Huns from the Caucasus made an incursion into the land. Goths and other barbarians trickled into it. In the mid-seventh century Slavs settled in parts of it. But its general character remained unchanged.

Asia Minor served as a battleground for Byzantine-Persian troops as they struggled for mastery over the Near East, and remained throughout steadfast in its loyalty to the imperial throne. It nurtured no separatist movements, as Syria and Egypt did. Fighting between East Romans and first the Sasanids then Arab Moslems was carried on through centuries but always indecisively. It was not until Saljuq Turks settled in the highland of the country in the eleventh century and rooted out its Greek civilization that the empire was struck in a vital part of its body. The decline after that was unmistakable and irremediable.

SYRIA

Although Christianity was born and reared in the southern part of the country and the Christians were so called for the first time in its northern part,[6] Syria remained in the grip of paganism until well

[2] Treated below, pp. 169, 176.
[3] Treated below, pp. 169-170.
[4] See above, pp. 160-161.
[5] Mentioned below, pp. 171-172.
[6] Acts 11:26.

into the fourth century. In one edict after another the first Christian emperor ordered the destruction of pagan temples and the prohibition of sacrifices. That great stronghold of heathenism with its licentious cult in Lebanon, Afqah,[7] was one of the first to be demolished. Constantine ordered also the conversion of the great temple at Baalbak into a Christian church. His devout mother Helena undertook a pilgrimage to the Holy Land and was traditionally credited with the discovery of the "true cross" buried on the site of the present-day Church of the Holy Sepulcher. She thereby introduced into Christianity the cult of holy pilgrimage, which accelerated the Christianizing process in the land. Native Christians, particularly in Lebanon, still celebrate on September 14 a feast with bonfires re-enacting Helena's traditional announcement of the discovery to her son at Constantinople by means of bonfires from hilltop to hilltop.

By the beginning of the fifth century Syria-Lebanon-Palestine must have presented the aspect of a Christian country. The Byzantine was the only period in its history in which this land could be called Christian

In its language and ritual the Syrian Church differed from the outset from the Byzantine. Gradually theological differences became emphasized. Aramaic (Syriac) was the language of the Syrian Church. Tradition ascribes its liturgy, which undoubtedly antedates any Greek or Latin liturgy, to St. James, a brother (cousin?) of Christ. Syria became first a stronghold of Nestorianism and later of Monophysitism, both of which served as an outlet for the political separatist movement of the people.

Nestorius, who was born in Cilicia, educated at Antioch and in 428 held the bishopric of Constantinople, taught that in Jesus a divine person (the Logos) and a human person were joined in perfect harmony of action but not in the unity of a single individual. His views were first condemned by the council of Ephesus (431). Edessa was the main center of Nestorianism. Monophysitism, next to Nestorianism the greatest schism the Oriental Church suffered, maintained that the human and the divine in Christ constituted but one composite nature. Hence the name from two Greek words meaning one nature.

Under the Byzantines Syrians and Egyptians must have become conscious anew of their ancient traditions. After a submergence of centuries under a wave of Greek culture, the native spirit was asserting itself. Alienation from Byzantium was due not only to ideological but to political and economic causes as well. Byzantine rulers were more autocratic in their administration, more oppressive in their taxa-

---

[7] Cf. above, pp. 104-105.

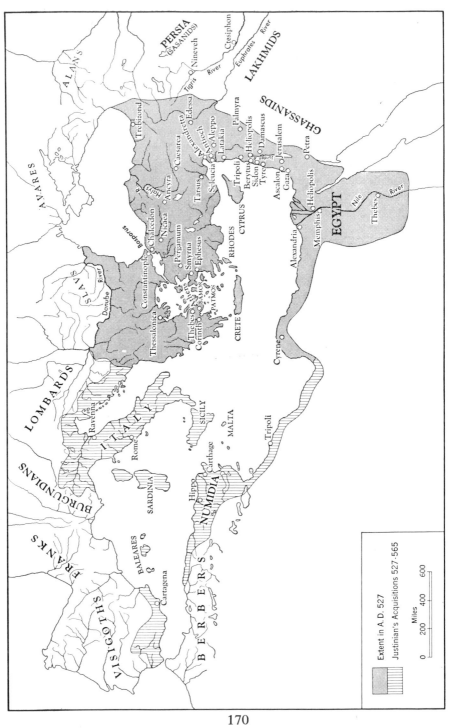

BYZANTINE EMPIRE AT ITS HEIGHT

Extent in A. D. 527

Justinian's Acquisitions 527-565

Miles

0   200   400   600

tion and less tolerant in their religious treatment than their Roman predecessors. In both Syria and Egypt hostility to the central government in Constantinople gave fresh impetus to ecclesiastical separatism.

The division of the empire does not seem to have adversely affected the prosperity of the country. In the Byzantine as in the Roman period the Eastern Mediterranean trade was almost entirely in the hands of Syrians. Their settlements dotted such commercial centers as Rome, Naples, Carthage, Marseille and Bordeaux. Through them wine from Ascalon and Gaza, purple from Caesarea, woven fabrics from Tyre and Berytus, sword blades from Damascus and embroidered stuffs from sundry towns found a European market. The traffic in silk, whether produced in the Near East or in China, was controlled by Syrian merchants. Chinese silk was first imported into some Phoenician seaport to be dyed and woven, or re-woven, before becoming acceptable to the Roman consumer. In those seaports it became linked with the purple industry. Besides silk spices and other semi-tropical products from South Arabia and India figured prominently in Syrian economy. Transit trade flourished no less than before.

EGYPT

Byzantine Egypt followed the same general pattern as Syria. In one respect it differed. Syria lay athwart the path of Persian troops as they battled with the Byzantines. Egypt was subjected to only one Persian invasion, in 616-18 when it was occupied for about ten years before Emperor Heraclius forced the withdrawal of the enemy.[8] The people evidently preferred Persian rule to Byzantine oppression. The temporary loss of the richest province of the empire and the granary of Constantinople was an economic blow. Besides, Egypt had a monopoly in the production of papyrus. Another but different blow was struck in 542, when a devastating plague originating in Egypt spread from Persia to Italy, threw the empire into confusion and left in its wake panic, famine, abandoned villages and depopulated towns.

The dawn of the fifth century found Egypt predominantly Christianized. This was the only period in its history in which it presented that aspect. Its Church claims foundation by Mark himself. In the fourth century it was seriously disturbed by Arianism.[9] In the fifth it embraced the Monophysite doctrine introduced from its neighbor to the north.[10] The condemnation of this doctrine by the council of Chalcedon (451) encouraged the Egyptian Church to adopt it officially. This

---

[8] See below, pp. 173-174.
[9] See above, pp. 160-161.
[10] See below, p. 177.

council also condemned Nestorianism. It formulated the doctrine of the two perfect and indivisible, but separate, natures of Christ, which became embedded in the Greek Orthodox as well as Roman Catholic— and later Protestant—creed.

As in Syria deviation from the Byzantine—the Orthodox—theology was one way by which opposition to imperial rule was expressed. Henceforward this church was in schism with the Greek Orthodox and the Roman Catholic Churches. Christianity released nationalistic tendencies, revived old traditions and gave new life to the native tongue, Coptic. Coptic, a descendant of ancient Egyptian (the two words are etymologically related) had adopted Greek letters supplemented by nine native signs. The new nationalism was hostile almost to everything Constantinople represented. In due course Greek was entirely abolished from church usage. The decline in Hellenism continued. By the beginning of the seventh century Greek had survived only as the language of the administration. Only a few Greek works, translated into Coptic, have been preserved in this language. Since the Moslem conquest in the seventh century Coptic has been superseded by Arabic except as the liturgical language of the church. Recent attempts at its revivication have failed.

SASANID PERSIA

The Sasanid (r. 226-651),[11] the third great dynasty to rule Persia, consisted of some forty rulers. It was more nationalistic, energetic and aggressive than its immediate Parthian predecessor. In its devotion to Zoroastrianism and claim to world dominion it was more a continuation of the earlier Achaemenid. Under the new dynasty the country was revitalized. It seriously challenged Byzantine hegemony in Western Asia and at least on two occasions came near restoring the old dominion of Darius I. But finally Persians and Byzantines fought one another to a standstill and to the point of mutual exhaustion, giving a new power in between—Islam—the chance to assert itself.

The first Sasanid who came near achieving a permanent conquest over Asia Minor was Shapur I (r. 240-271). Shapur invaded Mesopotamia, occupied north Syria and won the distinction of taking Emperor Valerian as a captive, after crushing his legions at Edessa (260).[12] Valerian died in captivity. The way was then open to Asia Minor. Caesarea in Cappadocia was taken. But no attempt was made to consolidate and hold the conquered territory. The day was saved for

[11] See above, p. 153.
[12] See above, p. 147.

Byzantium by an Arab prince of the Syrian Desert, Odenathus of Palmyra, who rushed to the succor of his sovereign, drove the Persians back across the traditional border line—the Euphrates—and even laid siege to the enemy's capital Ctesiphon.[13] Shapur considered himself an heir of the Achaemenids and assumed the pompous title "king of kings of the Persians and non-Persians." Under Shapur II (r. 310-379) Byzantium was forced to surrender several fortresses in Mesopotamia and the neo-Persian empire resumed its career of conquest.

Signal military successes marked the reign of Khosrau I (Chosroes, Kisra Anushirwan, r. 531-579), the most illustrious member of the dynasty. Khosrau was an able administrator and a reformer, particularly in the system of imperial taxation. His people called him the just. The year after his accession Khosrau concluded with Justinian, under whom the empire reached its greatest extent, the celebrated "eternal peace" treaty on the humiliating condition that the empire would pay the Persian king a large annual tribute. The treaty was prompted by Justinian's desire to free the imperial troops for operation in the West. Within seven years, however, Khosrau, alarmed by his foe's success in North Africa and Italy, violated the treaty and started a defensive war. His troops forced their way into Syria, sacked Antioch and reached the Mediterranean coast; northward the thrust reached the Caucasus and the Black Sea. With difficulty Justinian succeeded in buying a five-year truce by the payment of a large sum. In 562 another fifty-year peace was signed but proved no more definitive than the earlier one. One fact became clear: Byzantine influence in the Near East was on the wane.

A few years before the end of his reign Khosrau conducted what may be considered the most surprising military campaign of his long career, a naval expedition to southwestern Arabia. His large fleet sailed along the Arabian coast, routed the Abyssinians from what is called today Yemen and established Persian hegemony there. This was on the eve of the rise of Islam.

The second serious attempt at the conquest of Asia Minor was undertaken by his grandson Khosrau II Parviz (r. 589-628), the last famous Sasanid. Chosroes' forces broke the first time (605) through the frontiers, ravaged northern Syria, marched through Asia Minor and captured Caesarea. A detachment got as far as Chalcedon, across from the capital. A later attempt (611-617) penetrated deeper, resulting in the capture of Damascus, the sack of Jerusalem and the carrying away of the "true cross" to Ctesiphon and the subjugation of Egypt. Chris-

---

[13] For more details consult above, p. 147.

tian Syrians must have welcomed the Persians, whose treatment of Nestorians and Monophysites was more tolerant than was that of the Byzantines. In 617 Persian troops again reached the Bosporus and took Chalcedon (Scutari, Uskudar), within one mile from Constantinople. Meanwhile Slavs and Avars (ethnically allied to Huns) were attacking it from the north. The capital felt desperate; the empire appeared to totter. But fortunately for it a new leader arose to depose the tyrannical, untutored and incompetent Emperor Phocas (r. 602-610), end the chaotic condition, defend the realm and restore its unity. This was Heraclius (r. 610-641), able general, organizer and statesman, who rolled the Persian tide back, restored (628) Armenia, Roman Mesopotamia, Syria, Palestine and Egypt and was hailed savior of the empire. On March 21, 630 the conquering emperor entered Jerusalem and amid great rejoicing restored the holy cross. The solemn act symbolized the victorious conclusion of what may be considered the first great holy war of Christendom.

Under this Khosrau the neo-Persian empire attained its greatest extent and, strange as it may sound, suffered its final downfall.

BOOKS TO READ

Barker, Ernest, *Social and Political Thought in Byzantium* (Oxford, 1957).

Baynes, Norman H., *The Byzantine Empire* (London, reprint 1952).

Bury, J. B., *History of the Later Roman Empire,* 2 vols. (London, 1923).

Byron, Robert, *The Byzantine Achievement* (New York, 1929).

Byzantium, ed. Norman H. Baynes and H. St. L. B. Moss (Oxford, 1948).

Diehl, Charles, *Byzantium: Greatness and Decline,* tr. Naomi Walford (New Brunswick, N. J., 1957); *History of the Byzantine Empire,* tr. George E. Ives (Princeton, 1925).

Holsapple, Lloyd B., *Constantine the Great* (New York, 1942).

Hussey, J. M., *The Byzantine World* (London, 1957).

Jones, A. H. M., *Constantine and the Conversion of Europe* (New York, 1949); *The Cities of the Eastern Roman Empire* (Oxford, 1937).

Ostrogorsky, George, *History of the Byzantine State,* tr. Joan Hussey (Oxford, 1956).

Sykes, Percy, *A History of Persia,* 3rd ed. (London, 1930), vol. I.

Vasiliev, A. A., *History of the Byzantine Empire* (Madison, Wis., 1952).

Woodward, E. L., *Christianity and Nationalism in the Later Roman Empire* (London, 1916).

XV *Ecclesiastical, Literary and Artistic Achievements*

T HE early Byzantine age was a predominantly ecclesiastical age. The Church was its greatest institution, the saint its most revered hero. For two centuries beginning with Constantine's reign bishops, priests, monks, nuns, anchorites flourished as never before and as never after. They figured more prominently than scholars, secular writers and poets. Church buildings and monasteries were multiplied all the way from Egypt through Syria into Asia Minor. Visits to and prayers at shrines of saints were considered more efficacious than physicians' prescriptions.

Monasticism, a development of the Christian practice of asceticism, was then a favorite way of life. Founded in Egypt[1] the new style of Christian living, with its ideals of celibacy, poverty and obedience, found ready response in the entire area, where faith in secular institutions and confidence in the effectiveness of rational and intellectual processes were badly shaken. Maron, patron saint and founder of the Church that today flourishes in Lebanon and still bears his name,[2] was an ascetic monk who lived in the wilderness north of Antioch. Ephraem Syrus (the Syrian, *ca.* 306-*ca.* 373), the first great theologian and sacred poet of the Syrian Church, was responsible for fostering the monastic way of life in his communion. St. Ephraem organized at Edessa a seminary which became the first university of the Syrian (Suryani) Church.

EDESSA

Edessa became the Athens of the Syriac-writing people. In it Syriac was developed from Aramaic for Christian literary purposes and was enriched by translations from Greek. The Edessan school flourished until 489, when it was destroyed by the emperor Zeno, whose

---

[1] As noted above, p. 161.
[2] Discussed below, p. 450.

attempt to settle the theological controversies of the day were unsuccessful.   Its professors thereupon moved eastward to Nisibis (Nisibin), once a key city between the Romans and the Parthians, which became heir of Edessa as a Syro-Greek center of higher learning.   In both schools opposition to the types of Christian thought represented by Byzantium was the rule.

CHRISTOLOGY

Theological controversy was the breath of life among the learned of the fourth and fifth centuries.   It centered on the person and nature of Christ and cognate problems which agitate our minds no more than modern problems related to democracy, socialism and communism would have agitated the minds of those early Christian generations. The burning question was the determination of the relationship between the humanity of Christ and his divinity.   In due course the Syrian (that is, Syriac-using) Church split into two: East Syrian, commonly called Nestorian, and West Syrian or Jacobite.

EAST SYRIAN CHURCH

The Church of the East, as it proudly styles itself, claims foundation in the Apostolic Age and undoubtedly antedates Nestorius[3] by at least two or more centuries.   It counts him among the Greek, rather than the Syrian, fathers.   But since it refused to anathemize him his name was applied to it.   Cut off from the Roman Empire this church developed from the beginning its own doctrines and ritual.   From Edessa the communion spread into Persia where it throve.   It was a missionary communion with sufficient vitality to reach in later times India and China.   An extant stele in Sian Fu commemorates in Syriac and Chinese the names and labors of sixty-seven of its missionaries who arrived there in 635.   Through them were introduced the Syriac characters to be adapted to Mongol and Manchu use.   In India the Syrian rite struck root on the west coast especially Malabar, where the Syrian Christians claim the Apostle Thomas as founder of their church.

THE WEST SYRIAN CHURCH

If the East branch of the Syrian Church, anchored in Persia, was considered Nestorian in its theology, the West branch centered in north Syria was Monophysite.[4]   With its God-man Christology and the exal-

---

[3] See above, p. 169.
[4] Treated above, p. 168.

tation of the Virgin to celestial rank, this branch of the Syrian Church was comparatively lacking in missionary zeal. By the early sixth century the Monophysite doctrine had become deeply entrenched in Syria, where it became known as Jacobite, after the organizer of its communion Jacob Baradaeus, bishop of Edessa (*ca.* 543-578). Its adherents, however, prefer the name Orthodox or Old Syrians. From Syria Monophysitism spread northward into Armenia, where it is still the theology of its church (the Gregorian), and southward into Egypt to be adopted by the Coptic Church.[5]

MELKITES

Besides the Syriac-using Churches there was in Syria a relatively small body of Christians which felt the impact of Greek theology emanating from Antioch and Constantinople and wholeheartedly accepted the decrees of the council of Chalcedon.[6] This body was organized into the Orthodox Church which escaped religious excommunication, political persecution and even enjoyed a measure of protection from church and state. Hence the name they acquired Melkites (royalists). This communion drew its adherents largely from dwellers in cities and in ancient Greek colonies, gradually replaced Syriac by Greek in the ritual and followed the Byzantine liturgy. "Melkite," strangely enough, is used today as a designation not for the Greek Orthodox but for those of them who under the influence of Roman Catholic missionaries became attached to Rome in the early eighteenth century.

The liturgy which both of these churches of Syria use is ascribed to St. Basil (d. 379) bishop of Caesarea in Cappadocia and revised by John Chrysostom, patriarch of Constantinople (398-404). St. John began his religious career as an ascetic on a mount near his native Antioch. Soon he distinguished himself as an eloquent preacher denouncing laxity in morals and luxury in living. In strong terms he condemned the rich for resorting to deceit, usury, and monopoly and for their indifference to the needs of the poor. In an age of ecclesiasticism and theology his message was a social one, comparable to that of the prophets of Israel. His reputation spread to the capital of the empire and placed him on the patriarchal throne. Here his insistence on high moral standards and social reform brought him into conflict with the high-spirited empress Eudoxia, whom he publicly denounced for her wickedness. She sent him into exile near the Caucasus, where he died. The epithet Chrysostom (golden mouth) he received post-

[5] As cited above, pp. 171-172.
[6] See above, p. 171.

humously.   It was the work of Chrysostom, Arius, Nestorius and others that made Antioch the intellectual center of Syria.

BERYTUS' LAW ACADEMY

If Antioch was the theological capital of the area Berytus (now Beirut) was its educational capital.   This distinction was due to the school of Roman civil law which was founded at the turn of the third century presumably by a Syro-Lebanese emperor in Rome.[7]   Other provincial schools grew in the empire but Berytus' held the primacy. Its professors and students formed a brilliant galaxy attracted from all over the Near East, just as the population of the American University and the Jesuit University of that city now do.   The law school developed into a university.   Legal training was in those days a prerequisite for holding a government office.   Interesting snapshots of student life have been preserved.   Class exercises were suspended Saturday afternoon and Sunday.   Evenings were kept free for repeating the work done in the daytime.   New students were received by old ones with ridicule, to test their power of self-control—a sort of "freshman hazing."   Christian students fasted daily and indulged in the luxury of a bath once a year, on Easter eve.   A pagan Egyptian enamoured of a woman who did not reciprocate his affections resorted to magic to influence the demons and produce the coveted results.

The institution continued to operate until the mid-sixth century when a series of earthquakes and tidal waves demolished the city and with it the school.   When in 533 Justinian ordered a collection of legal opinions to be compiled to form the *Digest,* he summoned a law professor from Berytus to be a compiler.   The *Digest* comprises numerous excerpts from the writings of another professor Papinian, and about 2500 from the writings of another Ulpian—in all almost one-half of the whole.[8]   No wonder Justinian styled Berytus "the mother and nurse of laws."

ART AND ARCHITECTURE

Apart from the religious achievement, the most original contributions of Byzantine civilization were in art and architecture.   Diverse Greco-Roman, Hellenistic, Christian, Jewish and other Near Eastern elements blended in the fourth to the sixth centuries to produce an entirely distinctive artistic expression which spread from Armenia to Italy, maintained its vitality for over a thousand years and produced some of the greatest masterpieces of medieval times.   Particularly in architecture,

[7] Treated above, pp. 143-144.
[8] Cf. above, p. 146.

Courtesy of Arab Information Center

THE CHURCH OF THE HOLY SEPULCHER

decoration and minor arts, such as wood and ivory carving; manuscript illumination and enameling did this Byzantine or Eastern Christian art distinguish itself. With its extinction it left an enduring legacy discernible in later European as well as Moslem art. The importance of the roles played by Alexandria, Antioch and Ephesus in the evolution of this art is still hotly debated by scholars.

The formative stage covers the first two or three centuries beginning with Constantine's reign. In that period places of worship—churches, chapels, basilicas, monasteries—dotted the Christian Near East. Such buildings featured a new style of architecture with domes, bell towers and prominent crucifixes. From pre-Byzantine times we have the remains of a church, the earliest known, unearthed at Dura-Europos and dating from 232. From Constantine's time we have remains in the Church of the Holy Sepulcher and those of the Nativity. The present structure of the Nativity is Justinian's. From the end of the fifth century we have in north Syria the ruins of the monastery of St. Simeon (d. 459), one of the grandest and largest monasteries of the early Christian centuries. The lower part of the sixty-foot pillar, on which this Syrian ascetic is said to have perched for thirty years, teaching, preaching, and winning converts and disciples, stands in the midst of the ruins. First among pillar saints, Simeon was copied till early in the fifteenth century.

The first fruition of the Byzantine style of architecture took place in the sixth century under Justinian. His may be called the early golden age of art and architecture. Its masterpiece was, of course, Hagia Sophia ("divine wisdom," later St. Sophia) completed by Justinian in 537. In it the triumph of East Syrian art was recorded to be transmitted to Ottoman Turks, who plastered the cathedral's murals and converted it into a mosque. Under Mustafa Kemal it changed into a museum.

Syria was undoubtedly a fount of Christian art. It more than provided the theme. The early figure of Jesus is clearly an adaptation of that of Moses. The church drew upon the synagogue for its structure and symbolism. The Good Shepherd, an early popular subject, appears among other biblical figures on the wall of Dura-Europos church. The shepherd is usually portrayed with a lamb on his shoulder. Pre-Christian reliefs from north Syria and from Assyria show shepherds with gazelles on their shoulders, probably meant for sacrifice.

In painting and sculpture, as in architecture, the Eastern Christian sought novel ways of expression, independent of the traditional Greco-Roman models which since Alexander's conquest had dominated artistic production. The art of representing Christ, the Virgin or a saint by an image, an icon, began to thrive. In its gradual development iconography drew upon Hellenistic formulas for divinities, poets and orators. In 726 Leo III, the Isaurian, the first emperor to adopt the iconoclast view, prohibited the use of icons and religious paintings which ignorant Christians believed could work miracles when the intervention of the saint represented was invoked. Born in north Syria, this emperor must have developed hatred for images from early contact with Moslems and puritanical Jews.

Figure sculpture, however, was generally neglected because of its pagan association. Statues of emperors followed the Roman tradition. The Eastern Christian sculptor confined his art largely to columns, capitals, architectural ornaments, wood and ivory carving, book covers and reliquaries. From Egypt came a large number of carvings, displaying a wealth of decorative motive and merging into the Islamic art. Coptic Egypt also excelled in woolen textile decoration. From Mesopotamia we have some of the earliest Gospels' illuminated manuscripts, on purple-stained parchments, gold or silver lettering and intense coloring suggesting a mosaic. From Syria of the sixth century came some of the best silver vessels used in church services, including chalices and plates decorated with religious scenes. By that time artistic individuality and standardization had been attained and the way was paved for Christian medieval art.

UNDER SASANIDS

The language and writing of the Parthians were retained by the Sasanids and called Pahlawi (that is, Parthian). Pahlawi (Middle Persian), a descendant of Old Persian and parent of modern Persian. Written in Arabic characters it is rich in loans from Arabic and Islamic vocabulary. The Pahlawi script, as we learned before,[9] was drawn from Aramaic. Otherwise the Sasanids deliberately resumed the Achaemenid tradition considering it their richest legacy. The old sacred writings of Zoroastrianism, embodied in the Avesta,[10] were recorded several times, the final redaction was then made and commentaries were prepared. Zoroastrianism or Mazdaism remained the dominant state religion throughout the period. The supremacy of Ahura Mazda was more emphasized than in the classic dualistic system. At times rulers tried to enforce religious conformity among their subjects, Byzantine-like, and subjected Christians to persecution. But with the identification of local Christianity with Nestorianism, considered a heresy by Constantinople, its adherents were accorded full tolerance. The period is marked by complete disappearance of Greek and Hellenistic literary influences. Legends on coins were written in Pahlawi. The golden age of Pahlawi literature was attained under Khosrau I.[11] In 555 this king established at Jundi-Shapur an academy of medicine and philosophy, employing Christian professors who used Syriac as a means of instruction. Christians of course kept their intellectual contact with the West and translated Greek works. In Khosrau's reign the Bidpai fables were introduced from India and translated from Sanskrit into Pahlawi, which through an early Arabic rendition ultimately found its way into Spain and the rest of Europe.[12] From India at the same time the game of chess was also introduced. It was likewise picked up by the Arabs and carried over into southwestern Europe.

MANI

Two offshoots of Mazdaism reached the West, Mithraism[13] and Manichaeism. Mani (216-276) preached at Ctesiphon a synthetic system combining Zoroastrian and Christian elements and based on the avowed need of freeing the spirit from material bonds. He aimed at creating a new universal religion and proclaimed himself an apostle of

---

[9] P. 103.
[10] Treated above, p. 67.
[11] Treated above, p. 173.
[12] For further information see below, p. 245.
[13] Treated above, p. 163.

Christ but gave the Gospels a gnostic interpretation, involving emancipation of the initiates from the domination of matter through knowledge
(gnosis). Tolerated for a while, he was finally delivered to Mazdaean
priests to be put to death. His disciples carried on his teaching into
the Roman Empire, where its diffusion followed but fell short of
Mithraism. In North Africa Augustine was an adherent of Manichaeism for nine years.[14]

FINE ARTS

Of the architectural monuments of the period, whether temples or
palaces, only a few ruins are left. The rapid disintegration must have
been due to the unenduring material of construction, and in the case
of the fire temples possibly to deliberate destruction by the Moslem
conquerors. The style continues the Parthian tradition but manifests
reaction against earlier Greek influence. Iranian architects of this
period are credited with the feat of constructing the cupola on squinches

Courtesy of The Metropolitan Museum of Art, Fletcher Fund, 1934

SILVER PLATE, APPLIED REPOUSSE AND PARTIALLY GILT, WITH KHOSRAU I HUNTING
IBEXES

[14] Cf. above, p. 161.

over a square room and with the development of the arch on a high scale together with its use as a unit of construction.

Barrel-vaulted halls, used for palace entrance and as audience chamber, are the salient features of Sasanid architecture. The most famous of such structures is that of the royal palace at Ctesipton, whose 75-foot-wide vault, rises to a height of 90 feet and goes 150 feet deep. Presumably built by Shapur I (d. 272), though bearing the name of Khosrau (taq-i-Kisra), it was used as a ceremonial room and for state audience. Excavated by the Metropolitan Museum of Art in New York, its ruins are impressive. The Moslem conquerors viewed it with dilated eyes and Arab chroniclers with undiluted pride. The grander the prize, the more glory to Islam.

The pottery of the period achieved no special distinction but metalwork, carpets and textiles enjoyed a wide reputation. Specimens survive in European and American museums. Some notable silver bowls are now in the Hermitage Museum, Leningrad. The favorite themes in the representation are battle scenes, royal hunts and royal audiences. Many motifs of Persian art came to full fruition in the following Moslem period.

BOOKS TO READ

Bell, H. Idris, *Egypt from Alexander the Great to the Arab Conquest* (Oxford, 1948).

Byron, Robert, *The Byzantine Achievement* (New York, 1929).

Byzantium, ed. Norman H. Baynes and H. St. L. B. Moss (Oxford, 1948).

Diehl, Charles, *Byzantium: Greatness and Decline,* tr. Naomi Walford (New Brunswick, N. J., 1957).

French, Reginald M., *The Eastern Orthodox Church* (London, 1951).

Hitti, Philip K., *History of Syria, including Lebanon and Palestine,* 2nd ed. (London, 1957).

Hussey, Joan M., *The Byzantine World* (London, 1957).

Ross, E. Denison, *The Persians* (Oxford, 1931).

Runciman, Steven, *Byzantine Civilisation* (London, 1953).

Sykes, Percy, *A History of Persia,* 3rd ed. (London, 1930), vol. I.

Vasiliev, A. A., *History of the Byzantine Empire,* tr. S. Ragozin, 2nd ed. (Madison, Wis., 1952), vol. I.

Wilber, Donald N., *Iran: Past and Present,* 4th ed. (Princeton, 1958).

PART FOUR

THE ISLAMIC AGE

XVI   *The Arabian Prophet and the Koran*

THE conjoint rise of Islam with the appearance of the Arabians on the international scene radically changed the course of history in the Near East. It ended the Greco-Roman hegemony in politics and culture; introduced a new religion, Islam, still the predominant faith in the entire area; spread a new language, Arabic, still the daily tongue of eighty millions from Morocco to Iraq; and inaugurated a new way of life, itself a synthesis of old ways. The establishment of the new order may be taken as marking the end of ancient times for the Near East and the commencement of medieval times. Unlike medieval times in Europe, which comprised the "dark ages," this stage in Moslem world was on the whole characterized by splendor and glory. It all began in an unexpected little-known place, Hejaz, and with an unheralded person, Muhammad.

HEJAZ

Only the southwestern corner of the Arabian peninsula, favored with adequate rainfall and rich in spices and aromatic products, had thus far sustained an urban culture and figured in international relations.[1] The northwestern region, particularly Hejaz, was largely barren, with isolated oases as the chief support of settled life. Mecca, birthplace of Muhammad, lay forty-eight miles from the Red Sea in a rocky valley described by the Koran (14:40) as unfit for cultivation. The settlement owed its existence to a well, Zamzam, with tepid salt-bitter water, and its prosperity to its location on the spice route that linked South Arabia with Mediterranean seaports. Moslem tradition identified the well with the spring from which Hagar and Ishmael drank and saved their lives.[2] Thus favored with water and location Mecca became the

---

[1] Consult above, pp. 12, 133.
[2] Cf. Gen. 16:7, 14.

site of the Kaaba (*Ka'bah*, cubic structure), a pantheon of heathenism and object of pilgrimage, later Islamized. Medina, burial place of Muhammad and scene of his spectacular success, likewise lay on the south-to-north caravan route and was especially rich in date palms. It and its neighboring oases had attracted Jewish settlers, mostly of Arabian stock rather than from the seed of Abraham. The name (*al-Madinah,* the city, i.e. of the Prophet) was acquired after Muhammad had spent the last ten years of his life (622-632) in it. Judaeo-Christian ideas must have been trickling into Mecca from near-by settlements, traders, slaves, and other sources.

MUHAMMAD

Though born within the full light of history (*ca.* 571), the founder of Islam is but little known to us in his formative stage. Even the name his mother gave him remains unknown. She died when he was six years old and his father, a camel driver, had died before his birth. The name Muhammad ("most highly praised") sounds like an honorific title and is borne today by more people than any other personal name. The first significant fact in Muhammad's manhood was his marriage at the age of twenty-five to a wealthy high-minded widow, Khadijah, fifteen years his senior and a member of the Quraysh tribe, to a humble clan of which he belonged. The economic security thus acquired enabled the young man to pursue his inclination to meditate in an isolated cave on a barren hill outside Mecca. Amid the solemn grandeur of the wilderness and in the deep solitude of a cave he had opportunity to reflect upon the doubts and problems in his mind. It was there that he received his first revelation. It took the form of a "reverberation of a bell," later identified as the voice of Gabriel bidding him:

> Read: "In the name of thy Lord who created,
> created men of a clot of blood"
> Read thou! "And thy Lord is the most bounteous,
> who taught by the pen,
> taught man what he knew not." [3]

The call was purely auditory and had no visual aspects as in the case of Moses, Saul-Paul, and Isaiah.[4] From the wording of the first revelation we infer that the would-be prophet must have been burning with desire to bring his people a message similar to that of the "people of the book," the Jews and Christians, and that he was tormented with the realization of his inadequate schooling. The year was 610.

---

[3] Koran 96:1-5.
[4] Ex. 3:2 *seq.;* Acts 9:3-6; 26:13-18; Is. 6:1-4.

In his call and early message the Arabian prophet was no less prophetic than his Hebrew predecessors. God is one; he is all-powerful, creator of heavens and earth. There is a day of reckoning with splendid rewards for the righteous and terrible punishment for the wicked.

As messenger (*rasul*) the prophet (*nabi*) of Allah—originally one of the Kaaba deities—Muhammad did not make speedy headway. The aristocratic branch of his own tribe, who served as custodians of the heathen Kaaba and whose economic self-interest was involved, opposed him to the point of persecution. The early converts, with the exception of his wife and a couple of relatives, were recruited from among slaves and low classes. A change in scene and technique became imperative.

In the summer of 622 two hundred followers eluded the vigilance of the Quraysh and slipped quietly into Medina, which had sent a special invitation. Muhammad followed. This was a turning point in his career. Seventeen years later the *hijrah* (hegira, migration) was designated by the caliph as the official beginning of the Moslem era.

In his city of adoption the Prophet assumed new roles: those of a warrior, legislator, judge, and civil administrator. As the head of a band he led his followers on the battlefield from one victory to another against the Medinese Jews, Meccan Qurayshites, and other enemies. Gradually he broke off with both Judaism, and Christianity as well as with Arabian heathenism, replaced the Sabbath with Friday, substituted the muezzin's call to prayer for the sound of the gong, changed the direction (*qiblah*) to be observed during formal prayer from Jerusalem to Mecca, and sanctioned the pilgrimage to Kaaba. But wine and gambling, next to women the two dearest indulgences to the Arabian heart, were abolished in one verse.[5] Thus did Islam in Medina become itself. From the defensive it passed to the offensive and has since remained what the world has known it to be—a militant polity. Hitherto a religion within a state it now became more than a state religion; it became itself the state.

Toward the end of January 630 Muhammad entered Mecca triumphantly, rushed to its great Kaaba sanctuary and smashed the three hundred and sixty idols exclaiming: "Truth hath come and falsehood hath vanished!" In an ambiguous passage[6] he declared the area around the Kaaba *haram,* forbidden, which was later taken to mean forbidden to non-Moslems. Since then the number of Christian-born Europeans who have succeeded in visiting the place and escaping with their lives has been less than a score.

[5] Koran 5:92.
[6] Koran 9:28.

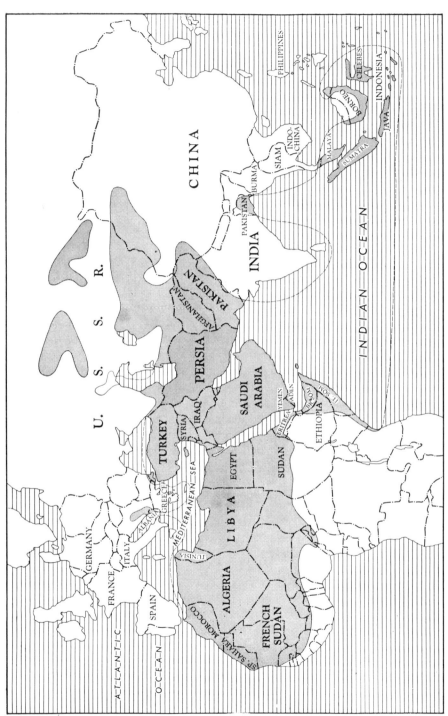

THE WORLD OF ISLAM TODAY

To the Medinese period in the career of Muhammad belong those lengthy chapters (sing. *surah*) in the Koran which comprise legislation and ceremonial regulations governing prayer, fasting, almsgiving, as well as ordinances relating to marriage, divorce, inheritance, treatment of orphans, slaves and prisoners of war.   The tiny religious community of Medina for which this legislation was originally intended has since then grown into the society of Islam, including men and women of all colors and races and numbering some four hundred million believers. This society today forms a solid block from Morocco to Pakistan and claims millions in India and Indonesia.   Every eighth living person is a follower of the Arabian prophet.   The community of Islam, as organized by Muhammad, was to have no priesthood, no hierarchy, no sacraments, and no central see.   It was meant to be a fraternity in which the religious bond took the place of the traditional bond of tribal kinship.   This was the first Arabian attempt at a socio-political organization based on religion.   The Medinese religious brotherhood was in miniature the subsequent world-community of Islam.

Within the span of a brief decade the son of an Arabian caravaneer established a religion that has superseded Christianity in vast areas of Asia and Africa, created the nucleus of a nation never before united, and laid the foundation stone of an empire that was soon to embrace a large part of the then civilized world.   His daily behavior became a canon which millions still consider standard behavior worthy of minute imitation.   Himself an unschooled man he was nevertheless responsible for the Koran, regarded by Moslems as the embodiment of all theology, law, science, and wisdom.

THE KORAN

To the Moslem the Koran (*al-qur'an,* reading, recitation) is the word of God as dictated in Arabic by the messenger angel Gabriel to Muhammad from an archetype preserved in the seventh heaven.   It is a rather small book, four-fifths the size of the Arabic New Testament in words.   Ninety of the 114 chapters were revealed in Mecca and are generally short and incisive, stressing the oneness of God, his attributes, the duties of man, and the inescapable final judgment of the individual. Though only 24 in number the Medinese chapters constitute the bulk of the book and include, besides the above-mentioned laws, ordinances governing the holy war (*jihad*),[7] theft, homicide, and adultery.   The prescription favoring plurality of wives[8] limits the practice of polygamy to four and authorizes concubinage.   Both polygamy and concubinage

[7] Discussed below, p. 204.
[8] Koran 4:3.

Courtesy of Princeton University Library

AN ARABIC MANUSCRIPT PAGE FROM THE KORAN (33:19-25)   Sixteenth century

were universally practiced in the ancient Near East.   Veiling also antedated Islam; it was considered a mark of the free woman as against
the slave and public ones and was recognized in the code of Hammurabi.   An Aramaean goddess appears on coins with a cover on her
face.   Rebekah veiled herself in the presence of Isaac[9] and Paul insisted

[9] Gen. 24:65.

that women should cover their heads while praying;[10] he evidently assumed the absence of veil indicated that the woman was of easy virtue, a presumption that lay behind the koranic injunction.[11]

Within the Medinese period falls the nocturnal journey in which Muhammad is credited with instant transportation from the Kaaba to Jerusalem and thence to the seventh heaven. The koranic reference to it is brief and vague.[12] Expanded and embellished by later accretions from Christian and Jewish parallels, as well as from the fertile Oriental imagination, the miraculous trip still forms a favorite theme particularly in mystic circles in Turkey and Persia. Modern research has established that material relating to this Moslem story was available in European languages in Italy, France, and Spain and became a major source of Dante's *Divine Comedy*. Parallels in style, characterization, narrative, and architectural description leave no doubt about the dependence of the greatest early Italian poet on the Arabic prototype. As the halting place of Muhammad's curious mount, Jerusalem acquired new sanctity in Moslem eyes. That the memory of the episode is still a living and moving force in the minds of Moslems is indicated by the Arab-Zionist riots of the 1920's centering on the Wailing Wall in Jerusalem.

It may come as a surprise to a non-Moslem reader to learn that almost all historical narratives and references in the sacred book of Islam have their biblical, particularly Old Testament, parallels. Abraham is cited no less than 70 times in 25 chapters and his name entitles a chapter (14). To Joseph is dedicated chapter 12, where the story is told with gusto and embellished with apocryphal details. The name of Moses occurs in 34 different chapters. The story of the creation and the fall of man is cited five times, the flood eight, and Sodom also eight. In most cases the story is told not for its own sake but for admonishing or teaching a moral lesson.

Of the Old Testament characters Abraham was particularly favored. He was a true Moslem, founder of the Kaaba, and Muhammad's ideal predecessor.[13] The new religion was made to look like a continuation of an old one. Of the New Testament characters Zachariah, John the Baptist, Jesus ('Isa), and Mary are the only ones mentioned. The last two are often in association. Mary, while still in the womb, was vowed by her mother unto God as a consecrated offering, but was confused

---

[10] I Cor. 11:5, 10.
[11] 33:59.
[12] 17:1.
[13] Kor. 3:60; 4:124; 3:61; 2:118 *seq.*

with Mary, sister of Aaron.[14]   Jesus' virgin birth is accepted[15] and non-canonical miracles, such as preaching while still in the cradle and creating birds out of clay, are ascribed to him.   Muhammad had a Christian (Coptic wife named Mary, a Christian slave whom he later adopted, and a Christian muezzin from Abyssinia.   Recognizing the Syrian Christian influence on Muhammad, an early Moslem legend takes him to Damascus at the age of twelve and establishes contact between him and a Nestorian monk in southern Syria.

The most impressive parts of the Koran deal with eschatology.   To Muhammad the judgment day was real and imminent.   Koranic references to it abound and chapters are dedicated to it.   Future life with its physical pleasures and bodily pains are depicted in glowing colors.[16]   Evidently neither Paul was known to Muhammad nor any of the Hebrew prophets.   But certain koranic passages stand in favorable comparison with the most sublime in the Old Testament.

> It is not righteousness that ye turn your faces
> to the east and to the west.
> But righteous is he who:
> Believeth in God and the last day,
> the angels, the Scriptures and the prophets;
> giveth of his sustenance, however cherished,
> to kinsmen and orphans,
> the needy, wayfarers and beggars
> and to ransom slaves,
> Who observeth the prayers, and payeth the alms.[17]

To the believers the Koran is the final authority not only in matters spiritual and ethical but in all other areas it touches or treats—theology, law, and science—all being aspects of the same thing.   The book made of Islam a literate religion.   In mosque schools it is still used as the text from which the student acquires his liberal education.   In theological colleges it forms the basis of the entire curriculum.   Due to its linguistic influence the various dialects of Arabic in vogue between Morocco and Iraq have not so drifted apart as to constitute different languages.   The earliest prose work in Arabic, it is still the standard which every aspiring Arabic writer today strives to follow.   By forbidding its translation, Islam imposed Arabic as the enduring cultural bond to hold the Moslem community together even after the religious bond had become loose.   In this it did not differ from Judaism, which by the use of Hebrew gave its adherents a spiritual and cultural unity,

[14] Kor. 3:35.
[15] Kor. 19:16-23.
[16] Kor. 56:8-56; 18:17-18; 22:5; 30:56; 15:35-6.
[17] Kor. 2:172.

and from Roman Catholicism, which by the imposition of the use of Latin gave Western Europe a cultural heritage of lasting value.

BOOKS TO READ

Andrae, Tor, *Mohammed: The Man and his Faith,* tr. Theophil Menzel (New York, 1936).

Arberry, Arthur J., *The Koran Interpreted,* 2 vols. (London, 1955).

Bell, Richard, *The Origin of Islam in its Christian Environment* (London, 1926).

Germanus, Julius, *Allah Akbar* (Berlin, 1938).

Hogarth, D. G., *Arabia* (Oxford, 1922).

Jeffery, Arthur, *The Koran as Scripture* (New York, 1952).

Katsh, Abraham A., *Judaism in Islam* (New York, 1954).

Lamsa, George M., ed., *The Short Koran* (Chicago, *ca.* 1949).

Muir, William, *The Life of Mohammed,* ed. T. W. Weir (Edinburgh, 1912).

Pickthall, Marmaduke, *The Meaning of the Glorious Koran* (London, 1930).

Roberts, Robert, *The Social Laws of the Qurán* (London, 1929).

Robson, James, *Christ in Islam* (London, 1929).

Rutter, Eldon, *The Holy Cities of Arabia,* 2 vols. (New York, 1928).

Torrey, Charles C., *The Jewish Foundation of Islam* (New York, 1933).

Watt, W. Montgomery, *Muhammad at Mecca* (Oxford, 1953); *Muhammad at Medina* (Oxford, 1958).

XVII *Islam the Religion*

THE system of beliefs and practices instituted by Muhammad and enshrined in the Koran constitutes the basic religion of Islam. The term is derived from a stem meaning to surrender: Islam is the religion of surrender, submission to the will of God. Its adherents generally enjoy a measure of contentment and resignation unattained in other faiths. Suicide is hardly known in their history.

DOGMAS

The basic dogma in Islam is expressed in the euphoneous formula: *La ilaha illa-l-Lah,* No god whatever but Allah. Belief in the unity of God forms the cornerstone of Islamic faith. God orders Muhammad:

> Say: He is God, the one
> God, the eternally sought.
> He beggeth not, nor was he begotten,
> And to him there is no equal.[1]

Ascribing plurality to the Deity seemed most abhorrent to Muhammad. Associating other deities with the one true God was the sin for which there was no forgiveness.[2] To the Moslems God is the supreme reality, pre-existent, omniscient, omnipotent, self-subsistent.[3]

God's tender attributes of love and mercy are overshadowed by those of majesty and might. In this he partakes more of the nature of Jehovah than of Christ's Father. In fact, the Islam of the Koran generally comes closer to the Judaism of the Old Testament than to the Christianity of the New. Nevertheless, all the chapters of the Koran are introduced with the same formula: "In the name of God, the compassionate, the merciful," a formula which is daily on the tongue of almost every Moslem.

[1] Kor. 112.
[2] Kor. 4:51, 116.
[3] Kor. 16:3-17; 13:9-17; 2:100-101, 256.

196

Second among the dogmas and closely associated with the first is the affirmation that Muhammad is the messenger (*rasul*) or apostle of God and his prophet.[4]   More than that, he is the "seal of the prophets." [5]

Moses was a prophet; so were Abraham, Noah, Christ, and others, each with a dispensation appropriate for a certain time or place. But Muhammad's dispensation sums up as well as supersedes all earlier ones. It is final. After it there is none. In the Koran, Muhammad is but a human being, his only distinction being his association with the "descent of the Koran" with its miraculous character demonstrated by the incomparable elegance of its style and unequalled sublimity of its contents. The veneration of Muhammad as a channel parallels that of Mary; the veneration of the Koran may be compared to that of the host by the Catholics. No one should touch the Koran unless

Hitti, THE ARABS, A SHORT HISTORY
(Princeton University Press)

A MEDALLION WITH THE MOSLEM PRO-
FESSION OF FAITH IN ARABIC: "NO GOD
WHATEVER BUT GOD; MUHAMMAD IS THE
MESSENGER OF GOD."

he is in a state of legal purity, induced by the ritual ablution.   In folklore and popular conception, however, the Prophet has no doubt been invested with divine aura, to the creation of which converts from Christianity must have contributed. In Islam as in other religions distinction should be made between the learned religion and folk religion.

The third dogma makes the Koran the word of God. This word is uncreated, coeternal, and in its Arabic form identical with a heavenly original.[6] The ancient Sumerian priests posited a celestial prototype for every temple on earth; the Hebrew sage considered Wisdom as "set up from everlasting, from the beginning;" when the Lord laid the foundations of the earth, Wisdom stood by him as one brought up with him.[7] The Epistle to the Hebrews[8] speaks of a heavenly Jerusalem, and so does the Revelation.[9] The koranic dogma belongs to this

[4] Kor. 7:156, 157; 48:29.
[5] Kor. 33:30.
[6] Kor. 9:6; 48:15; 17:170-78; 97:1.
[7] Prov. 8:22, 29-30.
[8] 12:22.
[9] 3:12; 21:2, 10.

cycle of thought, as do the Platonic concept of ideal[10] and the Gospel theory of the logos.[11]   Revealed in Arabic, "the language of the angels," the Koran should be recited, rather chanted in that language. A paraphrase for the benefit of a non-Arab is permissible, but that is not the Koran.   A quotation from it, properly made, should be introduced with "Saith Allah."   Muhammad's sayings constitute another collection, the *hadith,* of secondary authority.

A proper comprehension of the Moslem holy book presupposes general acquaintance with the Scriptures, knowledge of early Arabian culture, and some understanding of Arab character as well as of the genius of the Arabic language.   Unless projected against such a background, the book cannot be appreciated.   In its translated form it loses its artistic merit with its emotional appeal and becomes, as it did to a nineteenth century English litterateur, "a wearisom, confused jumble, crude, incondite," [12] the same impression a casual visitor might get from walking through a modern art gallery.

Other dogmas of Islam relate to a hierarchy of angels, headed by Gabriel; the nature of sin, in its moral and ceremonial aspects; and the immortality of the soul.

PRACTICES

The religious duties of a Moslem can be summed up under five categories, generally called the five pillars of Islam.   In fact they are acts of worship characterized by external legalism.

The first obligation is the profession of faith expressed in the double formula: "No god whatever but Allah, and Muhammad is the messenger of Allah."   To believe is not enough; one must profess the belief.   Profession is the first prerequisite of a convert into the religion. This formula is daily reiterated chantingly from the tops of minarets by muezzins calling the believers to prayer.   It is whispered in the ear of a new-born Moslem babe, uttered by him repeatedly throughout his life, and accompanies him to his grave in the funeral procession.

PRAYER

Then comes prayer prescribed five times a day in its formal type. When performing it the Moslem should be in a state of legal purity and properly oriented toward Mecca.[13]   Moslems are not ashamed of their God and are not ashamed to pray publicly to him.   Orientation

[10] Cf. above, pp. 159, 162.
[11] John 1:1-18.
[12] Thomas Carlyle, *Works,* vol. I (Boston, 1884), p. 295.
[13] Cf. above, p. 189.

Courtesy of Arabian American Oil Company

A PAUSE FOR THE EVENING PRAYER

in prayer must have been an early Semitic practice. Daniel opened the window of his chamber as he turned toward Jerusalem, knelt and prayed three times a day.[14] As a legally defined and prescribed act prayer follows an identical pattern of bodily postures, genuflexions, and prostrations. Arabic is the medium of expression. The formulas are stereotyped and abound in the mention of God's name. In each of the five prayers the opening chapter of the Koran, often likened to the Lord's prayer, is repeated four times, making it perhaps the most often-used prayer ever devised:

> In the name of God, the merciful, the compassionate.
>
> Praise be to God, lord of the universe,
> the merciful, the compassionate,
> ruler on the day of judgment.
> Thee alone we worship; Thee alone we ask for aid.
>   Guide us in the straight path,
> the path of those whom Thou hast favored,
> not of those who have incurred Thy wrath,
>   nor of those who go astray.[15]

In addition one is, of course, free to engage in private individual prayer or supplication. This form is spontaneous and unregulated, dictated by

[14] 6:10.
[15] Kor. 1.

the exigencies of events and circumstances. In its ritualistic form, including prostrations and genuflexions, Moslem prayer reflects Syrian Christian antecedents. Nestorian monks and hermits in Syria and its wilderness had developed an elaborate and impressive ritual of prayer long before Islam.

Friday noon prayer is the only congregational one. In large mosques a special area is reserved for women worshipers. The inside of the mosque is conspicuous by the absence of pews and pictures. The nearest substitute for pictures or icons is calligraphy, using passages from the Koran and names of the Prophet and his caliphs—all in Arabic characters, which lend themselves beautifully to decorative purposes. The simple dignified Friday noon prayer, in which worshipers arrange themselves in rows and follow the leader (*imam*) in their bodily postures and genuflexions, served to promote the sense of brotherhood in the Moslem community. The congregational mosque provided the first drill ground for this religion. A prominent feature of the Friday service is the sermon delivered by the preacher from a pulpit on which the artist usually bestows his best care. Both pulpit and sermon betray Christian influence.

Closely associated with prayer, as a manifestation of piety and love, is almsgiving. Originally prescribed as a voluntary act of worship,[16] almsgiving evolved into a regular tax on personal property, farm products, and merchandise and was collected by state officials. It was dispensed from the public treasury for the support of the needy in the Moslem community and for building mosques and defraying state expenses. Its exact amount varied according to time and place, but averaged two and a half per cent. Its historic background is probably the tithe paid by Semites to their gods. South Arabians could not market their spices before paying such a tithe. Today the obligation is left to the believer's conscience, but is observed throughout the Moslem world with particular scrupulousness, voluntary alms being considered especially meritorious. In the Arabian peninsula, however, its collection is still a government function.

Fasting constitutes the fourth pillar of Islam. It is likewise of pre-Islamic origin. Moses fasted,[17] as did Daniel[18] and Christ.[19] As a favorite practice among Syrian Christian monks and hermits it could not have escaped the notice of Arabian travelers and traders. Its Islamization restricted it—except when voluntary—to Ramadan, the

[16] Kor. 2:16-17, 263-9; 9:5; 2:40.
[17] Deut. 9:9.
[18] 9:3.
[19] Matt. 4:2.

month in which the Koran was first revealed, and stretched it over the long day, from dawn till sunset.[20]   Abstinence from food, drink, smoking, and sexual intercourse is ordained.   So strict is the interpretation of this obligation that a committee of the Azhar Mosque in Egypt found it necessary as late as 1949 to issue a ruling that injections of all kinds and medicine applied to a wound do not constitute a breaking of the fast.   Cases of subjecting a Moslem fast-breaker to violence on the part of the populace have been reported from Syria.   In the Arabian peninsula the obligation is enforced by law.

PILGRIMAGE

A visit to the holy city of Mecca is enjoined upon every able-bodied Moslem who can afford it once in a lifetime.[21]   The formal pilgrimage (*hajj*) should be performed at a fixed time of the year, the first half of dhu-al-Hijjah, a month which receives its name from this performance. Other visits can be made individually and personally but are less meritorious.   Thousands from Syria, Egypt, Iraq, Yemen, and other lands of Islam converge yearly by plane, train, automobile, and caravan early in this month to fulfill this great desire of their lives.   Until recent years the Egyptian caravan carried along with it a rich black brocade, with a gold embroidered band covered with koranic verses in fine calligraphy, to be used as a cover for the Kaaba.   Small pieces of the old curtain are sold as amulets.   In 1958 the official statement of Saudi Arabia put the total number of pilgrims at 600,000.

The holy ceremonies begin with the pilgrim donning a special garment of two seamless sheets of white cotton.   He starts on the sevenfold circumambulation of the Kaaba, kisses the Black Stone in its wall, drinks from Zamzam and continues with the sevenfold course between two adjacent mounds, after which he begins his march to Mount Arafat. En route to the mount he passes through a valley, Mina, and casts seven stones three times in commemoration, so Islamic tradition asserts, of Abraham's stoning of Satan, who appeared to him there.   Tradition also says that the sevenfold course between the two mounds commemorates Hagar's running in despair from one hill to the other when cast off by Abraham and seeing Ishmael perishing of thirst.   At Mina the ceremony ends with the sacrifice of a camel, sheep, or goat on the tenth of dhu-al-Hijjah.   This 'Id al-Adha[22] (feast of sacrifice) is celebrated as a three-day festival all over the Moslem world; it is the greatest festival in the Moslem calendar.   Tradition again relates it to Abraham,

[20] Kor. 2:178-81, 183.
[21] Kor. 2:192-6; 3:91; 5:1-2, 96.
[22] Kor. 22:3.

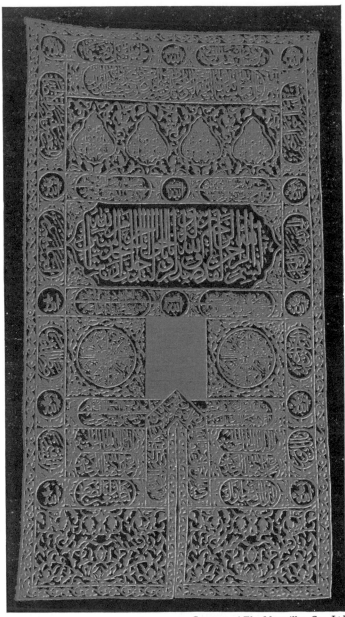

Courtesy of The Macmillan Co., Ltd.

A CURTAIN AT THE DOOR OF THE KAABA AT MECCA Bearing koranic inscriptions
which include surahs 1, 106, and 112. The prominent inscription above the
center is the first part of surah 48, verse 27.

Courtesy of Arab Information Office

PILGRIMS AROUND THE KAABA PERFORMING THE FRIDAY PRAYERS

specifically to his willingness to offer his son as a sacrifice. With the ending of the ceremonies, throughout which the pilgrim is in a sanctified state abstaining from all relations with women,[23] slaying animals, shaving his head, cutting his nails and uprooting plants, the pilgrim reverts to the secular state. He can then proudly affix to his name the title of hajj.

Echoes of early Semitic visits to holy places survive in the Old Testament,[24] and Moslem tradition endeavored to relate the Islamic practice to its Abraham. But it has all the earmarks of a heathen Arabian institution. The pilgrimage, Kaaba and Black Stone of meteoric origin were adopted by Muhammad from pre-Islamic heathenism and to that extent alienated his system from Christianity and Judaism, from both of which it was historically an offshoot.

Aside from the spiritual inspiration and religious uplift it imparts, pilgrimage in Islam has had an inestimable socializing effect. It provided the community with a unique opportunity for strengthening the sense of solidarity and revitalizing the unifying bond of brotherhood that makes of it a religious fraternity. Arabs, Persians, Turks, Pakis-

[23] Cf. Ex. 19:13.
[24] Ex. 13:14, 17; 34:22-3; I Sam. 1:3.

tans, Chinese, Indonesians, Filipinoes, black, white, and yellow, rich and poor, male and female, greet each other with *as-salamu alaykum!* (peace unto you!) and pray through Arabic, the language of the Koran. Of all the major religions of the world it is only Islam that has succeeded to a considerable extent in obliterating the racial and color lines. The line between believers and non-believers, however, has throughout been clearly marked. The common ground of the pilgrimage incidentally provided the zealous propagandist with an unparalleled chance to disseminate his teaching and thus spread his message far and wide. History records numberless cases in which leaders of sects and new schools of thought took advantage of the opportunity to win converts, make friends and turn them into disciples.

HOLY WAR

As a militant religion Islam enjoined holy war (*jihad*)[25] on believers in general; at least one sect gave this obligation the dignity of a pillar. The theory behind this institution divides the world into two potentially hostile camps: that of Islam (*dar al-Islam*), which is the abode of peace, and that of war (*dar al-harb*). It then becomes the duty of all free adult male Moslems, sane in mind and sound in body, to bear arms and push the wall that separates the two abodes. The theory has a modern parallel in international communism. A non-Moslem people is first invited to embrace Islam. If it is a "people of the book," particularly Christian or Jew, it is given the alternative of paying tribute and living as second-class citizens of the Islamic state but under its protection (*dhimmi*) or of fighting. In practice, however, the dhimmi status was granted to Zoroastrians, Berbers, and other peoples who were not Scripturaries. To this institution Islam owes much of its expansion as a world power. Death on the holy war battlefield, in the "path of Allah," is martyrdom, assuring the victim (*shahid*) Paradise and special privileges therein. Arabic has a special word for conquests achieved by Moslem arms: *fath* (opening), opening the path for the entry of Islam.

BOOKS TO READ

Arberry, Arthur J., *The Koran Interpreted,* 2 vols. (London, 1955).

Bell, Richard, *The Origin of Islam in its Christian Environment* (London, 1926).

Gaudefroy-Demombynes, *Muslim Institutions,* tr. P. MacGregor (London, 1950).

[25] Kor. 2:186-90.

Faris, Nabih A., ed., *The Arab Heritage* (Princeton, 1946).

Gibb, H. A. R., *Mohammedanism* (London, 1949).

Guillaume, Alfred, *Islam* (Harmondsworth, 1954).

Lammens, Henri, *Islam: Beliefs and Institutions,* tr. E. Denison Ross (London, 1929).

Levy, Reuben, *The Social Structure of Islam* (Cambridge, 1957).

Pickthall, Marmaduke, *The Meaning of the Glorious Koran* (London, 1930).

Smith, W. Robertson, *Lectures on the Religion of the Semites,* 3rd. ed., S. A. Cook (London, 1927).

Tritton, Arthur S., *Islam: Belief and Practices* (London, 1951).

Torrey, Charles A., *The Jewish Foundation of Islam* (New York, 1933).

XVIII   *The Caliphal State: In Medina*

O N THAT fateful June 8, 632, when Muhammad took ill and died complaining of a severe headache, the infant Moslem community lost its prophet, ruler, leader, and commander.[1] For he was all that in one. The question then arose who was to be his successor (*khalifah,* caliph), successor in all but his prophetic function, in which he, as the "seal of the prophets," [2] could have no successor. The caliphate was the first major political problem that confronted Islam. It remained a living issue until the mid-twentieth century, subsequent to its abolition of this institution by the Kemalist Turks. In the words of a twelfth century Arab historian of Islamic sects "no other issue in Islam brought about more bloodshed."

Soon conflicting groups arose. The Qurayshite emigrants who accompanied the Prophet on his hegira to Medina claimed the right of succession on the basis of blood kinship and priority in belief. The Medinese supporters counters with the claim that had it not been for the asylum they gave the Prophet and the emigrants, Islam would have perished in its cradle. In course of time these two groups coalesced to form one party, the companions. A third group maintained that Muhammad had designated Ali, his paternal cousin, husband of his only surviving daughter (Fatimah) and one of the earliest believers, as his successor. God and his messenger, they argued, could not have left such an issue to the determination of the community at large. After Ali, they added, the succession should be continued in his sons from Fatimah, Hasan, and Husayn. Herein lies the germ of divine, hereditary rule. Last but not least came the aristocratic branch of Quraysh, the Umayyads, who argued that they, as the traditional heads of the community, should be continued in power. Against them was the fact that they did not accept Islam until it had become firmly established,

[1] As noted above, p. 189.
[2] Above, p. 197.

which made their profession of it one of convenience rather than conviction.

The first group triumphed. The fifty-eight-year-old abu-Bakr, one of the first three believers and a father-in-law of Muhammad, was offered homage from the heads of tribes and chiefs of the gathered assembly—a sort of informal election. Abu-Bakr had conducted the congregational prayer instead of Muhammad when he was taken ill. In his unshakable belief in his son-in-law as the chosen instrument of divine revelation he probably had no equal. His faithfulness earned him the title of al-Siddiq.

ORTHODOX CALIPHATE

Abu-Bakr ushered in the first caliphate in Islam (r. 632-661). Located in Medina and consisting of four incumbents, each of whom was related to and intimately connected with the Prophet, it became known as the Orthodox (*rashidun*) one. During this period the luster of Muhammad's life continued to shed its influence over the thoughts and acts of his successors. It was the patriarchal stage of the caliphate, in which the successor had the tribal shaykh pattern, rather than the monarchical pattern that was to follow. Abu-Bakr, once a Meccan merchant, supported his family as a part-time businessman from his modest residence in a Medinese suburb. The four orthodox caliphs were:

Abu-Bakr	r. 632-634
Umar	r. 634-644
Uthman	r. 644-656
Ali	r. 656-661

The first problem confronting the nascent state was the "bringing back by force into the fold of Islam"—so Arab historians tell us—of the many tribes all over the peninsula who had seceded on the death of the Prophet and refused to pay alms. In reality the wars which occupied the early part of abu-Bakr's short caliphate were not to bring back apostates but to convert the Arabians, only a small fraction of whom could have heard of or accepted Muhammad in his lifetime. In a series of campaigns headed, among others, by a brilliant young Qurayshite general, Khalid ibn-al-Walid, central as well as southern and eastern Arabia were subdued. The caliph was adamant in his refusal to accept compromise. Arabia had to Islamize itself before it could Islamize other lands. It had to conquer itself before it could conquer the world.

In the course of these wars so many Koran memorizers and reciters were lost as to endanger the perpetuation of the sacred word. Abu-Bakr reportedly started the work of collecting the material which resulted in the compilation of the entire Koran in the days of Uthman (644-656). Uthman canonized the Medinese codex and ordered all others destroyed. The text, however, was not finally fixed in its orthography and diacritical marks until about three centuries later in Baghdad.

EARLY CONQUESTS

The military momentum generated by the domestic war had to seek outlets, especially since Islam discouraged Moslems' fighting against Moslems and frowned even on raiding each other, a favorite pastime of Arabian Bedouin life.

Soon two columns were on the march: one toward the northeast and Iraq, then in Persian hands, and the other toward the northwest and Syria, then under Byzantine rule. The Iraq column of some five thousand troops scored its first victory at Hira, seat of a Christian Arab kinglet under Persian suzerainty. Hira was the first acquisition outside of Arabia, a prelude to the conquest of all Persia. But Khalid, on orders from abu-Bakr, had to halt his advance and rush to the aid of his coreligionists hard pressed in Palestine by Byzantine defenders of the land. Khalid's perilous march of eighteen days through a five-hundred-mile almost waterless desert forms a favorite theme of Arab medieval saga. Water for the seven hundred troops was carried in skin bags, refilled a couple of times en route, but for the mounts the paunches of old camels served as reservoirs to be tapped either by inserting a stick and pressing down the animal's tongue or by slaughtering it. Its meat would then be eaten.

IN SYRIA

With dramatic suddenness Khalid appeared in eastern Syria and succeeded (July 634) in effecting a junction with the Arabian forces operating there. Arabian Christian tribes, the Ghassanids, domiciled in that area and speaking both Arabic and Aramaic, cooperated. In September 635, Damascus surrendered after a six-month siege. Treachery on the part of its civil authorities, headed by the grandfather of St. John of Damascus, facilitated the surrender. Umar ibn-al-Khattab (r. 634-644) then succeeded abu-Bakr. Umar, the greatest figure in early Islam after Muhammad and a Qurayshite emigrant, was the first founder of the Arab empire. The Byzantine capital of Syria was soon to become the Moslem capital of the Umayyad caliphate

(661-750), under which Moslem expansion reached its farthest limits.

But the battle to decide the fate of the country was soon to come. On a hot day of August 636, the two opposing armies faced each other on the banks of the Yarmuk, a Jordan tributary. The Arabians, 25,000 strong, were commanded by Khalid; the Byzantine army, twice as numerous and composed mostly Armenian and other mercenaries, was led by a brother of Emperor Heraclius.[3] The day was an excessively hot one clouded by wind-blown dust and presumably purposely chosen for the encounter by the Arabian generalship. The Byzantine fighters were cleverly maneuvered into a position where the dust storm struck them in the face. Only a few managed to escape with their lives. The fate of Syria, one of the fairest of the Eastern Roman provinces, was decided. "Farewell, O Syria," were Heraclius' parting words, "and what an excellent country this is for the enemy!" No further serious resistance was encountered until the natural limits, the Taurus, were reached. By 640 the entire country was firmly in Arabian hands. Khalid won his proud title "the sword of Allah."

EGYPT REDUCED

With Syria as a base, operations against Armenia and north Mesopotamia, on one hand, and Egypt, on the other, were facilitated. The Egyptian commander, Amr ibn-al-As, rivalled Khalid in dash and brilliancy of military achievement. Earlier a caravaneer on the Arabia-to-Egypt route, Amr, also a Qurayshite, had collaborated in the conquest of Palestine and repeatedly urged the caliph in Medina to authorize his leading a campaign against the valley of the Nile, granary of the Eastern Roman Empire and its richest province.[4] At last at the head of some four thousand, later greatly augmented, Amr followed the same beaten track along the coast anciently trod by Abraham, Cambyses, Alexander, Antiochus and the Holy Family, and lately by Napoleon and other conquerors. In December 639 he reached the Egyptian border. The Byzantine governor, who was also patriach of Alexandria, hurried eastward to check the unheralded advance. The usual three choices were offered: Islam, tribute, or the sword. With the surrender of the eastern fortress at Babylon, in the neighborhood of what subsequently became Cairo, the way to Alexandria was open. *Allahu akbar* (God is most great), battle cry of Islam, was soon to be echoed under the walls of the capital of the province and the base of its fleet.

---

[3] See above, p. 174.
[4] As indicated above, pp. 150-151, 171.

Early one summer day in 642 the Arabians found themselves at the seemingly impregnable line of walls and towers guarding the second strongest city in the empire.   On one side stood the lofty Serapeum,[5] the proudest monument of Egyptian heathen architecture; on the other loomed the beautiful cathedral of St. Mark, begun as the Caesarion temple by Cleopatra in honor of Julius Caesar; farther west raised their heads the two red granite needles, one of which now adorns the Thames Embankment in London and the other Central Park in New York. In the background towered the Pharos, one of the wonders of the ancient world.[6]   Against this city, guarded by a 50,000-man garrison and protected by a mighty fleet, a motley horde of 20,000 with no adequate siege equipment and not a single ship hurled itself.   In September 642, Alexandria capitulated.   "I have captured a city," reported Amr to Umar, "from the description of which I shall refrain.   Suffice it to say I have seized therein 4000 villas with 4000 baths, 40,000 poll-tax-paying Jews and 400 places of entertainment for the royalty."   The caliph entertained his general's messenger with bread and dates; they all joined in a thanksgiving service in the Prophet's mosque.   At this time Alexandria had no library of importance.   The great Ptolemaic one was burned as early as the days of Julius Caesar and its so-called daughter was destroyed later.   The often-repeated story, therefore, that by the caliph's order Amr fed the bath furnaces of the city for six long months with the book contents of the Alexandrian library is one of those tales that make good fiction but bad history.   It was first reported six centuries after the alleged event and bears the earmarks of fabrication.   The bulk of the volumes must have been parchment which does not burn.   From Egypt a push westward added Barca and Cyrenaica (642-643) in the northeast of modern Libya.   Later the road will lead to the rest of North Africa and from there to Sicily and Spain.

The loss of Syria and Egypt was a blessing in disguise to the Byzantines, as it was to the Turks at the end of the first World War.   It made them concentrate their energies on the defense of the realm that was properly theirs.   The Byzantines could then better ward off the repeated attacks of Slavs on Thessalonica and of Bulgars on the Balkans.   The Bulgars, of an origin related to the Turks, had advanced through southern Russia, crossed the Danube where they were fused with the Slavs and founded the first coherent Slavic power in the Balkans.

[5] Noted above, p. 129.
[6] Cf. above, p. 129.

PERSIA OVERRUN

While these operations were in progress in Syria and Egypt, the third front, Persia, was not neglected. The departure of Khalid left Sad ibn-abi-Waqqas, one of the Prophet's companions, in charge of the campaign. With reinforced troops Sad moved against al-Qadisiyah, in the vicinity of Hira, routed the Persian army and left its commander Rustam dead on the battlefield. The crossing of the Tigris without the loss of life was extolled by Arab chroniclers as a major feat. Lower Mesopotamia was incorporated. The Persian capital Ctesiphon (Madain of the Arabs) lay just across. Without determined resistance it was abandoned by its garrison and young Sasanid monarch Yazdagird III.[7] In June 637 Sad made his triumphal entry into the city which he made his headquarters. In a few years the whole country was overrun and consolidated, with the final victory at Nehawand (642). The booty seized at the capital dazzled the victors and provided the chroniclers with an opportunity to outdo themselves in their extravagant description of its treasures, estimated at nine billion silver pieces. Some of the warriors, unfamiliar with gold pieces, were willing to exchange them for silver ones. Others, who had never seen camphor before, took it for salt and used it in cooking. When blamed at Hira for selling an aristocratic woman who had fallen as his share of booty for only a thousand silver pieces, an Arabian replied that he never thought there was a number higher than ten hundred.

The ill-starred Yazdagird, grandson of Khosrau Parviz,[8] fell victim in 651, in a miller's hut near Marv, to the greed of one of his own people who coveted the crown treasures. His death marked the end of an empire that had lasted with little interruption for some twelve centuries and that was not to rise again for some eight more. When it rose again, the empire was a quite different version from the old.

The spectacular conquest of Persia marked the end of a period of history, but it could not have been the tragic affair represented by some. The land was not devastated and the people were not forced by the sword to accept a new faith. Those with vested interests in the old order naturally resented and resisted the change, but the masses must have found in the new religion a fresh source of inspiration, a quickening of the spirit, and a welcome relief from the artificialities of the official religion. Under the new order, as we shall see, Persian scholars, scientists, and artists attained heights hitherto unapproached.

---

[7] The Sasanids were described above, pp. 172 *seq.*
[8] Mentioned above, p. 173.

ISLAM THE STATE

Such easy conquest of so vast a territory—from Egypt to Persia inclusive—in a short decade is a historical phenomenon difficult to explain, especially when it is remembered that it was achieved at the expense of the two most powerful nations of the world by a people who had never before figured in military affairs. To the Arabs the explanation was simple: it was providential and in line with the clerical philosophy of the expansion of Christianity and the Old Testament interpretation of Hebrew victories in Canaan. To their historians the motivation was religious; the triumph was that of Islam. In fact what triumphed then was not Islam the religion but Islam the state, the Arab state. It was Arabianism and not Muhammadanism that expanded and spread. The outburst from Arabia was largely not one of zealous Moslems anxious to convert the world, but of nationalist Arabians, squeezed in an overpopulated barren area and eager to share in the larger life of the Fertile Crescent.[9] The new faith did, of course, provide the spark that lit an already loaded powder keg. It was a case of a hardy people feeling the pressure on its resources, developing the urge for expansion, conquest, dreaming of luxury beyond its own borders, and clothing its emotional unrest in religious concepts. A parallel case in medieval Europe appeared in the Crusades. In modern Europe the expansion of commerce, the development of technology, the discovery and peaceful infiltration of empty continents reduced the population pressure on its land resources and with it the impulse toward conquest. Viewed in its proper setting, the Arabian migration was the last phase of an age-long process of infiltration which began with the Assyro-Babylonians and carried the Hebrews and Canaanites to the other horn of the Fertile Crescent. Two or three centuries had to elapse before the bulk of the Syrian and Mesopotamian population began to profess Islam. When they did, it was primarily to escape tribute and seek identification with the ruling class. Egypt succumbed more readily. Mt. Lebanon persisted in its Christian character throughout the centuries.

ISLAM THE CULTURE

There was a third kind of Islam: Islam the culture. Its triumph was even more delayed. This was a synthesis of Syro-Aramaean, Persian, and Egyptian cultural elements maintained under the aegis of the caliphate and expressed through the Arabic tongue. The index of its victory was the substitution of Arabic for the native tongues. It was a

[9] Discussed above, p. 33.

slow process conditioned by the spread of Islam the religion. Northern Lebanon persisted in the use of Syriac till the seventeenth century and Anti-Lebanon still has three villages which use Aramaic.

By the conquest of the Fertile Crescent the Moslem Arabians entered upon the incomparably rich Semitic heritage of the ancient world with its Hellenistic accretions. The acquisition of Persia gave them vital contact with a worthy legacy of Indo-Iranian art, philosophy, and literature. On the other hand, the integration of Persia with the caliphate completed its withdrawal from the Hellenistic world, released it from its national isolation and offered it a world-wide field for its creative genius. Egypt introduced the Arabs to a still different civilization, the Hamitic, inaugurated by the Pharaohs and continued through the Ptolemies, Romans, and Byzantines. It is to the credit of the Arabians, that, unlike such other conquerors as the Vandals and Tartars, they appropriated more than they destroyed of the cultures of the peoples whom they conquered.

FAVORABLE EXTERNAL FACTORS

The enfeebled condition of the rival Byzantine and Sasanid states which had conducted internecine wars for generations,[10] the previous domestication of Arabian tribes on the Syrian and Mesopotamian frontiers,[11] and the hostility of the official Christian Church to the Monophysites in Syria and Egypt and to the Nestorians in Mesopotamia and Persia[12] all paved the way for the surprisingly rapid march of Arabian arms. As Semites the Fertile Crescent people must have sensed that the Arabians were nearer of kin to them than the Byzantines. The same, to a less extent, could be said of the Hamitic Egyptians. The Moslem conquest must have looked to many Near Easterners as a recovery by the area of its ancient domain. At last, after a millenium of submission to Westerners, Near Easterners were reasserting themselves. As for the new religion it must have looked more like a sect of Christianity. Moreover the tribute imposed by the new conquerors was less onerous than that of the old.

The Arabians constituted a fresh vigorous stock, fired with enthusiasm, imbued with the will to conquer, and emboldened by contempt of death under the influence of a new faith[13] and the promise of special reward for those who die in "the path of God." In their operations

---

[10] Discussed above, pp. 172-173.
[11] Cf. above, p. 208.
[12] Referred to above, pp. 169, 171.
[13] Cf. above p. 204.

they used techniques involving the use of cavalry and camelry which gave them a kind of mobility the Byzantines had never experienced.

CAMPAIGNS LACKED DESIGN

Equally fallacious is the Arab historians' assumptions that the campaigns were undertaken in accordance with prearranged plans on the part of caliphs in Medina. Far from being entirely or largely the result of cool and deliberate calculation the early expeditions to the Fertile Crescent started as raids for plunder and as outlets for the warring spirit of the tribes who were forbidden to engage in fratricidal combats.[14] Umar, under whom the bulk of the campaigns were conducted, enjoined his generals, "Let not the sea intervene between you and me." He further insisted on settling the men in camps of their own in preference to already existing towns. The camps of Iraq developed into the two cities of Kufa and Basra, brilliant centers of Moslem culture. That of Egypt, al-Fustat (from Greek for tent), was later incorporated with Cairo. When Mu'awiyah, one of the conquerors of Syria and then its governor, asked Caliph Uthman's permission to attack Cyprus, which was "so close that one could hear the roosters' crow," Uthman insisted that the governor should have his wife accompany him.

Systematic campaigning and the conscious creation of an empire followed inevitably. But both were due less to design and more to the logic of developments. The conquest of Egypt may belong to the systematic category.

ADMINISTRATION

Administering such a vast hastily acquired domain, with a heterogenous population of Arabians, Syrians, Mesopotamians, Armenians, Persians, Egyptians, and Berbers presented grave problems to the inexperienced conquerors. The natural procedure was to leave the Byzantine framework of the provincial government in Syria and Egypt, as well as the Sasanid administrative machinery in Persia, undisturbed and to work through it whatever new theories the Arabians had. Old functionaries and bureaucrats were not dismissed, as they could not be replaced.

Arab tradition ascribes, mainly to Umar, the basic facts of early Moslem political theory, starting with the assumption that in the Arabian peninsula none but Moslems could be tolerated. Moslem Arabians constituted a religio-military commonwealth keeping them-

[14] As noted above, pp. 191, 208, 212.

selves pure and unmixed in the conquered territory. Subject peoples were left in their varied professions and in the cultivation of the soil. Those of the conquered who persisted in their Christian and Jewish faiths were given the status of dhimmis,[15] subject to heavy tribute but not to military duty. Those who accepted Islam became free from the tributary obligation but in most cases continued to pay land tax. At the bottom of the socio-political ladder stood the slaves and prisoners of war.

This early setup, which assured ascendancy for Arabian Moslems and placed non-Arabian believers in an intermediate position between them and dhimmis, could not stand the test of time. Its breakdown began in the days of Uthman.

CIVIL STRIFE

The first wave of conquest covering the reigns of the first two Orthodox caliphs receded during the reign of Uthman and came to a standstill under the fourth, Ali. The interruption was brought about by domestic strife culminating in civil war, the first in Islam. The occasion was a struggle for the caliphate, the highest post in the state.

Compared to his two predecessors Uthman (r. 644-656) was a mediocrity. Seniority in age worked in his favor as against Ali. He was also a son-in-law of Muhammad. The only major operations in Uthman's time involved the occupation of Cyprus and Aradus (649-650) and a naval expedition against Constantinople which entailed the destruction of the Byzantine fleet on the Lycian coast (655). But all these campaigns were conducted from Syria by its able governor and caliph's kinsman, Mu'awiyah. By this time the Arabs had come into possession of two naval units, one in Acre[16] and the other in Alexandria, both built in Byzantine arsenals and manned by Syrians and Egyptians.

Originally a wealthy Umayyad merchant, Uthman lived in luxury, appointed his relatives as governors of provinces, and practiced other forms of nepotism. His official redaction of the Koran, entailing the destruction of all provincial copies,[17] brought on his head the wrath of readers who earned their living in the provinces as the receptacles and expositors of the sacred text. But the basic trouble was neither personal nor religious; it was rather the natural reaction of warriors and settlers abroad, largely of nomadic stock, to the system of centralized

---

[15] See above, p. 204.
[16] See below, p. 218.
[17] As noted above, p. 208.

government initiated by the second caliph and developed by the third. Disaffection among troops in Iraq and Egypt touched off a rebellion leading to Uthman's assassination.   In Iraq, Kufa was the center of disturbances that began among Ali's partisans.   The band that broke into his house and laid violent hands on him was led by a son of abu-Bakr.   The caliph's blood reportedly flowed over the copy of the Koran he was reading.   Ali maintained a malevolent neutrality.   The first murder of a caliph by a Moslem was by no means the last.

With Uthman's death the political unity of Islam was terminated. Soon Islam's religious unity was also to come to an end.   Islamic society entered upon a period punctuated with schism and civil strife that has not yet ended.

Of the first three candidates for the vacant post Ali (r. 656-661), the favorite of many, won.   But no sooner had he disposed of his two rivals, both companions of the Prophet, than he encountered a third and more formidable one, Mu'awiyah.   Mu'awiyah came out as the avenger of his kinsman Uthman.   In the mosque of his provincial capital, Damascus, he—as if taking a leaf from Antony's book—exhibited the "martyred" caliph's blood-stained shirt together with the chopped-off fingers of his wife who tried to defend him, and with shrewd eloquence aroused Moslem emotions.   The two horns of the dilemma on which he pinned Ali were: produce the assassins or accept the role of an accomplice.   To Ali's side rallied the Hejazis, who sensed in him a symbol of Arab chivalry, nationalism, and puritanical piety as well as the Iraqis whose city Kufa he had chosen as a second capital.   Under Mu'awiyah's banner gathered the Syrians— still mostly Christians—Neo-Moslems, and South Arabian tribes domiciled near by.

FIRST CIVIL WAR

War was unavoidable.   In Siffin on the west bank of the Euphrates the two armies stood face to face in July 657.   As the tide of victory turned in favor of the Alids, copies of the Koran were suddenly seen hoisted on lances high in the air.   The gesture was interpreted as an appeal from decision by arms to decision by the word of God.   The ruse contrived by the wily lieutenant of Mu'awiyah and conqueror of Egypt, Amr ibn-al-As, worked.   Hostilities were suspended.   Arbitration was agreed upon.   But the representatives did not meet until January 659.   The session was a public one held at a meeting place of caravans in southern Palestine and witnessed by a large crowd.   What exactly transpired there is not clear.   Ali seems to have lost the case before it was opened.   The mere fact of arbitration raised Mu'awiyah to the caliphal level and lowered Ali to the position of a mere pretender. Until that time Mu'awiyah had not dared announce his candidacy. He did not proclaim himself caliph until 661, after Ali had been struck with a poisoned sabre by one of his former followers. The lonely spot near Kufa where the caliph was interred, the present Mashad (shrine of) Ali at Najaf, has become one of the greatest centers of Moslem pilgrimages.

Ali dead proved to be more effective than Ali living. To his partisans, the Shiites, he became the patron saint, the vicegerent of God. A cult grew around him and a sect developed. This was the first great schism in Islam, one that has endured. Although basically political, the issue became religious; indeed the line between the two realms is not clearly drawn in Islam. By extremists among the Shiites, Ali was elevated high above Muhammad, was declared sinless and infallible, even the incarnation of the Deity. To Moslems in general he has lived in history as the paragon of Arabian nobility and Islamic chivalry. In tradition he is the Solomon around whose name countless proverbs, maxims, verses, wise sayings, and anecdotes have clustered.

On the political side his death marked the end of an era—the simple, patriarchal Orthodox one of Hejaz. It was followed by a brand new style of the caliphate—monarchical, worldly, and anchored in Syria. This was the Umayyad caliphate founded by Mu'awiyah.

BOOKS TO READ

Ali, *Maxims* (Lahore, 1946).

Arnold, Thomas W., *The Caliphate* (Oxford, 1924).

Brockelmann, Carl, *History of the Islamic Peoples,* tr. Joel Carmichael and Moshe Perlmann (New York, 1947).

Hazard, Harry W., *Atlas of Islamic History* 3rd ed. (Princeton, 1954).

Hitti, Philip K., *History of the Arabs,* 7th ed. (New York, 1960); *History of Syria, including Lebanon and Palestine,* 2nd ed. (London, 1957).

The Legacy of Persia, ed. A. J. Arberry (Cambridge, 1953).

Muir, William, *The Caliphate: Its Rise, Decline, and Fall* (Edinburgh, 1924).

Wellhausen, J., *The Arab Kingdom and its Fall,* tr. Margaret G. Weir (Calcutta, 1927).

XIX   *The Umayyad Caliphate*

T HE death of Ali did not entirely clear the way before Mu'awiyah. Iraq, hotbed of Shiism, declared Ali's eldest son Hasan as the legitimate successor of his father. Hejaz, seat of conservative Islam, was lukewarm in its loyalty to the Umayyads as represented by Mu'awiyah, but he was able to cope with the situation. Realizing that Hasan's interest lay more in the harem than on the throne, Mu'awiyah sent him what would be called today a signed blank check and thus satisfied him. The incident illustrates the kind of policy the caliph pursued. Its formulation as attributed to him reads: "I apply not my sword where my lash suffices, nor my lash where my tongue is enough. And if there be one hair binding me to others I let it not break: if they pull I loosen and when they loosen I pull." Death (*ca.* 669) at the age of forty-five, possibly poisoned through harem intrigue, removed Ali's son.

MU'AWIYAH, REAL FOUNDER OF THE ARAB KINGDOM

Secure in the caliphate, Mu'awiyah (r. 661-680) started building a new machinery of state within the earlier Byzantine framework. He stripped the Arabian system of many of its archaic features. Though inferior to Ali as a warrior he stood second to none among his contemporaries as a military organizer. The army, hitherto organized on tribal units, was whipped into a new fighting machine following the Byzantine model. Its core was Christian Syrians, Syro-Arabs, and Yemenites. Shipyards found in Acre ('Akka) at the time of the conquest were utilized for building a Moslem navy second in date to that of Egypt.[1] This makes Mu'awiyah an early admiral (word of Arabic etymology) in Islam. While still governor (655) he sent his fleet in conjunction with that of the Egyptians to destroy the Byzantine navy under Constans II, grandson of Heraclius, at Phoenix and score

---

[1] Cf. above, p. 215.

the first maritime victory in Islam.[2] By tying their vessels to the enemy's the Arabs converted the fight into a hand-to-hand one in which they excelled. Constans (r. 641-668) was an able and energetic emperor who, with a view to checking Arab advance, reorganized the provincial administration of the empire by establishing divisions under military governors who had wide powers over the civil authorities. This system remained in effect for centuries and strengthened resistance to Moslem attacks.

A couple of years before his assumption of the caliphate Mu'awiyah had to purchase from Constans a truce for a yearly tribute to be repudiated later. Hostilities against "the land of the Romans" was thereafter pressed by sea and land, with booty as the main objective, though the spectacle of Constantinople may have beckoned from the distant horizon. Annual summer razzias (from Ar. *ghazu*) kept the army physically fit. On two occasions the Syro-Arab army of Mu'awiyah stood before the high triple wall of the mighty capital. Between 668 and 669 it wintered at Chalcedon (the Asiatic suburb of Byzantium), but the siege was lifted through the energetic efforts of emperor Constantine IV (r. 668-685). The reign of Constantine, son of Constans, witnessed the high point of the Arab attack which was, as usual, synchronized with Slav incursions in the Balkans. In the Seven Years' War (674-680) the Arabs secured a naval base in the Sea of Marmora but were finally repulsed by the aid of a highly combustible compound "which would burn on water." This Greek fire was the invention of a Syrian refugee from Damascus. It may be considered the only first-rate technological invention produced by the Byzantine culture, which with the Moslem and Latin cultures formed the trinity of medieval civilization. To this period belong the temporary occupation of Rhodes (672) and Crete (674). Previously Rhodes had been pillaged and its once famous colossus sold for old metal. For the following two centuries the Byzantines and Arabs waged occasional wars for the mastery of the bridge lands of the Euphrates and the Cilician Gates. The physical boundaries raised by nature in the form of the Taurus and Anti-Taurus, the relatively cold climate of Asia Minor and the non-Semitic character of its population militated against giving the Arabs a permanent foothold in the area. The line of least resistance pointed in other directions.

From Egypt and Cyrenaica[3] the expansive movement of Islam continued its westward march. Kairwan, in what is today Tunisia, was founded in 670 as a stopping place for caravans and soon developed

[2] See above, p. 215.
[3] See above, p. 210.

into the capital of North Africa and a center of Moslem pilgrimages and learnings. In the east the Oxus was crossed and Bukhara in distant Turkestan was raided (674). Contact was thereby established with a new ethnic group and a different culture—the Turkish—of which we shall hear more later. With the extension of the territory of Islam went its consolidation.

NEW ADMINISTRATION

Mu'awiyah distinguished himself not only as a military organizer but as an administrator. The financial control of the state was left in the hands of St. John of Damascus' grandfather, who had figured in the surrender of Damascus.[4] This was the most important post in the government next to the supreme command of the army. Greek remained the language of the register.[5] The stability of the Umayyad throne was conditioned by the loyalty of its Christian subjects. For his favorite wife Mu'awiyah had chosen a Syro-Arab Christian who scorned Damascene court life and yearned for the freedom of the desert. Her son Yazid was nominated (679) by Mu'awiyah as his successor, thus introducing into the caliphate the hereditary principle pursued thereafter by the Abbasids and other major Moslem dynasties. The court physician was likewise a Christian; he could not have been but that. The court poet, al-Akhtal, would enter the audience chamber with a cross dangling from his neck. His poems, eulogizing the dynasty, are still studied and memorized by students throughout the Arab East. It was before the caliph that Maronites and Jacobites brought their religious disputes.

With Arab historians, writing mostly in the hostile Abbasid atmosphere, Mu'awiyah was no favorite though admittedly "one of the four geniuses of Islam." His collaborator Amr ibn-al-As was another. Historians regarded Mu'awiyah as the one who had destroyed the theocratic caliphate nurtured in Medina and who had built a secular state, a temporal sovereignty, with himself as its first king. Mu'awiyah was indeed the first king with a real throne and surrounded by a retinue of high officials and bodyguards following the Byzantine model. Beginning with his regime Islam looked less toward the desert for new inspiration and more toward the West. It lost its puritanical character. To his successors Mu'awiyah served as a model. He bequeathed to them a precedent of energy, clemency, and astuteness which many tried to emulate; but few succeeded.

[4] As related above, p. 208.
[5] See below, pp. 226-227.

HUSAYN AGAINST YAZID

Mu'awiyah's death and Yazid's succession served as the signal for Ali's second son Husayn to emerge from his retirement in Medina and claim the caliphate. Yazid (r. 680-683) was a drunkard, the first in caliphal annals but not the last. Husayn, at the head of a small band of relatives, harem, and followers—some of whom must have thought that he as the God-chosen imam was invincible—was met by an Umayyad army at Karbala, twenty-five miles northwest of Kufa, and peremptorily routed with his band. The head of the Prophet's grandson was sent to Yazid at Damascus but was forthwith returned to be buried with the body at Karbala. The Karbala shrine, like that of Najaf, became for the Shiites an object of pilgrimage more meritorious than Medina and even Mecca. The tenth of Muharram (October 10, 680) on which "martyrdom" was suffered is still commemorated as an annual passion day. Even now devout believers on that day cut their bodies with knives as they march in a procession of mourning.

Shiism was born on that day. Husayn's martyred blood, even more than his father's, was the seed of the new "church." "Vengeance for Husayn" became the battle cry of the new community; it contributed to the undermining of the Umayyad house and its final downfall in 750.

The destruction of Husayn and his band at Karbala did not mean the destruction of opposition everywhere. In Arabia, particularly Hejaz, and in Iraq, especially Kufa, anti-Umayyad and Alid forces had to be dealt with summarily. As Mu'awiyah was fortunate in having such a devoted and capable collaborator as Amr ibn-al-As, so was Mu'awiyah's successor Abd-al-Malik (r. 685-705) in having al-Hajjaj. Originally a school teacher in Taif, summer resort of Mecca, this one-eyed thirty-one-year man laid down the pen to take up the sword in support of the Umayyad regime. By drastic measures and in a few years he restored peace in Arabia, became its governor, and then moved against turbulent Iraq. No head there proved too high for him to reach. His victims numbered 120,000 we are told by prejudiced Abbasid historians. As viceroy of Iraq he dispatched his lieutenants "to open up new lands for Islam." Thanks to his and other generals' achievements the dynasty founded by Mu'awiyah moved to the meridian of its power and glory under the energetic Abd-al-Malik and his son al-Walid (r. 705-715). The first major wave of conquest, interrupted by civil strife,[6] was followed by a second and more extensive wave.

---

[6] See above, p. 215.

It netted the final subjugation of Transoxiana and western India, the Barbary states of North Africa, and the Iberian peninsula.

IN CENTRAL ASIA

In 700 Kabul (today capital of Afghanistan) was entered and its Turkish king forced to pay tribute. Four years later Khurasan was consolidated as a province of the caliphate with Marv as capital. In the first year of al-Walid's reign, permanent foothold was established beyond the Oxus, traditionally but not historically the boundary line between the Persian-speaking and the Turkish-speaking peoples. In the following years lower Tukharistan with its capital Balkh (Bactra of the Greeks), Sogdiana with its metropolis Samarkand, Khwarizm (now Khiva), and other lands were reduced. Bukhara, Balkh, and Samarkand, centers of Buddhistic cultures, were soon to become and remain centers of Islamic learning. The crossing of the Jaxartes added Ferghana. The push southward through what is today Baluchistan brought Sind (the lower valley of the Indus) and southern Punjab into the realm of Islam, a realm that as late as 1947 gave birth to Pakistan.

The Punjab and Sind in the southeast, Kashgar and Tashkend (now in Asiatic Russia) in the northeast mark the farthest Arab conquests in Asia.

AGAINST THE BYZANTINES

While these operations were in progress the eternal enemy to the northwest was not forgotten. In 692 the army of Justinian II (r. 685-695), son of Constantine IV and last of the Heraclian line, was shattered at Sebastopolis in Cilicia. Later campaigns netted Pergamum and Sardis among other cities and landed the Arab army for the third time at the gates of Constantinople. The siege of the capital was pressed for over a year beginning August 716. In the face of the Arab advance Theodosius III (r. 715-717), an obscure official raised to the throne by the army, stood helpless. The invaders were subjected to severe attacks by Leo, military chief of the Anatolian division, who was thereupon enthusiastically proclaimed emperor by the clergy and the populace of the capital. This was Leo III (r. 717-741), founder of the Isaurian dynasty and a distinguished general and organizer. A chain blocked the passage of Arab ships through the Golden Horn, the inlet of the Bosporus forming the city harbor. Scarcity of provisions, the rigors of an unusually cold winter, and attacks by Bulgars helped to force retreat. The capital was never again to

ARAB CONQUESTS IN THE FIRST CENTURY OF ISLAM

witness an Umayyad army. Leo, the soldier of humble north Syrian origin, was hailed the savior of Europe. The next and the last serious attack on Constantinople was in 782 under the Abbasids with Harun al-Rashid in command.[7]

NORTH AFRICA AND SPAIN

Meantime the Umayyads were attacking Byzantine possessions on other fronts. With Kairwan as a base and with cooperation from the Moslem fleet, the Byzantine forces were driven out of Carthage (698) and other coastal towns. The subjugation of the Berbers presented no serious difficulty. The hero of these campaigns was Musa ibn-Nusayr, son of a Christian captive taken by Khalid ibn-al-Walid in Iraq. The captive was seized with other boys in a church as they were studying the Gospels. Musa's horse "was the first Arab one to drink from Atlantic waters." Though for centuries under Roman and Byzantine domination, the Berbers, except those along the littoral, were but thinly affected by the European civilization.[8] But in a few generations they became and remained largely Islamized and Arabicized. Their Hamitic origin and nomadic background, which alienated them from Europeans, facilitated *rapprochement* with the Arabs.

IN SPAIN

The way was then open for the invasion of southwestern Europe. In 711 the viceroy Musa in Kairwan sent his Berber freedman and lieutenant Tariq on a marauding expedition. The narrow straits of water where he crossed, Gibraltar, still bear his name (Ar. *Jabal Tariq, the mountain of Tariq*). As in other cases the raid was the prelude of a conquest. Musa followed. Dissension in the royal house, discontent among the natives and disloyalty to the Visigothic rule facilitated the invaders' task. From the south to the north one city after another tumbled like a house of cards. Perturbed by such adventurous penetration into unknown lands Caliph al-Walid in distant Damascus recalled his viceroy to render an account of his conduct. At the head of a vast train of retinue, slaves and prisoners of war, including royalty, and loaded with undreamed-of treasures captured as booty, Musa made his long way through North Africa and Palestine. The triumphal procession, reminiscent of Roman processions, was officially received in 717 with pomp and dignity in the open courtyard of the Umayyad Mosque. This was indeed a high-water day in the annals of triumphant

[7] See below, p. 242.
[8] Cf. above, p. 161.

Islam. Never before had so many European prisoners and Western aristocrats offered homage to the commander of the believers. The first European territory was annexed to Islam, there to stay for centuries. One of the most sensational campaigns was concluded.

IN FRANCE

But the temptation to undertake a few incursions into Gaul could not be avoided. Lured by the stories of rich treasures in monasteries and churches in the "land of the Franks" and encouraged by reports of internal dissension in the Merovingian court, the attackers began crossing the Pyrenees in 718. Narbonne, Bordeaux, and other cities in the south and west succumbed. At a place between Poitiers and Tours, however, the invading army under Abd-al-Rahman al-Ghafiqi was met by Charles Martel (the hammer), mayor of the palace at the Merovingian court. It was a cold October Saturday in 732. Charles' foot soldiers wore wolfskins and stood shoulder to shoulder, forming a square, "firm as a wall and inflexible as a block of ice." Before Abd-al-Rahman had fallen among the victims. In the stillness of the night the Arab troops quietly vanished. This is the extent of the victory hailed by Western historians as one of the decisive battles of the world. Gibbon,[9] and following him many others, envisioned Paris and London mosques where cathedrals had stood and fezzes where hats had been worn—had the outcome of the battle been otherwise. In itself the battle decided nothing. The long, drawn-out Arab march of hundreds if not thousands of miles had reached a natural standstill. The city of Tours, however, marks the extreme limit of Moslem expansion in the West. Its date, 732 marks the first centennial of Muhammad's death. In it his followers were masters of an empire greater than any ancient or medieval one and comparable in our days to those of Great Britain and Russia. Throughout that extensive domain the name of the Arabian Prophet, joined with that of God, was called on five times a day from thousands of minarets.

DAMASCUS

The imperial capital rose to the occasion. In its center stood the Umayyad Mosque, a gem of architecture, built by al-Walid. Originally a Christian cathedral, it is today considered the fourth holiest sanctuary in Islam after Mecca, Medina, and Jerusalem. The Dome of the Rock (mistakingly called Mosque of Umar) was built by Abd-

[9] Edward Gibbon, *The History of the Decline and Fall of the Roman Empire*, ed. J. B. Bury, vol. VI (London, 1898), pp. 15 *seq.*

al-Malik. It is the oldest surviving Moslem place of worship. On this site Jews, Christians, and heathens have successively worshiped. Next to it stands al-Aqsa Mosque, also erected by Abd-al-Malik. In all these buildings of Damascus and Jerusalem, Christian natives and artisans trained in the Byzantine school were employed. Their mosaics are among the decorative masterpieces of the age. The north side minaret of the Umayyad Mosque is the oldest of its kind and has served as a model for later ones. Next to the Umayyad Mosque rose the caliphal palace with its green dome. No trace of it is left.

Courtesy of The Macmillan Co., Ltd.

AN IMITATION IN GOLD OF A BYZANTINE COIN WITH ARABIC INSCRIPTION AND COPPER
COIN OF ABD-AL-MALIK

The city was surrounded then as now by orchards (Ghutah) and watered by snow-fed streams arising in Anti-Lebanon. Barada (biblical Abana) was one of them. It was the early Umayyads who supplied the population with a water system unexcelled in its age. It is still functioning, and the name of Yazid is still borne by a canal dug, more likely widened, by him.

NATIONALIZING THE STATE

The Moslem state under Abd-al-Malik and al-Walid seems to have attained maturity. The time was ripe for replacing the Greek-writing officials of the public register in Syria and the Pahlawi-writing ones in Iraq with Arabs. The Arabicization of the register was accompanied with that of the coinage. In both the process was slow, conditioned by the existence of properly qualified personnel. The first step was to superimpose koranic inscriptions upon Byzantine coins current in Syria and Egypt. Then gold and silver coins imitating Byzantine and Persian types were struck. In 695 the first real Arab *dirham* and *dinar* were struck. The dirham, or unit of silver coinage, was generally one-tenth or one-twelfth of the dinar, or unit of gold currency, which weighed approximately four grams.

Abd-al-Malik is also credited with the development of a postal service initiated by Mu'awiyah. Designed primarily to meet governmental needs the system employed relays of horses and connected the imperial capital with the provincial ones. An interesting duty of the postmaster was intelligence, keeping the caliph and central authorities informed about significant happenings throughout the realm.

POLITICAL ADMINISTRATION

The administrative divisions of the caliphal empire under the Umayyads, based on the provincial system of the Byzantine and Persian empires, were organized under five units. With certain modifications the units were continued under the Abbasids. Syria and Palestine went together. Iraq with Persia and eastern Arabia formed a viceroyalty having Kufa as capital. Later the Iraq viceroy or governor general came to have one deputy governor—usually residing at Marv —over east Persia and Transoxiana, and another over Sind and Punjab. The Hejaz viceroyalty covered most of the Arabian peninsula. Northern Mesopotamia went with Armenia. Egypt constituted a viceroyalty by itself and so did North Africa west of it with Kairwan for capital. The amir of Spain ruled almost independently though nominally under the governor general of North Africa.

The three fold governmental functions of political administration, tax collecting, and religious leadership became differentiated and were entrusted to different officials, with the governor general responsible for the political and military administration. The caliph himself often appointed the tax collecting agent. In the early conquests Bedouins furnished the rank and file of the troops, but Meccans and Medinese furnished the leadership. The army was then made up mostly of Neo-Moslems and Christians. The judiciary system evolved slowly. First the conquering general would himself act as a judge. Tradition credits Umar with appointing the first judge, whom he sent to Egypt. In the provinces, the governors normally appointed the judges, but under the Abbasids the caliphs themselves often appointed these officials. In all cases the judges were recruited from among the theologians. Besides deciding cases judges administered pious foundations, wakfs (sing. *waqf*) and the estates of orphans and the insane. Expenses of local administration, soldiers' stipends, state annuities to Arabian Moslems (headed by the Quraysh and caliphal family) and miscellaneous services were met from local income; only the balance

went to the caliphal treasury.   Pensions and annuities were instituted
by Umar when he distributed the revenues of conquests among warriors,
the Prophet's relatives and companions, and all other Arabian Moslems.   Tribute from subject peoples formed the chief revenue of the
state in its first stage.   But our sources of information about revenue,
expenditures and the general economic situation betray a projection
backwards of the conditions of a later age.   As in the case of the conquests, the chroniclers read into the past the developments of later times.

The dhimmis remained under the jurisdiction of the spiritual heads
of their respective communities even in matters of civil and criminal
procedure.   Moslem law was not applicable to them except in cases
in which Moslems were involved.   Originally limited to Christians,
Jews, and Sabians (Mandeans, "Christians of St. John") the dhimmi
status was later extended to Zoroastrians, Berbers, and other non-
Scripturaries.   Cases relating to the personal status of dhimmis remained outside the jurisdiction of Moslem judges in the Ottoman Empire.

SOCIAL CLASSIFICATION

Society under the Umayyads was divided into four major classes.
At the top of the social ladder stood the ruling Arabian Moslems
headed by the caliphal household.   This was the aristocracy of the
Arabian conquests; it consisted of warriors, veterans, government officials, and town settlers.   It was more of a caste which one could
enter only by birth.   This group was greatly outnumbered by the
natives, who in villages and country places, especially where mountainous, naturally resisted Islamization and Arabicization and persisted
in their ancient culture patterns.   Next below came the Neo-Moslems.
In theory though not in practice, these people were admitted to full
citizenship in Islam. On conversion they found themselves still paying
the old land tax paid under Byzantines and Persians.   They had to
attach themselves to one or another of the Arabian tribes as clients—
a status which they resented on economic and social as well as cultural
grounds, for they represented the older and more highly developed cultural tradition.   It was these neophytes within the Moslem society who
became the first devotees of skilled crafts, specialized professions, and
the learned disciplines.   But to equalize them economically with
Arabian Moslems meant a double loss to the state treasury: decrease
in revenue and increase in expenditure.   This second-class citizenship
conditioned the new Moslems to the acceptance of doctrines inimical
to the state and led them to the espousal of unorthodox causes, such

as Shiism, which became in essence an expression in religious terms of political dissatisfaction.

Caliph Umar ibn-al-Aziz (r. 717-720) tried to remedy the situation. The fiscal measures he introduced made it possible, by a legal fiction, for a Moslem owner of land to pay only the tithe and not the higher rate. But time was a better healer. As Persian, Aramaean, Copt, Berber, and other Neo-Moslems attached themselves to Arabian tribes—who constituted but a small minority—intermarried, and contested the social and political leadership, the original nationality of the individual Moslem began to recede into the background and the follower of Muhammad began to pass for an Arab. An Arabian remained a native of the peninsula, but an Arab became one who professed Islam and spoke Arabic regardless of his national origin. This is the situation in the Arab world today from Morocco to Iraq.

As Umar II, considered the most pious of the Umayyads, introduced measures to alleviate the situation of the clients, he enacted others that worsened the condition of the third class, the dhimmis. As professors of revealed religions the dhimmis were protected. In consideration of the protection received they paid a poll tax in addition to the land tax. These measures, erroneously ascribed to Umar I, excluded Christians and Jews from public offices, prohibited their wearing turbans, required them to cut their forelocks, to wear distinctive clothes, to ride without saddle or only on pack horses, to erect no new places of worship, and to raise no voices while worshiping. The tone of these restrictions bespeaks a growing jealousy on the part of the Moslems of the political and social influence and economic prosperity of their non-Moslem subjects. The enactments must have been made in response to popular demand, but the necessity for their renewal in part or in full in later times[10] indicates the looseness with which they were enforced.

The slaves stood at the bottom of the social ladder. While canon law forbade the enslavement of a Moslem, it promised no liberty to him who after enslavement embraced Islam. By this time slaves must have become excessively numerous throughout the realm, some being prisoners of war, others captured by raids, still others purchased in the trade market. To these markets streamed black ones from inner Africa, yellow ones from Central Asia, and white ones from the Near East and southwestern Europe. Musa ibn-Nusayr is said to have captured 300,000 prisoners of war in his North African campaigns— one-fifth of whom he forwarded to al-Walid as a present—and 30,000

---

[10] See below, pp. 279-280.

virgins from the Visigothic nobility of Spain.   For an Umayyad prince, general, or governor to have maintained a retinue of hundreds of slaves did not seem extraordinary.   Even privates in the army had their shares from among the prisoners they captured.

Islamic law considered the offspring of a female slave a slave, but the offspring of a male slave by a freewoman as free.   Concubinage, but not legal marriage, was permissible between master and female slave. The children belonged to the master and were therefore free.   The last three Umayyads were the offspring of such unions.[11]   Some of the most distinguished Abbasid caliphs, headed by al-Mamun (r. 813-833), were also sons of concubines.   In such cases, the status of the mother was raised one notch: she could not be sold or given away and would be declared free on the death of her husband-master.

The liberation of slaves was considered a meritorious act in the sight of God.   The liberated one was then attached as a client to his former master who became his patron.   Slaves and ex-slaves wrote a brilliant chapter in the history of Islam the religion, the state, and the culture. At varied times and places, down to the Ottoman period, they rendered signal services in war, science, art, literature, and education.   For over two and a half centuries Egypt and for most of the time Syria were under a dynasty of Mamluk sultans.[12]

INTELLECTUAL ENDEAVOR

The Umayyad caliphate provided the Arabians—who brought with them from the peninsula no science, no art, and no philosophy—with the first opportunity to expose themselves fully and intensively to the influences of older and more highly developed civilizations.   In the Fertile Crescent, Egypt, and Persia the invaders sat as pupils at the feet of the peoples they conquered, and what apt pupils they proved to be! But the closeness of the period to the primitive pre-Islamic age, its preoccupation with wars and strife, and the instability of its economic and social conditions delayed the expected results.   The seed was then sown but the tree of knowledge did not come into full bloom until a century later, in the Abbasid period.[13]

In Hejaz the two sister cities of Mecca and Medina became the early home of studies relating to religion, theology, and law.   To Medina in particular flocked would-be scholars to devote themselves to the study of the mementos of its sacred past and to the compilation of legal and ritual enactments.   The result was the characteristically

[11] See below, p. 238.
[12] Treated below, pp. 315 *seq.*
[13] See below, pp. 244 *seq.*

Moslem science of tradition. Tradition (*hadith,* literally narrative) in this sense is an act or saying attributed to the Prophet or to one of his companions. The Koran and tradition provided the basis upon which the system of theology and law (*shariah*) were erected. The final compilation of the accepted-as-authoritative traditions was also made under the Abbasids.

In Iraq the twin cities of Basra and Kufa became animated centers of linguistic studies. Here on the borderline of Persia the scientific study of the Arabic language had its beginning, necessitated by the needs of Neo-Moslems to understand the Koran, qualify for government posts, and join the aristocratic conquerors. The first systematic textbook on Arabic grammar was composed by a Basrite Persian, Sibawayh (d. *ca.* 793), a book which is not yet considered obsolete by conservative schools in the Arab world.

In this period we can also detect the rudiments of those religio-philosophical movements that were to agitate Moslem minds for years to come. One of the earliest of such schools was the Qadarite, which taught that man had power (*qadar*) over his acts. This is the free-will doctrine in an embryonic form. The rise of the school represents a reaction against the harsh predestinarianism of Islam with its koranic stress of the almightiness of God. It also betrays Christian Greek influences. The Qadarite doctrine became a cardinal point in the teaching of a school which flourished in the early Abbasid period under the name Mutazilite (seceder, schismatic). Contact with Christianity in Syria, which had retained a residue of the questioning spirit, stimulated the critical thinking of Moslems who began to question the doctrine of the uncreated and eternal character of the Koran as inconsistent with the essential unity of God. The Mutazilites adopted a rational view toward this, too.[11]

The man who mediated Greek Christian thought then was John of Damascus (d. *ca.* 749), surnamed Chrysorrhoas (golden-tongued) on account of his eloquence. A Syrian, his native tongue was Aramaic but he wrote in Greek and knew Arabic. He was canonized by both the Greek and the Latin Churches. Young John served as a finance official in the caliphal court as his father and grandfather had done. At the age of thirty-one however, he abandoned the world and dedicated himself to a life of asceticism and devotion in a monastery near Jerusalem. His works include a dialogue with a Saracen dealing with the divinity of Christ and the freedom of human will and intended for the guidance of Christians in debate with Moslems. Tradition mistakenly ascribes to him the story of an ascetic Barlaam and a Hindu

[11] See below, p. 246.

From S. Joannes Damascenus,
OPERA, ed. J. Billium (Paris 1619)

ST. JOHN OF DAMASCUS

prince Josaphat, which is a Christian version of the life of the Buddha. This religious romance achieved unbounded popularity in medieval times and resulted in the canonization, under the name of Josaphat, of the Buddha by the Greek and Latin Churches.   The fame of St. John, however, rests upon the hymns he composed, which mark the highest attainment of beauty by Christian Church poets, the Byzantine art he codified, and the standard textbook of dogmatic theology he authored. As orator, polemic writer, hymnologist, and theologian he was an ornament to the Greek Christian Church.

SCIENCE

At the time of the Arab conquest of Western Asia, Greek science was more of a tradition in the hands of Greek- or Syriac-writing commentators than a living force.   The court physicians of the Umayyad caliphs were such men.[15]   Even Persian medicine was taught by Syrians transmitting the Greek tradition.   Around 683 a Persian-Jewish physician in Basra, Masarjawayh, translated into Arabic a Syriac treatise on medicine originally composed by an Alexandrian Christian priest.   This was the earliest scientific book in the language

[15] Cf. above, p. 220.

of Islam. Note the lengthy chain of transmission. Umar II is said to have transferred the schools of medicine from Alexandria to Antioch and Harran. A predecessor, al-Walid, is credited with making special state provision for isolating and caring for people afflicted with leprosy, blindness, and other chronic diseases. Medicine thus became the first science in which Moslems interested themselves. Their interest found expression in a tradition ascribed to the Prophet: "Science is twofold: that relating to religion (theology) and that relating to the body."

Closely related to medicine was alchemy, a word of Arabic etymology indicative of the contribution made in this field by later Arabs and transmitted to Europe. Legend credits a son of the second caliph with translating medical, alchemical, and astrological works from Greek and Coptic into Arabic. The legend is built around a small kernel of truth: Arab scientific thought had its inception in the Greek tradition.

ART

In art as in science Arabian Moslems started from scratch. Their military advance fanwise through Western Asia and North Africa put them in possession of standing and ruined structures representing a high artistic Byzantine and Persian development. More importantly it made available to them the skill and technical knowledge of the architects, artisans, and craftsmen who were then their subjects. This technique applied to the religious need of Islam and modified by Arab proclivities and local conditions produced what has been variously designated Saracenic, Arab, Moslem, and Mohammedan art.

The primitive mosque of Medina, consisting of an open courtyard enclosed by sun-baked clay, served as a general prototype. To protect the congregation against the sun, the Prophet had the flat roof of the adjacent building so extended as to cover the entire open court. When addressing the congregation, he stood on a palm trunk stuck in the ground, later replaced by a small platform with three steps copied from church pulpits seen in Syria. Atop the flat roof stood the first muezzin, originally an Abyssinian Christian, to call the believers to prayer.

The earliest mosques in conquered lands were the simple ones of Basra, Kufa, al-Fustat, and other camps. Where Moslems were settled in cities they first made use of already existing places of worship. Then the caliphs began to erect monumental structures. One of the earliest among these was the Dome of the Rock in Jerusalem built by Abd-al-Malik over the rock from which Muhammad ascended to heaven.[16] Those who worked on the structure were undoubtedly native architects trained in the Byzantine school. The lavishly used

[16] See above, p. 193.

Courtesy of The Bettmann Archive

THE DOME OF THE ROCK, JERUSALEM

mosaic decoration in the original structure was perpetuated in its repeated renovation.   The distinctive feature of the edifice was the dome,
copied from the church cupolas then in vogue in Syria and intended to
outshine that of the adjacent Church of the Holy Sepulcher.   It did.
The ensemble is a monumental structure of such noble beauty that it
has scarcely been surpassed anywhere.

Next in chronology and importance was the Umayyad Mosque in
Damascus.   The site was that of the basilica of St. John the Baptist,
originally a temple of Jupiter.   Al-Walid also used native builders and
artisans.   The model of its main feature, the minaret, traveled through
Egypt into North Africa and Spain and eastward into Iraq.   The semicircular niche (*mihrab*), which indicates the direction in which prayers
should be recited, first appeared in the Umayyad Mosque.   This
Syrian invention was in all likelihood suggested by the apse in the
Christian church.   Between the simple mosque of Medina and those
sumptuous ones of Jerusalem and Damascus the Moslem place of
worship completed its evolution.   The physical needs of the congregation are now amply provided for by a sheltered sanctuary, the ritual
needs are met by a minaret, pulpit, niche, and outdoor fountain for
ablutions.   The political considerations were met by a majesty of plan
and a splendor of ornament that served notice on the world that the

followers of the new faith were in nowise inferior to those worshiping in the grand cathedrals of Christendom.

The Arabians on the peninsula developed no feeling for either plastic or pictorial art. Islam's uncompromising monotheism and the Koran's strict prohibition of idolatry discouraged painting and sculpture. A traditional saying, ascribed to the Prophet, reinforced this view: "Those to be punished most severely on the judgment day are the painters." Painting and sculpture are a form of creation; creation is the privilege of God and God alone. Nevertheless Moslem art evolved in the course of time; it was eclectic in origin and motifs and was executed largely by the artistic genius of subjugated peoples under Moslem auspices and adapted to Moslem taste and needs. It was in Persia, Egypt, and Spain that Moslem art flourished. Its impress on European style may be attested by the term arabesque, common in most modern languages of the West.

The decorative motifs were derived largely from the vegetable kingdom and from floral designs. Even the flowers and plants are so stylized and conventionalized that they can hardly be identified with any existing plants or flowers. The representation of men and animals, which theologians insisted was the prerogative of God alone, was practiced under the Umayyads as exemplified in the mural decorations of their pleasure-houses along the fringe of the Syrian Desert. In one of these, built by al-Walid in Transjordan, there are pictures of the last Visigothic king of Spain and other enemies of the Arabs as well as of dancers, musicians, and other entertainers, executed no doubt by Byzantine Syrians. Another such house built by Hisham (r. 724-743) at Khirbat al-Mafjar near Jericho and recently excavated has walls decorated with human and animal motifs. Plump dancing girls appear with lipstick and scarlet-painted finger and toe nails. But places of worship remained free from such innovations; only mosaic and calligraphy have been used as ceiling and wall decorations in these buildings.

Most Moslem theologians frowned on music considering it religiously unpraiseworthy, but to the masses "wine continued to be the body, music the soul, and joy their offspring." No sooner had the first awe inspired by Islam worn off than musicians and singers began to appear in Hejaz. To one of them, ibn-Surayj (634-726), was ascribed the introduction of the lute from Persia and the first use of the baton in directing musical performances. Originally a Turkish slave, ibn-Surayj became a protégé of al-Husayn's daughter, famous for her beauty. His teacher was ibn-Misjah (d. *ca.* 714), a Meccan negro client who had

Courtesy of Department of Antiquities, The Macmillan Company

A MOSAIC FLOOR AT KHIRBAT AL-MAFJAR   A stylized pomegranate tree has two gazelles grazing under it, while a third is attacked by a lion. Brilliantly hued, the mosaic is surrounded by a border which gives it a tapestry-like effect.

traveled in Syria and Persia and is said to have been the first to put Byzantine and Persian songs into Arabic. The annual pilgrimage afforded Meccan and Medinese artists an international occasion to display their talents.

The Umayyad court patronized a galaxy of musicians, singers, and entertainers some of whom were drawn from Hejaz. Himself a composer, Yazid, son of Mu'awiyah, initiated the practice of holding grand festivities in the palace which featured wine and song. Yazid II (r. 720-724), successor of the austere puritanical Umar II, reinstated song and music in public favor. By his time the wood-bellied lute, coming from Persia through Hira, had superseded the skin-bellied one. The wind instruments included the flute, horn, and reed pipe. The percussion instruments were represented by the square tambourine, especially favored by women, and by the drum and castanets. So widely spread was the cultivation of the musical art under the Umayyads that it provided their rivals for the caliphate, the Abbasids, with one of their most effective arguments in their propaganda against their "ungodliness."

BOOKS TO READ

Arnold, Thomas and Alfred Guillaume, eds., *The Legacy of Islam* (Oxford, reprint 1947).

Brockelmann, Carl, *History of the Islamic Peoples,* tr. Joel Carmichael and Moshe Perlmann (New York, 1947).

Browne, E. G., *Arabian Medicine* (Cambridge, 1921).

Hell, Joseph, *The Arab Civilization,* tr. S. Khuda Bukhsh (Cambridge, 1926).

Hitti, Philip K., *History of Syria, including Lebanon and Palestine,* 2nd ed. (London, 1957); *The Arabs: A Short History* (Chicago, 1956).

Lane-Poole, Stanley and Arthur Gilman, *The Moors in Spain* (New York, 1911).

Levy, Reuben, *The Sociology of Islam,* 2 vols. (London, 1933).

Lewis, Bernard, *The Arabs in History,* 3rd ed. (London, 1956).

Macdonald, Duncan B., *Muslim Theology, Jurisprudence and Constitutional Law* (New York, 1903).

Mez, Adam, *The Renaissance of Islam,* tr. S. Khuda Bukhsh and D. S. Margoliouth (London, 1937).

Tritton, A. S., *The Caliphs and their non-Muslim Subjects* (London, 1930).

Von Grunebaum, Gustavo E., *Medieval Islam* (Chicago, 1946).

Von Kremer, Alfred, *The Orient under the Caliphs,* tr. S. Khuda Bukhsh (Calcutta, 1920).

Wellhausen, J., *The Arab Kingdom and its Fall,* tr. Margaret G. Weir (Calcutta, 1927).

Zaydan, Jurji, tr. D. S. Margoliouth, *Umayyads and 'Abbasids* (Leyden, 1907).

XX *The Rise of the Abbasids*

The successors of al-Walid, with two or three exceptions were unworthy caliphs, incapable if not dissolute or degenerate. Yazid II (r. 720-724), brother of al-Walid, spent more time in the chase or over the wine cup than on state affairs; music and poetry attracted him more than the Koran. The sudden increase in wealth and the superabundance of slaves made indulgence in luxury the rule of the day among the royalty and aristocracy. The eunuch system, picked up from the conquered Byzantine provinces, made the harem institution possible. A son of al-Walid, Yazid III (744), was the first caliph born of a slave mother. His two successors, with the second of whom, Marwan II (r. 744-750), the caliphate terminated, were also so born. The characteristic vices of urban civilization, against which the Arabians had not yet developed immunity, were beginning to sap their vitality.

Toward the end of the period the national structure of the Arabian society began to show cracks all along the walls. The old centrifugal forces, including individualism, particularism, and tribal loyalty were reasserting themselves. North Arabians were aligned against South Arabians. The northerners were the earlier Moslems and preserved a consciousness of basic cultural and ethnic difference from the southerners. They had settled mostly in Iraq and Persia; the Qays tribe was a leading one among them. The southerners, mostly Yemenites, had preferred Syria. Before long the entire Arabian society became polarized into two camps: the Qays and Yemen. For centuries, under different names and in innumerable places from the Indies to the Atlantic, this tribal dualism, transformed into an alignment of two political parties was responsible for strife, bloodshed, and even the downfall of dynasties, as it was in the case of the Umayyads. The issue remained a living one in such places as Lebanon and Palestine until the eighteenth century.

A more subtle threat to the Umayyad throne was the Shiite dissidents, who never acquiesced in the established order and considered the Damascus caliphs ungodly usurpers. Even Sunni pietists shared the view about the worldliness of the Umayyads, charging them with deviation from the puritanical origin of Islam. The wholehearted devotion of the Shiite to the Alid cause made them the center of popular sympathy. But the largest and strongest block in the opposition was that of the socially and economically discontented clients, new converts, especially in Iraq and Persia, where the reforms of Umar II had not solved the problem. When the wars of conquest had ended and the Arabian military aristocracy had become obsolete, the way was open for a new social order based on a peace economy of trade and agriculture represented by officials, landowners, businessmen, and religious scholars largely recruited from the client group.

All these elements of opposition awaited a leader to render their anti-Umayyad activity effective. The leader appeared in the person of abu-al-Abbas, a descendant of a paternal uncle of the Prophet named al-Abbas. His family claimed at least as much right to the caliphate as the Umayyad, for Umayyah was but a second cousin of Muhammad's grandfather. Abu-al-Abbas sought to unite all opposition groups under a feigned theocracy and a promise of the return to orthodoxy.

THE REVOLUTION SPREADS

In 747 the long-contemplated uprising broke out first in Khurasan under the instigation of a Persian client from Iraq, named abu-Muslim al-Khurasani, who had served as Abbasid agent. Under his leadership the insurgents captured the capital Marv and swept through the entire country. In the meantime the Iraq uprising was led by abu-al-Abbas, to whom public homage was paid as a caliph in a Kufa mosque (October 749). Before the black banner of the Abbasids the white banner of the Umayyads was in retreat everywhere, even in Syria. At last Marwan II (r. 744-750), the fourteenth and last of his line, resolved on a desperate advance to stem the rising tide. With 12,000 loyal Syrian troops he reached the Great Zab, a tributary of the Tigris, where in January 750 he was decisively defeated. The proud capital, Damascus, surrendered after a brief siege. The fugitive caliph was caught hiding in a church in an Egyptian town and decapitated. His head and the insignia of the caliphate were forwarded to the Abbasid general who pursued a policy of extermination against the fallen house. Eighty members of the royal family were invited to a banquet near Jaffa and, while eating, were treacherously fallen upon and cut down. Leather covers were spread on the dead and dying and the Abbasid officers continued their repast to the accompaniment of human groans. Centuries before a soldier named Jehu in the service of King Ahab had exterminated the royal family, piled the heads of seventy princes in two heaps and started a new dynasty in Israel. Centuries later Muhammad Ali invited the Mamluks to his castle overlooking Cairo, destroyed one after the other and started the Egyptian royal family which ended in 1952. Not even the dead were spared. Caliphal tombs in Damascus and elsewhere, with the exception of those of Mu'awiyah and the pious Umar, were opened and their contents exhumed and desecrated.

The only person to escape the massacre was the nineteen-year-old Abd-al-Rahman, grandson of the tenth caliph. Pursued by Abbasid cavalry he dashed through the Euphrates, trudged southward through Syria, and in disguise tramped through Egypt and North Africa. After five years of wandering he landed in Spain (775), where he established himself as the undisputed master of the peninsula and inaugurated in Cordova the brilliant Umayyad dynasty.

With the fall of the Umayyads the Syrian hegemony passed away. Arab-Moslem orientation changed; the center of gravity in Islam shifted eastward to Iraq and Persia. The early Arabian aristocracy was replaced by a hierarchy drawn from the whole gamut of nationalities in the caliphate. The old Arabian Moslems and the new foreign converts were coalescing. Arabianism fell, but Islam continued and in its new international garb marched triumphantly on with Iranianism.

FIRST ABBASIDS

Abu-al-Abbas (r. 750-754) introduced the Abbasid dynasty, the third after the orthodox and the Umayyad and the most celebrated and longest lived (750-1258). The title he assumed, al-Saffah (bloodshedder), foreshadowed the new policy of force to be pursued by the incoming regime. Representing itself as a substitution in the form of a theocratic state for a defunct secular caliphate, the new government gave prominence in state affairs to theologians and canon lawyers and ruled as if by divine right. But its piety was assumed and its religiosity feigned. The Baghdad caliphs were no less worldly than their predecessors of Damascus. The fundamental difference lay somewhere else: The Umayyad empire was more Arabian and the Abbasid more international. Al-Saffah took up his residence first in Kufa and then in a special capital he built farther north on the Euphrates. In his early thirties he died of smallpox. He was succeeded by his brother al-Mansur (r. 754-775), the real founder of the dynasty. All the thirty-five successors of al-Mansur were his lineal descendants.

As often happens in revolutionary coalitions, the party on top finds it necessary to liquidate the dangerous leaders of disgruntled parties. Abu-Muslim, to whose sword the Abbasids owed their initial success, was such a leader. On a visit from the province of Khurasan, which he ruled almost independently, abu-Muslim was unceremoniously killed during an audience with the caliph. Two grandsons of al-Hasan, who headed dissatisfied Shiites in Medina and Kufa were also slaughtered. The realm was gradually pacified and consolidated, a task which was made easier by the secession of Spain. Thereafter, Abbasid authority did not extend far beyond Kairwan; Islam and the caliphate were no more coterminous.

An enduring monument to al-Mansur was the city of Baghdad, which he founded on the site of a Persian village on the west bank of the Tigris. The site was a strategic one, lying in that valley which had seen the rise and fall of many a mighty and opulent capital. Within a few decades the city of al-Mansur had grown into an emporium of trade and industry and a political and cultural center of prime importance. It became a worthy heir of Ur, Babylon, Nineveh, and Ctesiphon, the ruins of which had served as a quarry for building the new city. In a century it numbered about a million people. After many vicissitudes Baghdad was resuscitated as a capital for the new Iraqi kingdom at the conclusion of the first World War.

In his new capital, surrounded by a high triple wall and a deep moat, the Abbasid caliph set up his throne surrounded by a Khurasanian bodyguard and ruling more like a Persian Chosroes than a Byzantine monarch or an Arabian shaykh. The system of government was patterned after that of the Sasanids. Persian titles, Persian wives and wines, Persian mistresses, and Persian garments became fashionable. Only in two fields did the Arabians hold their own; Islam remained the state religion and Arabic the official tongue. An important government institution that developed at this time was the vizirate, whose first incumbent was a Shiite Persian, Khalid ibn-Barmak, founder of the first vizirial family in Islam. Under the caliph, the vizir exercised the chief executive authority in the state. Khalid headed the department of finance under al-Mansur and served as his chief counselor. Fabulous fortunes were amassed by his successors, whose generosity matched their wealth. Canals, mosques, and other public works owed their existence to the munificence of a Barmakid. Their banquets and gifts to friends became proverbial. The phrase, "generous as a Barmakid," can still be heard in the Near East. Their popularity reached the danger point—from the caliphal standpoint. The task of doing something about this fell on the strong-willed Harun, grandson of al-Mansur, in whose political firmament no two suns could exist.   In 803 the severed head of the family leader was impaled on one of the Baghdad bridges and the two halves of his corpse on two other bridges. Other influential members of the family were apprehended and imprisoned for life; their property was confiscated.   The family became extinct, but the institution continued.

THE PRIME OF THE ABBASIDS

Like other dynasties in Islam the Abbasid reached the prime of its political life not long after its establishment.   In its case the zenith was reached under the fifth caliph Harun (r. 786-809) and his son al-Mamun (r. 813-833).   It was chiefly due to the courts of these two luminous caliphs that the Abbasids acquired a halo in the popular imagination that no other rulers in Islam ever acquired.

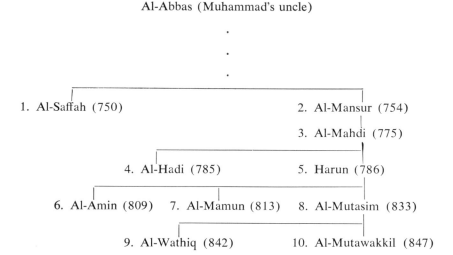

Al-Abbas (Muhammad's uncle)

1. Al-Saffah (750)   2. Al-Mansur (754)

3. Al-Mahdi (775)

4. Al-Hadi (785)   5. Harun (786)

6. Al-Amin (809)   7. Al-Mamun (813)   8. Al-Mutasim (833)

9. Al-Wathiq (842)   10. Al-Mutawakkil (847)

Harun had distinguished himself before coming to the throne.   In 782 he led the Arab forces for his caliph-father through Asia Minor to the Bosporus.   The weakened condition of the Umayyad caliphate in its last days and the capital's transfer eastward had encouraged the Byzantines to renew their century-old struggle against Islam.   Constantine V (r. 741-775), son of Leo the Isaurian, had in 745 taken the offensive and carried the war into Syria and in a subsequent campaign into Armenia.   The entire Moslem line of frontier fortifications from Armenia to Syria retreated as the imperial troops pushed back the Arab army along the entire border of Asia Minor.

Harun's father was the first Abbasid to resume the "holy war" against the eternal enemy of Islam. At that time Irene held the regency in the name of her nine-year-old son Constantine VI (r. 780-797) and was forced to conclude a singularly humiliating treaty involving the payment of a heavy tribute in semiannual installments. Harun won the honorific title of al-Rashid (follower of the right path). His was the fourth and last Arab army that threatened the Byzantine capital.[1] This final attempt to complete the conquest of the Greco-Roman Empire by the capture of its major city was no more successful than the earlier ones. Irene was interested in the iconoclastic controversy introduced by Leo III (r. 717-741), who as a north Syrian was probably influenced by Moslem iconoclasm. A Greek historian describes Leo as "Saracen-minded." In 721 the Umayyad caliph had issued an edict against "image-worship" which he tried to apply among his Christian subjects. The forbiddance of the religious use of images resulted from the Byzantine emperor's desire to check the alarming spread of monasticism which attracted an excessive number of men from active economic life and concentrated wealth in the monks' cloisters. Under Leo III's successors the controversy became violent. Images were whitewashed or destroyed; resisting monks were exiled, imprisoned, or even executed; and their monasteries were closed.

Irene, who blinded her son before putting him to death, replaced him (797-802) as the first empress in Byzantine history and was in turn deposed and banished by her minister of finance Nicephorus (r. 802-811). The new emperor repudiated the terms of the treaty with Harun signed by Irene as regent and again as empress and subjected his realm to a series of ravaging campaigns concluded in 806 by the imposition of an ignominious tax on the emperor himself and on other members of his household. The year 806 may be taken as marking the topmost point in Abbasid power, as 732 saw the Umayyad reach the pinnacle of their power.[2]

THE GLORY THAT WAS BAGHDAD

History and legend have conspired to make of the court of Harun al-Rashid and his son al-Mamun the most glamorous one in Islam. In the midst of the old city and covering about a third of its area stood the royal palace with its annexes for harems, eunuchs, and functionaries. Especially on festivals, weddings, receptions for foreign envoys, and other ceremonial occasions did the courtly wealth and splendor make their full display. The princely munificence of Harun, *beau idéal* of Islamic kingship, and of his immediate successors attracted

[1] As stated above, p. 224.
[2] See above, p. 224.

musicians, singers, dancers, wits, and poets from all over the realm.
Ibrahim al-Mawsili (of Mosul) headed the roster of musician-singers.
Arab chroniclers consider him the first in Islam "to beat the rhythm with
a wand and to be able to detect the ill-tuned instrument of a flute-player
among thirty ones and ask him to tighten the second string." His
patron caliph, they say, assigned him a monthly salary of 10,000 silver
pieces and for a single song rewarded him with 100,000 pieces. Here
is a rendition of couplets sung by him on the accession of Harun and
the appointment of Yahya al-Barmaki to the vizirate:

> Th' affrighted sun erstwhile had fled,
>   And hid his radiant face in night;
> A cheerless gloom the world o'erspread—
>   But Harun came and all was bright.
> Again the sun shoots forth its rays;
>   Nature is decked in beauty's robe:
> For mighty Harun's scepter sways,
>   And Yahia's arm sustains the globe.[3]

Other salaried musicians, singers, and entertainers furnished the theme
for many fantastic anecdotes immortalized in the *Arabian Nights* and
other works of Arabic literature.[4]

INTELLECTUAL AWAKENING: TRANSLATION

The luxurious scale of living, the dazzling bounty of the court, and
the victory of Moslem over Byzantine arms make this period a favorite
in Arab history and fiction. But what has rendered it significant in
world affairs is the fact that it witnessed the most momentous intellectual awakening in the history of Islam. The only period comparable
to it is the nineteenth to the twentieth century under the impact of the
West. The stimuli at this time came primarily from Hellenic sources,
although there were also Indo-Persian and Syrian ones. The awakening
was inaugurated by translations from Persian, Sanskrit, Syriac, and
Greek. In a few decades the Arabic-reading people had at their
disposal the most precious treasures enshrined in the literatures of these
languages. All this took place while Charlemagne and his lords in the
West were reportedly dabbling with the art of writing their names.
Through these new acquisitions Islam was enabled to absorb the main
features of the Semitic, Persian, and Hellenistic civilizations. In so
doing it no doubt lost much of its own primitive character, which
breathed the spirit of the desert and bore the stamp of Arabian nation-

---

[3] A. Clouston, ed., *Arabian Poetry for English Readers* (Glasgow, 1881),
p. 110.
[4] Cf. below, p. 267.

alism, but it meanwhile took its place in the medieval cultural unit which linked Europe with Western Asia. This entire culture, it should be recalled, was fed by a single stream, a stream with sources in ancient Egypt, Babylonia, Phoenicia, and Judaea flowing to Greece to receive new tributaries and then returning to the East in the form of Hellenism. That same stream, enriched by Moslem contributions, made its way back to Europe through Spain and Sicily and helped bring about the modern renaissance of Europe.

From India came the first impulse to Moslem study of the stars in the form of an astronomical treatise translated into Arabic under al-Mansur. An Arabic writing Persian, al-Khwarizmi (d. *ca.* 850), based his widely-known astronomical tables on this work and syncretized the Indian and Greek systems of astronomy, adding his own observations. Revised by a Moslem Spanish astronomer and translated into Latin by Adelard of Bath (1126) in Toledo, the astronomical tables of al-Khwarizmi served as a basis for other works in the West as well as in the East. Together with the Indian treatise came a mathematical one which introduced into the Moslem world the so-called Arabic numerals. These were used by al-Khwarizmi in his textbook on algebra (from Ar. *al-Jabr*), the first of its kind. This book was again translated in Spain in the twelfth century and was responsible for introducing into the West the numerals called Arabic by Europeans and Hindi (Indian) by Arabs.

From Persia came the earliest literary work in Arabic extant, a collection of delightful fables ascribed to Bidpai, the philosopher, and intended to instruct princes in the laws of polity by means of animal tales. The original work came to Persia from India, together with the game of chess, in the days of Khosrau Anushirwan (r. 531-578).[5] Since both the original and its Persian rendition were lost, the Arabic translation became the basis of translations into some forty European and Asiatic tongues. Icelandic was one of the last languages into which this work was put. La Fontaine, the French fabulist of the seventeenth century, acknowledges his indebtedness to Bidpai for the new material in his collection. Chess was likewise introduced into Europe by Arabs through Spain. The first description of this game in a European language appears in a book by Alfonso X, king of Castile and Leon (r. 1252-1284), one of the greatest apostles of Moslem learning in Christian Spain.

Of all the treasures available to the world of Islam at this time the intellectual legacy of Greece was unquestionably the most precious.

---

[5] Treated above, pp. 173, 181.

By appropriating it Islam entered upon its richest heritage subsequent to its earlier appropriation of the Hebrew-Christian cultural legacy. This made of the Moslems of the Arab caliphate, rather than the Christians of the East Roman Empire, the true successors and developers of the Hellenistic philosophy. Christian philosophy had driven out the Hellenistic one. But in Islam as in Christianity the fundamental notion of morality was obedience to divine law and the corresponding conception of God's will as essentially the enabling of righteousness to prevail remained unaffected. The Greek and Roman ideas of morality were far removed from these. It was only natural that the Syrians, who knew Greek, particularly the Christian Nestorians should serve as mediators and purveyors. The first translated Greek into Syriac and then into Arabic. The apogee of the translation movement was reached under al-Mamun, whose espousal of the Mutazalite doctrine[6] led him to seek justification for his position in Greek philosophy. He reputedly sent emissaries into Asia Minor and as far as Constantinople in quest of material. In 830 he established an institution of learning, "house of wisdom," which combined the functions of library, academy, and translation bureau. No more important institution of learning had been established since the foundation of the Alexandrian Museum over a thousand years earlier.[7] The importance of translation in the flow of human thought should not be underestimated; it provides the transport and without transport there can be no traffic.

Translators into Arabic showed no interest in Greek drama and poetry chiefly because of the close association of such material with Greek religion and mythology. Homer was translated into Arabic under Harun's father, but it did not survive. Arab interest took more practical form. Greek medicine, represented by Galen;[8] mathematics and allied subjects, for which Euclid and Ptolemy stood;[9] and philosophy, originated by Plato and Aristotle and expounded by Neo-Platonists, —these served as starting points on the Arab voyage of intellectual discovery.

The shaykh of translators was a Nestorian Christian from Hira named Hunayn ibn-Ishaq (Joannitius, 809-873). Hunayn was the superintendent of al-Mamun's library-academy. In this capacity he supervised the entire scientific work of the institution. His main interests were in medicine and philosophy. He was himself a practicing physician. The usual procedure was for him to do the initial translation from

[6] Treated above, p. 231.
[7] See above, pp. 128, 151.
[8] Cited above, p. 159.
[9] Cited above, pp. 129, 159.

Courtesy of Princeton University Library

GALEN IN ARABIC First lines of chapter in Hunayn's translation. Copied 1176-1177, this manuscript antedates any Greek or Latin ones extant and contains sections not yet translated into any European language.

Greek into Syriac and then have his son and nephew translate into Arabic. He and his school were responsible for rendering into the language of Islam the works of Galen and Hippocrates (d. ca. 377 B.C.) in medicine, Dioscorides (d. ca. A.D. 50) in botany, Plato's *Republic,* and Aristotle's *Categories* and *Physics.* The seven books of Galen's anatomy, lost in the original, have been preserved in the Arabic. Besides a monthly stipend of five hundred gold pieces, Hunayn is said to have received from his patron the weight in gold of every book he translated.

Hunayn was not only a great scholar but a fine character, a flower of Christian manhood under the caliphate. As private physician of al-Mutawakkil (r. 847-861), he was ordered by the caliph to concoct a poison for an enemy. On refusal he was committed to jail for a year at the end of which he was threatened with death if he persisted in his refusal. His reply was brief but uncompromising: "I have knowledge only in what is beneficial and have studied naught else." Surprised, the caliph, who then claimed that he was simply testing his physician's integrity, asked as to what prevented him from complying. Hunayn replied it was firstly his religion, which decreed that one should do good even to his enemies, and secondly his profession, instituted for the benefit of humanity and limited to bringing relief and cure.

In addition to Nestorians Syria produced a heathen community, the pseudo-Sabians of Harran, who labored in the translation field. This community was somehow included among the dhimmis. As star-worshipers, the pseudo-Sabians had special interest in the study of astronomy and mathematics. The dean of translators in this school was Thabit ibn-Qurrah (*ca.* 836-901), who had a patron in a successor of al-Mutawakkil. He is credited with having translated into Arabic—in collaboration with his son, grandsons, and other disciples—the bulk of the Greek mathematical and astronomical works including those of Archimedes (d. 212 B.C.) and Euclid. The work on Euclid was probably a revision of an early one by Hunayn.

ORIGINATION: MEDICINE

The period of translation, lasting roughly for a century ending in 850, was followed by one of original contributions. The two intellectual movements made of Baghdad a scientific capital of the world. They gave it a rank next to Jerusalem, its religious capital; Athens, its philosophical capital; and Rome, its legal one. The contention that the Arabs were transmitters of culture loses any derogatory implication when it is realized that from the standpoint of the history of thought transmission is of no less importance than origination. The impact of origination is on the here and the now. Of how much avail would the Decalogue, the Sermon on the Mount, the philosophy of Aristotle, the Code of Justinian have been to the world had they not been preserved and passed from one generation to another.

In theology, law, philology, and linguistics Arab scholars had started their creative work earlier.[10] Now they began to build up their scientific systems on the basis of material assimilated from the translated works and adapted to their needs and ways of thinking. The independent work they did in medicine, astronomy, mathematics, and geography was more conspicuous than that in philosophy.

Abbasid interest in scientific medicine began when al-Mansur, afflicted with a stomach ailment that baffled his physicians, summoned from Jundi-Shapur the dean of its hospital, ibn-Bakhtishu. The city was noted for its academy of medicine as well as for its school of philosophy.[11] Its science was based on the Greek tradition, but its language was Aramaic. Ibn-Bakhtishu, a Nestorian Syrian, became court physician and the founder of a brilliant family which for six or

---

[10] As noted above, pp. 230 *seq.*
[11] See above, p. 181.

seven generations almost monopolized the court medical practice. Scientific knowledge in those days, like jewelry making, was considered a family affair and passed on from father to son. A grandson of ibn-Bakhtishu was chief physician under Harun al-Rashid. He successfully treated a favorite slave of his patron for hysterical paralysis by pretending to disrobe her in public. The first hospital in Islam[12] was modeled after the Persian type. Other hospitals, about thirty, followed in the capitals of the provinces. Some of these had facilities for the study of medicine. The ibn-Bakhtishu family evidently maintained its Christian creed. Its founder had told the caliph he preferred the company of his fathers, be they in heaven or in hell.

The prevalence of eye diseases in Iraq and other Moslem lands made early Arab physicians concentrate on their study and treatment. Of all the organs of the body, the eye was the one best understood by them. The earliest extant textbook on ophthamology, recently translated into English, is ascribed to Hunayn ibn-Ishaq. Dissection was not encouraged by Islam. We hear of a Christian physician of a brother-successor of al-Mamun who dissected an ape which his patron had received as a present from Nubia.

Another distinguished physician of the Baghdad school was al-Razi (Rhazes, 865-925), so called after his birthplace al-Rayy (near Tehran, capital of modern Persia). In choosing a site for a new hospital in the capital al-Razi is said to have hung up shreds of meat in different places and selected the spot where they showed the least signs of putrefaction. This physician was the first to make a clinical distinction between measles and smallpox. His treatise on that subject is the earliest of its kind. His encyclopedic work on medicine *al-Hawi* (the comprehensive) was first translated into Latin in Sicily in 1279; and, under the title *Continens,* was repeatedly printed for use as a textbook. The last edition appeared in Venice in 1542. These and other works entitle al-Razi to his reputation as one of the keenest original thinkers and greatest physicians of medieval times. Another Arab physician of Persian origin was al-Majusi (d. 994), known to the West as Haly Abbas, a corruption of his first Arabic name. His last name, "the Magian," indicates his Zoroastrian origin. For his royal Buwayhid[13] patron, al-Majusi wrote *al-Kitab al-Malaki* (the royal book), a treasure-house of the science and practice of medicine. It advanced medical knowledge by presenting, among other points, a rudimentary conception of the capillary system and proof that, in delivery, the child does not come out by itself but is pushed by the muscular contraction

---

[12] Cf. above, p. 233.
[13] See below, p. 294.

of the womb. In its Arabic original and Latin translation the book was studied in both East and West until superseded by ibn-Sina's *al-Qanun* (the canon).

Arab science reached its highest point in ibn-Sina (Avicenna, 980-1037), physician, philologist, scientist and poet. He is best known as a philosopher-physician. Even now the designation *hakim* is used through the world of Islam for both wise man and doctor of medicine. Born into an Ismaili[14] family near Bukhara, ibn-Sina when still in his teens was accorded the privilege of studying in the library of a Samanid[15] ruler. He seems to have devoured its contents before embarking upon his professional career when he was in his early twenties. No less than ninety-nine titles are ascribed to him, covering philosophy, medicine, astronomy, theology, philology, and art. *Al-Qanun,* a codification of the entire Greco-Arabic medical thought, heads the list. It contains a clinical distinction between mediastinitis and pleurisy, a recognition of the contagious nature of tuberculosis, and of the spreading of disease by soil and water. Its materia medica considers some seven hundred and sixty drugs. Translated into Latin by Gerard of Cremona in twelfth century Toledo, the *Canon* gradually displaced the works of Galen, al-Razi, and al-Majusi as a text for medical education. In the last thirty years of the fifteenth century it passed through fifteen Latin editions. In the East it remained as the chief medical guide until the nineteenth century. A Spanish Arab, ibn-al-Khatib of Granada (d. 1374), wrote a remarkable treatise on the theory of infection as the Black Death devastated Europe and the people stood by helplessly considering it an act of God. From investigation and observation he described the spread of the disease from the one first afflicted to those with whom he had been in contact.

The Moslems of the East produced no internationally known surgeon, but those of the West did in the person of al-Zahrawi (L. Abulcasis, d. *ca.* 1013), court physician of the Umayyad caliphate at its height in Cordova. In his medical book al-Zahrawi included a surgical section in which he introduced or emphasized such then new practices as the cauterization of wounds and the crushing of stones inside the bladder. In its Latin translation this section held its own for centuries as the manual of surgery in such early schools of medicine as the ones in Salerno, Italy and Montpellier, France. In Oxford it was published as late as 1778. Al-Zahrawi is rightly considered the greatest surgeon medieval Islam produced.

[14] On this sect see below, pp. 282-283.
[15] See below, p. 292.

ALCHEMY AND BOTANY

Arabs excelled in alchemy and botany which were closely allied to medicine.   Alchemy (Ar. *al-kimiya*) was an Arab "science" [16] founded by a Kufan Jabir ibn-Hayyan (Geber, fl. 776).   Many of the physicians, including al-Razi, were also alchemists.   Jabir, more than any other worker in this field, clearly recognized the importance of experimentation.   He scientifically described the two principal operations of chemistry—calcination and reduction—and improved the methods of melting and crystallization.   Unfortunately he acted on the assumption that a base metal such as tin could be transmuted into a precious one such as gold by means of a mysterious substance—the philosophers' stone—in the search of which he wasted his time and energy.   Most of the hundred or so extant works in Latin and Arabic which pass under Jabir's name are no doubt spurious.   For generations after his death Jabir dominated alchemical thought.   His followers continued the quest for the two will-o'-the-wisps: the philosophers' stone and the elixir (Ar. *al-iksir*) of life intended to make young of the old and to prolong life indefinitely.   Nuclear scientists report progress on the solution of the metal problem, toward the realization of the other dream modern chemists offer only hormones and vitamins.

Al-Majusi, ibn-Sina and other medical authors devoted sections of their works to materia medica, but we know of no major scholars in the East who dedicated themselves to the study of plants.   The Arab West, however, produced one of the greatest botanists and pharmacists of the Middle Ages, ibn al Baytar of Malaga (d. 1248).   As a herbalist ibn-al-Baytar traveled in Spain, North Africa, Egypt, Syria, and Asia Minor.   The two books on materia medica and simple remedies, dedicated to his Ayyubid patron in Damascus, embody his researches supplemented with Greek data.   They comprise remedies from the animal, vegetable, and mineral worlds and include considerations of 1400 items, of which 200 plants were novelties.

No Arab did any serious work in zoology.   Two Arabic authors, one Iraqi and the other Egyptian, entitled their books "On Animals," but these were more literary than scientific works.   However, the Iraqi, al-Jahiz (d. *ca.* 868), knew how to obtain ammonia from animal offal by dry distillation and entertained a faint idea of later theories of evolution, adaptation, and animal psychology.   He was a radical Mutazilite, who founded a sect bearing his name, and a prolific man of letters, one of the most quoted in Arabic literature.   His learning, wit,

[16] Cf. above, p. 233.

and originality made him widely known in his day, but his unattractive-
ness (his name means the goggle-eyed) made al-Mutawakkil change
his mind about appointing him tutor to his sons.

ASTRONOMY AND MATHEMATICS

Next to medicine and its adjunct sciences the most conspicuous
creative work of the Arabs was in astronomy and mathematics. In
connection with his "house of wisdom" [17] al-Mamun erected in Baghdad
an observatory where scholars verified the length of the solar year, the
precession of the equinoxes, the obliquity of the ecliptic, and other
basic elements first discussed in Ptolemy's *Almagest*.[18] Al-Mamun also
built another observatory on the mount overlooking Damascus. Thirty
others followed. The equipment was simple: quadrant, astrolobe, and
dial globe. Al-Mamun's astronomers performed one of the most
delicate geodetic operations when they measured the length of a terrestrial degree. The study yielded fifty-six and two-thirds Arabic miles
as the length of a degree of the meridian—a remarkably accurate
result. The study assumed the roundness of the earth and was intended
to determine its size and its circumference. Al-Khwarizmi was among
those who participated in this operation. Another astronomer of this
period was al-Farghani (Alfraganus), born in Transoxiana and probably
a Turk. Al-Farghani was sent (861) by al-Mutawakkil to al-Fustat to
supervise the erection of a Nilometer. His book on astronomy, rather
short and readily intelligible, was rendered into Latin in Spain in 1135
and also into Hebrew; for a time it attained unparalleled circulation.

In astrology, a handmaiden of astronomy, men all over the world of
Islam continued to work. A Khurasanian, abu-Mashar (d. 886),
heads the distinguished list. The twelfth century translation of four of
his works into Latin made him the most cited authority on the subject
in the Middle Ages. Under the name Albumasar he figured as a
prophet in Christian iconography. Abu-Mashar held the popular belief
that astral influence controlled the events of life and the death of everything, but he rendered a major scientific service: He communicated to
Europe the fact that the laws of the tides were based of the relation to
the moon's rising and setting. Astrological research by abu-Mashar and
his successors necessitated the determination of latitudes and longitudes
of places all over the world and to that extent had scientific value.
Abu-Mashar's contemporary Muhammad ibn-Musa, one of three learned
brothers, was sent by the caliph to Ephesus on a curious research project: investigating the cave in which the Christian Seven Sleepers found

[17] Cited above, p. 246.
[18] Referred to above, p. 159.

refuge with their dog against Decius' persecution (250) and did not wake up for over a hundred years, when it became safe for Christians.

Building on the scientific foundations laid by Eastern Moslems, Western coreligionists advanced knowledge in this field as they did in medicine. Al-Zarqali of Toledo (L. Arzachel, d. *ca.* 1087), who revised the planetary tables of al-Khwarizmi, was probably the astronomer who reduced Ptolemy's exaggerated estimate of the Mediterranean as 62°—already cut by al-Khwarizmi to almost 52°—to the approximately correct figure of 42°. He was followed by ibn-Aflah (L. filius Afflæ) of Seville (d. *ca.* 1145), who sharply criticized Ptolemy and correctly asserted that Mercury and Venus had no visible parallaxes.

Arab astronomers have left on the skies immortal traces discernible to any reader of the names of the stars. Acrab (from Ar. for scorpion), Algedi (for kid), Altair (for flyer) Deneb (for tail), Pherkad (for calf) serve as illustrations. Besides there are such technical terms of Arabic origin as azimuth, nadir, and zenith. Our mathematical vocabulary includes such borrowed terms as algebra, algorism (from al-Khwarizmi), and cipher or zero as well as the translated ones illustrated by surd (deaf) and sine (pocket). An English mathematician, Robert of Chester (fl. *ca.* 1150), was the first to use Latin *sinus* in its Arabic trigonometrical acceptance. The diffusion of the Arabic numerals, including the zero from Spain in Europe, was slow. Throughout the eleventh, twelfth, and early thirteenth centuries Christian mathematicians persisted in the use of Roman numerals and the abacus or only made a compromise with the new system. An Italian Leonardo Fibonacci of Pisa published in 1202 a work which became a landmark in the introduction of Arabic numerals and marked the beginning of European mathematics. Leonardo had a Moslem for teacher and traveled in North Africa. The zero and Arabic numerals lie behind the progress achieved since then by the science of calculation.

In medicine translation from Arabic works was responsible for the introduction into European languages of such words as julep, rob, syrup, and soda. "Soda" is a corruption of an Arabic term meaning splitting headache; it was first used in Latin in that sense and latter used for a headache remedy. Other technical terms, such as dura mater and pia mater are translations. Chemical vocabulary abounds in words of Arabic etymology: alcohol, alembic, alkali, antimony, and tutty.

SOCIAL SCIENCE

In history, biography, human geography, and other social sciences Arabic authors made distinct contributions but their works found no translators in the period of translation. The first complete work in universal history was undertaken by a Persian from Tabaristan, al-Tabari (838-923), who arranged the material chronologically under the successive years of the hegira. For his monumental work al-Tabari drew from extant sources, translations from Persian oral tradition, and his own travels in Persia, Iraq, Syria, and Egypt. His history, published in fifteen volumes, is indispensable to any worker in this field. The first Arab historian to use the topical method, as against the annalistic, was al-Masudi of Baghdad (d. 956), styled the Herodotus of the Arabs. In common with other Moslem scholars of the day, al-Masudi engaged in a "journey in quest of learning" which took him in Asia as far as India and Ceylon and in Africa to Zanzibar. Such journeys were often undertaken in connection with the holy pilgrimage. His thirty-volume work, surviving only in an epitome, is an encyclopedic historico-geographical compilation characterized by unusual catholicity and intellectual curiosity. Especially noteworthy are his views on gradation between minerals, plants, and animals and his assertion that what is now dry land had been sea and what is sea had been changed into dry land in the course of time and as a result of physical forces.

Islam gave stimulus to the study of geography by the extent of its conquests, the institution of the holy pilgrimage, the orientation of the mosques, and the determination of the direction of the Kaaba for prayer purposes. Between the mid-seventh and the mid-ninth centuries Moslem traders had penetrated by land and sea eastward as far as China, westward to the farthest coasts of Africa and Zanzibar, and northward into Russia. In a work written in 851 a merchant from Siraf on the Persian Gulf gives us the earliest Arabic report on China and the coast lands of India. One interesting item therein is the use of fingerprints as signatures by Chinese. The cycle of stories around the name of Sindbad the Sailor was built up from the inflated and colored reports of travelers and traders. The earliest reliable account of Russia was given in 921 by an envoy of an Abbasid caliph to the king of the Bulgars along the Volga. The bulk of the account has been reproduced in the monumental geographic dictionary of Yaqut, considered the greatest of Arab geographers.

Yaqut (1179-1229) started his life as a slave of a Syrian merchant from Hama. His last name, al-Rumi, betrays his Greek origin. For his master Yaqut traveled as a salesman-clerk; after emancipation he continued his travels as a copyist and seller of manuscripts. The year 1219-1220 found him at Khwarizm at the time of the Tartar invasion before which, in the words of a biographer, he had to flee "as naked as he shall be when raised from the dust of the grave on the day of the resurrection." Finally he settled at Mosul to compile his encyclopedic dictionary in which place names are alphabetically arranged and the entries are enriched by valuable information from history, ethnography, philology, and natural science.

From Hindu geographers the Arabs picked up and perpetuated the notion that the known world had a center, a cupola or summit located in India and equally distant from the four cardinal points. This theory found its way into a Latin work published in 1410 whence Christopher Columbus acquired the doctrine that the earth was pear-shaped and that on the western hemisphere, opposite the Indian cupola, was a corresponding elevated center.

PHILOSOPHY

Moslem philosophy—if it could be so called—was in its early stage conditioned by and subjected to religion. The philosophers were theologians. The introduction of Aristotle, Plato, and their intellectual progeny produced a new type of philosophy and with it the term *falsafah*. The earliest representative of this type was al-Kindi, who flourished in ninth century Baghdad and was called "the philosopher of the Arabs" because of his pure Arab descent. Al-Kindi endeavored in Neo-Platonic fashion to combine the views of Plato and Aristotle and harmonize them with Islam. His principal work, however, was on geometrical and physical optics, which influenced Roger Bacon. Al-Kindi's treatises on the theory of music are the earliest extant in Arabic. The work of harmonizing Greek philosophy and Islam begun by al-Kindi was continued by a Turk, al-Farabi, and completed by a Persian, ibn Sina.

Al-Farabi (Pharabius, d. 950), who was born in Transoxiania, prospered in the Hamdanid[19] court at Aleppo. The system he worked out was a syncretism of Platonism, Aristotelianism, and Moslem Sufism;[20] it earned him the title of "the second teacher"—after Aristotle. In two works inspired by Plato's *Republic* and Aristotle's *Politics*, he presented his concept of a model city as a hierarchical organism analogous to the human body. The sovereign, who is perfect morally and intellectually, corresponds to the heart and is served by functionaries who are in turn served by others still lower. The happiness of the citizen is the object of the association in this ideal city.

The greatest Aristotelian philosopher Islam produced was ibn-Rushd (Averroës, 1126-1198) of Cordova and Seville. Ibn-Rushd was also

[19] Treated below, p. 306.
[20] Treated below, pp. 284-285.

an astronomer and a physician; he is generally considered the most eminent representative of Islamic culture in Europe. His work on medicine recognizes the principle of immunity in cases of smallpox and correctly explains the function of the retina. In philosophy he was more of a commentator than an originator. Using the works of Aristotle, in their Baghdad Arabic translation, and keeping the general framework and in part the titles, ibn-Rushd paraphrased the contents and made them palatable to his reading audience. His commentaries were rendered from Hebrew into Latin and have been chiefly preserved in those two languages. He was therefore more influential in the West than in the East. To the Europeans he became "the commentator," as Aristotle was "the teacher." Though Latin translations of Hebrew renditions of Arabic commentaries upon an Arabic translation of a Syriac translation of a Greek original, ibn-Rushd's works nonetheless agitated the minds of Christian schoolmen and scholars as no other works had. For four centuries beginning at the end of the twelfth, Averroism, ibn-Rushd's philosophy, held its own as the dominant school of philosophical thought despite opposition from Moslem, Christian, and Jewish orthodox circles. In fact the intellectual movement initiated by this Spanish Arab continued to be a force in the lives of Europeans until the birth of modern science.

Ibn-Rushd, last among the major Moslem philosophers, was a mild rationalist. He claimed the right to subject knowledge, except revealed dogmas of faith, to the judgment of reason. But he was by no means a free-thinker or unbeliever. His view of the process of creation by God, for instance, was evolutionary but in terms of eternity not in terms of days. It was in this borderland between religion and science that Arabs made original contributions to philosophy. Since they were not hampered by centralized ecclesiastical authority, Arab thinkers from al-Kindi down to ibn-Rushd were more free than their Christian counterparts to work toward harmonizing and reconciling traditional religious beliefs with the results of scientific research and rationalistic thinking.

A Jewish contemporary and fellow Cordovan of ibn-Rushd, Maimonides (1135-1204), had the same approach to Judaism. Prophetic visions he explained as psychical experiences. Maimonides was also an eminent physician and was invited to Cairo by Saladin to become the court physician. Indeed he stands out as the most distinguished of the Hebrew physicians and philosophers of the Arab epoch. His works, with one major exception, were written in Arabic, in which he is known as ibn-Maymun. On his death at Cairo he was carried, in accordance with his will, on hands over the route earlier traversed by his first namesake to be buried in Tiberias. His unpretentious tomb is still visited by throngs of pilgrims, while the Cairo synagogue bearing his name still provides a "cure" for ailing believers who spend the night in its underground chamber.

Translated into Hebrew and thence into Latin Maemonides' works exercised far-reaching influence in space and time. Traces of that influence are detectable in the writings of such celebrated scholastic philosophers as Albertus Magnus of the Dominican order and Duns Scotus, whose system long contended for supremacy with that founded by Thomas Aquinas, and in the writings among modern philosophers of the Dutch Spinoza and the German Kant. The works of ibn-Rushd and Maimonides rendered of medieval philosophy but one entity expressed in three languages—Arabic, Hebrew, and Latin.

JURISPRUDENCE

The Arabs were the only medieval peoples other than the Romans who cultivated jurisprudence as a science and thus evolved an independent system. But that system, called *fiqh,* was closely tied to the Koran and tradition (*hadith*).[21] These two formed the main and primary sources. Islam itself is a legislative system. Some 200 of the 6000 verses in the Koran are strictly legislative.[22] Numerous as they were these statutes, supplemented by a record of the sayings and doings of the Prophet, could not cover all civil, criminal, political, and financial cases that confronted the expanded Islam. New conditions and changing circumstances necessitated resorting to new principles: deduction from analogy, acceptance of the consensus of opinion (what we would call public opinion), and the equity of the judge. Soon different schools of legal thought arose and finally crystallized around four rites. While differing in their stress on the secondary principles, the primary one—the Koran—remained paramount throughout.

The school of Medina, naturally conservative, attached special importance to hadith as next to the Koran. Its leader was Malik ibn-Anas (715-795). The Malikite rite spread into and dominated Hejaz, North Africa, and Spain; it still holds its own today from the Suez to the Atlantic. The Iraq school was more liberal. Founded by a grandson of a Persian slave, abu-Hanifah (d. 767), it insisted on the right of juridical speculation—particularly analogical deduction—leading to what in modern terminology is called legal fiction. To the Hanafite rite almost one half of the world of Sunmite Islam belongs. Ottoman Turkey was its fort. Turkey together with India and Central Asia, still

---

[21] Mentioned above, pp. 198 *seq.*
[22] Noted before, p. 191.

adheres to it. Between these two schools arose a third, the Shafiite, which accepted speculation but with reservations. Al-Shafii (767-820), who was born in Gaza and who traced his descent to the Quraysh, studied under Malik in Medina, worked in Baghdad, and died in Cairo, where his tomb at the foot of the Muqattam is still the object of pilgrimage. His system dominates east Africa, Lower Egypt, Palestine, South Arabia, and the East Indies.

The last of the four orthodox rites to which the community of Islam —exclusive of the Shiah—belongs was founded by Ahmad ibn-Hanbal of Baghdad, a pupil of al-Shafii but a representative of uncompromising adherence to the letter of the hadith. His staunch support of conservative orthodoxy made him a natural enemy of the Mutazilites, then dominant in Iraq under al-Mamun,[23] and landed him in jail. To the inquisition he was led in chains and there scourged. His funeral, reportedly attended by 800,000 men and 60,000 women, attests to the veneration in which he was held, a veneration that is still manifest in the caravans of pilgrims to his tomb. The 28,000 hadiths he assembled, commented upon, and compiled enjoyed wide circulation, but today the Hanbalite rite claims no considerable following other than the Wahhabis of Nejd and Hejaz.

In a community—like that of Islam—with no church, no clergy, and no centralized authority, consensus of opinion naturally assumes high importance and serves as an expedient in adapting the institutional beliefs to varied and novel situations in a constantly changing world. A hadith was soon found—rather manufactured—to sanction the procedure. "My community," said Muhammad, "shall not agree on an error." The principle of agreement was invoked to canonize the vulgate text of the Koran, to authorize its lithographic reproduction, to perpetuate the pre-Islamic practice of circumcision, to approve the six canonical books of hadith,[24] to accept the miracles of the Prophet, to dispense with the necessity of descent from the Quraysh in favor of the Ottoman caliphs, and even to make saints of holy men and shrines of their tombs. The Shiites, however, reject the consensus principle. They held to the absolute authority of the infallible imams, Ali and his successors. They also differ from the Sunnites in another important respect. They maintain that the "door of interpretation" is still open and that Shiite interpreters can speak for the last imam, who is hidden somewhere and who will appear at an opportune moment.[25] So, while the imamate doctrine makes of the Shiite a more conservative and

[23] Treated above, pp. 231, 246.
[24] See below, pp. 260-261.
[25] Treated below, pp. 281-282.

authoritarian society than the Sunnite, the open door of interpretation provides it with a margin of deviation and liberalism which partially accounts for the rise of many sects in the Shiah as against the conformity of the Sunnah.[26]

The indebtedness of the Islamic legal system to the Roman-Byzantine system which was displaced by it in Western Asia and North Africa does not seem to be as great as expected. This is not surprising when it is remembered that as a religious institution the Islamic code would not, consciously and admittedly, borrow from an alien secular one. The fact, however, remains that Moslem statutes relating to taxation, commerce, finance, and other areas removed from the religious core bear the direct impress of Roman legislation, while other statutes relating to guardianship and will, hiring and letting might have passed through rabbinical and Talmudic channels. But we know of no Latin legal work translated into Arabic, despite the fact that Beirut was a great center of Roman legal education until a century before Islam,[27] and we are sure of no Latin terms borrowed for the Arabic legal vocabulary.

The prescriptions of the Islamic canon law regulate for the believer his entire life and conduct. Accordingly what constitutes right and wrong is the will of God as revealed in the Koran, and all ethical conduct derives its sanctions and inhibitions from the sacred law. Legists classify man's acts into five categories: absolute duty, involving reward if committed and punishment if omitted; commendable or meritorious actions, involving reward if performed but no punishment if omitted; permissible acts, which are legally indifferent; reprehensible ones, which are disapproved but not punished; and forbidden deeds, entailing punishment.

But as in the case of the other intellectual areas new streams of thought flowed from outside sources. Especially copious was the philosophical stream ultimately going back to Aristotle through Neo-Platonic and Neo-Pythagorean channels. The translation of Aristotle's *Ethics* by the Hunayn ibn-Ishaq school started the move toward a new type of moral philosophy divorced from religion and receiving its sanctions from no divine law. Several thinkers in Iraq and Persia took to the new school and contributed works on the subject. Meanwhile a third type of ethics was evolved, the mystico-philosophical, whose exponents were Sufis.[28] All the moral philosophers in Islam maintained admiration for the old virtues of resignation, endurance, and contentment; but they

[26] Treated below, pp. 281-282.
[27] As we learned above, p. 178.
[28] To be treated later, pp. 284-285.

treated vices as maladies of the soul—with the moral philosopher as the physician—and classified them according to an analysis of the faculties of the soul, each faculty having its own vice as well as its virtue.

THEOLOGY

Theology, a twin sister of law, was an early Moslem discipline and, at least in its orthodox form, developed along strictly Islamic lines. This intellectual activity was carried on largely by scholars of Arab descent in contrast to medicine, astronomy, mathematics, and alchemy which were mostly in Syrian, Persian, or Jewish hands. To Moslems in general the science of religion was science par excellence.[29]

Next to the Koran the *sunnah,* i.e. the deeds, utterances, and silent approval of the Prophet as recorded in the hadith, constituted the most important doctrinal source of theology. In this, theology did not differ from jurisprudence, but it did not admit other, secondary, sources as did jurisprudence. Hadith in both cases was expanded to include a record of actions and deeds of Muhammad's companions and their immediate successors. In a Prophetic hadith the meaning is inspired; in a koranic verse both meaning and words are revealed.

Transmitted first orally the avalanche of hadiths accumulated more material, genuine or spurious, as generations rolled on. Parties to a dispute—religious, political, social, or economic—found the temptation strong to fabricate a hadith, if one could not be found, in support of a particular view. National issues, such as the rivalry between Ali and abu-Bakr, the struggle, between Muawiyah and Ali as well as Ali's sons, the enmity between the Umayyads and the Abbasids, and the claim of superiority by Arab Moslems over non-Arab Moslems provided ample opportunities for creating or distorting hadiths and motivated their dissemination for propaganda purposes. All this necessitated the cultivation of a new science, unique in the case of the Arabs, the science of hadith. Criteria were worked out to determine the value to be attached to a hadith and to ascertain whether it was genuine, fair, weak, or spurious. The criteria were applied to the individuals in the chain of transmitters of a particular hadith to ascertain the piety, possible continuity, and proximity in time and person to the Prophet. Criticism was directed not so much toward the reported as toward the reporter.

By the third Moslem century six compendiums of hadith had been collected and were soon accepted as standard. These are the "six canonical books" which fix forever the traditional source of Moslem

[29] Cf. above, p. 233.

theology, just as the Koran fixes the revealed source. Of these six books that of a Persian, al-Bukhari (810-70), was the earliest and remained the most authoritative, attaining a rank second only to the Koran. Al-Bukhari is said to have selected 7275 items out of a total of 600,000 which he had assembled from 1000 shaykhs in the course of a sixteen-year journey through Persia, Iraq, Syria, Hejaz, and Egypt. He classified these items under such general topics as prayer, pilgrimage, and the holy war. Before recording a hadith the author reportedly performed the ceremonial ablution and prayer. His tomb outside of Samarkand is still visited by devout pilgrims who accord him the next rank after Muhammad.

The hadith literature did more than clarify and supplement the Holy Book. It furnished the community with apostolic precepts and example covering the minutest detail of man's duty. Such seemingly trivial matters as to how Muhammad ate a watermelon or used a toothpick became a norm.[30] A vague reference in a solitary koranic verse to a nocturnal journey was seized upon by hadith, elaborated and embellished and inflated to a prolonged visit to heaven and to hell.[31] This literature further served as a vehicle for introducing wise sayings, anecdotes, parables, and prayers in which converted Jews and Christians took part. Even a version of the Lord's Prayer was put in the mouth of Muhammad, who also commended "him who gives alms only in secret, so that his left hand knows not what his right does." In the hadith the Moslem home found its fireside literature and the Moslem community its Talmud.

Certain intrusive ideas and beliefs were domesticated and finally assimilated; others were too alien to Islamize and resulted in the formation of dissident groups outside the pale of Islam. Such groups often crystallized into sects, which will be treated in the next chapter. We have seen how early in Damascus the doctrine of free will began to agitate Moslem minds, resulting in the formation of a new sect and how in Baghdad a rationalist element began to challenge the uncreated character of the Koran.[32] As these heterodox groups increased in number and power, it became more imperative to defend, define, and perpetuate what was to be considered orthodoxy. Basra produced the man to do it. He was al-Ashari, who lived in Baghdad, where he died in 935.

Al-Ashari began his religious career as a student of the Mutazilite school, whence he acquired those weapons of logical and philosophical

---

[30] Cf. above, p. 191.
[31] See above, p. 193.
[32] Pp. 231, 246.

argumentation which he later turned against his former masters. "The Mutazilites," we are told, "carried their heads high until God sent al-Ashari against them." In pious Moslem eyes he not only exploded heretical theories but established, clarified, and transmitted the orthodox creed which has since become the fixed heritage of Sunnite Islam. He thus became the founder of its scholastic theology (*kalam*). His teaching attracted a large circle of pupils and his polemic and dogmatic writings made many more disciples; they are still used as texts in seminaries. Asharism and Islamic scholasticism have become almost synonymous.

Al-Ashari was outshone by a more brilliant disciple, al-Ghazzali (L. Algazel), who was born in Tus, Khurasan (1058), where he died in 1111. Al-Ghazzali is not only the greatest theologian Islam ever produced but one of the noblest and most interesting thinkers of medieval times. His was an inquisitive and penetrating mind. Al-Ghazzali and al-Ashari are the counterpart of the Greek and Latin fathers of the Christian Church. An autobiographical sketch left by him reminds us of St. Augustine's spiritual experience.

> Ever since I was under twenty (now I am over fifty) . . . no philosopher did I come across without desiring to learn the essence of his philosophy; no dialectical theologian, without striving to ascertain the object of his dialectics and theology; no Sufi, without coveting to probe the secret of his Sufism; no atheist without groping for the reasons for his atheism. Such has been the unquenchable thirst of my soul for investigation from my early youth—an instinct and a temperament implanted in me by God through no choice of mine.[33]

The quotation gives only a faint idea of the spiritual struggle through which this man went first as an orthodox Sunni, then as a Sufi, later as a skeptic, and finally, after physical and spiritual collapse, as a dervish living in isolation or roaming over the lands of Islam for twelve years in the course of which he restored his peace of mind. His stand became pragmatic: The only trustworthy knowledge is that gained by experience; intellect should be used to destroy trust in itself. Though intellectualism, as he had experienced it as a professor at the great Nizamiyah college of Baghdad,[34] failed him, al-Ghazzali at last wrote a highly intellectual work on "revivification of the sciences of religion," which won him the title "the great authority on Islam." In it he combated the theory that the mere imparting of knowledge was the primary object of education, insisting on the necessity of stimulating the moral consciousness of the student and thus bringing for the first time in

[33] Hitti, *History of the Arabs,* pp. 431-432.
[34] Discussed later, pp. 270.

Islam the problem of education into organic relation with a profound ethical system. In his works this Arab writer employed Greek dialectics to strengthen the structure of scholasticism, gave the *coup de grâce* to philosophy—except for elements palatable to orthodox theology—and made mysticism acceptable to the canon law. His works promise to maintain their hold on Moslem readers everywhere for years to come.

FINE ARTS

In the development of their architecture, painting, and industrial arts the Abbasids did not follow Umayyad patterns, which were basically Byzantine Syrian; they adopted native and Persian ones—particularly Sasanid. The impact of Persian culture on Baghdad was all-embracing.

Unfortunately, however, hardly a trace is left to give us an inkling of the splendor of the royal and vizirial palaces of the capital and of its mosques and other public buildings. The destruction wrought by civil wars, Mongol invasions, floods, and other natural causes has been so complete that even the sites of most of these structures, about which we read in the *Arabian Nights* and other literary works, cannot now be identified. Outside of Baghdad the most conspicuous ruins are those of Samarra, temporary Abbasid capital (836-889). Its great mosque, built by al-Mutawakkil at a cost of 700,000 dinars, was rectangular in shape with multifoil arches and windows displaying Indian influence—which came through Persia. Neither in this nor in an adjacent town mosque, also of the mid-ninth century, does the prayer niche, appearing first in Syrian mosques,[35] figure. Outside of the Samarra mosque rose a tower analogous in structure to the Babylonian ziggurat[36] rather than the Damascus' minaret. The scanty remains of al-Raqqah on the Euphrates, part-time residence of Harun al-Rashid, display influences from an easterly rather than westerly direction. The Sasanids, it will be recalled,[37] had developed a distinctive type of architecture with ovoid or elliptical domes, semicircular arches, spiral towers, indented battlements glazed wall tiles and metal-covered roofs, all of which became factors in the formation of Abbasid art.

In Samarra its builder (836) Caliph al-Mutasim, son of Harun al-Rashid, ornamented the walls of his palace with frescoes of nude female figures reminiscent of those in al-Walid's hunting lodge in Transjordan.[38] His son al-Mutawakkil, under whom the temporary capital reached its zenith, even had a picture of a church with monks among many other

---

[35] As noted above, p. 234.
[36] Cited above, p. 79.
[37] Above, 183.
[38] Described above, p. 235.

Courtesy of Worcester Art Museum

THE UNFORTUNATE CAMEL IN THE BIDPAI FABLES   Persian, 14th century

representations on his palace walls.   These were undoubtedly the work
of Bzyantine-trained artists.   Manuscript representations, such as those
of the strange mount on which Muhammad ascended to heaven,[39] seem
to have taken for their prototype Greek centaurs or Assyrian human-
headed winged bulls coming, of course, through Persian. Jacobite
and Nestorian Christians contributed another element derived from
book-decoration.   In miniature illustrations the Manichaean influence
is often evident.

Among the earliest manuscripts illustrated with miniatures are the
fables of Bidpai[40] and the essays of al-Hariri of Basra (d. 1122) still
esteemed among the chief treasures of literary Arabic.   These miniatures, dating from the early thirteenth century, suggest the artists were
trained in Christian schools.   Subsequently Moslems, especially those
of Persia with their centuries-old Indo-Iranian tradition, began to
develop arts of their own.

[39] Cited above, p. 193.
[40] Mentioned above, p. 245.

Courtesy of The Bettmann Archive

A SCENE FROM AL-HARIRI, ESSAY 19   A sick man, his son behind his head, is
visited by his friends.   Manuscript dated 1334.

Persians excelled in all types of decorative design and color including
those pertaining to industrial arts.   The pre-Islamic Sasanid period
witnessed the development of the potter's craft which later produced
the equal of the ceramics of any country at any time.   Examples
of luster painted Persian pottery became highly prized.   There then
emerged, under Persian auspices, those delicate geometrical and floral
patterns which became dominant in and typical of Moslem art.   Abstract
style was not a new discovery in Western Asia but under Islam it was
brought to its supreme fulfilment.   Human, animal and plant forms,
as well as geometric and epigraphic figures on vases, plates, and tiles
attained a beauty of style unsurpassed by any other Moslem people.
Kashani (Qashani) tiles, first produced in Kashan, south of Tehran,
were imitated in Baghdad, Damascus, Cairo, and Cordova; they finally
became popular in Turkey, Spain, India, and other lands.   These are
square or hexagonal glazed tiles, sometimes figured with conventional
flowers and employed in exterior and interior building decoration.
The predominant colors are indigo and turquoise blue, green, and less
often red and yellow.   This industry survived in Damascus until the
eighteenth century.

In Antioch, Damascus, Tyre and, other ancient Phoenician towns the

Courtesy of The Louvre

PANEL OF LUSTRE TILES FROM AL-RAYY, 13TH CENTURY

processes of enamelling and gilding glass were almost perfected. The Louvre, British Museum, Arab Museum of Cairo, and the Metropolitan Museum of New York include among their treasures plates, cups, vases, ewers, and lamps from these and other early Moslem centers. For centuries Egypt vied with Persia in metalwork and rug decoration. Hunting and garden scenes were especially favored in carpet decoration. Kashan also gave its name to a type of rug of soft color and fluid floral design often in medallion form. Egyptians and Syrians distinguished themselves in decorated silk fabrics, the Egyptians perpetuating the Coptic tradition. Crusaders and other Europeans used such pieces as wrappings for souvenirs and saints' relics and thus introduced them into the West, where they began to be imitated.

In tombs, schools, mosques, and dervish fraternity lodges mosaics and calligraphy remained the favored forms of decoration. Arabic letters lent themselves more admirably to ornamental purposes than did any other characters with the possible exception of the Chinese. Gradually and as a result of their close association with the Koran, they acquired a semi-holy character. After the substitution by Mustafa Kemal of the Latin for Arabic-Turkish characters,[41] faint voices were heard advocating the same treatment for Arabic but they fell on deaf ears.

The legists' frowning on music[42] was as ineffective as their disapproval of painting. The courts of Harun al-Rashid and his immediate successors would not have been half so dazzling without the scores of musicians, singers, dancers, and other entertainers. The pages of the *Arabian Nights,* the twenty-one volume work entitled *Book of Songs* (*Kitab al-Aghani*), and many other literary works would lose much of their color and attractiveness if stripped of the fantastic anecdotes and portrayals of musical festivals held under caliphal patronage. On one such occasion, presided over by Harun, two thousand performers are said to have taken part. Not to be outdone his son al-Amin (r. 809-813) held a festival in which the personnel of the palace, male and female, danced till dawn.

Harun's favorite artist was Ibrahin al-Mawsili,[43] a musician whom he made a boon companion. His name was derived from al-Mawsil (Mosul), where as a kidnapped boy Ibrahim was detained. During his detention he began his career learning brigands' songs. His pupil and successor, Mukhariq (d. ca. 845), also started his life as a slave. A woman singer bought him from his butcher father when she heard the boy advertising his father's meat in a melodious and powerful voice. She trained him. On passing into Harun's possession the young singer so ingratiated himself with his master that he was freed, rewarded with 100,000 dinars, and honored with a seat by the caliph's side. An anecdote tells how one evening as he was walking along the Tigris and began to sing, torches started to flit in the street. They were carried by Baghdadis who left their homes eager to enjoy his voice.

Harun's successors, al-Mamun and al-Mutawakkil, patronized al-Mawsili's son Ishaq. Ishaq, like his father and many other artists of

[41] Treated below, p. 370.
[42] Above, p. 235.
[43] On him see above, pp. 243-244.

the day, was not only a musician-singer but also a composer, poet, and scholar—as scholars went in those days. Because he was well versed in the scientific lore of the age, he won the position of boon companion to these caliphs. More than anyone else Ishaq personified the spirit of classical Arabic music and was considered the greatest all-round musician Islam had produced. "The jinn prompted his melodies" in the judgment of Arab art historians. For a slave girl singer, bright and beautiful, whom he had trained, a governor of Egypt offered 30,000 dinars and a ruler of Khurasan 40,000, but Ishaq solved the problem by freeing the girl and marrying her.

These early virtuosos were mostly practical performers and singers following generally indigenous models. They were not musical theorists. The scientific mathematical side of the art had to wait until the proper works in Greek became available. Two Aristotelian treatises on speculative music were translated by Hunayn ibn-Ishaq (d. 873). Other Greek works followed. From them Arabic authors gained their earliest scientific ideas on music and on the physical and physiological aspects of the theory of sound. The Arabic term *musiqi* (later *musiqa*) was borrowed from Greek to be applied until the present to the scientific aspects of music. Meanwhile such Arabic names of instruments as *qitar* from guitar, and later *urghun* from organ were introduced. The masters favored the lute (from Ar. *al-'ud*), others the viol (*rabab*).

Al-Kindi (d. *ca.* 873), whom we have mentioned as a philosopher,[44] pioneered the Arab school of Greek music. He is credited with the first use of notation in Arabic. Several other Arab philosophers and physicians were, like him, musical theorists. Among these al-Farabi (d. 950),[45] himself an accomplished lute performer, was the greatest writer on the theory of music not only in Islam but in the Middle Ages. His translated works together with the musical studies of ibn-Sina and ibn-Rushd were used as textbooks in Western Europe.

Most of the technical Arabic works in this field have regrettably been lost. For a time Arabic notation, with its two constituent elements of melodic modes and rhythmic modes, was transmitted orally and finally lost. The little surviving material on musical theory is fully intelligible to no one living today.

EDUCATION

Education, as a formal purposeful activity, received its first impulse in Islam—as in other cases—from religion. The first school must

[44] See above, p. 255.
[45] Above, p. 255.

Courtesy of Princeton University Library

FROM AL-FARABI'S BOOK ON MUSIC   Sample of notes.   Manuscript copied in 1421.

have been an adjunct of the mosque, if not the mosque itself, and many schools have so remained throughout the centuries. The curriculum centered on the Koran as a reading text. Together with elementary reading and writing went grammar, stories relating to the Prophet and his companions, poetry, and principles of arithmetic. In its initial stages the educative process was practically all memory work. Street parades honoring young pupils who have memorized the Koran are not rare in Moslem cities even today. Girls were welcome to religious instruction only on a low level. Children of aristocratic families generally had special tutors who instructed them in religion, polite literature, and the art of versification.

The elementary school teacher was usually a low grade student of theology and did not command the respect of the community. The teachers of more advanced material were more highly educated and, evidently under the Abbasids, were organized into a sort of guild. Such masters could grant a personal certificate acceptable in academic circles. Works on pedagogy do not make their appearance until the late Abbasid period when a style of development was attained in which theories could be discussed. Two sayings supposedly by Muhammad testify to the high regard in which education came to be held: "The ink of scholars avails more than the blood of martyrs," "Seek ye learning even if in China." Ali is claimed to have said, "I am the slave of him who taught me even a letter"—an often-quoted saying today. That Moslem society did not betray the presumed intentions of its founder may be proved by a comparison of Baghdad, Cairo, or Cordova as intellectual centers, with their European counterparts in the ninth to the eleventh centuries.

Al-Mamun's "house of wisdom" in Baghdad could be called the first higher institution of learning in Islam, but the first real college, with provision for scholarships and for the physical needs of its students, was the Nizamiyah in Baghdad. Established in 1065-1067 by Nizam-al-Mulk, Persian vizir of the Saljuq court,[46] this school became a model for later ones. Primarily a theological seminary dedicated to the study and promulgation of Sunnite Islam according to the Asharite system. the Nizamiyah used the Koran, hadith, and poetry as the backbone of its curriculum. These subjects corresponded to Greek and Latin in their relation to the humanistic curriculum in European universities. Among the distinguished professors of this school was al-Ghazzali. Al-Nizamiyah survived the destruction of Baghdad by Hulagu in 1258, as it survived later invasions by Tartars, and was finally merged with another institution of Baghdad in 1395.

In its spread the Nizamiyah type of theological school (*madrasah*) covered Khurasan, Iraq, and Syria, receiving impetus from the idea that the founding of such institutions was a meritorious act in the eyes of God. The Andalusian traveler ibn-Jubayr on his visit in the late twelfth century counted about thirty such schools in Baghdad, twenty in Damascus, and six in Mosul. In all of them theology and allied subjects remained the basis of instruction.

Aside from schools with their formal education there was the congregational mosque with its "circles," where a learned theologian, sitting on a cushion, would lecture on the Koran, hadith, or literature to any audience squatting on the floor in front of him. Any visitor or passer-by could avail himself of such opportunity. The system tied in admirably with the institution of travel in quest of learning.[47] Traveling geographers and other scholars benefitted from such circles. Al-Shafii presided over such a circle in al-Fustat. Mosques also functioned as libraries; their collections were generally donated in perpetuity (*waqf*) to the Moslem community by scholars and men of wealth or royalty. They therefore often included books on philosophy, astronomy, medicine, and logic. Mosul before the mid-tenth century boasted a library, built by a citizen, where readers were supplied with writing paper gratis. Basra did better. The donor of its library granted subsidies for scholars

---

[46] See below, pp. 295-296.
[47] Above, p. 254.

working in it. The library of Shiraz, founded by the enlightened Buwayhid Adud-al-Dawlah (r. 977-982),[48] had its books listed in catalogues, properly arranged in cases and administered by a regular staff. At about the same time al-Rayy had a "home for books" with four hundred camel-loads of manuscripts listed in a ten-volume catalogue. Ibn-Sina, we learned before, acquired his medical self-education in a royal library. Yaqut spent three years collecting material for his geographical dictionary from the libraries of Marv and Khwarizm.

Though commercial in purpose the bookshop, a place where knowledge could be bought and sold, served as an important agency for the dissemination and advancement of knowledge. We first hear of book-shops in Abbasid Baghdad. An Arab geographer claims that at the time he was writing, 891, the capital boasted a hundred book-dealers congregated in one street. Their shops, like their successors in Baghdad, Cairo, and Damascus, must have been small booths like the ones which today adjoin mosques. Some were certainly large enough to accommodate connoisseurs and bibliophiles and to serve as centers for intellectual discussions and literary debates. Certain booksellers themselves had at times more than commercial interests and served as copyists, calligraphers, literati, and authors. To more than one of them we owe solid contributions especially in literature. Yaqut, it will be recalled, started his career as a book-dealer's clerk.

Bookstores and libraries could not thrive beyond a certain point so long as parchment and papyrus were the only writing material. Paper, one of the boons China bestowed upon the world, was for a time imported to Baghdad from the Far East. Its manufacture from flax, linen, or hemp rags was learned by Moslems in Samarkand in the mid-eighth century, from Chinese prisoners of war. Before the end of that century Baghdad had its first paper mill. From Iraq the industry spread into Arabia, Syria, and Egypt. By the end of the tenth century paper had almost entirely displaced papyrus and parchment throughout North Africa and Western Asia. By the middle of the twelfth century the industry had passed from Morocco to Moslem Spain, where Yaqut names Játiva as its earliest center, and thence into Christian Europe. A philological reminder of this interesting and significant contribution is English "ream," which ultimately comes from an Arabic word for bundle. Without this new writing material Europe could not have achieved the measure of intellectual progress it has achieved since that century.

That Moslem society was privileged in having a sizable body of learned men and an elite of cultured laymen cannot be gainsaid, but

[48] Treated below, p. 294.

to assume that a large segment of the society enjoyed the benefits and shared in their knowledge would be unjustified. The answers submitted by the educated slave girl Tawaddud to the savants' questionnaire reported in the *Thousand and One Nights* (nos. 438-461) may be taken as a fair index of the knowledge of a cultured person between the ninth and twelfth century: The planets are seven—the sun, the moon, Mercury, Venus, Mars and Jupiter. Intellect has its seat in the heart, where God deposits it and whence it ascends to the brain. The human body has 360 veins, 260 bones, and 5 senses. It is compounded of four elements: water and earth, fire and air. The stomach lies in front of the heart, which is served by the lungs as ventilators. The liver is the seat of compassion; the spleen, of laughter; the two kidneys, of cunning. The stomach is the home of all diseases; diet is the source of all healing. But not much of this knowledge, quasi-scientific as it was, could have infiltrated through the thick wall that separated the privileged from the masses saturated with ignorance. The bulk of the society, whether urban or rural, must have lived under unsanitary conditions, in intellectual and material poverty, and in an atmosphere dominated by jinn, superstition, and antiquated tradition. The plight of the peasant may be epitomized in the words lately used to describe the Egyptian fellah, "He could sink no lower because the earth was there to retain him."

BOOKS TO READ

Arnold, Thomas and Alferd Guillaume, eds., *The Legacy of Islam* (Oxford, reprint 1947).

Browne, E. G., *Arabian Medicine* (Cambridge, 1921).

Faris, Nabih A., ed., *The Arab Heritage* (Princeton, 1946).

Farmer, Henry G., *A History of Arabian Music to the Thirteenth Century* (London, 1929).

Hell, Joseph, *The Arab Civilization,* tr. S. Khuda Bukhsh (Cambridge, 1926).

Le Strange, Guy, *Baghdad during the Abbasid Caliphate* (London, 1924); *The Lands of the Eastern Caliphate* (Cambridge, 1905).

Levy, Reuben, *A Baghdad Chronicle* (Cambridge, 1929).

Mez, Adam, *The Renaissance of Islam,* tr. S. Khuda Bukhsh and D. S. Margoliouth, (London, 1937).

O'Leary, De Lacy E., *Arabic Thought and its Place in History,* rev. ed. (London, 1954); *How Greek Science Passed to the Arabs* (London, 1949).

Pope, Arthur A., *An Introduction to Persian Art since the Seventh Century A.D.* (New York, 1931).

Totah, Khalil A., *The Contribution of the Arabs to Education* (New York, 1926).

Von Grunebaum, Gustave E., *Medieval Islam* (Chicago, 1946).

Wilber, Donald N., *Iran: Past and Present,* 4th ed. (Princeton, 1958).

XXI *Society in Abbasid Days*

THE stratification of society under the Abbasids retained its Umayyad framework,[1] but it was marked by wider fusion between its Arabian and non-Arabian Moslem components. By this time the primitive tribal system, formerly the basic pattern of social organization in Arabia, had been virtually obliterated and the gulf between old and new Moslems was being bridged. Polygamy, concubinage, and slavery served as the arches. Of the caliphs only three —abu-al-Abbas, al-Mahdi and al-Amin—were sons of free women; and only one, al-Amin, had both parents of the Quraysh. All three were early Abbasids. The rest had first Persian and later Turkish mothers and wives, mostly of slave origin.

WOMEN, WINE AND SLAVES

In the first Abbasid century and a half the Moslem woman enjoyed a measure of freedom comparable to her Umayyad predecessor; but, with the grafting of the Buwayhid regime[2] on the caliphate, segregation of the sexes and strict seclusion of the female were enforced. We no more read of women playing a conspicuous role in state affairs or competing with men in intellectual endeavor or in social life. In the golden prime of the Abbasids as in that of the Umayyads, several queens exercised marked influence over their husbands; others added grace and luster to the court. Al-Saffah, for example, took no decisive step without his wife's approval. He had promised her on oath never to marry another nor even to have a concubine. Al-Mahdi's wife sponsored researches to locate the house in which Muhammad was born and dedicate it as a hallowed spot. More glamorous and famous was al-Rashid's queen Zubaydah, who supplied Mecca in Hejaz and other water-thirsty cities in Palestine and Iraq with waterworks that bore

---

[1] Analyzed above, pp. 227 *seq.*
[2] Treated below, pp. 293-294.

her name. Her influence determined the precedence in accession to her son al-Amin, though inferior in intellect and ability to his half-brother al-Mamun.

But shortly after that the picture changes. In the *Thousand and One Nights* the woman is the personification of cunning and intrigue and the repository of all base sentiment and every unworthy thought, reflecting the degree of her degradation in the late Middle Ages. The times were generally marked with excessive concubinage, lax sexual morality, and self-indulgence. Restrictions against drinking, formerly a distinctive feature of Islam, were all but forgotten in high society. Indulgence in alcoholic drinks, in both company and in privacy, was common. Jewish dealers provided facilities for winebibbers and Christian monasteries offered sheltered "bars" for those seeking privacy. "The old wine of the monastery" became proverbial. The debauched poet and boon companion of Harun and al-Amin, abu-Nuwas (d. 810), son of a Persian washerwoman, sang the praises of wine in poems which are still popular. He and other erotic poets gave public expression to their perverted passion; they addressed their amorous compositions to "beardless youthful boys." The *Thousand and One Nights, Aghani,* and similar works contained many stories of licentious revelry that modern puritanical publishers have expurgated from their editions. The Persian practice of using poets, musicians, singers, and scholars as boon companions led to the development of professionals and became an established institution in the court.

Perhaps no other Eastern society of this period enjoyed the high standard of living that Baghdad society enjoyed. In the West, Moslem Cordova had no match among Christian capitals. Its people indulged in public baths and walked on paved streets illuminated by lights from bordering houses centuries before a Londoner saw a public light or a Parisian could step on a street without getting his shoes soiled with dust or mud.

Sports and physical exercise, could not have been popular entertainment in those semi tropical lands. Those of high status engaged in such indoor games as chess,[3] dice, and backgammon. Harun, by whom many other innovations were fathered, was presumably the first to play and encourage chess. He is credited with having included a chessboard among his presents to Charlemagne. On the list of outdoor sports hunting came first. Umayyad caliphs, it will be recalled, built special lodges for that purpose on the margin of the Syrian Desert. Falconry and hawking were Persian contributions. Other notable items in the list were archery, polo—also of Persian origin—fencing,

---

[3] On its introduction see above, p. 245.

javelin-throwing, and horse racing. Dexterity in hunting, archery, and chess playing were necessary qualifications of a boon companion.

Such a luxurious scale of living as that enjoyed by royalty and the aristocracy would not have been possible without an abundance of slaves. As in medieval modern society, even the middle class evidently had gadgets in plenty. Slaves were black, white, and yellow—Sudanese, Greek, Armenian, Turkish—boys and girls, men and women, all originally non-Moslem. They could be kidnapped, taken as prisoners of war, or bought in the market. Generals and governors habitually included among their presents to the caliph or vizir girls received or exacted from among their subjects. The boys were mutilated before they were attached to the harem. The court of al-Muqtadir (r. 908-937) is said to have housed 11,000 Greek and negro eunuchs. Oher boys, also possibly mutilated, were dressed in rich attractive uniforms, beautified, perfumed, and trained to perform in an effeminate fashion. Following the Persian precedent the use of effeminate lads for the practice of unnatural sex relations became an established institution with al-Amin. This caliph sketched the reverse of the picture by creating a corps of female pages, dressed like boys, who bobbed their hair and put on silk turbans. Caliphs, judges, governors, poets, theologians, scholars unshamefacedly used such boy or girl slaves. Al-Mamun sent as presents to his subordinates and lieutenants trusted slaves who would spy on the officials and if necessary do away with them.

ECONOMY

The maintenance of a high scale of living and a retinue of slaves carried with it a presumption of wealth. The upper layer of the commonalty—consisting of merchants, craftsmen, scholars, and other members of the learned profession—must have bordered on the aristocracy in its standard of life and social prestige. It gradually superseded the old aristocracy, based on blood and priority in Islam, and deposed the Arab warrior caste. The lower layer comprised farmers, herdsmen, manual workers and simple country folk, representing in general the native stock persisting in its old faiths, together with the mass of the Moslem community. The early merchants were Christians, Jews, Zoroastrians, and professors of other non-Moslem faiths; but these were in due course largely superseded by Moslems and Arabs. Arabs did not look upon trade with the same disdain as they looked on agriculture. The wide extent of the empire entailed trade on an international scale by both land and sea. Baghdad, Basra, Siraf, Cairo, and Alexandria were centers of active commerce.

Moslem traders of the ninth and following centuries ventured as far East as China. There is evidence that even Korea was reached. Silk, the earliest of Chinese gifts to the world, was their main quest. The land route leading through Samarkand, Bukhara, and other Turkestan towns was called "the great silk way," but caravans picked up the merchandise of Transoxiana and Turkestan en route. It was traders, travelers, and Sufi wanderers, rather than warriors, who carried Islam into what has become Indonesia and thence into the Philippines. Indonesia was made a Moslem state in 1949. Diplomatic relations between the Abbasid court and the Far East preceded commercial interaction. Chinese records of the eighth century contain references to the first Abbasid and to Harun al-Rashid. Westward Abbasid merchants covered North Africa and reached Spain. Harun entertained the idea of digging a canal through the Isthmus of Suez.[4]

Egypt maintained the tradition of high-class linen and cotton fabrics, glassware, vases and other products of the industrial arts which were shipped to all parts of the Moslem world. Africa offered ebony, ivory, and negro slaves. But on the whole trade in the Mediterranean was not brisk. The Black Sea was even less hospitable, though we read of business relations with the peoples of the Volga regions in the tenth century. Coins found along the Volga and as far north as Sweden confirm the evidence of literary sources. The Caspian provided better opportunities. Transoxiana yielded rubies and lapis lazuli, Turkestan was noted for its rugs, furs, felt cloaks, amber, honey, swords, and slaves. Syria offered to the international market tables, sofas, lamps, earthenware, kitchen utensils, and the time-honored glass of Sidon and Tyre. Al-Bahrain had its pearls then as now; and southern Arabia continued its trade in spices as India did. In Persia several towns won distinctions as centers for the manufacture of carpets, brocades, embroideries, and robes of honor. Shiraz produced striped woolen cloaks which were in special demand. Khurasan yielded highly prized gold, silver, and marble works and Naysabur turquoise articles. The bulk of this industrial activity was carried out with infinite patience and skill by hand, with no deviation from tradition and no contribution of original ideas or methods in technology. A rich and careless class continued to demand objects of elegance and was ready to pay for them, to the enrichment of merchants and business owners, while the actual workmen—slaves and manual laborers—remained underpaid, undernourished, and in unsanitary living conditions. The concept of a labor-saving power, technology, a pillar of our modern society was born in the middle ages of the West.

[4] Cf. above, pp. 92-93, 128.

An idea of the fortunes amassed by industrial magnates and merchant princes of the day may be gained from certain cases recorded—probably exaggeratedly—in the chronicles of the day. A jeweler in Baghdad remained wealthy after al-Muqtadir (d. 932) had confiscated 16,000,000 dinars of his property; a Basra marine merchant had an annual income of over 1,000,000 dirhams; another Basran, an uneducated miller, could afford to distribute 1000 dinars a day as alms to the poor; many Siraf maritime merchants lived in 30,000-dinar homes and possessed 4,000,000 dinars each.

Several words of Arabic derivation in European languages perpetuate the memory of this medieval Moslem trade and industry. Some of these words were borrowed in the Crusading period (to be treated in a forthcoming chapter), others went through Spain. "Taffeta" originally Persian, "satin" originally Chinese, and "tabby" may be taken as illustrations. An Umayyad prince named Attab, who resided in Baghdad and gave his name to a quarter which won distinction in the manufacture of a high-grade, striped fabric (*attabi*), has left us the word now used in describing a striped cat. "Satin" is a corruption of the name of a Chinese town whence silk was imported. From Damascus came the product and the word damask. In Lower Egypt a city, Tinnis, which manufactured cloth and cloth balls, gave us the name of our game tennis.

AGRICULTURE AND DHIMMIS

The tilling of the land remained in non-Moslem hands for a long time even after the landowners had become Moslems. Since it constituted the main item of the state revenue and sustained the bulk of the population, agriculture was the object of special care on the part of the central government. The Tigro-Euphrates valley, next to that of the Nile, was the richest territory in the realm and the center of the Abbasid caliphate which thus improved its agriculture. Extensive irrigation works were undertaken. Canals were opened or reopened to form in the lower valley a veritable network and to join the two rivers. Some of the canals date from Babylonian days. Staple among the crops produced were dates, rice, cotton (originally an Indian plant), flax, and sesame. In certain areas fruits, vegetables, and other plant products—such as oranges, sugar cane, lupines, nuts, eggplants, roses and violets—were abundant. Distilled rose petals yielded the fragrant volatile oil which became known throughout the world as attar (Arabic word from Persian). The preparation of perfumes from roses, water lilies, violets, oranges, and the like flourished as an industry not only there but also in Damascus, Shiraz and other Persian towns. The

Persian province of Faris included in its annual land tax 30,000 bottles of the essence of red rose.

For centuries on their farms and in their country places the old folks clung to their ancient culture patterns and preserved their native tongues—Aramaic and Syrian in Iraq and Syria, Iranian in Persia, Coptic in Egypt, and Turkish in Central Asia. Though suppressed as a group, the dhimmis produced occasional individuals who rose to eminence in governmental and professional positions. Open jealousy on the part of the Moslem community found expression in discriminatory legislation. Harun was the first Abbasid to re-enact or re-enforce the Umayyad measures of Umar II.[5] In 807 Harun ordered that all churches erected subsequent to the Moslem conquest be demolished and that all members of the tolerated sects don the prescribed garb. His grandson, al-Mutawakkil, passed even more stringent decrees. In 850 and 854 this caliph commanded that Christians and Jews should affix wooden images of devils to their houses, level their graves to the ground, wear outer garments of specified colors, and ride only on mules with wooden saddles marked by two pomegranate-like balls on the cantle. The jurists of the period imposed a new disability which became more enduring that the caliphal ones: the testimony of a Christian or a Jew was not acceptable against a Moslem. The ground for the legislation was that Christians and Jews had falsified the Scriptures (Koran 2:70; 5:16).

Abbasid anti-dhimmi legislation precipitated mass movements in favor of Islam which ended in giving the entire area the Islamic aspect it still maintains. Egypt was subjected to further enactments under a Fatimid caliph.[6] With that the conquest of Islam the religion[7] was achieved. Concomitant to it was the conquest of language. In Iraq and Syria the transition from one cognate language to another was relatively easy. Arabic as the language of learning had won the day before Arabic as the vernacular. In out-of-the-way places, such as Mount Lebanon, the struggle for survival by native Syriac continued until only a few centuries ago.

The Christian subjects of the Abbasid caliphs were, as under the Umayyads, mostly Nestorians concentrated in Iraq; Jacobites, Greek Orthodox, and Maronites in Syria; and Copts in Egypt. The Nestorian patriarch was accorded the privilege of residing in the capital, a privilege denied the Jacobite patriarch who received his investure from the caliph and was recognized as the official head of all Christians in the

---

[5] Treated above, pp. 229-230.
[6] As will be noted below, p. 303.
[7] Consult above, p. 212.

empire.   The Jacobite patriarch had his seat at Antioch.   Jacobites were suspected of pro-Byzantine sympathy.   The Copts belonged to the same communion as the Jacobites but used and still use Coptic, rather than Syriac, in their church service.   The Maronites used Syriac, as they still do.   The Greek Orthodox and Greek Melkite persist in the use of Greek.

A surprising fact about the Nestorian Church under the caliphs is that it possessed enough vitality to send missionaries as far as China. A stele at Sian Fu, erected in 781, commemorates the names and labors of sixty-seven missionaries.   A more enduring bequest than the religious has been the Mongol and Manchu characters derived from the Syriac.   The Christian Church of India, on the southwest coast, dates from earlier times and maintains its affiliation with the Nestorian patriarchate.

As a less conspicuous minority the Jews presented no serious problems to the Moslems and on the whole fared better than Christians. In 985 an Arab geographer found most bankers and money-changers in Syria of the Jewish faith and many of the clerks and physicians of the Christian community.   As late as 1169, according to a Jewish Spanish traveler, the Jewish colony in Baghdad supported ten rabbinical schools and seventy-three synagogues.   Its head exercised the same measure and type of jurisdiction over his community that the Christian patriarch did over his.   On his way to an audience with the caliph the chief rabbi, dressed in rich ornamented clothes, was preceded by a herald calling out, "Make way before our lord the son of David."

ZOROASTRIANS

The Zoroastrians, mentioned only once in the Koran (22:17), were not strictly "people of the book," but practical politics and expediency dictated that they be treated as such.[8]   Their religion ceased to be the state religion but its fire temples continued to be used for some time in Persia and neighboring lands.   Those of its adherents who early in the eighth century fled to India are represented today by the Parsis. Manichaeanism,[9] an offshoot of Zoroastrianism, was likewise accorded the status of a tolerated sect but became the object of intense persecution because it evidently held some special fascination for the followers of Muhammad.   A number of crypto-Manichaeans were crucified in Aleppo in 780 by al-Mahdi who further instituted an inquisition against this community in Baghdad.   The only other major inquisition in Islam was that of his grandson al-Mamun, who used it to test candidates to

[8] Cf. above, p. 228.
[9] On Mani see above, pp. 181-182.

judgeships with views differing from his on the created character of the Koran.[10] Al-Mahdi's son Harun appointed a special officer to deal sternly with Moslems tainted with the doctrines of Mani.

Persia remained unconverted to Islam until well into the third century. Even today it counts a few thousand adherents of the old faith. Shortly after the Moslem conquest Arabic established itself as the language of learning and society. Some of the brightest luminaries in the intellectual, spiritual, and artistic firmament of Islam were of Persian stock. But the vernacular Arabic never succeeded in superseding the Iranian, which in due course reasserted its supremacy.

SHIITES

The two major branches of the Moslem community—the Sunnite and the Shiite, with their subdivisions—took their final forms in the course of the Abbasid period. The Sunnites adopted the Asharite system[11] and generally conformed to it throughout the ages, hence they experienced no fragmentation. In this particular sense they may be compared to Roman Catholics. The Shiah on the other hand provided refuge for the discontented and frustrated—whether politically, economically, or socially—and broke up into several splinter groups. In this respect it corresponded to the Protestant Church. But in its insistence on the imam (leader) doctrine as the core of its creed and the "apostolic" succession to the imamship in the Alid family it resembled the Catholic Church. Since in Islam the state and the religion were different aspects of one and the same thing, whenever a conflict of interests created a faction that faction expressed its doctrines in theological terms and presented itself as a sect. The Shiah provided fertile soil for the growth of such sects, but all formed the opposition party.

The Shiite imam differed from the Sunnite caliph in his inheritance from the Prophet not only his temporal sovereignty but his spiritual authority as well. In that capacity he was an infallible leader,[12] exacting unquestionable obedience and possessing the divine gift of impeccability. His was the prerogative of interpreting the law and in his absence the door of interpretation was left for certain learned men.[13] Ultra-Shiites went as far as deifying Ali. The founder of Islam imposed a revelation, the Koran, as the intermediary between God and man; all Shiites made a man, Ali, the intermediary. From Ali the imamship passed on to his son al-Hasan and then to his other son al-

[10] See above, p. 231.
[11] Treated above, pp. 261-262.
[12] Cf. above, p. 217.
[13] Referred to above, p. 258.

Husayn.   The succession was continued in nine descendants of
al-Husayn.   The bulk of the Shiah owe allegiance to these twelve
imams, whence they are called Twelvers.   Most of these imams were
either poisoned or fell fighting the constituted authority.   Though they
contributed significantly to the success of the Abbasids in their struggle
against the Umayyads, the Shiites suffered no less under the new regime.
Their last imam Muhammad disappeared in 878 under obscure circumstances in a Samarra mosque, leaving no progeny to become the "hidden imam."   He also became the "expected imam."   Since then in a
state of occultation, he is certain to appear in due time as the *mahdi*
(divinely guided one) to restore true Islam as the universal religion of
the world and usher in a short millennium before the final end.   This
idea belongs to the same cycle of thought as the Messianic; it similarly
represents a psychological reaction of a suppressed minority and a
personification of hope on the part of its leaders.   A startling Shiite
doctrine that developed concurrently was that of dissimulation, making
it not only ethical but obligatory on the believer, as a measure of protection, outwardly to profess another religion whenever necessary.

Next to the Twelvers came the Seveners.   The two parties agreed on
the succession of the first six imams.   The addiction of number seven,
Ismail (d. 760), to wine provided the occasion for a serious split.   The
Twelvers passed him by for his younger brother, but the Seveners
reasoned that he was above the law and considered him the last visible
imam.   To his followers, also styled Ismailites, Ismail also became the
hidden and expected imam.   The imam-mahdi concept is central in all
Shiite schools of thought.

The Ismailites became less tolerant than other Shiites and adopted
Neo-Platonic and gnostic ideas leading to an esoteric interpretation of
the Koran.   They assumed that only the exoteric or literal meaning of
a verse can be known to the public and that the esoteric or inner meaning is known only to the initiated few.   As a frustrated, persecuted
minority the sect resorted to underground organization and violent
methods of implementation.   One of their early orders, led by an
Iraqi named Qarmat (*ca.* 890), swelled in numbers and effectiveness
and became a malignant growth in the body politic of Islam.   Based
on communistic principles involving property and even wives the order
found special favor in the eyes of Iraqi peasants.   The extent to which
such strange doctrines were put into practice cannot be ascertained.
The Qarmatians considered the shedding of Moslem blood in the attainment of their purposes legitimate.   At the beginning of the 900's they
became strong enough to carve for themselves an independent state
along the western shore of the Persian Gulf, posing a real threat to the

caliphate. Their raiders reached Oman. In 930 Qarmatian atrocities culminated in the seizure of the Black Stone and the removal of it from Mecca. After twenty years of exile the sacred relic was restored to the Kaaba by a Fatimid caliph. The Fatimids had Ismailite origins. Before the Qarmatian furor subsided Syria, Yemen, and Khurasan were drenched in blood through its propaganda and subversive activity.

ASSASSINS

Social upheaval and economic unrest expressed themselves religiously in a Neo-Ismailite movement headed by a Persian, Hasan al-Sabbah (d. 1124). After a sojourn in the Fatimid court Hasan broke with the Egyptian imam and started what he called the "new preaching." In 1090 he gained possession of a strong fortress which was inaccessible, strategically located on a spur of the Alburz 10,200 feet above the sea, and commanding important routes. From this "eagle's nest," as the name probably means, the grand master conducted a campaign of terrorism that was felt throughout the Near East. Branches sprang in the mountains of Syria with headquarters in castles some of which are still standing. The order was a secret organization with a grand master at the head below whom stood a grand prior in charge of a district. At the bottom were the "self-sacrificers" who dared all, risking their lives while making assassination an art. One of their distinguished victims in Baghdad was the illustrious vizir Nizam-al-Mulk (1092).[14]

In Syria the "old man of the mountain," as the grand master was called, struck awe and terror in the hearts of Crusaders as they made their way up and down the coast. It is said that Richard Coeur de Lion was spared because the Assassins did not want to make it easy for his Sunnite adversary Saladin. The name Assassins (from Ar. *hashish*) was given them by the Crusaders because the self-sacrificers were allegedly drugged by the grand master preparatory to their adventurous missions. A graphic but second-hand account of the drugging was left by Marco Polo, who passed in the neighborhood of Alamut in 1271 or 1272, sixteen years after its destruction by Hulagu. The scene is enacted in a superb garden surrounding the elegant palace of the grand master.

He [the grand master] kept at his Court a number of the youths of the land, from 12 to 20 years of age, such as had a taste for soldiering. . . . Then he would introduce them into the Garden, some four, or six, or ten at a time, having first made them drink a certain potion which cast them into

[14] Treated below, pp. 295-296.

a deep sleep, and then causing them to be lifted and carried in. So when they awoke they found themselves in the Garden:

When therefore they awoke, and found themselves in a place so charming, they deemed it was Paradise in very truth. And the ladies and damsels dallied with them to their hearts' content. . . .

So when the Old Man would have any prince slain, he would say to such a youth: "Go thou and slay So and So; and when thou returnest my Angel shall bear thee into Paradise. And shouldst thou die, natheless even so will I send my Angels to carry thee back into Paradise." [15]

The Syrian order was destroyed by a Mamluk sultan, Baybars, in 1272. But remnants, known as Ismailite, can be found not only in northern Syria but also in Persia, Oman, Zanzibar, and India. Bombay produced the late leader of the group, Aga Khan, who spent most of his last years in France and England.

The Druzes, who owe their name to a missionary of the Fatimid al-Hakim,[16] and the Nusayris of Syria are other surviving offshoots of the Ismailite school. Both practice the rites of their religion, open only to the initiate, in secret; but more of the Druze books, all in manuscript form, have been exposed to public eye than of the Nusayri. The Nusayris probably bear the name of an ibn-Nusayr who flourished at the end of the 800's. They retain relics of heathen belief which evince passage from paganism directly to Ismailism. They seem to have absorbed Christian elements from their environment, including Christian names and the celebration of Christmas and Easter. Their deification of Ali gave them the name Alawites, which was popularized under the French mandate. Today they number a few hundred thousand, mostly peasants, concentrated in and around Latakia.

SUFISM

Sufism is more a way of life than a sect; it is the form which mysticism took in Islam. It relies on intuition, emotion, and the "inner light" rather than on intellect, tradition, and revelation as a means of knowing God, and on asceticism and love as a means of approaching and uniting with him. Its devotees were drawn from both Sunnites and Shiites. The rise and spread of Sufism represented reaction against the cold intellectualism of the philosophers and the superficial formalism of orthodox Islam. The approach was personal. What it primarily sought was personal union with the Deity. Like other Islamic movements it sought justification for its position in the Koran and found it in such passages as those that condemn "greed after the chance good

---

[15] *The Book of Marco Polo, the Venetian,* tr. Henry Yule, 2nd ed. (London, 1875), vol. I, pp. 146-9.

[16] Below, pp. 303-304.

things of this present life," those that commend "those who turn to God," and those that emphasize "trust in God, for God is a sufficient guardian" (Kor. 4:96; 9:113; 38:47). The Sunnites interposed between man the finite and God the transcendent a book, the Koran; the Shiites interposed a man, the imams; and the Sufis interposed a personal emotion, love.

In the course of its evolution, however, the Sufi system took diverse forms as it adopted asceticism—rampant in Oriental Christianity—and absorbed elements from Gnosticism, Neo-Platonism, and Buddhism, including the theosophic and pantheistic ones. Their very name, derived from Arabic (*suf*) for wool, betrays the favored dress imitating that of Christian monks. Celibacy, encouraged by certain of their orders but discouraged by Islam in general, reflects a monastic institution. Asceticism and mysticism, however, came to be regarded by devotees of Sufism as an emotional means of purifying the soul, preparatory to knowing and loving God and finally effecting union with him, rather than as a means of gaining his reward in a future world. In its pantheistic form Sufism worked out the doctrine of *fana,* self-annihilation in God, reminiscent of Buddhist Nirvana—a heresy in Islamic eyes. A Persian Sufi al-Hallaj was flogged, exposed on a gibbet, decapitated and burned by the Abbasid inquisition in 922 for having declared, "I am the Truth," identifying himself with God. He was the first great Sufi martyr. His mystic theory shines in these couplets of his composition:

> I am He whom I love, and He whom I love is I.
> We are two souls dwelling in one body.
> When thou seest me, thou seest Him:
> And when thou seest Him, thou seest us both.[17]

In its excessive veneration to the heads of its fraternal orders, Sufism was also condemned by orthodox Islam.

Sufi orders, developed after the twelfth century, were the nearest approach Islam made to Christian monasticism. In the practice of solitary meditation and prolonged vigils, aspects of Christian monastic life are reflected. A fraternity would normally be housed in a "monastery" of its own, headed by a shaykh under whose guidance novices could be instructed and initiated into the particular order. Besides neophytes a fraternity could have affiliated members who attend services at their convenience. A master ruled the order. Each order had its own religious services, some quite elaborate and many betraying Christian litanies as a source. The usual ritual involved a circle of devotees

---

[17] Cf. R. A. Nicholson, *Studies in Islamic Mysticism* (Cambridge, 1921), p. 80.

repeating in unison and with uniform peculiar breathing and bodily movements such formulas as "no god whatever but God" so many times as to induce self-intoxication or hypnotism. Songs and dances, both abhorrent to puritanical Islam, were often practiced.

First in chronology among the orders was the Qadirite, founded by Abd-al-Qadir al-Jilani (d. 1166) of Baghdad. One of the most tolerant and charitable orders, the Qadirite now claims adherents from Algeria to Java. The Rifai, bearing the name of Ahmad al-Rifai

Garnett, MYSTICISM AND MAGIC IN TURKEY (Isaac Pitman, London, 1912)

A MAWLAWI NEOPHYTE LEARNING THE WHIRL DANCE

(d. 1175), also an Iraqi, has won distinction in the field of strange feats on the part of its members, such as swallowing glowing embers, live serpents and, glass and passing needles and knives through their bodies. The Mawlawis, or whirling dervishes, owe their origin to Jalal-al-Din al-Rumi, a Persian who died in Konya (Konieh, classical Iconium) in 1273. Originally applied to a member of any religious fraternity, the term dervish (of Persian etymology) was later narrowed down to members of a wandering mendicant religious order (fakirs, Ar. for beggars) whose conduct and looks, in Moslem eyes, brought discredit to the entire system. The Mawlawi order featured music in its ritual. Its superior enjoyed the privilege of girding the new sultan-caliph of the Ottoman Empire with his symbolic sword. Another Turkish order was the Baktashi founded around 1500 and noted for its connection with the Janissary corps. The Baktashis encouraged celibacy, revered Ali, and displayed traces of Christian influence in their theology. Mustafa Kemal decreed that all orders in Turkey be abolished.

Other fraternities arose in different parts of the world and assumed local colors. The native one of Egypt was that founded by Ahmad al-Badawi (d. 1276) and concentrated in Tanta. Today it has branches all over the land. Al-Badawi is still considered the greatest saint Egypt produced. When an offer of marriage was made to him, he replied, "I have resolved not to marry other than a maid of Paradise" (Kor. 56:22). The remaining years of his life he spent hermit-like, communicating by signs only and falling into trances in which he saw visions. In Libya the native order is the Sanusi, to which the royal family belongs. This was founded by an Algerian shaykh in 1837 and is distinguished by being a congregation state with political and military as well as religious aims. It reminds us of the Crusading Templars.

Besides contributing the warm personal element to religious life and a form of ritual, Sufis are credited with the introduction of the rosary into Islam. Of Hindu origin this instrument of devotion was presumably borrowed by Sufis from Eastern Christians and then made its way through the Crusades into the West to become a feature of Roman Catholic ritual. The cult of saints was another innovation in Islam for which Sufis were responsible and which reflected Christian impact and was necessitated by the desire to bridge the gap between the worshiper and the worshiped. The founder of the order and, to a lesser degree, his successors were accorded sainthood in a sort of apostolic chain. The cult spread into non-Sufi circles. No canonization was connected with it; popular acclaim prompted by the performance of "miracles" on the part of a living or dead pious shaykh or ascetic sufficed. Among the Moslem denominations only the Wahhabi of Saudi Arabia are completely opposed to the saints' cult.

Even women were accorded the rank of "friends of Allah" by Sufis. An early example was Rabiah al-Adawiyah (717-801) of Basra, a mystic lady of noble birth and lovely character. When young she was sold as a slave but her master freed her on noticing a radiance around her as she prayed. Declining offers of marriage Rabiah lived a life of extreme asceticism and otherworldliness, devoting herself to the guidance and instruction of a circle of followers in the "mystic way," and inculcating the stock virtues of penitence, patience, gratitude, poverty, and utter dependence upon God. Asked whether she hated Satan, Rabiah replied, "My love for God leaves no room for hating Satan." When in a dream the Prophet asked her whether she loved him, her reply was, "My love to God has so possessed me that no place remains for hating aught or loving any save Him." [18]   Several of the saintliest characters in Islam were bred in the bosom of Sufism.

Perhaps the tenderest and most exquisite poetry in Islamic literature has been produced by Sufi mystic poets—particularly Persian. Notable among them was Jalal-al-Din al-Rumi (d. 1173), many of whose works have been done into English. In fact almost all Persian poets of the first order, like Sadi[19] and Hafiz (of Shiraz, d. 1389) had strong mystic strains. The following couplets from ibn-Arabi (1165-1240), the leading mystic philosopher of Spain, are a sample of the universality achieved by Moslem Sufi:

> My heart is capable of every form:
>   A cloister for the monk, a fane for idols,
> A pasture for gazelles, the votary's Kaaba,
>   The tables of the Torah, the Koran.
> Love is the creed I hold: wherever turn
>   Its courses, love is still my creed and faith.[20]

In the field of philosophy Sufism can claim at least three of the greatest intellects Islam ever produced, al-Farabi, ibn-Sina, and al-Ghazzali. It was al-Ghazzali who reconciled Sufism and its multi-unorthodox practices with orthodoxy and grafted mysticism on intellectualism in Islam.

The rise, flourish, and spread of such institutions as Shiism and Sufism and the establishment of such systems as Ismailism with its Assassins, Nusayrism, Druzism, and other heterodoxies may be taken as symptomatic of a malady in the body politic of Islam. They represent dissatisfaction with the existing order—religious, political, and social—together with desperate attempts to introduce change. At least the extremist movements were sign posts along the path the caliphate was pursuing toward its disintegration and final downfall.

BOOKS TO READ

Arberry, Arthur J., *An Introduction to the History of Sufism* (London, 1943?); *Sufism: An Account of the Mystics in Islam* (London, 1950).

[18] Margaret Smith, *Rabi'a the Mystic and her Fellow-Saints in Islam* (Cambridge, 1928), p. 99.
[19] On him see below, pp. 298-299.
[20] Cf. Reynold A. Nicholson, *A Literary History of the Arabs* (Cambridge, reprint 1953), p. 403.

Attwater, Donald, *The Christian Church of the East* (Milwaukee, 1946).

Browne, Laurence E., *The Eclipse of Christianity in Asia* (Cambridge, 1933).

Donaldson, Dwight M., *The Shiite Religion* (London, 1933).

Hitti, Philip K., *The Arabs: A Short History* (Chicago, 1956).

Hodgson, M.G.S., *The Order of Assassins* (The Hague, 1955).

Levy, Reuben, *Persian Literature* (London, reprint 1928); *The Sociology of Islam,* 2nd ed. (Cambridge, 1957).

Nicholson, Reynold A., *The Mystics of Islam* (London, 1914).

Smith, Margaret, *Readings from the Mystics of Islam* (London, 1950); *The Sufi Path of Love* (London, 1954).

Tritton, A. S., *The Caliphs and Their Non-Muslim Subjects* (Oxford, 1930).

XXII   *The Caliphate Dismembered: Successor States*

The Umayyad empire was coterminous with Islam, but the Abbasid was not; it began to shrink early in its career.   Spain was the first province lost.   There the young fugitive prince, Abd-al-Rahman I,[1] inaugurated (755) in Cordova a rival Umayyad regime that carried on the enlightened tolerant tradition of his Damascus ancestors.   A few years later Morocco followed, with a Shiite dynasty that endured for almost two centuries.   This was the first successful Shiite attempt of its kind.   While Shiites were carving for themselves a domain in western North Africa, Sunnites were doing likewise in mid-North Africa, Tunisia of today.   The governor whom Harun al-Rashid appointed there in 800 ruled as an independent sovereign—content with the title of amir but seldom bothering to inscribe the caliph's name on the coinage as a token of his spiritual authority.   This experience became a recurring theme in Moslem annals: The caliph appoints a governor to a distant province, the governor would usurp sovereign authority, assume the title of amir or sultan, content himself with an occasional mention of the caliph's name in the Friday sermon or on the coins and send him a present, and finally bequeath the authority to his progeny.   In this case the new amir extended his domain eastward beyond the western frontier of Egypt.   His successor pushed on into Sicily (902), ruled it for a century and a half, and used it as a base for operations against Malta and Sardinia, both of which were likewise seized.   Arabs held Sicily until the Norman conquest began in 1060.

[1] Mentioned above, p. 240.

The Sicilian Normans produced a line of Arabophile kings culminating in Roger II (r. 1130-1154). Roger dressed like a Moslem, built a chapel decorated with medallions bearing Kufic inscriptions, and was dubbed by his critics the "half-heathen king." In fact he was an Occidental edition of an Oriental monarch. The chief ornament of Roger's court was the distinguished Arab geographer and cartographer al-Idrisi (d. 1160), who dedicated a book to his patron summing up the main features of earlier works in Greek and Arabic and adding original material collected by special research workers. Al-Idrisi assumed the sphericity of the earth and correctly located the sources of the Nile in the lakes of equatorial Africa. Roger's grandson, Frederick II (r. 1215-1250), ruled both Sicily and Germany, took part in the Crusades, and was considered the second of the "two baptized sultans" of Sicily. In Frederick's court scholars and philosophers from Syria and Baghdad flourished, as did Oriental dancers and singers. His interpreter-astrologer, a Christian from Antioch, translated for him an Arabic treatise on falconry which Frederick used for his book, the first modern natural history. Other Arabic works, originally Aristotelian, were done into Latin for the emperor by Michael Scot. Thus did Sicily take its place, after Spain and Syria, as the third of the bridges through which Arab culture found its way into Europe.

IN THE EAST

While the western wing of the Arab eagle was being clipped, the eastern also suffered. The civil war between al-Amin, son of the Arab wife of Harun al-Rashid, and al-Mamun, son of his concubine, presaged the forthcoming conflicts between Arabs and Persians. Beginning with the ninth century, in which the caliphate was at its apogee, the centrifugal forces in Islam—involving nationalistic tendencies as well as aristocratic and regional aspirations—started to express themselves in the creation of local dynasties. A trusted general of al-Mamun, named Tahir, who had won laurels in the civil war, was rewarded by his master with the governorship of Khurasan in 820. Tahir was descended from a Persian slave. Though one-eyed, he wielded the sword so effectively that he became known as the "warrior with one eye plus an extra right arm." As governor, Tahir acted independently; he did not even mention the caliph's name in the Friday prayer. The Tahirids moved their capital from Marv to Naysabur, extended their sway to the Indian frontier, and remained in power till 872.

At about that time they were superseded by the Saffarids, who held Persia for the next thirty-two years. The founder al-Saffar was a coppersmith by profession, as his name indicates, and a brigand by avocation.   Though short-lived his regime posed more of a threat to the caliphate because it was more nationalistic than its predecessor.   The Saffarids were followed by the Samanids (*ca.* 874-999), with whom the old Persian aristocracy was restored to power and to the full enjoyment of its former privileges.   Saman was a Zoroastrian noble of Balkh.   His Moslem great grandsons had started as sub-governors under the Tahirids and became founders of the dynasty.   They ruled from the borders of India to Baghdad and from the desert of Transoxiana to the Persian Gulf.

The Samanid was one of the most enlightened regimes Persia ever experienced.   Under it the capital city Bukhara came near eclipsing Baghdad as an intellectual and political center.   Thither turned the stream of authors, poets, and other bounty or patronage seekers. Samarkand ranked second.   It was to a Samanid ruler, Mansur, that al-Razi[2] dedicated one of his medical works, *al-Mansuri,* in 914.   Another Samanid, Nuh II (r. 976-997), was the one who accorded ibn-Sina access to the scientific treasures of his library and started the teenager on his way to authorship and world fame.   It was during this period that Persian literature experienced its early renaissance.   In its course poetry grew from infancy to full manhood.   The first and last Persian epic poem, the *Shah-Namah* (Book of Kings) of Firdawsi (the Paridisiaie, 940-1020), was largely drafted.   Firdawsi was born near Tus, birthplace of al-Ghazzali and other great intellects of Islam.   He spent thirty-five years composing the 60,000 rhyming couplets of his epic, recounting the glorious deeds of Iranian kings and heroes, historic and legendary, from Adam down to the Arab conquest.   Though a Moslem, Firdawsi sang the glory of Zoroastrian days and became the living embodiment of national pride, self-respect, and patriotic feeling. The *Shah-Namah* was a source of perennial inspiration to later Persian poets.   One of its finest tales was admirably retold by Matthew Arnold under the title "Sohrab and Rustam."   This epic is one of the masterpieces of world literature; it has been done in part or in full into almost all living languages.   By this time the real political power had fallen into the hands of Turks, originally slaves with whom Samanids had staffed the court.   To one of them, the great Mahmud of Ghaznah, Firdawsi dedicated his work but received meagre reward.   Turks had not reached the stage at which they could appreciate poetry.   In return Firdawsi penned a bitter attack on Mahmud and had to take shelter outside his reach.   The rise of the Ghaznawid dynasty introduced into the struggle for power a third element, the Turkish.   It further marked

[2] Treated above, pp. 249-250.

the first victory of this element over the Iranian for the mastery of Islam, as we shall learn later.

TURKISH BODYGUARD

While the wings of the Abbasid eagle were being clipped at both extremities, a dagger held by Perso-Turkish hands was pointed at its very heart. In caliphal hands, Baghdad had hitherto remained secure in control of the international trade routes and revered as the head-quarters of Sunnite Islam. But all this was soon to change. Al-Mutasim (r. 833-842), eighth caliph and son of Harun, began the use of Turkish slaves and mercenaries as caliphal bodyguards to counter-balance the mounting influence of the Persian soldiery. But the remedy proved to be worse than the malady. Soon the number of these guards rose to four thousand and its conduct became so unbearable to the populace that the capital rose in arms against it. In 836, the caliph had to move his seat of government up the Tigris to Samarra. This Assyrian name was Arabicized into Surra Man Ra'a, "pleased is he who sees it," which the cynical wits of the day claimed it to mean, "He who sees it with the Turks settled therein is pleased with Baghdad well rid of them." The rise of this royal guard of predominantly Turk-ish soldiers parallels the praetorians in Rome and the Janissaries in Constantinople. The path led from slavery, through soldiery, to mastery. In this as in the other cases it was indicative of the deterioration of the central power.

The restoration of Baghdad as the capital under al-Mutadid (r. 892-902) changed the scene but not the course of events, as the real power continued to slip from caliphal to military hands. Army commanders could now do and undo caliphs at their pleasure. At one time Baghdad presented the spectacle of three personages who had once held the highest office in the state but were then deposed, blinded, and objects of public charity. The international prestige of the caliphate fell so low that in 909 a Shiite in North Africa, Ubaydullah al-Mahdi, dared declare himself an imam-caliph—thus starting the powerful Fatimid line. A Sunnite amir in Cordova, Abd-al-Rahman III, had no hesi-tancy in proclaiming himself caliph in 929, thereby initiating the rival Umayyad line of Spain. For the first time the world of Islam had three rival caliphates in different areas of that world.

BUWAYHIDS

With the central authority in Baghdad undermined, the green light was flashed for the advance of a new regime, the Buwayhid. Buwayh was a Persian in the service of the Samanids. As his masters weakened he gained strength. To bolster his dynastic aspirations he claimed descent from the Sasanid royal house. Gradually he and after him his sons established mastery over western Iran, which the sons partitioned among themselves. One of them advanced against Baghdad in 945, was received by the caliph, made "commander of the commanders," and honored with the title of Muizz-al-Dawlah (he who renders the state mighty). Indeed he was the one rendered mighty at the expense of the state. Instead of being a puppet of Sunnite Turks, the caliph therewith became a puppet of Shiite Persians. But Muizz kept the caliph's name in the Friday sermon and on the coinage, inscribing his own name with it. The caliphate under the Buwayhids (r. 945-1055) experienced its darkest period of humiliation and eclipse.

This, however, does not imply that the regime itself was wicked. Under at least one Buwayhid, Adud-al-Dawlah (the supporting arm of the state, r. 977-982), notable benefits accrued to the state. Adud consolidated the several provinces under members of his house in Iraq and Persia into a state over which he ruled from Shiraz. He undertook a number of public works such as repairing canals, founding hospitals, and building mosques in several cities of the empire. He beautified Baghdad. Scholars and poets flocked to his court. It was to Adud that al-Majusi dedicated his great medical work entitled "royal." [3]

SALJUQS

The life-cycle followed by the Buwayhid state did not differ in essence from that of its predecessors. Incompetency and discord among Adud's successors made their domain fall piecemeal to Turks— Ghaznawids, and Saljuqs. The stage was then set for a new ethnic group, the Turkish, to play the leading role in the political drama of Islam.

The newcomers started as rude nomads, unspoiled by town life and uncontaminated by the vices of civilization. As tribes they moved westward from Turkestan, adopted Sunnite Islam in or around Bukhara, swarmed over Persia and Iraq, spilled over Syria, and finally overran Asia Minor. No dynasty in their way remained standing. Endurance, mobility, and valor marked their advance. When fully established their sway extended from the western frontiers of Afghanistan to the eastern borders of the Mediterranean. Once more Moslem Asia was unified, but this time under a Turkish sultan rather than an Arab caliph. Once more vitality began to throb in the veins of the body of Islam. It was the Saljuqs who held back any further encroachment on the part

[3] Cited above, pp. 249-250.

of the Byzantines, dealt the first blows to the Crusaders, and paved the way for the success of their Ottoman kinsmen. This experience of barbarian infidels, setting their feet on the necks of the followers of Muhammad, accepting the religion of the conquered, and becoming its ardent champions was repeated by their Mongol cousins in the thirteenth century and again by their Ottoman relatives in the fourteenth. In the darkest hours of Islam the state, Islam the religion achieved its most brilliant victories.

December 18, 1055 was a memorable day in Saljuq annals. That day saw a grandson of Saljuq, Tughril by name, standing at the head of his Turkomans, knocking at the mighty gates of Baghdad. Instead of resisting him the caliph received him as a deliverer. Tughril was recognized as regent of the empire with the official title of sultan (he with authority) and the honorific title of "king of the East and of the West." "Sultan" remained in use by the Ottomans till the end of their regime. Tughril (r. 1037-1063) was fortunate in his two immediate successors; the three were the grand Saljuq sultans. Under Tughril's nephew Alp Arslan (hero-lion, r. 1063-1072) the decisive battle of Manzikart (Malazkird, in Armenia) was fought in 1071 in which the Byzantine emperor Romanus Diogenus was taken prisoner. The battle gained for the Saljuqs, in fact for the Moslems, a permanent foothold in the "land of the Romans," which they had coveted ever since Mu'awiyah's days. Tribes poured in and settled, and the basis of the Turkification of Asia Minor was laid. Seven years after Manzikart the Saljuq sultanate of Rum (from "Romans") was created with Nicaea (Niqiyah, Izniq), not far from Constantinople, as center. This was the first Moslem state the Crusaders encountered on their long way to the Holy Land. After 1084 the capital shifted southeast to Iconium (Quniyah, Konieh), the richest and most beautiful Byzantine city in Asia. In the meantime a son of Alp, Tutush, had started a dynasty (1094-1117) in north Syria which did its share in hindering the progress of the Crusaders.

Tughril kept his seat of government in al-Rayy. Alp chose Isfahan, but Alp's son Malikshah (r. 1072-1092) moved from Isfahan to Baghdad. All three sultans relied on able Persian viziers supported by Persian bureaucracy. At Baghdad the caliph was kept on the throne, a shadow of his former self, bedecked in all the regalia of his high office but shorn of its duties. When a daughter of Malikshah was married by a caliph, Saljuq power hit its meridian. The realm extended from Kashgar—the farthest eastern point to which the Moslem empire ever reached—to the proximity of Constantinople. Malikshah's efforts, seconded by those of his Persian vizir Nizam-al-Mulk, provided the realm with new or repaired roads, mosques, city walls, canals, and caravan-serais. A biographer claims that all roads in the empire from Trans-oxiana to Syria were so safe that even one or two travelers could go anywhere alone.

Nizam symbolizes the ascendancy of Persian culture over the Saljuq. Untutored if not illiterate, Malikshah at the suggestion of his cultured vizir summoned a meeting of astronomers (1074) in his newly erected observatory to reform the Persian calendar. This they did with such brilliant success that a modern scholar claims it is superior to the Gregorian one we use. One of those who collaborated in its revision was the astronomer-poet Umar al-Khayyam (d. 1123). Although he is known to the West as a poet of wine, mainly through the successful translations into English, French, German, and Italian, Umar is more known in the East as a mathematician. His mystic poetry tinged with skepticism bordering on agnosticism discouraged Moslem use of it. The quatrains were originally composed for the author's own entertain-ment. Another significant reform inspired by the vizir related to the military feudal system, which he based more on land than on money. Land was granted to an army officer on condition that he furnish a specified number of armed men. In theory the land was offered only for a term of years and was revocable.

The revised calendar, called Jalali, perpetuates the first name of Sultan Malikshah. The remarkable college built at Baghdad and named Nizamiyah, perpetuates the name of his learned vizir. This was the institution in which al-Ghazzali held a professorship.

With the termination in 1092 of Nizam's life by an assassin's dagger, the period of glory that covered the reigns of the first three Saljuqs ended. The weakening of central authority led to the breakup of the house, for a state built on a tribal basis by a nomadic people could be held together only with some dominant personality at its head. The military fief system organized by Nizam became hereditary and led to the establishment of independent states. The main line, the Great Saljuqs of Persia, maintained a form of suzerainty down to 1117. The Saljuqs of Rum in Iconium were superseded after 1300 by the Ottoman Turks. Saljuq domination in Baghdad lasted till 1194 in the caliphate of al-Nasir. The Saljuqs and Ottomans bequested to the Islamic reli-gion a mystic coloring that manifests itself in the various dervish orders that have flourished in Asia Minor and that also display elements of shamanistic origins mixed with Christian and indigenous beliefs of the land. In their new homeland the Saljuqs adopted the double-headed eagle of Sumero-Hittite origin as an emblem and passed it on to Constantinople, whence it reached Austria, Prussia, Russia, and finally the United States of America.

ENTER THE MONGOLS

Caliph al-Nasir (r. 1180-1225), whose caliphate was one of the longest in Moslem annals, made a feeble but belated attempt to restore his office to something of its former self. His was the flicker of an expiring flame. With the hope of shaking off the Saljuq hold on Iraq and Kurdistan, he instigated one of the Khwarizm shahs against them. The founder of this dynasty was a Turkish slave from Ghaznah whom Malikshah had appointed to the governorship of Khwarizm. In the battle of 1194 the Saljuq power was crushed only to be replaced by that of the shahs. One of them adopted Shiism and resolved to put an end to the Abbasid caliphate and install an Alid. His plans were frustrated by the sudden appearance on his borders of a new threat to him and to the caliphate in the person of Chingiz Khan, redoubtable chief of pagan Mongolian tribes.

In the way of an appalling swarm of some sixty thousand Mongolians, augmented en route by levies extracted from conquered peoples, nothing could stand. Riding fleet horses, armed with strange bows, and determined to share in the higher life to the west of them Chingiz' hordes spread havoc and destruction wherever they passed. A crimson stream marked their trail. Khwarizm was utterly devastated. Bukhara's mosques, famed for piety and learning, were turned into stables. Thousands of the inhabitants of Herat, Samarkand, and Balkh were either butchered or carried into captivity. Chingiz, according to a late tradition, boasted of being "the scourge of God sent to men as a punishment for their sins." By the early thirteenth century he and his hordes had shaken to its foundation every state from China to central Europe. Russia was partly overrun. Fortunately his route took him north of Baghdad. At his death in 1225 he left a hodge podge of an empire the like of which the world had never before experienced.

THE CALIPHATE DESTROYED

Al-Nasir and his successors, the last Abbasids, lived in a state of alarm; they feared the lull was the kind that preceded a storm. In 1253 a grandson of Chingiz, Hulagu, again swept westward. What economic or military pressure at home was responsible for wave after wave of these Mongols or Tartars being sent out cannot be determined, but the fact that a sick man lay on his deathbed in Baghdad and sundry heirs were scrambling for parcels of his estate offered an attractive invitation. In 1256 Hulagu reached Alamut, the Assassin "mother convent," demolished it and dealt a crushing blow to the dreaded order from which it never recovered. In January 1258 the Mongol mangonels began battering the walls of Baghdad. Caliph al-Mustain (r. 1242-1258) commissioned his vizir and the Nestorian patriarch— Hulagu had a Christian wife—to negotiate terms of peace. Hulagu would not receive them. Nor would he pay heed to the traditional warning "if the caliph is killed the whole universe is disorganized: The sun hides its face, rain ceases, and plants grow no more." He knew better, thanks to his astrologer's advice. On February 10, his men swarmed into the city through a breach in the tower. The unhappy caliph and three hundred of his officials were summarily slaughtered. The capital was given over to plunder and flames. Such was the pestilential odors emitted from the accumulated heaps of corpses in the streets that the conqueror had to evacuate the city temporarily.

The kingdom which Hulagu on his death in 1265 passed on to his successors, the Il-Khans (subordinate rulers), extended from the Oxus to Syria and from the Caucasus to the Indian Ocean. The caliphal capital was reduced to a provincial capital.

Like their Saljuq predecessors, the Mongols were quick to appreciate and utilize the administrative and artistic ability of their Persian subjects and to patronize cultivated savants. Less than half a century after Hulagu's merciless attempt to exterminate all vestiges of Moslem culture, a great-grandson of his, Ghazan, embraced Islam (1295) and devoted himself to the revivification of its culture—another instance of the conquest of Moslem religion where Moslem arms had failed. In a suburb of his capital city Tabriz, Ghazan started the construction of a group of buildings set within gardens and including a dervish home, hospital, observatory, library, academy of philosophy, religious schools, and administration building. Under the Il-Khans laws were codified, taxes more equitably levied and collected, and internal security was maintained. Ten thousand men policed the numerous caravan roads. Genoese and Venetian merchant colonies grew in Tabriz. The seventy-five years of Il-Kanid rule was rich in economic and literary achievements. Many historical works were produced then.

To this period belongs Sadi (*ca.* 1184-1291), one of the brightest jewels in the literary crown of Persia. In the course of his travels in Syria, Sadi was taken prisoner by the Crusaders. He was found digging ditches in Tripoli by an acquaintance from Aleppo who ransomed him and gave him his daughter in marriage with a hundred-dinar dowry. Sadi returned to his birthplace, Shiraz, where he composed his two masterpieces the *Gulistan* (rose garden), a classical model for later Persian prose, and the *Bustan* (orchard), which includes some of his Sufi poems. Sadi also wrote in Arabic. In his *Gulistan* he comments on his experience with the Franks:

> Better to hang in chains, when friends are there,
> Than dwell with strangers in a garden fair.[4]

He further reports on his Aleppine wife who, once in a torrent of abuse said to him, "Are you not the man whom my father bought back from the Franks?" "Yes," replied Sadi, "I am that man whom he bought back from the Frankish chains for ten dinars, and delivered into your bondage for a hundred dinars."

Beautiful Shiraz in southwest Persia was the scene of the nativity and activity of another great poet, Hafiz, the greatest lyric poet the country produced. His name, meaning "memorizer of the Koran," was a title he received in his youth on accomplishing that feat. He later held a chair of koranic exegesis in a school of his native city. The theologian turned a poet, specializing in singing the joys of youth —including love, wine, and women—and the beauty of nature particularly when awakened from its winter slumber. Copiously irrigated by a canal opened by a mid-tenth century Buwayhid, Shiraz was counted by Moslems one of four terrestrial paradises. While not introducing many new ideas, Hafiz so excelled in the felicity of expression, the depth of feeling, and the beauty of imagery that he was rated by his people as the incontestable master of the poetry of love and wine— even above Umar al Khayyam. In his love scenes boys are not excluded, but the treatment is with restraint and the obscene avoided. Sham and hypocrisy are treated with disdain. The following verses illustrate his depiction of a scene in spring:

> Thus spoke at dawn the field-bird to the newly wakened rose:
> "Be kind, for many a bloom like you in this meadow grows."
> The rose laughed, "You will find that we at truth show no
>   distress,
> But never did a lover with harsh words his love so press,
> If early wine from jewelled cup it is your wish to drink,
> Then pearls and corals pierced with eyelash you must strive
>   to link.
> Love savour to his nostrils to entice he ne'er can seek,
> Who on the tavern's earthly floor has not swept dusty cheek." [5]

Hafiz' love poems, perhaps meant half sensually, half mystically, were later interpreted in the Sufi fashion and thus gained entree into pious

[4] Arthur J. Arberry, *Classical Persian Literature* (London, 1958), p. 189.
[5] Reuben Levy, *Persian Literature* (London, impression 1928), p. 77.

circles and widened their sphere of influence. That was what had happened earlier in the case of the Song of Songs. His works served as a guide for future generations of Persian and Turkish poets and were translated into German and English. Goethe was one of those inspired by them. Hafiz died in his native town in 1389, two years after the city had suffered an invasion from Timur. An alleged dialogue between the two men revolves on a discussion of one of the poet's verses.

Timur started a line which lasted almost a century (1405-1501). The period was dominated by Jami (1414-1492), so named after a village in Khurasan. Jami was prolific in both poetry and prose. From his pen we have three *Diwans* and several other works. One of his poems treats the story of Joseph and Potiphar's wife (*Yusuf u-Zulaykha*), treated earlier and more realistically by Firdawsi. Jami also wrote a *Diwan* and a long poem on spring in imitation of Sadi's *Gulistan.* He is usually regarded as the last of the Persian classical poets. His admirers claim that Firdawsi was the greatest in epic poetry, Nizami in romances, al-Rumi in mystic poetry, Hafiz in lyrics, and that Jami was great in all these genres. Nizami, who died at the beginning of the thirteenth century, made his reputation as the undisputed master of romantic poetry through a collection of five poems (*Khamsah, quinte*), also styled the five treasures, one of which treats the old theme of Majnun (one who went mad) and Layla, the two desert Arab lovers who were kept apart by a family feud until death united them.

The rejuvenation of Islam under Saljuqs and Mongols manifests itself abundantly in the fine arts. Tabriz, Shiraz, and Herat developed centers for calligraphy and manuscript illumination. The *Shah-namah,* among other works, was then illuminated. Painting, textiles, and all other varieties of decorative art felt the throb of this new life. It is possible that in the train of the Mongols came specimens of the arts and crafts of China and certainly some of its artisans. Chinese influence in the physiognomy of the painted subject becomes apparent. The new elements modified the traditional rigidity, injected more ease and grace, and imparted greater flexibility to the composition. As if to make up for their early ravages Mongol rulers, after embracing Islam started religious building programs that produced some of the most magnificent structures of their kind. The Saljuq mosque assumed the standard form of an open court surrounded by arcades with columned and vaulted halls on two sides. The congregational mosque of Isfahan, built in 1088 by a political rival of Nizam-al-Mulk and enlarged under

Courtesy of The Metropolitan Museum of Art, Dick Fund, 1939

MIHRAB OF FAÏENCE MOSAIC FROM A SCHOOL AT ISFAHAN, DATED 1354

the Mongols, is the most spacious place of worship in the land and perhaps its most important religious architectural monument. In it the problem of effecting union between the dome, which is round, and its base, when it is square, is solved in an ingenious way. The two are united by, strange as it may seem, the motif of the pointed arch.

The blending can be said to be perfect.   It represents the carrying of the principle of the squinch to a high development.

Saljuq and Mongol potters with sensitive hands, lively imaginations, and delicate taste carried their craft to a fuller realization of its possibilities.   They were no doubt inspired and helped by poets, painters, and calligraphers.   Many of the most beautiful specimens of Saljuq and Mongol pottery come from al-Rayy.   At times Mongol pieces tend to be over-elaborate.

The rash of states which began erupting all over the body of the caliphate in the eighth century was not entirely of Persian and Turkish origin.   Some were or claimed to be Arab.   Of these, the Fatimid in Egypt and the Hamdanid in Syria deserve special consideration.

THE FATIMIDS

The Fatimid dynasty was born (909) and reared in Kairwan, Tunisia, displacing the Arab power in control,[6] but attained its maturity in Cairo, Egypt, to which it moved in 973, displacing a petty Turkish dynasty which had in turn superseded an earlier Turkish one.   These two Turkish dynasties had ruled Egypt and southern Syria from al-Fustat.   The course they pursued was analogous to that of their contemporaries.   The caliph sent a governor to Egypt in 868; the governor acted independently and energetically; his incompetent successors indulged in luxury; they gave way to another dynasty which turned out to be just as ephemeral as its predecessor.

The founder of the Fatimid caliphate, more strictly imamate, was Ubaydullah al-Mahdi (r. 909-934), who claimed descent from Fatimah through al-Husayn and Ismail.   He was, therefore, not only a Shiite but an Ismailite and his second name indicates that he claimed to be the expected imam.[7]   The hero of the Egyptian conquest was originally a slave who, under the name of Jawhar al-Siqilli, became commander of the Fatimid army.   His second name suggests Sicily as his birthplace. In 972, three years after his entry into al-Fustat, Jawhar began to lay out a new quarter, al-Qahirah (whence Cairo), to become the seat of the government.   He also began building the great mosque al-Azhar, with which was associated an institution of higher learning that is today the oldest university extant and a main source of Islamic learning.   An Azhar representative marching in an international academic procession even today is entitled to the senior position.   Al-Aziz (r. 975-996), fifth in the dynasty, was the first Fatimid to commence his rule at Cairo.   Under him the empire reached its zenith, extending

[6] Treated above, pp. 290 *seq.*
[7] Cf. above, pp. 281-282.

Courtesy of the Metropolitan Museum of Art,
Bequest of William Milne Grinnel, 1920

MINIATURE OF RUSTAM, HERO OF A *SHAH NAMAH* TALE, CAPTURING THE HORSE, RAKHSH

*Courtesy of the Metropolitan Museum of Art,
Rogers Fund, 1912*

WALL TILE, EARLY 14TH CENTURY

Courtesy of the Metropolitan Museum of Art,
Gift of Alexander Smith Cochran, 1913

MINIATURE PAINTING OF A HUNTING SCENE FROM A MANUSCRIPT OF JAMI, *DIWAN*, 15TH CENTURY

from the Red Sea to the Atlantic. The mention of his name in the Friday prayers throughout that territory as well as in Sicily, Yemen, Mecca, Damascus, and once even in Mosul indicates nominal recognition of his sovereignty. Clever Ismailite propaganda contributed to the success of the regime, as did the Fatimid fleet, which had no competitor in the Eastern Mediterranean. This posed a grave threat to the rival caliphate in Baghdad. So sure was al-Aziz of his ability to exterminate that caliphate that he is said to have commenced preparations in Cairo for housing his captured rival. But he would even then have another Sunnite rival at Cordova, whom he began verbally to attack. The Cordovan answer was prompt and supercilious, "You, having heard of us, denounce us. Had we ever heard of you we would have done likewise."

Al-Aziz was probably the ablest in the line. He accorded his Christian subjects a measure of tolerance never enjoyed before. In this he was no doubt influenced by his Christian vizir and Russian wife, sister of two Melkite patriarchs and mother of his successor al-Hakim. Al-Aziz adorned his capital with palaces and mosques, enriched it with bridges and canals, and started the Azhar on its way to becoming a great academy. Being a poet and lover of learning, he desired to attract scholars but the fact that his court was heretical militated against that. He committed one serious mistake; the importing of Turkish and negro troops had the same results as it had had in Baghdad.

In contrast his blue-eyed eleven-year-old successor al-Hakim (r. 996-1021) inaugurated a reign of terror. Al-Hakim killed one vizir after the other; demolished the Church of the Holy Sepulcher (rebuilt later to become one of the greatest architectural monuments of Christendom); and reactivated the old regulations forcing Christians and Jews to wear black robes, use only donkeys as mounts, dangle from their necks a cross, if Christians, and a kind of yoke with bells, if Jews. This enigmatic caliph established and endowed a "hall of learning" for teaching medicine and astronomy in addition to the strictly Islamic subjects with stress on the Shiite variety. His court was illumined by ibn-Yunus (d. 1009), the greatest astronomer Egypt ever produced, and ibn-al-Haytham (Lat. Alhazen, d. *ca.* 1039), the leading physicist and student of optics Islam produced. Ibn-Yunus' astronomical tables, bearing the name of his patron, corrected the then current tables by original observations. In his work on optics, translated in twelfth century Spain, ibn-al-Haytham opposed the Euclid-Ptolemy theory that eyes send out visual rays to the object of vision and presented the results of experiments testing the angles of reflection. In his attempt to regulate the annual flow of the Nile for al-Hakim, however, he failed and simulated madness to escape the caliph's wrath.   The culminating act in al-Hakim's strange career was to declare himself, in accordance with ultra-Ismailite doctrine, the incarnation of the Deity.   He was so accepted by a small band which survives today mainly in Lebanon and called Druzes after al-Hakim's Persian missionary Darazi.   Al-Hakim's eccentricities were considered evidence of his divinity.   One dark night on his way to a hill overlooking his capital, he disappeared probably through a conspiracy hatched by his sister whom he had charged with infidelity.   But to his followers this was only a voluntary and temporary disappearance.

The decline in Fatimid fortunes followed closely on the attainment of the summit.   For a time, under al-Mustansir (r. 1035-1094), the decline seemed reversed when a pro-Fatimid general succeeded in seizing Baghdad and proclaiming Fatimid sovereignty.   The disruptive forces were not very different from those that had operated elsewhere before.   The succession of immature, incapable, or disinterested caliphs invited the rise of ambitious seekers after power in the heart of the empire as well as on its periphery.   As viziers contended for supreme power they were backed by factions in the army.   In the army itself trouble was continually brewing between Turkish, Berber, and Sudanese battalions.   The economy of the country became paralyzed; the efflorescence of the early period, supported by international trade, had gone.   Famines due to misbehavior on the part of the Nile or neglect of its canals became frequent.   One lasted seven years. North Syria fell into Saljuq hands; and before the close of the eleventh century the empire had shrunk to little more than Egypt.   At that time an unexpected non-Moslem enemy was advancing from the northwest.   The destruction of the Church of the Holy Sepulcher, the most sacred object of Christian pilgrimage, was one of the episodes that prompted the Crusaders to move.   The establishment of Latin Kings in Jerusalem brought the danger nearer home.   In 1167 one of the Crusaders stood at the very gates of Cairo, but the final blow to the decrepit caliphate came from the hands of a Sunnite Moslem.   In 1171 Saladin ordered the Friday preacher to cite the name of the Abbasid rather than that of the Fatimid al-Adid (r. 1160-1171), lying sick on his bed.   Saladin therewith added Egypt to his Syrian domain offering lip allegiance to Baghdad.   So smoothly was the historic change accomplished that, according to the chroniclers of the period, "no two goats locked horns."

Fatimid architectural monuments and artistic relics long outlived Fatimid political institutions.   Egypt is today a solidly Sunnite country. But the Azhar and al-Aqmar Mosques, three of the city gates, and other public buildings today constitute "must" items on a tourist itinerary. In al-Aqmar, built in 1125, we recognize the earliest appearance of the corbelled ("stalactite") niche and the bold designs of Kufic inscriptions, which became major features of Moslem architecture. The stalactite pedentives and deep niches introduced by Fatimid architects were adopted by their Ayyubid and Mamluk successors, developed and passed down. Likewise the Fatimid treatment of Kufic inscriptions on stone or wooden panels foreshadowed the glories of the later age. The practice of associating a tomb, usually of the founder, with a mosque also began during this period.

The Arab Museum of Cairo counts among its treasures several panels of carved wood dating from Fatimid days. Some display such Persian, originally Sasanid, animal motifs as deer attacked by monsters and hares seized by eagles. The ceramic art also followed Persian models.

NORTH SYRIA

The Fatimid hold on Syria was precarious and unstable. The northern part of the country was contested by Qarmatians, Turks, Saljuqs, and Byzantines. During al-Hakim's reign, Bedouins from the Syrian Desert began to encroach on the land. The chief of one of them wrested Aleppo and with his line held it for over half a century. The spirit of the age with its political anarchy, social decay, intellectual skepticism, and religious uncertainty found expression in the poetry of abu-al-Ala al-Maarri (973-1057).

Born at Maarrat al-Numan, southwest of Aleppo, al-Maarri lost his sight early in life as a result of smallpox. In Baghdad he had contacts with Mutazilites, philosophers and freethinkers, and possibly with Hindus who converted him to vegetarianism. On his return home he lived in seclusion, referring to himself as the double-prison (blindness and home) inmate. Unlike most poets of the day he did not waste his talent eulogizing princes with a view to monetary reward. Al-Maarri made his mark as one of the rare poets of Islam who freed themselves from the shackles of tradition. Especially interesting to us is a treatise of his which peopled limbo with reported heretics enjoying themselves discussing textual criticism. This is one of the works whose stimulating effect is noticeable in Dante's *Divine Comedy.* Here is a sample of his irreligious thinking:

> Moslems are stumbling, Christians all astray,
>   Jews wildered, Zoroastrians on error's way.
> We mortals are composed of two great schools—
>   Enlightened knaves or religious fools.[8]

[8] Cf. R. A. Nicholson, *Literary History of the Arabs,* p. 318.

Another and more distinguished dynasty of bedouin origin in north Syria was the Hamdanid (r. 944-1003). Though Shiite this family was so tolerant as to preserve for a time the caliph's name in the Friday prayer. The dynasty made its mark under Sayf-al-Dawlah (the sword of the state, r. 944-967), a title bestowed on him by the Baghdad caliph to convey the impression that the recipient was under his control. In reality Sayf fully controlled a domain embracing, in addition to north Syria, part of Cilicia and a large portion of upper Mesopotamia. Border clashes with the eternal enemy to the west were inevitable, and Sayf was the first—after a long interval—to take up the cudgels seriously against the Byzantines. In Nicephorus Phocas (r. 963-996) he encountered more than a peer. This emperor and his successor John Zimisces (r. 969-976) temporarily occupied not only the capital Aleppo and Antioch but several coastal towns as far south as Beirut. The advance of Zimisces, Armenian by birth and one of the greatest of Byzantine generals, was halted at the gates of Jerusalem by Fatimid forces. The victories of these two emperors helped to raise the empire to its greatest glory.

Sayf's fame, however, rests on other than military considerations. His court was ornamented with a galaxy of literary and artistic talent that compared on a small scale with that of Harun and al-Mamun. Among them was the renowned philosopher-musician al-Farabi, the outstanding historian of literature abu-al-Faraj al-Isfahani (d. 967), and the poet laureate al-Mutanabbi (d. 965). For an autographed copy of his monumental *al-Aghani* (book of songs) abu-al-Faraj received from his patron a thousand gold pieces. The last of the major classical poets, al-Mutanabbi, has left odes that are still memorized in Arab schools. To his poet's eulogies Sayf owes perhaps more of his fame than to his own military achievements. The Byzantine-Hamdanid conflict, however, may be considered a significant chapter in the prehistory of the Crusades.

BOOKS TO READ

Brockelmann, Carl, *History of the Islamic Peoples,* tr. Joel Carmichael and Moshe Perlmann (New York, 1947).

Dimand, M. A., *A Handbook of Mohammedan Decorative Arts,* 3rd ed. rev. (New York, 1958).

Hitti, Philip K., *History of the Arabs,* 7th ed. (New York and London, 1960).

Hodgson, Marshall G. S., *The Order of Assassins* (The Hague, 1955).

The Legacy of Persia, ed. A. J. Arberry (Cambridge, 1953).

Levy, Reuben, *A Baghdad Chronicle* (Cambridge, 1929); *Persian Literature* (London, reprint 1928).

Lewis, Bernard, *The Arabs in History,* 3rd ed. (London, 1956).

O'Leary, De Lacy E., *A Short History of the Fatimid Khalifate* (London, 1923).

Pope, Arthur U., *An Introduction to Persian Art* (New York, 1931).

XXIII *Crusaders, Ayyubids and Mamluks*

THE eleventh century witnessed the establishment of a Moslem state in Byzantine territory within striking distance of Constantinople, another in Sicily whose incursions reached Rome and Genoa; and a more powerful one in Spain, whence raids into France had been carried on for two centuries. Europe had been threatened or attacked in its front, rear, and soft belly. It was time to react. Action and reaction between Europe and Asia had antedated Islam and Christianity. The Crusades wrote the medieval and most spectacular chapter in the history of that drama.

The motivation was complex. French and Norman princes were hungry for territorial acquisition. Italian merchants from Genoa, Pisa, and Venice were interested in commercial expansion. The restless and romantic adventurers were eager for a new outlet for their ambitions. The devout and sinful sought penance through the holy pilgrimage. The Roman Catholic Church, whose aid was solicited by the Byzantine emperor against the encroaching Saljuqs, seized upon the opportunity as a means for healing the recently effected schism with the Greek Church.

The spark was set by a speech delivered in 1095 in southern France by a French-born pope, Urban II. In it the pope recited tales of Moslem atrocity, made open allusions to the opportunities for personal profit, and distributed crosses, thereby raising the enthusiasm of his audience to a high pitch and clothing the project in religious concepts. Perhaps no more effective speech was delivered in medieval times. The cross became a badge worn by the would-be Crusaders. Like wild fire a strange psychological wave, centering in France, spread through Europe engulfing high and low, old and young and in some cases emptying whole villages of their populations. To the economically and socially depressed masses in France, Italy, and Sicily taking the cross was more of a relief than a sacrifice.

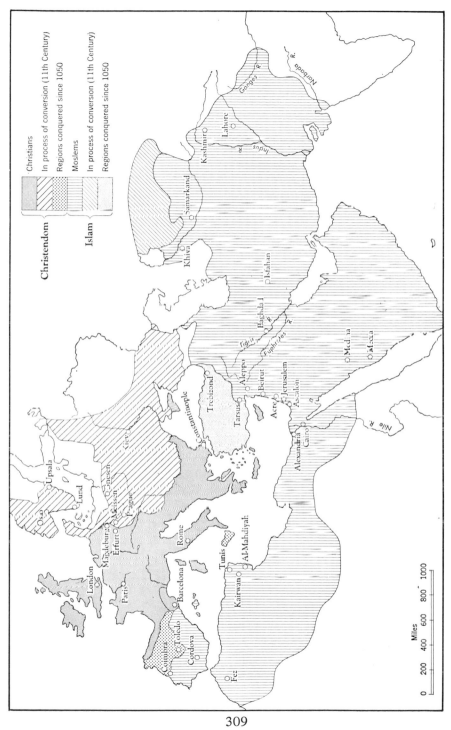

ISLAM AND CHRISTENDOM ON THE EVE OF THE CRUSADES

In three great divisions the French converged on Constantinople as the rendez-vous: one of Normans under Bohemond, the shrewdest and most effective of the leaders; another of Provençals under Raymond of Toulouse, the most devout; and a third of Lorrainers under Godfrey of Bouillon and his brother Baldwin, future king of Jerusalem. Emperor Alexius Comnenus exacted an oath of fealty from the leaders to insure his title to any recovered "lost province" of his realm. Only Raymond refused.

PERIOD OF CONQUEST

The route of the first Crusaders led across the Saljuq domain. Its head city Nicaea was captured in June 1097 and a large part of its territory was restored to the Byzantine emperor. By the time the marchers reached north Syria their leaders were already squabbling among themselves and seeking conquests each for himself. Instead of moving southward toward the ultimate goal, Jerusalem, Baldwin swung eastward and in 1098 occupied Edessa (Ar. al-Ruha, Tur. Urfa), then an Armenian Christian principality. The first Latin state was established. Tancred, a leader of Italian and Sicilian Normans, turned westward and occupied Tarsus, also in Armenian hands. His kinsman Bohemond, chief Norman leader, aimed at Antioch. As the cradle of the first organized Christian church (Acts 11:26) and key to the entire Syrian region, the city was of special significance to the Crusaders. But the siege, though supported by the Italian fleet, was arduous and long, lasting from October 1097 to June 1098. No sooner had the besiegers, through treachery of an Armenian general of the Saljuq amir, gained entry into the city than they found themselves besieged by a Saljuq reinforcement. For twenty-five days the beleaguered suffered from plague and starvation. Only a miracle could save the day. The miracle came through the discovery, under a church altar, of the "holy lance" that had pierced the Savior's side as he hung on the cross. Emboldened by this celestial sign, the Crusaders effected a sortie resulting in the besiegers' repulsion. Bohemond established himself in control of the new principality. Disappointed, Raymond, whose men had made the new discovery, parted company and pushed south to seek his own fortune in some other adventure. In 1109 he succeeded in wresting Tripoli from the hands of its Arab amir and there built a castle, the first of its kind, and still one of the grand sights of that ancient town.

Godfrey of Bouillon followed Raymond and both took the coastal route once taken by Alexander and other great conquerors. They thereby maintained easy communication with the fleet which supplied

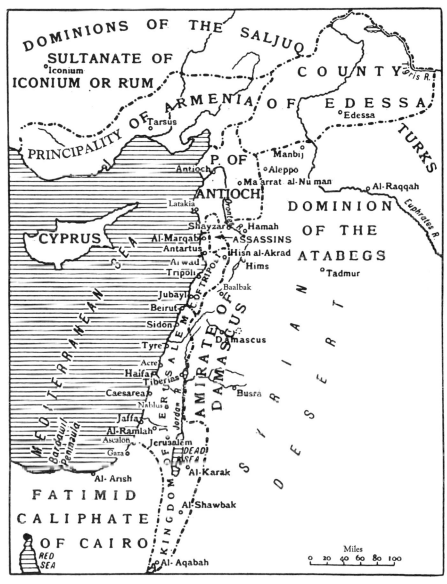

CRUSADING STATES OF SYRIA *ca.* 1140

supplies and recruits and they avoided contact with towns that had large Moslem concentrations such as Hamah, Hims, and Damascus. The march was almost a promenade. The Maronites of Lebanon even served as guides and later as archers in the Crusading ranks.

COAT OF ARMS OF THE KINGDOM OF JERUSALEM On a field of silver a cross potent between four crosslets, gold.

At last Jerusalem was reached. It was then held by a Fatimid garrison of about a thousand men. After a month's siege conducted by Godfrey, Raymond, and Tancred the holy city was stormed July 15, 1099. Its population was given to the sword. "The heaps of heads and hands," in the words of a Latin chronicle, "could be seen throughout the streets and squares." A new Latin state, by far the largest and most important, came into being. Godfrey served as its head for one year. He was followed by Baldwin (r. 1100-1110), who assumed the title king of the Latin kingdom of Jerusalem. Under Baldwin and his successor Baldwin II (r. 1110-1118) the kingdom was extended to include territory from Beirut to the Red Sea. It was fortified by castles and received the nominal allegiance of the three Latin states (Tripoli, Edessa, and Antioch which for a time included Cilicia).

These were the first and last acquisitions by Crusaders. They were due more to weakness and disunity on the part of the invaded than to strength and unity on the part of the invaders. The end began with the appearance on the eastern front of a new leader, a Turk named Zangi, lord of Mosul then of Aleppo. His were the first blows under which the Latin states were ultimately to crumble. The introductory blow fell on Edessa in 1144; it was the first city to be lost and the first to be regained. With that the spirit of the holy war began to animate Moslem rather than Christian fighters. On Zangi's death two years later, the championship of Islam passed to his more capable son Nur-al-Din (the light of the faith). In 1154, Nur wrested Damascus from another Turk and made it his seat of government. Therewith the one remaining barrier between Zangid and Latin territories was removed. Realizing the decrepit condition of the Fatimid regime and eager to put Jerusalem between an upper and a lower millstone, Nur commissioned an able lieutenant to proceed to Cairo and do what he could by peaceful or forceful methods. The emissary succeeded in receiving the vizirate from the caliph al-Adid. Two months later the vizir died leaving his young nephew Salah-al-Din (the rectitude of the faith, Saladin) in his place.

ENTER SALADIN

Born in Iraq of Kurdish parents Salah, when a year old, moved with his family to Baalbak, where his father served as commander for Zangi. In his boyhood he cherished only one ambition, to be a theologian. Only reluctantly did he accompany his uncle to Egypt. There, however, his military career began; he developed a threefold ambition: substituting Sunnite for Shiite Islam in Egypt, uniting that country with Syria under one rule, and pressing the holy war against the Franks. The first was attained in 1171 on the deposition of al-Adid.[1] With Egypt went Cyrenaica and Hejaz. The death of Nur-al-Din three years later provided Salah with the opportunity to realize the second ambition. With the first two goals attained the third entered the range of possibility. Nur's dream of encircling and then crushing the intruders was beginning to be realized under an abler successor.

After nibbling at the Latin state the time came for decisive action. The place was Hattin, an extinct volcano 1700 feet above the Sea of Galilee, which tradition makes the site of the delivery of the Sermon on the Mount. The date was July 3, 1187. For almost two days the Latin army—exhausted by the march, laden with heavy armor, and crazed with thirst—was subjected to an incessant shower of arrows the like of which they had never experienced. Of the 20,000 knights and footmen only a few remained alive through apostasy or capture. The long procession of captives was headed by the king of Jerusalem, Guy de Lusignan, seconded by Reginald of Châtillon, lord of al-Karak, a mighty fortress southeast of the Dead Sea. Reginald, an unscrupulous adventurer, had not only harassed pilgrims on their way to Hejaz but reportedly laid out fantastic plans for attacking Medina and carrying away the body of Muhammad for exhibition purposes. Saladin had sworn to kill him with his own hand and he did. But Guy was treated in a manner worthy of his royal state and freed after having pledged never again to bear arms against Moslems —a pledge he failed to fulfill.

Jerusalem was left defenseless. It soon yielded and its Christian population received a humane treatment compared with the way the Moslem population had been treated. All those who could ransom themselves on the spot or after a period of grace were allowed to do so; the rest were sold as slaves. The tide of conquest continued, engulfing one city after another, until only Tripoli and Antioch, besides minor towns and castles, were left.

[1] Noted above, p. 304.

The loss of the holy city aroused Europe to a new pitch of Crusading fervor. A new campaign was organized under the three mightiest sovereigns of Europe—Philip Augustus of France, Frederick Barbarossa of Germany, and Richard the Lion-Hearted of England. Legend and history have united to make of this campaign one of the most spectacular episodes in the military annals of medieval times. The particular battlefield was Acre (Akka), decided upon by the Frankish command as providing the key for the restoration of the lost territory. The city was besieged. Saladin rushed to its rescue. Though put between two fires the besiegers persisted for two years (1189-1191) with remarkable feats of valor performed on both sides. At last the city fell and 2700 of its prisoners were slaughtered on their failure to pay the ransom money. Haifa was also seized by Richard and a firm foothold was regained in the land. Peace was then concluded on the general basis that the coast from Tyre south belonged to the Latins, while its hinterland remained in Arab hands.

AYYUBIDS

In 1193 Salah-al-Din died and was buried outside the Umayyad Mosque in the Syrian capital, where his shrine is still frequently visited. The legacy he bequeathed was not only one of shining chivalry and

A COIN OF SALAH-AL-DIN   Obverse and reverse of a silver dirham of Salah-al-Din struck at Damascus, A.D. 1177-1178.

staunch championship of orthodox Islam but also of the patronage of learning. The schools, hospitals, mosques, and seminaries he founded in his Syro-Egyptian realm served as models for his Ayyubid and Mamluk successors. The citadel he built in Cairo and used as residence while there still dominates the city. But after his death the kingdom was parceled out among his sons and brothers, giving rise to a number of petty Ayyubid branches in Egypt, Damascus, Hamah, and other Syrian and Mesopotamian cities. The anti-Crusading spirit aroused by him lay dormant for half a century. The Moslems lost the unified command and the united domain. The Christians were in as weak a position with quarrels among leaders, rivalries between Genoese and

Venetians, and friction between Hospitalers and Templars, the two militant orders.

In the first half of the thirteenth century the center of interest shifted from Syria-Palestine to Egypt. Al-Kamil (r. 1218-1238), nephew of Salah-al-Din and his successor there, loomed as the leading Ayyubid figure and received the homage of the dynasts in Syria. Shortly before his accession Crusaders landed in Egypt and occupied Dimyat (Dami- etta). The invasion was prompted by the realization by the maritime republics of Italy that Egypt was then the head Moslem state and that only by its conquest could their ships reach the Red Sea and share in the opulent commerce of the Indian Ocean. Al-Kamil, formerly a friend of Richard, signed commercial treaties with European countries and showed unusual interest in irrigation and agriculture. He was favorably disposed toward his Christian subjects, received St. Francis of Assisi (founder of the Franciscan order) and discussed religion with him. In 1229 he concluded with Frederick II of Sicily[2] a treaty yielding Jeru- salem. The city, however, was restored under his second successor al- Salih (r. 1240-1249).

As al-Salih lay on his death-bed he received the news that Louis IX, king of France, had directed a fresh Crusade against Egypt. As the French army moved toward Cairo, however, pestilence thinned its ranks and its line of communication was destroyed, the Nile inundation being at its height. The king was taken prisoner. After a month of captivity Louis was released on the payment of a ransom and proceeded to Syria, where he remained for four years (1250-1254). There he fortified several coast towns one of which was Sidon, where the ruins of his castle are still standing. In nobility of character, genuine piety and devotion to ideals, St. Louis stood in a class by himself among Crusading leaders. His canonization was indeed well deserved.

MAMLUKS

The death of al-Salih in 1249 left his widow Shajar-al-Durr (the tree of pearls) as the virtual head of the state. Shajar, the only Moslem queen to rule Egypt and Syria, was originally a Turkish or Armenian slave in the harem of the last Abbasid caliph. A daring and energetic woman she inscribed her name on the coins and had it mentioned in the Friday sermon. When her former master al-Mustasin wrote to the notables of Egypt, "If you have no man to rule over you advise us and we shall send you one," they chose the army commander Izz-al-Din Aybak for sultan. Shajar did the next best thing; she married him.

[2] Treated above, p. 290.

Originally a slave (*mamluk*) in al-Salih's bodyguard, Aybak (r. 1250-1257) started the line of Mamluk sultans of Egypt-Syria, which lasted until the conquest of the Ottoman Turks in 1516-1517. The line was mostly Turkish and Circassian. When a sultan died it was usually not his son but his slave or a mercenary in his bodyguard who succeeded him. The bondman of yesterday might become the army commander of today and the monarch of tomorrow. Although they were generally uncultured, untutored, and bloodthirsty, members of this oligarchy adorned Cairo with architectural monuments of which it still rightly boasts, cleared Syria of the remnant of the Crusaders, and definitely checked the advance of the redoubtable Mongol hordes of Hulagu and Timur (Tamerlane). But for that, the entire course of history and culture in the Near East might have been different.

It was the fourth Mamluk, al-Zahir Baybars (r. 1260-1277), who resumed the anti-Crusading activity that was begun by Nur-al-Din and continued by Salah-al-Din. He inaugurated the series of sultans that dealt the final blows to Latin Syria. His first military feat was the checking of the Mongol wave which after the fall of Baghdad had swept as far south as Palestine. He then firmly reunited Egypt and Syria under his control. One after the other of the Frankish-held towns fell into his possession. Even some of the formidable castles garrisoned by the mighty orders of Templars and Hospitalers could not withstand his and his successors' onslaughts. Originally organized to protect pilgrims on their way to the Holy Sepulcher, the knights that were called Templars acquired their name from their headquarters in King Baldwin's palace next to the building known as Solomon's Temple. The knights called Hospitalers started as a body of monks under whose auspices a hospital in Jerusalem was conducted.

The strongest and most significant among the cities was Antioch, which surrendered in 1268. Of its garrison and people 16,000 were put to the sword and some 100,000 were led to captivity. The slave market became so glutted that a boy would fetch only twelve dirhams and a girl five. The city itself with its citadel and venerable churches was set to flames—a blow from which it has never recovered. Today it is in Hatay, acquired by Turkey from Syria on the eve of the second World War. Three years after Antioch's fate, tenacious Crac des Chevaliers (Hisn al-Akrad, "citadel of the Kurds"), garrisoned by Hospitalers, yielded. This is the most admirable of all medieval castles in preservation. For years the castle, under the count of Tripoli, stood sentinel over the Hims-Tripoli road linking the coast with the interior. It could house as many as two thousand at a time. In modern times a whole town was housed in it, but it was cleared under the French

HISN AL-AKRAD, CRAC DES CHEVALIERS, ONE OF THE STRONGEST AND LARGEST OF THE
CRUSADER CASTLES

mandate. The Crac headed the list of mountain-type castles set to
dominate the passes leading from the Moslem hinterland to the Frankish
seaboard. Equally formidable and impressive was al-Marqab ("watch-
tower," Castrum Mergathum), also held by Hospitalers, which made
peace in 1285 after a thirty-eight-day siege. This fortress represents
the coastal type designed to control the important maritime roads and
ports and defend them against the Egyptian fleet. Al-Marqab is still
perched like a dreadnought on a hill overlooking the Mediterranean
with arrowheads embedded in its walls as a souvenir of past experience.
Many other Crusade structures, secular and religious, have surrendered
to the crushing impact of time.

Al-Marqab was reduced under Qalawun (r. 1279-1290), worthy
successor of Baybars. Like his predecessor, Qalawun was a Turkish
slave whose title al-Alfi (thousander) bespeaks the high price of a
thousand dinars paid for him. Four years after the capture of al-
Marqab Tripoli, the largest city still Frankish held, succumbed and
was left in ruins. Acre was the only place of military importance left.
It was stormed in May 1291 by Qalawun's son and successor. Its
Templar defenders were all massacred, a promise of safe-conduct notwithstanding. The city was plundered, its fortifications were disman-
tled, and its houses set on fire. Therewith the curtain fell on the last act
in the East-West medieval drama.

THE IMPACT OF THE CRUSADES

In their wake the Crusades, despite the fact that the periods of truce in them were longer than those of war, left havoc and destruction. Almost all cities held by them, especially those along the coast, were left in ruins. Fearing the Franks' return, Mamluks followed the policy of "scorched earth." Today there is not much to remind us of the Crusaders beyond ruined castles on hilltops unless it be some of the ill feeling generated and maintained between Christians and Moslems. As for Western Europe the results were on the whole more beneficial. This was its major expansion and it brought it in touch with a higher civilization from which lessons could be and were learned. In law, medicine, astronomy, philosophy, art, and other intellectual fields the Crusaders had little to impart and much to acquire, despite the fact that Moslem culture had lost its creative character and was already on the decline. Language was a barrier, irresponsiveness and lack of appreciation on the part of the Europeans was another. Only one major medical work, that of al-Majusi,[3] was done into Latin at Antioch in 1127 by a Pisan. Hospices and hospitals, chiefly lazar houses sprang up in twelfth century Europe suggesting at least Oriental stimulation.[4] Stories, some of Persian origin, were transmitted and appear in the contemporary Latin literature. Chaucer's *Squiere's Tale* has an *Arabian Nights* antecedent. In military art the Crusaders acquired the knowledge of conveying military intelligence by courier pigeons, the use of fire for signaling at night, and certain aspects of chivalry. The fleur-de-lis, for instance, which appeared in Moslem heraldry as the blazon of Nur-al-Din, was adopted by the Franks and passed on to France and Canada. The Church of the Holy Sepulcher and the Dome of the Rock were imitated in several ecclesiastical buildings of England, France, Spain, and Germany. The Crusading movement opened new markets for European merchants, widened horizons for the intellectuals and accelerated other forces already in operation. It popularized such Oriental products as rice (*arizz*), lemon (*laymun*), attar (*itr*), ginger (*zanjabil*), and sugar (*sukkar*). Until then honey was the only ingredient—and a rare one—used by Europeans for sweetening foods and drugs. With sugar was introduced the sugar cane, today one of the chief products of the islands of the West Indies. Ambergris (gray amber, from Ar. *'anbar*), as a highly valued element in perfumery, originated in Arabia, where it was found floating in the Indian Ocean. It was also widely used throughout the East for flavoring drinks and

[3] Noted above, pp. 249-250.
[4] Cf. above, pp. 248-249.

for burning as incense. Warriors, pilgrims, sailors and merchants returned with rugs, carpets, and fabrics which were later imitated. Such fabrics as damask (from Damascus), muslin (from Mosul), baldachin (from Baghdad), taffeta (Ar. *tafta,* from Per.), satin (Ar. *zaytun,* corrupted from a Chinese place name) testify to Europe's industrial indebtedness to the Near East of this period.

ARMS OF FRANCE Early coats of arms of France showed fleurs-de-lis on a blue field.

While this infiltration was taking place through Syria, cultural streams were passing through Moslem Spain and Arab-Norman Sicily-Italy, as we have had occasion to note repeatedly before. It is therefore difficult at times to ascertain the exact course of borrowed culture in Europe of that period. The first Italian textile workers acquired technical skills and models for designs from Sicily. Boccaccio, known as the father of classical Italian prose, indirectly derived several tales in his *Decameron* from Oriental sources. Fables from the Bidpai collection and stories from the *Arabian Nights* must have been transmitted and recounted by innumerable Europeans. Boccaccio's writings were used as source material by Chaucer, Shakespeare and others Among the names of agricultural products that of the tomato called in Italian "apple of the Moors" (*pomo di moro,* corrupted into *pomo d'oro,* "apple of gold") betrays Arabic transmission. To our Italian immigrants in America we owe the solid-fleshed common tomato varieties we eat; the real American tomato (the word is Aztec) is watery-fleshed and does not keep well.

An interesting by-product of the Crusading activity was the initiation of Christian work among Moslems. The military failure of the Crusades prompted another and more peaceful approach. Converting the Moslem seemed easier than exterminating him. The Carmelite order, still active in the Near East, was founded by a Crusader in 1154 and bears the name of a mountain in Palestine. Two other monastic orders, the Franciscan and the Dominican, were later established in Europe and sent representatives to the area, where they still operate. A Catalan ecclesiastic, Raymond Lull (d. 1315), was the earliest European to stress Oriental studies for implementing the new effort. Having studied it himself from an Arab slave, Raymond taught it and encouraged others to do likewise. He founded a college of friars for the study of this language and was probably influential in bringing about the resolution of the council of Vienne to create chairs of Arabic and Tartar in the Universities of Paris, Louvain, and Salamanca.

AYYUBID AND MAMLUK CONTRIBUTIONS

Salah-al-Din received from his predecessor Nur-al-Din a tradition of architectural and educational patronage which he enriched and passed on to his successors. The period was the first phase of a long era of general decline in which the sources of original intellectual work were drying or already dried up and scholarly activity was generally limited to compilation, annotation, and imitation. With it came the end of the period of efflorescence, which began around the mid-eighth century, and beginning of the dark ages of the Arab world, which lasted until the nineteenth century.

The type of school organized and promoted by Nurids and Ayyubids was more of an intellectual descendant of Nizam-al-Mulk's institution rather than al-Mamun's academy in Baghdad. It was a collegiate mosque comprising a theological seminary, a law academy, and a school of letters, all endowed and supported by the state. Both teachers and students received pay and as a rule lodged in or around the institution. The literary works of the period were generally biographical collections, dictionaries, historical compendiums, and legal manuals. Special mention should, however, be made of an Ayyubid ruler of Hamah, abu-al-Fida (1273-1332), whose geographical treatise in favor of the sphericity of the earth contains the argument of the loss or gain of one day as one travels around it. As a lad abu-al-Fida had witnessed the Mamluk capture of Tripoli to which he refers in his historical work, itself a redaction of an earlier one.

Some progress was made in the field of medicine especially as it relates to the treatment of eye diseases. A remarkable achievement of Nur-al-Din was the hospital he built, equipped and endowed in his capital. Free diet and drugs were prescribed to patients by its physicians. The hospital was furnished with a library and served as a medical school. The building is today used for housing a school of commerce. There is evidence to indicate that physicians, oculists and druggists were required to pass a test before receiving licenses to practice. A noteworthy product of the Nuri hospital was the Damascene ibn-al-Nafis (d. 1288), who became dean of the Qalawun hospital in Cairo, modeled after that of Damascus. Ibn-al-Nafis contributed a clear conception of the pulmonary circulation of the blood three centuries before the Spanish Servetus, who is credited with the discovery.

He is described as one "who would not prescribe medicine when diet sufficed." Qalawun is said to have received his inspiration while lying sick with colic in the Nuri hospital. In a way his hospital was an improvement. It was open to the sick of both sexes, employed male and female attendants, and contained special wards for segregating various diseases. The whole was endowed to yield a million dirhams annually. Its remains are the oldest extant in Egypt.

Salah introduced the Syrian type of dervish monastery and collegiate mosque into Egypt, where it became domesticated, and was continued by the Mamluks. As an alien oligarchy in a land in whose soil they had no roots, the Mamluks evidently resorted to public works to ingratiate themselves with their subjects. The collegiate mosque of Qait-Bay

Courtesy of The Bettmann Archive

THE COLLEGIATE MOSQUE OF QAIT-BAY, CAIRO

(r. 1468-1495) is a memorial one containing his tomb as well as the school he built.   In addition to its symphony of color, the dome is decorated with a charming network of conventionalized foliage and rosettes.   The building maintained the tradition of vigor and virile elegance established by the Ayyubid school of Syria.   The sultan-builder of this mosque, originally purchased by one of his predecessors for fifty dinars, had no scruples about blinding his alchemist for his failure to turn dross into gold.   Royal patronage was not limited to architecture.   The museums of Egypt, Europe, and America exhibit exquisite vases, ewers, trays, chandeliers, perfume burners, and other copper and brass utensils of the period.   There are also superb specimens of iron work, wood carving, and glassware.   Mamluk industrial arts show no decline.

Courtesy of The Walters Art Gallery, Baltimore

A BRASS INCENSE BURNER MADE IN MAMLUK SYRIA, SECOND HALF OF 13TH CENTURY
Inlaid with silver, its lower part is decorated with units of scrolling stems symmetrically composed and coalescing with water fowls.

Economically, however, the period was far from being a happy one. To meet the expenses of their frequent campaigns, public works, and extravagant courts, sultans resorted to extortions from their subjects. Basically the Mamluk system was a feudal and self-perpetuating oligarchy working to the advantage of the Mamluks not the natives.   The sultan would offer an amir or officer a grant of land, in lieu of pay, with the stipulation that the recipient would maintain five to a hundred Mamluk soldiers.   The grants were not intended to be hereditary; they were for life or a part of it, with the result that the Arabicized descendants of Mamluk officers were excluded from sharing in the accrued benefits in favor of newly imported slaves.   Natural causes added their quota of misery. Drought, famine, and pestilence occurred frequently.   A chronicler reports four plagues of considerable severity in the fourteenth century, one of which (1348) raged for several years and reached Europe, where it became known as the Black Death.   The epidemic is said to have carried away 300,000 Cairenes in the first three months.   Considering it a sign of God's wrath, the sultan sought to make atonement by fresh exactions from Christians and Jews.

END OF THE MAMLUKS

The last Mamluks were an especially sad lot. They wrote one of the darkest chapters in the history of the land. Some were so greedy and selfish as to monopolize sugar, spices, and other commodities and realize excessive profits from their subjects. Others were drunkards, homosexuals, and depraved. One could not recite the first chapter of the Koran, as part of the prescribed prayer, without committing a mistake; another could not sign his name without tracing it on one previously written by his secretary. One sultan had his two physicians beheaded for their failure to bring him relief from a fatal malady. The moral and political deterioration was not confined to the highest in the oligarchy. Amirs, officers, ambitious leaders, and chiefs of bodyguards organized factions, started revolutions, and struggled to grasp all possible wealth and power. Soon new factors from outside were to operate and add trouble to the domestic affairs.

In 1498 a Portuguese navigator, Vasco da Gama, found his way round the Cape of Good Hope to India. He returned to Europe the following year with a cargo of its greatly desired and highly priced spices. His expedition was followed by others. A new, cheaper, and safer route was found to link Europe with the Far East. The Near East was by-passed, the Moslem world outflanked. A blow was dealt to its transit trade in particular and international trade in general from which it was not able to begin recovering until the opening of the Suez

Canal and the introduction of modern means of travel and communication. A different and more serious threat was concurrently forming in the north.

While Mamluks were building up their state, Ottoman Turks were organizing theirs on Saljuq-Byzantine ruins. These two powers were bound to clash especially at the border where Asia Minor and Syria met. As they clashed a third major power was rising to the east, Safawid Persia, rejuvenated and aggressive. The Safawids were Shiites, natural enemies of Sunnite Turks. Squeezed between Safawids and Ottomans, the Mamluk sultan Qansawh al-Ghawri (r. 1500-1516) chose what seemed to him the lesser evil and sided with Shah Ismail (r. 1502-1524), founder of the Safawid line. The Ottoman throne was then occupied by an energetic warrior sultan Salim I (r. 1512-1520). On a battleground north of Lake Urmia in 1515, the Janissaries' superior artillery cut down the Persian cavalry and routed the entire army. Salim pushed on and occupied not only Mesopotamia and part of Armenia but Tabriz, Ismail's capital. In the spring of the following year Qansawh proceeded from Cairo to north Syria under the pretext of acting as an intermediary. To make his mission seem peaceful he brought in his train several judges headed by a puppet caliph, named al-Mutawakkil, whose predecessor—a scion of the defunct Abbasid family—had been picked up by Baybars and set up at Cairo as a nominal caliph to bolster the Mamluk regime. But Salim would not be fooled. He shaved the beard of Qansawh's envoy —a grave insult—and sent him back on a mule with a declaration of war.

The two armies met at Marj Dabiq north of Aleppo. Khair Bey, Mamluk governor of Aleppo, deserted with his troops. The aged Qansawh, stricken with apoplexy, fell dead from his horse. The Egyptian army, wedded to antiquated weapons and counting on personal valor, gave way before the Ottomans using artillery, muskets, and other long-range powder machines. The Mamluks were among the first Easterners to make use of gunpowder (1370), only two or three decades after its effective use in Europe, where it began to be granulated around 1429. A predecessor of al-Ghawri built an arsenal and cast cannon on a large scale, but al-Ghawri revived the Arab tradition of horsemanship and chivalry, which at Merj Dabiq was detrimental. A French traveler reports seeing cannon in Beirut's citadel in 1432. The Turks employed the new weapon with great effectiveness against Christian powers on sea and land. The Chinese invented gunpowder and used it as an incendiary. Around 1240 the Mongols introduced it into Europe where the application of its explosive force to the propulsion of missiles, i.e. the invention of firearms, was later made. The result of Marj Dabiq was decisive. Salim entered Aleppo and was received with rejoicing. All Syria lay at his feet. Early in the following year (1517) his men stood before the walls of Cairo, defended by Qansawh's successor and ex-slave Tuman-bay (r. 1516-1517). Before the Ottoman guns stationed on the Nile banks the city's fortifications readily crumbled. Tuman fled to a bedouin camp but was caught and hanged on one of the capital's gates. The Mamluk sultanate was thus exterminated. A new one took its place, that of the Ottoman Turks, under whom Egypt, Syria, and Hejaz were to linger for four long centuries.

With Salim's conquests the Arab and quasi-Arab era, whose vicissitudes we have traced through nine hundred years, ended. In the course of that era the Near East experienced changes that took place and radically affected every aspect of its life. Christianity and Zoroastrianism, the two predominant religions, were replaced by Islam. Aramaic and Coptic were superseded by Arabic, which came near superseding Persian, too; Turkish displaced Greek in Antatolia. In its turn the Moslem Near East experienced a number of radical transformations. Its society first based on a commercial monetary economy passed to an essentially military feudal one based on subsistence agriculture. Then gradually but surely the ascendancy of sedentary Arabs and Arabic-speaking peoples was replaced by that of Saljuq Turks and Mongols. Now a third change is imminent. The center of gravity shifts to Ottoman Constantinople, and in the east to native Persians. Turkish- and Persian-speaking rulers inherited Arab thrones. With the loss of Arab political power the last gleams of Arab glory vanish.

BOOKS TO READ

Arnold, Thomas and Alfred Guillaume, eds., *The Legacy of Islam* (Oxford, reprint 1947).

Grousset, René, *The Civilizations of the East,* vol. I, *The Near and Middle East,* tr. Catherine A. Phillips (New York, 1931).

A History of the Crusades, The First Hundred Years, vol. I, ed. Marshall M. Baldwin (Philadelphia, 1955).

Hitti, Philip K., tr., *An Arab-Syrian Gentleman and Warrior in the Period of the Crusades* (New York, 1929); *Syria: A Short History* (New York and London, 1959).

Lane-Poole, Stanley, *Saladin and the Fall of the Kingdom of Jerusalem* (New York, 1898).

Muir, William, *The Mameluke, or Slave Dynasty in Egypt* (London, 1896).

Monro, Dana L., *The Kingdom of the Crusades* (New York, 1935).

Poliak, A. N., *Feudalism in Egypt, Syria, Palestine and the Lebanon* (London, 1939).

Runciman, Steven, *A History of the Crusades,* 3 vols. (Cambridge, 1951-1954).

PART FIVE

*IN MODERN TIMES—OTTOMANS
AND PERSIANS*

XXIV   *The Ottoman Empire*

THE Ottomans who dominated the Near Eastern scene in modern times had their dim ethnic origins as Turks in Central Asia, where nomadic Turkish states had risen as early as the sixth Christian century. Pushed westward by some undetermined forces Turkish-speaking peoples established themselves in Turkestan, where they first came in contact with Indo-Iranians. It was there that the Arab-Moslem invaders of the seventh to the eighth century found them. Between the eleventh and the thirteenth centuries Turkish tribes flooded the entire northern territory of Islam from the Oxus to Anatolia. To them the horse served the same purpose as the camel did to the Arabians. They drank its milk, ate its flesh and, using stirrups and armed with bows and arrows, rode on its back to victory. Mobility and endurance characterized their march. Those who founded the Ottoman family penetrated into the heart of Anatolia, where they found their kinsmen, the Saljuqs—both belonging to the Ghuzz federation of tribes—already established. Nomadic Turkish speakers drifting into Anatolia from the east served as a perennial source of replenishment. Their language was a branch of the Uralic-Altaic group, but produced little or no written literature. Originally their religion was a primitive form of shamanism, which peopled the unseen world with gods, demons, and ancestral spirits responsive only to the shaman, or mediumistic conjurer. Somewhere en route they embraced Islam, at first perhaps only in name.

RISE OF THE OTTOMAN STATE

The Saljuq power which they found in Anatolia had decayed as a result of attacks from Mongols on the east and Byzantines on the west. In the ensuing struggle the newcomers assumed find supremacy. Their first leader had a Moslem name Uthman (Osman, Ottoman; r. *ca.* 1299-1326). a semi-historical figure who became the eponymous founder of the state and the dynasty. All thirty-six sultans, ending

329

with Muhammad VI Wahid-al-Din (r. 1918-1922), were his lineal descendants. The principality had its first important center at Brusa (Bursa), only thirteen miles from the Sea of Marmara. For about forty years beginning in 1326 this city served as capital and subse-

THE FLAG OF THE OTTO-
MAN EMPIRE

quently as base for attacks on Europe. In these attacks Constantinople was by-passed, Adrianople (ancient Hadrianopolis, after its founder Hadrian; Tur. Edirneh, Edreneh, now Edirne) was seized and used as another royal residence beginning in 1366. Thereby was the route from Constantinople to its Balkan hinterland blocked and the capital of eastern Christendom isolated from its potential allies, especially the Slavs. Its final doom was assured. The Turks' situation in Europe enabled them to acquire knowledge of the use of firearms which, as we learned, served them well in the struggle against Persians and Mamluks for supremacy in Western Asia. The principality of Brusa, which evolved into a kingdom in Adrianople, then became an empire and developed into one of the most powerful and enduring states ever built in Islam.

Courtesy of Turkish Information Office

ONE OF THE TOWERS OF THE FORTRESS RUMELIHISAR Built by Muhammad the Conqueror as a prelude to the attack on Constantinople, the ruins stand on the Bosporus below the campus of Robert College.

With authority consolidated over the Balkans, the turn of Constantinople came. The hero of its reduction was the twenty-four-year-old Muhammad II (r. 1451-1481), seventh sultan after Uthman. In 1953 the Turkish capital celebrated its five-hundredth anniversary. Muhammad earned the title of Fatih, Conqueror. The city that had defied repeated attacks from Arab Moslems yielded at last to a Turk, a new champion of Islam. The end of the Byzantine Empire marked the beginning of the fully evolved Ottoman Empire. A new era in history began and a fresh map of the eastern hemisphere had to be made. Constantinople served as Ottoman capital till 1923, when Mustafa Kemal chose Ankara for his seat of government.

Courtesy of American Numismatic Society

A COIN OF SALIM I   Struck in Serez, accession date 1512, gold.

Now it was time for expansion. Its hero on the Asiatic front was a grandson of Muhammad, Salim I (r. 1512-1520), whose military exploits netted the Arab East and Egypt.[1] The acquisition of the territory gave the Turks control of the oldest seats of culture and the meeting place of international trade routes between East and West. With Egypt went Hejaz. The incorporation of the holy cities of Islam enhanced the prestige of the Ottoman sultan in all Moslem eyes. The successors of Salim claimed to be the legitimate successors of the Arab caliphs.

THE SPLENDOR THAT WAS CONSTANTINOPLE

The hero of expansion on the western front was Salim's son Sulayman (r. 1520-1566), under whom the empire reached its zenith. Known to his people as the Qanuni (lawgiver) and to Europeans as the Magnificent, Sulayman codified, on the basis of the sacred law of Islam, and promulgated a system that remained supreme until the reforms of the nineteenth century. His court was magnificent indeed. He adorned his capital with palaces, mosques, and other public works, undertaken by his architect Sinan, originally a Christian slave from Asia Minor. Other cities in the realm benefited by Sulayman's munifi-

[1] Treated above. pp. 324-325.

THE SALIMIYAH MOSQUE AT CONSTANTINOPLE, A MASTERPIECE OF SINAN

cence and Sinan's talent.   Mecca and Jerusalem had their water supply
improved.   Sinan's two architectural masterpieces were the mosques
bearing the names of his two patrons, Sulayman and his son Salim
II.   Designed to eclipse Saint Sophia (Tur. Aya Sofya), the Sulaymaniyah's exquisite structure is topped with a dome eighty-eight feet
in diameter considered the handsomest and most impressive one in the
capital.   The edifice is decorated with mosaic and faïence in the Persian
style, and its tiles, which followed Saljuq models, display the height of
artistry in structure and color.   Sinan is credited with three hundred
and twelve buildings including mosques, palaces, schools, hospitals,
public baths, and burial "chapels."

Under Sulayman, Turkey expanded its sea power.   Two years before his accession two Ottoman Corsairs of Greek birth, Khayr-al-Din Barbarossa and his brother, had invaded Algeria (roughly Numidia of the Romans), warded off Spanish encroachments, and bestowed it on the Sublime Porte, so called from the gate of the sultan's palace at which justice was administered. Khayr-al-Din built up for Sulayman a well-equipped fleet, manned largely by Italian and Greek renegades, and made it an instrument of imperial aggression throughout the Mediter-

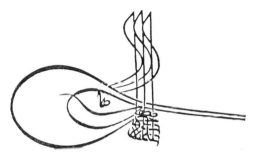

CALLIGRAPHIC EMBLEM OF SULAYMAN THE MAGNIFICENT, BEARING HIS NAME

ranean. Hitherto the Janissaries (Tur. for new troops), the infantry corps recruited first from slaves, conscripts, and sons of subject Christians seized as tribute, had represented the military force of the state. The fleet carried the terror of the Turkish striking force westward to the coasts of Spain as the Janissaries carried it eastward to Persia In 1534 Khayr-al-Din invaded Tunisia (Africa of the Romans), which, however, was not reduced to a Turkish province till 1574. Its reduction was achieved by the Ottoman governor of Egypt who had also to his credit the addition of Yemen to the domain of the house of Uthman. An Ottoman admiral of probable Christian origin, Piri Reis, conducted operations on the southern and eastern coasts of the Arabian peninsula and netted Aden and Muscat. A recently discovered map, used by Piri and called the Columbus map, shows the Atlantic Ocean and America. The conquest of Tripoli (1551) completed the acquisition of the Barbary states with the exception of Morocco (roughly Roman Mauretania), too far removed from the center of operation.

Meanwhile the land forces were not idle. Under Sulayman the frontier of the empire was pushed westward to include the greater part of Hungary. Vienna was besieged in 1529 and later in 1683, when it was relieved by a German-Polish army. It was presumably in the course of this last siege that the Turks left bags of coffee and thus introduced this drink into Central and Western Europe. Its first

THE OTTOMAN EMPIRE

AT ITS HEIGHT *ca.* 1550

mention in European literature was in 1585.   In Constantinople itself the first appearance of coffee was in 1554, when an Aleppine and a Damascene opened two coffeehouses which soon became a rendez-vous for wits, literary men, and gentlemen of leisure.   There they sought distraction, playing chess or backgammon, while novices in poetry submitted their latest compositions for the verdict of acquaintances. Theologians objected to the drink and sultans prohibited its use, but Sufis found it an aid in vigilance for night prayers, poets sang its praise, and the masses became more and more addicted to it.

The two horns of the Ottoman crescent under Sulayman came near making a junction; one stretched from beyond Budapest to the head of the Persian Gulf and the other from the western frontier of Algeria to the Red Sea coast of Arabia.   To the king of France, this Turkish ruler would address himself in this style: "I, who am the sultan of sultans, the sovereign of sovereigns, the dispenser of crowns to the monarchs on the face of the earth . . . to thee who art Francis, king of the land of France."

IMPERIAL SETUP

The empire set up by the Ottomans was basically a military dynastic institution with no deep support from the loyalty of its subject peoples— a conglomeration of religious and ethnic groups.   Slavs, Greeks, Albanians, Kurds, Armenians, Arabs, Jews, Christians, and Moslems with separate provincial loyalties were held together by the sword of Uthman. The empire produced an artificial unity and imposed indefinite stability on the area, but the situation remained precarious especially when the hand holding the sword was weakened.   Throughout, the Turks remained a minority, a class by themselves.   The class accepted him only who professed Sunnite Islam, spoke Ottoman Turkish, and conformed to the social pattern considered by it to be correct.   It will be recalled that the Arab Umayyads and Abbasids had followed the same general principles, but in their case the rush on the part of the conquered was so great that it became overwhelming.   With the Turks, however, the movement never assumed mass proportions.   The only exception was provided by Anatolia, seat of early Greek civilization centered in Troy, Sardis, Pergamum and other celebrated towns, and land of the "seven churches" of the Book of Revelation (chap. 1 *seq.*). Here Turkification was eventually almost complete.   Anatolia was to provide the only solid base for a Turkish state.

Under the sultans the power of the state resided in the military, representing force, and the ulema (theologians), representing religion.   As early as the fourteenth century sultans began the practice of imposing

a regular levy of boys, who were augmented by war prisoners and purchase and drawn into the capital to be Islamized, Turkified, rigorously
trained and pressed into the service of the state. The boys were all
from Christian families, as the religious law forbade the enslavement of
Moslems. Government officials as well as army officers and soldiers
came from this group. In the first centuries of the empire prime
ministers, vizirs, admirals, generals, and provincial governors started
their lives as slaves and so remained—in theory at least, holding their
positions, properties, and even lives at the pleasure of the sultan-caliph.
In the eighteenth century the personnel of the corps recruiting these
officials radically changed in favor of young men from Moslem families.
Many were Sufis. Sufism was a feature of Turkish Islam and colored
its many aspects. It linked the two mighty institutions: the religious
and the military.

In contrast to the military and governmental hierarchies, the theological in Constantinople recruited almost to a man from persons of
Moslem origin. This group took it upon itself to supply the diverse
Moslem denominations in the empire with a common ideal on which
they could meet. What brought the Arabs and Turks together was
religion, not language. The religious hierarchy was headed by the
shaykh al-Islam. Originally the mufti, chief judge, of the capital, the
shaykh al-Islam acquired religious and political importance that has no
parallel in other lands of Islam. Early Turkish muftis studied under
Syrian and Egyptian ulema. In the nineteenth century the shaykh's
office handled all institutions having a religious basis. He thus stood
on a par with other vizirs; only the grand vizir was considered higher
in rank. As head of the religious hierarchy the shaykh could pro-
nounce the *fatwa* (religious opinion) that would depose a sultan.

The ulema did not oppose the mystic tradition of Turkish Islam.
In the face of a combination between them and the Janissaries the
sultan had no way of imposing his will.

THE MILLET SYSTEM

Social stratification in the empire followed religious lines. From
time immemorial religion and nationality in the Near East have been
inextricably interwoven. In Turkey the religious grouping was termed
millet (Ar. for religion, nationality). The two major millets were
Islam and Rum (Roman, Greek Orthodox). Armenians and Jews
were also millets. The religious head of the millet was officially recognized by the government as the one to administer the laws pertaining to
personal status within the community. Moslem law was not applicable
in marriage, divorce, inheritance, and adoption cases. This organiza-

tion of the dhimmis into self-centered communities militated against inter-community exchange and had its adverse effect upon the political, social, and economical institutions of the state.   On the whole the Ottoman society may be pictured as consisting of a number of almost self-governing groups with a vast gap between the governing class of political, military, and religious officials headed by the sultan-caliph and a governed class of merchants, artisans, and cultivators.

The millet system was extended to European residents of the state. In 1520 Sulayman signed with the Venetians a treaty in thirty chapters (from L. *capitula,* whence capitulations), which confirmed privileges previously enjoyed under Byzantines and added new ones.   Fifteen years later the French acquired their first capitulations, with the British following in 1580.   Originally given as a concession by a strong monarch, the capitulations bestowed extraterritorial rights upon foreigners, eventually enabling them to interfere unduly in Turkey's internal affairs. These rights were not shaken off entirely until the first World War.

PROVINCIAL GOVERNMENT

The Ottoman principle of provincial administration did not differ much from the preceding Byzantine and Arab principles.   Its main function was to provide the central government with revenues for its treasury and manpower for its army.   Besides collecting taxes the governor was responsible for internal security; external security was the concern of the Sublime Porte.   The practice of farming out tax collection was, of course, retained as were the Mamluk administrative divisions of Syria and Egypt.   Each province had its governor, entitled pasha, appointed and sent by the Porte.   Lebanon, mountainous and difficult of access, with its liberty-loving Maronites and Druzes, deserved different treatment.   On its conquest Sultan Salim confirmed its Druze prince Fakhr-al-Din I al-Mani in his post as the leading feudal lord. Others, all natives, remained in their posts.   As a rule these vassals acted independently of Constantinople, transmitting their fiefs to their progeny, offering no military service to the imperial army, and even exercising the power of life and death over their subjects.   In 1608 one of them, Fakhr-al-Din II, concluded a treaty with a foreign power, the Medicis of Florence.[2]

The system of taxation was one of exploitation for the benefit of the imperial court.   Tithes and dues collected by feudal landlords constituted the principal revenue of the state.   Other items in the revenue included war spoils, tribute from Christians, and tribute from European dependent states.   No successful attempt was made to exploit the na-

---

[2] For more on him see below, pp. 451 *seq.*

tural resources of the land or to improve the economic status of its people.

BEGINNING OF THE DECLINE

The plateau at the peak attained by Sulayman's empire did not stretch far. Not long after his time decline began. His son Salim II (r. 1566-1574), whose succession was secured through the intrigues of his mother Roxelana, reportedly captive daughter of a Russian priest, had more taste for wine and women than for state affairs. During his reign dissipation, bribery, and corruption became rife. His son and successor Murad III (1574-1595) sired more than a hundred children. In Murad's and his successors' reigns wars were fitfully carried on with

Courtesy of American Numismatic Society

A COIN OF MURAD III   Struck in Constantinople, accession date 1574, gold.

enemies on the eastern and western frontiers including the Persians, Venetians, Hungarians, Austrians, and Poles. The unsuccessful siege of Vienna in 1683 is usually marked as beginning the end of the empire. A series of prominent grand viziers and statesmen provided by the Koprulu family, probably of Albanian extraction, in the second half of the seventeenth century retarded the process of decline but could not stop it. Their attempts at reforming the Janissary corps, stamping out corruption, and raising the morale of the bureaucracy brought only temporary relief.[3] Other viziers owed their positions to court favoritism rather than competence. Hitherto the Ottoman Empire had generally been on the offensive side; hereafter it moved to the defensive side. Its concern was no longer acquiring new territory but holding on to already acquired territory.

Degeneracy in the royal line, harem influence in the palace, corruption in high circles, and the decline of the military continued to push the state on its downward course. A state unwieldy in character, heterogeneous in population, far flung in area, and organized primarily for warfare rather than its people's welfare is not likely to stand the shock of changed conditions. Other elements of weakness were embedded in

[3] On the achievement of one of them see below, p. 343.

its dynastic system: the centralization of supreme authority—at least in theory—in the hands of the sultan-caliph, and ambiguity in the line of succession. The traditional nomadic and early Moslem principle gave the right of succession to the senior member of the tribe or family. Early Ottoman dynasts adopted the principle of the succession of son to father, but not necessarily the eldest son. In the early seventeenth century, because of special considerations, the practice was altered to provide for the succession of the eldest male member of the family. In accordance with this principle a feeble-minded prince, Mustafa I, succeeded to the throne in 1617. Three months later he was declared incompetent, forced to yield in favor of his nephew, and then dragged again to the throne in 1622 by Janissaries. In the following year he was once more compelled to renounce the throne in favor of another nephew, Murad IV (r. 1623-1640), an eleven-year-old boy. It was this Murad who abolished the tribute in Christian children, thus further opening the way for the admission of Turks to the Janissary corps. During his reign Baghdad (1638) and lower Mesopotamia were definitely annexed after having passed between Ottoman and Persian hands several times.

This lack of an established rule of succession led to endless intrigues and civil strife. Sulayman had his eldest son strangled to clear the way for his favorite concubine's son. Imperial fratricide had been legalized by an ordinance of Muhammad the Conqueror. Murad III opened his reign (1574) by murdering five of his brothers; his son Muhammad III (r. 1595-1603) did him one better by murdering fifteen of his brothers. The law of fratricide was extended, mainly by sultans newly ascending to the throne and anxious to strengthen their position against all possible rivals, to other male members of the royal family not excluding fathers, uncles, cousins, and nephews. The problem of succession led to the debilitating practice of confining the oldest male relative in a special pavilion, surrounded by a high wall, under strict surveillance. This practice began around 1603. When one such "caged" prince became sultan, he often showed signs of arrested growth and marked mental deficiency. Abd-al-Hamid I (r. 1774-1789) was kept in seclusion for forty-three years and was mentally affected, as was Muhammad V Rashad (r. 1909-1918).

Misrule at headquarters was bound to have its repercussions throughout the realm. The governors of provinces generally bought their appointments at Constantinople and entered upon their duties primarily motivated with the promotion of their personal interests. To them their subjects, especially when non-Moslems, were in reality what they were in name, raya (Ar. *ra'ayah,* herd), a human flock to be shepherded, milked, and fleeced.   Until the middle of the eighteenth century the Turkish usage of "raya" was extended to cover even the peasant population of the empire that was Moslem.   With no tenure or security in office governors had no time to lose in exploitation.   The governor who returned to the Porte to face dismissal, confiscation of property, or forfeiture of life was not a rarity.   Syria had no less than a hundred and thirty-three viceroys in the first hundred and eighty years of its life as an Ottoman province.   Egypt's record was even worse.   As the central authority declined, respect for its provincial representatives proportionally decreased and the temptation on the part of ambitious local chieftains increased, with the result that certain provinces lapsed into anarchy while others passed under local control.   Autonomy was not always an improvement over the autocracy it replaced.

With no serious attempts, governmental or indigenous, to improve the ancestral methods of agriculture and techniques of home industry, or even to keep the old system of irrigation in repair, the economy of the Arab lands deteriorated.   North Syria between Aleppo and the Euphrates, anciently fertile enough to support kingdoms, had been reduced to a desert by the mid-eighteenth century.   So it had remained until the present time.   The area of Syria-Lebanon-Palestine which in Roman days supported six million people had by the end of that century about half that number.[4]   Iraq, whose bloom under Nebuchadnezzar in ancient days and under Harun al-Rashid in medieval times is well-known, sank to a new depth.   When in the early twentieth century a British irrigation engineer was commissioned to study its problem he could recommend no better solution than to reopen and repair the ancient canals.   In Egypt the situation was rendered worse by the frequency of famine and pestilence.   One epidemic, that of 1619, carried away about half a million of a population which could not have been more than a few million.   Another, twenty-four years later, is said to have left two hundred and thirty villages desolate.   By the end of the eighteenth century the entire population was two and a half million as against some eight million in Roman days.

RUSSIAN AGGRESSION

The Ottoman Empire was partly in Europe but hardly of it.   Straddling the Bosporus with one foot in the Balkans it was nevertheless largely oriented eastward in its language, religion, ethnic relations, and ways of life.   Established at the expense of European states, it found itself in a perennial state of warfare with Balkan and then with Central European neighbors.   At times it even warred against Spain because

[4] Cf. above, p. 141.

of Tunisia, and often against Venice because of Crete, Cyprus, and navigation rights. In the seventeenth century first Austria-Hungary and then Russia loomed as formidable foes. The Ukraine, Azov, other frontier territories, and trading rights in the Black Sea were the bone of contention with her northern neighbor, with whom the struggle was carried on into the eighteenth and nineteenth centuries. Access to the warm Mediterranean waters was and still is considered vital for the existence of Russia with her ice-locked northern ports. Under Peter the Great and Catherine the Great rejuvenated Russia embarked upon a career of aggression. In 1696 Peter wrested Azov from Turkish hands. Between 1768 and 1774 Catherine conducted successful campaigns ending with the treaty of Kuchuk Kainarji. No more humiliating treaty had been signed by Turkey. Besides the imposition of a heavy indemnity the treaty exacted the right of free navigation in Turkish waters—thus opening the way to the Mediterranean, laying the basis for the right of interference in the protection of the Greek Orthodox Christians of the empire, and providing an opportunity for Russia to meddle in the internal affairs of her neighbor. A few years later Russia signed a treaty with Austria aiming at driving the Turks out of Europe. The Byzantine Empire was to be restored, with a young grandson of Catherine at its head, and Austria was to receive the western half of the Balkans.

A principal cause of the Crimean War (1854-1856), in which Great Britain and France fought on Turkey's side, was Russia's claim for protecting the holy places of Palestine. Ostensibly fought for the preservation of the integrity of the Ottoman Empire, the war was actually fought for the curtailment of Russia's growing influence which had virtually displaced that of the two Western powers at Constantinople. Neither of these two powers relished the prospect of another imperialist installed on the Bosporus. Rivalry between these powers, which began seriously with the Kuchuk Kainarji treaty, gave decadent Turkey a new lease on life. The treaty then may be considered as marking the first manifestation of the so-called Eastern question—in reality a Western question involving the desire of European powers, each jealous of the other, to carve for themselves spheres of influence in a temptingly weak state. Britain and France had an interest in the area in itself and as lying athwart their imperial "life lines"; Austria and Russia had ambitions of territorial annexation. Once the terror of Europe, the Turk in 1853 was called by Nicholas I of Russia "the sick man of Europe." It was this emperor's designs on Constantinople which provoked the Crimean War.

ATTEMPTS AT REFORM

The need for curbing official abuses and introducing drastic reforms was first felt and implemented by the Koprulus, of whom Mustafa was grand vizir from 1689 to 1691. Mustafa reduced the number of high officials and endeavored to improve the finances of the state by regulating its currency and farming out the tobacco tax. These and other wise measures for the better treatment of non-Moslem subjects foreshadowed later legislation.

Among the sultans the point of departure for reform was military considerations. They and those responsible for defense awoke after the treaty of Kuchuk Kainarji to the realization of the fact that they had been far outstripped in military science and art by Europeans. Until then there had been no clear realization that the outstripping included other aspects of culture. Salim III (r. 1789-1807), who had not been

Courtesy of American Numismatic Society

A COIN OF ABD-AL-MAJID   Struck in Constantinople, 1858, silver, 40 paras.

immured as had his predecessors, made an attempt to enforce discipline among the Janissaries, establish a new militia modeled after the French, reorganize under French and English direction the military engineering school founded by his predecessor, and add a new navigation school. In all this he was opposed by Janissaries who first forced him to abdicate and later murdered him and other advocates of reform.

Salim's nephew and disciple Mahmud II (r. 1808-1839), the sole surviving male of the house of Uthman, removed a huge roadblock from the path of national progress when on a spring day in 1826 he had his new corps turn its artillery on the Janissaries' barracks and demolish them, destroying therewith some eight thousand of the troops. Those in the provinces were likewise exterminated. Another notable achievement of Mahmud, greatest of the reforming sultans, was the encouragement of the study of French, which began to become widespread at this time. Introduced for implementing a military program this foreign language unwittingly came to serve as a key for unlocking a treasury of new thoughts—political, social, economic, scientific, and philosophic. Once the barrier of language was broken through there could be no limit to cultural cross-fertilization. Mahmud's reign would have been more notable for its reform had it not been for the Balkan wars which ended with the independence of Greece (1828) and for the uprising in Egypt which established Muhammad Ali as a semi-independent dynast.[5]

Courtesy of American Numismatic Society

A COIN OF MAHMUD II   Struck in Constantinople, 1822, gold.

Mahmud's son Abd-al-Majid (r. 1839-1861), who ascended the throne at the age of sixteen, followed in the footsteps of his father. The regulations he promulgated under the title of "noble script" and "imperial rescript" aimed at guaranteeing the lives, property, and honor of all Ottoman subjects regardless of creed and nationality; abolishing the farming out of taxes and enforcing their equitable apportionment; removing the disabilities under which non-Moslem subjects labored; and guaranteeing the treatment of all as equal before the law. Certain measures, such as improving the condition of prisons, abolishing torture, allowing the acquisition of property by foreigners were unexpectedly new. More revolutionary were those aimed at the annulment of the civil powers of the Christian Churches' heads, and investing certain powers in synods and lay councils, allowing full liberty of conscience and enforcing the eligibility of Christians—who had been excluded or permitted to buy themselves off—for military service. But these regulations, like earlier ones, remained ink on paper. Mostly premature they lacked effective implementation. Conservative ulema, with a narrow interpretation of Islamic law, opposed them; foreigners, enjoying extraterritorial rights, objected to them; Jewish and Christian money-changers were set against the non-farming out of taxes; the youth among them did not favor the military provision. In pursuance of his new

[1] Treated below, pp. 431-434.

regulations Abd-al-Majid attempted to introduce the Code Napoleon and reconcile it with Islamic laws. He also launched a new policy of centralizing the government. Meanwhile he instituted provincial councils, mixed tribunals for cases in which litigants were of different religious persuasions, and established technical schools, all of which entitle him to a high place of honor among the Ottoman sultans.

Courtesy of American Numismatic Society

A COIN OF ABD-AL-MAJID Struck in Constantinople, 1850, silver, 20 piasters.

Abd-al-Majid's brother Abd-al-Aziz (r. 1861-1876) visited the great exposition at Paris and stopped at Vienna and London in 1867. He was the first sultan to travel abroad. In the three following years the Lycée of Galata Serai, the University of Constantinople, and a school of law were established, indicating a continuation in the processes of modernization.

THE HAMIDIAN REGIME

Beginning with the nineteenth century the political reform movement was reinforced by liberal Turkish thinkers and writers who had fallen under the spell of French writers. The two streams would have moved with greater speed and effectiveness had it not been for the setback received under the reign of Abd-al-Hamid II (r. 1876-1909), one of the longest and most reactionary reigns in Turkish annals.

Abd-al-Hamid had a good start. In the second year of his reign his troops, entrenched at the small town of Plevna, Bulgaria, checked for a hundred and forty-three days (ending December 10, 1877), Russian advance against Constantinople. The czar had declared war in support of Turkey's rebellious subjects in the Balkans and, of course, with a keen eye to his country's interest. The battle of Plevna gave the Ottoman Empire forty years of life and left the Turks—where they still are —in control of the straits, with Russia still imprisoned behind the Black Sea.

For grand vizir the sultan had Midhat Pasha, a champion of liberalism and reform.   For years Midhat had worked secretly with a few like-minded young Turks to create a constitutional regime.   On July 15, 1876 Murad V issued a proclamation in which the Turkish word for constitution (adapted from Arabic) was used in an official document. After a three-month reign Murad was declared insane and his brother Abd-al-Hamid was installed in his place.   On October 23 Abd-al-Hamid, under the inspiration of Midhat, solemnly proclaimed the promulgation of a constitution and the institution of a representative parliament.   The draft was modeled after French and Belgian originals. The new regulations ordained that all subjects were to be known as Ottomans and enjoy freedom of thought and conscience within the limits of the law.   While Islam was recognized as the state religion, protection was guaranteed to all other religions in the state.   But shortly after that the sultan dismissed his minister and in February 1878 dissolved the parliament, which he had evidently proclaimed to ward off encroachment on his sovereignty and to invite Western European sympathy.

Courtesy of American Numismatic Society

A COIN OF ABD-AL-HAMID II   Struck in Constantinople, 1899, gold, 100 piasters.

Living under constant fear for his life and throne from liberal Turks and for the entire state from uprisings in Bulgaria, Armenia, and other provinces, the sultan retired to a life of seclusion behind the walls of his palace and began to rely on force, secret police, and censorship of the press.   He assumed that his personal rule was essential to the preservation of his life and throne.   Repressive measures were taken against societies, whether Moslem or Christian, plotting against the sultan or the state.   These measures produced opposite results and ended in massacre.   The first Armenian massacre of 1894, having failed to frustrate nationalist aspirations, was followed by another in 1895, a wholesale one in which a hundred thousand Armenians perished.   Abd-al-Hamid won the title of red sultan.

Meanwhile his foreign policy began to take an Eastern orientation based on the antiquated theory of Pan-Islam. The most articulate advocate of this theory, Jamal-al-Din al-Afghani,[6] was welcomed to the capital. For the head of the most powerful state to pose as a champion leader of Moslems everywhere, including North Africa, Egypt, and India was not far fetched; it provided him with a club over the heads of the imperialist powers. In 1908 his project of linking Syria with the holy city of Medina by rail was completed. A million guineas, one-third of the cost, was raised from voluntary Moslem contributions the world over. The engineers were Germans.

By then Germany had replaced Britain, France, and Russia as the dominant influence at the Sublime Porte. Its emperor Kaiser Wilhelm had initiated the "drive-to-the-East" policy, visited Constantinople, Beirut, Jerusalem, and Damascus (1898) and acquired certain concessions for his country. Chief among these were the concession for the Baghdad railway and the sending of military missions to train the Turkish army. The new railway linked Turkey and her provinces to Berlin and was soon called the Berlin-Baghdad railway, although it had not yet reached Baghdad. Later it connected with Tripoli (Lebanon) and Cairo. The project was viewed by Britain as a threat to her favored position in the Middle East and even beyond the Persian Gulf to India. It became the focal point in the Eastern question.

The attempt of Abd-al-Hamid to check the stream of progress, dam the flow of Western ideas, and turn the hands of the clock permanently back was at last frustrated by a coup of young officers in his army in 1908. They represented the Committee of Union and Progress of the secret society of Young Turks, intellectual descendants of the group to which Midhat once belonged. Their primary aim was the achievement of a Western-style constitution for the empire and the fusion of its heterogeneous nationalist groups into one homogeneous democratic nation. Abd-al-Hamid was ready to "cooperate." He immediately announced the restoration of the constitution he had abrogated and ordered the abolition of censorship and espionage and the release of all political prisoners. No more welcome news could have been received. With the velocity of an electric current jubilation spread throughout the land. Christians and Moslems embraced each other in the streets of Beirut. "Liberty, equality, fraternity" were the key words of the new order. Utopia was around the corner.

But wily Abd had no more intention of preserving the constitution of 1908 than that of 1876. Caught intriguing with his palace officials he was deposed in April 1909. His doddering brother Muhammad V

---

[6] On him see below, pp. 405-406.

Rashad (r. 1909-1918) was installed in his place.   Authority rested in the hands of the Young Turks.

Therewith a new era in Ottoman history began.

BOOKS TO READ

Alderson, A. D., *The Structure of the Ottoman Dynasty* (Oxford, 1956).

Brockelmann, Carl, *History of the Islamic Peoples,* tr. Joel Carmichael and Moshe Perlmann (New York, 1947).

Earle, Edward M., *Turkey, the Great Powers and the Bagdad Railway* (New York, 1923).

Fisher, Sidney N., *The Foreign Relations of Turkey 1481-1512* (Urbana, 1948); *The Middle East: A History* (New York, 1959).

Great Britain, *Turkey in Europe* (under the direction of the Foreign Office, London, 1920).

Jackh, Ernest, ed., *Background of the Middle East* (Ithaca, 1952).

Lane-Poole, Stanley, *The Story of the Barbary States* (New York, 1891).

Lybyer, Albert H., *The Government of the Ottoman Empire in the Time of Suleiman the Magnificent* (Cambridge, Mass., 1931).

Marriott, J. A. R., *The Eastern Questions* (Oxford, 1917).

Merriman, Roger H., *Suleiman the Magnificent* (Cambridge, Mass., 1944).

Pears, Edwin, *Life of Abdul Hamid* (New York, 1917).

Ramsaur, Ernest E., *The Young Turks: Prelude to the Revolution of 1908* (Princeton, 1957).

Royal Institute of International Affairs, *The Middle-East: A Political & Economic Survey,* 2nd ed. (London, 1954).

Scherill, Ferdinand, *The History of the Balkan Peninsula* (New York, 1922).

Stavrianos, L. S., *The Balkans since 1453* (New York, 1958).

Wittek, Paul, *The Rise of the Ottoman Empire* (London, 1938).

XXV *Ottoman Culture*

W<small>HAT</small> goes under the name of Turkish Ottoman culture was basically a striking blend of a few Central Asian elements with disparate others, mostly Arab and Persian, partly Byzantine and Anatolian. The language remained Altaic despite its unlimited borrowings from Arabic and Persian. From Central Asian nomadism the predisposition to war may have lingered as did the hospitable assimilative tendency.

FROM BYZANTIUM

The Byzantines directly or through the Saljuqs of Rum furnished the general pattern for some military and governmental institutions especially in Anatolia and the Balkans. Byzantine ecclesiastical hierarchy is reflected in the ulema organization with muftis presiding over territorial jurisdiction under the supreme authority of the mufti of Constantinople—shaykh al-Islam—who corresponded to the Greek patriarch. Such organized hierarchy was not known before in Islam. The expression "in mufti" (not in uniform, in civilian dress) is an Anglo-Indian one referring to the loose robe of the Moslem mufti. The legal and social segregation of the dhimmis became more accentuated than ever before. In Umayyad Syria, Abbasid Iraq and Fatimid Egypt Christians mingled more freely with Moslems than they did in later Turkey. Since cross-fertilization from the West was likely first to affect the Christian community, its segregation made its contribution to national life rather difficult. One may speak today of a Christian Arab but a "Christian Turk" sounds like a contradiction in terms. An Armenian, a Greek, or a Jew is a Turkish citizen, formerly subject, but not a Turk.

On the more cultural side the impact of Byzantium was not impressive. Muhammad the Conqueror gave his troops free reins for three days in the conquered city after which he took measures to safeguard its manuscripts, relics, and architectural monuments. His entourage

MEDALLION DECORATING THE BACK OF THE MANTLE OF MUHAMMAD THE CONQUEROR
(1451-1481)   The mantle is of cotton tissue with gold.

included Greek-speaking scholars. He himself had some knowledge
of Greek and kept a library of Greek books, but after his time Greek
faded away.   This sultan forced Christians who had fled at the time of
the conquest to return to their homes.   Some of them were architects,
skillful artisans, and textile weavers who kept the tradition of local art
and industry alive.   Byzantine woven silks were highly prized in

Europe. Other Byzantine artistic motifs are clear in Turkish architecture especially in the interior decoration of mosques and palaces. Traces of the Italianate style are also apparent.

The tulip flower figured prominently in mosaic, textile, and other decoration especially in the sixteenth century. The plant itself was introduced into Vienna in 1554 by an ambassador to Turkey and in 1591 to the Low Countries, where it achieved great success and popularity. Between 1634 and 1637 the production of new varieties and speculation on their prices became such a craze that a single flower was sold for the equivalent of $5,200. Ownership of one flower, at times even non-existent, was often divided into shares. Today the cultivation of tulip bulbs and their exportation have become an established industry in Holland.

FROM PERSIANS AND ARABS

The main inspiration for Turkish artistic development came from Persia. Before migrating into Western Asia the Turks had firsthand contacts with Persian culture which were reinforced in the course of the many campaigns conducted from Constantinople. Among the trophies carried away by Salim I and other Ottoman invaders were objects of art which served as models. Persian borrowing is clear in mosaics, architectural decoration, miniatures, woven silks, and textiles. In all these fields Turkish artists, first imitators, developed their own techniques and a style of their own. Among the textiles of the Near East those of sixteenth century Turkey achieved distinction due to their fabric, coloring, and design. They succeeded the silks and velvets of Byzantium. Genoese and Venetian merchants introduced the products of Constantinople and Brusa into Italy, whence they reached France and attained some vogue in Western Europe. A large number of Ottoman sultans were patrons of art and literature.

Equally important was Persian influence in the fields of mysticism, poetry, and general literature. The exaltation of the monarch is one of many political ideas reflecting Persian antecedents. The Ottoman sultan assumed among other Persian titles those of shah and shahan-shah.[1]

The richest bequest, however, came from the Arabs, the two channels being religion and language. With the adoption of Islam went theology, law, hadith, and related sciences. The stream inevitably carried with it numberless technical terms to become embedded in the language. Having arrived in Western Asia with little written literature

[1] See above, p. 54.

TEXTILE WORKERS OF THE PALACE IN THE LATE SIXTEENTH CENTURY They are printing plain stuff with a mixture of gold and silver at the ceremony of the circumcision of Prince Muhammad (Muhammad III, 1595-1603), son of Murad III (1574-1595).

the Turks adopted the Arabic characters which they retained until the Kemalist reforms. Arabic literature in its varied aspects—poetical, historical, linguistic, and lexicographical—offered ready models which could at least in the early stages be imitated. All that, of course, swelled the borrowed vocabulary. Several of the early Turkish authors even found it easier to compose their works in Arabic. After all, they wrote to a limited audience and the use of Arabic contributed to authorship pride; it was a sign of erudition. As late as the seventeenth century one of the most renowned of Ottoman men of letters, Hajji Khalifah (d. 1658), wrote his many-volumed bibliographical masterpiece in Arabic. The work arranges alphabetically the titles of all Arabic, Persian, and Turkish books of whose existence he was aware. Other Ottoman authors preferred Persian as a medium of expression.

Together with borrowing and imitating went translation. Down to the fifteenth century Turkish literary activity featured translation from

Persian and Arabic. In the sixteenth century the translation movement reached its height.

OTTOMAN CONTRIBUTIONS

In statecraft and law, architecture and other artistic fields, poetry, mystic literature and historiography Ottoman writers made worthy contributions. The sixteenth century produced the first Turkish poet of distinction, Muhammad Fuzuli (d. 1556 or 1562). Fuzuli was born in Baghdad of Kurdish origin and wrote in the Azerbaijani idiom. His style is marked with originality and lacks the artificiality that characterizes earlier works. He sang the glories of love, love in more than a profane sense. His poetry reflects the mystic tinge that colors Turkish Islam especially in its folk variety. From the thirteenth century to his time Turkish versifiers had striven to adapt the Persian-Arabic metrical system to the Turkish idiom. In the sixteenth century the pre-classical period in Turkish literature, during which writers were dependent upon foreign patterns, may be said to have ended; the classical period began. By the time of Ahmad Nadim (d. 1730), Turkish poets were consciously composing verses that were free from foreign accretions. Nadim sang in colorful, vivacious verse the "tulip age" of Constantinople under Ahmad III (r. 1703-1730), who was especially fond of tulips and birds. The cultivation of this flower became a fashion among the well-to-do. This sultan spent much of his time entertaining his wives with frivolities, festivities and illuminations.

The classical period lasted until the impact of the West in the mid-nineteenth century. In prose it featured religious works—including mysticism and the lives of holy men—chronicles, and geographies.

BEKTASHI LITERATURE

The Sufi literature produced by members of the Bektashi order was peculiarly Turkish. While other dervish orders spread in Turkey, none attained the vogue of the Bektashi variety. Mawlawi (whirling) dervishes and Rifai (howling) dervishes[2] drew their ideology from Persian and Arabic sources and made extensive use of those two languages, but the Bektashis favored the native idiom. Their literature reflects national customs and points of view. Their ritual was practiced in absolute secrecy.

In their general philosophy of the original equality of all religions and the emphasis on love as the means of achieving mystic union of the individual with God, the Bektashis do not deviate from the Sufi norm. All Sufis pictured love as the nostalgic longing of man to go back to

[2] On these orders see above, pp. 285 *seq.*

God, whence he derived his being. It was God's love which caused the world to be made and which made Adam. A poem, ascribed to an unknown author identified by some with Hajji Bektash, describes the cycle of emanation from and back into the godhead and sums up the Bektashi philosophy of creation and the mystical experience of union with the divine reality:

> Before the world came into being in the hidden secret of non-existence,
> I was alone with Reality in his oneness.
> He created the world; because then
> I formed the picture of Him, I was the designer.[3]
>
> I became folded in garments made of the elements;
> I made my appearance out of fire, air, earth and water.[4]
> I came into the world with the best of men [Adam];
> I was of the same age even as Adam.
>
> The blessed rod I gave to Moses.
> I became the Holy Spirit and came to Mary.
> I was guide to all the saints;
> To Gabriel the Faithful I was the right hand companion.
>
> To this world of "being annihilated in God" I have often come and gone.
> I have rained with the rain and I have grown as grass.
> I have guided aright the country of Rum;
> I was Bektash, who came from Khurasan.[5]

The last quatrain brings out the pantheistic strain in ultra-Sufi philosophy.

The order derives its name from a Hajji Bektash whom legends bring from Persia (Khurasan) in the days of Uthman's son. He led an exemplary life, worked miracles, and blessed the Janissary corps which legend asserts was then founded. The blessing is, no doubt, a projection of the later connection between the two orders—the military and the religious. In fact there is no clear reference to the order by this name before the sixteenth century. Bektashis throughout the centuries served as chaplains for Janissaries; a head chaplain lived in the barracks. They participated in the frequent revolts. It was but natural, therefore, for the blow administered by Mahmud II (1826) to fall also on Bektashi heads, especially in the capital and environs where their lodges (monasteries) were destroyed. Revived later, the order flour-

---

[3] Cf. Prov. 8:22-31, where Wisdom plays the role played here by the Sufi.
[4] These are the four elements of Empedocles and other Greek philosophers.
[5] Adapted from John K. Birge, *The Bektashi Order of Dervishes* (Hartford, 1937), pp. 122-25.

ished again but never regained its former prestige. In 1925 Mustafa Kemal gave it along with other dervish orders the *coup de grâce*.

Among other borrowings from pre-Islamic pre-Christian beliefs mention may be made of the doctrine of transmigration of souls and the mystic doctrine of numbers. Hinduism, too, embraced metempsychosis. The Pythagorean origin of the cult of numbers is unquestionable. Among Bektashis the numbers twelve and four were the center of special interest. Excessive veneration of Ali and recognition of the twelve imams, his descendents, betrays rich Shiite heritage, despite Sunnite profession. The cap of the chief of the order has twelve triangular stripes with a green turban wound around it. The battle ax, staff, amulet, and Husayni crown are other Bektashi insignia. The amulet, worn around the neck, is made of stone which memorializes the rock that, when struck by Moses, yielded twelve springs of water for the twelve tribes of Israel (Kor. 2:57). If the stone comes from a quarry near the Hajji Bektash monastery its reddish coloring is accounted for by a touch of blood from Bektash himself. The Husayni crown is that of Ali's martyred son and is represented by twelve pleats radiating from a common center.

Of special interest to us are the glaring Christian elements which gave rise to the hypothesis that the early adherents of the order were Christians who professed Islam as subterfuge. The Bektashi trinity consists of Allah—Muhammad—Ali, with Ali replacing Christ. Confession of sins to the head of the order is practiced as is a form of communion in which wine, bread, and cheese are shared. Some Bektashis practiced celibacy and often lived in lodges by themselves. Bektashi women did not veil. Though dead in Turkey the order still has cells, one of which is flourishing on al-Muqattam in Cairo.

An outstanding prose work of the classical period is an account of the observations, experiences, and adventures of Evliya Chelebi (1612-1679), who for forty years engaged in a series of journeys within the Ottoman Empire. Written in simple and unaffected style this work, though rich in exaggerations and legends, is a veritable storehouse of information on the history, geography, and folklore of the period. In historiography Ottoman authors were highly successful. The royal palace supported an official historian and supplied him with facilities for research. The historian of the reigns of Salim and Sulayman, Mustafa Naima, who was born in Aleppo (1655) and died in Constantinople (1716), displays a high sense of accuracy, thoroughness, and devotion to truth that gives his work superiority over all others of this and the preceding periods.

In general literary life in the seventeenth and eighteenth centuries, which were marked by political decline, continued to follow the lines it had followed in the sixteenth century. But in the nineteenth century, with the increased impact of the West, the course was changed. The break with the past became more pronounced under the Young Turks and Mustafa Kemal.

IMPACT OF THE WEST

Turkish response to military Western stimuli came earlier and moved more rapidly than did their response to intellectual stimuli. Until the nineteenth century, most borrowings from Europe were of material or techniques and were conditioned by military considerations. Gunpowder came first, in the fourteenth century[6] and was followed by shipbuilding, navigation, artillery, and military engineering. The printing press was introduced in 1728 by a Hungarian renegade, Ibrahim, and its first product was a Turkish translation of an Arabic lexicon. The literary themes, patterns of thought, and style continued to display traces of the old Persianizing or Arabicizing school until the nineteenth century. The turning point was in the reign of Mahmud II (r. 1808-1839) when the study of the French language began to be diligently pursued, though not yet as an integral part of the school curriculum. In fact until the 1850's the Koran and religious instruction monopolized elementary and secondary school education. After that other textbooks were introduced into the curriculum; in 1861 the first high school for girls was opened; eight years later the University of Constantinople was founded to succumb two years later to a storm of reaction from which only the schools of medicine and law survived. Students who had studied in France then began to appear on the scene.

With the introduction of the press, the more general use of French, and the increased patronage of European institutions of learning by Turkish students, Turkey became aware that Europe had already by far outstripped her in all fields of endeavor and that the traditional synthesis of religion, state, and sword had failed to meet the challenge of a new era. That era was marked by European coalescing into new nationalistic states, based on unprecedented economic and industrial growth, and on rapidly expanding trade, and political influences. More than that, these states had striking power adequate to reach any part of the inhabited world. At last the belief of the Ottomans in the excellence of their way of life, engendered by national pride and fostered by phenomenal success, was deeply shaken. Cultural provincialism began to yield to cultural pluralism.

[6] Cf. above, p. 330.

An early student in France, Ibrahim Shinasi, went there at the age of twenty-four to specialize in linguistics. Shinasi published in 1859 a small volume of translations from French poets. He then became editor of the first nongovernmental newspaper in the Turkish language (1860). Turkish flowed from his pen with less artificiality and pomposity and with more simplicity and comprehensibility. Soon other translations by other Turkish writers from Molière, Victor Hugo, La Fontaine, Rousseau, and Lamartine followed. For the first time the Turkish reader gained a glimpse of an entirely different philosophy of life and a new outlook on it. The Turkish writer discovered that his mother tongue was not after all impervious to change and could be adapted to modern literary and scientific thought. Shinasi was followed in his editorial work by his disciple Namik Kemal (1826-1871), who had also fallen under the spell of French authors and philosophers and pursued the less involved and burdensome and more direct style— the style and structure of the people's speech. The old school would have probably expired had it not been for the oppressive reign of Abd-al-Hamid (1876-1909), in which writers vacillated between the old and the new.

LAW REFORM

Legal institutions, both courts and codes, varied little from what they had been in the time of Sulayman the Magnificent until the nineteenth century. During his reign a jurist of Aleppine nativity, Ibrahim al-Halabi (d. 1549), held the position of preacher-teacher in Constantinople and composed a work which became the handbook of Hanafi law, Hanafi being the rite considered official by the Ottomans. There was hardly a legal innovation until the reigns of Mahmud II and Abd-al-Majid. In 1839 a judicial body emerged and began to encroach upon the jurisdiction of the shariah hitherto considered all-embracing. The encroachment, however, was limited to commercial cases involving non-Moslems. Under Abd-al-Majid (r. 1839-1861) special commissions were gradually established throughout the empire to settle commercial conflicts between Ottoman subjects as well as between them and foreigners. In 1851 the commissions were replaced by commercial courts, based on French usage. A new institution thus arose depriving the ulema of segments of their domain. The step was especially welcomed by Westerners.

With the wedge driven in by reforms in the commercial courts, it became easier for the criminal court reforms to follow. In 1858 a new criminal code was promulgated, again after a French model, but questions of personal status remained within the sole jurisdiction of the courts presided over by theologians. The civil court judge was normally trained in the Western tradition. The dichotomy between the civil court and the religious court then became open and clearcut. All the reforms involving commercial and penal codes were also borrowed largely from Napoleonic legislation. But until 1915 the principles of reform did not extend to the sacred sphere of family relations. It was left to the Young Turks to take that audacious step.

EDUCATION

Early Ottomans must have followed the educational procedure evolved under Saljuqs and Arabs into whose cultural legacy they entered. Throughout the then Moslem world elementary education was carried out in mosques and was restricted to the study of language, the Koran in Arabic, and the "sciences" related to it. Advanced work was done largely in the private homes of learned men who offered courses in theology, law, linguistics, and mathematical sciences. Then there was the madrasah[7] type initiated by Sunni rulers to combat Shiah propaganda, which became especially vehement under the Fatimids. Though basically a theological seminary, the madrasah of Nizam-al-Mulk[8] did some justice to the humanities and concerned itself with training for public careers. After Nizam, Salah-al-Din was the greatest builder of such institutions. Early Ottoman scholars patronized institutions of higher learning in such renowned centers of education as Mecca, Damascus, and Cairo.

By the early sixteenth century Ottoman theologians had become organized into a hierarchy and had begun a trend toward conservatism, a trend from which they never recoiled. In the second half of that century three of their members, one in the capital, were executed on charges of freethinking. The purge left the extreme right wing in control. Under its direction the madrasah declined into an inefficient seminary of the narrow type dedicated to theology and sacred law with no physical sciences and no foreign languages. Persian was frowned upon because its literature was tainted with unorthodox mysticism. Even Turkish poetry based on Persian models was excluded from the curriculum. An enlightened grand vizir of Ahmad III (d. 1730) who founded a school and encouraged its use of Persian and mathematics was frustrated by a revolt which cost him his life and the sultan his throne. Insulation against the penetration of European thought was, of course, of the double kind. The import of printed books was

---

[7] Discussed above, p. 270.
[8] See above, p. 270.

banned.   Coming at a time when contemporary Europe was making its basic advances in science, technology, and industry the results were especially disastrous.   A French advisor to the Porte in the late eighteenth century reports that the ministers were so ignorant of European geography as to suppose that Russian ships could not enter the Mediterranean from the West.

No creative work was expected and none was forthcoming.   Such rare scholars as Hajji Khalifah who made an original contribution were not the product of the madrasah system; they were even disavowed by the ulema.   Printing by Moslems was forbidden and so remained until the second quarter of the eighteenth century.   By that time Christian subjects had introduced Greek, Armenian, and Arabic presses. There were also Jewish ones.   When the newly converted Ibrahim was permitted to introduce a Turkish press, he was directed by a legal opinion (*fatwa*) to publish only dictionaries, historical and scientific— but not religious—works.   Ibrahim set up a committee for choosing Persian and Arabic works for translation.   After his death (1745) the press lay practically idle until the end of the century.   In all he had published seventeen books, one of which was a cosmology by Hajji Khalifah.

Even schools established for training the slaves of the sultan's household surpassed the madrasahs in the richness of the curriculum and the quality of teaching.   They included instruction in Arabic and Persian and offered courses in calligraphy, music, architecture, painting, and sculpture.   Lodges of all Sufi brotherhoods were centers of specialized education.   The Bektashi ones emphasized music, while the Mawluwis laid stress on Persian precisely because of the mystical element in its literature.   The military schools opened their doors to the French language before the madrasahs did.

Outstanding among the military slave schools was that founded by Muhammad the Conqueror in the palace shortly after the conquest of the city.   It developed into one of the most remarkable institutions of learning in its time.   Founded for training men for military and government service the school was continued for over three and a half centuries, until the time of Mahmud II.   The course covered twelve to fourteen years.   It combined in almost equal proportions courses in liberal arts and courses relating to physical training as well as the sciences and arts of war and government.   It was a stiff course requiring rigorous discipline.   Competition was keen and the screening minute.   Those physically distinguished were drafted into the cavalry or Janissary corps.   Those who were mentally superior were further trained for civil and political careers.   In the first two centuries of its existence the school of the palace supplied the empire with the majority of its court officials and military officers.   Of sixty-eight grand vizirs whose careers have been studied, forty-eight were its graduates.   An idea of the measure of success achieved by this institution may be gained from the fact that though the first generations of its students were wholly alien in race, creed, and language[9] yet the recorded instances of renegades or rebels from among them were rare—so thorough was the assimilation.

In the second half of the nineteenth century European schools gained admission into the capital.   One of the earliest was the Lycée of Galata Sarai, mentioned above.[10]   Outstanding among them was Robert College, the first American college established overseas.   Founded in 1863 through the efforts of an American missionary-educator, Cyrus Hamlin, and the generosity of a New York merchant, Christopher R. Robert, the institution had as its primary purpose the education of the youth of the Christian minorities.   Nevertheless it never came under the control of a mission board.   For the first half century of its existence the student body consisted largely of Bulgarians, Greeks, and Armenians.   There was a time in which the entire cabinet and diplomatic corps of the Kingdom of Bulgaria were Robert College graduates. Since the founding of the republic by Atatürk the character of its student body and faculty personnel has changed in favor of the Turks. For a time it was a junior college.   In addition to liberal arts and business courses, the college maintains a school of engineering that attracts students from all over the Near East.   Eight years after the founding of Robert College the American College for Girls was established on a nearby campus; both occupy picturesque sites on the Bosporus overlooking the Asiatic shore.   This institution has provided training for women in government service, the professions, and education.   The two colleges have merged and operate under a joint board of trustees in New York.

BOOKS TO READ

Brown, John P., *The Derwishes,* ed. Horace A. Rose (London, 1927).

Gibb, Elias J. W., *Ottoman Literature* (New York, 1901); *A History of Ottoman Poetry,* 6 vols. (London, 1900-1909).

Gibb, H. A. R. and Harold Bowen, *Islamic Society and the West,* Vol. I, pt. 1 (London, 1950), pt. 2 (Oxford, 1957).

[9] As noted above, p. 336.
[10] P. 345.

Hasluck, F. W., *Christianity and Islam under the Sultans,* ed. Margaret Hasluck, Vol. I (Oxford, 1929).

Miller, Barnette, *Beyond the Sublime Porte* (New Haven, 1931); *The Palace School of Muhammad the Conqueror* (Cambridge, Mass., 1941).

Patmore, Derek, *The Star and the Crescent: An Anthology of Modern Turkish Poetry* (London, 1946).

XXVI *The Young Turks and the Republic*

THE Young Turks revolution of 1908 and their assumption of fuller power in 1909 [1] marked a turning point in the history and nationalistic consciousness of the Turkish people. The decline of the Ottoman system, which began toward the end of the seventeenth century and continued slowly through the eighteenth, acquired momentum in the following century by the twin forces of European imperialism and nationalism operating on a supranational state. Nationalism until then had been limited to Balkan peoples under Ottoman sovereignty.

TROUBLES: FOREIGN AND DOMESTIC

The Young Turks embarked upon their stormy career with more good intentions, enthusiasm, and patriotic zeal than wisdom and experience. Theirs was a colossal task: transforming a decrepit outmoded state into one competent to meet the challenge of the day. The task was rendered more difficult by hostility on the part of the neighboring nations and opposition on the part of the constituent nationalities of the empire. Cooperation came from nowhere.

Three months after the successful coup of July 1908, Austria, taking advantage of the situation, annexed Bosnia and Herzegovina; Bulgaria declared her full independence. In 1911 and 1912 Italy, embarking upon her colonial career under pressure from its continually growing population, marched her troops against Ottoman provinces in North Africa and occupied Tripoli and Benghazi. Two Young Turkish officers who assumed the defense were Enver Bey (later pasha) and Mustafa Kemal. In the meantime the three Slav powers of Serbia, Montenegro, and Bulgaria had allied themselves against their former sovereign and were joined by Greece, which seized Salonika. In the following year (1913) an alliance between Bulgaria and Serbia for the partition of Ottoman Macedonia led to a second Balkan war, with the

---

[1] Discussed above, p. 347.

result that Turkey was stripped of most of her European possessions. Even Adrianople, next to Constantinople in strategic and commercial importance and from 1366 to 1453 residence of the sultans,[2] was seized and held temporarily by Bulgarian forces.

Concurrently disorders and outbreaks convulsed the empire from Albania to South Arabia. The main issue was decentralization and the position of Turkish as the official language. In April 1909 Armenian demonstrations provoked a massacre in Adana and neighboring places. In eastern Anatolia Kurds attacked their Turkish neighbors and were attacked by them. A series of disorders in Yemen ended with the Porte's guaranteeing its autonomy in 1912. In Paris in the following year there was an Arab congress which demanded decentralization of the Arab provinces.[3] More serious was an insurrection (1910) in Albania whose people's demand for autonomy was met with violent bloodshed. The repressive measures did not stop the proclamation of Albania on November 28, 1912 as an independent principality. In 1928 the principality evolved into a monarchy under Ahmad Zogu. A mountainous country, Albania had offered stiff resistance (1443-1468) to the Turks before it succumbed. It retained a substantial Christian minority. By 1913 the net loss to Turkey under the new regime had included Bulgaria, Serbia, Albania and most of the districts with Greek-speaking populations.

Amidst this sea of internal and external disturbances the Young Turkish ship of state floundered. In the second year of their assumption of power the Young Turks revised the constitution, deprived the sultan of his authority to dissolve the parliament, and made the cabinet responsible to it. Weak and helpless, Muhammad V was left as a figurehead. Once a secret society, now a political party, the new regime remained a minority. Its policy was first polarized toward Ottomanism, infusing into this term a nationalistic connotation. Until then Ottomanism had been used chiefly as a dynastic term, in the same sense as Abbasid or Umayyad were used. The presumption for the new policy was that all communities of the empire could be fused into one nation, owing loyalty to the sultan and the constitution, using one language, and accepting Turkish leadership. The immediate result was the stimulation of the separatist movements and the encouragement of nationalist loyalties among their Greek, Arab, Armenian, and other subjects. Even Moslem Arabs began to manifest separatist tendencies. With the failure of this policy, revision was made to Hamidian Pan-Islam. The inspiration came from sympathy expressed by Moslems in

[2] Cf. above, p. 330.
[3] Discussed below, p. 497.

India and Egypt during the Italian and Balkan wars.   But Pan-Islam
turned out to be as dead a corpse as it had been under Abd-al-Hamid.
The proof came when the sultan declared a holy war (*jihad*) upon the
entry of Turkey into the World War on the side of the Central Powers
and no response whatever was evoked.   The theoricians of the regime
concocted a new pan-, Pan-Turanianism.   One immediate inspiration
came from Turkish refugees from Russia.   The Pan-Turanian thesis
maintained that the Turkish speakers of the Volga and other parts of
Russia, of Azerbaijan and other provinces of Persia, and of Central Asia
could be united under the primacy of those of Turkey.   It proved to be
an academic thesis.   Any tangible results consisted of further alienation
of non-Turkish elements in the empire.

Frustrated, the Turkish leaders resorted to forceful measures.   The
martial law proclaimed at the deposition of Abd-al-Hamid was strengthened with stricter censorship, a wider network of espionage, and immediate destruction to all those who dared publically oppose them.   The
regime which overthrew the Hamidian took a leaf from its register.
With the involvement of Turkey in the war, terrorism took a new lease
of life; the Young Turks could hardly be said to have remained masters
in their own house.

THE GREAT WAR

In the summer of 1914, at the outbreak of the international conflict
which ultimately involved the principal nations of the world, the Young
Turks threw themselves into the arms of the one power, Germany,
which they thought could help them against their ancestral enemy,
czarist Russia.   The step was taken under a triumvirate of Talaat as
prime minister; Enver, minister of war; and Javid, minister of finance.
Talaat began his career as a telegraph operator.   Javid belonged to a
Jewish community of Salonika (Dönmeh, turn-over), which professed
Islam but maintained aspects of Jewish life and belief.   This community had helped subsidize the Union and Progress movement.   What
precipitated Turkey's entrance was the admission on August 11, 1914
of two powerful German cruisers into the Bosporus, where they were
given Turkish names and incorporated into the Ottoman fleet.   In the
following month the capitulations were unilaterally abrogated.   Germany acquiesced.   In October these two cruisers took part in the bombardment of Odessa and other Russian Black seaports, whereupon
Russia declared war and was followed by her two allies Britain and
France.

Though unprepared and enfeebled, Turkey, which soon found herself
engaged in combat on four fronts, proved to be of immense value to the

Central Powers. On her frontiers she tied up over a million Allied troops and sent her men to three theaters of war outside of her territory —Persia, the Balkans, and Galicia (now in Poland). For four long years Turkey held out, collapsing in October 1918, months after Russia's collapse. On the Caucasian front she faced only Russia; on the Iraqi front she faced Anglo-Indian troops; on the Palestine-Egyptian front she met the Arab, British and French forces; and on the Dardanelles front there were Australian, New Zealander, and French forces. Russian troops had no difficulty in penetrating into Anatolia and capturing Trebizond, Erzurum, and other important towns thus arousing the nationalistic aspirations of Armenians behind Turkish lines. This resulted in a general deportation of the Armenian community, sixty thousand of whom, after years of deprivation, homelessness, and wandering found a new home in Lebanon. Certain members of the Armenian refugee colony, which first settled on the outskirts of Beirut and improvised shelters of petroleum cans, have since risen to positions of eminence in industry, commerce, and even the politics of Lebanon.

The obstinate and long-drawn-out defense of the Dardanelles under Marshal Liman von Sanders, chief of the German military mission to Turkey, assisted by Colonel Mustafa Kemal, was one of the memorable episodes of the first World War. The Allied campaign started in February 1915 as a naval operation to establish easy communication with the Russian partner. Both sea and land operations ended in January 1916, leaving Russia as deadlocked as before. Three months later General Charles Townshend, leading an Anglo-Indian force in southern Iraq, was forced to surrender at Kut al-Amarah. This operation had begun in 1914 and was designed to occupy the territory at the head of the Persian Gulf; protect the Anglo-Iranian petroleum installations, which had not then been highly developed; and impress the Arabs under Ottoman rule. Another German, von der Goltz, held the supreme command on that front. The following year, however, the Anglo-Indian forces under General Maude entered Baghdad and occupied Mosul and Kirkuk. Mesopotamia was forever lost to Turkey.

For over two years Palestine served as a Turkish base for operations against Egypt. These were under Jamal Pasha, whom the Young Turks had sent as governor general of Syria and commander in chief of the army corps stationed there. Two attacks on the Suez Canal in 1915 and 1916 were repulsed and were followed by an offensive launched from Egypt by General Edmund Allenby which was no less successful than that of Maude in Mesopotamia. In the meantime the sharif (descendant of the Prophet) of Mecca, Husayn, had started a revolt in Hejaz against his Turkish suzerain, proclaimed himself "king of the Arabs" (1916), and sent contingents to cooperate with the Anglo-French forces in Palestine. The Allied army occupied Jerusalem in 1917 and reached Beirut and Damascus in 1918. Palestine, Lebanon, and Syria were forever lost to Turkey. An English inscription on the rock at the mouth of the Dog River adds the name of Allenby to a roster of great conquerors including Ramses, Esarhaddon, and Nebuchadnezzar.[4]

The Franco-British troops were well received by the inhabitants. Their advent marked the dawn of an era of relief, after four years in which particularly Syria and Lebanon suffered privations hardly known in their history. Suspected of anti-Ottoman, pro-Arab, or pro-French sympathies these two countries were ruled by Jamal Pasha with a rod of iron. Christian and Moslem leaders were imprisoned, banished, or hanged in the public squares of Damascus and Beirut. Jamal, who had his headquarters in Damascus, lost no time in abrogating the internationally recognized autonomy Lebanon had enjoyed since 1861.[5] Martial law was declared and enforced. For the defense of the area and in preparation for the abortive attempts on Suez he imposed military conscription on the Lebanese, requisitioned beasts of burden, and gave priority of provisions to his troops. As the Allied fleet tightened the blockade, imports of food, drugs, and cloth vanished. Epidemics of fatal diseases reaped their human harvests while swarms of locusts reaped their green harvests. As early as the winter of 1916 the population faced starvation. Out of 450,000 inhabitants of Lebanon no less than 100,000 were reportedly lost.

AN UNEASY TRUCE

For the Turkish population of the empire, however, relief was not yet in sight. The armistice signed at Mudros (in Lemnos Island, October 30, 1918) ended the four-year World War, but started a new series of wars which lasted for another four years. Allied fleets and troops occupied the capital and its straits and stretched the truce terms to the point of violation. With the advent of the Bolsheviks secret treaties were disclosed by which Britain, France, Russia, Italy, and Greece would partition the empire, not excluding the Turkish homeland proper. Czarist Russia was to receive Constantinople and the straits, which Bolshevik Russia forthrightly renounced. In fulfillment of the terms of the secret treaty Italy proceeded to land troops in Adalia (Antalya, southwestern coast of Anatolia) which had been apportioned to her and the Greek fleet—equipped and supported by British, French, and American

---

[4] See above, p. 7.
[5] Treated below, p. 455.

units—landed its troops farther north in Smyrna, dreaming of reestablishing an Ionia. Greek troops penetrated inland and took Brusa and other towns.

The truce treaty was followed by the peace treaty of Sèvres (six miles southwest of Paris), which was accepted by Sultan Wahid-al-Din on August 10, 1920. By now the Young Turks' leaders had left the country. Enver landed in Turkestan, where he was killed in a struggle between two factions; Talaat was assassinated in Berlin by an Armenian; and Jamal found refuge in Afghanistan. At Sèvres Turkey renounced all claims to her non-Turkish territories and agreed to let her islands go to Italy and Greece. Syria and Lebanon were to be mandated to France; Iraq and Palestine to Britain; Hejaz and Armenia were recognized as independent; and the straits were to be internationalized. This would dismember the empire and reduce Turkey to Constantinople and environs in Europe and the remainder of Anatolia.

The peace treaty brought no more peace than the truce treaty had brought truce. Frustrated and helpless the sultan's government, under the thumb of the Allies, pushed the country into a state of anarchy. Opposition by the nationalists mounted and soon developed into defiance and resistance which began to take organized form. Nothing could have aroused the nationalist consciousness of the Turks more than the landing of foreign troops in Anatolia. The leadership fell on one man —Mustafa Kemal. "Turkey for the Turks" became the slogan of the new movement. Ottomanism, Pan-Turanianism, and Pan-Islam were all discarded like worn-out coats.

MUSTAFA KEMAL

In April 1920 the grand national assembly, meeting at Ankara and claiming to represent the Turkish nation, rather than the sultan— "prisoner of a foreign army of occupation," set up a provisional government with Mustafa Kemal as its head. Two years later this government abolished the sultanate but kept the caliphate in the house of Uthman. Muhammad VI was the last representative of this house, and the fetwa by which he was deposed was the last to be issued by a Turkish religious leader. Constantinople, capital since its foundation in the fourth century, ceased to be a capital; even its name gave way to its Turkish form, Istanbul, in 1923. The caliphate bestowed on Abd-al-Majid, son of Abd-al-Aziz, was abolished in 1924. Attempts to revivify the institution were made by King Husayn of Hejaz and in his behalf, but man could not put life into what history had condemned to death. The remnants of the house of Uthman were banished. In the meantime Mustafa had rolled back the Greek army to the sea,

THE VICTORY MONUMENT IN ANKARA WITH MUSTAFA KEMAL ON HORSEBACK

whence it came, and won the title of Ghazi (warring champion against
unbelievers). His comrade at arms Ismet won the title of Inönü, after
the site of a decisive battle he fought. Smyrna became Izmir. The
Italian invaders were easier to handle. On July 24, 1923 the Lausanne
peace treaty was signed by Ismet Inönü in which Turkey renounced all
claims to non-Turkish territories, recovered eastern Thrace and certain
islands, paid no reparations, abolished the capitulations, and was
recognized as a fully independent state within her ethnic frontier—
a far cry from the treaty of Sèvres. On October 29 the Turkish re-

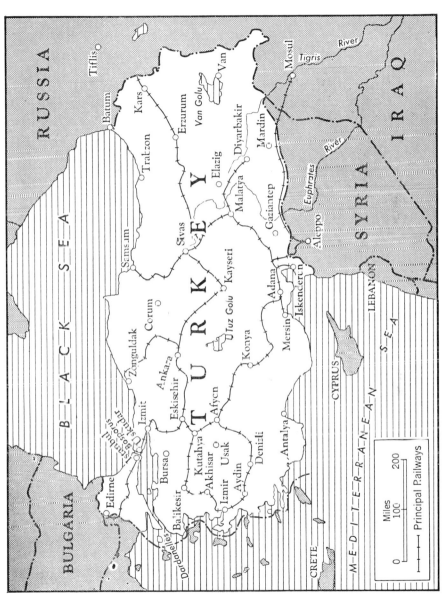

REPUBLIC OF TURKEY

public was proclaimed, with Mustafa as president and Ismet as prime minister. This is the date that is celebrated as independence day.

All pre-Kemalist reformers had assumed the necessity of the continuity of the sultanate-caliphate and the inseparability of religion and state. The Young Turks had taken faltering steps toward the secularization of education and the removal of the shariah from the jurisdiction of the shaykh al-Islam to the ministry of justice. They further introduced a family law in reformation of marriage and divorce regulations; until then laws of personal status and family relations had remained untouched. The Turks were more clearly realizing that the Western military superiority, which was driving them to change, was not an isolated phenomenon. They saw that it was closely related to achievement in technology and education and based on a developed economic and social structure. The doors of the University of Constantinople, many of whose principal chairs were soon occupied by German professors, were opened to women students. For the first time it was fully appreciated that no thoroughgoing abiding reform could be effected with two major roadblocks in the way: the sultanate-caliphate and the union between Islam and the state. Once such a radical break with the past was achieved progress toward secularization, modernization, and adoption of Western institutions and ideas would be greatly facilitated. Accordingly all religious orders were prohibited; Latin script replaced the Arabic in writing Turkish; polygamy was legally abolished and the laws of divorce altered; the veil was ordered removed; and the hat was substituted for the fez. The old code of laws with its religious sanctions was discarded in favor of a new judiciary system based mainly on the Swiss civil code. When it was legislated that all Turks should adopt Turkish family names, Mustafa took as his family name Atatürk, father of the Turks. In fact, as in name, he was the father of the new Turkey. A cult rose around his name to fill the vacuum created by the relinquishing of certain elements in the Islamic heritage.

The new legislation was issued in the name of the national assembly meeting at Ankara, but it was largely initiated and inspired by one man. The constitution of 1934 guaranteed for all citizens individual rights and civic liberties; it placed all legislative power in the hands of the national assembly and gave it the right to choose the president. In a six-day speech (1927) the president outlined his policies and announced the abolition of Islam as a state religion. Sporadic outbursts of opposition to certain measures among reactionary Turks and more serious ones among Kurds in eastern Turkey were all ruthlessly crushed. A dictator who was reelected three times (1927, 1931,

FIRST BUILDING OF THE UNIVERSITY OF ANKARA   The building houses the faculties of history, geography, and language.

1935), Atatürk yet regarded his dictatorship as a temporary necessity pending further education of his people. He built up potentially democratic machinery and operated through it. Under his regime complete equality to all citizens was assured, universal education was introduced, and a university was founded in the capital. English joined French in replacing Arabic and Persian in the school curriculum. Technical and professional education was not neglected. Attempts were made to modernize the economy and industry of the country, leaving no aspect of life untouched.

In his foreign policy Atatürk was equally enlightened, as indicated by the Balkan pacts he concluded and the cordial relations he established with Britain and France as well as the Soviet Union. Peace with Greece was facilitated by the exchange—subsequent to the Lausanne treaty—of Greek population in Turkey for Moslem population in Greece. By this radical operation one of the thorniest of minority problems was practically solved.

THE SECOND WORLD WAR

The new era ushered in by Atatürk was assured of continuity when on his death in November 1938 he was succeeded by his close collaborator Ismet Inönü. In internal affairs *étatisme,* state socialism, remained the cardinal point, though Inönü proceeded more cautiously and deliberately. Étatisme, as explained by Atatürk himself, differed from that of nineteenth century European theorists in holding to the principle of the individual's private initiative while putting in state hands the nation's economy. But foreign relations were subjected to new strains with the outbreak of the second World War.

As the dark clouds began to thicken on the Western horizon, France, the mandatory power over Syria, conceded to Turkey the right of incorporating the district of Alexandretta, partly populated by Turks. Hatay, as it then came to be called, gave Turkey further access to the northeastern corner of the Mediterranean. Both Great Britain and France proceeded to sign with Turkey a pact of mutual assistance in case of war in the "Mediterranean area." The entry of Italy on the side of Germany introduced war into the area, but the new ally failed to implement the pact. Impressed by the initial show of military superiority of Germany, startled by the early collapse of France and uncertain British prospects of success, Turkey continued throughout to straddle the fence.

The declaration of war by the United States on Japan, December 8, 1941, the day after the Japanese sneak attack on Pearl Harbor (Hawaii), was an encouraging but not a decisive development. A few days before the attack President Roosevelt had declared the defense of Turkey vital to the security of the United States and extended to her lend-lease aid. But even in the following summer Turkey fearfully faced the prospect of German troops on her Balkan and Caucasian frontiers as well as on her Egyptian-Arab frontier. German conquest of Greece and the occupation of her islands left Turkey isolated, a small neutral state amidst mighty antagonists. Ankara became a paradise for propagandists and spies, but its government stood steadfast in the belief that there was nothing to lose and everything to gain by a policy of passivity. As American successes began to dispel doubt about the final outcome of the conflict, Turkey's neutrality became more beneficent to her anti-Axis Allies. Her declaration of war on Germany and Japan in February 1945 was a mere token designed to meet the deadline stipulated by the Allies for a seat at the proposed United Nations charter meeting at San Francisco.

Before then Turkish economy had been moving from bad to worse. Armed neutrality strained it to the breaking point. Essential imports had practically ceased, prices soared, currency depreciated, and rationing was extended to most staples of life. By the end of the war prices were five times as high as they had been at the beginning. The government imposed a war tax, a high per cent of the citizen's wealth, under penalty of forced labor in an eastern province. The local enforcement was rather light on Moslem Turks but heavy on Jews, Greeks, and other Christians. The Armenians had dwindled into an insignificant minority. Social unrest, a corollary of the economic situation, necessitated a stricter enforcement of martial law and press censorship which had been in operation for years.

American economic, military, and naval aid continued on an increasing scale even after the cessation of hostilities. The polarization of world power into two principal centers—capitalist America and Communist Russia—and its cold war corollary raised the strategic importance of Turkey in Western eyes. As Russia's close neighbor, with one foot in the Balkans and the other in the Near East, Turkey with its stable and relatively reliable government and its traditional antipathy to Russia, loomed as a valuable Western ally in the cold war. In 1947 Congress approved the granting of $100,000,000 to implement the Truman doctrine. Benefits also accrued from the Marshall plan which ensued. In 1950 the International Bank for Reconstruction and Development accorded a credit of $12,500,000 for improving the ports of Istanbul, Izmir, and other cities. The United States Economic Cooperation Administration offered a generous sum for the promotion of industry and commerce. Hundreds of American technicians and experts were sent to cooperate with their Turkish counterparts.

Throughout Atatürk's regime and a large part of Inönü's the country had but one party, known as the Republican People's Party. Yielding to pressure from enlightened public opinion and pressure from abroad, Inönü ended martial law and the single-party system and proclaimed a new law guaranteeing free elections. The May 1950 election resulted in a landslide in favor of the opposition, the Young Democratic Party, headed by Jelal Bayar. Although of humble origin, Bayar had had a distinguished career as a member of parliament. His regime pursued a moderately more liberal policy as expressed in encouraging private enterprise and investment of foreign capital, abandoning the salient features of étatisme, and easing press censorship. But in its foreign relations, despite internal difficulties, there was no deviation from the clear path of identifying national interests with those of the West.

In the spring of 1953 the president paid a state visit to the United States, where he was warmly received as a representative of a valuable ally. His Prime Minister Menderes followed him. Two years later, subsequent to the Communist aggression in Korea, Turkey was the first to announce its determination to join the United Nations forces. Its troops served with distinction on the battlefield. Early in that year she had joined the North Atlantic Treaty Organization (NATO) as a full member. Turkey took the initiative in concluding with Iraq a defensive treaty which was joined by Britain, Pakistan, and Iran (1955) and became known as the Baghdad Pact, Baghdad having been chosen as headquarters. The pact was set up, on the lines of NATO, as a northern Near Eastern tier against possible Soviet aggression and was vehemently denounced by Russia. The Soviet Union threatened its southern neighbors and regarded the setup as a link forged by the West to join NATO and the Southeast Asia Treaty Organization (SEATO). The United States refrained from joining the organization but offered moral and financial support. In 1955 the United States military aid to Turkey was stepped up to $200,000,000 plus economic assistance; it was to continue at an annual rate of $70,000,000. In August 1958 the sum of $359,000,000 was extended by way of aid. Other than with Russia Turkey faced problems with two of her neighbors, Syria and Greece. The Syrian problem was occasioned by Syria's leftist move in 1956; the Greek problem related to Cyprus, which has a considerable Turkish minority. Turkey's solution of dividing the island between herself and Greece has been found unacceptable and she yielded. In the spring of 1960 the Bayar-Menderes regime was overthrown by a military coup.

A NEW LITERATURE

A new Turkey required a new literature. The rupture with the past in her literary life was no less pronounced than in her political life. The way was prepared under the Young Turks.

The victory of 1908 insured the modernization of the trends in writing.[6] In the prewar period the Young Turks freed the press from the shackles of censorship and inspired a new national literature. Even men like Tevfik Fikret (1867-1915), who had been in the traditional pattern, now waxed eloquent in their appeal to Easterners to abandon old ways and follow in the path of progress. Fikret discovered new ideals in French literature and began to write lyrics with love and pity as themes. Echoes of the past lingered, though in a revised form. Islamism, based on the assumption that the maintenance of the empire depended on the maintenance of its religious tradition, found a spokesman in Mehmet Akif (1873-1936). Himself a poet, Akif held that the poetical medium was the most effective in influencing and instructing the common people. Turkism also, which emphasized the ethnic basis, attracted a number of writer-advocates after the two disastrous wars, when Turks began to worry about their survival as Turks. This literary movement was then used to arouse national consciousness vis-à-vis the rising Bulgarian and other Christian nationalities in the Balkans. Ziya Gök Alp (1875-1924) became the exponent of this movement. More than anyone else Ziya gave the Turkish national ideal its clearest literary expression; he was the intellectual father of Turkish nationalism. In his articles in a Salonika periodical (*young pens*) he strove to approximate the written to the

---

[6] Pp. 352-353, 356.

spoken medium. His patriotic poems and his lectures at the resuscitated University of Constantinople inflamed the youth with the new ideology. So dangerous was he considered by the Allies on their occupation of the capital that they had him banished to Malta.

With the changing of script under the Kemalist regime the trend toward the simplification of the Turkish idiom and its purification from Arabic and Persian influences gained momentum. Along with that went attempts to utilize the unexplored riches of native folklore and to utilize indigenous themes. Fiction writers invariably chose themes from the people's lives. While the Republican period gave rise to a few poets of distinction, no such playwrights arose then. French literary influence, which began to be noticeable in the mid-nineteenth century,[7] found new channels after the 1908 revolution, when a group of young graduates of the Galata Serai Lycée[8] emerged, assuming the designation "dawn of the future." They introduced French symbolism and stressed colorful description of local scenes. But English influence was not well marked until quite recently. In 1912 Halidé Edib (1883-   ), an alumna of the American College for Girls,[9] published her first novel. Twenty-three years later she published an English novel, *The Clown and His Daughter,* in which skillful characterization and richness of plot and atmosphere recall English works. Halidé also wrote patriotic poems. Turkish classical meters and vocabulary have remained until now somewhat resistant to adaptation to the people's demands, but at last they have yielded to the Muse of a Constantinople fisherman's son, Mehmed Emin (d. 1944). Emin's popular lyric poems served as an accompaniment to the victory of the Young Turks and the new Turkey.

BOOKS TO READ

Frye, Richard N., ed., *Islam and the West* (The Hague, 1957).

Herslag, Z. Y., *Turkey: An Economy in Transition* (The Hague, 1960?)

Hoskins, Halford L., *The Middle East,* 2nd ed. (New York, 1959).

Lenczowski, George, *The Middle East in World Affairs,* 2nd ed. (Ithaca, 1956).

Lewis, Bernard, *Turkey Today* (London, 1940); *The Emergence of Modern Turkey* (Oxford, 1961).

Lewis, G. L., *Turkey* (New York, 1955).

Ostroróg, Leon, *The Angora Reform* (London, 1927).

[7] As discussed above, p. 357.
[8] Cited above, p. 336.
[9] Mentioned above, p. 360.

Parker, John and Charles Smith, *Modern Turkey* (London, 1940).

Price, Clair, *The Rebirth of Turkey* (New York, 1923).

Royal Institute of International Affairs, *The Middle East: A Political and Economic Survey,* 2nd ed. (London, 1954).

Thomas, Lewis J. and Richard N. Frye, *The United States and Turkey and Iran* (Cambridge, Mass., 1951).

Tongas, Gérard, *Atatürk and the True Nature of Modern Turkey,* tr. F. F. Rynd (London, 1939).

Toynbee, A. J. and D. P. Kirkwood, *Turkey* (London, 1926).

Webster, Donald S., *The Turkey of Atatürk* (Philadelphia, 1939).

White, Wilbur W., *The Process of Change in the Ottoman Empire* (Chicago, 1937).

Yale, William, *The Near East: A Modern History* (Ann Arbor, 1958).

XXVII   *Safawid Persia*

AFTER eight and a half centuries of national eclipse under Arab and Mongol domination Persia emerged as a great independent state led by a native dynasty, the Safawid (r. 1501-1736). The family's ancestor Safi-al-Din (d. 1334) was a Sufi who claimed descent from Ali, acquired a wide reputation for sanctity and a considerable following in the country. This was the only dynasty in Persia which claimed Arab descent. It started at the summit of one of those ever diminishing heights of power which have punctuated the political history of the country. Safawid Persia presented a radically different look from Sasanid Persia. Moslem in faith, Neo-Persian in language—using Arabic script and an abundance of Arabic loan words—, the new Persia was farther alienated from its Hellenistic and antique heritage.

Courtesy of American Numismatic Society

A COIN OF ISMAIL I   Struck in an ambulatory military mint in 1508, silver.

The founder of the new dynasty was Ismail I (r. 1501-24) who, following the careers of his father and grandfather, added the role of warrior to the profession of sanctity. Marriage between religion and the sword was not a novelty in Islam. In one battle after another Ismail subdued the different Timurid and Turkoman petty states and became master of all Persia. The descendants of Timur (d. 1405), who had ruled from his capital Samarkand the area from Delhi to

Damascus and from the Aral Sea to the Persian Gulf, retained their hold on north Persia until this time. They were preceded by their relatives the Il-Khans, founded by Hulagu about 1250.[1] Ismail chose Tabriz, for capital, proclaimed himself shah and made Shiah the official religion of the country. Persia is still Shiite. With his kingdom consolidated he extended his conquests from the Oxus to the Persian Gulf and from Afghanistan to the Euphrates. Only the Ottoman Turks were left as rivals.

If the Sasanids were inspired by Zoroastrianism,[2] the Safawids were inspired by Shiism, which they endeavored to propagate westward beyond their realm. This brought them into religious conflict, additional to the political, with the Sunnite Ottomans. A duel between the two great powers into which the Near East was then polarized thus began and was carried on for years. It recalls the earlier duel between Persians and Romans. In the first round the Turks came on top. Salim's forces after the battle of Chaldiran north of Lake Urmia (1515) invaded Persia and occupied its capital.[3] Far from weakening Shah Ismail's position the episode served to rally his people around his new throne with intensified loyalty. Nor did the repeated occupation of Tabriz and other Persian towns by Salim's successor Sulayman undermine the power of Ismail's son, who had succeeded him at the age of ten.

THE MERIDIAN OF POWER

Safawid power attained its meridian under the fifth shah Abbas I (r. 1587-1629). Abbas was unquestionably the most highly esteemed in his dynasty and one of the ablest modern shahs Persia produced.

Courtesy of American Numismatic Society

A COIN OF ABBAS I   Struck in Kashan, 1599, gold.

He belonged to an epoch which produced such great figures as Sulayman the Magnificent, Queen Elizabeth and Akbar, third Mogul emperor of India, whose very name means great. Three of this galaxy were Moslems. "Great" became Abbas' title and great he was in

[1] See above, p. 298.
[2] See above, p. 172.
[3] Discussed above, p. 324.

energy, determination and even in ruthless jealousy. He murdered one of his sons and blinded two others, as their popularity reached a point which did not suit his convenience. The rest of the royal princes he immured in the harem under the tutelage of eunuchs. Patricide was practiced by one of his predecessors; fratricide was also practiced by the shahs though not to the same extent as among Ottoman sultans. The unusually long reigns of the Safawids may be explained by the practice of killing all possible pretenders among the royal family.

In his early career Abbas was himself under the domination of Persianized Turks (Kizil-bash) while the western part of his territory was under Ottoman domination. He gradually built up on the Ottoman model an army of Armenian and Georgian converts comprising infantry and artillery forces, all on a paid basis. Hitherto the army was composed of tribes under tribal leadership. His artillery was supplied by a cannon foundry started by two English adventurers, the Sherley brothers. Feeling secure at home he started campaigns against the Turks, retook Tabriz, chased them out of the land and pursued them to Mesopotamia where he occupied Baghdad, Mosul and Diarbakr. More than a warrior Abbas cultivated the arts, fostered trade, and pursued an unusually enlightened policy with his European contemporaries. The mosques, palaces, and public baths he built in Isfahan, his capital, made it a "wonder of the world." Isfahan still

Courtesy of Iranian Information Center

THE IMPERIAL MOSQUE AND PALACE GATEWAY AT ISFAHAN BUILT BY ABBAS THE GREAT The imperial square is in the foreground.

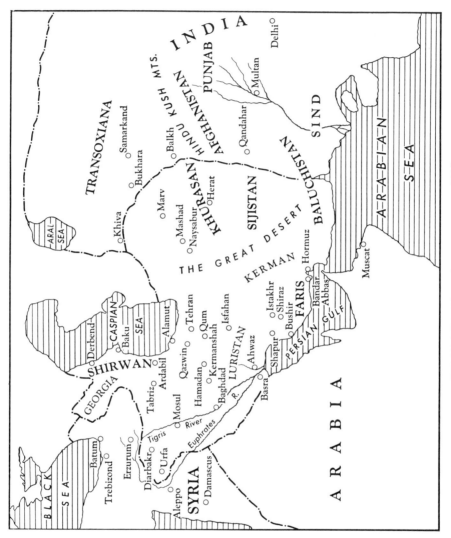

THE SAFAWID EMPIRE AT ITS HEIGHT *ca.* 1515

attracts more sightseers from abroad than any other town in Persia. What Abbas did was to construct a new imperial town outside of the old one. The new development centered on a great square around which were ranged the imperial palace and mosque, a smaller mosque and a monumental entrance to the covered bazars. On one side of the square stretched a wide garden area studded with royal palaces and pavilions. An avenue led across the river to garden palaces on the opposite side. The shah in person supervised some of the construction work. The capital is said to have grown to enclose within its mud-brick walls some 600,000 inhabitants, 162 mosques, 48 seminaries, 1802 caravanserais and 273 public baths. It is claimed that almost every house had its garden court. Other public works of Abbas outside the capital included schools, roads, caravanserais and public baths.

Of the Europeans the Portuguese were the first to establish themselves firmly on Persian soil. Before them Venetian dealers had the monopoly of what there was of international trade. In the reign of Shah Ismail Portuguese seized Hormuz, the leading mart on the Persian Gulf and a trade center for overland trade to India. Carpets, cotton and wool, fruits and gum were its chief exports. The city remained in Portuguese hands until 1622, when it was recovered by Persians aided by forces supplied by the Dutch and English East India Companies. This was the first display of British military might in Asia. For this service the British naturally received special privileges. The company had been in operation for years in India and had begun invasion of the Persian market in the sixteenth century, but in 1616 it was brought into conflict with the Portuguese. After 1622 British influence in the shah's court and the Persian Gulf began to outweigh all others. In 1763 the English established a factory in Bushir, seven years later another in Basra. Since then they have been the paramount power in the Gulf. Close by Hormuz Abbas founded another base of trade, Bandar Abbas, which outstripped its neighbor. The French did not secure permission to trade in Persia until 1664.

INEPT SHAHS

Abbas the Great was followed by a series of inept rulers who set the dynasty on its downward course, a one-century course from which it never recovered. Abbas' immediate successor, his grandson Safi (r. 1629-1642), distinguished himself by a wholesale execution of members of the royal family, male and female, together with most of the generals and counselors who had contributed to making his grandfather's reign the illustrious reign that it was. Safi was in good company with his Ottoman contemporary Murad IV. The harem began to dominate the imperial court. Two later successors were dissolute and addicted to drink. Another was so meek and pious as to give the Shiite theologians an opportunity to seize power and persecute Sunnite minorities. This dark picture had one bright spot, a relative economic prosperity, thanks to the brisk international trade mainly through European activity. Travelers flocked to the country and gave us a dazzling picture of the pomp and pageantry in the aristocratic and royal life.

Internal weakness encouraged external aggression. The Turks reiterated their attacks, again temporarily occupied Tabriz and in 1638 annexed Baghdad and with it all Mesopotamia, which remained in their hands until the first World War. This was accomplished under Murad IV, one of the last warrior sultans of the Ottoman dynasty. Russia, on the other hand, was starting its series of ambitious conquerors. Cossack raids on the Caucasus established a precedent. Its czar Peter the Great captured the key-fortresses of Derbend and Baku (1722-1723), and in 1724 entered into an agreement with Turkey to dismember Persia, Russia to annex the three Caspian provinces already occupied and Turkey to receive the western provinces.[4] The death of Peter the Great and the ensuing war between Russia and Turkey interfered with the consummation of the agreement.

While security against external danger was assured for the time being, internal security was further imperiled by the upsurge of minorities: Afghans and Turks, both Sunnites. Afghanistan had been till then alternately a part of India or of Persia; in fact it had no independ-

Courtesy of American Numismatic Society

A COIN OF ABBAS III   Struck in Tabriz in 1734, silver.

ent existence until about the mid-eighteenth century. Ethnically related to the Persians, the last Afghans spoke largely a sister language of Persian, Pushtu (Pashtu), written in an alphabet modified from Persian-Arabic. Under local chieftains one Afghan tribe after another began to assert its independence and build up petty states. Chieftain

[4] Cf. above, pp. 341-2.

Mahmud seized Herat and Mashad, marched against Isfahan and in 1922 captured it. Members of the Safawid dynasty maintained a hold on certain territories but they had to face another uprising, this time by a Turkoman tribe, the Afshar, while Ottoman and Russian invasions were renewed. Anarchy prevailed. The veneration in which the early Safawids were held was no more sufficient to hold the state together. Out of the chaos emerged a new figure, Nadir Quli, the Afsharid chief. He was the man destined to restore the state and give it a new strength. Nadir in 1731 deposed the ruling shah and proclaimed the shah's son Abbas, still in the cradle, in his place, with himself as regent. Five years later, on the death of Abbas III, the regent won the unanimous election of an assembly of leading Persians as the new shah. Thus was started a new dynasty, the Afsharid.

THE AFSHARIDS

The hero of the new day was born in a tent in Khurasan and earned his living first as a leader of a robber band and then as a camel driver. He later entered the military service of the Safawids and won distinction as a warrior. After seizing power Nadir conducted a series of brilliant military campaigns which not only freed his country from Afghans, Ottomans and Russians but pushed its boundaries into India, Turkestan and Iraq, far beyond any point attained before. Having destroyed the petty Afghan state, which had arisen on the ruins of the Safawid, he marched his troops against Afghanistan proper and pushed on to Delhi. Among the spoils he brought back from this city were the fabulous Peacock Throne and Koh-i-noor ("mountain of light"), the famous diamond now among the jewels of the British crown in the Tower of London. When obtained by the British from the Punjab in 1849 the diamond weighed 186¼ carats. The throne was constructed (about 1630) by the Mogul emperor Shah Jahan, more celebrated for building the Taj Mahal. The throne had twelve pillars, each bearing a gem-incrusted peacock and was used by later shahs. North of India, Nadir, who has been called the Napoleon of Iran, captured Bukhara and Khiva, important centers of eastern Turks. All these military exploits, however, were raids and resulted in no permanent annexation. Westward Nadir moved against Iraq and seized Mosul and Basra. Taking advantage of the Russo-Turkish war he threatened to join Turkey unless Russia returned the Caspian provinces. Russia yielded. Again the Persian Empire, united under one lord, stretched from the Indus to the Caucasus and the Euphrates, but the unity was not on a firm foundation; it was of a short duration. Nadir was lacking in statesmanship and his regime in administrative ability and experience. His unsuccessful efforts to make Shiah a fifth orthodox school as a preliminary to the renunciation of Sunnah resulted in a growing discontent which he tried to suppress by ruthless measures.   Despotic exploitation added to restlessness and impoverished the land.   Also unsuccessful was the attempt he made to build a fleet in the Persian Gulf.   The military exploits overtaxed the manpower as well as the economy of the country

Courtesy of American Numismatic Society

A COIN OF NADIR SHAH   Struck in Isfahan in 1741, silver.

and not enough was received in return.   At last the war lord fell victim to the dagger of one of his officer tribesmen, leaving very little by way of cultural legacy or of enduring value.

The Afsharid dynasty (r. 1736-1796) founded by Nadir consisted of only four shahs.   Shortly after its founder's death the country was again plunged into a state not less anarchic than that preceding him. Nadir's son, who succeeded, was dethroned after one year.   Nadir's second successor, a grandson, was defeated and blinded by a Shiite rival.   Afghanistan won its independence.   The rest of the country was hotly disputed by different chieftains.   Torn by internal strife the southwestern part was taken over by the head of a nomadic Iranian tribe, the Zand, named Karim Khan (r. 1750-1779).   The

Courtesy of American Numismatic Society

A COIN OF AGHA MUHAMMAD   Struck in Resht in 1788, gold.

triangular contest between Afghans, Qajars and Zands ended in favor of the Zands.   The new dynasty (r. 1750-1794) comprised seven rulers, who contented themselves with the title of regent.   Shiraz was made the capital and was adorned by the dynasty's founder with fine buildings.   For a time the country enjoyed a sorely needed rest.

Karim's benevolent rule seemed more benevolent in contrast with those preceding and succeeding. The memory of his name is still cherished by Persians. But no sooner had he passed away than the usual struggle for power among brothers and other relatives began. At last in 1794 another tribal chief, Agha Muhammad of the Turkoman Qajar tribe, which had been bidding for power for some time, seized it. In the accession of the Qajar dynasty a new leaf was turned in Persian annals.

ARTISTIC AND INTELLECTUAL ACTIVITY

The political revival under the Safawids was reflected in the arts of the time. The entire period, more particularly that of Abbas the Great, was marked by considerable architectural and artistic activity. In general Safawid products followed the Mongol Timurid patterns but fell short of them in excellence. The preceding period had featured huge vaulted arches, melon-shaped domes and minarets, all faced with vari-colored tiles and with calligraphic ornamentation. Likewise the Safawid artisans featured color, glazed tiles, polychronic and mosaic taïence. Their attempts to revive metalwork and the ceramic art were not successful. Of the royal and aristocratic residences only few examples have survived, chief among them are those of new Isfahan by Abbas the Great. Examples of such public works as aqueducts and bridges are also extant. Of the mosques, seminaries and shrines many have come down to us. In religious architecture more durable material was used.

Abbas the Great invited from China some three hundred potters with their families, who left a manifest impression on Persian porcelain with its delicate coloring and refined designs. The country, it should be recalled, was favorably situated astride the few passes that linked the Near East with India and the Far East along the "silk road" flanked with centers of commerce and culture which at times were destroyed by Mongol invaders. Three centuries earlier, when the Mongol Il-Khans were Islamized,[5] Chinese cultural currents began to flow copiously into the Persian stream. Marks became clearly apparent in decorative motifs including the introduction of the dragon, the lotus, the phoenix and cloud symbols. Pottery, textiles and carpets of the Safawid age show such influence. Carpet weaving served as an outstanding medium of the period's decorative arts. Largely in the past a home or a small workshop industry, carpet weaving now began to rise to higher cooperative levels. Weavers, painters and illuminators joined hands with talents to produce pieces worthy as royal gifts to foreign

---

[5] Consult above, p. 298.

Courtesy of The Metropolitan Museum of Art, Gift of Samuel H. Kress Foundation, 1946

MEDALLION RUG, TABRIZ COURT MANUFACTURER, CAPTURED AT THE TURKISH SIEGE
OF VIENNA IN 1683

rulers or as furniture for mosques, mausoleums and holy shrines.   The
material was wool or silk, usually with a centralized design, the center
being a medallion.   Other designs presented an over-all pattern.
Trees, flowers and animals—real or fictitious—were often used; rarely
were human beings depicted.   The garden was the favorite theme.
Tabriz, Kashan, Isfahan, Kerman and Herat became and have remained
the main weaving centers.   The carpet products of the sixteenth and
seventeenth centuries have not been since excelled.

Painting, a court art, was another activity which strongly felt Chinese
impact.   Its miniature variety, born in the Il-Khanid days out of the
union of Persian, Mesopotamian and Chinese elements, was continued

Courtesy of The Metropolitan Museum of Art, Rogers Fund, 1930

SILK VELVET BROCADE WITH PLANTS GROWING OUT OF ROCK FORMS Butterflies and clouds scattered between. First half of 17th Century.

under the Safawids. Miniatures, in bright opaque colors covering the entire picture area, were used to illustrate epic or romantic poetry. Illustrated manuscripts usually had an elaborately decorated frontispiece in which blue, derived from lapis lazuli, and gold predominated. Such designs as the flowering shrub or a rose with a nightingale or a butterfly were generally favored in painting. Miniature painting kept on a high level until the end of the reign of Abbas the Great. Miniatures were not executed separately and then inserted in a book as is the practice in modern illustrations. They were rather interpenetrated with the text and blended with the calligraphy. Sketches featured foliage, animals and at times included persons illustrative of the text. Then comes the leather worker to collaborate with the calligrapher and the painter in producing an embossed and tooled cover that would, with the text and the inside miniature, present one pleasing harmonious ensemble. The cover layout followed in general that of the carpet. Manuscript covers were highly prized not only as an external protection but also as an artistic part of a possession to be cherished and prized for genera-

Courtesy of The Metropolitan Museum of Art, Gift of Alexander Smith Cochran, 1913

EXTERIOR OF A BOOK COVER, 16TH CENTURY

tions.   Before the end of the sixteenth century the art of bookmaking was already on the decline.

The masterpieces of Persian literature—those of Firdawsi, Sadi, Nizami,[6] and the fables of Bidpai—were among the first to be illustrated. The story of Joseph and Potiphar's wife, treated among others by Jami, was especially popular among miniaturists, particularly the scene in

[6] See frontispiece.

Courtesy of The Metropolitan Museum of Art, Rogers Fund, 1917

DANCING DERVISHES, STYLE OF BIHZAD, *ca.* 1490

which Joseph's admission to Potiphar's wife's salon so overcomes the attendant ladies with his resplendent beauty that they unconsciously cut their fingers instead of the fruits they were eating. The master miniature artist, Bihzad, was born in Herat in 1440 and was still alive in 1524. He was patronized by the Timurid as well as the Safawid court. Shah Abbas reportedly considered him as worth half his kingdom.

In Bihzad the miniature art culminated. Schools following his style arose in Tabriz, Herat, and other places and his name was at times forged to the embarrassment of later scholars and collectors. Among the authenticated paintings bearing his name is a copy of Sadi's *Bustan* in the Egyptian national library at Cairo.

Literary and intellectual life did not respond to the rejuvenating political stimuli generated by the Safawid dynasty as the artistic life did. The last of the classical poets was Jami (d. 1492),[7] who dominated the fifteenth century as Hafiz had dominated the fourteenth and Sadi the thirteenth. The Safawid period represented a hiatus between the classical and the modern. In earlier times several of the most brilliant belletrists, historians, geographers, philosophers, physicians, scientists in Islam were of Persian nationality, as noted before, but they wrote in Arabic and were therefore treated with other Arab authors.

Poetry no less than painting was then a court art. Such talent required leisure and patronage to develop. Safawid rulers did not encourage secular praise. They built and endowed theological seminaries and fostered the praise of the imams. A new hierarchy of theologians arose which acquired authority on doctrinal matters and assumed the exclusive rights to new interpretation of the Koran and tradition beyond anything attained or claimed by Sunni theologians. This is the nearest institution that Islam ever produced comparable to the Roman Catholic hierarchy in its highest echelon, and this is the institution that now attracted young ambitious intellectuals and diverted them from possible belletrist pursuits. The abuse of power by the Shiite hierarchy and its intolerance toward Sunnites contributed to the downfall of the dynasty and its replacement by Turks and Afghans.

On raising the Shiah to the rank of a state religion and finding a dearth of competent theologians Ismail I invited or encouraged teachers and scholars from abroad to come, teach, propagate and establish the tenets of the creed. Among those who responded was a Lebanese whose son, Baha-al-Din al-Amili (1542-1622), had a distinguished career. His last name indicates origin in Amil east of Tyre. Baha-al-Din was elevated to the shaykdom of Islam in Isfahan under Abbas the Great. Jurist, theologian and to a less extent philosopher and mathematician Baha attempted to encompass the totality of contemporary Moslem lore. His best known work was a book of legal opinions and decisions which served as a text for many school generations.

Equally prolific and even more influential was his pupil Sadr-al-Din al-Shirazi. After receiving his license from the master in Isfahan Sadr-al-Din returned to his native Shiraz and occupied a chair in one

---

[7] Treated above, p. 300.

of its seminaries.   He restored ibn-Sina (Avicenna) to the curriculum
—which orthodox divines had banned—but under cover, using deliberately obscure expressions.   Sadr's twenty volumes comprise commentaries on the Koran, dissertations on tradition, treatises on polemics,
theology, and metaphysics and accounts of his travels.   He is said to
have made the holy pilgrimage to Mecca seven times, all on foot.   He
died at Basra (1641) returning from the seventh pilgrimage.   His
metaphysics became a source of Shaykhi and Babi theology to be treated
in a later chapter.

Three or four theologians of the period laid the basis of Shiah
theology today prevalent in Persia and the rest of the Near East.   Most
of the works of the others were sterile and ineffective.   Several theologians wrote in Arabic, Arabic being the Latin of Islam, and in ornate
style beyond the comprehension of the masses.   In this their prose
was even farther removed than poetry with its artificially elegant and
affected idiom.

Certain Persian poets of the sixteenth and seventeenth centuries, attracted by the Mogul court of north India, especially that of Akbar
the Great (r. 1556-1605), migrated there and made Persian poetry
dominant in the court.   India became a second center of Persian
poetry with a peculiar style of its own.   A new channel was found
through India for reaching Central Asia.   A noteworthy emigrant poet
was Jamal-al-Din al-Urfi, who was born and educated in Shiraz, where
his father, a government official, administered the customary law
(*'urf*).   At the age of twenty Jamal suffered a severe attack of smallpox which left his face badly disfigured and evidently soured his life.
By way of psychological compensation he became possessed by self-
conceit and arrogance that made him intolerable to his colleagues.
Emperor Akbar took him into his service but Urfi died soon after at
Lahore (1591) aged thirty-six.   Urfi was credited with the invention
of a new style of poetical composition featured by novel expressions,
original metaphors and avoidance of Arabic vocabulary.   He was one
of the early Persian writers to seek to purge the native tongue from
Arabic loan words and became especially popular with the Turks.

In other than political and religious fields the writers of the period
labored in history but achieved no distinction either by the sheer bulk
of output or by the quality of the slender content.   What they left
is mostly monographs on special periods or localities, biographies of
shahs and accounts of princes and notables with little heed to the
people with their religious, political, social and economic problems.
European travelers' accounts come to our aid here.   The last century
of the Safawid period was extraordinarily calm in so far as wars and

invasions were concerned, but the state existed on its acquired reputation and inspired no meritorious historians. Even the style used was usually stilted, overloaded with Arabisms and abounding in ornamentation. From this period we have accounts of the lives of Safi-al-Din, ancestor of the family, Ismail, its founder, and Abbas, its greatest representative. That of Abbas was written in 1616 by his own secretary-writer (*munshi*), Iskandar. Iskandar Munshi was born in 1560 and worked as an accountant before devoting himself to the art of composition. The following quotation from the biography he wrote illustrates the inflexible severity of its hero and the kind of material the biographer presented:

should he command a father to kill his son, the sentence would be carried out immediately, even as the decree of destiny; or should the father, moved by parental tenderness, make any delay, the command would be reversed; and should the son then temporize, another would slay both. By such awful severity the execution of his commands attain the supreme degree of efficiency and none dared hesitate for an instant in the fulfilment of the sentence inevitable as fate.[8]

BOOKS TO READ

The Legacy of Persia, ed. A. J. Arberry (Oxford, 1953).

Lockhart, Lawrence, *Nadir Shah* (London, 1938); *Famous Cities of Iran* (Brentford, 1939); *The Fall of the Safawi Dynasty and the Afghan Occupation of Persia* (Cambridge, 1958).

Pope, Arthur U., *An Introduction to Persian Art* (New York, 1931).

Ross, E. Denison, *The Persians* (Oxford, 1931); *Sir Anthony Sherley and His Persian Adventure* (London, 1933).

Sykes, Percy, *A History of Persia,* 3rd ed., vol. II (London, 1936).

Wilber, Donald N., *Iran: Past and Present,* 4th ed. (Princeton, 1958).

[8] Edward G. Browne, *A History of Persian Literature in Modern Times,* vol. IV (Cambridge, 1924), p. 108.

XXVIII *Qajars and Involvement in European Politics*

T HE dynasty founded by Agha Muhammad (r. 1779-
1797)[1] counted seven shahs and lasted till 1925. The Qajar was one
of several Turkoman tribes which settled in the Safawid period and
furnished troops for the army. The founder tragically suffered castra-
tion at the age of five by a political enemy of the family. He is the
only eunuch known to have founded a dynasty. After serving as a
hostage in the Zand court of Karim, young Agha Muhammad started
on his military career. He seized Tehran in 1779, made it his residence, and engaged in incessant warfare that ultimately gave him control
over the country. But he displayed none but military ability. His
mutilation had left him a pathological personality dominated by vindic-
tiveness and sadistic lust for domination. The only authority he refused
to challenge was that of the religious hierarchy. When two of his
servants, whom he had condemned to death for some trivial reason,
assassinated him, a sigh of relief spread among his subjects. His name

Courtesy of American Numismatic Society

A COIN OF FATH ALI SHAH   Struck in Ganjeh, 1801, silver.

still lives as the synonym of inhumane treatment. None of his successors, with the exception of Nasir-al-Din (r. 1848-1896), showed any
marked ability or serious concern for the welfare of their people.
Starting with Agha's immediate nephew-successor, Fath Ali (r. 1797-
1834), they ruled the country as though it were an enemy land to be

---

[1] Mentioned above, p. 385.

exploited for the benefit of the royal family.   Fath appointed his sons as governors of provinces and established bad precedents in favoritism and a high life of pomp and splendor, while denying his troops their rightful pay.   Under him Tehran was definitely fixed as the capital— a position it still holds—though in summer he followed his forebears' model and lived in a tent on a plain.

It was during this shah's reign that the door was opened for the infiltration of foreign political influences that put the country in the orbit of Western European powers and ultimately made of her a tool for imperialist designs.   Europeans had discovered Persia in the six-teenth century,[2] but the contacts had been preponderantly commercial. Until this time only Turkey and Russia had lain within the horizon of Persia's foreign policy.   But in the nineteenth century Western Eu-rope's urge for political and economic expansion became especially impelling and acquired competitive aspects.   Britain came first with her concern in Persia primarily as a buffer state to her Indian posses-sion.   Britain first considered France of Napoleon as her rival, though French activity had hitherto been cultural and limited to the interior. The activity dated from the time of Abbas the Great, who permitted stations for the Carmelites.   As Russia after the Napoleonic period and subsequently began her thrust toward Central Asia, she became the rival.   The thrust was interpreted as a threat to British interests.   By the 1880's Russia's conquest of Khiva, Bukhara, Marv and the subjuga-tion of the Turkomans was complete.   The encirclement of the victim by these two great powers was practically accomplished.   By strange combinations the rivals of today may become the partners of tomorrow in the division of the spoils.

BRITISH-FRENCH-RUSSIAN RIVALRY

British authorities in India began the nineteenth century by inciting Fath Ali to attack Afghanistan as a means to diverting that country from attacking India.   Two years later, from Egypt, Napoleon made the first of his overtures to Persia to join him in an attack on British India, the Persian expeditionary force to be trained by his men.   The British took the grandiose scheme seriously.   The shah welcomed French support for his contemplated attack on Georgia, wrested in 1801 by Russia.   Georgia was a Christian Caucasian province.   In 1807 a French general with seventy officers arrived in Tehran, but in the following year the French mission was replaced by a British one that had been invited in return for a British subsidy to Persia.   The Anglo-Persian treaty of 1814, directed against Russia, left Persia

[2] Above, p. 381.

dependent on Britain in its foreign policy. The Russo-Persian treaty (Turkoman-Chai) of 1828 put her at the mercy of Russia. It ceded to Russia the largest part of the Caucasian territory, imposed capitulations in the model of those enforced on Turkey, and put Persia's foreign trade in the hands of Russia. Soon other European powers demanded similar privileges as in the capitulations, which were not abolished till 1928. Six years after the signing of the Turkoman-Chai treaty an Anglo-Russian agreement was reached guaranteeing the independence of Persia and revealing the degree of distrust between the two contracting parties. The shah's country became a mere pawn in the game of world politics. Imperialism took a new turn: it involved controlling the natural resources and trade of the undeveloped country rather than changing its color on the map to conform to that of the ruling country.

Courtesy of American Numismatic Society

A COIN OF NASIR-AL-DIN SHAH Struck at Tehran, 1880, gold, 10 tomans.

In the long reign of Nasir-al-Din (1848-1896) the trend toward foreign control of the country's economy continued unchecked. The shah, who ascended the throne at the age of sixteen, was capable, patriotic, and open-minded; but had neither the purse nor the sword that was necessary. Besides, he had to contend with internal disorders occasioned by a new intellectual life.

The steadily growing impact of the West on his country aroused Nasir's curiosity about the source of influence. No Persian ruler had ever before stepped on foreign soil except as an invader or exile. In his three visits (1873, 1887, 1889) Nasir stopped at London, Paris, St. Petersburg, Munich, and other important centers. In Paris he visited the international exposition of 1889. The simply written account of his experience was widely read and favorably affected modern Persian prose. What he desired most to learn was probably how to reinforce his power as a ruler and increase the state's revenues. But the high expenses involved in the trip left such a strain on the country's finances that a state monopoly of the tobacco industry was instituted. In 1890, the monopoly, with the right of cultivation and trade, was transferred to a European group of capitalists. It aroused a national storm of indignation, tobacco being one of the most widespread pleasures in which the public indulged. At the instigation of theologians abstention from smoking was practiced and civil disturbances broke out, necessitating buying back of the concession. But the half million-pound-sterling price had to be borrowed, and the foundation of a long-standing state debt was thus laid. The 1890 tobacco uprising is especially significant; it was the first time the people had defied the will of the shah. Fifteen years passed before the second and more serious uprising was staged.

Concessions, mainly to British interests, ensued one after the other; none produced the expected result. The one for telegraph lines was given in 1864 first from Bushir to Baghdad and later to connect with London—through Odessa and Tiflis—with ramifications reaching the main cities in the provinces. In 1889 British interests received a concession for founding the Imperial Bank of Persia. Other British interests opened the Karun River for navigation. Arising near Isfahan, this river flows first west then south to join the Tigris-Euphrates at Shatt al-Arab. It is navigable, except for the Ahwaz rapids to Shushtar. Unsuccessful attempts were made to interest the State Department in Washington and Wall Street in New York in a trans-Caspian railway and other projects. Earlier a British subject had been granted a gigantic package of monopolies in return for a commitment to found a national bank, open mines, and construct railways; but the grant was withdrawn.

The country was sinking deeper and deeper into debt. A loan from Britain (1892) was followed by one from the Russians in 1900, guaranteed by customs receipts except from the Persian Gulf ports. The Russians further stipulated the liquidation of the British loan and no borrowing from any other foreign power for the next ten years, thereby establishing virtually a financial monopoly over the country. A Russian bank was opened in Tehran. In 1902 the Russian government offered another loan, receiving in return the concession to construct a railway from Julfa (now Djulfa, Dghulfa) on her southern border to Tabriz and Tehran. Two years before that plans were considered for the construction of a major trunk from Russia through Persia to the Gulf coast, but these plans were vehemently opposed by the British.

One bright spot in this period of financial strain was the relative peace the country enjoyed. Except for Nasir's attempt to recover Herat and other parts of Afghanistan—a national dream of the Persians —no major military project was undertaken. In fact the occupation of Herat was the last foreign campaign carried out by Persia. Britain immediately declared war and landed troops at a Persian Gulf port, forcing the shah to withdraw his troops from Afghan territory. The cardinal point in British policy presumably was to keep Persia weak. Russia established a naval base at Astrabad on the southeasternmost bay of the Caspian. The Persian army remained weak though successive missions from France, England, Russia, Austria, and Italy tried to train it. Only the Cossack brigade, founded and officered by Russia, could be counted on as an effective instrument of warfare.

Russia's domination of Persian affairs received a setback as a result of her surprising—to Near Easterners—defeat at the hands of Japan in the 1904 to 1905 war. In that first decade of the century the latest competitor for empire building, Germany, entered the Near Eastern field. While Britain had assembled her possessions piecemeal and almost haphazardly, Germany followed a carefully calculated scheme, using a Teutonic or Nordic wedge through Central Europe and the Baghdad railway[3] wedge through Western Asia. The extension of German influence into this area was construed as inimical by both British and Russian interests. The two powers soon compromised their differences and signed an entente (August 1907) which recognized the northern half of the country as the Russian sphere of influence and the southern part as the British sphere. The central zone was left open to concessions for either party. The agreement reaffirmed the "independence and integrity" of Persia—the usual lip service political hypocrisy pays to sincerity—which misled none, least of all the people concerned. The country was then under Muhammad Ali (r. 1907-1909), as weak and ineffective a ruler as his father predecessor Muzaffar-al-Din (r. 1896-1907) and with no more pressing desire than to fill his empty treasury with loans. It was under Muzaffar that the absolute monarchy was, at least in name, transformed into a constitutional monarchy (to be treated later) with a constitution and a national assembly which Muhammad Ali, with the support of Russia, tried to overthrow three times. He was finally forced to abdicate by the nationalists and revolutionaries,[4] emboldened by the success of the Young Turks movement. When some factions in the nationalist group expected to pit German against Anglo-Russian interests, the national assembly turned to the United States for financial advice.

[3] Discussed above, p. 347.
[4] Cf. below, p. 414.

MUZAFFAR-AL-DIN SHAH

On the recommendation of the Department of State a young official of the Union Trust in Washington, W. Morgan Shuster, was invited to Persia as treasurer-general and given almost a free hand. He arrived in the spring of 1911 with four American assistants but with no knowledge of the economic, social or political situation. With energy and the best intentions he tackled the problems, but in the autumn of that year Russia served two ultimatums for his withdrawal. He had planned to appoint a military attaché of the British embassy as chief of the newly organized gendarmerie to enforce taxation. The country was then under a young shah Sultan Ahmad (r. 1909-1925), who succeeded his father Muhammad Ali (r. 1907-1909) at the age of twelve. Russian forces moved against Tabriz, where they slaughtered a number, and bombarded Mashad, the holy site of one of the imams. The American mission was withdrawn in 1912.

PETROLEUM

One of the last and what turned out to be most significant concession ever given to a British subject was the one given to William K.

D'Arcy, a New Zealander, for oil in 1901. It was a sixty-year ex-clusive concession covering the country with the exception of the northern provinces, in return for which the government was to receive £20,000, an equal amount in paid-up shares and 16 per cent of the annual profits.

Oil and gas seepage on the Near East surface must have been as early a phenomenon as man himself. References abound to it in ancient writings. Its products were evidently used for painting, mortar mixing, waterproofing, lamp fuel, and medical purposes. Noah covered the inside and outside of his ark with pitch (Gen. 6:14). Seeping oil or gas on the Iranian plateau, ignited by such a natural cause as lightning, must have so impressed its primitive onlookers that it became an object of wonder and finally of worship. Later, when Zoroastrian-ism under the Achaemenids became the official religion, its temples housed eternal flames, utilizing springs of oil or gas. It was near the site of a Parthian temple, today called Masjid Sulayman, about a hun-dred and twenty-five miles north of the head of the Persian Gulf that oil was struck at a depth of 1100 feet and found to be in commercial quantities. This was after seven years of expenditure of energy and money on a seemingly futile project and at a time when the board of directors was on the point of issuing orders to stop the operation. Not until the first decade of the twentieth century was the exploration and exploitation of this "liquid gold," the future main source of revenue for many Near Eastern lands, earnestly pursued.

In 1909 the Anglo-Persian (later Iranian) Oil Company was formed in London and proceeded with the construction of roads, buildings, a pipeline to Abadan, an island at the mouth of Shatt al-Arab, and a refinery on it. The Abadan refinery can handle 700,000 barrels and is still the largest in the world. An area of some two hundred square miles, hitherto barren and used by Bakhtiari tribesmen for their flocks, was before long converted into a modern industrial settlement, with gigantic electric installations, up-to-date housing and medical facilities, and a population of about 60,000. Labor was recruited mostly from Bakhtiari nomads. Other areas were exploited by ramifications of this company and by other companies that made of Persia one of the major oil fields of the world. Quick to realize the importance of the new product, the British Government purchased a majority of the shares in 1914. The new Persian product proved invaluable to her and her allies in the four-year war effort. The increasing dependence of England upon this product strengthened the bargaining power of the Persian government and increased its royalties. In 1933 a new con-tract was signed, stipulating that royalty payments should reach a total of at least £750,000 each year. In the 1940's they mounted to £10,000,000.[5]

THE GREAT WAR

At the outbreak of European hostilities in the summer of 1914, Persia proclaimed a state of neutrality which neither she had the might to implement nor any of the belligerents the desire to respect. The Cossack brigade was still under Russian officers, but the gendarmes were under Swedish command which tended to sympathize with the Germans. Persian territory was freely violated by both sides in the conflict. The capital became a hotbed of international intrigue in which Russians, Germans, and British were the leading participants. Its imperial court was spineless; it shifted with the wind. Russia and Britain, now allies, tightened their hold on their respective spheres of influence. Britain was given a free hand in the neutral zone between. The Central Powers—headed by Germany and Austria—used Turkey as spearhead against neighboring Persia.

In January 1915 Turkey opened a front against Russia through northwestern Persia on her border. Kurds joined Turks in the attack. Tabriz changed hands more than once as Russian troops advanced or retreated. The Germans started operations in the south and along the gulf coast. Their early display of military might and their initial success on the European battlefield had so impressed Near Easterners that most of them believed in the final victory of German arms. Besides Persians and other Near Easterners had no grudge or grievance to harbor against the new Central European power. A former German consul at Bushir, popular among the tribesmen and conversant in their language, arrived at Shiraz to stir up the people as his counterpart T. E. Lawrence was doing among the Arabs. But this "German Lawrence," as he was styled, met with less success. Equally unsuccessful were other German agents in the area who aimed at a thrust through Afghanistan, with the hope of drawing that country into war, and ultimately into India to foment trouble and divert British troops. The familiar propaganda line was followed: ill feeling against the traditional oppressors of the people were inflamed, full and complete independence was promised, and most importantly cash payments were pledged. The British counteracted by having Major Percy Sykes of India move to Bandar Abbas (1916) and organize a force of 11,000, known as the South Persian Rifles. Order was reestablished and the pipelines to the gulf defended.

In that year the smashing defeat of the Anglo-Indian expeditionary

[5] See below, p. 421.

force at Kut al-Amarah in Iraq[6] encouraged the Turkish troops and released more of them for the Persian front. The frontier was crossed and even Tehran was threatened, but the thrust was halted by Russians. In 1917 the tide of war turned against Turkey; Baghdad and lower Mesopotamia were lost and her troops were withdrawn from Persia. In November of that year, following the Bolshevik (later Soviet) revolution and the overthrow of the czarist regime, Russia retreated from Persia. The collapse of Russia freed the northern territory; but the presence of foreign troops there, and to a less extent in the south, left the country in a state of famine, with her finances shattered and the morale of her people at its lowest depth.

Persia sent a delegation to the Peace Conference at Paris in 1919 to present her grievances and demands. Chief among the demands were the restoration of Caucasian and Caspian territories annexed over the years by Russia, the abrogation of the humiliating Anglo-Russian treaty of 1907, the cancellation of the capitulations with their extra-territorial rights, and reparation for damages caused by war. But at the instigation of the British the delegation was not officially received. Instead the British proposed a bilateral treaty prefaced by the usual formula for respecting independence and integrity and continuing with the offer of military and civil advisers; the revision of the customs tariff; and a £2,000,000-loan, guaranteed by revenue from customs and used for the construction of roads and railroads—terms which would have reduced the country to a protectorate. A young incompetent and irresponsible shah, seconded by a weak and corrupt cabinet, signed the agreement; but the national assembly, responding to public opinion and emboldened by an American diplomatic protest, refused to convene for ratification. The British had failed to sense the strength of the nationalist spirit which for years had been stirring and was on the point of explosion. On the other hand, in 1918, Russia reversed the traditional policy by offering a treaty of amity renouncing all earlier treaties, concessions, and interests inherited from the defunct regime; cancelling all outstanding debts; and voiding all extraterritorial rights for Soviet citizens. The Julfa-Tabriz railroad, and many docks, harbors, and installations were accordingly turned over to the Persian government. Caspian fisheries were excepted, but navigation was opened to Persian shipping. In 1920 Persia was accepted as a fully independent member of the League of Nations, and in January of the following year British troops began to withdraw from the southern part of the country.

The first World War may be said to have sealed the fate of the Qajar

---

[6] See above, p. 365.

dynasty. Irresponsive to the demands of the surging patriotic and nationalist feelings, it passed away unlamented, with Shah Sultan Ahmad writing the last inglorious chapter in its biography. The hero of the coup was Reza Khan, commander of the Cossack brigade. Early on the morning of February 21, 1921, Reza at the head of 4,000 men appeared in the capital, occupied its state offices, and took control. Hardly a shot was fired. Sultan Ahmad's reign of seventeen years was beset from the start with serious internal disturbances and international problems. Ascending the throne as a lad, the choice of a regent was hotly contested by reactionaries and liberals. His father the ex-shah returned from Odessa, to which he went when deposed, and made a vain attempt to recover the throne. His lament as expressed by a local poet ran:

> Could I to Tehran once an entry gain
> Its people butcher-like I'd cleave in twain.

Indifferent and effeminate Sultan Ahmad made long sojourns in Europe, becoming a hibitué of night clubs in Paris and leaving state affairs in the hands of a ring of courtiers living on the spoils of the government and people. In 1923 he, apparently fearful for his life, left Persia for Europe, where he died seven years later. He had been deposed since 1925. Reza Khan ended a dynasty and started a new one; more importantly, he ended an era and started a new one.

BOOKS TO READ

Brockelmann, Carl, *History of the Islamic Peoples,* tr. Joel Carmichael and Moshe Perlmann (New York, 1947).

Elwell-Sutton L. P. *Modern Iran* (London, 1941).

Haas, William S., *Iran* (New York, 1946).

Martin, Bradford G., *German-Persian Diplomatic Relations, 1873-1912* ('s-Gravenhage, 1959).

Shuster, W. Morgan, *The Strangling of Persia* (London, 1912; New York, 1920).

Sykes, Percy, *A History of Persia,* 3rd ed., vol. II (London, 1930).

Wilson, Arnold, *The Persian Gulf* (Oxford, 1928); *Persia* (London 1932).

XXIX   *Stirrings of a New Life*

ARLY in the reign of Nasir-al-Din (1848-1896) the solidarity of the Shiah structure began to show cracks in its walls. A split in the official religion amounted to one in the state. Until then no one had dared challenge the spiritual authority of the ulema whose leaders, mujtahids (interpreters of theology and law), exercised undue influences on state affairs. The ranking mujtahids lived and taught at Najaf and Karbala, holy burial places of Ali and al-Husayn.

BABISM

The first to effect a schism in the Shiah was the son of a merchant, Ali Muhammad, who had been born in Shiraz in 1819 and received the usual education. His title sayyid indicates claim of descent from Ali and Fatimah. On a pilgrimage to Karbala this young Persian became acquainted with Shaykhi doctrines, so called after Shaykh Ahmad ibn-Zayn-al-Din al-Ahsai (of east Arabia, d. 1826), who had worked at Yazd under the patronage of its governor, a son of Fath Ali Shah. The Shaykhis taught that while the twelve imams had no power in themselves, they were in reality the instruments for the transmission of divine knowledge and will. As such they were the intermediary through which God could be understood. This made of them the hypostases of the supreme being. Though it took an ultra-Shiite position, Shaykhism remained within the pale of Islam, though close to the periphery. Its successor, Babism, stepped outside and with its offshoot Bahaism was considered heretical.

On May 23, 1844, the thousandth anniversary of the disappearance of the twelfth imam, whose appearance was awaited, Ali Muhammad proclaimed himself the expected mahdi and assumed the title Bab (door), the gateway to the esoteric knowledge of the divine truth. The second step was to consider himself the "mirror" through which believers could behold God himself and learn his will, a position easy to confuse popularly with that of the incarnation of the supreme being.

403

The Bab adopted the age-old technique of giving allegorical interpretation to koranic passages.   Therewith points could be stretched to any desired extent.   He taught the equality of sexes and denied the obligation of veiling and even of circumcision and ritual ablution.   The prescribed month of annual fast was reduced to nineteen days and the daily reading of the sacred book he wrote was set at nineteen verses. His community was to be under nineteen elders.   The number nineteen became an especially favored number as he, in Neo-Pythagorean style, attached hidden significance to it.

Starting as a mystical spiritualized movement Babism—like other movements in Islam—served as a rallying center for political, economic, and social malcontents.   Its followers increased explosively.   Particularly sensational was the conversion of a beautiful and poetically gifted young lady in Qazwin, Qurrat-al-Ayn ("the eye's satisfaction"), who cast off the veil and started to preach in public.   She incurred the curse of her uncle, an esteemed theologian, who was subsequently murdered in a mosque by a Babi.

Disturbances followed in Mashad, Zanjan, Tabriz, and other areas. In 1850 the Bab was shot on orders from the government at Tabriz; one of his prominent disciples, Qurrat-al-Ayn, was executed later.   In the capital "seven martyrs" fell.   Subsequent to an attempt on the shah's life, several leaders were banished to Baghdad, whence they were transferred farther inland to Adrianople by the Porte at the request of the Persian government.   One of them Baha-Allah ("splendor of God") claimed that he was the next manifestation of the divine will foretold by the Bab.   Baha arrogated to himself the mission of revising his precursor's system.   What he really did was to found a new one, with himself as the latest revelation not only to Moslems but to all mankind.

BAHAISM

In 1868 the place of Baha's exile was changed to Acre (Akka) in Palestine.   The system he formed combined such Christian elements as love for one another and doing harm to no one with elements of liberal thought then current in Europe.   These were grafted on the mystical Shiite heritage of Islam.   It condemned war, preached human brotherhood, and advocated a universal language.   On Baha's death in 1892 his eldest son Abbas Effendi Abd-al-Baha (the slave of Baha) assumed leadership.   Abbas advanced the movement and explained its relationship to modern demands. He stressed the humanitarian, cosmopolitan, pacifist aspect and aspired to make Bahaism a universal religion.   In this he was emboldened by the vogue his writings, translated into English and French by a British lady follower, had in Europe.   The mystical flavor and Oriental flowery expression made them especially attractive to a certain audience. Bahaism was introduced into the United States in the early 1890's; it attracted public attention at the Chicago fair (1893) and won converts from all classes, including Negroes. One of its early propagators was of Lebanese Christian origin. At present Bahai activity centers at Wilmette, Ill., where a beautifully designed temple stands, and in New York, where it issues a periodical. Other Bahai communities arose in Europe, particularly in Germany, but the most interesting religion modern Persia gave the world has been denied a place in the land of its origin.

JAMAL-AL-DIN AL-AFGHANI

More influential than any of these nineteenth century Persian, perhaps any modern, teachers was Jamal-al-Din al-Afghani (1838-1896),

JAMAL-AL-DIN AL-AFGHANI, PAN-ISLAMIST AND REFORMER

a rare combination of a Pan-Islamist and a liberal modernist. Jamal expounded the thesis of the modernization and internal development of Moslem states, by the adoption of Western science and technology, and their union under one caliphate into an empire capable of coping with European powers and resisting their interference and exploitation. His travels through Afghanistan, India, Egypt, Turkey, Russia, Paris,

London, and according to one reliable source, the United States, gave him a world-wide platform which his eloquent tongue, facile pen, and impressive personality exploited to the full.

Jamal's career began in Afghanistan where, according to his own account, he was born. Critics, however, say that the Asadabad in which he said he was born was not in the district of Kabul but in the province of Hamadan, Persia, a fact he disclaimed because of the treatment Persia accorded him. After the death of his patron, governor of Kabul, Jamal-al-Din al-Afghani went first to Cairo, where he lectured at the Azhar, and then Constantinople, where he preached at Aya Sofia. In Egypt his ideas contributed to the revolution which led to the British occupation in 1882 and they won him a brilliant disciple, Muhammad Abduh, future mufti of the country.[1] With him he published in Paris (1884) a short-lived Arabic newspaper whose copies are still in demand and fetch high prices. While there he engaged in a polemic with Ernest Renan, who in a lecture at the Sorbonne had stressed Islam's opposition to science. While in St. Petersburg he induced the czar to allow his Moslem subjects to print the Koran and other religious books. In response to a telegraphic invitation from Shah Nasir-al-Din Jamal went to Tehran to occupy a high political office. But the shah's concern about the growing popularity and prestige of his guest outweighed his interest in the idea of reform, and he cast him aside. On his last journey to Europe (1889), however, the shah met Jamal in Munich and extended a new invitation. This time the guest aroused the jealousy of the grand vizir and had to seek asylum in a shrine considered inviolable but whence, nevertheless, he was expelled, glad to escape with his life. From Basra he continued his agitation in favor of reform and in criticism of the existing order. On his prompting, an Iraqi mujtahid issued a fetwa forbidding the enjoyment of tobacco so long as its cultivation and trade were in the hands of a European monopoly.[2] Al-Afghani's attacks on the shah's absolute government and corruption in high places as well as his demands for immediate reform were echoed by religious leaders; they strengthened the nationalist cause.

When in London in 1892 the Turkish ambassador extended to the Pan-Islamic agitator an invitation to settle in Constantinople as the guest of Abd-al-Hamid under a life pension and in an elegant mansion. The sultan-caliph hoped to use him for his designs involving a different brand of Pan-Islam. But the guest's continued sharp attacks on the Persian government and the assassination of Shah Nasir-al-Din in 1896 by a disciple of his aroused suspicion in high places. Babis were first

---

[1] On him see below, pp. 443-4.
[2] Cf. above, p. 396.

unjustly charged with the crime. The last five years of al-Afghani's life were spent in this "guilded cage," subject to endless machinations by the sultan's entourage and whence he repeatedly sought permission to depart. The end came through cancer, though some claim through poison administered by an aide of Abd-al-Hamid. The impress he made on the liberal constitutional movement in the Near East is still a living force.

EUROPEAN MISSIONS: CATHOLIC

Before the birth of the Shaykhi-Babi movement, which drew its inspiration from internal Islamic sources, foreign intellectual and cultural stimuli were beginning to operate though their cumulative effect did not become apparent until the nineteenth century. Political rather than religious considerations prompted Abbas the Great to allow Christian European missionaries to work in his realm. For years popes had summoned Christian sovereigns against Ottoman Turks, the Safawid's worst enemy. The first Safawid, Ismail, had made overtures to the grand master of the Knights of Rhodes for joint action against the common enemy. Earlier still Mongol rulers and popes had exchanged views on this subject. Dominican and Franciscan embassies were sent to the court of the Il-Khans. For a time before making their final choice in favor of Islam (1295),[3] these rulers of Persia had flirted with Christianity. Dim echoes of history resound in the legendary tale of Prester (priest, presbytery) John, who in the twelfth century carved from Moslem lands an empire beyond "Persia and Armenia."

The papal Carmelite mission to Persia was organized and started work in 1604, after Abbas had promised to put all Christians in his domain under the Apostolic See. Isfahan was made the headquarters. In the 1620's residence was established in Shiraz and the Capuchins joined. There were also members of the Society of Jesus. The work was directed toward Christians, particularly Armenians, who had refugee settlements in central Persia. One, called Julfa near Isfahan, originated in refugees from the homeland and carried the name of a Caucasian city on the Russian borderland. The unkind geography of Armenia placed its inhabitants in the unenviable war path of three enemy nations—Turks, Russians, and Persians—and subjected them to endless disabilities, persecutions, and dispersions. The new Julfa served as a base for Carmelite activity.

For a time all went fairly well. Capuchins extended their work into Moslem areas but the base in general remained non-Moslem. One tangible result was the creation of the two Uniat communities: the

[3] Cf. above, p. 298.

Armenian Catholic Church, split from the Gregorian, and the Chaldean, split from the East Syrian Church or Nestorian.[4] The esteem in which certain missionaries were held may be evidenced by the attendance of the shah and his court at the funeral (1660) of Father de Rhodes of Avignon, the "Francis Xavier of Persia." So promising did the prospects then look that Isfahan was created an episcopal see. Later the tide turned. The century which opened auspiciously for European missions ended ominously. The anarchic period marking the demise of the Safawid dynasty and the intrusion of the Afghans and of the Afsharids practically liquidated the work. Shah Sultan Husayn (1694-1722) was overriden by reactionary religious leaders who persecuted even Sunnite fellow Moslems. He ordered forced circumcision of the remnant Zoroastrians and sought a similar treatment for the Armenians. The Afghans destroyed churches and convents. Christian minorities fared no better at the hands of Nadir, the first Afsharid.

A fresh start was made by Lazarists in 1840, reinforced by Sisters of Charity. The center of operation shifted north to the Nestorian district of Urmia. Residences were established in Tabriz, Tehran, Isfahan, and other towns. Urmia developed into an episcopal see. The work took on different aspects: the educational work was implemented by schools, and humanitarian ends were expressed through hospitals and orphanages. Seminaries were founded, but these were patronized exclusively by Syrian and Armenian Christians. In 1862 Lazarists established a permanent foothold in the capital city of Tehran by the construction of a house and a church. Twelve years later the Sisters of Charity added a hospital and two schools. Shah Nasir-al-Din offered an annual contribution, the equivalent of four hundred dollars, to the first hospital and orphanage.

PROTESTANT

It was time for Protestant missions to begin work. The band of pioneers was led by Henry Martyn, chaplain of the East India Company, who arrived in Shiraz in 1811. There he completed the translation of the New Testament into Persian, which was less successful than his earlier translation of the book into Hindustani. It was revised by a worker of the Church Missionary Society, which was established in Isfahan in 1866. Martyn also translated the Psalms into the native tongue and sought in vain to present copies to the shah. His involvement in animated discussions and heated arguments with high officials

---

[4] Discussed above, pp. 176-7.

and theologians as to the relative merits of Christianity and Islam, Christ and Muhammad, forced his withdrawal from the country. Another German Lutheran missionary was expelled for the same reason. Broken in spirit and health, Martyn died in 1812 in an Asia Minor town on his way back home. He was buried in an Armenian cemetery.

The Church Missionary Society chose south Persia, the British political zone of influence. Again it stressed educational and medical work in which Moslems could more freely participate. It built stations in Kerman, Yezd, Shiraz, and Isfahan. William Glen of this mission rendered the Old Testament into Persian; his text is still in use. Glen, a Scotchman, entered the country in 1838 and spent four years in Tabriz and Tehran working on his translation.

Meanwhile American missionaries had found their way into the area. The first were sent in 1834 by the American Board of Commissioners of Foreign Missions (Congregationalist). Urmia, in the Syrian Christian area, was again chosen for base. By this time, however, missionaries were allowed to live and work freely. The American mission settled in the north where it built schools and hospitals.

In 1871 the work was transferred to the Presbyterian Church of the United States and extended through its board of Foreign Missions into wide areas. Urmia remained the center. It soon had a high school, a hospital, and a printing press in Syriac movable type. Stations were developed in Tabriz, Tehran, Hamadan, Resht, and Qazwin. By 1900 Protestant work had extended over all the north except for the extreme eastern part. Mashad was opened in 1910. The American Bible Society collaborated in the publication and distribution of religious works, including a translation of the Scriptures into Syriac, the tongue of the Nestorians.

American educational work culminated in the American College of Tehran (1925), which grew out of a primary school in the capital city founded in 1873. In 1932 the regents of the University of the State of New York granted the college a charter empowering it to confer bachelor's degree in arts and sciences. Eight years later it was absorbed by the Persian ministry of education. In its pioneering days the institution's enrollment was almost exclusively of Armenians, Zoroastrians, and Jews; but with the opening of the twentieth century the Moslem student body steadily increased. At its height the total enrollment reached about eight hundred and fifty. Several assistant ministers of state, members of the majlis, lawyers, physicians, professors, and businessmen did their undergraduate work in this institution. Subsequent to its incorporation by the state it acquired a new name, Alburz

College, after the mountain which is the most prominent feature of the landscape as seen from the campus.

The educational track laid by Western teachers became a double-lane track.   Persian students, not waiting for teachers to come to them, began to go to the teachers.   England and France were the goal and professional studies the attraction.

Early in the nineteenth century the government started to sponsor student education in Europe, the first recorded case was that of one sent to England in 1810 to study medicine.   Others followed in small groups to prepare for civil service and professional careers.   Student migration continued on the increase in the twentieth century reaching over ten thousand in 1958-1959.   Germany claims the largest share of these students, about 4,000, and then the United States about 3,700.

A POLYTECHNIC INSTITUTE

In 1851, shortly before the dismissal of Nasir-al-Din's enlightened vizir, Mirza Taqi Khan, the first school of higher education founded by this vizir was completed.   This polytechnic institute (Dar al-Funun), a combination of state college and military academy, subsidized its students which were mainly drawn from aristocratic families.   The courses offered were in the military sciences and to a less extent in engineering, medicine, and pharmacy.   Its professors were understandably neither English nor Russian but Austrian, assisted by native scholars who translated books and lectures.   For about fifty years, after which it became a secondary school, this institute remained the main channel for transmitting Western science.   Its graduates held high offices in government and in the professional fields.

Mirza Taqi Khan had developed the idea for the institute from his observations first in Russia, where he accompanied his master, a government official, and later in Turkey.   The son of a cook, he did menial work before his talents were discovered and utilized.   His surname was in reality a princely title (lord) and his first name was likewise a title, meaning writer.   Under Nasir-al-Din, Taqi performed the functions of a grand vizir but, either because of humility or prudence, refused to hold the title.   He married the shah's sister.   Taqi had the rare distinction in the Persian hierarchy of having been not only inamenable to bribery but a fighter against it among his colleagues.   He stood against the sale of justice and appointments, the granting of pensions to favorites of the court, and other abuses in government and religion. Enmity on the part of his colleagues and jealousy on the part of the shah's mother led to his dismissal and eventually to his execution on the ground that he was becoming too powerful.

INTELLECTUAL PRODUCTION

The Qajar regime brought with it no literary revival. In the field of poetry, where Persia had earlier excelled, the first half of the nineteenth century was as barren as the preceding century. The second Qajar, Fath Ali (r. 1797-1834), was himself a versifier and sought to attract to his court literary and learned men, but with no tangible result. His collected poems (*Diwan*) were lithographed about 1860. His poet laureate composed, besides a *Diwan,* an imitation of Firdawsi's classic, neither of which was of special merit. A more talented court poet was Qaani (d. 1853), considered the most notable poet of the century. Qaani was born in Shiraz and given the name Habib-Allah; "Qaani" was his pen name. His language is marked with grace and melody but reveals no touches of genius. He was one of the rare Persian poets who condescended to reproduce the colloquial enunciation and speech of two stammering characters in a dialogue. The poet knew French and English and even translated several works from these languages, but he maintained his position in the old school. An interesting contemporary poet was Yaghma, whose life was an unbroken chain of sorrow. Yaghma is celebrated for his obscene and abusive verses; but in his pessimism and in his satire of the notables, he represented the spirit of the age. He went so far as to deny the possibility of a happy life. He was one of those who tried to rid Persian of its Arabic words, a movement which did not attain the dimensions of the parallel Turkish movement.

It was not until the second half of the nineteenth century that the old literary form, both verse and prose, began to change and its contents to show a new spark of life. The determining factor was the break through the linguistic barrier which had isolated the people intellectually and placed them in political provincialism and scientific stagnation. Exposure to fresh currents of thought, with its resultant cross-fertilization, shook their confidence in the perfection of their way of thinking and acting, as it had done the Ottomans before them. The first authors to strike a new note in science and technology were teachers in and graduates from Dar al-Funun together with scholars who had studied in Europe. In the last half of the nineteenth century about a hundred and sixty books were printed, some original others translations, dealing with mathematics, medicine and physical sciences, philosophy, history, literature, and other humanities. The first director of Dar al-Funun was Reza Quli Khan (d. 1871), one of the most learned and respected men of the age. He enjoyed the patronage of Nasir-al-Din, who also appointed him as head of the ministry of science, created in

1858, and entrusted him with the education of Crown Prince Muzaffar-al-Din.   Reza published a number of historical and geographical works and two voluminous books on the lives and works of Persian men of letters from earliest times to his.   The institute was fortunate in having other able directors who also headed the ministry of justice.   One of these was Itzad-al-Saltanah (d. 1881), who published in 1863 for the administration of the institute the first scientific gazette in Persia.

Translation of fiction came later and remained on a limited scale. Three of Molière's works—*Le médicin malgré lui, Tartuffe,* and *Le misanthrope*—made their appearance in Persian but neither they nor others enjoyed any popularity.   *Le misanthrope* was printed in Constantinople (1869-1870) by an anonymous translator.   Acquaintance with Turkish dramatic literature may have made this Persian translation possible.   The translations of original Azerbaijani Turkish plays which appeared at this time were more popular.   The original Persian plays written by Malkom Khan were in the Turkish fashion.   Persia, it will be recalled, had passion plays centering on the martyrdom of Ali and al-Husayn but no stage.   This lack made further development of the drama difficult.

The printing press, even in its lithographic form, was late in entering Persia.   The first native press of this kind was set up at Tabriz about 1816 by Abbas Mirza, eldest and favorite son of Fath Ali.   The Carmelites had had one earlier, but it was ineffectual.   In 1851, Nasir-al-Din printed his decrees in what might be termed a journal.   Other journals followed, all lithographed sheets, short-lived, issued at irregular intervals and run by the government or for it.   They carried laudatory reports about princes and rulers with no news or observations of popular interest.   The center of gravity was still in the hierarchy; the common man had not yet begun to count.   So slow was the growth of journalism that no newspapers in the real sense were issued until the first decade of the twentieth century, the decade of the constitution and national assembly.

Outside the country—in Constantinople, Cairo, Calcutta, and London—a higher standard was achieved in Persian journalism, but its product could not enjoy wide circulation in the country.   The weekly *Akhtar* (star) in Constantinople was suppressed by Abd-al-Hamid in 1896, its twenty-first year, following Nasir-al-Din's assassination.   For a time the editor was a Babi.   The London *Qanun* (law), founded in 1890 by Malkom Khan and al-Afghani, was more positive and articulate.   It stressed the people's grievances and in unmistakable terms spelled out their demands: a fixed code of laws and a parliament wherein people's representatives would be free to discuss all matters related to the welfare of the state while enjoying the privilege of immunity in what they say or do in the discharge of their function. The circulation of the journal was prohibited in Persia.

Malkom was an Armenian born in Julfa (Isfahan) and educated in Paris. He is credited with introducing freemasonry into the country. Its membership was recruited largely from alumni of Dar al-Funun and European universities. When an imperial decree dissolved the organization, closed its lodges, and banned even the use of the term freemasonry, Malkom turned his activities to another channel. He preached what he called a religion of humanity and claimed 30,000 followers. From 1872 to 1889 he served as his country's minister at the Court of St. James.

THE CONSTITUTION

The Qajars began their rule in the pattern of former dynasties as an absolute monarchy of the autocratic dictatorial type. There was no other pattern to follow. They ended it in the Western pattern as a limited monarchy with a constitution and a parliament. The historic transformation was not due to their efforts unless their abuses could be so considered. The shah regarded himself as the chosen of God; until this time, the people had shared the belief. General discontent with irresponsible administration, with corruption in high places, and with exploitation by foreign powers and concessionnaries was not new, what was new was the awareness of a different system and of the people's having the power to make a change. This awareness was the product of a higher level of education and familiarity with Western thought. Graduates of Dar al-Funun and of European universities, al-Afghani and other writers and journalists, and Persians living abroad contributed to that end. Magazines, sporadic and ephemeral as they were, provided centers for the gathering of young writers, nationalists, and admirers of Western culture.

The event which triggered the explosion was not so important in itself; it was the flogging (December 1905) of seven or eight Tehran merchants for profiteering in sugar by order of the government. This kind of punishment was not uncommon in those days; but its reception was uncommon. Several merchants took sanctuary in a mosque, the same in which Jamal-al-Din had defied Nasir-al-Din, and became the nucleus of a daily increasing group of malcontents. In this they were encouraged by religious leaders, disgruntled high officials, British agents, and reportedly by the crown prince himself. The target was Grand Vizir Ayn-al-Dawlah ("eye of the state"), whose eye was evidently blind to the condition of the people and whose ear was deaf to their entreaties. When the shah promised dismissal of his obnoxious vizir, the crowd dispersed; but when the shah failed to do as he said, the people repeated the performance on a grander scale. When Ayn-al-Dawlah threatened to use force to compel merchants to open their shops, several thousand revolutionaries sought refuge in the British legation. The shah was obliged to yield. But the dismissal of his vizir was no longer enough. On August 5, 1906, he agreed to the convocation of a national assembly (*majlis*). On October 7 the majlis—consisting of elected representatives from the royalty, aristocracy, ulema, businessmen and landholders—was convened in the capital. It drew up a constitution of the liberal type. Shortly after signing it the sickly and incompetent Muzaffar-al-Din died.

Muhammad Ali (1907-1909) was no more willing to live with the constitution than his father had been willing to sign its birth certificate. In his hostility to the new instrument of democracy Muhammad Ali had the blessing of Russia, with whose aid he organized a new brigade of Cossacks and made more than one attempt to destroy the parliament. But the nationalists were equally determined to maintain their new position. In this the support came from public opinion. In 1907 a rash of newspapers, ninety or more, covered the country. There was no public library until 1904, when the national library was founded in Tehran. It became the rendez-vous of reformists. Semi-secret clubs were organized, calling themselves nationalist societies and in some cases entertaining anarchistic ideas. A fanatic assassinated the shah's vizir, and another threw a bomb at the shah's automobile, killing an escort. In June 1908 the shah had his brigade bombard the parliament building, kill a number of the liberal leaders and place the capital under martial law. The timing was bad. This was the month in which the Young Turks succeeded in their coup against the tyranny of Abd-al-Hamid. Tabriz, heart of Azerbaijan, the Turkish-speaking province, rose in revolt. It had sent to the parliament some of its ablest and most enlightened members. With the aid of Russian troops the government forces occupied the city, but no sooner was that done than the horns of the revolution popped up somewhere else. Bakhtiari tribesmen in the south, under a chieftain who had just returned from a European trip, marched against Isfahan then Resht and, joined by a brigade of Armenians, Turks and Caucasians from Resht moved on to Tehran. The nationalists' three-day street fight in the capital made the shah's position untenable. Muhammad Ali fled to Odessa, leaving his twelve-year-old son, Sultan Ahmad, as his successor. Two years later he returned to stage a coup but failed.

The new shah was under the control of a clique of reactionary politicians headed by a regent. In December 1911 the majlis was dismissed and the parliament house locked. The northern part of the country, where the capital lay, was then under Russian domination in implementation of the 1907 entente.[5] The majlis was not convoked again till July 1914, in order to accept the speech from the throne by the shah then attaining his majority and receiving the crown. This was the eve of the World War. When in August 1919 the government negotiated a new treaty with Britain the national assembly refused to convene to ratify it.[6] The assembly after that was tied to the career of another dynasty, the Pahlawi.

BOOKS TO READ

Elwell-Sutton, L. P., *Modern Iran* (London, 1941).

Ferraby, John, *All Things Made New* (London, 1957).

Groseclose, Elgin, *Introduction to Iran* (New York, 1947).

Lambton, Ann K , *Landlord and Peasant In Persia* (London, 1953).

Shoghi Effendi, tr., *Bahá'í World Faith* (Wilmette, Ill., 1943).

Shuster, W. Morgan, *The Strangling of Persia* (New York, 1920).

Sykes, Percy, *A History of Persia*, 3rd. ed., vol. II (New York, 1930).

Wilson, Arnold T., *Persia* (London, 1932).

[5] See above, p. 397.
[6] See above, p. 401.

XXX   *The Pahlawis and Modernization*

THE era inaugurated by Reza Khan (r. 1925-1941) marked a clear-cut break with the past, similar to but not as thorough-going as that of Mustafa Kemal in Turkey. Both leaders were dictators of the first order, but their dictatorships differed from the ones superseded in being less egotistical and more directed toward the public good—as subsequent results showed. In both cases the door was left open for the resumption of democratic processes.

SHAH REZA

Before the majlis in December 1925 had proclaimed Reza Khan shah, with the right of successorship to his heirs, he had exercised dictatorial powers and had been invested by the assembly with those powers. In April of the following year the new shah ascended the Peacock Throne still glittering with jewels from the Indian plunder by a predecessor, Nadir Shah. When Reza dashed into Tehran, he found a chaotic political situation. With destructive guerilla warfare he crushed Soviet-agitated opposition in the northwest and uprisings under Kurdish and other local chieftains, disarmed the semi-independent tribes, put the powerful Bakhtiari tribe under military officers, and restored the central government authority to the south, wherein it was undermined by British presence. The last to yield were the Arabs of Khuzistan, under a chief who had entered into direct treaty relations with the British. His territory covered the left bank of Shatt al-Arab and the lower reaches of the Karun from Ahwaz downstream—an area which was strategic because of its oil wells and the pipeline. Bringing the tribes under government control was a feat no previous shah had achieved.

Reza was then free to launch a program of reforms parallel to and partly inspired by that of his Turkish contemporary, but executed with more restraint and caution. The Persian task was made infinitely more difficult by limited exposure to Europe, the lack of officials with admin-

416

istrative experience, and the existence of a religious body that in a Shiite society executed spiritual power as pronounced as that of the medieval Christian clergy. The shah was aware of the value of a ready-to-fight armed force, loyal to him, and satisfied in its compensation. Weapons and equipment were supplied by France. The number was raised to 40,000. The importance of facile communication was equally appreciated. With the aid of American engineers old roads were improved and new ones laid out. The telegraph line begun by a British company in 1864 was extended. Wireless stations were installed and made available to the public. But the project closest to the shah's heart was a trans-Persian railway line from the Persian Gulf to the Caspian Sea. In 1927 he turned the first soil of this huge undertaking which took twelve years to complete. It was financed by a sales tax on tea and sugar—with no money borrowed. To meet the mounting expenses, state monopolies were expanded to cover most fields of production and business. This amounted to turning merchants into government employees. The United States was requested to recommend a financial mission. Headed by Arthur C. Millspaugh the mission reorganized and systematized the finances of the country (1922-1927) but those of the military were kept beyond its control.

The removal of intellectual impediments to insure the free flow of ideas was of no less urgency than the removal of the physical impediments of communication. The man who was hardly cultured himself and who had no clear understanding of Western civilization set out to build up the modern culture of his country and to introduce Western techniques. Perhaps the fact that he was not deeply rooted in Persian culture made the program less painful to him. The privileges of the religious class were curtailed, their extensive possessions were seized, dervish orders were suppressed, and public religious pageants and sacred plays were prohibited. A system of elementary and secondary education on modern lines was introduced. Until that time elementary education had practically been in the hands of religious men and had been organized around the Koran. After 1926 students, averaging a hundred a year, were sent to Europe and America. By 1941 all educational institutions erected by foreigners had become thoroughly nationalized. In 1935 the University of Tehran was organized by joining the faculties of law, science, literature, theology, and medicine which had been under the ministry of education, and putting them under the administration of a chancellor of the university. European instructors were increased. The same year saw the foundation of a school of engineering. Later the college of agriculture was transferred from the ministry to the university. Today the university has in addition schools of fine arts, teacher training, nursing, dentistry, and pharmacy. The student enrollment rose from about 2000 in 1937 to 9321 in 1958, of whom 998 were women.

Like Mustafa Kemal, whom he admired and visited at Ankara, Reza Shah was the first leader among his people to be convinced that Western institutions could not sit comfortably on Oriental medieval economic and social substructures. He did not overthrow the constitution nor dissolve the majlis but reduced it to a ratifying body. By this time the early enthusiasm for representative government had subsided. To ease the process of weaning from the present, the government decreed (1935) that the ancient name of the country, Iran, be substituted for Persia originally the name of a southwestern province. The shah took for his family name "Pahlawi," from Old Persian "Parthian." He was the first leader of genuinely Persian stock in a century and a half. "Urmia" was changed to "Rezieh" to commemorate his first name. Mustafa Kemal had tried to connect his people with the early Hittites and to relate Turkish to the mother tongue of Europe.

Social change, because of the amount of emotion involved, creates more tension than economic change. The abolition of titles of nobility and the replacement of sons of aristocratic families by more meritorious officials presented serious problems. More serious problems resulted from legislation relating to the status of womanhood. This was the most sensitive area because religion was also involved. New laws discouraged polygamy, facilitated divorce by a wife, raised the girls' marriageable age to fifteen, and removed the veil, the outward symbol of isolation and subordination. Juridically women were given the same rights as men with certain reservations. The emancipation of women meant the end of the patriarchal family and the introduction of a new element into the man-dominated cultural and economic life of the country. In out-of-the-way places such legislation could not be enforced.

In his foreign relations the shah was equally enlightened. The century-old capitulations, incompatible with independence and self-respect, were abolished in 1928 after a year's notice. Five years later the Anglo-Iranian Oil concession given in 1901 was extended in time and revised in favor of more royalty for the government. In 1937 a five-year pact of non-aggression was signed with Turkey, Iraq, and Afghanistan further guaranteeing each other's borders and binding each country to refrain from interference in the others' internal affairs. The pact was signed at the summer residence of the shah, Sadabad, outside of Tehran, and bore its name.

SECOND WORLD WAR

With the memory of the preceding war still haunting the government and people, Iran was determined to remain free from entanglements. While they tried to keep the country out of war they could not keep the war out of the country. The advance of German troops into the Ukraine was considered in British and Russian eyes as a move endangering the Caucasus, Iran, oil, and the supply route from the Persian Gulf to Russia. No such chance could be taken. In August 1941 Russian troops occupied the northern part and British troops the southern. British naval units entered through the Persian Gulf and landed troops from Iraq through Khorram Shahr. The two zones were already delimited. The shah admired in Hitler and Mussolini those strong qualities that he possessed and that stood out in contrast to the timidity and indecisiveness of Allied leadership particularly in the initial stage. He and a number of his officers leaned Axis-ward. The German occupation of Paris in 1940, only nine months after the start of hostilities, convinced Iran of the doom of the democratic cause.

One month later, to save the throne for his son, the shah abdicated and left the country. He died three years later in Johannesburg, South Africa. His twenty-two-year-old son Muhammad Reza (1941-   ) succeeded. The new shah immediately announced the resumption of constitutional rule. His government entered into a treaty alliance with the two occupying powers who promised to respect the territorial integrity and independence of the country and to withdraw all troops six months after the cessation of hostilities. A few months later Iran declared war on Germany. The importance of the move was dramatized by the conference in Tehran in 1943 and headed by Churchill, Stalin, and Roosevelt. Iran was then promised substantial material aid for and after the war period.

Aid was needed badly. The cessation of traffic between the two occupied zones, the utilization of transport facilities primarily for military needs, and the stoppage of the importation of certain essential commodities resulted in a drastic shortage of consumers goods and a soaring of prices to at least ten times their prewar level. Although, the working class profited by increased opportunities and higher pay and the middle by profiteering and other means, these effects were more than counterbalanced by inflation. The demoralizing effect of the occupation by foreign forces added to the discontent and resulted in widespread disturbances. The free press with its forty new journals, mostly like the earlier ones ephemeral and irresponsible, did not contribute much to stability. Soviet-inspired leftists made capital of the situation and the religious group, hoping to recapture its former status, was not eager to see Western prestige established. American aid was slow in coming and inadequate in quantity. For a second time Millspaugh was invited and granted broad powers to reorganize the finances. But, after two years' work (1943-1945), he withdrew with his mission, leaving at least one tangible contribution—a graduated income tax system. Another American, Colonel Norman Schwartzkopf, was invited to reorganize and direct the gendarmery. An army aid mission started its work in 1943. In 1949 the shah initiated a program of distributing lands inherited from his father among the peasants living on them, or selling them to landless farmers at low prices and on long-term payments. The landlord class, not eager to expose its possessions to such hazards, viewed the affair with alarm.

With the termination of hostilities, tension eased. In compliance with the bipartite treaty British forces of occupation withdrew in March 1946; after some hesitation and after receiving some concessions, the Russians followed. American non-combatant forces which had entered the country (1942-1943) for expediting military supplies to the Soviet Union by building and utilizing roads, railways, airports, and seaports withdrew in 1945 on completion of their work. The Allied troops left valuable electric and other installations together with an enlarged and improved system of communication. The Soviet Union left in addition a leftist movement which crystallized into a vigorous party called Tudeh (masses). This party's heirs sponsored a separatist movement in Turkish-speaking Azerbaijan, contiguous to Russia; the case was brought before the security council of the United Nations in 1946. Three years later, following an attempt on the shah's life, the party was proscribed and the leaders who did not flee the country were jailed. The party went under ground. In the autumn of that year (1949) the shah came to the United States on a state visit. He was warmly received everywhere, but the expected amount of aid and of investment of private American capital did not materialize. The Export-Import Bank offered loans for the purchase of supplies and equipment in the United States, Point Four gave aid for technical assistance, the Mutual Defense Assistance Program supplied military material, the United Nations provided some technical aid, but there was little coordination among these varied projects. Restoration to any semblance of self-sufficiency remained illusive. Economic conditions continued to worsen after the majlis, in April 1951, passed a bill nationalizing the oil industry in defiance of the British government and company. Oil was the main source of national revenue, and Iran stood fourth among the oil-producing areas in the world.

OIL NATIONALIZED

The author of the nationalization bill was septuagenarian Muhammad Mosaddiq, who as deptuy, government official, cabinet member, and prime minister had persistently preached the anti-foreign pro-nationalist gospel. His histrionic antics and eccentric showmanship gave him country-wide publicity. After the passage of the bill and his assumption of power he, pajama-clad, chose one day to seek refuge in the parliament house, against some imaginary danger, and went to bed. The national front he headed drew to itself rabid nationalists, leftists, and malcontents. The British government, the largest shareholder in the company, brought the case before the International Court, but Mosaddiq's government contested the court's jurisdiction. The case was brought before the United Nations upon which Mosaddiq visited the United States. All attempts at compromise or submission of the dispute to arbitration failed. By that time the Abadan refinery had been cleared of the British and the country of British diplomats and businessmen. Other oil companies in the Near East profited by the situation, but they did not welcome nationalization. The acclaim with which nationalization was received by Iranians would not have been so universal had the company followed a more enlightened policy and put a more liberal interpretation upon its legal obligations. To the Iranians its conduct seemed like old-time imperialism applied to industry and business. The list of long-standing grievances included charges that too many foreigners were employed, that natives were excluded from high technical and senior executive posts, that local employees were treated as of a lower breed, and that the company yielded inadequate royalty. Time was when such behavior could have been tolerated but not in the mid-twentieth century.

While the problem assumed international significance and seemed insoluble, the economic situation continued to deteriorate. The closing of oil operations left some fifty thousand wage earners unemployed. Reactivation of the Abadan refinery and putting its products in the world market did not prove to be as easy as the nationalist proponents had expected. In reply to a message President Eisenhower made it clear to Mosaddiq that the United States was not in a position to extend further aid or to purchase the country's oil products. As unrest increased martial law was extended. The premier aimed at disposing of both shah and parliament and appropriating all authoritarian power to himself. In August 1953 the shah and the queen had to leave the country.   A royalist revolutionary coup supported by General Fazollah Zahedi succeeded in arresting Mosaddiq and putting him in jail, where he spent the next three years.   Some of his aides were tried and condemned to death on a charge of treason.   The triumphal return of the shah was received with jubilation.

A new regime headed by Premier Zahedi reached a solution to the knotty problem.   In the spring of 1954 an international oil consortium of the Anglo-Iranian Company and seven others, of which five were American, was formed under the new name of British Petroleum Company, Ltd.   A few months later an emergency grant of forty-five million dollars was made by the United States to restore economic stability, and the continuation of military and technical assistance was promised. The aid was to enable the country to carry on pending the receipt of oil revenues.   New commitments were made after the acceptance of the Eisenhower doctrine early in 1957.   The International Bank for Reconstruction and Development offered a loan of seventy-five million dollars.   In March 1959 a bilateral defense agreement was signed at Ankara between the United States and Iran whereby the United States promised in case of aggression to take such appropriate action as might be mutually agreed upon.

REFLECTION IN LITERATURE

The political revolution of the first decade of the twentieth century, ending in the introduction of a representative government, hastened the literary revolution for which the last decades of the preceding century had prepared the way.   It also released long-suppressed intellectual energies as manifested in the volume and variety of the new products. No more was the bard to sing the eulogies of shahs and governors and subsist on their bounty, nor was the artist to flourish on court patronage.   The much more numerous writers and journalists had to address themselves to a wider audience than ever before.   To that end they had to speak clearly and simply.   Prose gained preponderance over poetry, which since the beginning of Islamic days has been the classical expression of the Persian mind.   Both struggled to free themselves from the thousand-year-old classical traditions which were older and more deeply entrenched than they had been in Turkey.   In addressing themselves to the common man, both poet and prose writer had to use common-day language and style.   The process of eliminating from Persian words of foreign origin, particularly Arabic, was accelerated. Reza charged the Iranian Academy with the task.   According to a study made by this academy in 1937 more than fifty per cent of the Persian words were of Arabic etymology, an almost incredible fact unless it is remembered that for over a thousand years Arabicism was a display of erudition. The new poetry followed the folk ballad as exemplified in the compositions of abu-al-Qasim Arif Qazwini (b. 1880), a pioneer in this field. His ballads became especially popular in the revolutionary period. Satirical poetry was cultivated at this time perhaps as never before.

As new genres in prose writing appeared the vernacular found its way into them without strain. New themes, such as the liberation of women, became subjects of polemics. Short-story writing, a favorite genre in early times as evinced by the originals of the *Arabian Nights,* took on new aspects under Western stimulation. In 1922 a collection of such stories was published. Three years before, the first historical novel, the work of Musa Hamadani, had appeared. Evidently inspired by the great war, its hero was the Achaemenid Cyrus. This and other works were intended to remind modern generations of the glory of their ancient ancestry. Comedies after European models also made their debut. A fictitious travel book by Hajji Zayn al-Abidin of Maraghah (d. 1910) imitated the *Divine Comedy* but treated an entirely different subject. Under the title *Ibrahim Bey's Books of Travel* the author depicts scenes and experiences that exaggeratedly mirror the bad administration and sad social conditions under Shah Muzaffar-al-Din. The work was clearly intended as a satire on the methods of the old regime, with the hope of arousing discontent and speeding reform. Readers could not but sense that. Written in simple but forceful style, the three-volume book had great success. The first volume has been translated into German.

Arts were not able to recover from the decline reflected in the political situation beginning with the turn of the eighteenth century. All the new artists could do was to emulate the products of the sixteenth and seventeenth centuries. Relief work, a classic art revived in the days of Fath Ali, was apparently neglected, but practically all other modes of artistic expression were cultivated. Modern sculpture was introduced. New academies arose for fine arts but their products show no originality. The academy of music has sought to cultivate European music and at the same time transpose native music into polyphony, making it most agreeable to modern generations without losing its identity. Some success has been achieved in combining traditional songs and themes into melodic sequences. New students of the history of music have sought to trace the origins of their music to Sasanid rather than Arabic antecedents.

The first Pahlawi put in motion a plan to rebuild the capital. Most of the new public buildings follow the European style. The entrances to the museum of archeology and to the medical building in the new university, however, display ancient Persian influence; but the columns of the national bank building imitate those of Persepolis.

Not much original work has been done in the industrial arts either. Carpet weaving and pottery making followed the traditional line back to the sixteenth and seventeenth centuries. Safawid patterns were imitated but never excelled. The same could be said of surface decoration by mosaic and silver inlaying and of wood and ivory work. Under the onslaught of modernization in industry all such handwork has suffered with no prospect of recovery.

BOOKS TO READ

Browne, Edward G., *The Press and Poetry of Modern Persia* (Cambridge, 1914).

Elwell-Sutton, L. P., *Persian Oil: A Study in World Power* (London, 1955).

Fatemi, Nasrollah S., *Diplomatic History of Persia 1917-1923* (New York, 1952); *Oil Diplomacy* (New York, 1954).

Frye, Richard N., ed., *Iran* (New York, 1953).

Haas, William S., *Iran* (New York, 1946).

Hoskins, Halford L., *The Middle East,* 2nd ed. (New York, 1959).

Lambton, Ann K. S., *Landlord and Peasant in Persia* (London, 1953).

Lenczowski, George, *The Middle East in World Affairs,* 2nd ed. (Ithaca, 1956); *Russia and the West in Iran, 1918-1948* (Ithaca, 1949).

Millspaugh, Arthur C., *Americans in Persia* (Washington, 1942).

Royal Institute of International Affairs, *The Middle East: A Political and Economic Survey,* 2nd ed. (London, 1954).

PART SIX

THE ARAB STATES

XXXI *Ottoman Background and Heritage*

T HE Arab states under study form a part of the Near East and at the same time part of the Arab world. This world consists of a continuous area stretching from Morocco through North Africa and Western Asia to the Persian Gulf and the Zagros Mountains, a distance of some three thousand five hundred miles. The area is studded with arid or semi-arid deserts, interspersed with oases, and marked by diversified ethnic elements and varied social and economic stages of development. There are, however, two major unifying bonds: religion and language. Islam is the prevailing faith everywhere—except in Lebanon—and Arabic is by far the preponderant language. Islam, it should be recalled, is more than a religion; it is a way of life. In most of these countries Islam is at least nominally the religion of the state or the religion of the head of the state. Bedouins provide the liaison between the cultivated land and the desert. All these countries, again with the exception of Lebanon, have a nomadic population. The area may be roughly divided into four units: North Africa, Egypt, the Arab Crescent, and the Arabian peninsula. The North Africa block is not included in the Near East under study. Geographically Egypt lies in North Africa, but historically and culturally it is in the Near East. Throughout the ages it has been oriented in that direction.

NORTH AFRICA

Proximity to Europe, distance from the heart of Arabism and Islam, and a largely Berber and European population characterize the North Africa block. This is "white Africa" which is separated from black Africa by the Sahara. Basically the population was Berber. Of these countries Tunisia, with an earlier Semitic element centering in Carthage, was the one most thoroughly Arabized, only one per cent of its population retaining Berber customs and speech. Its Phoenician coloniza-

427

tion marked the dawn of the historical age in North Africa. The Berber element increases in the direction of the west, constituting thirty per cent in Algeria and sixty per cent in Morocco. It also increases in the direction of the hinterland, the coastal region and urban centers having been fully Arabicized. Morocco was the only country not subjugated by Ottomans. Anchored exactly opposite Gibraltar it overlooks the Atlantic and the Mediterranean and flanks the water gate to southwestern Europe and to the Near East. In the middle ages it was the seat of two mighty empires, Almoravides (r. 1056-1147), whose sway extended into Algeria and Spain, and its successor Almohades (r. 1130-1267), which added almost all North Africa. Morocco has preserved a tradition of national life. Libya (formerly Tripolitania) has a large proportion of Italian colonists and so has Tunisia. Tripolitania, the land of three cities, takes its name from the three cities, Oea (now Tripoli), Leptis Magna (Labdah) and Sabratha (Sabratah). The first two were founded as Phoenician colonies, Sabratha as a Carthaginian one. The territory formed the eastern part of the Carthaginian empire. Under the Romans and Byzantines these cities continued to develop as trading centers and starting points for caravans to the interior. The ruins of Leptis Magna, Sabratha and Cyrene, next to those of Egypt, are the most impressive in Africa. Tunisia and Algeria have extensive French colonists. Algeria's central position gives it added importance. The North Africa countries were the first to fall under European domination and the last to feel the stirrings of Arab nationalism. They were all, one after the other, taken over by the Latin states of south Europe. Algeria was the first.

In 1830 the French expelled the Turks from Algeria,[1] leaving it without a ruling class and with a chaotic society. The motivation for the conquest was evidently not so much to suppress piracy as to reassert French hegemony in the Mediterranean, where it had received a staggering blow subsequent to the British naval victory at Trafalgar in 1805. The French proceeded to assimilate and colonize the country and eighteen years later formally declared it French territory. According to the 1954 census the country's population was 9,529,726 of whom 934,052 were French. The prolonged bloody conflict between Algerian nationalists and French forces which started in 1954 has been a constant source of irritation to the already-strained French-Arab relations. In 1959 President Charles de Gaulle took a bold step offering the Algerians, after a four-year period of pacification, the opportunity to vote for secession, which implies independence, for complete Frenchification,

---

[1] For the acquisition of North Africa by the Turks consult above, pp. 332-3.

which amounts to integration with France, or for autonomy, which gives Algeria a community status. In March 1962 a peace treaty was signed providing a settlement on the basis of self-determination to be registered in a referendum a few months hence.

Tunisia's turn came next. Its occupation in 1881 was dictated by the desire for security on the eastern border against growing Italian ambitions. A French protectorate, Tunisia was accorded internal autonomy in 1955 and full independence the following year. In 1957 the monarchy was abolished and a republic declared.

Its eastern neighbor Libya, the Turkish province of Tripoli, was seized by Italy in 1911 and ceded by Turkey the following year.[2] The new name was given it in 1934 by the Italians as a revival of the ancient Greco-Latin name. The new colony incorporated Cyrenaica, Tripolitania, the Fezzan, and a major portion of the Libyan desert. The country is but sparsely populated. In the course of the second World War, in 1942 and 1943, the Italians and Germans were expelled; Tripolitania and Cyrenaica were put under British and the Fezzan under French military administration. In December 1951 the country was declared an independent sovereign kingdom in pursuance of resolutions passed by the United Nations. In 1958 oil was discovered in Libya in commercial quantities.

Of the North African states Morocco is the only one to have cherished a long tradition of national independence. In medieval times it was the seat of two mighty Arab-Berber empires that included Moslem Spain and extended east of Morocco. Morocco's conquest by France began in 1901, but the French zone was not fully acquired until 1912. Meanwhile Spain was busy acquiring her zone in the territory across from its coast. In that year the country was divided into a French protectorate and a Spanish one. In 1956 both France and Spain relinquished their protectorates in favor of the sultan, now king.

The Ottoman era for the Arab lands of the Near East was an unhappy one signalized by corruption in administration, feudal exploitation, scarcity in economy, and intellectual stagnation. The downward course starting under the Mamluks continued precipitately. Egypt was one of the worst sufferers.

EGYPT

Sultan Salim (r. 1516-1517), destroyer and inheritor of the Mamluk empire, left an army of occupation in Egypt consisting of some five thousand Janissaries; put the country under a viceroy, entitled pasha; but kept the twelve districts (sing. *sanjaq*) into which the coun-

[2] See above p. 362.

try was divided under Mamluk governors.   No radical changes were introduced into the administration then or later.   Each Mamluk governor, or bey, to use his title, had his own troops and slaves but acknowledged Turkish suzerainty by the payment of annual tribute.   Powerful ones among them made puppets of the Ottoman viceroys and defied Constantinople by failing to remit what was due.   Though a caste by themselves replenished by the importation of fresh slaves from the Caucasus, the beys had an advantage over the pashas, who were on temporary appointments, remote from the base, and ignorant of the language and customs of the people governed.   At best a pasha's tenure of office, which he had very likely bought, was of short duration. His chief concern was often how to replenish his own resources.   In the two hundred and eighty years ending in the conquest of Napoleon and the rise of Muhammad Ali, no less than a hundred such pashas succeeded one another.

Under this dual form of control the natives sank deeper and deeper into the abyss of poverty and misery.   Poor sanitary conditions and low human vitality made of the area a playground for famine and pestilence.[3]   Deprived of the daily means of sustenance, beaten and oppressed by overlords, villagers deserted their farms and turned to a life of brigandage on the waste lands between settlements.   Thus was the valley of the Nile, once a granary of Rome and supporter of a ten-million people, barely able to support two and a half million people by the mid-eighteenth century.   In his sonnet "Ozymandias" (Ramses II), Shelley accurately portrays the sad state of Ottoman Egypt:

> And on the pedestal these words appear—
> "My name is Ozymandias, king of kings:
> Look on my works, ye Mighty, and despair!"
> Nothing beside remains. Round the decay
> Of that colossal wreck, boundless and bare
> The lone and level sands stretch far away.[4]

As the central authority represented by the Ottoman pasha waned, that of the Mamluk bey waxed.   In 1769 Ali Bey, reportedly son of a priest from the Caucasus who had found his way as a slave through brigands into Egypt, took the logical step and expelled the pasha.   He then declared himself independent, struck coins in his name, had it mentioned in the Friday noon sermon, and launched a double-attack on Arabia and Syria.   His general and son-in-law, formerly his slave, occupied Mecca; captured several cities in Syria, headed by Damascus;

---

[3] See above, p. 340.
[4] *The Complete Poetical Works by Percy Bysshe Shelley,* Cambridge edition (Boston, 1901), p. 356.

but then betrayed his master and entered into secret negotiations with the Porte. Ali was murdered in 1873 but other Mamluks, equally rapacious, seized power. Ephemeral as it was the rise of Ali Bey demonstrated the vulnerability of the Ottoman Empire at its Arab-half in the latter part of the eighteenth century. The century ended with the invasion of Napoleon Bonaparte.

NAPOLEON'S INVASION

Napoleon sensed the situation well. In his Arabic proclamation on landing in Egypt in 1798, he said that he was there to punish the Mamluks, who were not as good Moslems as he and his fellow-Frenchmen were and to restore the authority of the Sublime Porte. Whether his real purpose was to strike a mortal blow at the British Empire by interrupting her communication with the Orient or to fight his way through Western Asia into Constantinople and the Balkans remains undetermined. In either case his bid was for world domination through the Near East. The French general had no difficulty in capturing Alexandria, defeating the Mamluks at the battle of the pyramids outside of Cairo. There he demanded from the shaykh of al-Azhar a fetwa enjoining submission to his rule. The shaykh requested a prior submission to Islam to which Napoleon offered only two objections: lack of circumcision and addiction to wine. He then proceeded through Gaza and Jaffa to Acre where he had his first "Waterloo" at the hands of the local governor al-Jazzar[b] assisted by a British squadron. Meanwhile Napoleon's fleet had been destroyed by Admiral Nelson (Horatio) at Aboukir (Abuqir) Bay—only two frigates escaped—and line of supply had been cut. He rushed back to France leaving a French force which by 1801 was overwhelmed or evacuated.

The Napoleonic armed inroad into Arab territory was the first of its kind following the Crusading days. It set a chain reaction—on both the political and intellectual levels—that has not yet ceased. The year 1798 may be marked as the year in which Western powers discovered the Arab East leading to their rivalry for domination or spheres of influence. The impact of the West in the following century and a half is the most pregnant fact in the recent history of the area.

MUHAMMAD ALI

In the Ottoman army which helped frustrate Napoleon's designs was a Turkish officer of Albanian nativity named Muhammad Ali, destined to gain mastery over the country and initiate the line terminated

---

[5] On him see below, pp. 446-7.

in 1952 with King Farouk (Faruq). Four years after the expulsion of
the French forces, the Sublime Porte appointed this officer as pasha
over Egypt and in 1841 the pashalik was made hereditary in his family.
By that time he had become virtually independent but nominally under
Ottoman suzerainty. The acknowledgment was expressed in the usual
tribute payment.

Reforms and innovations introduced by the new pasha in the course
of that half-century leave him without a peer among his Moslem
contemporaries; they entitle him to the honor of being called father of
modern Egypt—efforts of post-1952 Egyptian historians to "debunk"
him notwithstanding. The viceroy confiscated properties with irregular
titles; cancelled land grants upon which payments to the state were in
arrears; and expropriated fiefs making himself practically the sole
proprietor of the country. He then established monopoly over the
export of grain, sugar, indigo, and other products becoming almost
the sole producer and contractor. This is the first case of nationalization in an Arab land. Muhammad Ali put special effort to improving
agriculture and industry by introducing up-to-date methods, opening
canals, and bringing in new crops, such as cotton from India and the
Sudan. Rice was also introduced. The cultivation of cotton revolutionized the country's agrarian economy and remains to the present
day the main source of Egypt's national revenue. He imported textile
plants and a sugar refinery. The rebuilt barrage north of Cairo bearing
his name testifies to his interest in irrigation. By effective quarantines
he combated the spread of plagues.

Although illiterate, speaking Turkish and unable to identify himself
fully with his people, Muhammad Ali started a ministry of education,
founded the first school of engineering in that part of the world, the
first school of medicine, and the earliest Arabic press. The press at
Bulaq is still functioning. The press idea was inspired by the example
set by Napoleon, who had plundered one from the Vatican and brought
it along for his proclamations in the tongue of the natives. The director
of the new press was a Syrian, Niqula al-Masabiki, who had spent four
years in Italy, particularly Milan, where he cast type. In its first twenty
years (1822-1842) the Bulaq press put out two hundred and forty-
three books, mostly texts. Napoleon's Arabic sheet inspired *al-Waqa'i'
al-Misriyah* (daily happenings), founded in 1828 as the official organ
of the government. The medical school, also still a going concern,
was headed by a French physician, Clot Bey. Napoleon had also
brought along engineers, architects, mathematicians, chemists, historians,
archeologists and Egyptologists and started a sort of academy of science
with a library in Cairo. This has survived to the present. On his

Courtesy of The Bettmann Archive

MUHAMMAD ALI, FOUNDER OF MODERN EGYPT

orders the engineers made a survey with a view to digging a Suez canal and reported a twenty-five-foot differential between the Red Sea and the Mediterranean precluding such a possibility. These manifestations of intellectual phenomena and the military aspects of the invasion began to shatter the Arab belief in the superiority of their Islamic culture. In the Bulaq press, translations of French works were published. European professors were invited to Egypt, and promising young Egyptians were sent to France, England, Italy and Austria to pursue further study. Between 1813 and 1849 (the year of Muhammad Ali's death) three hundred and eleven such students were sent to Europe at the expense of the state.

The military, of course, was not neglected. Again a Frenchman, Colonel Sèves, modernized the army. The colonel professed Islam; assumed the name of Sulayman Pasha, now borne by one of the main streets of the Egyptian capital, and left a progeny which married into the Alid family. The first venture of the army was made (1811), in response to an appeal from Constantinople, into Arabia against the Wahhabi power.[6] North Arabia was occupied till 1840. To celebrate the departure of the first contingent, the viceroy invited to his residence at the citadel, built by Saladin on a hill overlooking Cairo, the leading

[6] To be treated later, pp. 461-2.

Courtesy of United Arab Republic Tourist Agency

MUHAMMAD ALI MOSQUE INSIDE THE CAIRO CITADEL BUILT BY SALADIN

Mamluks of the city. Coffee drinking over, these honored guests filed out through a narrow passage toward the main gate and were then and there felled down, one after the other, by the host's bodyguard. Their remnant were ferreted throughout the land and liquidated. At last the six-hundred-year-old Mamluk problem was solved. The second venture was into the Sudan, the eastern part of which was occupied and held in some form or the other until the middle of the twentieth century. The fact that the Nile had its sources in the Sudan made the territory of strategic significance to Egypt.

Once more did Sultan Mahmud II appeal to his powerful vassal, this time against the Greeks in their war for liberation. The viceroy obliged by sending land and sea forces under his able son Ibrahim Pasha, conqueror of Wahhabi Arabia and future conqueror of Syria. Victory was snatched from the Turko-Egyptian army in 1827 when the combined fleet was destroyed at Navarino by European intervention. As a price the pasha of Egypt expected the annexation of the pashalik of Syria and when that was denied in 1831, he sent his son against it. With the aid of Bashir Shibab,[7] semi-independent prince of Lebanon, Ibrahim in two years occupied the entire country. His capture of Acre, seizure of Damascus, and victory over the Turkish army at Hims opened

[7] To be treated later, pp. 453-4.

the door to the heart of the land of the Turks. Before the end of 1833
he had routed the army at Konya and pushed to within about a hundred
and fifty miles of Constantinople. Panic-stricken, the sultan appealed
to Britain; France had encouraged the Egyptian invasion as a countermove to British influence. The sultan was also ready to receive aid
from Russia. The prospect of Russian intrusion, however, impelled
the French to side with the British. Moreover, both preferred a
decrepit Ottoman state in which they could gain spheres of influence
to a youthful vigorous one which might, in addition, endanger their
lines of communication. Once again Western European intervention
deprived the Egyptians of the fruit of their victory. Anatolia was
evacuated, but Syria remained under Egyptian control until 1840. The
dream of creating an Arab empire with Muhammad Ali at its head
was shattered. There was no national foundation for it in the consciousness of the people at that time. Even when revived by the Sharif
Husayn of Mecca three-quarters of a century later, it turned out to be a
daydream. However Muhammad Ali was confirmed in the viceroyalty
of Egypt-Sudan with hereditary rights.

SUEZ CANAL

The tide of progress ebbed with the accession of Abbas I (r. 1849-
1854), grandson of Muhammad Ali. The grandfather had lapsed into
senility two years before his death in 1849 and his son, Ibrahim, had
died one year before. Muhammad Ali and Ibrahim had been the new
Egypt. Their disappearance from the scene left the country leaderless,
with a vacuum no one could fill. Hostile to Western culture in general
and to the French in particular, Abbas plugged the inflow of new
ideas, abolished trade monopolies and factories, closed Western-style
schools, and halved the army. In 1851 he granted an English company
a concession for constructing a railway, but he would not grant even
an audience to a French company interested in building a Suez canal.
The Alexandria-Cairo line, completed in 1856, was the earliest in this
part of the world. In his effort to turn the hands of the clock back
he was seconded by theologians, reactionairies, and conservatives. Too
hurried and shallow to endure by themselves his grandfather's reforms
lapsed. Abbas' successor Said (r. 1854-1863) tried to swing the pen-
dulum back in the direction of progress. Cotton cultivation was
stimulated by shortage of this product in the United States due to the
Civil War. Said granted his subjects the right to own landed property
and freely dispose of it, combated trade in negro slaves, gave concession
for a telegraph line, and more importantly granted a concession to
build the Suez Canal. He encouraged foreign capital investment and

did not hesitate to incur foreign loans. The canal concession was given to an early friend of his, Ferdinand de Lesseps, a French diplomat and engineer. The viceroy was to receive preference shares, yielding fifteen per cent of the net profit of the company, and to provide four-fifths of the required labor. The concession was for ninety-nine years from the date of the opening. Labor was first supplied by conscription of peasants. The British took the position that the project was a physical impossibility and objected to the use of forced labor. Digging began in April 1859. The city erected at the north entrance of the canal, Port Said, bears the viceroy's name; Ismailiyah, halfway station on the canal, was founded as headquarters for building operations and named for his successor Ismail. Said's public works, travel in Europe, the military aid given the sultan in the Crimean War, luxurious living, and bestowal of bounties on favorites and grandees caused the first Egyptian debt, over £3,000,000 to a London bank. This was the first step on the disastrous path that led to state bankruptcy and foreign intervention. Muhammad Ali incurred no debt.

Work on the canal proceeded more effectively when Ismail Pasha (r. 1863-1879) discontinued forced labor and indemnified the company. Ismail, son of Ibrahim, generously increased the tribute paid the sultan from £376,000 a year to £720,000 and was rewarded by the title of khedive (from Per., lord, ruler) and the right of primogeniture in his own line. This was almost an acknowledgment of full sovereignty. Two successors of Ismail were styled khedive, but the third one, Husayn Kamil, was made sultan by the British in 1917.[8] Ismail had been educated in France and was sent by his predecessor on diplomatic missions to the Vatican and the court of Napoleon III. He is credited with having said that Egypt was a part and parcel of Europe. Pursuing the modernizing activity initiated by his grandfather, he replaced the old system of consular jurisprudence by creating mixed courts, started a post office, introduced gas and water into his capital, and extended

---

[8] Genealogical tree of the royal Egyptian family:

1. Muhammad Ali (1805-1848)

| 2. Ibrahim (1848) | Tusun | 4. Said (1854-1863) |
| | 3. Abbas (1848-1854) | |

5. Ismail (1863-1879, khedive 1866)

| 6. Tawfiq (1879-1892) | 8. Husayn Kamil (1914-1917, sultan, 1917) | 9. Fuad (1917-1936, king, 1922) |
| 7. Abbas II (1892-1914) | | Farouk (1936-1952) |

MODERN EGYPT

the railway and telegraph lines. The number of public schools under him rose from 185 to 4817. For the mixed courts and other reforms Ismail's minister Nubar Pasha (d. 1899) should be given credit. An Armenian by birth he came to the country at the age of seventeen. "Give Egypt water and justice," he argued, "and the country will be happy and prosperous." The mixed tribunals established uniformity of jurisdiction and served as a model for native courts. Their civil code was translated into Arabic (published 1866) along with adaptations from other European—mainly French—codes and introduced into the native courts when established in 1883. This meant as in Turkey radical reduction of the jurisdiction of the religious courts and of the customary and often arbitrary jurisdiction of local agents. The translating was mainly done by Rifaat al-Tahtawi (d. 1873), one of the early scholars to go to France, chief translator of the school of medicine, and editor of *al-Waqa'i' al-Misriyah*. He pioneered in the transmission of Western thought to the Arab world. Copts, Jews, and other minorities maintained their religious courts for cases relating to marriage, divorce, and other personal status issues.

The cost of projects undertaken by Ismail was beyond anything the state could pay. By this time a new class of Alid princes, pashas, and officials, largely of non-Egyptian origin, had taken the place of the Mamluks and was as busy exploiting the country. The viceroy himself was given to ostentation in both public and private affairs. The opening of the canal in 1869 provided the occasion for pomp and magnificence that is said to have cost £1,000,000. The guests of honor were led by Emperor Francis Joseph of Austria; Empress Eugenie, leader of fashion in Europe and shedder of glamor at the court of Napoleon III; and crown prince of Prussia. The khedive had the satisfaction of feeling on a par with the crowned heads of Europe. At the newly-built Opera House at Cairo, the first of its kind in that part of the world, *Rigoletto* by the renowned composer Guiseppe Verdi was brilliantly performed. *Aïda* followed two years later. Written at Ismail's invitation on the basis of a sketch by the French Egyptologist Auguste Mariette Bey, *Aïda* typified Italian opera at its best. Marriette was one of the earliest archeologists in the Near East field.

The Nile-Red Sea canal, dug by early Pharaohs around 2,000 B.C. and redug by Darius, Ptolemies, Abbasid, and Fatimid caliphs[9] gave birth to a hundred-mile daughter which marked the greatest impression and the most influential change man had thus far made on the face of the earth. It was meanwhile the greatest abbreviation of distance

[9] Cf. above, pp. 52, 92-3, 128, 277.

Courtesy of Arab Information Center, New York

THE OPERA HOUSE, CAIRO

Built by Khedive Ismail in 1859, this was the first house of its kind in the Moslem East and marked the birth of its theatrical art.

between the Far East and the West. The canal speeded the Near East's re-entry into the main stream of world trade and international affairs and offered it compensation for the loss sustained by the discovery of the route around the Cape of Good Hope some three hundred and seventy years earlier.

But for the time being there was no considerable return for the viceroy on the twelve million-pound sterling investment in the project. This, added to the other millions recklessly spent on state and personal affairs, raised the total debt to a staggering hundred million. On behalf of the loanholders, the British and French established a dual control over the finances of the country by appointing an English controller general of the revenue and a French controller general of expenditure. The British government itself had become the largest single shareholder through the purchase of Ismail's shares and thus gained control of the canal. In 1878 she fortified her position in the area still further by acquiring control of Cyprus. In the following year Ismail was deposed with the half-hearted consent of Abd-al-Hamid and was replaced by his son Tawfiq (r. 1879-1892).

NATIONAL UPRISING

Foreign powers and investors were at least temporarily satisfied but the people's condition worsened. The presence of Christian European high officials aroused popular resentment even animosity on political and religious grounds. It sparked the explosive reservoir of discontent of the army, officered largely by Turkish Circassians who neither spoke the native tongue nor understood their troops, and by peasants suffering from burdensome taxation and subjected to a system of *corvée*. The government could force any able-bodied male to work for nominal pay or no pay at all. The army and the peasants found a champion in a colonel, former student of theology at the Azhar and later a pasha, Ahmad Arabi. Son of an eight-acre land cultivator, Arabi headed the resistance movement consisting of young educated men, theologians, civil servants. He soon became a national hero leading Egyptians against Christian foreigners and Turkish rulers and officers. The movement was vaguely aimed at a constitutional monarchy and an assembly. Meantime riots had broken out in polyglot Alexandria, originating in a petty squabble between a British Maltese and a Moslem donkey boy and ending in the massacre of about fifty-seven Europeans and a hundred and forty Egyptians. This incident provided the British with an excuse for shelling Alexandria in July 1882, landing troops in Port Said, and seizing the canal. Abd-al-Hamid's support was sought but was not received. The French dissociated themselves from the British action.

At al-Tell al-Kabir, a village north of Cairo, the hastily-assembled army of Arabi was routed (September 1882) and its leader was sent to exile in Ceylon. Premature as it was, Arabi, was the first definite expression of nationalist feeling in modern Egypt with grass-root origins. Its ideology of resistance to control by the West but adoption of its methods was clearly inspired by Jamal-al-Din al-Afghani, who had taught in Cairo after 1871. Arabi proudly added "al-Misri" (the Egyptian) to his name; his party took for a slogan "Egypt for the Egyptians," a slogan that was to reverberate over Egypt for years to come.

BRITISH OCCUPATION

The developments of 1882 left England in sole control of Egypt. In an early declaration she expressed desire to withdraw her troops "as soon as the state of the country and the organization of proper means for the maintenance of the khedivial authority will admit of it." Under the unpretentious title of resident and consul general Lord Cromer (Evelyn Baring) was the virtual ruler of the country, his main support being the army of occupation. The suzerainty of the sultan-caliph was nominally maintained, as a diplomatic fiction, but the annual tribute was applied to the Ottoman debt of Egypt. Ministers and provincial governors could maintain their posts as long as they heeded the "advice" or "recommendation" of the British resident. A legislative assembly was created consisting of thirty members, fourteen nominated by the khedive and sixteen elected; but it was more a consultative and deliberative body. Beyond that no effective machinery was set up for preparing the country for self-government. Under Lord Cromer (1883-1907) the *corvée* was abolished, taxation was revised in favor of the peasants and reduced in some needy places by thirty per cent, the finances ordered, and the national debt cut down to manageable size. The construction of the Delta barrage (1890) and the Aswan dam (1902) increased the cotton crop. Exports and imports trebled and the standard of living was appreciably raised. Local justice and police, national courts, and provincial administration were retained by native Egyptians. But public education was left in no-man's land; illiteracy remained widespread. Private and foreign schools contributed their share in combating it. Only secondary education was relatively promoted not so much for its liberal values as for preparing candidates for civil service.

International complications served to strengthen England's foothold in the land and prolong her occupation. Dissatisfaction in the Sudan provided an organizer and a symbol in an ascetic religious leader who proclaimed himself the expected mahdi. Between 1881 and 1885 the Mahdi at the head of an excessively enthusiastic band of dervishes and followers succeeded in destroying the Egyptian garrison, killing the British general Charles George Gordon (also called Gordon Pasha and Chinese Gordon), and occupying Khartoum. Gordon Memorial College of Khartoum, now the University of Khartoum, bore his name. Egypt itself felt uneasy. But between 1896 and 1898 Lord Kitchener (Horatio Herbert), leading a joint Anglo-Egyptian force, recovered the Sudan and re-insured the sources of the Egyptian water supply. Kitchener of Khartoum, as he was then called, was appointed governor. The Anglo-Egyptian Sudan, as it was after that called, was put under condominium government (joint sovereignty), headed by a governor general with supreme military and civil command appointed by the khedive on the recommendation of the British government. The administration worked satisfactorily and after 1924 it was Sudanized step by step until January 1, 1956, when the British and Egyptian flags were ceremoniously lowered, in the presence of representatives of the two countries and the Sudanese flag was hoisted.

In the first decade of the twentieth century, when higher education especially of the Western type had been received by a numbr of young Egyptians, nationalist feeling began to assert itself The French encouraged the agitators but in the Anglo-French entente cordiale of 1904 the French agreed to end the obstruction of British policy in Egypt in return for support for French policy in Morocco. One school of the Egyptian nationalist movement was attracted by Hamidian Pan-Islamism, but another, led by Mustafa Kamil, a French-educated lawyer, concentrated on national independence and constitutional government. The spectacular success of the Young Turks in 1908 raised the hopes of the constitutional nationalists.

Khedive Abbas II Hilmi (r. 1882-1914), barely eighteen at his accession, wavered between these two schools, but was more attracted by the Pan-Islamic ideal. But in his resentment to British tutelage as expressed in Cromer's domination he was consistently resolute. After the death of Mustafa Kamil (1908) the movement was led by another lawyer, Azhar-educated, Sad Zaghlul. Zaghlul took part in the Arabi revolution and held several high positions in the government including the ministry of education, the ministry of justice, and vice presidency of the assembly. With the appointment of Kitchener as resident a faint attempt was made to satisfy, at least appease, nationalist demands. In place of the old legislative assembly a new body was created consisting of eighty-three members, sixty-six of whom were elected by indirect suffrage and seventeen nominated by the government. This was in

1913 on the eve of the great war, when no such assemblies could survive.

No sooner had Turkey taken a position of hostility than a state of war was declared (November 1914), Egypt was pronounced a protectorate—thus terminating its anomalous situation—, Abbas II was deposed and his brother Husayn Kamil (r. 1914-1917) was named sultan. Martial law and censorship were applied. The use of the canal was denied to enemy shipping. The failure of the Allies' attempt to force the Dardanelles heightened Egypt's importance in the prosecution of the war against Turkey and her possessions. The country served as a base for British military operations. It supplied grain and other cereals, fodder, beasts of burden, and recruited a large labor and camel corps. Where these commodities and services could not be acquired by regular means, they were requisitioned against inadequate compensation. The cost of food, clothing, drugs, and other necessities of life rose to prohibitive heights, while the average wages of laborers did not rise correspondingly. The onus of the hardship, of course, fell on the peasants and working class.

By the end of the war British control, though eased, seemed more odious than ever. Nationalism, temporarily quiescent, was aroused. The abortive attempt of Turkey at the Suez and other developments in that country weakened the Pan-Islamic wing of the nationalist movement. Allied victory in November 1918 and the preceding Anglo-French declaration that in waging war on Turkey the Allies contemplated the enfranchisement of peoples under its rule strengthened the other school. So did the novel doctrine of self-determination enunciated by Woodrow Wilson. Enthusiastic hopes were raised among the nationalist leaders headed by Sad Zaghlul. Of peasant stock Zaghlul was an Azharite who had studied law, participated in the Arabi insurrection and served as judge and minister of education. No sooner had the war ended than he requested permission to lead a delegation (*wafd*) to London to press his party's demands for full independence. He was denied the opportunity and in March 1919 deported to Malta with three other leaders. Though a signal for murderous outbreaks at Cairo and riots in the country, the deportation was repeated two years later by Lord Allenby, hero of Palestine and now British resident. Zaghlul was sent among other places to Aden and the public reaction was so strong that the term Wafdist became equated with nationalist.

At last the British yielded. In 1922 they pronounced the protectorate ended, declared Egypt a sovereign state of the monarchic type and appointed the sultan's brother Fuad (r. 1922-1936) king. There were four reservations, however, relating to British communications, national defense, protection of foreign interests and native minorities, and the status of the Sudan. Nonetheless Egypt therewith may be said to have attained a new stage in its modern career. Under Muhammad Ali elements of Western civilization were introduced largely in the military and political field by way of example and with the help of advisers and renegade Europeans. In the second stage the main borrowings were financial and legal arenas. They comprised loans and codes. The third stage, covering the protectorate,was marked by Britishers managing all aspects of government administration.

INTELLECTUAL CENTER

British Egypt developed into a leading center of Arab intellectual activity. The abundance of opportunities it provided educated men for lucrative employment and the relatively free climate it furnished for the expression of thought attracted American- and French-educated young men from Lebanon and Syria.[10] Presses, learned magazines, and modern newspapers flourished there as nowhere else in Arab lands. The country reared not only patriotic and political leaders but intellectual ones whose influence was felt beyond its narrow confines. Among them were religious reformers and revivalists.

Earlier attempts to rethink Islam in the light of modern developments and to revivify its decadent spirit were made in Persia and Arabia;[11] but the Egyptian attempt, led by Muhammad Abduh (1849-1905), differed from both. Born to a peasant family in Lower Egypt Muhammad had the good fortune to attend the Azhar when the Persian reformer al-Afghani was lecturing there. The two became close associates. The young scholar espoused the nationalist cause, but moderately. He opposed excessive Europeanization of his country, participated in the Arabi revolution (1882), and landed an exile in Lebanon and Syria. There and later in Paris, where he collaborated with al-Afghani in editing an Arabic newspaper, he was exposed to Western influences. On his return to his homeland he worked as teacher and writer and rose to the two highest religious positions in his country: the rectorship of al-Azhar and the muftyship of Egypt. Starting from identical premises as had his two predecessors—ibn-Abd-al-Wahhab and al-Afghani—namely, that the condition of contemporary Islam was unhealthy and that there was need for its reformation, the Egyptian theologian arrived at different conclusions. He deprecated the use of

[10] Discussed below, pp. 486-7.
[11] See above, pp. 403-4, 461-3.

force as a means of reform, extended hospitality to the products of scientific research, and stressed the intellectual and spiritual rejuvenation of Islam.   He endeavored to separate religious from political issues so that each category might be judged on its own merits.   His writings were singularly free from xenophobia.   His flexible interpretation of koranic passages that seemed to be in conflict with modern thought opened a new way to the solution of the problem of Islam by reading into it ideas and attitudes that were not exactly or fully contained therein.   This was precisely what Christian theologians had been doing for centuries: trying to remodel their spiritual fathers rather than abandoning them.   Qasim Amin[12] and other liberal writers owed their inspiration to the grand mufti of Egypt.

BOOKS TO READ

Ayrout, Henry H., *The Fellaheen,* tr. Hilary Wayment (Cairo, 1945).

Bonné, Alfred, *State and Economics in the Middle East,* 2nd ed. (London, 1955).

Crouchley, Arthur E., *The Economic Development of Egypt* (London and New York, 1938).

Dicey, Edward, *The Story of the Khedivate* (New York, 1902).

Dodwell, Henry, *The Founder of Modern Egypt: A Study of Muhammad Ali* (Cambridge, 1931).

Elgood, P. G., *Bonaparte's Adventure in Egypt* (London, 1931); *The Transit of Egypt* (London, 1938).

Hoskins, Halford L., *British Routes to India* (New York, 1928).

Issawi, Charles, *Egypt at Mid-Century: An Economic Survey* (London and New York, 1954).

Marlowe, John, *A History of Modern Egypt and Anglo-Egyptian Relations, 1800-1953* (New York, 1954).

Warriner, Doreen, *Land and Poverty in the Middle East* (London and New York, 1948).

Wilson, A. T., *The Suez Canals Its Past, Present, and Future* (London, 1933).

Wood, Jarvis H., *Pharaoh to Farouk* (New York, 1955).

Young, George, *Egypt* (London, 1931).

[12] On him see below, pp. 521-2.

XXXII *The Arab Crescent*

THE lands of the Arab Crescent in varying degrees shared with Egypt the general disabilities imposed by Ottoman rule. Lebanon fared best. Generally corrupt administration, high taxation, neglect of natural resources, failure to introduce improved methods of agriculture, industry, and communication began to tell heavily as the centuries rolled by. These were the centuries in which Europe was taking long strides forward in many fields of endeavor. The Ottoman curtain which shut off the Arab East from the West and isolated it materially and intellectually may be considered the most serious single disservice rendered the area.

For certain radical changes in the world routes of international trade that adversely affected the economy of the region, the Ottomans were not responsible. Their advent almost synchronized with the opening of the first all-sea voyage to India by Vasco da Gama in 1498, subsequent to Diaz' discovery of the Cape of Good Hope. His was the first voyage from Western Europe around Africa to India, resulting in the building of a Portuguese empire in Asia. Much of the transportation, hitherto funneled through the Eastern Mediterranean, was diverted to southern channels. Portuguese replaced Near Easterners as the middlemen, and the Mediterranean was by-passed. Another relevant event was the discovery of the New World only a half a dozen years before the discovery of the cape. Gradually the center of world events shifted westward. The Mediterranean ceased to be in the middle of the civilized world as it had from early history.

SYRIA

Sultan Salim, who in 1516 to 1517 incorporated Syria in the Ottoman Empire, introduced no radical changes in its administrative system inherited from the Mamluks. The country was administered as three provinces, now called *walayahs*—Damascus, Aleppo, and Tripoli—each under a wali entitled pasha. Sidon was created walayah in 1660 as a check on the growing autonomy of Lebanon. Damascus was entrusted to its former Mamluk governor, Jan-Birdi al-Ghazali who, following his colleague at Aleppo, had betrayed al-Ghawri.[1] This made al-Ghazali virtual viceroy of Syria. He who betrayed the first master did not hesitate to betray the second. On Salim's death in 1520 the Damascus wali proclaimed his independence at the Umayyad Mosque, assumed the title of al-Malik al-Ashraf (the most noble sovereign), and struck coins in his name. But Sulayman lost no time. His Janissaries attacked the Syrian capital and meted out such a punishment to it and its inhabitants that has since associated the Janissary name in the country with terror.

Turkish walis followed one another in breathless sequence, but the sphere of their control was limited to towns and their environs. Out-of-the-way places remained under local chiefs, the desert population under bedouin shaykhs. As noted above, Damascus experienced no less than a hundred and thirty-nine pashas in the first hundred and eighty years of Ottoman rule. In three years Aleppo witnessed nine different ones. As the economy declined, uncertainty of life increased and the population shrank to less than a third of its height in Roman days. Villages by the hundreds in northeast Syria, depopulated in Mamluk days, disappeared in Ottoman times.[2]

In 1724 a Damascene, Ismail al-Azm, was entrusted with the walayah of his city. The office was passed on to his son Asad, starting a line of native governors. Other members of this family were appointed over Tripoli and Sidon. Ismail spent some of the last days of his life in jail; Asad was treacherously killed in the bath on instructions from the Porte. Sumptuous palaces of the Azm family, with woodwork, mosaic and other elaborate decorations typifying eighteenth century Arab architecture, are still among the show places of the Syrian capital and Hamah. The palace in Damascus was partly destroyed in the course of an uprising against the French mandate in 1925. The Hamah palace today houses a school.

More adventurous but less legitimate was the career of Ahmad Pasha al-Jazzar. His surname, meaning butcher, was acquired from his efficient work as an executioner in the service of the Egyptian Mamluk Ali Bey.[3] Ahmad, of Christian Bosnian origin, was sold by a Jewish slave dealer after having committed a sex crime and fled to Constantinople. From Cairo he went to Sidon, where he distinguished himself in the military service of the sultan and received the governorship of

[1] Cf. above, p. 324.
[2] Cf. above, p. 341.
[3] On him see above, pp. 430-31.

the city as a reward. Southward he extended his authority to Acre, where he succeeded its native governor. This city became his capital. He fortified it by forced labor, monopolized its trade, and organized a cavalry corps of eight hundred Bosnians and Albanians and an infantry corps of about a thousand Moroccans. In it he defied Napoleon, checked his advance and sent him back whence he had come. The sultan considered it prudent to send his intensive wali (1780) a firman bestowing on him the additional governorship of Damascus. Until his death in 1804 al-Jazzar ruled as a virtually independent viceroy of Syria. An unprincipled dictator, he lived up to his early reputation and ruthlessly cut down foe and rival, leaving a name that has lived to the present as a synonym of cruelty. His rise exemplifies the rule: the power of the provincial governor increases in direct proportion to the decrease of the central authority.

IRAQ

Iraq was incorporated into the Ottoman Empire in 1638 after zig-zagging for over a century between Persian and Turkish occupation.[4] It remained in that empire until the first World War. In its Ottoman career Iraq wavered between the Syrian and Egyptian models, maintaining its peculiar features and problems.

Distance from and communication difficulties with Constantinople, proximity to Persia, a preponderance at least in large areas of the Shiite element to whom Persia was of special attraction, and the presence of unwieldy Kurdish tribes in the north and Arab tribes in the south and the east—all these beset its administration with difficulties and created special problems. Ottoman interest was essentially in tribute and the use of the land as a base of operation against Persia and east Arabia. The country suffered two serious invasions in this period. One invasion was by Nadir Shah, who in 1733 laid siege to Baghdad and ten years later to Mosul,[5] and the other was by the emerging Wahhabis of Nejd, whose intensified raids culminated in sacking the shrine of al-Husayn in Karbala (1801) and that of Ali in Najaf (1802), the two most sacred sanctuaries of Shiite Islam. In addition Iraq boasted al-Kazimayn, outside of Baghdad, where the seventh and ninth imams were entombed. Pilgrimage to these sanctuaries was a main source of revenue which was considerably reduced by these wars. There was a partial compensation in the seventeenth century advent of the East India Company into the Persian Gulf; it put the country on the East-West overland route.

[4] Cf. above, pp. 340, 382.
[5] Cf. above, p. 383.

For eighty-one years beginning in 1750 Mamluks ruled the land. The first one of them was in the service of the governor whom he succeeded. The Porte's attempts to impose its nominees were not successful. Communications between the federal and the provincial capitals were at the mercy of desert wanderers and hill tribesmen. These Mamluks were recruited for the most part from Christian slaves of Circassian (Georgian) origin. The historic theme revolved on personalities and intrigues in Baghdad. Under Mamluks as under pashas

MIDHAT PASHA, WALI OF IRAQ, 1869-1872, AND AUTHOR OF OTTOMAN CONSTITUTION

the people suffered from insecurity, oppression, corruption, and the miscarriage of justice. Outstanding in the Mamluk oligarchy was Sulayman, styled al-Kabir (the great, 1780-1802), who received aid from the East India Company in securing the pashalik and remained friendly to the British. Sulayman united the three pashaliks of the country—Baghdad, Basra, and Mosul—and in so doing curbed Kurdish chieftains in the north and Arab shaykhs in the south. The Kurds, mountaineers and Sunnites but affiliated with the Persians in language and blood, have remained a thorn in the side of Iraq as well as Turkey. This Mamluk had in addition to deal with Wahhabi raids. Sulayman did not renounce allegiance to the Porte; he was generous in the frequency of his reports, but less so in sending gifts, and least in paying the expected tribute.

Not until 1831 did Constantinople succeed in reasserting its authority. The Mamluks were exterminated. A strong garrison was stationed at Baghdad. In 1869, to keep away a dangerously liberal high official, a reactionary grand vizir sent Midhat Pasha as wali over Baghdad and commander of its army corps. Any resemblance between the Baghdad Midhat entered and that of Harun al-Rashid must have been accidental. But the new governor was not deterred. With energy and farsightedness he set in motion an undreamed-of program of developing and improving the land. Clogged-up canals were cleared, roads were opened, and a horse tramway line was started; more surprisingly a savings' bank was founded and a "Euphrates railway" was contemplated. He even tried to induce individuals of the powerful Muntafiq combination of Arab tribes in the south to settle on a life of agriculture. He brought Nejd and a part of east Arabia under Turkish authority, thereby winning admiration from Iraqis; but official jealousy and increased hostility in Constantinople resulted in his recall. To stress his incorruptibility a story was circulated that he had to sell his watch to pay his travel expenses back. There he wrote the constitution under Abd-al-Hamid.[6] Midhat ended his days an exile in al-Taif (Hejaz), where he was strangled in prison (1883) after unsuccessful attempts to poison him.

LEBANON

Lebanon traced an independent course of its own basically differing from any other. The mountainous character of its land, the nature of its inhabitants, and the ingrained tradition of individualism and liberty-loving dictated that course. As in Phoenician days the two mountain ranges continued to shut off communication with the east, while the sea continued to invite intercourse with the west. Lebanon is the only country in the Arab area, with no desert and no bedouin population but with a variety of small communities made up of originally unhappy minorities in neighboring lands that sought and found refuge there. Such was the case of Maronites, Druzes, and Shiites. It is also the only country in which a majority of the Christian population has survived in the face of Islam. Its people have resisted Arabicization as they have resisted Islamization. As late as the seventeenth century some north Lebanon villages were still speaking Syriac. The Maronite Church has maintained that ancient language in its liturgical works and insists on writing Arabic, when used in them, in Syriac letters

---

[6] Treated above, p. 346.

Young scholars from this sect were the only ones who succeeded in penetrating the Ottoman curtain and pursuing their education in Rome.

The Maronites owe their name to a semi-historical ascetic monk, Saint Maron (Marun), who lived east of Antioch and died in 410. Under pressure from hostile neighbors his disciples and followers moved south, first to a monastery they built on the Orontes and then to the heights of north Lebanon. There they blended with the scanty Syriac-speaking population to form in the early eighth century a quasi-nation, defying the Damascus caliphate and holding friendly contacts with Byzantine emperors. They came first to Rome's attention in the period of the Crusades.

As Maronites were expanding in the north, Druzes of Fatimid origin,[7] were penetrating its southern part. Subjected to persecution from the Sunnite majority the Druzes resorted to secrecy in the maintenance of their religious beliefs and the practice of their rites. Access to the sacred writings, always in manuscript form, was limited to the initiated few. Religious knowledge became esoteric. But the sense of solidarity they developed surpassed even that of the Maronites. Even now the community has no public places of worship, ignores the five daily prayers, and takes no part in the fast of Ramadan or the holy pilgrimage to Mecca. It observes strict monogamy but authorizes easy divorce.

On Maronites, Druzes and their feudal lords, Manis, and Shihabis much of the history of Ottoman Lebanon revolves.

UNDER THE MANIS

No sooner had Salim victoriously entered Damascus than a delegation of Lebanese, headed by Fakhr-al-Din I al-Mani, presented itself before the sultan to offer its allegiance. Fakhr-al-Din, feudal lord of the Shuf district (southeast of Beirut), had with his colleagues followed the wait-and-see policy while Mamluks and Ottomans battled for Syria. Salim confirmed Fakhr and other lords of the mountain in their fiefs, allowing them the same privileges as they had had under Mamluks and imposing a relatively light tribute. He had more dangerous potential enemies to heed. For a hundred and eighty-one years the Manis, who were of uncertain origin and who had entered Lebanon in the early twelfth century and settled in the Shuf with Baaqlin as center, ruled over a large part of Lebanon. There they embraced Druzism, the religion of their subjects. As amirs they exacted taxes and duties at their pleasure, acted independently in all domestic affairs, exercised the right of life and death over their subjects, and transmitted their offices

---

[7] See above, pp. 303-4.

to their descendants. They could deal directly with the Porte or through its representative in Damascus, Tripoli, or (later) Sidon. One of these lords went so far as to sign a treaty with a foreign power, the Medicis of Florence. The treaty included a military clause against his suzerain. This was Fakhr-al-Din II (r. 1590-1635), under whom Manid hegemony reached its apex.

Twelve-year-old Fakhr-al-Din succeeded his father who was killed by the Turks, in the amirate. He developed a threefold ambition: building a greater Lebanon, severing the last link in the chain that tied it to Constantinople, and setting it on the path of "modernism" and progress. In all three he achieved spectacular success. One after the other of the outlying districts, beginning with Sidon, which was once under his father, and Beirut, were annexed to his tiny state. The reigning sultan Ahmad I (r. 1603-1617), a weakling, had his hands full warring unsuccessfully against Austrians, Hungarians, and Persians. By 1610 the Mani prince had extended his authority from the Dog River to Mount Carmel and inland to Tiberias. By the addition of fertile Biqaʻ, he increased the state revenue and acquired enough funds to organize an efficient army. Meanwhile Fakhr had gained possession of some of the formidable castles of Crusading repute. By way of promoting agriculture and commerce he encouraged the flax and silk industry; built caravanserais (khans); constructed bridges over the coastal rivers; and sought new channels of trade with Florence, Venice, and France. To Europeans he extended capitulary privileges identical with those inaugurated by Sulayman the Magnificent. By this time the suspicions of the Damascus' wali had been aroused. In 1613 the Porte sent against his audacious vassal a land and sea force. Prudence dictated withdrawal from the scene. Accordingly Fakhr with a small entourage left the country on three vessels and landed in the court of his ally Cosmo II, duke of Tuscany. After two years in Florence, Naples, and other places he returned home, disappointed at having received no military aid but more determined to carry out his ambitious scheme.

Not satisfied with the greater Lebanon he had created, Fakhr wrested Tripoli from its Turkoman amirs and extended his sway north into Syria and south into Palestine and Transjordan. The Turkish forces that moved against him from Damascus were cut to pieces in al-Biqaʻ and the wali himself was captured. Constantinople accepted the *fait accompli* and designated Fakhr lord of Arabistan. Feeling free to develop his country's resources further, the overlord invited engineers, architects, irrigation and agricultural experts from Tuscany and ordered the importation of cattle to improve the local breed. Of more enduring value was the permitting of European Catholic missions to settle in the land and carry on their educational and religious work. Fakhr is said to have been baptized by his Capuchin physician.

Once more the suspicious eye of the Porte was turned against him. By now Murad IV was in a stronger position than he or his two predecessors had been before. The walis of Damascus and Cairo moved against the Lebanese rebel. The fight he put up was faint and futile. His requests for aid from Tuscany went unheeded. In 1635 he was led captive to Constantinople, where he was strangled in the square of a mosque by two mutes.

Thus ended the career of the first modern Lebanese, the one who pointed out to Lebanon its destiny.

UNDER THE SHIHABIS

The Manis were succeeded by the Shihabis, their allies and relatives by marriage. The Shihabis trace their origin to the noble Quraysh family which had entered Lebanon half a century after the Manis. The first in the amirate was Bashir I (r. 1697-1707), son of a sister of the last Mani. Bashir was elected by a national assembly of elders and shaykhs and reported to the sultan by the Sidon wali with the assurance that the usual taxes would be paid. For seat he chose Dayr al-Qamar, capital of the last Manis.

For almost a century and a half (1697-1842) the Shihabis maintained, through a feudal hierarchy of princes and shaykhs, the two principles of home rule and hereditary succession. They kept their hold by pitting one local party against another and maintaining a balance between Maronites and Druzes, the two major elements in the population. From an enfeebled Porte, they had little to fear. Their feudal power rested on universal military service which they enforced on their untrained subjects. It was extemporaneous. The fourth governor, Mansur (r. 1754-1770), embraced Christianity in its Maronite variety. Some Shihabis remained Moslem. Fuad Shihab, elected as president of the Lebanese Republic in 1958, is a Christian member of the family.

The Shihabis promoted the policy of tolerance toward Europeans initiated by their predecessers. Capuchins and Jesuits as well as European traders became firmly established in the land. Being mostly of French nationality, these Europeans wittingly or unwittlingly served to implement the policy inaugurated by Louis XIV (1643-1715) to promote French trade in the Levant and protect its Catholics. This brought the Maronites, who had established cordial relations with France earlier through Crusaders,[8] closer to that country. Members

---

[8] See above, p. 312.

of a Lebanese family, al-Khazin, were given consular offices in Beirut and Sidon and accorded French citizenship. In 1734 a Lebanese priest, graduate of the Maronite College at Rome, put a high school he had founded under Jesuit administration. In 1789 another high school in a Lebanese town was founded by a graduate of Rome. These were the first two European-style educational institutions in the area. The Maronite College in Rome was founded in 1584 by Pope Gregory XIII. It was in fact a seminary. Some of its graduates returned home to occupy positions of leadership in church and education. Others remained in Rome or moved on to various European cities to introduce Oriental studies abroad. Istifan al-Duwayhi (d. 1704) became Maronite patriarch and left the first important history of the sect. Al-Samani (L. Assemani, d. 1768) made the Vatican library a repository of one of the greatest collections of Oriental manuscripts and books. His *Bibliotheca Orientalis* (4 vols., Rome, 1719-1728) remains a major source of information on the churches of the East. In 1736 al-Samani represented the pope at a synod in Lebanon which sealed the union between the Maronites and Rome. Al-Sahyuni (L. Sionita, d. 1648) held the chair of Semitic languages at the Collège Royal, Paris, served as interpreter for Louis XIII, and contributed to the compilation of the Paris Polyglot Bible, the first to include Syriac and Arabic.

BASHIR II

Shihabi power culminated in the amirate of Bashir II (r. 1788-1840), who followed in the footsteps of Fakhr-al-Din II. Shrewd in politics, most impressive in features and personality, and of ferocious dignity, Bashir schemed and labored to maintain a Lebanon that was autonomous, enlightened, and modernized. His iron-rod long rule, tempered with stern justice, gave the country a measure of security that has since become proverbial in the local saga. Napoleon solicited his aid against Acre, promising more independence, lighter taxes, and additional territory, but Bashir waited to see. To the Turkish forces checking the Wahhabi advance in 1810 he contributed 15,000 fighters; the time was not yet opportune to break off with the Porte. Later, however, he bet on the wrong horse when he sided with the Sidon wali against the Damascus viceroy and had to retire to Egypt in 1821. There he struck up a friendship with Muhammad Ali which bore fruit in the cooperation Bashir later offered Ibrahim in the conquest of Syria. After the bombardment of Beirut, headquarters of Egyptian operations, by the Anglo-Austrian-Turkish fleet, the lord of Lebanon delivered himself to the British and was taken to Malta.

Christian by baptism, Moslem by matrimony, and Druze to his
subjects, Bashir opened the Lebanon's door wider than ever to Western
educational influences and commercial contacts. He equipped the
magnificent palace he built at Bayt al-Din (Btaddin), across a picturesque valley from Dayr al-Qamar, with both chapel and mosque. The
palace, a show place in Lebanon, is still used as a summer residence for
the president of the republic. Italians and Greeks hastened to Beirut
to open hotels; British and French firms struck roots in the city. Ships
began regular service between England and Lebanon. In 1841 a

Courtesy of The Macmillan Co., Ltd.

BASHIR AL-SHIHABI II, AMIR OF LEBANON, 1788-1840

Frenchman built the first silk factory in the country; soon an English-
man built another. The country prospered. Sericulture became and
remained to the first World War a leading Lebanese industry. In the
1820's, American missionary enterprise found a lodging in the country
and contributed immeasurably to the intellectual renaissance of the
area.

Ibrahim Pasha's expulsion and Bashir's withdrawal from the land
left it in a state of disturbance and gave the Porte a chance to assert its
direct authority. In 1842 the last Shihabi amir was deposed and replaced by a renegade Hungarian, Umar Pasha, the first Ottoman governor to be sent from Constantinople. Lebanese party polarization—
until then political and tribal rather than denominational, began to take
on religious aspects, with Christians and Druzes aligned against each

other. This gave Western powers a new chance; the British patronized Druzes as a counterbalance to French patronage of Maronites. The Russians continued to favor the Greek Orthodox. Civil wars between Christians and Druzes began in 1845 and after periods of uneasy truce culminated in 1860. In that year about 12,000 Christian lives were lost with the connivance if not cooperation of the Turkish authorities. The spark flew to Damascus to ignite a deposit of ill feeling generated by Ibrahim's liberal policy toward Christians. Finally the country was pacified through European intervention and the landing of 7,000 French troops.

MOUNT LEBANON A MUTASARRIFIYAH

In 1861 Lebanon, stripped of its seaport and the Biqa' plateau, was created an autonomous district under a governor general (*mutasarrif*), nominated by the Porte and confirmed by the European signatories of its new statute: France, Britain, Russia, Prussia, Austria, and (later) Italy. The new regulations provided that the mutasarrif be a Catholic Ottoman subject responsible to the Porte and assisted by an elective administrative council of twelve members representing the religious communities. His tenure, first for three years, was later extended to five, and was renewable. The country was to have its own militia, to contribute no troops to the imperial army, and to pay no tribute to the treasury. Its taxes were to meet its local needs. Justice was left entirely in the hands of local courts, and cases of personal status were kept under the jurisdiction of the respective religious authorities. In the more than a half century of its existence the mutasarrifiyah of Mount Lebanon had seven different governors of Armenian, Italian, Polish, and Levantine origins and enjoyed a measure of self-rule, prosperity, security, and stability denied to or unattained by any of its neighbors. The saying went around: Happy is he who owns even a goat's enclosure in Mount Lebanon. Its Maronite feudal lords disintegrated, but the Druze held on. A network of highways linking its main towns spread over the country. In 1863 a French company completed the Beirut-Damascus highway. the first of its kind in the area, and a regular diligence service was established between the two cities. Another French company completed in 1895 a Beirut-Damascus railroad which later connected these two cities with Turkey, Iraq, and Egypt.

Lebanon became an open arena for the interplay of Western cultural forces. To the new material and intellectual sources its people responded more spontaneously and wholeheartedly than any of their neighbors. Sons of Lebanon migrated into all parts of the civilized world, building new bridges for contact with the rest of the world. In the summer of 1915, Jamal Pasha[9] abolished the privileged position of Lebanon and put it under a Turkish mutasarrif whose tenure, like that of Umar Pasha, was brief. This was in the second year of the first World War.

FIRST WORLD WAR

The war period was the darkest in the modern history of Lebanon. In it Jamal Pasha perpetrated a reign of terror on the assumption that its Christian population was pro-Western and its Moslem population pro-Arab. Seized correspondence in the Beirut French consulate provided the most copious source of charges against French sympathizers. Membership in one of the many secret societies sufficed to label a person as a King Husayn sympathizer. The court martial at Alayh, a favorite summer resort, was primed to establish guilt by association or hearsay. The gallows at the main square of Beirut were ready to treat anyone condemned. Eleven were hanged in 1915 and fourteen the following year. In this year about a hundred Lebanese and Syrian leaders, representing prominent and influential families, were sentenced to prison, exile, or death. Meanwhile the main sources of national income were drying up. Tourists and summer visitors vanished; the silk industry dwindled; remittances from friends and relatives abroad were delayed. The gold and silver coinage was replaced by depreciated Turkish paper money never used before. Disease and starvation took their toll, almost a fourth of the population perished.[10] Relief came in 1918 with the occupation of the land by Allied troops under General Allenby.

The dark clouds of 1860 and 1914 to 1918 did not lack a silver lining. They aroused, especially in Great Britain and the United States, increased Western interest in Lebanon and stimulated new activities. Measures intended to bring temporary relief through orphanages, schools, hospitals, and the like tended to become institutionalized and finally to be taken over or copied by indigenous agencies.

BOOKS TO READ

Bliss, Frederick J., *The Religions of Modern Syria and Palestine* (New York, 1912).

Brockelmann, Carl, *History of the Islamic Peoples,* tr. Joel Carmichael and Moshe Perlmann (New York, 1947).

[9] Above, p. 366.
[10] Cf. above, p. 366.

Haddad, George, *Fifty Years of Modern Syria and Lebanon* (Beirut, 1950).

Hitti, Philip K., *Lebanon in History* (New York and London, 1957); *Syria: A Short History* (New York and London, 1957).

Hourani, A. H., *Syria and Lebanon* (London, 1946).

Longrigg, Stephen H., *Four Centuries of Modern Iraq* (Oxford, 1925); *ᶜIraq, 1900-1950* (London and New York, 1953).

Miller, William, *The Ottoman Empire and Its Successors* (Cambridge, 1936).

Ziadeh, Nicola A., *Syria and Lebanon* (London, 1956).

XXXIII *The Arabian Peninsula*

A̲RABIA holds a unique place among Arab lands and occupies a warm spot in the hearts and minds of Moslems everywhere. This is particularly true of Hejaz, cradle of Islam, heartland of Arabism, and the annual meeting place of hundreds of thousands of pilgrims. But the halo of sacred associations was extensive enough to encompass Hejaz' neighbors and to keep them isolated and insulated until a few decades ago. Even in pre-Islamic days the peninsula was never exposed to as strong political and cultural influences as the other Arab lands were. The Roman invasion from Egypt (24 B.C.) and the temporary occupation of the southwestern corner by Persians and by Ethiopians left no enduring impression.

YEMEN

On the peninsula only two states may be considered really independent: Saudi Arabia, centering on Nejd and Hejaz, and Yemen. The others are in varying degrees dependent upon the British. Hejaz did not figure prominently in history until the rise of Islam. It was southwestern Arabia, centering on Yemen, that first stepped on the threshold of civilization. Hejaz' and Nejd's population have been largely pastoral and nomadic. Yemen received enough rain to make the cultivation of soil rewarding. Its products and those of its neighbor Hadramaut—including spices, myrrh, and frankincense—were from earliest times in great demand in Egypt and the Fertile Crescent and later in the Greco-Roman world. In addition the country lay on the route to India, whose minerals and typical products were also highly prized.

South Arabians were the Phoenicians of their area, except that their trade was mainly by land caravans. As early as the twelfth century before Christ a highly organized society with a stable monarchy appeared in Yemen. The semi-legendary queen of Sheba bears the name of the Sabaean people and kingdom.[1] The still unexplored ruins of

[1] See above, pp. 133-4.

the capital city Marib and the impressive remains of its dam—an extraordinary engineering feat of the sixth pre-Christian century—give us a glimpse of the grandeur of ancient Yemen. This rain-favored, felicitous land was the Arabia Felix of classical writers. Of the three countries Yemen has remained more self-contained and medieval than Hejaz and Nejd, which, because of the discovery of oil in the 1930's, have opened a window on the world of the West.

Northwestern Arabia was inherited by the Turks from the Mamluks in the early part of the sixteenth century, but the southwestern part was acquired by conquest later under Sulayman the Magnificent.[2] At different times Yemen owed allegiance to the Sublime Porte but actual control was remote and ineffective. The imams, descendants of Zayd, great-grandson of Ali were the rulers in temporal as well as in spiritual matters. They were the counterparts of the sharifs of Mecca who, however, enjoyed the advantage of being custodians of the holy places besides being descendants of the Prophet. In Yemen, as in Hejaz and other parts of the peninsula, the area was divided and subdivided into innumerable units under tribal chiefs and shaykhs living in tents, or under lords and amirs in walled towns. Shaykhs, sharifs, and imams were in a constant struggle for existence or mastery.

Zayd, from whom the Sana imams descended, was "martyred" in 740 as he led an uprising against the Umayyad caliphate. An offshoot of the Shiah, the sect named after him stood closer to the Sunnite community than did any other Shiite sect.

In 1633 an imam, Qasim by name, expelled the Ottoman wali from Sana and started a line of rulers that with interruptions lasted until 1871. In 1849, however, the Porte succeeded in imposing its nominee as wali. For over fifty years the walis' chief concern was to keep down insurgent tribesmen by force.

The modern kingdom of Yemen was born in the first World War and fathered by its imam Yahya, an unusually energetic man, who rose to power in 1904. After 1914 the Turkish garrison at Sana was almost isolated from other Turkish forces and became ineffective. On the cessation of hostilities, the remnant of the garrison with the Turkish officials withdrew from the country. In the Anglo-Italian rivalry for ascendancy in the new kingdom, Italy—which had occupied Libya and Ethiopia—won, mainly because of the British occupation of Aden, considered Yemeni territory. In 1926 Italy succeeded in signing with the imam a treaty of friendship and commerce, and in the following year received from him a mission headed by his second son. The

[2] Cf. below, p. 470.

mission was welcomed by King Victor Emanuel and Mussolini and was impressed by the country's industrial development. An agreement followed for the purchase of arms from Italy, intended for use mainly against the British neighbors.

Independent Yemen was not successful in reclaiming any territory from the British to the south. On the north lay tiny Asir, which was disputed by a more powerful neighbor, Saudi Arabia. By a bloodless military campaign Yemeni troops were driven out, and Asir was annexed to Saudi Arabia (1934).

The imam-king who, as signified by his double title, combined the supreme spiritual and temporal authority in his person, continued to rule in the old-fashioned way, enforcing the shariah and unreceptive to outside demands. He was assisted by a council of ministers appointed by himself. Although he invited Italian physicians to man his new hospital at Sana and a few engineers to undertake projects of irrigation largely on his estate, on the whole he kept his country in isolation. Naturally he showed preference for the Axis in the second World War, but with the British victory at al-Alamain in Egypt he changed his mind. In 1943 Yemen severed diplomatic relations with Germany; two years later it joined the League of Arab States and in 1947 was accepted for membership in the United Nations.

In 1947 Imam Yahya received the first diplomatic mission from the United States and signed a treaty of friendship and commerce. The following year a former minister and governor of Hudaydah executed a *coup d'état* in which the imam, two of his sons, and his prime minister were assassinated. In a counter coup, however, the imam's eldest son, Crown Prince Ahmad, governor of Taiz, recovered the throne and captured and executed the conspirators. Ahmad allowed American interests to build a road in his country and permitted other to explore for oil and minerals. In the last few years, mainly because of the British presence in Aden and American support of Israel, Ahmad leaned in the direction of Soviet Russia. In March 1958 he signed an agreement establishing a federal union with the United Arab Republic, from which he seceded following Syria's secession. The earlier murmurings against old-fashioned autocratic rule and isolation from world currents of thought and trade again found expression in the 1955 uprising, engineered by Ahmad's younger brother Abdullah. Abdullah had traveled extensively in Europe, represented his country at the United Nations, and arranged for the first Yemeni students to come to America. The coup ended in the beheading of Abdullah, the would-be imam, as well as of another brother, al-Abbas, governor of Sana; the instructor general of the army; and other leading conspirators.

HEJAZ

Hejaz enjoyed its only heyday, a short one, under the Orthodox caliphs (632-661). With the rise of the Umayyads and the transfer of the seat of government to Syria, the center of gravity in Islam and Arabism shifted north, never to return. The spotlight began and continued to shine on Damascus, Baghdad, Cairo, and Cordova. The entire peninsula went into a state of eclipse. Mecca and Medina attracted scholars devoted to the study of mementos of the sacred past and involving traditions relating to the life of the Prophet and his companions, law enactments, and ritualistic procedures. Fresh currents of science, philosophy, and art by-passed the peninsula. Schools of hadith, shariah, and theology flourished there, where schools of medicine, astronomy, mathematics, and architecture developed in the Fertile Crescent, Persia, Egypt, and al-Andalus. Even in Arabic linguistics and grammar, the masterpieces were produced not in the two sister cities of Hejaz but in those of Iraq, Basra and Kufa. Such works were inspired by the needs of non-Arab converts to Islam and were carried out by them. From its medieval slumber Arabia did not begin to wake until a few years ago.

Politically Hejaz, as the Abbasid caliphate deteriorated, followed the successor states which arose in Egypt, ending with the Mamluks. That was where the Ottoman Turks found it. The appending of the holy land to a state gave that state special prestige in Islamic eyes. The sultans left in command the sharifs, whose family had ruled the country since the eleventh century. No occurrence of international import was experienced until the Wahhabi upheaval in the second half of the eighteenth century.

WAHHABISM

This movement began as a puritanical religious revival initiated by a Nejdi, Muhammad ibn-Abd-al-Wahhab (d. 1792). Young Muhammad studied at Medina, Mecca, and Damascus. He visited other places outside of his native land and returned home distressed by the impression that Islam as practiced had deviated widely from orthodox theory and observance prescribed by the Koran and the Prophet. Specifically it had acquired an accretion of "innovations," such as the cult of saints, veneration of shrines, visitation to tombs, and the use of the rosary—all savoring of idolatry. An adulteress should be stoned; a thief's hand should be amputated; the use of alcoholic drinks, tobacco, and silk clothes strictly prohibited. For inspiration he evidently drew on the founder of the conservative school of Moslem jurisprudence, ibn-Hanbal of Baghdad (d. 855), as interpreted by the Syrian theologian ibn-Taymiyah (d. 1328), both of whom he must have particularly studied while abroad. Abd-al-Wahhab and his followers were to be the real Muwahhids (unitarians); their opponents, however, styled them Wahhabis.

The new prophet was driven out of his home town by his own people. His interdictions against time-honored practices were not acceptable. In a petty chief of a neighboring tribe, Muhammad ibn-Saud (d. 1765), he at last found an ally and a son-in-law, ready not only to defend the new cause but to propagate it. This was the first ibn-Saud in history. Sword and religion marched together. Moslems who practiced the forbidden innovations forfeited their claim on Islam and should be fought, it was agreed, to the point of conversion or extermination. Converts were made in mounting numbers in an ever-widening area. Every new convert of ibn-Abd-al-Wahhab was a recruit to the fighting machine of ibn-Saud. In 1773 Riyad was captured; it later became capital of Wahhabism. Central and eastern Arabia served as the heartland of a new kingdom, indeed an empire. By the opening years of the nineteenth century the Wahhabi movement had acquired enough power to burst upon unsuspecting neighbors and overrun their lands. Karbala was sacked and its inhabitants massacred; its sister Najaf was not spared. The Sunnite shrines in Mecca and Medina correspondents of Karbala and Najaf, two most cherished shrines of the Shiah, were not spared. They were captured and relieved of some of their venerated tombs, relics of paganism. Damascus was attacked. A new empire, loose and ephemeral, extended from Palmyra and Damascus to Oman, and from al-Hasa to Hejaz. For the first time since the Orthodox caliphate such an area fell under the scepter of one ruler.

It was time for Constantinople to act. Mahmud II entrusted his powerful Egyptian viceroy with the task. In a series of campaigns led first by his sixteen-year-old son, then by himself and by his eldest son Ibrahim, Wahhabi power was suppressed at its source though it was not utterly destroyed. How could a half-bedouin force stand against a trained and disciplined army? The Wahhabi headquarters Dariyah was razed in 1818; and the leader, Abdullah ibn-Saud, was taken to Constantinople and beheaded. Other members of the royal family were banished to Turkey or Egypt. The first Wahhabi attempt at an empire was terminated.

In 1836 a Saudi ruler refused to pay tribute to the sultan. Another Egyptian expedition was dispatched but had to be withdrawn to reinforce the Egyptian campaign in Syria. Determined to rule directly, the Turks sent a wali with a garrison to be stationed at Medina in 1845.

No wali's arm in Hejaz was long enough to reach central Arabia. Here disorder reigned. Squabbles among Saudi contestants gave a new leader in the north his chance. He was ibn-Rashid, head of the powerful Shammar tribe. In the 1870's ibn-Rashid's power was firmly established and expanded; al-Hasa with its neighboring coast[3] was occupied by the Turks, and the Turks and Rashids entered into friendly relations. In 1891 Muhammad ibn-Rashid occupied the Saudi capital Riyad. His amirate was then the mightiest in the peninsula.

RESTORATION

A Saudi family with a ten-year-old son, Abd-al-Aziz, found asylum in Kuwait, where the future leader first came to know and esteem the British and to dream and scheme for the reclamation of the Wahhabi heritage. At the age of twenty and at the head of a band of two hundred followers, Abd-al-Aziz struck through the intervening desert, entered Riyad by night, and stealthily forced his way into the residence of the Rashidi governor. They reached the bedchamber by climbing one over another's shoulders. The governor happened to be out but the next morning as he stepped into the outer yard of his house, he was engaged in a hand-to-hand combat with the intruders. He and his guard were slaughtered January 16, 1902. Abd-al-Aziz thus became master of his ancestral capital, ending a story that has become an epic in Saudi saga.

This master stroke was a preview of more daring and extensive ones to follow. The outlying districts had to be added and consolidated despite Turkish support to the Rashid house. It was however evident that no successful operations could be launched outside the immediate vicinity without changing the patriarchal tribal organization, with its centrifugal tendency, pastoral economy, and nomadic way of life to a non-tribal or pan-tribal structure based on agriculture and settled life, and aspiring to a quasi-national development. To this end the new leader started the Ikhwan (brotherhood) colonies, each under strict Wahhabi discipline and responsible for a contingent of armed force. In 1913 he, at the head of his Ikhwan, suddenly descended upon al-Hasa and seized it from the Turks who had held it for over forty years. The new acquisition opened a window onto the Persian Gulf and through it onto British India. It brought ibn-Saud closer to the British-dependent Arab states on the coast. The outbreak of the first World War found ibn-Saud still confronted with two rivals, ibn-Rashid in the north and Husayn in Hejaz.

[3] Cf. above, p. 449.

HUSAYN IBN-ALI

While ibn-Saud was laying the foundation for a solid kingdom, his future adversary Husayn ibn-Ali of the Hashimite house was cherishing a vision of a united Arab nation under his leadership. The grand sharif counted heavily on his blood, ibn-Saud on his wits. Husayn was installed in the hereditary amirate of Mecca in 1908 after having spent many years in Constantinople where he had become versed in the intricacies of contemporary Turkish policies. In that same year the Constantinople-Hejaz railway line, a pet scheme of Abd-al-Hamid, reached Medina.[4] The new amir opposed its extension to Mecca because of the political-military advantage it would give his suzerain over him. Alienation between Mecca and Constantinople was widened as the Young Turks launched their Turkification policy. Arab nationalist organizations in Damascus, Baghdad, Beirut, and Cairo turned to the descendant of the Prophet for leadership. The miscarriage of the Anglo-Indian government attempt to involve Abd-al-Aziz in the war against Turkey through Iraq made the Anglo-Egyptian government concentrate on Husayn. In October 1914 it offered him a conditional guaranty of independence. Husayn was ready to bargain. In his correspondence with McMahon, British resident in Cairo, he spoke in the name of the "Arab people," demanding recognition of the independence of the Arab country in the area from Mersin-Adana in the northwest to the Persian frontier and south as far as the Indian Ocean. McMahon took exception to the Alexandretta district and to the area west of a line between Aleppo, Hamah, and Damascus where French interests were paramount. In June 1916 Husayn raised the standard of rebellion, proclaimed the independence of Hejaz under his kingship and attacked the Turkish garrison at Medina. He proclaimed himself king of the Arabs but was not so recognized by Britain and France. The action forced on Turkey another front. The spectacular emergence of T. E. Lawrence, the liaison officer who held the purse of English sterlings, and of Faysal—Husayn's third son as organizer and leader of guerrilla battalions—gave the Arab campaigns dramatic overtones. Railroad bridges were dynamited; Turkish garrisons driven out of Hejaz; and, in a climactic move, al-Aqabah was occupied (1917). The occupation of this seaport dislodged the Turks from their last foothold in the Arabian area. Since then the Hejaz railway south of Transjordan has been in disuse. Plans were made to cover and facilitate General Allenby's advance through Sinai and Palestine as

[4] As noted above, p. 347.

though with a right flank. But Allenby took the Turks in Palestine by surprise, and Faysal, reinforced by an Australian division, moved inland into Damascus entering it on November 30, 1918.

To the peace conference at Versailles (1919) Husayn sent his son Faysal to press his claim. By this time the Arabs had learned that as early as the spring of 1916 the British, French, and Russians had reached a preliminary secret understanding embodied in the secret Sykes-Picot agreement parceling out Turkey, Syria, and Iraq among themselves. Mark Sykes was a British Oriental expert and traveler, and Georges Picot was the French consul at Beirut in 1914. This agreement, first divulged when the Bolsheviks came to power, provided for Palestine an international administration, put Syria west of an Aleppo-Hamah-Damascus line in the French sphere of influence, Iraq south of Mosul in the British sphere, and whatever was left was to be organized into an independent state or a federation of states. Faysal had no chance at Versailles, and Husayn would neither compromise nor yield on the mandates over the Arab Crescent and other issues. The temporary enthronement of Faysal over Syria and more promisingly over Iraq, together with the appointment of Abdullah as amir over Transjordan, brought him some solace but no reconciliation.

ABD-AL-AZIZ IBN-SAUD

In the international conflict ibn-Saud's part remained passive but locally he was active, consolidating his possessions, pushing his colonization plan and awaiting his chance. In 1921 he renewed operations against the house of ibn-Rashid, eliminated their remnant and occupied their capital Hail. All central and eastern Arabia were then under his sole control. When three years later Husayn, while visiting Transjordan, took advantage of the deposition of the last Ottoman caliph[5] and laid claim to the vacant high office, a pretext was provided for opening hostilities. Husayn's claim was considered a usurpation by believers especially in India and even in Syria. The Ikhwan met no strong resistance in Hejaz. Disillusioned and disappointed Husayn abdicated in favor of his eldest son Ali, left on a British vessel and ultimately landed in Cyprus. In December 1924 ibn-Saud entered Mecca. A year later he seized Medina. Ali took refuge in his brother's court at Baghdad. The Hashimite house of Hejaz was destroyed. In January 1926, the Wahhabi conqueror was proclaimed king of Hejaz, at the grand mosque of Mecca. He acquired the title of sultan of Nejd and dependencies the following year. The acquisition of the land of the

---

[5] Discussed above, p. 367.

holy pilgrimage was a great economic asset.   In 1932 the two realms
were combined into the Saudi Arabian Kingdom.   It was the first time
after the rise of Islam that such an extensive area had been organized
into one state.

With his desire for further expansion satisfied, the first king of Saudi
Arabia devoted his undivided attention to the economic and social
development of his realm.   To a land dominated from time immemorial by tribal warfare, raids, pillage, and lawlessness he introduced a

Courtesy of Arabian American Oil Company

KING ABD-AL-AZIZ IBN-SAUD

measure of unity, orderliness, and security never before enjoyed.
Rebellious tribal chiefs were suppressed by force, enticed by subsidies,
or brought into alliance with the royal family through intermarriage.
Full advantage was taken of the Islamic liberal laws of marriage, concubinage, and divorce.   The time-honored practice of holding hostages
was also exploited.   Theologians and obscurantists in Hejaz and among
his own Wahhabis had to be reconciled, convinced, or silenced.   Tele-
phones, radios, and telegraphs which were essential for efficient administration, were first opposed on the ground of being instruments of the
devil.   The chanting of a few koranic verses on the radio during an
audience in the royal palace attended by the divines neatly demonstrated the emptiness of their argument.   Of no less importance in a
country with widely scattered settlements were modernized facilities

ARABIAN PENINSULA

for transportation and communication. Motor vehicles began to re-place camel caravans, pilgrims rode to Mecca and Medina in buses and at last a railway linked the capital with the oilfield in the east and extended to the port of Dammam on the Persian Gulf. A few hospitals and clinics brought the blessings of modern hygiene and the sorely needed art of healing to an undeveloped, uneducated society. For physicians and pharmacists, teachers, engineers, and other professional and skilled men, the king had to draw on neighboring countries, particularly Egypt, Lebanon, and Syria. Several of his ministers and ambassadors were also recruited from those lands.

To meet the expenses of the new projects ibn-Saud could at least draw not only upon the ordinary revenue of the land but on his new and ever-mounting royalties from the Arabian American Oil Company. A mining concession given to American and British interests in 1934 yielded some gold in Hejaz but not in sufficient quantities, but ibn-Saud could count on the advice of the company in establishing contacts with American concerns. Large-scale plans for land reclamation and irrigation were carried out. The government's interest was mainly on the technological rather than the educational side. About ninety-five per cent of the people remained illiterate.

Saudi Arabia maintained generally cordial relations with its Arab neighbors despite a dynastic feud with the Hashimite house represented by the two monarchs of Jordan and Iraq. It joined the League of Arab States at the time of its formation (1945), but played no conspicuous part in the evolution of its policy. Friendly relations with the West were at times strained as a result of the Zionist activity and the creation of Israel. Both ibn-Saud and his son-successor Saud were critical of the preferential treatment given the new state. In the summer of 1948 a small Saudi contingent joined other Arab forces in the fight in Palestine. Early in the 1940's, when war necessities and priorities curtailed Arabian oil operations and difficulties of communication sharply reduced the pilgrim traffic, the country was threatened with bankruptcy. At the request of the United States Great Britain made available to ibn-Saud grants from the $425,000,000 just given her by the American government. The annual payments increased progressively until in 1945 they reached $2,500,000. Direct supplementary aid came from the United States by way of lend lease, Point Four, Mutual Assistance, or in the form of loan. In 1946 the Export-Import Bank granted Saudi Arabia a $10,000,000 loan and four years later a $15,000,000 one. In 1942 an American agricultural mission was sent to survey the possibilities and make recommendations. In the following year the United States was authorized to establish an American air base at

Dhahran, where the oil company had its wells and installations. It took four years to construct the base, one of the best equipped abroad. In that same year (1943) the American legation at Jidda, later elevated to an embassy, was established on a firm basis.

On his way back from Yalta (February 1945) President Roosevelt met ibn-Saud on board an American warship in the Bitter Lake, Egypt. This was the first and last trip abroad the king ever made. In the following month Saudi Arabia declared a token war on Germany and sent a representative, Faysal, to the San Francisco conference.

Saud, who succeeded his father in 1952, had visited the United States four years earlier and established firsthand contacts with the West. On the whole he followed the track blazed by his great predecessor. In internal affairs, however, he deviated from the one-man rule and developed a cabinet with new ministries. His younger brother Crown Prince Faysal, who represented his country at the United Nations, was appointed minister of foreign affairs and chairman of the council of ministers. Faysal began to exercise more power as relations between the king and President Nasser (Jamal Abd-al-Nasir) of Egypt were strained. Subsequent to the triple Israeli-British-French attack on Egypt in the autumn of 1956, Saudi Arabia stopped shipment of oil to Great Britain and her possessions. In January 1957 King Saud paid an official visit to the United States but no tangible results accrued by way of removing misunderstanding between his Arab neighbors and Washington.

Saud's government has shown some interest in modern and higher education. At Jidda a royal palace with its environs has been converted into a "city of learning." In 1957 Saud inaugurated the new University of Riyad with two faculties of science and letters, the latter comprising departments of Islamic law and religion and of Arabic language and literature. An increasing number of students began going abroad, especially to Cairo and Beirut and even to England and the United States. A small middle class of modern businessmen, industrialists, teachers, technicians, and other professionals started emerging and threatening the traditional social structure. The new spirit of Arab nationalism has been working through this class. Upheavals are sure to follow.

OMAN AND ADEN

The coastal territory of southern and eastern Arabia—al-Hasa excluded—with its shaykhdoms and territories is British dominated. Britain's interest stems form its concern for the security of India, desire to ward off all competitors, and to control the area's trade routes.

Oman, the only state in the group with a history, was the first to fall into the British sphere of influence, in fact, to fall into European hands. Its capital Muscat, commanding the southeast entrance to the Persian Gulf, was held by the Portuguese from 1508 to 1688. When Sulayman the Magnificent occupied Baghdad and Basra,[6] he found the Portuguese in ascendancy around the Persian Gulf blocking its southern exit. His admiral Piri Reis conducted campaigns against Aden (1547) and Muscat (1551) from Suez and besieged Hormuz then in Portuguese hands[7] but withdrew upon receiving news of the approach of a hostile fleet. Shipwrecked on the Bahrain Islands he returned to Cairo to be sentenced to death because of his mishap.

This great sea captain was the first Ottoman cartographer. He prepared a manual of his sailings and two maps, one sketching the coasts of the Mediterranean, which he gave to Sultan Salim, and one, based on the map used by Columbus, described the Atlantic Ocean including the America coast and the western coasts of Europe and Africa. The place names on this map appear in Italian form, betraying the source of information. Piri Reis' geographic works were evidently kept a secret in the imperial palace the contents of whose library were not divulged until 1929. The Portuguese soon found a more formidable rival than the Turks in the British. Having lost Hormuz to them in 1622 the Portuguese made Muscat, hitherto a naval base and factory, the headquarters of their fleet. It became their most valuable possession.

In 1741 a native ruler Ahmad ibn-Said, a descendant of the imams of Yemen, established a line of rulers still in control. British treaty relations with Muscat began early in 1798, the year of Napoleon's invasion of Egypt. The treaty was concluded by the East India Company, which two years later sent its agent as the first British resident in this city. Other treaties followed involving suppression of slave trade and customs agreements. A new one was signed in 1891 in which the sultan bound "himself, his heirs and successors never to cede, to sell or to mortgage, save to the British Government, the dominions of Muscat and Oman or any of their dependencies." Similar terms were exacted later from the states of eastern Arabia. In 1939 a new treaty of friendship, commerce, and navigation was signed. During the first half of the nineteenth century Oman, under Sultan Said ibn-Sultan (r. 1804-1856), was the outstanding country in the peninsula. It controlled Zanzibar and a part of east Africa. But on this sultan's death the sultanate was divided between his two sons and the African possessions

[6] Cf. above, p. 447.
[7] Cf., above pp. 333, 381.

were separated from the Arabian mainland. Increasing bedouin attacks from inland weakened the sultanate still further.

In the second half of the nineteenth century the center of international interest shifted from the eastern corner of the peninsula to the western—from Muscat to Aden. The Napoleonic attempt on Egypt, the development of steamship navigation, and the revival of Red Sea trade subsequent to the opening of the Suez Canal contributed to that end. Aden had the only good harbor between Egypt and India. It lay a hundred miles from Bab al-Mandab, the southern gate of the red Sea. Built in the crater of an extinct volcano and surrounded by precipitous rocks, it was a naturally fortified town. Its strategic importance did not escape early conquerors. Albuquerque in 1513 made an unsuccessful attempt at its capture. The Turks raided it later and seized it in 1547, but their hold on it and its Yemen hinterland remained precarious. Yemeni imams freed themselves from Turkey and in 1735 a local shaykh, that of Lahaj, freed himself from Yemen and started a new line of independent rulers. In 1839 a British force from Bombay, sent by the East India Company, captured Aden from the sultan of Lahaj and brought it under the British flag. Since then Aden has developed into a chief entrepôt and coaling station on the maritime highway between the West and south Asia. In 1937 it was declared a crown colony.

With one foot planted at Aden the British took a six-hundred-mile stride eastward—about the length of England, Wales and Scotland put together—reaching the Oman boundary. This was constituted into the Aden Protectorate, consisting of numerous shaykhdoms and sultanates (in reality principalities) under Arab chiefs who between 1882 and 1914 were brought into treaty relations with His Majesty's Government. All these rulers acknowledged the authority of the governor of the Aden colony, who was at the same time governor of the protectorate. The defense of the realm became the responsibility of the United Kingdom. Hadramaut, of ancient renown as a source of spices, frankincense and other tropical products, covers an extensive area in the eastern part of the protectorate. In marked contrast to her policy elsewhere Britain has tightened her hold on Aden since the second World War. This further aroused the Yemen authorities, who have never ceased to consider the entire area as *terra irredenta*. When the Eisenhower doctrine of 1957, promising military and economic aid to any Near Eastern country seeking it against international communist aggression, was offered Imam Ahmad, he made his acceptance contingent upon America's resolving the Anglo-Yemeni dispute in his favor.

To forestall nationalist agitation the British prompted a "Federation of the Emirates in the South" which on February 11, 1959 was started by six of the twenty-five states constituting the Aden Protectorate. The British hoped the federation would develop into an economically and politically independent entity with friendly relations to the United Kingdom. The members of the new federation considered the step as marking the conception of a larger state and the first stage in progress toward unity and full independence. The remaining units in the protectorate have thus far abstained from joining the federation on the ground that being British-sponsored it is not likely to fulfill their aspirations.

EASTERN ARABIA

While Britain was consolidating her position in southern Arabia, the eastern part of the peninsula was not overlooked. In the course of the nineteenth century the Persian Gulf became virtually a British lake with His Majesty's Government as its warden. The modern history of the eastern coast would have been uneventful, had it not been for the advent of the British and the discovery of inestimable underground wealth in the form of petroleum. Before then the main sources of income had been pearl fishing, boat building, and date growing; a large part of the population had been nomadic. The establishment of British control and the production of oil have been the most significant events in the area since the rise of Islam. Human settlements are today sprinkled along the coast, up the valleys and in oases, but deserts and plains are left to the nomad to roam from one source of water and pasture to another. In Kuwait and Bahrain oil and other commercial and industrial ventures have given rise to, among other things, a largely urban population.

At the head of the Persian Gulf, bordering on Iraq, lies tiny Kuwait. The name, meaning small castle, may relate to a sixteenth century Portuguese castle whose remains can still be seen on the coast. Kuwait's rule has been in the hands of the Sabah family since 1756. The shaykhdom acknowledged Ottoman sovereignty in 1871; but in 1899, when it was considered a desirable terminus for the Berlin-Baghdad railroad and the Turks planned to occupy it, its shaykh, Mubarak al-Sabah, signed a treaty placing his interests under British protection and binding himself not to grant a concession to any foreign interest without British consent. In 1961 Kuwait became fully independent, joined the League of Arab States, but remained free to call on Britain for protection.

With a population (1961) of 322,000 (half of whom are foreign born), it claims the largest proportion of urban settlers along the coast.

Bahrain and the Trucial States maintain the special treaty relation with Great Britain making them protected (not protectorate) states. The British government assumes full responsibility for their protection and conduct of foreign affairs, otherwise their local rulers are practically independent. This responsibility is exercised through a political resident (not a governor) with headquarters at Bahrain and political agents in the different states subordinate to him. Of these states only Bahrain has a British adviser.

Bahrain is the principal island in an archipelago named after it. Because of its position and function as center of the pearl industry in the gulf, Bahrain was the first territory in the area to fall into European hands and has since been coveted by neighboring and distant powers. Portuguese, Persians, British, Dutch, Turks, and Wahhabis have at times contested its possession. The Portuguese held it from 1507 to 1622, when it was seized by Safawid Persians. About a century and a half later the Khalifah family of an Arab tribe crossed over from Kuwait and seized the islands which they have held since. In 1820 treaty relations were established with the British binding the shaykh to suppress piracy and forbid the sale of property gained by plunder. Other treaties followed. In 1880 a final agreement was made binding the shaykh and his successors "to abstain from entering into negotiations or making treaties of any sort with any State or Government other than the British without the consent of the British Government." This was followed by a further agreement (1892) in which the ruling shaykh promised not "to cede, mortgage, or give for occupation any part of this territory save to the British Government." Periodically the Persians have revived their claim to sovereignty on the islands and Kuwait, on historic grounds and supplemented by the presence of a minority of population of Iranian origin and a sizable community of the Shiah. Through Bahrain and Kuwait modern Iran has interfered in Arab affairs. The Palestine problem was of no special concern to her.

THE TRUCIAL COAST

The Trucial, formerly the Pirate-Coast, is a four-hundred mile territory extending from the southern frontier of Qatar to the boundary of the sultanate of Muscat and Oman. It comprises seven thinly populated shaykhdoms with a large bedouin population. Qatar is a thumb-shaped peninsula projecting into the Persian Gulf. Its development from 1940 onward resulted from the exploitation of oil, in which it exceeds Bahrain. Of its estimated 40,000 population, 10,000 are pastoral. Rain in sun-baked Qatar and the Trucial States is scanty and capricious, averaging about three inches per year.

In 1959 Qatar's ruler received close to $50,000,000 as his half of the earnings of the Eastern Petroleum Company, a subsidiary of the Iraq Petroleum Company. This put the per-capita income in competition with that of Kuwait for the highest position in the Persian Gulf area. Part of the income is deposited in a reserve fund, which assumes added importance from the fact that at the present rate of production Qatar, like near-by Bahrain, is likely to run out of oil in twenty-five years. Bahrain has international commerce, but Qatar has no alternative sources of income. Qataris belong to the same school of theology as Saudis, but—thanks to British influence—do not enforce Wahhabi law with the same rigidity. Public school education for girls in the shaykdom began earlier than in the kingdom.

The seven states are termed Trucial because of the truce and other agreements binding them to Great Britain. These agreements, effected in the course of the nineteenth century, bound them to curb piracy, slave trade, and all hostile acts at sea. The estimated population is eighty thousand. Ruling shaykhs exercise absolute authority over their subjects. Their relations with each other, as well as with foreign states, are administered by the protecting power. In contrast to other territories in the neighborhood, no oil in commercial quantities has thus far been unearthed. Consequently no sudden developments have been experienced.

ARABIAN OIL

The man to locate the site of the first productive oil well in an Arab land other than Iraq was an American geologist in the employ of Standard Oil Company of California. This was in Bahrain, where oil was brought to light on June 1, 1932. The discovery encouraged this company to seek a concession in Saudi Arabia, where oil in commercial quantities was found in 1938. Kuwait followed in the same year; then came Qatar.

No one in the early 1930's could have foreseen the far-reaching effect of the discovery of this strategic resource. Desert lands which had been little known suddenly jumped to the center of world attention, not only the world of finance but of politics, too. Gradually the site of the major oil product shifted from the Caribbean to the Persian Gulf. Since then more private American dollars have been invested in the area than in any other single foreign activity. In twenty years the

Near East became the world's largest oil reservoir, having an estimated 174,000,000,000 barrels of reserves, against 40,000,000,000 barrels in North America. Between 1948 and 1959 the revenues of Near Eastern governments from oil operations increased from about $1,000,000,000 to about $1,250,000,000. This billion-dollar income is expected to double in the foreseeable future as the area is called upon to supply about a half of the free world's demand for liquid fuel, natural gas resources, and other petroleum products which still remain untapped. The proved reserves of Kuwait alone, now considered the richest oilfield in the world, exceed all those of the United States. Oil in Kuwait is more plentiful than fresh water; a gallon of distilled oil is not much more expensive than one of distilled water.

The leading company is the Arabian American Oil Company operating in Saudi Arabia and now jointly owned by Standard of California, Texas Oil Company, Standard Oil of New Jersey, and Socony Vacuum. Its product in 1958 totalled 49,339,605 metric tons. Its payments to the government in 1957, roughly half of its income, amounted to approximately $323,400,000, about 90 per cent of the entire state revenue. An up-to-date refinery at Ras al-Tannurah was built in 1945 and a Trans-Arabian Pipeline (Tapline) to Sidon on the Mediterranean was completed five years later. The Kuwait Oil Company, jointly owned by the British Petroleum Company (formerly Anglo-Iranian) and Gulf Oil Corporation, had an even more spectacular development. In April 1953, when oil operations in Iran were temporarily suspended, the Kuwait production began to exceed the Saudi Arabian. Kuwait ranks presently as the fourth largest oil-producing field in the world. Its income is distributed through a development program involving schools, hospitals, asphalted roads, and the construction of low cost housing. In proportion to the population the revenue is perhaps the highest in the world.

Of all Near Eastern lands Kuwait comes nearest to being a welfare state. A child of Kuwaiti parents is entitled to free tuition from kindergarten to secondary or technical school and to free books, clothing, and food. He may even continue his studies abroad on the same basis. An unemployed Kuwaiti is, with his dependents, supported by the state. A resident of the country (the immigrants from Iran, Iraq, and other Arab lands perhaps equal the natives in number) can hardly find a private physician to whom a fee would be due or a public pharmacist from whom he could buy a drug, all such services being offered by the state. A number of the teachers and physicians are Palestinians and Egyptians.

The effect of such a sudden and overwhelming increase in wealth and on the society and economy of a community psychologically unprepared to receive it cannot yet be evaluated. It generated new and difficult problems which are still unsolved. While in the past the ruling class was the one to benefit largely from the new resource, seepage to the lower strata is progressing. The standard of living in the oil producing Arab countries has become appreciably higher than that in the other Arab lands. Improvement is noticeable in the means of communication, facilities for education, and sanitary conditions. Oil has served to introduce that part of the Arab world to the West and to establish close cultural relations.

BOOKS TO READ

Armstrong, H. C., *Lord of Arabia* (London, 1938).

Caroe, Olaf, *Wells of Power* (London, 1951).

Dickson, H. R. P., *The Arab of the Desert* (London, 1949).

Hazard, Harry W., ed., *Eastern Arabia* (New Haven, 1956); *Southern Arabia* (New Haven, 1956).

Lawrence, T. E., *Revolt in the Desert* (New York, 1927).

Longrigg, Stephen H., *Oil in the Middle East* (London and New York, 1954).

Lenczowski, George, *The Middle East in World Affairs* 2nd. ed. (Ithaca, 1956).

Mikesell, Raymond F. and Hollis B. Chenery, *Arabian Oil* (Chapel Hill, 1949).

Philby, H. St. John B., *Arabia of the Wahhabis* (London, 1928); *Arabia* (London, 1930).

Sanger, Richard H., *The Arabian Peninsula* (Ithaca, 1954).

Williams, Kenneth, *Ibn Sa'ud* (London, 1933).

XXXIV *The Arab Crescent and the West: Modernization*

I N SAUDI ARABIA, we have learned, the historical double theme for the last century and a half has been Wahhabism and oil; in eastern Arabia, it has been Great Britain and oil; but in the Arab Crescent the one theme under which most of the meaningful events of the period may be directly or indirectly grouped has been the impact of the West with its two ultimate consequences: nationalism and democracy. Since its formative period Arab culture, in all its political, economic, social and intellectual aspects, did not undergo such radical changes as it has experienced in the nineteenth and twentieth centuries. Indeed, the chain reaction generated by the inflow of new ideas and the introduction of institutions from Western Europe and later from the United States has not yet ceased. Of the lands of the Crescent only Iraq has thus far been richly productive of oil.

The story of the impact had early beginnings in medieval times but contact between the two cultures then was sporadic. It was not until the 1820's in Lebanon under Bashir II and in the 1830's in Syria under Ibrahim Pasha that the impact assumed serious proportions and became continuous. Unlike other areas in the Near East the impact was first cultural and was initiated by Western enterprise, its agents being Christian missionaries, first Catholic then Protestant. In Turkey the introduction to Western culture was prompted by military-political considerations; in Saudi Arabia by economic relations; in Egypt by political and economic through loans, concessions, and subjecting the means of communication to European control. In Syria-Lebanon-Palestine, however, the approach was through schools and other educational institutions.

Lebanon provided the locale. Its salubrious mountainous climate, autonomous government, accessibility by sea and preponderance of Christian population with their tradition of tolerance and freedom were the factors determining its choice. The Holy Land, with its historic background and religious associations, offered faint competition.　The Lebanese were the most responsive to cultural influences emanating from the West.　Their land had been oriented in that direction from its earliest days, and it soon developed into a center of radiation to neighboring lands.

CATHOLIC ACTIVITY

Catholic missionary activity in the area may be said to have had its inception as early as the Crusading period.　Convinced of the futility of force as a means for winning Moslems, internationally-minded Christians then began to think in terms of peaceful devices.　A friar order, founded (1154) by a Crusader on the Carmel, whence it took its name, spread into the West, secured papal endorsement in 1226 and established centers of activity in Damascus and Tripoli.　Carmelite legend associates the foundation of the order with Elijah and Elisha, both of whom were "monks."　Franciscans followed the Carmelites.　The disciples of St. Francis of Assissi landed in Acre in 1219, the year he visited Cairo, and started operations.　By the nineteenth century they could claim eleven convents and seven parishes scattered between Tyre and Aleppo.　For centuries after 1328, Franciscans held the "custody" of the Holy Sepulcher and the Church of Nativity.　Capuchins were stationed in Lebanon in 1627 and found a patron in its enlightened and tolerant Druze amir Fakhr-al-Din II.　He was allegedly baptized by his Capuchin physician.[1]　If there is a question about Fakhr's conversion to Christianity, there is none about the conversion of his late Shihabi successors,[2] particularly the great Bashir II.　The Capuchins today have their principal center in Beirut, where their church stands conspicuously in the heart of the town.

The Jesuits, destined to become the most effective channel for transmitting French culture, appeared on the scene later.　In Mount Lebanon they found ready collaborators in the Maronites.　In 1734 in cooperation with a priest and former student of the Maronite College at Rome,[3] they founded the Ayn Turah academy, the first modern European-style school in the Arab Crescent.　This was followed (1848) by a seminary at another Lebanese village, Ghazir, which was later moved to Beirut to serve as a start for their celebrated university.　In 1774, when their order was suppressed by papal authority, the educational work continued under Lazarists.　The Jesuits returned with renewed vigor under Bashir II and Ibrahim Pasha.

[1] See above, pp. 451-2.
[2] Consult above, p. 452.
[3] Cf. above, p. 453.

Beginning in the 1840's schools for girls, orphanages. and other charitable institutions were founded by Sisters of St. Joseph of Marseille, Sisters of Nazareth of Lyon, and other orders. Beirut, Sidon, Tyre, Nazareth and other towns were the beneficiaries. The Nazareth school at Beirut is today one of the most flourishing in that city of learning. In 1853 an order of indigenous nuns was founded on the French model. Its educational work now extends into a number of towns and villages in Lebanon and Syria.

PROTESTANT ACTIVITY

The latter part of the long reign of Bashir II (1788-1840) was a crucial period in the political and cultural history of Lebanon. In it the Catholic missions were firmly established and the Protestant missions were introduced to find permanent lodging.

It was July 1823 when the first American missionary. Pliny Fisk, landed in Beirut. He was sent from Boston, by the American Board of Commissioners for Foreign Missions, with a companion who took a post at Jerusalem. The work in Palestine was later taken over by the Church Missionary Society of England. These two pioneers were followed by others—teachers, social workers, nurses and physicians. By way of implementation primary and secondary schools for boys and girls were planted not only in such leading towns as Beirut, Tripoli, Sidon and Zahlah but in such mountain villages as Suq al-Gharb and Abayh. Between 1834 and 1860 more than thirty-three such schools were founded by Americans in Syria-Lebanon. Although the original aim was not to found a new sect, converts—mainly from the Greek Orthodox community—were organized into the Syrian Evangelical Church in 1848. Syria then geographically included Lebanon and Palestine. Two years later the enlightened sultan Abd-al-Majid in an imperial decree recognized, through the influence of England, Protestants as one of the legal religious bodies in the empire. In 1958 the American Mission as such ceased to exist. More strictly, in recognition of the rising tide of nationalism, it was incorporated into the Evangelical Church of Syria and Lebanon. The national church has assumed administrative responsibility for missionaries and indigenous churches. Until then and since 1871 missionary work had been in the hands of the Presbyterian Board of Foreign Missions with headquarters in New York. Its emphasis has been shifting from the religious to the broad cultural.

If the reign of Bashir II and his alliance with Ibrahim Pasha marked the first stage in the development of Western cultural penetration, the civil disturbances culminating in the massacre of 1860[4] ushered in the second stage. The aroused sympathy and interest of Christian Europe found practical expression in orphanages, dispensaries, boarding schools, and other benevolent institutions which became a permanent feature of the land. Other institutions were added later. Before the year of the massacre was over Beirut witnessed the founding, by the newly organized British Syrian Mission, of a training teachers' college for girls, and Sidon saw the founding of a center for hospital and orphanage work by the Prussian Deaconesses of Kaiserwerth. The British school is still turning out qualified teachers, and the Deaconesses' center, transferred to Beirut, served as the hospital of the medical school of the Syrian Protestant College, known since 1920 as the American University of Beirut. Beirut became the site of another modern school for girls, opened by Americans in 1862, and of a junior college for women, known since 1924 as the Beirut College for Women.

Later noteworthy institutions of pioneering character were an insane asylum and a tuberculosis sanitarium. The Lebanon Hospital for Mental and Nervous Disorders was started in two houses in a Beirut suburb (al-Asfuriyah, 1897) by a German Swiss, Theophilus Waldmeier. Today it occupies twenty-five buildings. Waldmeier had been associated with the Society of Friends (British) that had entered Lebanon twenty years earlier and founded a still-flourishing boarding school for boys and girls at Brummana. The Society of Friends (American) today operates chiefly in Palestine, mainly a British field. In Jerusalem an Anglican bishopric was first established in 1842; its titular was for a time alternately English and German. In the course of time all large Protestant missionary societies were represented in the Near East, all using the same techniques for delivering their message: educational institutions, distribution of religious literature, dispensaries and other medical means, and charitable means.

Until the end of the nineteenth century close confinement, at times with chains or manacles, was the classical treatment for the mentally ill. Christians sent their insane to a cell in a secluded monastery where prayers would help exorcise the possessing evil spirit. The tuberculosis sanitarium was established near Juniyah north of Beirut by a member of an American missionary family, Dr. Mary Eddy, reputedly the first licensed woman practitioner in the Ottoman Empire. Since then the institution has moved to a higher village in Lebanon. For decades these two institutions remained the only places where up-to-date treatment could be administered. They attracted patients from even out-

---

[4] Treated above, pp 454-5

side Arab lands. In 1948 the first nursing school for psychiatric nursing was added to the Asfuriyah hospital.

THE PRINTING PRESS

To further implement the educational process, the American Mission moved their Arabic printing press from Malta to Beirut in 1834. It is still in operation. The Jesuits matched it, on the other side of the city, with their Imprimerie Catholique, today one of the best equipped publishing establishments in the Arab East. Prior to this time Lebanon had had printing machines with movable type, but they were primitive. A Syrian deacon in the Greek Catholic Church, Abdullah Zakhir, had introduced (1733) such a machine from Aleppo. The ancestry of the Aleppo press, established in 1702 by a Christian patriarch, may go back through Wallachia (now Rumania) to Italy. There, in 1514, an Arabic font was cast for the first time under papal auspices in the interest of the propagation of the faith. Its first product was a book of prayers of which only four known copies have survied. As early as 1610 a Maronite monastery in Lebanon owned a press which could produce Arabic works, but in Syriac characters. Throughout this early development of printing the motivation was entirely religious. This may help to explain the tardiness of Moslems—with their excessive veneration to the word of God as handwritten in the Koran—in adopting the new invention. Even today Moslems in general and Arabs in particular refrain from publishing their holy book by other than multigraphic or lithographic processes. Kemalist Turks provided the exception in printing as well as in translating it.

Both Jesuit and American Mission presses in Beirut made their first major project the translation of the Bible into what may be termed neo-classical Arabic, comprehensible to the layman and nevertheless correct in grammar. Until then the only Arabic versions were unattractive and scarce. They were reprints from a 1571 edition published by the Vatican.

The Protestant version, of which the New Testament was published in 1860 and the Old Testament in 1865, was done from the original languages by Eli Smith, a graduate of Yale, and Cornelius Van Dyck in collaboration with three local scholars. Van Dyck—a physician, linguist, mathematician, and scientist—was one of the most respected and beloved of the missionaries. Two of these three, Butrus al-Bustani and Nasif al-Yaziji, were Christians, and one, Yusuf al-Asir, a Moslem. Later revised, this translation still enjoys wide vogue wherever Arabic is used. The American Bible Society in New York has borne the cost

FIRST PAGE OF *al-Sawa'i* (BOOK OF HOURS). This is the first Arabic book to be printed. It is dated 1514 from Fano, Italy.

of its printing. Nasif al-Yaziji's son, Ibrahim, collaborated in the Catholic translation, which used the Vulgate.

TWO UNIVERSITIES

American educational effort culminated in the founding (1866) of the college known (since 1920) as the American University of Beirut. The Jesuits matched it fifteen years later with the Université Saint-Joseph. Educational rivalry was therewith raised to the highest level. Both institutions have continued to meet the demand for an education

COLLEGE HALL, AMERICAN UNIVERSITY OF BEIRUT   Oldest building on the campus, first occupied in 1873.

and culture; both have served as nurseries for the earliest scientific thinkers and leaders of the area. Less conspicuous but no less important has been the army of teachers, civil servants and professionals who have labored in all sectors of the Near East and contributed their share in improving them. The American University, chartered in the State of New York, is today under a self-governing board of trustees in New York City. Considered the most influential American institution of learning outside the United States this university counted in 1959 about 9000 living graduates, of whom 2250 resided in the land of its location, 5500 in the rest of the Near East and 1250 in other parts of the world. In 1924 the university became coeducational. It registered in the autumn of 1959, 2661 students, of whom 1726 were in the school of arts and sciences, and the rest in the schools of medicine, pharmacy, nursing, public health, engineering, and agriculture. Since old Ottoman laws forbade dissection of cadavers and Moslems in general frowned on it, the early medical professors had to rob graves under cover of darkness and smuggle corpses on donkey-back. At its charter meeting in San Francisco (1945) the United Nations had thirty graduates of this university among its delegates; since then this world organization has included in its membership more delegates trained in Beirut University than in any other university anywhere.

St. Joseph University also maintains schools of liberal arts, medicine, pharmacy, engineering. In addition, it has colleges of theology, dentistry and law. While administered by Jesuits, it receives an annual subsidy from the French ministry of education. Some of its schools are patronized by the University of Lyon. All Catholic missions in the Near East were considered under the official protection of France.

Other noteworthy American institutions in this field are the American University at Cairo, which since 1921 has maintained a distinguished school of Oriental studies; the Assiut College (junior) in Upper Egypt, where most pastors of the Coptic Evangelical Church as well as many professional men and government employees had their early training; and Aleppo College, organized as a junior one in 1937.

As the wave of new ideas splashed on the eastern shore of the Mediterranean, Iraq remained in backwater. Its schools of Najaf and Karbala, a Gibraltar of medievalism, continued to attract students from all the Shiite world and intellectually dominate the local scene. Latin missionary work in Persia and Syria, among Nestorians, Armenians, and Jacobites naturally affected Christian Iraqis. As early as 1663 a Syrian Uniat Church was organized and later (1830) recognized by the Porte. Another Uniat community, the Chaldean, was established in 1552; its patriarch of Babylon chose Mosul for his residence. Carmelite and Dominican missions established stations, with schools and dispensaries at Mosul and Baghdad. They also established a printing press at Baghdad mainly for work among Uniats. The Jesuits entered the capital city later (1932) and founded a secondary school which opened its door to all faiths. This was preceded by an American mission secondary school at Basra which was also patronized by Moslem pupils. Southern Iraq benefited from Protestant work in the Persian Gulf area organized in 1889, when the American Arabian Mission opened stations with schools and hospitals at Bahrain and Muscat. Five years later the Reformed (Dutch) Church in America adopted the earlier missionary work including that at Basra. The Church Missionary Society was mostly Protestants, almost entirely converts from Christian communities in the two large cities of Baghdad and Mosul.

But the bulk of the Iraq population, Sunnite and Shiite, remained untouched. Its schools were for a time impervious to modern scientific knowledge and critical approach. A limited number of young men had a glimpse of Western culture through the back door of Constantinople where they had military training. But military training is not exactly liberal, nor conducive to the liberation of the recipient from the treble-shackle of ignorance, prejudice, and provincialism. The father of the first Shiite student to seek education at the American University of Beirut after the first World War had first to solicit an opinion from the spiritual head of his community. It was justified on the ground that such education would prepare the young man to combat Christianity more effectively. As it turned out Fadil al-Jamali continued his higher education in the United States, married an American girl, rose to the highest position in the government of his country, the premiership. Essentially because of his espousal of the Western cause, he was jailed under death sentence by the regime which came to power July 1958 but pardoned and released three years later.

Measured in terms of dollars, American investment in and contribution to Near Eastern education from 1820 to 1959 is second only to American investment in oil. It is estimated at about four hundred million dollars. Today from Constantinople to Mosul and from Bahrain to Assiut some thirteen thousand students are enrolled in American institutions of higher learning—liberal and professional. More than that number are registered in primary and secondary schools. Some of these institutions, like that of Suq al-Gharb, have passed into indigenous hands; others, like the American University of Beirut, have a faculty composed mostly of its own graduates, but the approach and the technique remain American.

INTELLECTUAL RENAISSANCE

As the eighteenth century passed into the nineteenth, the educational institutions of the Arab East—whether governmental or religious—were till in the traditional, conventional pattern, mirroring the stagnant culture of the age. The society they served was living in the past and its educators were so overawed with respect for their heritage that they felt no urge to venture onto new paths. The forty-five madrasahs (theological schools) in Aleppo and the many others in Damascus, as well as the more numerous congregational mosque schools in both cities, mentioned by an eighteenth century Syrian scholar, did not differ

radically in their curricula and methods of instruction from their antecedents in the twelfth century.[5]   They in general practiced the educational ritual of the past with little regard for the standards of its high
priests.   The late standards were degenerate and artificial, putting
premium on style rather than content.

Throughout the eighteenth century literary productions displayed
the characteristic feature of a decadent intellectuality: concentration on
scholasticism and theology, lack of originality, and an exaggerated sense
of complacency.   Egypt was especially self-centered; its sons rarely
traveled and its shaykhs monopolized intellectual output.   Besides such
scholars, Syria and Iraq maintained clerks and secretaries who did
editorial work and shared in poetical and belletrist composition.   Support for educational institutions everywhere continued to come from
endowments of lands and buildings established by generations of pious
believers.   Ottoman sultans made it a practice to supplement the income from endowments with contributions from state revenues.   The
practice of medicine, like other crafts, was still hereditary.   Its art and
science were a curious blend of ancient Greek science, Moslem Prophetic tradition, astrology, and magic.   Iraq was in an even less favored
position, having been subjected to numerous invasions of Mongols and
conquests by Persians.   A limited number of pupils pursued their
higher studies at al-Azhar, the two Harams (Mecca and Medina), and
Constantinople, all in the theological category.

In response to the new stimuli native schools on the Western model
began to appear after 1860.   In the absence of adequate Arabic texts
most of them used French or English as the language of instruction in
the sciences.   In 1864 Beirut became the seat of such a secondary
school established by the Greek Catholic patriarchate: This was followed by a Greek Orthodox school and in 1874 by a Maronite one.
All three are still flourishing.   Three years before the end of the century the same city saw the foundation of another such school by an
Azharite shaykh.

Concurrently literary and scientific societies, drawing their inspiration
from and patterned on Western societies, were organized.   One, the
Syrian Literary Society (al-Jam'iyah al-Ilmiyah al-Suriyah), claimed
Christian, Moslem and Druze members, residents of Beirut as well as
Lebanese and Syrian emigrants in Cairo, Constantinople, and other
cities.   Its monthly bulletin included papers on literary, scientific, industrial, and agricultural subjects, representing a unique collective
effort of learned men of this time in the Ottoman Empire.   It was in a

---

[5] Cf. above, pp. 270-71.

secret session of this society held at Beirut in 1868 that a twenty-one year-old poet, Ibrahim al-Yaziji, recited original verses which, transmitted by word of mouth, incited Arabs to rise against their oppressors, thus sounding the first clarion call to Arab nationalism and independence.

A native pioneer in what may be termed the modern school was Butrus al-Bustani (1819-1883), who was born in a Maronite Lebanese village and educated at Ayn Waraqah. He became an associate of American missionaries from whom he learned Hebrew and Greek—to assist him in the Bible translation—in addition to English. Al-Bustani founded in Abayh a school, later incorporated with the Syrian Protestant College; edited in Beirut one newspaper and three periodicals; authored textbooks in grammar and mathematics that deviated from old patterns and are still in use; and compiled six volumes of an encyclopedia which, until a few years ago, was the only work of its kind.

Two years before al-Bustani issued his newspaper, a fellow countryman, Khalil al-Khuri, had founded in Beirut (1858) what may be identified as the first real Arabic newspaper in the world. This *Hadiqat al-Akhbar* (orchard of news) was preceded by a journal published (1854) in Constantinople by an Aleppine and by the government organ of Muhammad Ali.[6] Iraq had an analogous publication, *al-Zawra* (1870), influenced by Midhat Pasha. Soon *al-Hadiqah* had many sisters, mostly in Beirut and Cairo, with editors versed in one or more European language. They played a significant early role in popularizing knowledge and spreading news about the world outside. By 1892 Beirut had seen the birth of twenty eight papers and periodicals of which sixteen had suspended publication or moved to Cairo. In the decade beginning 1904 the number of newspapers in Lebanon rose from 29 to 168 and in Syria from 3 to 87. Those early publications emphasized literary and scientific articles and news of the world; local politics was, of course, taboo. For a time they provided almost the only opportunity for the bright and talented of the rising generation of literati. By the early twentieth century, Lebanese emigrants had carried printing presses and Arabic papers to the many lands of their adoption.[7]

Egypt after 1882 provided a more congenial climate for intellectual activity. To it was moved in 1885 a learned magazine, the first of its kind, founded by two early graduates of the American University of Beirut, Yaqub Sarruf and Faris Nimr. Rich in translations from

[6] Cited above, p. 432.
[7] Treated later, pp. 493-4.

European languages and well edited, *al-Muqtataf* (choice pieces) developed into a sort of extension school for modern scientific and literary learning. For a long time during its seventy-six-year career it had no rival in the Arabic world. The two learned editors of the journal also published a newspaper *al-Muqattam* (1889-1952), which at the turn of the century commanded the widest distribution of any Arabic daily. Its first rival, *al-Ahram* (the pyramids), was likewise founded (1875) by two Lebanese scholars, Salim and Bisharah Taqla, who were of French-native education. *Al-Ahram* introduced modern methods of journalism and printing. It also established bureaus or planted correspondents in the leading cities of Western Asia, North Africa, Europe and America. It is still a leader in its field. *Al-Muqtataf* had a contemporary in *al-Hilal* (the crescent), now (1959) in its sixty-seventh year. It was also founded by a former student of the American University of Beirut, Jurji Zaydan. Zaydan was not only the first critical historian in the Arab world but the father of the historical novel. New editions of his history of Moslem civilization and history of Arabic literature appeared as late as the 1950's.

LITERARY ACTIVITY

Alongside the new types of scholarship, journalism and historiography, there arose a new type of poetry. Its authors strove to free themselves from the shackles of the past which lay even more heavily on them than on prose writers. In due course new genres sprang up including novels, short stories and dramatic compositions with new themes, new styles, and a different outlook on life. Dependence on European models was clear. The first drama was presented in 1848 by a Sidon-born writer, Marun al-Naqqash, who had journeyed in Italy and who used a room in his home as a theater. The title *al-Bakhil* (the miser) betrays relationship to Molière's *L'Avare*. Two years later al-Naqqash presented another play *Harun al-Rashid*. For an emblem for his theater and actors Marun chose the cedar tree, which in 1943 was adopted as the emblem of the Lebanese Republic. There was opposition to the theater on the familiar grounds of its corrupting the youth's morality; but the art was given an enduring boost, especially in Moslem eyes, when Khedive Ismail built at Cairo the Opera House (1869).[8] By 1915 the tongue of the Arabs was in possession of no less than 900 dramatic pieces, some translations but mostly originals. The intuitive, imaginative element in European romanticism rather than the rationalist element in its literatures was the one congenial to Arab

---

[8] Above, p. 438.

borrowers. French literature—a Mediterranean product—exercised a larger measure of fascination on Arab writers than "cold" Anglo-Saxon literature. Long before such names as Shakespeare and Milton, Goethe and Whitman were heard in the literary circles of the Near East, the names of Corneille, Hugo, and Lamartine had become familiar.

For centuries Moslem Arabs had generally regarded Western Europe as a land of barbarians from which the world of Islam had nothing to learn. No effort whatsoever was made to study a European language; in fact such study was deprecated. Ibn-Khaldun, one of the greatest minds Islam has ever produced, argued magisterially that the acquisition of a foreign language is a hindrance to the knowledge of good Arabic. The literature, like any other thing living in indifference to forms not of its creation, ran the risk of ultimate paralysis. In the judgment of these authors as in that of an earlier writer, there was no new thing under the sun.[9]

Under Ottoman domination the literary class had lost whatever was left from Mamluk days of intellectual curiosity and of sensitiveness to new ideas. In response to the new stimuli, however, a radical change in outlook came about, necessitating a change in language. And Arabic again did it! Precisely a thousand years earlier the language of the Koran and poetry responded to the challenge of philosophical and scientific translations from Greek and yielded adequate material. Confronted with a parallel problem, modern European tongues had no alternative but to resort to Greek and Latin to express modern scientific concepts. But Arabic, too proud to borrow except terms phonetically harmonious and morphologically assimilable, offered from its triconsonantal verb roots the raw material from which new words could be coined to convey with precision up-to-date concepts in science, philosophy, and art. Without undue strain it served as a hospitable host to a myriad of new thoughts that sought admission into the minds of its users. Arab minds, like other minds, once stretched by new ideas refused to recoil to old dimensions. By the early twentieth century the intellectual renaissance of the Arab East had reached dimensions that remind us of the European renaissance in the early sixteenth.

STRAIN AND CONFLICT

The intrusion of new ideas—religious, political, scientific, and socio-economic—was bound to generate conflict between the old and the new. The conflict went through all the stages characteristic of the confrontation of one culture with a less highly developed one. Individual strands

[9] Ecc. 1:9.

of the encroaching culture, rather than the whole, are first admitted by the host culture.   Once a strand is admitted it invites other strands. The penetrative force of each is normally in inverse proportion to its value: An ideological strand is apt to penetrate faster and farther than a political one, the political faster than the religious.   Economic change involves less emotion and consequently less strain than social change, but these involve both less emotion and less strain than religious change.   Giving up camel riding in favor of cadillac riding constitutes less of a problem than giving up loyalty to a tribe or a church in favor of another social organization or a religious denomination.   In Baghdad of Harun and al-Mamun, when Arabs first borrowed generously from Greek sources, they could pick and choose without imperiling the entire structure of their society.   They borrowed only philosophic, scientific, and artistic ideas.   Islam then was at its peak.   It entertained a feeling of superiority vis-à-vis the then decadent Greek culture. But the reverse was true when the West made its impact.

When the Arab economy confronted the industrialized Western European economy, it was at a decided disadvantage.   Arab economic activity was almost entirely limited to the small, single, independent institutions based on handwork and crude machinery.   Agriculture, the dominant activity was largely of the subsistence variety.   A typical farmer produced a sufficiency for his family use, as the typical craftsman produced enough for his village.   Urban settlements were still small.   The handloom stood in the place of the factory.   Partnership in business enterprises was usually restricted to members of the same family.   The onslaught of wholesale, technological products on such an economy was indeed devastating.   Before the flow of factory-produced textiles from Manchester and machine-made home articles from Paris and other centers of industry in Europe the local market stood helpless.   Town and village handicraft dwindled if they did not vanish.   An economic adjustment in trade and industry was necessitated and in turn necessitaed an adjustment in the distribution of the population.   Urban settlements offered new and richer opportunities for work and education and were immediately augmented.   Migration from the village to the city continued well into the twentieth century.

A new class appeared, it included the new type of businessmen and Western-educated lawyers, physicians, teachers, and other professionals. It lodged itself as a middle class between the traditional group of government officials, landowners, aristocrats, and ecclesiasts and the underprivileged class of manual laborers and soil tillers.   Thus was the gap widened between the high and the low, the rich and the poor.   The wider the gap grew the greater was the source of dissatisfaction.   In its early stages this middle class was recruited mainly from minorities, but it was later augmented from the majority group and it gathered into its hands the forces of control in the society not excluding the political.

Movement of goods and men necessitates improvement in means of communication and transportation. Even before the epoch-making opening of the Suez Canal, a steamship company in England had established regular service (1836) with Egypt and Lebanon.[10] French, Austrian and Italian companies followed. The first record of a ship flying the United States flag entering the Beirut harbor was of a chartered vessel, *The Pilgrim,* which arrived in 1832 under a twenty-nine-year-old seafaring American, George C. De Kay. In its internal and external communications, Egypt[11] developed faster than the countries on the Eastern Mediterranean seaboard. Iraq trudged behind. In 1863 the Beirut-Damascus highway, still the main artery between the two capital cities, was completed by a French company. From this trunk line paved roads later radiated into the remotest villages of Lebanon. Before the end of the century another French company had opened the Beirut-Damascus railway.[12]

Iraq enjoyed no improved facilities of communication until the first decades of the twentieth century. The first major project was the Baghdad Railway.[13] The British army of occupation expanded and modernized the Basra port (1916). From it extended paved roads and light railways, well protected against the ever-threatening floods. River channels were cleared or straightened. Roads were fitted for heavy mechanical transport on a large scale. Airports were later created and Iraq took its rightful place as a link in the East-West chain of communication.

The structure of the social order was not the only institution to be altered by the creation of a middle class; the structure of the social unit, the family, was also changed. The Arab family organization had remained patriarchal and endogamous since biblical days. Three consecutive generations lived under the same roof and under the tutelage of the senior member of the family, usually the grandfather. When married, girls lost their membership in the ancestral family and acquired membership in their husbands' families. All family property was held by the patriarch as a joint possession. Marriages were normally arranged by parents. Traces of endogamy are embedded in "my cousin" (*ibnat 'ammi*), still applied by a husband to his wife. The common

[10] Cf. above, p. 454.
[11] Cf. above, p. 435.
[12] Cf. above, p. 455.
[13] Discussed above, p. 347.

word for father-in-law even today is "uncle," no matter how unrelated he may be to the son-in-law.

Family loyalty was one of three dominant forces in community life, the other two being devotion to ancestral religion and attachment to the local soil. The three were interrelated, to an extent interdependent. Disruption in one entailed cracking in the others. In the scale of values "belonging" and conforming stood higher than freedom in individual thought and action. By the opening of the twentieth century Western-style education was beginning to challenge the validity of this scale of values and to wreak havoc on the family institution. Young men and women demanded the privilege of choosing a mate; she or he could be outside the kindred circle. The smaller family unit, the biological, replaced the older expanded family. With the disruption of the family unit, time-honored loyalties and homely virtues were strained to the breaking point.

As the lure of new ideas and the invitation to think and act independently attracted the youth, fear of subversion harassed the old. The improved status of women, entailing new temptations and new perils, aroused special opposition. Religious institutions were by no means immune. As the secular point of view developed, more than religious traditions were questioned. The new view offered rational scientific explanations for happenings in life and nature hitherto considered the exclusive domain of the divine. Religious sanctions began to decline.

Modernization, or Westernization, in the sense of the adoption—with adaptation—by Near Easterners of the up-to-date style of life developed in Western Europe, could not therefore be considered an unmixed blessing. As a process of cultural diffusion, it was all-embracing. The lower classes imitated the upper who had assimilated Western thought and in turn had imitated European ways. As its evil results became more apparent, reaction against it became more widespread and more determined. The ranks of the opposition swelled by recruitment from different categories of the society, as the evils touched all aspects of its life. In addition to the adverse results noted above—the decimation of small productive units in agriculture and industry, the uprooting of the rural population, the breakdown of the inherited system of social values, and the weakening of the religious institutions—there was the effect on the political institutions.[14] Underlying the opposition to Westernism was a creeping feeling of insecurity on the part of the leaders of the established order. They feared that the intruding elements might undermine their ideal of the good life. Three types of persons emerged

---

[14] To be considered later.

with respect to the influences working in the direction of modernity: the traditional, the modernized, and the transitional. The three are still discernible. In the Arabian peninsula the traditional group is preponderant; in Lebanon the modernized is the predominant type. The rest of the Arab countries lie in between.

EMIGRATION

One factor which contributed considerably to the modernization of Lebanon has been emigration.

The bulk of Arabic-speaking emigrants to the four quarters of the world has come from Lebanon. Emigration worked as a safety valve to an overpopulated mountain whose women were more productive than its soil. Besides, the Lebanese, because of their seafaring tradition and Christian background, felt more predisposed to adventure and to feel at home in Europe and America than other Near Easterners. Syria stood next as a source of emigration. Egypt and Iraq offered no considerable quota.

Egypt, itself relatively overpopulated, was in the 1880's and 1890's on the receiving end of the line. Before 1890 Ottoman authorities permitted emigration only there. To Egypt under the British flocked Western-educated Lebanese and Syrians in quest of wider and more remunerative fields for their activity. Interpreters, clerks, government officials, physicians, pharmacists reaped the new harvest not only in the valley of the Nile but in the Anglo Sudan. Literary men founded magazines and newspapers.[15] Emigrants bent on business sought such places as Manchester, Paris and Marseille. In due course merchant settlements flourished in these and other centers of trade and industry. America was discovered as early as the seventies, but that it was the "land of opportunity" was not realized until the nineties. It attracted the less educated and more mundane who, with intellectual baggage as light as their material baggage, flocked with increasing numbers. The Lebanese wave that rolled on the shores of New York and Rio de Janeiro sent splashes into every other country, indeed into almost every city in the two Americas. Australia, New Zealand and West Africa came next. The number of settlers there swelled after the mid-1920's, when the United States imposed quotas on its newcomers. A traveler in such regions as Nigeria and Ghana is struck by the number of streets bearing the name of Lebanon and by road signs reading "Lebanese Quarters." Rare indeed is the Lebanese village which cannot lay claim to at least one American citizen as its

---

[15] Cf. above, pp. 487-8.

son. Contemporary Lebanon speaks of itself as divided into two numerically equal halves: the resident and the emigrant. Syrian and Lebanese Americans, first and second generations, number about a quarter of a million in the United States and a little more in Brazil. A Lebanese government census released in December 1958 makes the Lebanese abroad total 1,250,000, of whom 450,000 (!) live in the United States, 250,000 in Brazil, 150,000 in Argentina and 60,000 in Mexico. Their colonies are primarily commercial colonies. That of São Paulo is both commercial and industrial; it ranks as the wealthiest in that prosperous city.

Pioneer emigrants considered their lands of adoption as of sojourn. They sent home money to be used for building red-roofed houses or purchasing lands for their future use. In most cases these plans did not materialize. Remittances, however, continued to flow to the folks back home and helped boost the economy of the country. In the first World War remittances were responsible for saving numberless lives.[16] Even as late as 1952, twenty-two million dollars, Lebanese government statements claim, were contributed by Lebanese abroad to relatives and friends and to religious, charitable, and educational institutions.

Wherever Arabic-speaking emigrants went, there went with them their cuisine, their churches, and their printing presses. A 1929 census lists 3023 Arabic newspapers and periodicals, extant or extinct in the world. Of these 102 were born in North America, 166 in South America, and 14 in Great Britain. New York boasted a literary circle clustered on Jubran Khalil Jubran (Kahlil Gibran, d. 1931), whose influence was felt wherever Arabic was written. The circle published an organ which survived until the 1950's; Jubran's works have been translated into several European and Asiatic languages. São Paulo had its *al-Usbah al-Andalusiyah* (Andalusian band), whose magazine likewise survived to the 1950's. By their return visits, private correspondence, and publications, emigrants immeasurably enhanced and accelerated the Westernizing movement in Arab lands. They encouraged opposition to Ottoman domination as well as the mandates, meanwhile strengthening the urge for self-government under democratic institutions.

TWO DYNAMIC FORCES

Of all the ideas introduced from the West two stand out among the most dynamic: nationalism and the urge for independence. The two have been interrelated. Their introduction set in motion a chain

---

[16] Cf. above, p. 456.

reaction that promises to continue in operation for generations to come.

Nationalism in the modern sense implies loyalty to a territorially and politically defined unit that transcends all other forms of loyalty —not excluding the denominational. Such a concept could have no roots in Arab tradition or in Islamic ideology which puts spiritual values above economic ones and sets the religious fraternity against the outside world. Modern nationalism is purely secular with predominantly economic ends. Until the second half of the nineteenth century Arabic literature had no adequate phraseology for such terms as nation, nationalism, fatherland (*patrie*), patriotism. French provided the concepts and served as a guide. The French Revolution of 1789 gave birth to the French nation. French nationalism, based on the "rights of man," spread its precepts through the Napoleonic wars eastward. As the armies of Napoleon swept over Europe, they carried with them a newly codified system of laws and new ideals of political equality. In the Balkans, the Greeks, Bulgarians, and Rumanians were indoctrinated before their Ottoman rulers. In its primitive stage the new Ottoman spirit, expressed itself in a nationalist reform movement aiming in vain at modernizing a medieval empire.[17] The Young Turks were equally unsuccessful in their attempt to reconcile a multi-national empire with the requisites of a modern nation-state. The Republic of Mustafa Kemal set high social aims—perhaps too high—which it strove valiantly to attain. This probably accounts for its enduring value.

In Persia nationalist self-consciousness asserted itself in the struggle for freedom from Persian tyranny within and for independence from imperialist pressure without. Even today, after more than half a century of existence, the nationalist spirit there has not set high and clearly-defined social goals. What gives modern nationalism its force is the passion it evokes; the passion is comparable to that evoked by religion or war.

Arab nationalist development took a different course, though like the Turkish and Persian it stemmed from the French. Based on a vague feeling of ethnic relationship, its rise was due not only to Ottoman oppression, but also to resistance to assimilation by Moslem Turks or by Turanians. Until the rise of the Young Turks the main bond between Arabs and Turks was Sunnite Islam personified by its temporal and religious leader the sultan-caliph. The pseudo-ethnic Arab base gave a sense of common identity and an incentive for coordinating activity toward a common goal. Except in Egypt it was not until after the imposition of the mandates that nationalist reaction

[17] See above, pp. 345-6.

against "Western imperialism" became pronounced.[18] It then focused
on a main objective: expelling the intrusive foreign authority.   Even in
the following period of independence, Arab nationalism did not set
sufficiently high social aims.   Nor has it yet articulated or clarified
its new goals and worked out plans for their attainment.   Literary Arab
nationalism had even a less pronounced social message than its political
aspects.   One can search in vain in the writings of the first two or more
generations for a consciousness of responsibility for ameliorating the
poverty, ignorance, and disease under which the masses lived.   Such
themes hardly ever came within the purview of writers.   The reconciliation of nationalism with Islam the religion has not yet been effected.

Before Arab awakening took on political aspects it was purely intellectual.   The distance between the two was not difficult to cover.   As
Arabs realized more fully the might and dimensions of the medieval
empire set up by their ancestors and the volume and quality of the
contribution they had made to science and literature, they felt more
and more the urge to restore that glory and to revive that culture.   The
memory of the past colored the present and spurred action for the
future.   That faint undercover spark struck by a Lebanese youth at
Beirut in 1868[19] had more inflammatory opportunities at Cairo.   There
journalists and literati, mostly Lebanese and Syrian Christians, wielded
pens in behalf of the new idea but they had to wait long for tangible
results.   The Arabi uprising in Egypt[20] was outside this stream.

Thus starting from a theoretical Pan-Arab base and depending upon
a community of language to hold it together, the infant and fragile
movement suffered fragmentation as it encountered local road blocks.
In Egypt opposition to British occupation became the touchstone of
the nationalist spirit, which therewith assumed a provincial aspect.
Egyptian nationalism then and there parted company with Pan-Arab
nationalism.[21]   By the same token Syria under the French mandate
developed a local brand of nationalism, as Iraq developed its in opposition to the British mandate.   This, however, does not imply that Arab
nationalism would have otherwise succeeded in achieving Arab unity.
The main stumbling block has always been local tensions rather than
foreign interference, a fact not readily admitted by Arab politicians
and writers.

The rapid growth of Arab nationalism in the inter-war period synchronized with the decline of internationalism.   Despite the novel

[18] Treated below, pp. 512-13.
[19] See above, pp. 486-7.
[20] Sketched above, pp. 439-40.
[21] Cf. above, p. 441.

machinery provided by the creation of the League of Nations, the early 1920's was the time in which Western imperialism soared to its highest modern peak. It was the time in which the secret agreements among the great powers to parcel out the Ottoman Empire among themselves,[22] and the Balfour declaration favoring a national home for the Jews in Palestine[23] reached their overt development. It was also the time when the mandates were imposed. Perhaps no other period in history heard so much talk of cooperation among nations and saw so little action in that direction.

The urge for independence, a corollary of the nationalist spirit, did not become a moving force until after the first World War. As late as 1913, when the first Arab congress, a six-day one, was held at Paris. Arab demands centered on decentralization and the recognition of Arabic as an official language where it was the mother tongue. Decentralization was the theme of a party (*Hizb al-Lamarkaziyah*), which had risen in Egypt the year before and had secret branches in Syria and Iraq. Another interesting underground organization, named after Qahtan (a legendary ancestor of the Arabs), went one step farther and advocated a dual Turko-Arab empire, on the Austro-Hungarian model, where a form of union between the two peoples could be achieved while remaining separate. The Paris congress was called and chaired by a Christian Lebanese immigrant in France, eleven of its twenty-four delegates were Christians, of whom three were immigrants from the United States. The assumption by the Sharif Husayn of the title of king of the Arabs (1916)[24] made him the rallying focus of the rising movement, despite the fact that his mind was blank so far as modern concepts of nationalism were concerned.

In his revolutionary proclamations Husayn explained his break with the Young Turks on the ground that they had dethroned the shariah and replaced it with constitutionalism and such laws as those which changed the status of women and absolved soldiers from the fast of Ramadan. To him the only lawful state was the Islamic one, a caliphate embracing as large a part of the community as possible. He, of course, aspired for the headship of such a state. His sons Abdullah and Faysal, however, had established in 1915 contacts with the secret societies of Syria and Iraq, particularly the Young Arab Association (*al-Jam'iyah al-Arabiyah al-Fatah*), founded in Paris by seven students. It was this association which first approached Husayn through a special emissary.

[22] See above, pp. 366-7.
[23] Treated later, p. 507.
[24] Referred to above, p. 464.

Turks were then launching their Turkification policy. On November 9, 1917 a joint Anglo-French declaration, emanating from the headquarters of their expeditionary force at Cairo, asserted that the goal envisaged by these two powers was "the complete and final liberation of the peoples who have for so long been oppressed by the Turks, and the setting up of national governments and administrations that shall derive their authority from the free exercise of the initiative and choice of the indigenous populations." This, as well as the doctrine of self-determination enunciated by Woodrow Wilson were taken seriously and literally by the Arabs. As a matter of fact Wilson was more specific in the case of the Arabs. According to his "point twelve," "The non-Turkish nationalities under Turkish rule should be assured an undoubted security of life and an absolute opportunity of autonomous development." As early as October 1914 the British, in return for Arab support against the Ottomans, had committed themselves to a course of emancipating "the Arabs" and recognizing them as an "independent nation." Independence, however, had to await the mandates.

BOOKS TO READ

Antonius, George, *The Arab Awakening,* 4th impression (New York, 1946).

Fisher, Sydney N., ed., *Evolution in the Middle East: Reform, Revolt and Change* (Washington, 1953).

Hourani, A. H., *Minorities in the Arab World* (London, 1947); *Syria and Lebanon* (London, 1946).

Kohn, Hans, *Nationalism: Its Meaning and History* (Princeton, 1955); *Nationalism and Imperialism in the Hither East* (London, 1932); *Western Civilization in the Near East* (London, 1936).

Matthews, Roderic D. and Matta Akrawi, *Education in Arab Countries* (Washington, 1949).

Middle East Institute, *Nationalism in the Middle East* (Washington, 1952); *The Arab Nation: Paths and Obstacles to Fulfillment* (Washington, 1961).

Yale, William, *The Near East: A Modern History* (Ann Arbor, 1958).

Zeine, Zeine N., *Arab-Turkish Relations and the Rise of Arab Nationalism* (Beirut, 1958).

XXXV *The Mandates*

WHILE Syrians and Iraqis were day-dreaming about independence the Allied Powers were agreeing to partition the area in their own interests. Their prime ministers conference at San Remo (April 1920) drew the main lines of the terms to be imposed on Turkey. In the treaty of Sèvres, signed four months later, the sultan's government renounced all claims to non-Turkish territory: Hejaz was recognized as independent, Syria and Lebanon were assigned as mandates to France, Iraq and Palestine with Transjordan to Great Britain—the two powers thereby acknowledged as heirs of the Ottoman Empire. The renunciation of all non-Turkish territories lost as a result of the World War was reaffirmed by the Kemalist government in the Lausanne treaty of July 1923.[1]

The mandate concept was a novel feature in political thought attributed to the initiative of General (Jan C.) Smuts of South Africa and President Wilson. Syria, Lebanon, Palestine, and Iraq were styled class A mandates administered under the League of Nations. The relevant article in the covenant of the League acknowledged such communities as having reached a stage of development where their existence as "independent nations can be provisionally recognized, subject to the rendering of administrative advice and assistance by a mandatory until such time as they are able to stand alone." This made France and Britain trustees. The same thought was reiterated in the act of the mandate—a seemingly noble thought but ignobly executed.

The act itself was rather carelessly drawn. It set no objective criteria for measuring the mandated peoples' capacity for self-government, offered no implementation for the attainment of the professed goal, and failed to specify a time limit for the withdrawal of the mandatory powers. In the British act, acknowledgment was made of the Balfour declaration and the obligation of its implementation. In the French

---

[1] Cf. above, p. 368.

499

act, Syria and Lebanon were included in one document in which an article made French and Arabic official languages, reserving the right of public instruction to Arabic. Of the twenty articles only one—dealing of all things with archeology—is analyzed into sections covering a sixth of the whole text. In both acts insufficient heed is paid to the development of economic sources in the mandated areas.

SYRIA

French administration in Syria was for years entrusted to generals who had won distinction in the World War and to aides drawn from the colonies. To them the mandate was but a version of the Sykes-Picot agreement of 1916.[2] Though the personnel was as unstable in its tenure as the Paris government was, the policy remained the same, proceeding on the assumption that the mandate was to last forever, while the people were determined that it should not.

Even with the best intentions and qualifications, any mandatory power would have found its path bristling with thorny difficulties. Emerging from a calamitous long-drawn-out period of war, the mandated territories were at the lowest ebb in their modern history politically, economically, socially, and spiritually. They had—Lebanon excepted—no experience in self-government, no institutions for self-rule, no tradition of liberal administration, and no effective instrumentalities of democratic procedure. A modern civil service class was conspicuous by its absence. The population included a considerable unruly nomadic element, a peasantry ridden with ignorance and poverty under a still primitive landowning system and methods of farming, and a landlord's class generally lacking in incentive to improve conditions and in the consciousness of social responsibility. As late as 1932 over forty-one per cent of the total population was estimated as illiterate. Besides, Syrians had already openly committed themselves as opposed to the French mandate. This was in the summer of 1919 when an American commission, sent by Wilson to ascertain the wishes of the people, visited the country. Britain, France, and Italy had agreed to be represented on an international commission but failed to cooperate. The commission had gained the impression that Iraq was safe for the British and therefore did not visit the country. But, beginning the following year, the result discredited the source of the commission's information. The commission found the majority of the Lebanese, being Christians and fearful of submergence in a Moslem greater Syria, favorably inclined toward France. It interviewed no British officer in

---

[2] Discussed above, p. 465.

Palestine who believed that the Zionist program could be carried out
except by use of arms.   All thought it would require no less than 50,000
soldiers even to initiate the program.   The American government pi-
geonholed the commission's report, as it ran counter to plans already
declared by her two allies.

First in a series of French high commissioners to Syria and Lebanon
was General Henri Gouraud, one-armed hero of the Marne.   In
December 1919, two months after his arrival in Beirut, his troops
were engaged in fighting dissident Syrians.   On March 11 of the following year a national Syrian congress at Damascus declared for complete independence and proclaimed Faysal king of a greater Syria.
In the following month the supreme council of the Allied Powers
assigned the mandate for Syria to France; the approval of the League
of Nations was made two years later.   On July 28, 1920 Gouraud sent
his troops against the Syrian capital.   The newly crowned king fled and
was the following year installed by the British over the equally improvised throne of Iraq.   This episode is indicative of the jealousies and
rivalries that continued to plague Anglo-French relations in the area.

Free to establish a firm regime, the French then organized the Syrian
territory into three autonomous and loosely federated units centering
on Damascus, Aleppo, and Latakia.   These so-called *états* were later
so shuffled and reshuffled in number and constituency that it made the
people suspect a policy of "divide and rule," especially since two of the
états, that of the Alawites (Latakia) and the new one of the Druzes,
were based on a religious distinction.   Lebanon augmented by the
addition of the maritime coast and the interior plain, both of which
formed parts of it under Mans and Shihabs—was proclaimed on
September 1 Grand Liban and given a separate status.   This Greater
Lebanon became the Lebanese Republic of today.

Repressive measures were taken against Syrian leaders as they
reactivated nationalist societies that had operated underground in the
late Ottoman period.[3]   Such men as Shukri al-Quwatli, future president
of the Syrian Republic, and Faris al-Khuri, its prime minister, were
jailed or deported.   Popular dissatisfaction broke into open revolt in
1925 to 1926, in the course of which Damascus was bombarded twice.
In 1926, a new high commissioner, fifth in a rapid succession, promised
a general amnesty and authorized elections.   The constituent assembly,
elected in April 1928, drafted a constitution which gave no recognition
to the French mandate.   The constitution was rejected and the parliament indefinitely adjourned.   In 1930 the high commissioner himself

[3] Consult above, p. 497.

introduced a constitution making Syria a republic with a five-year-term president elected by the parliament. A new parliament, elected in 1932, was again indefinitely prorogued two years later. The rise to power of the Popular Front Party in France temporarily improved the situation. A Franco-Syrian treaty of friendship and alliance was signed in Paris September 9, 1936, providing the ending of the mandate within three years and pledging the facilitation of Syria's admission to the League of Nations. The Syrian parliament ratified the treaty, but the French government did not submit it to ratification, thus abandoning it entirely. The more liberal British attitude toward Iraq added fuel to a highly inflammable situation. Evidently the French were over-sensitive about the possible effect on the North African situation.

Syria's reaction to the high commissioner's declaration in 1939 that his government had denounced the treaty and intended to reestablish the mandatory regime was obscured by the outbreak of the World War. After France's surrender to the Axis forces and the high commissioner's following of the Vichy regime, both Syria and Lebanon, as detailed in a later paragraph,[4] had to be reoccupied by British and Free French troops. They were thereupon declared independent. Syria's independence was formally recognized in September 1941, but she could not exercise the full privileges pertaining thereto till five years later.

The French could justly point to valuable contributions they made to the welfare of the country and its people. They set up the framework of a modernized government, maintained a certain measure of law and order, improved communications, widened the areas of cultivation. and extended the facilities of modern education. But no due credit was given by the people in view of the accumulating grievances. The charges included the use of the native government as a façade, censorship and espionage, manipulating elections, discouraging the employment of Arabic in favor of French, unduly promoting French commercial interests, depreciating the native currency by tying it to the inflated franc, pitting one party or sect against another, and above all suppressing nationalist feelings. Of no less importance was the psychological factor: resentment on the part of the "natives" at being treated as inferiors by Europeans, whose superiority was acknowledged only in material civilization.

The many highhanded measures were finally topped by the signing with Turkey of an agreement giving Turkey a free hand in the border

[4] P. 504.

sanjak of Alexandretta.   This was done in the face of vehement protests by the Syrian government and people and in violation of the provision of the mandate to safeguard the integrity of the territory entrusted to its care.   The arrangement was the first step leading to the ceding to Turkey by France of the sanjak which was incorporated, under the name of Hatay, by the Turkish Republic.[5]   All this came about in 1939, on the eve of the second World War.

LEBANON

Mandated Lebanon was not as restless as its neighbor.   The first fifteen years or so were a period of peaceful progress.   Some sections of the population demanded the return of the territory to its pre-1920 dimensions.   Syrian strikes, agitations, and uprisings had some repercussion particularly in Moslem quarters, but the situation remained under control.   Lebanon received a larger share of the benefits in the form of improved roads and other means of transportation and of educational facilities.   French investors increased and largely owned and operated the railways, public utilities, and banks.   New concessions and contracts usually went to French concerns or to Lebanese ones with French connections.   Beirut was a special recipient of such benefits.   Lebanon could assimilate a heavier dose of French culture and language.   Its reaction to what the French called their "civilizing mission" was not as violent as Syria's.   Improved conditions were reflected in the decline in emigration despite a striking increase in population.

In 1926, six years after its enlargement and recognition as an entirely separate state, Lebanon was proclaimed a republic, the first in the Arab world.   At the request of the high commissioner, a representative council, drew up a constitution providing for a parliament, chose a president of the republic, and a responsible cabinet.   Though suspended at times by French authorities and amended several times, this constitution of 1926 has remained in force to the present day.   Unlike the constitutions of Lebanon's neighbors it contained no provision for any state religion.   A convention, however, has developed requiring a Maronite president of the republic, a Sunnite prime minister, and a Shiite speaker of the house.

The year 1936 may be considered the watershed in Franco-Lebanese relations.   The failure of the French chamber to ratify the treaty signed then by the president of Lebanon and the high commissioner started the decline.   It was a twenty-five-year treaty of amity and alliance—

[5] Cf. above, p. 372.

similar to the Franco-Syrian one—acknowledging the independence of Lebanon and pledging sponsorship for its admission to the League of Nations. It differed from the other chiefly in allowing the French to maintain armed forces in Lebanon for the duration of the treaty.

The advent of the war blanketed both mandated territories with an atmosphere of calm, hiding currents of discontent. Both countries were put under martial law; all parliamentary procedures were, of course, suspended. The people faced the prospects of a new war with fear and trembling, memories of the preceding war having not been entirely forgotten.

But the second World War turned out to be much kinder than the first. Public health was maintained on a high level, the food situation was alleviated through the activity of the Anglo-American Middle East Supply Center stationed at Cairo, inflation was curbed, and the downward trend of depression stopped. In fact the productivity of both countries was increased and their economies improved, thanks to the demand on food, building material, and other necessities required by the presence of thousands of British and French troops who guarded the area from the Axis.

On the political side the picture was less rosy. After France's collapse (summer of 1940), High Commissioner Gabriel Puaux sided with the Vichy government, received the German commission sent to the area, and closely cooperated with Axis troops. In June of the following year, British and Free French armed forces attacked by sea and land and occupied both countries after some resistance. On May 27, a few days before the assault, Georges Catroux, commander in chief of the Free French troops in the Levant and delegate-general under General de Gaulle, had announced to the Syrian people that he was sent "to end the mandatory regime and to proclaim you free and independent." The United Kingdom government associated itself publicly with "the assurance of independence given by General Catroux on behalf of General de Gaulle to Syria." November 27 has since been celebrated as the Syrian day of independence. On November 26 Catroux proclaimed in the name of his government and its ally Great Britain the termination of the mandate for Lebanon and the independence of the country.

Both statements were taken by the people on their face value. But in Syria no constitutional life was restored until August 1943, when a newly elected chamber chose Shukri al-Quwatli president of the republic. Even then the national government was not able to gain powers and prerogatives pertaining to independence. On April 12, 1945 Syria was admitted to the League of Nations. Twenty days earlier she had become a member of the League of Arab States. The evacuation of French troops was not completed till April 1946.

Lebanon had a harder time. When its chamber elected Bisharah al-Khuri (Khoury) as president of the republic in 1943 and proceeded to delete from the constitution references to the mandate, the new delegate-general of the Free French arrested the president, his prime minister, and other members of the cabinet and sent them to a castle on the frontier. Nothing could have more infuriated the public. Strikes, demonstrations, and disturbances spread and continued for days. Under pressure from within and from without—especially from Lebanese emigrants—France yielded. The exiled officials were returned on November 21 and reinstated the second day, since then celebrated as the national holiday. Lebanon joined the League of Nations and the League of Arab States simultaneously with Syria. A plaque on the Dog River rock commemorates the evacuation of the last French troops December 31, 1946.

IRAQ

Though less developed than either Lebanon or Syria, British-mandated Iraq fared better than both. It was fortunate in passing from a military to a civilian administration early in its career and in having in its administration persons versed in the lore of the people and cognizant of their psychology. These included Miss Gertrude Bell, H. St. John Philby, and High Commissioner Percy Cox. An early experience must have taught the British a lesson: One month after the British government obtained the mandate, tribesmen in the south broke out in an insurrection that spread into the north and was not suppressed until early the next year (1921). The prospect of independence held out by the Allies in the period of war had aroused more nationalistic feeling, nourished by the Syrian example, than expected. The cost to Britain was the lives of over 400 British and Indian troops and an expenditure of £20,000,000, to Iraq 8450 casualties and the loss of more than £400,000 in revenue and by damage to railways.

In March 1921 a Cairo conference called by Colonial Secretary Winston Churchill chose Faysal as king of Iraq. His reception at Baghdad was lukewarm. Faysal had led the Arab forces against the Turks and was a favorite of T. E. Lawrence. Five months later Faysal was crowned at the capital. The king was to be guided by the advice of the high commissioner. The general setup was comparable to that of Egypt at the turn of the twentieth century. The choice turned out to be a happy one. Despite initial local opposition by anti-

Westerns, extreme nationalists, and aspirants to the highest office and in face of difficulties inherent in his anomalous position as king over a mandated country; Faysal, in eleven years, managed to lead his country through the steps toward full sovereignty and the dignity of independence while receiving the benefits of a mandatory power. In October 1922 the council of ministers ratified a twenty-year treaty providing that every royal act was to receive the previous approval of the high commissioner and every ministerial order that of the political adviser. The constitutional assembly, in March 1924, declared Iraq a sovereign state under a hereditary monarch and a responsible system of government. In 1930 a new alliance with Britain provided "full and frank consultation in all matters of foreign affairs for twenty-five years." It also stipulated mutual aid in time of war. Attached to the treaty were annexes giving Britain advantages in matters relating to business, finance, and education. British advisers were to be preferred to others. In October 1932 Iraq qualified as an independent member of the League of Nations. The British high commissioner who had signed the treaty became ambassador.

Iraq prospered in the inter-war period as never before in its modern history, oil being the main reason. By the time political independence was attained, the country was fast becoming economically independent. The first oil concession was given in 1925 to what is now the Iraq Petroleum Company. On the night of October 14, 1927 a gigantic gusher of this precious liquid shot out of an experimental well near Kirkuk a hundred and fifty miles north of Baghdad. The field turned out to be a rich one. Local legend places in Kirkuk the tomb of Daniel, whose book (3:23) relates the story of the "burning fiery furnace." Four years later the company began constructing pipelines to conduct the product to Haifa, Tripoli, and Baniyas on the Mediterranean. The Haifa line was rendered inactive in the course of disturbances marking the rise of Israel. The company also began annual payments of £400,000 against future royalties, fixed at four gold shillings a ton for a twenty-year period. Approximately fifty per cent of the Iraq government revenues accruing from oil royalties enabled it to carry out a sizable development program. Hitherto the principal product of the Iraq soil had been dates, Iraq being one of the foremost date producers of the world. Its crop yields annually 400,000 tons, two-thirds of which are exported. This was the fruit that probably attracted early man to the Tigro-Euphrates valley. It is considered one of the most nutritional products of nature, three pounds of dates supposedly provide the daily calories of a manual laborer. Oil in Kuwait and Bahrain transformed these two countries from centers of pearl fishing to centers of petroleum, but Iraq maintained its leadership in dates while it developed into a leading oil center.

PALESTINE

Palestine was the unhappiest of all. Its mandate, committed to the Balfour declaration, was not recognized by the people, in fact, it was stubbornly resisted throughout its duration. Strikes, demonstrations, riots, disturbances, and insurrections punctuated the period. The three-corner struggle—Arab against British, against Zionists—ended in 1948 with the forced termination of the mandate, the expansion of the amirate of Transjordan, the creation of the state of Israel, and the displacement of a million refugee Arabs, still huddled in camps in adjoining lands and living as wards of the United Nations relief agency.

The mandate for Palestine and Transjordan was assigned—simultaneously with the French mandates—to Great Britain on April 25, 1920. Britain considered Palestine essential for the security of its position at the Suez Canal and in Egypt. The League of Nations approved the mandate on July 24, 1922 on terms set forth in the Balfour declaration, with its ambiguous and contradictory phraseology, but excluded Transjordan from its application. The act of the mandate thereby held the germ of all the troubles that were to ensue. Britain amputated Transjordan and instituted it as an autonomous amirate under Abdullah, son of King Husayn. This declaration, issued in November 1917 in the name of the British minister of foreign affairs, reads:

His Majesty's Government view with favor the establishment in Palestine of a national home for the Jewish people and will use their best endeavours to facilitate the achievement of that object, it being clearly understood that nothing shall be done which may prejudice the civil and religious rights of existing non-Jewish communities in Palestine.

What "national home" precisely meant was not clear. That it could be established without prejudicing the rights of the "non-Jewish communities" was not practicable unless those communities were a minority. At that time the Arabs of Palestine outnumbered the Jews by ten to one—700,000 against 70,000. As a pledge, it conflicted with other pledges given to Arabs and made of the once "promised land" a multi-promised one.

The declaration echoed the thought first formulated in 1896 by a Hungarian-born Viennese journalist, Theodor Herzl, in a pamphlet titled *Der Judenstaat* (the Jewish State). Deeply stirred by the homelessness and the unhappy condition of his people, particularly in Rumania and Russia, Herzl advocated the creation of a Jewish state and organized international congresses at Basel "to establish a publicly and legally assured home in Palestine." He did not insist on Palestine as the only site, but through the ages zealous Jews have never ceased to pray for the return to Zion. The Zionist movement thus fused the religious aspiration with the social need for an asylum from discrimination and the political dignity of a state. The movement soon became world wide.

In response to an article in the act of the mandate, providing for "the cooperation of all Jews who are willing to assist in the establishment of a Jewish national home" the Zionist organization set up the Jewish Agency for Palestine. The agency took it upon itself to promote Jewish immigration, purchase new lands, foster the Hebrew language and culture, and provide for the religious needs of the new community. For years, the agency was headed by Haim Weizmann, who also headed the World Zionist Organization. Born in Russian Poland, Weizmann lectured on biochemistry at Manchester University and was credited with inspiring the Balfour declaration. Under his leadership the two pillars on which the Zionist state was to rise became clearly defined: the "in-gathering" of the Diaspora and the provision of land for their settlement. Thus could the Jews attain a majority and obtain political and economic control. To this end a national fund was set up to which Jews and sympathizers the world over contributed. The Jewish Agency gathered so much power into its hands that it became a government within a government.

The reaction of Palestine Arabs was not slow; but it was disorganized, inadequately supported, and generally ineffective despite the fact that hostility to Zionism was unanimous among the Arabs of Western Asia and North Africa. Local disturbances began early, and the appointment in 1920 of a Jew, Herbert Samuel, as first high commissioner did not allay the growing fear. The constitution promulgated in August 1922 confirmed the dual British policy; made English, Arabic, and Hebrew official languages. This concession was practically the only recognition of the preponderant element in the population. But the Arabs would not cooperate.

One of the first major outbreaks (1928) centered on the Wailing Wall; for the Jews the wall marked the site of Solomon's Temple, but for the Arabs it was the face of the outer wall of their holiest sanctuary in Palestine, third holiest in Sunnite Islam. The tempo of Jewish immigration and colonization reached its crescendo in the mid-1930's, subsequent to Hitler's rise to power and his persecution of German Jews. The outbreak it provoked in 1936 assumed the dimensions of a civil war lasting for three years. In 1939 an Arab high committee was formed, a number of whose members were deported to the Seychelles, but its leader, the mufti of Jerusalem, fled to Lebanon. The government's sporadic attempts to halt the influx of immigrants were temporary because of outside pressure, the last phase of which was exerted by President Harry S. Truman. In the first World War the Zionist center of gravity had shifted from continental Europe to England, and in the second from England to the United States.

With rare faith, courage and singleness of purpose Zionists pushed their aggressive designs forward. They built schools and hospitals, started industries, introduced modern methods of agriculture and pioneered numberless projects of enduring social and cultural value. Some of the most productive lands were purchased, often at inflated prices, from absentee landlords in Beirut and Damascus; the lure of the prices offered was irresistible even for the Amir Abdullah. Their publicized achievement won the acclaim of the West and added to the host of admirers and supporters. Between 1919 and 1939 Zionist groups spent an estimated $79,000,000 on agricultural and other pursuits in Palestine.

In the meantime Arab economy in general worsened as a result of unsettled conditions, inflation, as well as discrimination against and displacement of workers. Largely by natural growth Arab population had increased by 1939 to about 1,044,000, but it had seriously reduced its majority; it then outnumbered the Jewish population by only two to one. In its struggle for existence it remained disorganized, impoverished, under benighted if not obsolete leadership and received no adequate support from outside sources. Short-sightedly it extended its negative non-cooperative policy to boycotting even royal commissions sent to Palestine to investigate as well as a round table conference at London.

ISRAEL

Even before the outbreak of the World War in the summer of 1939, the Arab rebellion had spent itself. Its key figure, the mufti of Jerusalem, was ousted from Lebanon by the French and given asylum in Baghdad in October. There he made it his business to stir up further ill feeling against the Allies. He no doubt contributed to the pro-Axis coup in Iraq. In 1942 the official Zionist position was outlined at a conference at the Biltmore Hotel, New York City: converting Palestine into a Jewish commonwealth, conducting unlimited immigration under Jewish Agency control, and organizing a Jewish army to implement the general program. The underground army of about 60,000 men and women from the settlements became more active.

The British had given it tacit recognition and even furnished it with weapons in the 1936 to 1939 uprising. Its activities included smuggling arms and illegal immigrants. The British hoped to use it for defense against possible German attack. Extreme Zionist gangs became more active in acts of terrorism and guerrilla warfare, especially in 1945, when the tide of war began to recede from the area. In July of that year the Labor Party, whose executive had committed the party to the Zionist program with its unlimited immigration, came to power. In London as in Washington and New York politicians sought to woo what they considered the Jewish vote. The authorities opened the door for Jewish influx even wider whether it was legal or not, they took no measures to check the growing aggression.

Palestine became a principal source of grave concern to the United Nations. Its general assembly on November 29, 1947 approved a recommendation by its committee to partition Palestine into two states. By this time neighboring Arab states had not only gained full independence but started national armies. To the Arabs in general, who had hardly shaken off what to them was the yoke of imperialism or the inferiority feeling it had bred, the mere thought of an exotic state planted by the West in the heart of their land was unbearable. An "army of liberation" was hastily called forth to fight on the spot. Although dignified by the blessing of the two-year-old Arab League, the detachments were ill-equipped, poorly trained, and officered by inexperienced men were no match to the mechanized enemy forces. They lacked unity of command and purpose, and were recruited largely from volunteers. The heads of the states—with their dynastic feuds, jealousies, and personal aims—were equally disunited. Only the Arab Legion of Jordan, trained and officered by Britishers, could have effectively performed, but under pressure from the British and for reasons of his own, King Abdullah ordered action limited to the area not included in the Jewish share of the partition plan. The jinni let loose by the British could not be contained again. As Arabs attacked Jews, Jews attacked Britishers. On May 14, 1948 a provisional government in Tel Aviv declared the birth of an independent state to be known as Israel. The United States was the first to recognize the new state, but she was followed by Russia and her satellites. The British announced the termination of the mandate and withdrew, leaving the country in a state of anarchy and civil war and registering upon themselves perhaps the greatest failure in the history of their Oriental policy.

The head of the new government who made the proclamation was Russian-Polish-born David Ben-Gurion, chairman of the Jewish Agency since 1935 and organizer of the peaceful and military Zionist activities in the land. Weizmann was invited from London to assume the presidency, an office of honor but not of authority. From 1949 on, with two years (1953-1955) excepted, Ben Gurion has held the prime ministry of the state. Israel in April 1958 counted 2,000,218 inhabitants, of whom 216,139 were non-Jews. Arabs left at home felt no more at home. They were considered a security menace.

All Arab states have persisted in their policy of political non-recognition and economic boycott of the emerging state. For a time they carried on their futile war. Truces were arranged by the United Nations, but the victory-drunk army in violation of the terms thereof continued its conquests, thereby adding an area approximately half of the partition share allotted. In February 1949 an armistice arranged by a United Nations commission was signed in Cyprus by Egyptian and Israeli representatives. The other warring Arab states signed later. But it was an uneasy armistice. These states still consider themselves in a state of war with their enemy. Tension and border clashes have continued to mark their relations. Artificial serpentine frontiers, undiminished flow of arms and subsidies from the West—especially the United States—to Israel and the blight of the refugees—a particularly sore spot—have been the perennial sources of friction. Israeli bond sales in the United States for 1959 amounted to $42,648,-000, bringing total sales—since 1951—to $368,668,000 and augmenting the grand total from sales and charitable contributions from the United States over the decade ending in 1959 to about a billion dollars.

A most spectacular episode took place on October 29, 1956, when Israeli forces crossed into Sinai and were seconded a few days later by Anglo-French forces bombarding Egyptian airfields and landing troops at Port Said. The immediate provocation was a military alliance presumably against Israel signed by Egypt, Syria, and Jordan and intensified raids by Egyptian-trained death volunteers (*fida'is*). Russia threatened to send volunteers in support of the friendly four-year-old Egyptian regime. Under pressure from the United States and the United Nations the three invading armies were withdrawn from Egyptian soil.

TRANSJORDAN

One other state benefited materially from the Palestine debacle, Transjordan, which grew into Jordan. Transjordan, with a biblical name but no historical existence, was called into being and put in 1920 under Amir Abdullah, who was then threatening to attack French Syria, whence his brother King Faysal had been ejected (as noted before). Amman was chosen as capital. To the British the emerging state would serve as a buffer against bedouin and Saudi raids and link their mandate to Iraq. To Abdullah it was not only a gesture of appeasement to him personally but also a make-up for what he considered British betrayal to his father. Hence it was a step towards building a new Hashimite dynasty over a greater Syria, which was his cherished dream.

At the close of the Cairo conference in the spring of 1921 Churchill visited Jerusalem, where he confirmed Abdullah as *de facto* ruler with the proviso that he would abandon inimical intentions against the French and accept British financial aid and military protection. The terms of the new dispensation were not specific enough to avert occasional misunderstandings leading at times to strained relations between amir and high commissioner, but on the whole it worked to the satisfaction of both parties. On May 25, 1946 Amir Abdullah was proclaimed king over Transjordan, which the treaty of London signed two months earlier had declared independent. Two years later the treaty of 1928 was replaced by an up-to-date one with certain reservations related to military bases and defense measures. In the Palestine war the Arab Legion was busy occupying new territory and adding to a state which was hardly viable. In 1948 Abdullah was proclaimed king of All-Palestine and Transjordan and in the following year the country was renamed the Hashimite Kingdom of Jordan.

IMPERIALISM AND INDEPENDENCE

Unwittingly the mandatory powers rendered the cause of Arab nationalism a service while combating it. From the intelligentsia the movement trickled down to the lower levels of society and developed a new aspect: uncompromising opposition to the West. Nationalist feeling was no more the property of an intellectual group seeking to assert for itself a place in society. The struggle to shake off the mandates gave birth to political parties and established a tradition of open revolt. For the first time the Arabic word for imperialism, colonialism (*isti'-mar*), became current on tongues and in literature.

The mandates to the people became the embodiment of imperialism —the attempt of industrially and militarily developed societies to insure their security and continued development by extending control over less developed societies and thereby gain markets, raw materials and strategic positions. In the process the society intruded upon benefits materially, but the benefits are often lost sight of by the psychological complex generated by the general attitude and behavior of the agents of the intruding society.[6]   In the case of the Arab lands as the nationalist spirit seeped from the higher into the lower strata of society, it gained in mobility and emotionalism but was fused with Pan-Islamism. However it provided a wider and firmer base and awakened the consciousness of self-responsibility fundamental for independence.   As this consciousness clashed with colonialism it sparked what has been styled the revolution of rising aspirations in the face of which no imperialism or colonial devices could stand.

BOOKS TO READ

Cumming, Henry H., *Franco-British Rivalry in the Post-War Near East* (London, 1938).

Haddad, George, *Fifty Years of Modern Syria and Lebanon* (Beirut, 1950).

Hanna, Paul L., *British Policy in Palestine* (Washington, 1942).

Hoskins, Halford L., *The Middle East*, 2nd ed. (New York, 1959).

Hourani, A. H., *Great Britain and the Arab World* (London, 1945); *Syria and Lebanon* (London, 1946).

Hurewitz, J. C., *The Struggle for Palestine* (New York, 1950).

Ireland, Philip W., *Iraq: A Study in Political Development* (London, 1937).

Jeffries, J. M. N., *Palestine, the Reality* (London, 1939).

Kirk, George F., *A Short History of the Middle East*, 6th ed. (New York, 1961).

Kohn, Hans, *Nationalism and Imperialism in the Hither East* (London, 1932).

Longrigg, Stephen L., *Iraq, 1900-1950* (London, 1953).

Nuseibeh, Hazem Z., *The Ideas of Arab Nationalism* (Ithaca, 1956).

Royal Institute of International Affairs, *The Middle East: A Political and Economic Survey*, 2nd ed. (London, 1954).

Wright, Quincy, *Mandates Under the League of Nations* (Chicago, 1930).

Ziadeh, Nicola A., *Syria and Lebanon* (London, 1957).

[6] Cf. above, p. 502.

XXXVI *Independence*

T HE second World War, no exception to other great wars, resulted in the burial of states and dynasties and the birth of others.   In the area concerning us the Ottoman Empire was demolished and on its ruins rose four states: Iraq, Syria, Lebanon and Jordan. Egypt had attained virtual independence in the inter-war period.[1]

RADICAL CHANGE IN WORLD POWERS

Meantime a shift in the world balance of power had taken place. Great Britain and France, hitherto predominant in the area, had lost their status as the two leading world powers.   Throughout the nineteenth century Great Britain, by virtue of her industrial preeminence, financial power, and naval supremacy was able to maintain her position as the greatest colonial empire.   For a time before that France was the strongest power in Europe.   The new polarization was around the United States and Soviet Russia.   Heading a formidable bloc of satellite nations in Europe and Asia, Russia entered the Eastern Mediterranean, a prize coveted since the days of Peter the Great.   In the East-West tug of cold war which dominated postwar world politics, the infant Arab states occupied a medial position.

The creation of Israel, which the Arab states considered enemy number one, and the phenomenal production of petroleum in the Persian Gulf area have posed new and complicated international problems to the Arab states.   In the twelve years since 1948 hostility to the Zionist state has not appreciably abated.   Repeated bloody border raids and reprisals have marked the period.   Of all the 7,000,000 refugees who have appeared on the international scene since the end of the second World War, this one-seventh has been unswerving in its stand for repatriation.   In the ten years beginning 1946 the production of crude oil has increased from 16,000,000 tons to 145,000,000, supplying about seventy per cent of the needs of Europe.[2]   Externally

[1] See above, pp. 442-3.
[2] Cf. above, p. 7.

514

it has made the area more of a coveted prize than ever; internally it has created social, political, and economic problems of vast dimensions.

These newly liberated countries have found themselves in a state of transition from colonial dependence to political and economic independence calling for the adaptation of an obsolete socio-economic structure to modern technical and organizational requirements. All were nationally aroused and politically inexperienced and all had populations that were preponderantly illiterate and poor. Unluckily for them the world situation absorbed their energies to the neglect of the domestic situation. Nationalism became more concerned with the development of self-respect than with social progress, economic improvement, and narrowing the gap between the privileged few and the underprivileged many. As the masses awakened the gap became—at least looked like—a gulf with the bridges few and far between.

EGYPT

The independence of Egypt, declared in 1922, was more nominal than real. The first stage, ending in 1936, was marked by a triangular struggle in which the contestants were the king, who owed his throne to the British but who could not be too subservient to them and maintain it; the Wafd, organized for revolutionary purposes but now in control of state affairs; and the British, who were not willing to relinquish their hold on the land. By temperament, tradition, and training King Fuad was an authoritarian ruler with no sensitiveness for the needs of his people and more particularly the common among them. The clash with a democratically elected parliament was inevitable. Elections, except when rigged, invariably gave Wafdists a parliamentary majority from whom cabinets were formed. Egypt held the life line of its occupying power, short-cutting its access to India. Of the three contestants the Wafd continued to advance in popular favor as against the other two.

Aside from the issue of defence the Sudan stood out as a principal stumbling block in that path of mutual understanding. The Egyptians claimed right of conquest[3] and considered its possession vital to insure their water supply and their intra-area communication. Their country, owed its fertility to the river that was a moving highway. In the three years ending in 1930 British warships made three appearances in the port of Alexandria to exert political pressure on the Egyptian government or to be ready in case disturbances got out of hand.

In 1936, after years of wrangling, a new threat was felt by both

[3] See above, pp. 434, 435.

sides. Italy, which had been an aggressive Mediterranean power since its occupation of Libya in 1912, then entered the Red Sea, as an imperialist force, with the invasion of Abyssinia (1935). The Anglo-Egyptian treaty of 1936, a new milestone on the way to complete independence, was, in effect, a mutual defense agreement in which the occupation was formally terminated but the British were empowered to maintain bases and garrisons for the protection of the canal, pending the development of adequate local forces. The Anglo-Egyptian condominium of 1899 over the Sudan was continued, with a new provision that the Sudan government would not employ British or Egyptian officials except in those cases where Sudanese were not available. This set the Sudan on its path to full independence which was not realized until 1956.

In 1937 the capitulations were abolished and Egypt was admitted to the League of Nations. In that year Farouk (Faruq) who, as a minor, had succeeded his father in the preceding year assumed full powers. The son followed in the steps of the father, adding luxurious and licentious living.

Egypt did not exercise its prerogatives of sovereignty long before the world crisis began to throw its dark shadow across its path. Soon after the outbreak of European hostilities in the summer of 1939, Egypt broke off diplomatic relations with Germany, declared a state of siege, and proceeded to implement its treaty obligations with Britain. Italy's entry into the war in June 1940 brought the conflict closer to home. Italian aircraft bombarded Egyptian objectives. Both Cairo and Alexandria were subjected to repeated air raids by Axis planes. The crisis was reached in the autumn of 1942 when General Erwin Rommel's Africa corps—especially trained for hot desert warfare— swept through Libya to al-Alamain (El Alamein) in north Egypt, sixty-five miles west of Alexandria. For days, as the battle raged, the fate of Egypt hung in the balance. The decisive victory, won by General Bernard L. Montgomery, checked the enemy's advance. A memorial erected there for the 13,000 Allied troops who made the ultimate sacrifice reads:

They preserved for the West the link with the East and turned the tide of war.

In addition to its strategic importance in defense, war-time Egypt served as a supply center for the entire Near Eastern region and as a base in preparation for the Allied campaign against Japan.

Economically the country did not suffer; in fact it prospered. The presence of troops from the British Commonwealth, and later from the United States, with high purchasing power boosted its economy. The entire 1940 cotton crop was bought by England. The country emerged from the second World War as the strongest and most influential Arab state. Its capital, most populous of all African and Western Asia cities, pushed forward as a center of industry, commerce, and international aviation. With the passing of war danger, the struggle between the palace and the Wafd was reactivated; so was the agitation, mainly by students and Wafdists, against the British, whose troops of occupation were more evident than ever. The last of these troops were not withdrawn till 1951. Alexandria ceased to be a British base. A new Egyptian trend became noticeable in the increased interest in Pan-Arab affairs, signalized by the initiative the government took in organizing at its capital the League of Arab States (1945). Hostility to Zionism was one of the inspiring factors. Other motivating forces were the urge for freedom, unity, and collective recognition. With headquarters at Cairo and an Egyptian secretary general, the league fell under local influence.

In February 1945 the Egyptian government made a token declaration of war on Germany and Japan and was subsequently admitted to the United Nations. In common with other members of the league—particularly Iraq, Syria, and Jordan—its forces crossed the Palestinian border to check the emergence of the State of Israel. Egyptian troops remained in occupation of the Gaza district, a strip about a hundred and fifty square miles in area. The discreditable performance of the Egyptians on the battlefield was attributed by army officers to corrupt government officials, including members of the royal palace clique, who supplied the troops with defective weapons. This alleged scandal precipitated the military coup of July 23, 1952, which ended the monarchy.

REVOLUTIONARY REGIME

The coup, aimed at the discredited regime, was hatched in the Officers Club at Cairo by a small secret group of "free officers." Its abrupt, complete, and bloodless success bespeaks careful and prolonged planning. Its result was a clean sweep of the symbols of the past. One after the other of the established institutions tumbled down. On July 26, 1952—three days after the coup—the scion of the century-and-a-half ruling family abdicated and went into exile in Italy. Before the year was over the constitution had been abolished. Early the following year political parties were dissolved. On June 18, 1953 the monarchy was abolished, and General Mohammed Naguib (Najib), a hero of the Palestine war, was made president and prime minister of the new republic. The titles of pasha and bey were banned and soon passed into oblivion together with that of his majesty.   No public tears were shed over them.

A new era dawned on a land that probably had witnessed more eras than any other land.   To the world at large the revolutionary command council proclaimed that it was a three-in-one revolution: a French revolution to rid the country of the king with his corrupt regime and form a republic, an American revolution against the British in occupation, and a Turkish Kemalist revolution to transform and regenerate the social and economic aspects of the old culture.

Less prone to extreme measures in dealing with foes and new contestants for power, Naguib was bound to clash with his younger and more dynamic and hitherto little-known deputy, Colonel Gamal Abdel Nasser (Jamal Abd-al-Nasir).   Chief among these contestants was the Moslem Brotherhood (al-Ikhwan al-Muslimun).   Founded by a minor government school teacher in 1928 as a puritanical movement, the Brotherhood aimed to reform Islam by return to the rejuvenating teachings of the Koran and hadith.   In the second World War it developed a terrorist wing and spread outside the land of its birth.   Naguib was a sympathizer, if not a member.   In its aspiration for supreme power it made common cause with Wafdists, fascists, socialists, and communists.   Nasser emerged victorious.   Before the end of 1954, Naguib was overthrown and put under house arrest, where he presumably still lingers.   An unsuccessful attempt on the life of Nasser by a Brotherhood member resulted in its being outlawed again.   It has since been underground.   With the passing of leadership from Naguib to Nasser an apocalyptic vision of the destiny of Egypt and the role it was to play in Arab and world affairs began to loom in youthful Egyptian eyes.

On June 23, 1956 Nasser, with only his name on the ballot, was elected president of the republic for a six-year term.   Since then he has led his country through more than one international crisis.   On June 13, 1956 he and his people celebrated the withdrawal of the last British troops from the country in accordance with an agreement signed two years earlier, providing for such action and for transferring the Suez Canal base to Egyptian authorities.   Hailed as a national hero, he was soon to develop into a Pan-Arab hero.

He first turned to the West in quest of financial aid particularly for executing a gigantic scheme involving the construction of a high dam at Aswan and thus reclaiming a vast territory from the desert and providing for the needs of a mounting population characterized by a descending standard of living.   The census of 1917 gave the Egyptians 12,700,000, citizens with 5,500,000 cultivatable acres; the 1947 census figures are 19,000,000 and 6,000,000. By 1956 the population had reached 22,000,000 and was increasing at the rate of 500,000 a year without a parallel increase in the national economy. Lands seized from wealthy owners and distributed among tenants and farmers could not solve the problem. After receiving approval for his $1,300,000 application for loan from the International Bank (February, 1956), Nasser was brusquely rebuffed by the Department of State which expressed some doubt about the soundness of his country's economy. England followed with the same decision. The Egyptian President struck back by proclaiming the nationalization of the Suez Canal with a view to raising the required capital from its income. The statue of Sesostris III,[4] which is to be erected in 1960 on the site of the demolished one of de Lesseps symbolizes the complete Egyptianization of the canal. Vociferous protests and threats, particularly from England and France, went unheeded. Using an abrupt military campaign by Israel through Sinai on October 29, 1956 these two powers attacked Egyptian objectives by air and landed troops at Port Said as noted above. Russia rallied to the support of harassed Egypt by offering to send volunteers. President Eisenhower took the initiative in condemning the triple attack and, under pressure from the United Nations, the reckless venture was given up. Apparently London counted on a repetition of its 1882 performance with Arabi Pasha.

The Israeli campaign was launched a year after Egypt, Syria, and Saudi Arabia had signed a military agreement and unified their commands. This agreement indicated the ineffectiveness of the League of Arab States and reflected the inherent disunity of the Arab world—a disunity that was not created by the West, as usually claimed, but one undoubtedly exacerbated by it. Arab nationalism was not strong enough to hold Arabs together. Of the ten members in February 1960, two—Tunisia and Iraq—refused to attend a meeting in Cairo because of hostility to Nasserite Egypt.

Ever since the rise of Israel, Egypt had shared with other Arab neighbors a feeling of frontier insecurity prompted by Zionist expanionist policy; continued unlimited immigration; and increasing armament from the West, particularly from France. Unable to secure weapons from the same source, Nasser turned to the only other alternative left and signed with Czechoslovakia (September 1955) an agreement which opened the door for other transactions—including those involving machinery, raw material, and consumers' goods—from the Soviet bloc. Two years later an agreement was signed with the Soviet Union whereby the Union undertook to advance 60,000,000 Egyptian pounds

[4] See above, p. 40.

for a development program including the Aswan Dam. For the first time the Arab East discovered an alternative to doing business with Western Europe. The setback to England and France in the economic field paralleled the setback in the political and military fields. Loans from Russia culminated, in February 1960, with an offer of a hundred-million dollars to carry on the construction of the dam through the second and final stage.

The new discovery, followed by the evacuation of the last foreign troops from Egyptian soil, the nationalization of the canal connecting the two seas, and the bold stand against the triple invaders sent Nasser's stocks rocketing sky high. The barrage, mostly unjustified, of violent attacks by Western politicians and newspapers, built Nasser into an Arabian superman. The remembrance of his triumphs and achievements were kept fresh and shiny by the powerful radio and widely-read newspapers of Cairo. No other Arab since Crusading days, they reiterated, had dared defy the "Franks." Nasser's pictures began to adorn walls of barber shops, editorial offices, public buildings from Aden and Sana to Aleppo and Mosul and from Baghdad to Fez. A personality had emerged around which the inflamed mass feeling could cluster. Arab nationalism was equated with Egyptian nationalism. An Egyptian champion looked upon himself and was looked upon by others as the Pan-Arab champion.

One other leader posed a challenge; he was Nuri al-Said, elder statesman of Iraq and many times its prime minister. Nuri was also an Arab nationalist, but his nationalism was of a different brand and was "tainted with imperialism." He cooperated with Great Britain and had behind him the Hashimite throne. The first open break between the two rivals came in February 1955, when Nuri served as the local architect of the Baghdad Pact. The pact, as we learned above, was an outgrowth of an improvised Anglo-American policy to build up a "northern tier" of Turkey, Iraq, Iran, and Pakistan to hinder, if not stop, a Soviet frog leap to the southern tier with its oil fields, international highways, and the Suez Canal, as well as unexploited mineral and other resources of Africa. The pact tied up the four Moslem states through England with NATO. It received the blessing and aid of the United States but was denied its membership. Although it was professedly a military alliance against the threat of danger from the north, the pact received arms as well as dollars and pounds.

As Iraq was alienated from Egypt, Syria—Iraq's natural ally—was drawn closer to Nasser. Damascus had independently followed the track of Cairo and ended in its embrace. It declared a policy of neutrality, refused "aid with strings attached," patronized the Soviet market for arms and goods, and under its President Shukri al-Quwatli entered into a series of economic and military agreements with Egypt which were climaxed in an historic merger.

SOCIAL PROGRESS

Until the 1940's Arab national feeling aimed squarely at independence as if independence were an end in itself. In the forties and early fifties the dominant chords in the orchestration were negative: anti-Zionism, anti-imperialism, and anti-colonialism. A new positive chord was thereafter struck: a social one involving the welfare of the common man and emphasizing industrialization. At no time in the history of the land had the worker, the peasant, become the subject of so much concern on the part of the governing class. General public welfare, for the first time, became a lively issue. A "nationalist, democratic, socialist, cooperative society" was repeatedly declared to be the revolutionary objective. Judging by the implementation, democracy meant freeing the national—rather than the citizen's—will to act independently, and by socialism employing the state machinery to achieve public welfare, industrial development and social legislation. Agrarian reform, involving the parcelling out of large estates among landless peasants, was one feature of the new trend.

In 1958 and 1959 Egypt opened about a hundred factories (sugar, cotton, machinery, chemicals) and hoped to use its industrial potential to strengthen her political as well as commercial ties with Africans. By assuming the task of industrialization, improving educational and sanitary conditions, and raising the level of general income, the new regime sought to bring the rural masses within the political orbit on its side. In February 1960 the two leading banks of Cairo were "nationalized." Small industries were introduced, old ones encouraged, improved agricultural methods fostered, and reports about them were featured in the daily press. The Arabic equivalents for such terms as centers for rural teacher training, programs for social workers, and classes for village inspectors were almost unheard of before. The report of the Ford Foundation for 1959 shows grants for these and other educational projects in the southern region of the United Arab Republic (Egypt) in the amount of $318,000, and in the northern region (Syria) $473,480.

Social change, unlike material change, is slow, rigid and, multi-dimensional. A Cairo judge, French educated and follower of Muhammad Abduh,[5] Qasim Amin (d. 1908), published in 1898 a book *Tahrir*

---

[5] Sketched above, pp. 443-4.

al-Mar'ah (liberation of the woman) in which he tried to read liberal
ideas into the relevant koranic passages and to reinterpret traditional
opinions in the light of modern thought.   Qasim's attack was aimed
at polygamy, divorce, and the practice of veiling.   His attempt was
received with a storm of opposition.   An Azharite critic sarcastically
remarked that he would welcome an opportunity to meet the author's
wife.   Twenty-seven years later another judge, Ali Abd-al-Raziq, but
Azhar trained and connected with a shariah court, wrote a book on
Islam and the fundamentals of faith in which he maintained that, after
all, the Prophet's message was religious rather than governmental and
political.   He was forthrightly condemned by a disciplinary council of
al-Azhar and dismissed from his post.   The attorney general ordered
confiscation of all copies of the first edition.

In 1950 another Azhar shaykh, Khalid Muhammad Khalid, in a book
titled *Min Huna Nabda'* (tr. Isma'il R. el-Faruqi, *From Here We Start*),
went further than any of his predecessors in attempting to separate state
and religion, and in advocating equality of sexes, reinterpretation of koranic precepts and the reformation of religious instruction.   He provoked less violent reaction under the revolutionary regime than his predecessors had under the monarchy.   The attorney general rescinded the
order banning Abd-al-Raziq's work.

The Wafdists had taken earlier steps (1946) toward liberalizing laws
governing marriage, divorce, and inheritance.   But it was not until
1957 that a radical operation was performed on the problem of the
dichotomy between the religious law as applied in personal status cases
and the modern civil law introduced over the years.[6]   The operation
consisted of abrogating the shariah courts, as well as the religious
courts of non-Moslem communities, and providing that all litigation
thereafter be conducted in the ordinary courts but under the relevant
personal law.   Judges presiding over ordinary courts were as a rule
trained in the Western tradition.   In 1960 a special judicial committee
of the United Arab Republic imposed new restrictions on the Moslem
husband and decreed new rights for the wife.   A man's divorce can be
obtained only in a court of law with fair provision for the wife.   If he
wishes to avail himself of the privilege of having more than one mate,
he must prove his need for that.   If a woman leaves her husband he
cannot use the police to force her return.   She can sue him for divorce
if he takes on an additional wife.   In connection with the fast of
Ramadan, 1960, Egypt's mufti expressed the opinion that brushing the
teeth with paste was permissible when fasting, provided paste is not

---

[6] Cf. above, p. 438.

swallowed, and so wife-kissing, even on the lips, so long as it is chaste rather than passionate.

Even in legislation on personal status, the United Arabic Republic lagged behind the Tunisian. This young state abolished polygamy outright. Its code of family law (1956) departs from traditional Islamic law as radically as the up-to-date Turkish legislation. It should, however, be remembered that this traditional law of Islam, which has been riddled with shots by modernist-oriented Moslem states, had been for centuries the main guarantee of law and order throughout the world of Islam. Tunisian President Habib Bourguiba (abu-Ruqaybah, "short necked"), the most Westernized of Arab Moslem rulers, initiated in February 1960 a series of explosive attacks on one of Islam's strongest pillars the month-long daylight fast of Ramadan. His argument was that since Islam absolves the believer from this obligation for reasons of health or holy war, it should absolve the undernourished worker whose productivity is lowered by fasting. He failed to impress the grand mufti and his fellow ulema. Bourguiba thereupon ordered the concert-halls, coffeehouses, and restaurants closed at midnight throughout this month.

IRAQ

Independent Iraq (since 1932)[7] like independent Egypt, passed through a monarchic stage into a military republic, but under entirely different circumstances. In Iraq the monarchy was British imposed and its overthrow was due to disparate reasons. Of its three Hashimite monarchs Faysal I was outstanding in personal charm, statesmanship and, broad tolerance; these made him generally acceptable to his heterogeneous subjects.[8] He ranks high among the leaders the Arab world produced in the potwar period. Faysal had spent his boyhood with his exiled father in Constantinople under Abd-al-Hamid, led the Arabian army with distinction during the revolt, and experienced Western diplomacy at Versailles. But the domestic and foreign problems with which he had to cope defied ready solution and overtaxed his energy. Broken in health he sought rest and cure in Switzerland, where he died in 1933, leaving his twenty-one-year-old son Ghazi as his successor.

Inexperienced and lacking his father's ability, Ghazi let the government under him degenerate into intrigues of political cliques. Cabinets rose and fell at an average of four a year. The practice of dividing state-owned lands among tribal shaykhs to win them over built up a

---

[7] See above, pp. 504-5.
[8] Cf. above, p. 504.

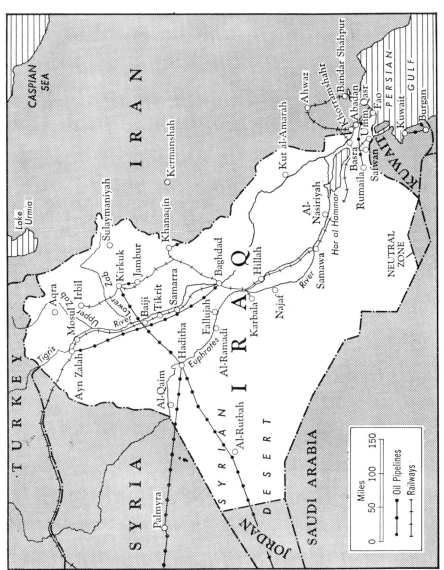

KINGDOM OF IRAQ

new feudal aristocracy to the detriment of the peasantry and contributed to the downfall of the monarchy. Ghazi's addiction to fast motoring cost him his life. On his death in an accident in 1939 his four-year-old son was proclaimed his successor under the name of Faysal II.

Pending Faysal's attainment of majority on May 2, 1953, his maternal uncle Abdul-Ilah, son of Ali (eldest son of King Husayn), assumed the regency, was nominated crown prince, and remained for years the power behind the throne. The future king received some education in England before assuming his royal duties. His was the saddest lot. On the occasion of the military coup of July 14, 1958, headed by Abdul-Karim Kassem (Abd-al-Karim Qasim), the young king, together with his regent uncle, other members of his household, and his prime minister Nuri al-Said, were slaughtered. A republic was declared.

PROBLEMS AND PROGRESS UNDER THE MONARCHY

Uppermost among the foreign problems which confronted Faysal I and his two successors were the relations with Britain and the tension with Israel. The two sets of problems were interrelated. The difficulty with Britain revolved on the possibility of maintaining the prestige of independence and the dignity of sovereignty while receiving financial and military aid from a foreign power—a difficulty aggravated by the rising tide of nationalism. From 1937 on Anglo-Iraqi relations began rapidly to deteriorate as the anti-Zionist feeling and resentment at British espousal of Zionist cause mounted. The decline of British influence gave the Germans their chance, a chance favored by early developments of the second World War. In 1941 an army coup established a temporary regime at Baghdad with a non-belligerent policy. Baghdad and Basra were reoccupied by British forces after which the country, considered vital for the Allied cause particularly as a base for the movement of supplies and material to Iran and Russia, fulfilled its obligation as its British ally. Two years after the pro-German coup, Iraq declared war on the Axis Powers and in 1945 signed the United Nations charter.

In Baghdad hostility to Zionism and Israel was more pronounced than in most other Arab capitals, so was the support of the Palestine Arab cause. On May 15, 1948 Iraqi troops were rushed to the Palestine battlefield. Subsequent to the establishment of the new state a law was passed in Baghdad making Zionist activity liable to the same penalty as Communist activity. In 1949 the secretary general and three leaders of the Communist Party were hanged in the capital. In the course of 1951 to 1952 close to 130,000 Iraqi Jews emigrated mostly to Israel.

The domestic scene, complicated by the fact that nine-tenths of the population was illiterate and one-sixth nomadic, was aggravated after the British withdrawal. In the north were Sunnite Kurds, linguistically and ethnically related to the Iranians, who conspired against the established authority and aspired for union with fellow tribesmen in Iran and Turkey in a new Kurdistan. They provided fertile soil for Soviet and other foreign propaganda. Leading a nomadic or semi-nomadic life, these Kurds paid no taxes and shunned settlement. Throughout the 1920's and 1930's Iraq had to take punitive measures against them in the mountainous region of Mosul and Sulaymaniyah.

Equally disturbing but more resentment-provoking was the Assyrian (Nestorian Christian) community. In its original habitat by Lake Van, under the jurisdiction of its hereditary patriarch, this Moslem-persecuted community was a thorn in Turkey's side. Not being Catholic or Protestant it had no protector in France or Russia. For generations the Anglican Church had favored it. In the closing years of the first World War and thereafter the British, recognizing the fighting qualities of these hardy mountaineers, raised levies from them and used them for their purposes. They spread in Iraq, acquired a reputation for invincibility, and meanwhile dreamed of an autonomous state. With the termination of the mandate their position became precarious. Eight hundred fighters crossed the Tigris (1933) into Syria but, refused settlement by the French, they recrossed the border and made the mistake of attacking an Iraqi post. This gave the Iraqi army a chance to settle old accounts. Assyrian fighting power was crushed, the rest of the community was disarmed, and forty of their sixty-four villages were sacked and totally or almost totally destroyed. King Ghazi decorated the commanding officer, who was of Kurdish origin. The problem of this turbulent minority was thus settled.

INTER-ARAB RELATIONS

Baghdad's relations with Amman and Beirut were consistently warm and cordial, but those with Damascus and Cairo varied from warm to cold. A charter member of the League of Arab States, Iraq played an important role in its early development. Its close relations with Jordan were formalized in a ten-year treaty, assigned in 1947, providing measures for joint military training, common defense, and economic cooperation. If King Abdullah cherished a greater Syria project, Iraqi statesmen cherished a more comprehensive one: an Arab Crescent union.

Iraq's economy was sounder than that of almost any other state, which enhanced her prestige and put her in a position to aid such a needy ally as Jordan. The rapid development of her oil industry was combined with wise and economic planning. In 1932 and 1938 new concessions were given oil companies in Mosul and Basra. In 1934 Kirkuk oil, discovered ten years earlier, was flowing through two twelve-inch pipelines, one to Tripoli and the other to Haifa. The Haifa line was cut in the Israeli war. In 1950 its Kirkuk-Tripoli pipeline was duplicated by a sixteen-inch one, and plans were laid for a new thirty-inch one to Baniyas on the Syrian coast. In that year the government created a development board and assigned seventy per cent of its future oil revenues to be used for such major projects as digging canals, building dams for flood control, bridges, highways, airports, and for educational and military purposes. By 1957 the board had laid plans for improvements to cost $500,000,000.

For a time relations with Syria were so cordial as to encourage belief in an immediate merger of the two countries. This was particularly true in 1949 under the short military regime of al-Hinnawi. But estrangement set in early in 1955, when Iraq joined Turkey in what came to be called the Baghdad Pact. Prompted by Egypt the League of Arab States endeavored in vain to dissuade Iraq. Egypt was infuriated. The four Moslem states on the flank of Russia—Turkey, Iraq, Iran, and Pakistan—were to form with Great Britain a cordon against Russia's feared advance southward. Arms and money were to be supplied by the European ally. Accordingly in 1956 to 1957 Iraq received from Britain arms valued at £2,000,000. In 1957 the sum of $12,500,000 was pledged to the four Moslem members of the pact from money appropriated for the implementation of the Eisenhower doctrine.

In the Suez crisis, however, Iraq sided squarely with Egypt, broke off diplomatic relations with France and attendance at the pact's session was made conditional on Britain's abstention. Iraq even rushed troops to Jordan. But the blowing up of its oil pipelines and pumping stations in Syrian territory entailed an estimated loss of $5,000,000 a month. For months Syria would not allow repairs, which were not completed till June 1958.

MILITARY REPUBLIC

That was an eventful year in the history of the Arab East. The Syrian-Egyptian union destroyed the Arab states' precarious equilibrium and set off a chain reaction that promised to last for years. As a countermove Iraq on February 14 hurriedly consummated the long-talked-of plans of union with Jordan and declared an Arab Federation of the two states. The federation was to be under King Faysal, with Husayn maintaining his throne over Jordan. The capital was to alternate between Baghdad and Amman. Provision was made for the unification of armed forces, foreign policies, educational systems, and customs administrations.

As it turned out the federation was one of governments rather than peoples. It lacked the appeal of social progress and national upsurge which marked the birth of its southern rival. Besides, the Iraqi regime seemed already outdated to many, while the Egyptian regime enjoyed the advantage of a popular and trusted youthful leader and embodied the social aspirations of the Arab masses. Arab nationalists in both Iraq and Jordan who favored merger with the new United Arab Republic became more active and vociferous than ever. So were anti-monarchist and anti-Western groups. Leftists were also aroused in both countries. Unfortunately the development board program, specializing on long-range projects as it did, had failed to ameliorate the sad condition of the low-income group which did not see much hope in the new federation.

Amelioration, they thought, was forthcoming on that day of July (14, 1958), when radio Baghdad announced a successful military coup. Excitement reached delirious dimensions. Overnight the monarchy was obliterated. The pro-Western regime was wiped out. Other than the leading members of the royal family and the prime minister, some two hundred were killed. Others were apprehended and imprisoned. A republic was declared.

Out of the melee a brigadier (later general), Abdul Karim Kassem (Abd-al-Karim Qasim), emerged as leader of the coup and head of the new government. Iraq, his proclamations reiterated, remained an integral part of the Arab nation, but was to be governed in its foreign policy by a neutral attitude that would take no sides in the cold war, and guided in its internal policy by the principles of nationalism and democracy. Its efforts would be directed toward raising living standards through industrialization and land redistribution. Political freedom would be withheld pending the successful completion of the revolutionary task. The Iraqi-Jordan Federation collapsed. The Baghdad Pact could not so remain without Baghdad; it became the Central Treaty Organization with headquarters at Ankara.

Thus did revolutionary Iraq express its ideology, involving Arab nationalism, international neutralism, democracy and social welfare, in terms almost identical with those of revolutionary Egypt. The goal to be aimed at was national rather than individual democracy, and social equality rather than political freedom. In the scale of values national power stood high, subordinating other values. But in implementation the Iraqi course diverged from the Egyptian and the two dominating leaders found themselves in opposition to one another, each vehemently supported by his native radio and press. The Iraqi brand of Arab nationalism differed from and would not mix with the Syrian-Egyptian brand. Kassem's regime sensed no incompatibility between Iraqi national interests and Communism. Baghdad became the only important base from which Soviet Russia could operate. Cairo was provoked more than ever against Baghdad and against Communism. The year before Syria had looked like a promising field. Despite the fact that Soviet Russia served in Arab eyes as a catalyst accelerating the driving out of Western imperialism and as a model for industrial and social modernization, none of the Arab states has thus far embraced the Communist ideology, nor is one likely to become a satellite in the foreseeable future. As long as Islam the religion has its hold on the people, it will act as a deterrent, though maybe not a decisive one. Throughout 1959 Kassem had endeavored to steer a middle course between the two opposing groups of Leftists and pro-Egyptian Arab nationalists struggling for control of his regime. The unsuccessful attempt on his life (October) was generally attributed by Baghdad press to pro-Egyptian conspirators. Disappointment with the performance of Russian technicians in the refinery and other oil installations was beginning to express itself in the early months of 1960. Iraq's oil revenues for this year are estimated at $280,000,000.

JORDAN

Tiny Transjordan, created a principality by the British in the early 1920's and put under its Palestine mandate, evolved into an independent kingdom in 1946 and was expanded to become the Hashimite Kingdom of Jordan in 1948 and 1949—all under the leadership of Abdullah ibn-Husayn.[9] As son of the sharif of Mecca and king of Hejaz, as head of the noble Hashim family, and as a leading figure in the Arab movement, Abdullah exercised influence out of proportion to the size and importance of his realm. His blood kinship to the occupant of the Iraq throne drew him close to that country. His pet scheme of a greater Syria, uniting his country with Syria, Palestine, and possibly Lebanon as a nucleus for a Pan-Arab empire gave him contacts with that entire area. One fact, however, discredited him in nationalist eyes: Abdullah was a British collaborator. Worse than that he was suspected of dealing with Zionists on the basis of dividing the spoils.

[9] As discussed above, pp. 511-12.

The king was adept in Near Eastern politics. He had spent his young manhood with his father in political exile at Constantinople under Abd-al-Hamid and served as deputy in the Ottoman parliament. He knew Turkish well but took pride in his knowledge of Arabic literature and history. In his memoirs (unsatisfactory English translation, New York, 1950) he quotes a letter to him from King ibn-Saud and within parentheses corrects its Arabic. The memoirs reveal no feeling of responsibility toward his subjects. An assassin's bullet cut short his enjoyment of the newly-expanded realm as the king was entering the Aqsa Mosque (Jerusalem) for Friday prayer on July 20, 1951. The motive behind the crime was related to Abdullah's reputed softness toward Israel, although that never came out in the accessories' testimonies. Abdullah's forty-two-year-old eldest son Talal, who succeeded him, had his career terminated by mental illness. When the government's request for abdication was communicated to this genial and cultured man, he said only, "Please, thank the government" and retired to a sanitarium near Istanbul, where he still lives.

On May 2, 1953 his son Husayn (Hussein), having come of age, discontinued his studies in a military academy in England to ascend the throne. Like his royal cousin of Iraq, Husayn had to become a man before he stopped being a boy. The inexperienced but energetic and courageous king inherited a realm the eastern part of which was semi-desert, semi-nomadic, with a 400,000 population; the western part was peopled by about 1,000,000, half of whom were refugees. The country was not blessed with any special physical resources. Jordan lay closest to Israel and contested with it not only frontiers but the rights to use the Jordan water. The flow of visitors from abroad to the holy places, a main source of national income, was adversely affected by unsettled local conditions. Attempts to discover oil of any commercial importance have been unsuccessful. Valuable deposits of minerals, particularly potash and bromine in the Dead Sea, over half of whose shores lie in Jordan territory, require for production more capital than the country and its Arab neighbors have been able to afford. The Yarmuk offers hydroelectric and irrigation possibilities that have been worked out into a joint long-range project with Syria; the United Nations relief and works agency pledged £18,000,000 for refugee settlement on the realization of the project.

Politically weak, economically anemic and heterogeneously peopled, Jordan invited aggression from its Arab neighbors. Its king could well pray to Allah to help him against his friends, as he could well take care of his enemies. Plots against him and his throne were habitual. But he and his kingdom have thus far survived. In his struggle for survival

HASHIMITE KINGDOM OF JORDAN

he could count on the unswerving loyalty of his well-trained, well-disciplined Arab Legion, particularly of the bedouin element in it. Jordanian Bedouins have held his house in special reverence. The summary dismissal of the legion's commanding officer, Lieutenant General John B. Glubb (1956), in deference to nationalist opinion, reduced its morale, but regardless of that the legion could not be strong enough to cope with the Arab-world-shaking developments of the ensuing two years.

FROM CRISIS TO CRISIS

Disruptive forces—sparked by pro-Nasser Arab nationalists, leftists, anti-monarchists, political, and economic malcontents—came near wrecking the state in 1957. The government declared martial law, created military courts and dissolved all political parties. The dispatch of the sixth fleet to the Eastern Mediterranean by the United States and her declaration that the integrity and independence of Jordan were of vital interest to her steadied the shaky throne. Amman repudiated its seven-year-old Syrian-Egyptian agreement, involving unified command, and abandoned plans to exchange diplomatic relations with the Soviet Union. As the government turned to the United States for financial aid—despite its earlier condemnation of the Eisenhower doctrine—it was subjected to a barrage of explosive radio and press attacks from Damascus and Cairo. The king was represented as a traitor to the Arab cause and his subjects were incited against him.

Even more perilous was the crisis of 1958 precipitated by the Iraq upheaval of July 14 and the summer-long disturbances of normally-stable Lebanon. In response to Husayn's appeal for military help against threat of foreign interference British troops were promptly flown there from Cyprus as American marines were being landed on the Lebanese shore. The Iraqi coup was decisive in prompting both the British and American measures. By November the British troops had been completely withdrawn from Jordan and in the following March the king, emerging from the crisis with enhanced prestige and popularity, felt free to undertake a visit to Washington and London. On his return, however, it was disclosed than an officer in his company was implicated in a conspiracy and was sentenced to death. While the trip did not succeed in interesting private foreign capital, it did produce results. In March 1960 Jordan received $4,000,000 in the seventh and last installment of budget aid for the fiscal year 1959, the total aid having amounted to $40,500,000.

SYRIA A REPUBLIC

Young independent Syria set out in 1946 [10] on a tortuous and dark path which led it through three republican and three military regimes before it landed in the embrace of Egypt. Of all the governments of the new Arab states, its was the least stable. Its political and economic instability reflected internal and external conditions peculiar to itself.

Religion had splintered the country's population to a greater extent than any other Arab land, with Lebanon excepted. Christians constituted about an eighth of the total, and Nusayris—in the Latakia region—about a tenth. Druzes, not numerically but otherwise strong, held southern Hauran. The country produced political groups which came nearer than in any neighboring Arab land to be considered parties, but failed to produce national leaders able to cope with the complicated problems. There were the traditional Nationalist Party, which came to power in 1943 and elected al-Quwatli as first president; the People's Party, favoring the Fertile Crescent scheme; an influential group advocating King Abdullah's Greater Syria; the Syrian Nationalist Party, founded by a Christian Lebanese on the assumption that there was such a nationhood as "Syrian" (independent of and unrelated to Arabism); the Arab Renaissance Party, committed to a socialistic program. As the modern heirs of a most glorious period in Arab history, Syrian Moslems could not forget the treatment accorded them by Westerners who were—in their estimate—still barbarians when Damascus was the Umayyad capital. Such was the xenophobia engendered that any cooperation with the West was disfavored. Some even considered de-Europeanizing the entire educational system. In its neighboring Arab lands the systems remained ambivalent in their general attitudes: hospitable to Western science, technology and methodology, while hostile to their proponents and professors.

Equally intense was the animosity toward Israel. The Syrian-Israeli frontier was the scene of more bloody conflicts than any other Arab-Israeli frontier. The last encounter to threaten a full-scale war occurred in February 1960. One of the sources of the Jordan, whose waters Israel planned to divert, lay in Syrian territory. The only other non-Arab neighbor was Turkey, against which a grudge was harbored on account of Alexandretta. [11]

The nationalists government under al-Quwatli, even more than nationalist governments in other Arab states, concerned itself with the

---

[10] Cf. above, p. 502.
[11] Treated above, pp. 502-3.

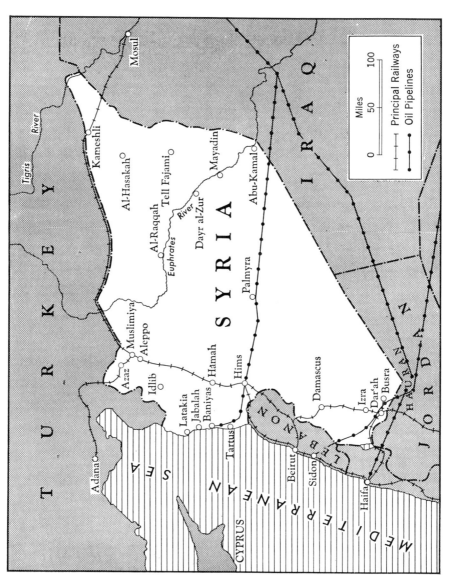

establishment of dignity and self-respect and with measures of defense, particularly vis-à-vis Israel's expansionist policy—to the neglect of problems relating to social justice, economic and industrial development and the general welfare of the people. Consequently the financial problems moved from bad to worse. Currency was still tied to the unstable French franc. As prices soared, sales dipped. The humiliating performance of the military in Palestine catalyzed the revolutionary spirit against the established authority, as it did in Egypt. The high expectations of the era of independence were far from realized. This was all at a time when awareness of the extent of the gap between what is and what ought to be was growing sharper, and the feeling of helplessness and mystic submission to a superior will on the part of the masses was giving way to a practical determination to change the *status quo*.

MILITARY REGIMES

A series of military regimes marked the year 1949. President al-Quwatli found refuge in Egypt. Colonel Husni al-Zaim, who displaced him, introduced progressive reforms, including granting electoral rights to women of elementary education and placing privately-endowed charitable institutions (*waqfs*) under state control. He also introduced a modern commercial law. But his French leanings proved his undoing. A bullet ended his career as abruptly and dramatically as a coup started it. Colonel Sami al-Hinnawi, who displaced him, enjoyed even a shorter term. He favored union with Iraq. His chief of staff, Lieutenant Colonel Adib al-Shishakli, gradually gathered the reins of executive power into his hands and held them for about four years.

Except for its duration, the Shishakli regime achieved no distinction. The downward curve in economy, morale, and prestige acquired momentum. Newspapers were suppressed, political parties abolished and a new party, the Arab Liberation Party, was created. The defense item in the national budget continued to climb higher and higher. The government refused American aid "with strings attached." Secretary of State Dulles' visit to the area (1953) with its subsequent promise of "equal friendship to both sides" [Arabs and Israelis] was discounted. The rupture of the Syrian-Lebanese customs union, a heritage from the mandate, severed the last economic link with its twin sister republic. The Lebanese frontier was temporarily closed (1950) to Syrian exports. Syria, in contrast to Lebanon, embarked upon a protective tariff policy. Long-range schemes for draining a swampy part of the Orontes valley and provide hydroelectric power for a vast area at a cost of $280,000,-000, as well as elaborate projects for drainage and irrigation connected with the Euphrates and the Yarmuk, at a cost of $200,000,000, could not be pursued. In February 1954 al-Shishakli, faced with a Druze uprising in Hauran and an army rebellion in Aleppo, fled to Saudi Arabia and later to France. The aged Hashim al-Atasi, who had for a time served as head of the government, was restored to the presidency by the army. He retired in August 1955 and by vote of the chamber of deputies al-Quwatli was elected president for the second time. Democratic rule was resumed. Military rule was tested and found wanting.

CONSTITUTIONAL GOVERNMENT RESTORED

Al-Quwatli returned with a renewed determination to follow in the Egyptian track. By that time the Soviet Union had idetnified its interests with Arab interests. Aside from the over-all "anti-imperialist, anti-colonial, anti-Western" professed ideology, Russia assumed an anti-Israeli attitude, encouraged Arab nationalism, claimed friendship, and proffered support to the Arab cause. The West failed to seek or find a common ground for meeting the Arabs. Technical, economic, and financial aid, more importantly arms, began to flow from the north. The flourishing Arab Renaissance Party, which had by this time spread into Jordan and Iraq, failed to distinguish clearly between socialism and communism. After 1955, in which the Soviet Union gained its first foothold in an Arab land, the Union started offering more of such aid than the United States was giving all Arab states. America was then aiding Egypt to the extent of $60,000,000, Jordan $44,000,000, Lebanon $35,000,000, Iraq $12,000,000 and Syria nil because of her refusal to accept. In the summer of 1957 Moscow offered Damascus $100,-000,000 at two and one-half per cent interest for the development of its resources and the improvement of its means of communication. In that summer American embassy officials in Damascus were charged with plotting, in conjunction with opposition leaders, the overthrow of the Syrian government. Turkey was also charged with preparations for attacking her southern neighbor.

Communist infiltration awakened the leading civil authorities to the growing danger. On Syria's initiative the long-standing plans for union with Egypt were hurriedly consummated. Twenty days later a plebiscite in the two countries confirmed the merger. The second day, February 22, was designated a national holiday. The Syrian leader of the Communist Party, a member of the chamber of deputies, fled to Moscow. It was five months later that Russia found a new base in Iraq. The estimated population of Egypt was 24,000,000, of Syria 4,080,000. Of the members of the new cabinet 20 were Syrians and 34 Egyptians.

The northern region of the United Arab Republic was soon brought under laws of the southern region. Foreign policy and national defense were unified. Plans for coordinating the two economies were set in motion. The Egyptian agrarian reform law, fixing a maximum individual land-holding at 200 acres of irrigated land, was introduced into Syria. Lands in excess of limits were to be taken over by the state during the next five years with compensation. Both regions joined in fighting Communism, on the ground that it disrupts Arab unity, and in accepting American aid. Restless under the new restrictions the northern region staged in September 1961 a bloodless military coup, seceded from the Union and called itself the Syrian Arab Republic.

LEBANON

The infant Lebanese Republic, covering an area (3470 square miles) not much larger than Yellowstone National Park and sustaining a population (approximately 1,000,000) not exceeding that of a good-sized American city, embarked upon its fully independent career[12] with serious liabilities but a favorable balance of assets all of its own. Religious loyalty had splintered its people. The situation was further aggravated by the fact that neither the Christian nor the Moslem community constituted a preponderant majority. It was natural for the Lebanese Moslem to feel a greater sense of identification with other Moslems beyond the borders of the state, as it was natural for the Christian to draw nearer to Christian Europe. Its first president, a Maronite Christian, and his prime minister, a Sunnite Moslem, worked out a formula which became known as the Lebanese national covenant, to the effect that Moslems would hereafter compromise their Arabism as Christians would compromise their Westernism and thus establish a common basis for a rising Lebanese nationhood.

A fledgling though it was, Lebanon had had experience in striking out for itself in autonomous rule since 1861.[13] The backbone of its population was its Maronite and Druze mountaineers, each community as proud as it was tiny. Hardened by cold climate, imbued with love of freedom, daring and individualistic, Maronites and Druzes developed a Lebanese tradition. Lebanon was farther removed from the desert than any other Arabic-speaking land. It had no nomadic population. Without the benefit of rich natural resources it had attained a high standard of living through free enterprise, domestic and international trade, tourism, and remittances from its sons overseas. In the dis-

[12] See above, pp. 504-5.
[13] Treated above, pp. 455-6.

tribution of wealth there has been less disparity in Lebanon than anywhere else in the Arab area.

As a summer resort it attracts Iraqis, Kuwaitis, Saudi, and other Arabians with more money than they can spend or invest in their respective countries. Its relatively mild and varied climate, mainly a product of the proximity of its mountains to the sea, as well as its modern schools and hospitals, and the reputed tolerance of its people draw lovers of sports, students, convalescents and estivators from near and far. Since the second World War its mountain has become a winter playground. Its people boast that theirs is the only country where one can swim and ski on one and the same day. Without the benefit of an elaborate public system of education it has achieved a remarkably high degree of literacy by means of private and foreign schools. Its state university, not a well-developed institution, was not founded until 1951. More attuned to Western cultural influences by its Christian ties to Europe, its colonies overseas, and Western institutions of learning within its territory, Lebanon has made a relatively early transition from medievalism to modernism. It has become, in fact, a show window through which the hinterland could look to the West. Its capital, a gateway to the East, developed into an entrepôt for its neighbors, a market for exotic goods, and a station for businessmen from the West. In modernist orientation the Tunisian Republic may be rising to a second position.

RELATIONS WITH NEIGHBORS

For a few years after their liberation from the mandate, Syria and Lebanon lived like two neighbors with one front door—the Beirut port. But Syria's new economic policy clashed with Lebanon's long-standing commitment to free trade. Amidst a world of currency control and at a time of trade restrictions, the merchant republic has stood by its adherence to the traditional law of supply and demand as determinants of the price of a commodity. To the pattern of economic development throughout the surrounding area, it remained an exception. The customs controversy spearheaded a prolonged Syrian-Lebanese dispute involving problems of frontier control, tobacco monopoly, and concessionary companies which under the mandate operated jointly in both hands. Subsequent to the divorce of the two economies (1950) under the Shishakli regime, Syria closed the border for two years and imposed economic boycott.

Lebanon had to seek new markets or expand old ones for its transit and export trade, responsible for a considerable portion of its national income. The increased revenues of the oil-producing neighbors offered new opportunities. Lebanon itself received considerable revenues from the Iraq pipeline terminating in Tripoli and Saudi Arabian ones terminating in Sidon. It is the only country where the production of services—transportation, insurance, investment yield, and profits from tourism and transit trade—amounts to almost two-thirds of the national income, leaving one-third to the production of agricultural and industrial goods.

More pressing were the political problems. The Lebanese government viewed with concern the Greater Syria and the Fertile Crescent projects. It cherished the policy of cooperating wholeheartedly with its neighbors but not to the extent of losing its identity. While in the Arab-Moslem world, it was not entirely of it. The founder of the Syrian Nationalist Party, himself a Lebanese, was executed in Beirut (1949) on a charge of treason, uniting Lebanon with Syria. His party was for a time banned. The country could develop no solid political parties which would cut across confessional lines. While the constitution of the republic made no provision for the religious affiliation of the president, a tradition grew that he should be Maronite, his prime minister Sunnite, and the speaker of the chamber of deputies a Shiite. At least one ministry was occupied by a Druze. Seats in the chamber were distributed among the various religious denominations in proportion to their numerical strength. Other than Maronites the Christian community comprised half a dozen or more denominations.

BETWEEN EAST AND WEST

In the East-West tug of war the Lebanese government leaned in a direction that alienated it further from Syria and from Egypt. While it kept its political and economic relations with the Soviet Union, it took progressive steps in the opposite direction. In the summer of 1955 it negotiated a loan from the International Bank for Reconstruction and Development in the amount of $27,000,000 for its major project, that of the Litani, the only good-sized river that has both source and mouth in its territory. When completed the project will double the electric power available within the republic and will also increase the total irrigated area by about two-fifths, mostly in the coastal region. In the following year Lebanon received from the United States a pledge of $3,670,000 for improving its Beirut international airport and other means of communication. Later in that year it did not break diplomatic relations with Britain and France, as a sequel to the Suez episode, although it took a firm stand in favor of Egypt.

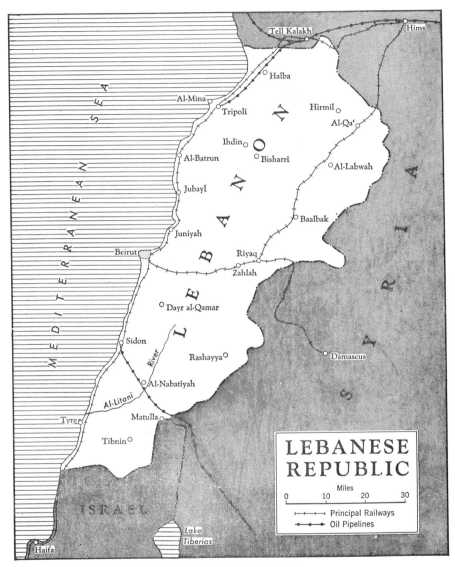

LEBANESE REPUBLIC

When the Eisenhower doctrine was announced early in 1957, Lebanon was the only one to accept it formally and did so even before its approval by congress. Under the doctrine's program it was to receive $20,000,000 mainly for defense purposes.

TWO INTERNAL CRISES

The apparently stable republican regime inaugurated by Bisharah al-Khuri in 1943 did not prove to be so stable in 1952. Stability was the price paid by sectarianism at the expense of efficiency. Sectarianism demanded not the man for the job but the Greek Orthodox, the Shiite, the Druze for the job. Worse than that family loyalty, a relic of tribal society, required a man in high position to favor relatives and friends.

Charges of nepotism, favoritism, corruption, and inefficiency were given voice as the president entered upon his second term. The political situation was aggravated by economic problems. Rise in the cost of living; increased unemployment; devaluation of the French franc with which the Lebanese pound was tied, and the rupture of customs relations with Syria—created economic difficulties for the regime. A peaceful revolution spearheaded by the politically and economically discontented ended in the downfall of Bisharah al-Khuri. The whole procedure was conducted within the constitutional framework: strikes of businessmen and service men spreading from the capital to other cities, refusal of the army to use force against strikers, inability to form a new cabinet. On his resignation in September 1952 the chamber of deputies elected a leader of the opposition Kamil Shamun (Camille Chamoun) as the second president of the republic. In contrast to the prevailing revolutionary pattern in the Near East, conducted by army officers and stained with blood, this was a rose-water revolution.

The issue of the Shamun regime's failure to introduce the promised administrative, judicial, and electoral reforms was before long overshadowed by a more urgent one: the retention of the state's sovereignty while cooperating with "neutral" Arab neighbors and maintaining a Western orientation. Performance on such a tightrope became more hazardous after 1955. The Shamun regime took a non-equivocal stand. In its minister of foreign affairs, Charles Malik (future president of the United Nations general assembly), it found an eloquent spokesman who upheld the country's pro-American alignment as fervently as he condemned international communism. An element in the Lebanese population reacted unfavorably. The emergence of the United Arab Republic in 1958 stimulated the reaction while it aroused fear of absorption in a larger Arab state by another body in the population. The delicate Christian-Moslem balance was destroyed. The gap between Lebanon and the new state was widened into a gulf.

The anti-Shamun movement in different parts of the country found ready leaders in three Sunnite ex-prime ministers, a former Druze cabinet member, two Shiite ex-speakers of the house, and other influential Christians many of whom maintained they were deprived of their chamber seats through rigged elections for which the government was held responsible. Cabinet members were normally recruited from among the deputies. The president was suspected of seeking a third term which the constitution discouraged. In July 1958 the government found itself confronted with widespread strikes, disturbances, terrorism, and bloody conflicts which reduced the country to a state of political chaos and economic paralysis. The Iraq explosion added fuel to the blaze. On July 14 Shamun appealed to the United States for troops to maintain security and preserve the independence and integrity of Lebanon which was threatened by foreign interference. Ten thousand marines were immediately landed on the beach near Beirut.

On the last day of July the chamber of deputies elected General Fuad Shihab (Fouad Chehab), commander in chief of the army, as third president. By the end of October all United States forces had been withdrawn. A soldier by training and a descendant of the aristocratic family that had ruled Lebanon for a century and a half, Shihab has nevertheless strictly adhered to constitutional democratic rule. Under him and a coalition cabinet, headed by a leader of the opposition from Tripoli, stability has been restored and no marked deviation has been noted from Lebanon's Western alignment.

As members of the Mediterranean branch of the Caucasian race, rockers of the cradle of our civilization, inventors of our alphabet, founders of our religion, co-sharers of our classical heritage, contributors to our medieval science and intellectual renaissance, inhabitants of the nearest part of the East to Europe, the Near Easterners come closest to us ethnically, historically, culturally, and geographically. An ancient Near Easterner would have felt less strange in Greece or Rome than elsewhere in the then known world, and so would a medieval Near Easterner. By the same token a European would have felt more at home in Near Eastern culture than in any other Asian or African culture. The realm in which Europeans and Near Easterners share has always been vastly larger than that in which they differ. As early as 1819 the poetic pen of Goethe inscribed:

> Whoever knows himself and others
> This he will also know
> That East and West
> Are not separable any more.

BOOKS TO READ

Anderson, James N. D., *Islamic Lands in the Modern World* (New York, 1959).

Badeau, John S., *The Emergence of Modern Egypt* (New York, 1953).

Bonné, Alfred, *State and Economics in the Middle East,* 2nd ed. (London. 1955).

Glubb, John B., *Britain and the Arabs: A Study of Fifty Years* (London, 1959).

Haddad, George, *Fifty Years of Modern Syria and Lebanon* (Beirut, 1950).

Harris, George L., *Egypt* (New Haven, 1957); *Iraq: Its People, its Society, its Culture* (New Haven, 1958).

Hitti, Philip K., *Lebanon in History* (New York and London, 1957); *Syria: A Short History* (New York and London, 1959).

Lenczowski, George, *The Middle East in World Affairs,* 2nd ed. (Ithaca, 1956).

Longrigg, Stephen H., *Oil in the Middle East: Its Discovery and Development* (London, 1954); Longrigg and Frank Stoakes, *Iraq* (London, 1958).

Meyer, A. J., *Middle Eastern Capitalism* (Cambridge, Mass., 1959).

Patai, Raphael, ed., *The Republic of Syria,* 2 vols. (New Haven, 1956); *Jordan* (New Haven, 1957).

Peretz, Don, *Israel and the Palestine Arabs* (Washington, 1958).

Qubain, Fahim I., *The Reconstruction of Iraq, 1950-1957* (New York, 1958).

Royal Institute of International Affairs, *France and Britain* (London, 1945); *Great Britain and Egypt, 1914-1951* (London, 1952); *The Middle East: A Political and Economic Survey,* 2nd ed. (London, 1954).

Ziadeh, Nicola, *Syria and Lebanon* (New York, 1957).

Index